# Reflexive Governance for Sustainable Development

# Reflexive Governance for Sustainable Development

*Edited by*

Jan-Peter Voß

Dierk Bauknecht

*Öko-Institut – Institute for Applied Ecology, Germany*

and

René Kemp

*MERIT, Maastricht University, The Netherlands*

**Edward Elgar**
Cheltenham, UK • Northampton, MA, USA

Published by
Edward Elgar Publishing Limited
Glensanda House
Montpellier Parade
Cheltenham
Glos GL50 1UA
UK

Edward Elgar Publishing, Inc.
136 West Street
Suite 202
Northampton
Massachusetts 01060
USA


A catalogue record for this book
is available from the British Library


ISBN-13: 978 1 84542 582 1
ISBN-10: 1 84542 582 0

Printed and bound in Great Britain by MPG Books Ltd, Bodmin, Cornwall

# Contents

## INTRODUCTION

## REFLECTIONS ON REFLEXIVE GOVERNANCE

## STRATEGIES FOR SUSTAINABLE SYSTEM TRANSFORMATION

# Figures

# Tables

# Contributors

**Peter Balogh** is a geographer and head of research of the Floodplain Management Pilot Project in Nagykörü, introducing the principals and practice of sustainable water and land use in the Tisza-region.

**Dierk Bauknecht** is a research fellow and project leader with the Energy and Climate Group, Öko-Institut, Institute for Applied Ecology, Germany. He works on the transformation of energy infrastructures, innovation studies and transdisciplinarity.

**Ulrich Beck** is professor of sociology at the University of Munich and at the London School of Economics. He is editor of the Second Modernity Series published by Suhrkamp Verlag. Research foci are theories of modernity and the sociology of risk.

**John Grin** is a professor of policy science, in particular system innovation, at the Department of Political Science of the University of Amsterdam. His current research focuses on system innovations, that is, reflexive modernisation of socio-technological practices, especially in the areas of agriculture, water management and health care.

**René Kemp** is a senior research fellow at MERIT (Maastricht Economic Research Institute on Innovation and Technology). He has been working since 1988 on innovation and environmental policy issues, as an economist and policy analyst. He has a broad range of expertise, covering various sectors (manufacturing, transport, energy, waste and to a lesser extent services).

**Kornelia Konrad** is with the research group CIRUS (Centre for Innovation Research in the Utility Sector) at EAWAG (Swiss Federal Institute for Aquatic Science and Technology) in Switzerland. The CIRUS research focus is on sustainable transformation of infrastructure sectors from a social science perspective.

**Marie Céline Loibl** is with the Austrian Institute for Applied Ecology. Her research interests include: methods for interdisciplinary and transdisciplinary research projects, team-coaching in environmental research, consultation for designing and organising environmental research-programs, process evaluation and participatory methods for integrating representatives from municipalities, enterprises and private initiatives into research projects.

**Derk Loorbach**  is a researcher at Dutch Research Institute for Transitions (DRIFT) in Rotterdam. He graduated in political sciences in 2000 and is currently working on his PhD on the subject of transition management. In addition he is involved as scientific advisor in a number of projects. His main research interests are complex and evolutionary governance, sustainable development and transitions.

**Piotr Magnuszewski**  is an adjunct professor in the Institute of Physics, Wroclaw University of Technology and research associate in the International Institute for Applied Systems Analysis. His research interests are qualitative and quantitative modelling, adaptive management and complexity science.

**Ines Oehme**  is with the German Environmental Protection Agency, where she deals with product related environmental protection. Before that, she was with the Inter-University Research Centre for Technology, Work and Culture in Graz (Austria). She has expertise in issues of technology and society and ecological product policy. Recent research projects dealt with strategies for transition towards sustainable production and consumption systems and on green public procurement.

**Arie Rip**  is a professor of the philosophy of science and technology at the University of Twente in the Netherlands. He works and publishes extensively on science policy, technology dynamics and technology assessment, and forms of expertise.

**Harald Rohracher**  is director of the IFZ: the Inter-University Research Centre for Technology, Work and Culture in Graz, Austria and research fellow at the Department of Research on Technology and Science, Faculty for Interdisciplinary Studies (IFF), at the University of Klagenfurt. His main fields of research are the social shaping of technology, diffusion and adoption of environmental technologies, and the role of end-users in technological innovations.

**Jan Sendzimir**  is a systems ecologist and works in research and project development at the International Institute for Applied Systems Analysis (IIASA) on applications concerned with 'wicked' problems, problems with apparently unsolvable combinations of ecological, economic and socio-political factors, that occur over relatively large areas such as river basins, major watersheds and mountain chains. The theoretical framework includes theories of resilience, catastrophe, complex adaptive systems and chaos.

**Adrian Smith**  is a research fellow at SPRU (Science and Technology Policy Research Unit) at the University of Sussex, Brighton, UK. His research draws upon various social science perspectives in order to better appreciate the relationships between technology, society and sustainable development.

**Philipp Späth** is a senior researcher at the IFZ: the Inter-University Research Centre for Technology, Work and Culture in Graz, Austria. He is lecturing in the social studies of technology at the Universities of Graz and Klagenfurt. His main fields of research are new modes of governance and cross-cutting issues of technology- and innovation policy, energy- and environmental policy. His work focuses on strategies for transitions towards sustainable energy systems and sustainable production systems.

**Andy Stirling** is a senior lecturer at SPRU (Science and Technology Policy Research Unit) at the University of Sussex, Brighton, UK. He works on practical and theoretical issues around scientific uncertainty, precaution, divergent values and public engagement in risk and technology policy.

**Bernhard Truffer** heads the research group CIRUS (Centre for Innovation Research in the Utility Sector) at EAWAG (Swiss Federal Institute for Aquatic Science and Technology) in Switzerland. The CIRUS research focus is on the sustainable transformation of infrastructure sectors from a social science perspective.

**Anna Vári** is senior research fellow in the Institute of Sociology, Hungarian Academy of Sciences and Professor at the Department of Environmental Management at the Budapest University of Technical and Economic Sciences. Her fields of research and teaching include health and environmental policy, risk analysis, conflict management and public participation.

**Bas van Vliet** is a lecturer and researcher at the Environmental Policy Group at Wageningen University, in the Netherlands. His research interests are environmental sociology, infrastructure management and consumer perspectives.

**Jan-Peter Voß** is a research fellow and project leader with the Energy and Climate Group, Öko-Institut, Institute for Applied Ecology, Germany. His research interests are governance studies, innovation and technological change, methodology of transdisciplinary research.

**K. Matthias Weber** is head of the Department of Technology Policy at ARC Systems Research, one of the institutes of Austrian Research Centres ARC, and lecturer in innovation economics and technology policy at the University of Economics in Vienna. He works mainly on issues of priority-setting and governance of science, technology and innovation policy, but also on foresight and transitions in production-consumption systems and in information society technologies.

**Katy Whitelegg**   is a researcher in the Department of Technology Policy at ARC Systems Research, Seibersdorf, Austria. Her research interests are in policy integration, research for sustainable development and women in research.

**Franziska Wolff** is a research fellow and project leader with the Environmental Law Group, Öko-Institut, Institute for Applied Ecology, Germany. Her research interests focus on the analysis of institutional arrangements and governance structures, policy instruments and processes as well as German and international environmental politics, especially agriculture and biodiversity.

# Preface

We make our own history but we do not choose it. An indication of this statement is the fact that policy and public debate are primarily concerned with problems that arise from past economic, political, scientific and technological activities. Unemployment, social disintegration, ecological destabilisation, globalisation, migration, and proliferation of weapons of mass destruction are all examples of systemic effects of past decisions that individuals and collectives made to deal with problems for the actors concerned. Successively, the central and most pressing problems of modern society are those which are caused by the side effects of past problem-solving. Cognitive and institutional patterns of society build up around these problems. Their consequences bring about adaptations, and capacities are developed to restore where possible. Social policy, innovation assessment, environmental policy, humanitarian and development aid represent examples.

The notion of *reflexive modernisation* as developed by Beck, Giddens and other authors captures this dynamism through a reconceptualisation of society which spirals around itself, stumbles over its own feet, and busies itself with self-created problems rather than heroically conquering the world, unfolding civilisation, and progressing towards truth and ideal order. The insight of reflexive modernisation gives rise to an understanding of societal development in which instrumental rationality and the search for best solutions take on an uncertain direction in shaping the course of societal development. If progress gets overthrown by unintended side effects, the ideals of certain knowledge, unambiguous evaluation as well as planning and control become revealed as illusionary. Governance practices, which are based on these illusions, appear as problem producers rather than problem solvers. An alternative orientation for governance is needed – as are new methods that can fill the gap which scientific prediction, analytic assessment, and control-oriented management approaches have left. Like society in general, governance is also thrown back on itself and forced to reflect its cognitive and institutional foundations in the idea of modernisation. But what could an alternative understanding and respective strategies and practices look like which might create a better future?

This is the topic that this book confronts. It explores the concept of reflexive governance as a course for the shaping of societal development, which incorporates uncertainty, ignorance, heterogeneity, ambiguity, unintended effects, error and lack of control. These qualities are all aspects that modern problem-solving procedures try to eliminate. Incorporating these indeterminacies implies looking for ways to work with them. This means developing strategies and methods for problem-handling and institutional arrangements, which can make productive use of them as constitutive elements of societal development.

Our discussion under the heading of reflexive governance relates to recent discussions in technology studies, policy studies and science studies. In technology studies, impact assessment emerged as its own professional field, which is oriented towards the anticipation of possible 'side effects' of new technologies. In this field, methods have emerged that involve scientists, citizens, and practitioners in mutual learning with technology experiments. In policy studies, new modes of governance have been conceptualised to capture informal interactions and self-organisation as important factors for regulating societal development. Participatory policy analysis takes distributed knowledge as a basis for policy advice. In science studies, including in the philosophical and more empirically oriented strands, a shift in focus can be observed from academic disciplines to heterogeneous networks as places of knowledge production. The embedding of knowledge in social contexts of interaction raises fundamental methodological questions about the possibility and usefulness of value-free knowledge that can be generalised. Reflexive governance may provide a concept through which these discourses can join together. It offers a general concept of societal problem-handling; that is, interaction in which a group of interdependent actors constructs problems and tries to influence ongoing developments to make them disappear. As such, reflexive governance comprises cognitive and social dynamics and is directed at knowledge, technology and institutions alike.

A characteristic of the reflexive governance concept is that it is also concerned with itself. It understands reflexive governance to be part of the dynamics which are governed. Governance processes can become the object of shaping strategies. At the same time, broader dynamics, which are not usually considered to be part of governance, are acknowledged to play an important role in shaping societal development and therefore become part of governing (such as science, public discourse, social networking, and technological development). Reflexive governance puts itself up to probing. It acknowledges that governing activities are entangled in wider societal feedback loops and are partly shaped by the (side) effects of its own working. It incorporates such feedback by opening problem-handling processes for diverse knowledge, values and resources of influence in order to learn about appropriate problem definitions, targets and strategies of governance for sustainable development. As such, reflexive governance is about the organisation of recursive feedback relations between distributed steering activities. In this book we make first steps in articulating the concept of reflexive governance by elaborating some theoretical aspects and pointing out practical ways of putting it in to practice.

As such it can be the beginning of a path of thinking and acting. The book presents a specification of the concept of reflexive modernisation with respect to theoretical and practical problems of governing. It differs from other works about reflexive modernisation in that it investigates concrete empirical practices in policy and management, which take up the repercussions of reflexivity: uncertainty, ambiguity and dispersion of social control. Reflexive strategies are examined in empirical fields such as utility transformation, energy policy, renaturalisation of river basins, research policy, research management, technology policy and agricultural policy. This volume presents a link between abstract theoretical discussion and the very specific forms in which reflexivity is played out as practical experience. At the same time, it includes critical theoretical discussions, which relate to other general concepts such as globalisation, structuration, postmodernism, planning theory, risk assessment and epistemology.

A unique feature of the book is the systematic link that is developed between the theory of reflexive modernisation and the concept of sustainable development and practices which refer to it. Sustainable development is analysed as a *chiffre* by means of which reflexive modernisation becomes politically negotiated and by means of which practical governance innovations can join together.

After saying what this book is about, we should also say what it is not about. The book is not a discussion of political science or a comparative analysis of changing governance patterns nor a discourse analysis of reflexive modernisation. The core themes focus on the rationale of a specific type of governance rather than a systematic analysis of the governance of certain sectors of society. Its impetus is towards revised concepts and logic of steering and problem-solving and how these play out in practice.

The book developed out of a series of workshops which brought together researchers from nine European countries with an interest in boundary-crossing between disciplines and practical societal problem-handling. Accordingly, the people involved came from both academic and transdisciplinary research sectors and from different home disciplines. The broad subject of the workshop series included questions that were connected to the shaping of sustainable transformation processes. Such questions entail problems of knowledge production of interactions between society, technology and nature, the assessment of alternative options and transformation paths, and the development and implementation of strategies which can effectively influence the course of socio-ecological transformation processes.

The book project took shape only gradually. It started as a compilation of abstracts for chapters in which workshop participants would elaborate their perspective on sustainable transformation and elaborate links to other papers. This was an occasion to reflect on the differences in perspectives when presented side by side and to lead into the preparation of a draft version for an introductory chapter, which would draw out the common questions and general lines according to which the specific governance issues from the empirical cases could be arranged. This is where the concept of reflexive governance first emerged. At this point the book began to take on a life of its own. Over the course of iterated revisions, the book took on new shape, with important new contributions from Beck, Grin, Rip and Stirling on reflexive governance. Some characteristics of the book may hint at the prevalence of uncertainty, ambiguity and the lack of complete control during the production process. Yet we did not make a strong attempt to streamline chapters according to any ex-post rationalisation of what has happened to bring us where we are. Instead, we decided to let the book tell the story of reflexive governance as an emerging concept, a concept which has a high degree of interpretive flexibility, which is not closed down but open to interaction with several other concepts and empirical problem areas, and which as a result of these interactions is expected to change its shape. For this reason we decided to include the original version of the introductory chapter (presenting the conceptual outline of reflexive governance), which the authors used to develop their discussion in the subsequent chapters. Only in the concluding chapter do we make an attempt to draw together what we have learned for the overall concept. This enables the reader to follow the concept of reflexive governance on the path of its evolution and become tempted to engage in taking it further.

It would be interesting (and possibly rewarding in terms of insights about appropriate ways to organise research processes) to trace the various interactions – small talks, jokes, drawings, discussions of more and less structured types, presentations, comments and amendments to draft texts – which form the history from which the product in hand emerged. Because this could grow into another book project, we name just a few outstanding ingredients to the production process without which this book would not have been possible. The Socio-ecological Research Programme at the German Ministry for Education and Research (BMBF) needs to be mentioned at the outset, not only with respect to the funding for a truly experimental project of knowledge networking,[1] but also for the sake of representing an inspiring example of reflexive governance in the field of research policy. This refers to the combination of strategic foresight and flexible adaptation to unforeseen developments which exemplifies the programmatic idea of the 'learning research programme' and is purposefully put into practice by Ingrid Balzer, Angelika Willms-Herget, and Bernd Fischer. Further credits go to the Industrial Transformation Project of the International Human Dimensions Programme on Global Environmental Change (IT-IHDP), which endorsed our project and provided a platform to connect with a wider community of sustainability researchers worldwide.

We also want to mention the people who have been involved in the workshop series and its preparation, but do not have a contribution to which their name is credited in this book. Regine Barth, Bettina Brohmann, Susanne Bruppacher, Dirk Bunke, Frank Ebinger, Miklós Fule, Irmgard Hubauer, Måns Nilson, Tamás Pálvölgyi, Susanne Schidler, Claus Seibt, and Jørgen Wettestad have contributed in various ways to the discussion from which this book emerged. We especially appreciate the work of Isabella Kessel who made important contributions to bringing about integration at the workshops and thus prepared the ground on which this product has grown. Bernadette Kiefer did an impressive job in grappling with the heterogeneity of contributions in terms of formatting and making them converge into one coherent document. Olivia Voils and Tom Walker did the best they could to make the English of us non-native speakers comprehensible to a broader public.

**Dierk Bauknecht**
**René Kemp**
**Jan-Peter Voß**
Freiburg, Maastricht, Berlin, May 2005

# NOTE

1.  The German Research Ministry funded the workshop series within the programme on 'socio-ecological research' as a measure to develop the research infrastructure for sustainability research. It was chaired by the Öko-Institut the Institute for Applied Ecology, as part of the project 'Schnittstellenentwicklung für die Integration akademischer und praxisbezogener Forschung im Bereich Sozial-Ökologie (knowledge interfaces)'.

# Introduction

# 1. Sustainability and reflexive governance: introduction

## Jan-Peter Voß and René Kemp

## INTRODUCTION

Disappointment abounds in public discourse about sustainability. Many say that the outcome of sustainability strategies has been meagre compared to the outpouring of rhetoric regarding the concept towards the end of the last century. The long-standing definition of the Brundtland Commission – 'development that meets the needs of the present without compromising the ability of future generations to meet their own needs' – is accepted everywhere as a general normative orientation (WCED 1987), as is the criterion for a good society of equal consideration for ecological, economic and social development goals (UNCED 1992, Ch. 8). But when it comes to practical implementation, the concept seems to dissolve into rhetoric that masks familiar conflicts over concepts, goals and instruments that for decades have dominated societal action in problem areas such as energy, transport, agriculture and housing.

A widespread attitude is that the concept of sustainability adds nothing new for the treatment of practical problems. It is said that the concept waters down the new parameter of political decision making introduced by the concept of ecological carrying capacity (see Matthes 2002). The organisational and technological arrangements of modern society are said to be reproduced with all their ambivalences under the banner of sustainability (Conrad 1997). The vague label diffuses concrete challenges and presents a veil behind which particular interest groups can evade responsibilities and commitments that they had previously been urged into through public pressure and political struggle. For many, sustainability appears at best an empty phrase and at worst a Trojan horse for the redefinition of the public interest by a powerful few.

This book takes a different standpoint. It argues that the multi-dimensional and dynamic concept of sustainability (Rammel et al. 2003) has fundamental implications for the governance of modern society.

The systemic and long-term nature of social, economic and ecological development brings complexity and uncertainty to the fore as key issues for sustainability. Sustainability cannot be translated into a blueprint or a defined end state from which criteria can be derived and unambiguous decisions taken to get there. Instead, it should be understood as a specific kind of problem framing that emphasises the interconnectedness of different problems and scales, as well as the long-term and indirect effects of actions that result from it. Societal discourse on sustainability has highlighted the ambiguity of social goals, uncertainty about cause and effect relations and the feedback that occurs between steering activities and social, technological and ecological development. Sustainability calls for new forms of problem handling. These differ from the forms that are adequate for delimitable, decomposable problems that can be managed in a linear way. The concept of sustainability has brought with it recognition of the limits of rigid analysis and the inadequacy of policy approaches that aim at planning and achieving predetermined outcomes.

From this perspective, sustainable development is more about the organisation of processes than about particular outcomes. It is about the modes of problem treatment and the types of strategies that are applied to search for solutions and bring about more robust paths of social and technological development. We set out to explore these new modes of societal problem treatment under the heading of 'reflexive governance'.

## REFLEXIVE GOVERNANCE

Reflexive governance refers to the problem of shaping societal development in the light of the reflexivity of steering strategies – the phenomenon that thinking and acting with respect to an object of steering also affects the subject and its ability to steer. Examples of such reflexivity include research policies bringing up new knowledge that shifts policy objectives, or subsidies increasing the lobbying power of supported industries and thereby changing political force fields. Reflexive governance thus implies that one calls into question the foundations of governance itself, that is, the concepts, practices and institutions by which societal development is governed, and that one envisions alternatives and reinvents and shapes those foundations.

As suggested by Beck's notion of reflexive modernisation (Beck 1994; Beck et al. 2003), the reflexivity of governance also includes the possibility that certain governance patterns undermine themselves by inducing changes in the world that then affect their own working. Rationalist problem solving (being central to modernity and past and present governance) undergoes change to deal with problems overlooked in past problem solving. It is easy to understand why this is so. Rationalist problem solving depends on both the analysis of system dynamics to predict the effects of alternative options and the precise definition of goals and assessment of options to determine which is the best to be implemented through powerful interventions and sophisticated control systems. This kind of problem solving seeks to eliminate uncertainty, ambivalence and interference from uncontrolled influences. Using this approach, it was possible to achieve tremendous technological developments, sophisticated patterns of social regulation and high economic efficiency of production. The trick is simple: to decide and act rationally, one needs to isolate discrete dimensions of complex reality, that is, to select relevant elements, express cause and effect in linear form, establish the priority of goals and assign responsibilities. This pattern of productive reduction of complexity orchestrates modern science, technology development, bureaucratic organisation, project management, policy making and broader patterns of social organisation such as the differentiation of functional subsystems for economics, law, science, politics and so on (see Luhmann 1990; Schimank 1996; Mayntz 1999). This problem-solving approach yields tremendous power because it constructs a multitude of specialised perspectives, enabling more precise targeting of purposes, concentration of action capacities and control over processes within the system boundaries thus defined (Schimank 1988). At the same time, however, this kind of problem solving leads relentlessly to unintended consequences (Dörner 1989; Böhret 1990). The more problem solving is disengaged from the full, messy, intermingled natural reality and oriented towards the worlds of specialists, the larger is the share of interdependencies and dimensions of embeddedness ignored in the development and implementation of supposed solutions. The more evasive such problem solving is, the more effective it becomes with respect to particular instrumental purposes and the stronger the impacts of unintended consequences become.

These impacts are perceived either as 'externalities', from the perspective of other specialised problem orientations or, from the problem solver's own perspective, as 'side-effects' or 'repercussions'. Examples include interference between different policy or corporate departments – such as transport and environment or R&D and marketing – as well as traffic congestion, technological risks, environmental problems and individualisation as results of industrialisation. These unintended consequences cause new, often more severe problems that are more difficult to handle because they require setting aside specialised problem solving. These can be called second-order problems (Jahn and Wehling 1998). Sustainability is one, if not the main second-order problem of modernist problem solving. Second-order problems work successively to disrupt the structure of modernist problem solving because to grasp them – to reconstruct them cognitively, to assess them and to get competences together to act on them – they require putting aside the isolation of instrumental specialisation, widening filters of relevance, trading off values and engaging in interaction with other specialists. In short, these problems require transgressing the cognitive, evaluative and institutional boundaries, which, paradoxically, undermines the modernist problem-solving approach. Problem solving becomes paradoxical in that it is oriented towards constriction and selection to reduce complexity but is forced into expansion and amalgamation to contend with the problems it generates (see Beck 1993). This is what we call the constellation of reflexive problem handling or, on the societal level, reflexive governance.

Reflexivity has two different but related meanings here that are often confused in accounts of reflexive modernisation. The first meaning of reflexivity refers to how modernity deals with its own implications and side effects, the mechanism by which modern societies grow in cycles of producing problems and solutions to these problems that produce new problems. The reality of modern society is thus a result of self-confrontation. This can be called first-order reflexivity. The second meaning of reflexive modernisation refers to the cognitive reconstruction of this cycle in which problem solving through instrumental rationality generates new problems. The impacts of technology, scientific knowledge production and the legitimacy and effectiveness of democracy are examples of problem areas where such reflection has brought up critical reassessments of rational problem-solving methods and led to the development of alternative methods and processes of problem handling that are more open, experimental and learning oriented. Often these approaches aim to foster interaction between different perspectives and actively explore the uncertainties, ambivalences and control problems articulated in such a confrontation of rationalities. Constructive technology assessment, deliberative policy making and transdisciplinary research are alternative concepts to rational problem solving that all underlie concrete practices. New problem-handling paradigms and institutional arrangements based on critical assessments of modern problem solving and its reflexivity have themselves become characteristic features of reflexive modernisation. But these phenomena are reflexive in a different way from that of the self-confrontation of modernisation with its own side-effects. They represent a second-order reflexivity that entails the application of modern rational analysis not only to the self-induced problems, but also to its own working, conditions and effects. In this way, second-order reflexivity interrupts the automatism of executing problem-solving routines. It transcends particular rationalities, and breaks the vicious circle of first-order reflexivity. Reflexive modernisation, or reflexive governance, comprises both the condition of being shaped through its own side-effects and the transcendence of this cyclic pattern through reflection of the modern understanding of rationality itself. It is shaped by the interplay of first-order and second-order reflexivity. This book focuses mainly on second-order reflexivity and particularly on the emergence of an additional level of integrative, unrestrained and open-ended 'second-order' governance that reflects, orients and supervises diverse specialised problem-solving processes. In this way, the powers of specialisation and integration can check and balance each other. The benefits of rational problem solving can be exploited while the fact that problem solving is embedded in more complex contexts and their dynamics is accepted as a constraint. Such second-order governance, however, can no longer be called problem solving. Only unambiguous and confined problems can be 'solved' in a deliberative manner. Second-order governance consists of a procedural approach towards reflecting the interdependencies, understanding aggregate effects of specialised concepts and strategies, and engaging in the modulation of ongoing societal developments by establishing links and organising problem-oriented communication and interaction among distributed steering activities (for related ideas about steering see for example Rip 1998; Beck 1993; Dobuzinskis 1992).

Various reflexive governance approaches can be identified that confront the challenge of shaping sustainable development by reflecting the complex interactions underlying problematic development. By initiating procedures through which problem perceptions, assessment criteria and action strategies of different actors can be exposed to each other, actors can begin mutually to adapt their perceptions, criteria and strategies before such adaptation is imposed in a much more costly way as a consequence of the external effects of specialised problem-solving processes.

Such governance approaches often focus on specific dimensions of problem handling such as analysis, goal definition, assessment or strategy implementation. Constructive technology assessment, foresight exercises, transdisciplinary research, participatory decision making and cooperative policy making are examples of those approaches. Others, such as transition management and adaptive management, are more comprehensive. However, they all share a general understanding, which is related to the concept of reflexivity as outlined above. By creating interaction between various rationalities, they take account of the complexity of interlinked social, technological and ecological development, the fundamental uncertainty with respect to system dynamics, the ambiguity of sustainability criteria and assessment and the contingency of the effects of human action in the context of long-term system change. Reflexive governance modes are therefore geared towards continued learning in the course of modulating ongoing developments, rather than towards complete knowledge and maximisation of control.

Practical instances of reflexive governance can be found in different parts of society – in general ways of producing knowledge and making policy and in production-consumption systems such as energy and agriculture. They can also be found at different levels of problem treatment – from the management of an individual organisation to networks and sectors and up to the global level. Governance practices within these different contexts follow particular streams of historical development and are usually discussed within the framework of professional concepts and language. Similarities are therefore not easily recognised. One concern of this book is to develop a perspective in which the similarities and linkages between these approaches become visible. This will help us to take stock of governance innovations in various practice areas that reflexively deal with the complexity and ambivalence inherent in sustainable development, to compare the conditions and historical paths from which they have emerged and to enable mutual learning in terms of concepts and practical experience. Finally, an integrated review of reflexive governance innovations helps to shift the debate about the usefulness of the concept of sustainability from immediate outcomes to more hidden process innovations and ways of structuring and handling problems. Even if their effects are of a more diffuse and long-term nature, they should not be overlooked in assessing what has come out of the sustainability concept and in discussing strategies to develop its potential.

To establish a common frame of reference for diverse kinds of governance innovation for sustainability, we elaborate some strategic cornerstones of the concept of reflexive governance. We do this by first defining a broad notion of governance as the patterns of processes by which society handles its problems and shapes its own transformation. We then discuss the specific problems of governance for sustainable development along the dimensions of systems analysis in the light of complexity, goal formulation in the light of the ambiguity of sustainability and strategy implementation in the light of distributed control. In the course of this discussion, we derive cornerstone strategies that help to identify adequate ways of handling governance problems of sustainable development. A compilation of these strategies represents a practically-oriented framework of reflexive governance that can serve as a common reference for the diverse conceptual aspects and practical instances discussed in the remaining chapters of the book.

**Governance as Problem Handling**

In this volume, we use the term 'governance' to describe the characteristic processes by which society defines and handles its problems. In this general sense, governance is about the self-steering of society.

Problem handling and self-steering, however, do not imply that governance is a linear process that follows a plan or is controlled by a specific actor or group of actors. Rather, governance is understood as the result of the interaction of many actors who have their own particular problems, define goals and follow strategies to achieve them. Governance therefore also involves conflicting interests and struggle for dominance. From these interactions, however, certain patterns emerge, including national policy styles, regulatory arrangements, forms of organisational management and the structures of sectoral networks. These patterns display the specific ways in which social entities are governed. They comprise processes by which collective problems are defined and analysed, processes by which goals and assessments of solutions are formulated and processes in which action strategies are coordinated. We use the term governance to describe the process of societal problem handling that comprises these three dimensions. As such, governance takes place in coupled and overlapping arenas of interaction: in research and science, public discourse, companies, policy making and other venues. To understand how specific patterns of social change come about or to assess the performance of problem handling, it is important to take into account interdependencies across various arenas of governance.

**System Analysis and Complexity**

A principal feature of the problems confronting sustainable development is that the systemic interconnections to which these problems refer are enormously complex. With the exception of quite narrowly defined disciplinary or professional situations, the problems of sustainable development cannot be grasped by means of simple models. Sustainable development focuses the long-term dynamics of particular forms of social organisation within a global context. Even single companies or local communities consist of a large number of very different elements of a social, technological or ecological nature. They contain subsystems or are themselves differentiated at various levels of organisation. The unfolding of processes within these structures – even more so the change of the structural configuration itself – is thus not sufficiently grasped by models that have only a few independent and dependent variables and assume clearly-defined, linear relationships of cause and effect. The understanding, explanation and analysis of the problem of sustainable development thus becomes a problem in itself. With sustainability problems it is difficult to isolate a unique cause or to predict the effects, both desired and undesired, of a particular intervention (Funtowicz et al. 1998). Three specific features associated with the complexity of sustainable development problems are discussed in the next three sections: first, the heterogeneity of elements, which precludes relying on disciplinary expert knowledge; second, the impossibility of predicting system developments and the effects of interventions, which makes errors unavoidable; and third, the irreversibility of social development, which embeds a strong path dependency in decision making.

**Heterogeneous interactions**

The understanding of long-term transformations in socio-ecological systems such as, for example, energy production and use, transport or agriculture requires knowledge about the very heterogeneous elements of these systems. Such elements include technological artefacts and networks, chemical substances in soil, water and the atmosphere, the organisation of firms and markets, political institutions, scientific theories and cultural values and attitudes. Knowledge is needed about the processes in which they each change and about how they relate and interact with each other. Conventional disciplinary science does not deliver this kind of knowledge about the 'interlinked and complex nature of reality' (Gallopín et al. 2001: 228). Instead, it concentrates on a very specific selection of elements and interactions – analytical 'slices' of reality. In real world entanglements, however, there is no clear boundary between these categories and the networks of cause and effect that cut across them. Each specialised perspective defines the systemic embedding of the particular analytical abstraction with which it is concerned as non-existent. In specific cases, this may be methodologically justifiable because linkages have been found to be insignificant. Parts of reality can sometimes be viewed in isolation without losing important aspects. In most cases, however, especially in the area of sustainability problems, linkages extend well beyond the scope of the problems as they are defined by disciplines and the cognitive models that are used to understand them.

The knowledge restrictions of specialised perspectives relate not only to scientific disciplines but also to the scientific method of knowledge production in general. The full set of factors and interactions that are relevant in real world problem settings cannot be handled through systematic modelling alone. More synthetic kinds of knowledge, gained from practical experience, are an important complementary source. Knowledge production for sustainable development cannot therefore rely only on scientific knowledge produced within the institutions and along the methodological guide rails of formal science. It also needs to integrate the tacit knowledge of societal actors. This tacit knowledge often cannot be subjected to conventional methods of scientific inquiry. It can only be generated in interactive settings in which knowledge is co-produced by scientists and actors from respective fields of societal practice. But also with respect to practice, it is important to integrate a diversity of perspectives because professional roles also entail selective perspectives.

Considering the heterogeneity of the elements that play a part in sustainable development, effective problem treatment calls for the use of methods of integrated knowledge production that transcend the boundaries between disciplines and between science and society. Practical and conceptual steps in this direction have been taken under the heading of transdisciplinary knowledge production (Nowotny et al. 2001; Hirsch Hadorn 2003; Bechmann and Frederichs 1996; Thompson Klein et al. 2001; Bergmann 2003).

**Uncertainty**
The interdependence of social, technological and ecological elements makes system transformation a complex and uncertain process. The overall process, its factors and drivers, cannot be analysed by linear models of cause and effect because feedback is pervasive. If the process of sustainable transformation – for example, of electricity provision or agriculture – is further understood as a process that takes place within a multi-level structure of nested subsystems at the local, regional and global level, the interaction on each level adds to the overall complexity. The result is that socio-ecological transformation cannot be predicted. Unpredictable interactions may give rise to self-stimulating processes like self-organisation, or to destructive resonance. Examples of such contingencies include topics in public discourse, social movements, BSE, strategic action under regulation and stock market crashes. Thresholds for catastrophic change cannot be defined by a single parameter but rather are driven by a confluence of many factors, not all of which can be sufficiently ascertained to determine corridors of safe levels of activity. Examples of this kind of difficulty include ecological pressure that causes a breakdown of ecosystem resilience, social injustice that causes upheaval or tax increases that lead to an economic depression. This is a fundamental constraint because of the impossibility of measuring all incremental factors that are relevant, especially the human factor. Non-linear system dynamics may give precisely those apparently minor factors a significant voice in where the system will go, as in the 'butterfly effect' (Gleick 1998; Byrne 1998). Here an apparently small effect tips the balance (examples can be found in Gladwell 2000).

This is why it is not possible to rely on simple models of the causes underlying sustainability problems. Even if complexity is excluded from cognitive models, the world still remains as complex as ever and the connections that are ignored will still be effective (Dörner 1989). Inadequate problem constructions thus return in the form of unexpected consequences when strategies are implemented in the real world (Böhret 1990). This means that for processes of socio-ecological transformation, we face fundamental uncertainty about the effects of policy interventions or management decisions (see Dobuzinskis 1992; Stacey 1996).

The only way 'out' of this dilemma is to remain within it – but to do so consciously: to accept that there will always be a high degree of ignorance and uncertainty connected to societal action within socio-ecological systems. Unintended consequences will persist because no comprehensive and exact model for the prediction of socio-ecological dynamics is possible. With a growing impact through the scale and depth of human intervention, a high probability of unintended consequences needs to be assumed as an essential condition of problem-solving strategies. This would mean that ignorance and uncertainty are actively dealt with rather than being denied by pretending complete knowledge and the existence of 'best solutions' (Walker et al. 2001).

A second requirement for the adequate treatment of sustainability problems can therefore be stated: because of inherent uncertainty about long-term dynamics and systemic effects, strategies as well as cognitive, institutional and technological structures need to be adaptive to allow for error and learning. This process necessitates the capacity to respond to unexpected effects and developments. Strategies should feature experimentation, monitoring and evaluation so that they may respond systematically to new experiences, altered interpretations and changed circumstances.

**Path dependency**

In addition to being unpredictable, socio-ecological developments and the effects of human activity within them feed into a continuous process of structural changes. These ongoing transformations are sometimes more subtle, hidden in the background of system structures, and sometimes more visible as in the overthrowing of established patterns. Increasingly, it is human activity that shapes world development – including its ecological dimension – even when it is not the intention to do so. The global climate is a prominent example. Deep-rooted changes associated with modernisation cannot be attributed to particular policies or other strategies. Instead, such changes are brought about as the aggregate and long-term effect of unsuspected daily practices in production, consumption and political regulation (Rip and Kemp 1998). Metaphorically speaking, one could say that future socio-ecological system structures grow behind the backs of the actors who create them.

In this continuous process of development, patterns emerge in which social values and institutions, technology and ecological systems become interdependent. Positive feedback may occur between developments in technology, corporate organisation, regulation, consumption habits and ecological factors. This response leads to a mutual stabilisation of the various elements within a given socio-ecological regime (compare the notion of regime in Kemp 1994). In addition to stabilisation, positive feedback can also give rise to structural dynamics that give regions or key industrial sectors a 'life of their own' beyond the control of any single actor. Initially minor changes and marginal developments may evolve into massive structural configurations that then restrict the variety of directions open to future changes. The cognitive, institutional, technical and economic patterns thus established become a selection environment for innovations and future change. In this way, socio-ecological transformation is path dependent. Future developments are influenced, enabled and constrained by structures that have grown out of particular historical developments. Both the fossil fuel-based electricity system and the individual transport-based mobility system are examples of such path dependency. Even the renewable energy component within the electricity system can be seen as a regime developing according to its own path dependency.

Path dependency imposes severe constraints on the transformations needed to achieve sustainability. Because certain social and technological functions must be maintained, revolutionary disruptions are to be avoided. This means that even when an extreme hazard of certain regimes become apparent – as is now the case with greenhouse gas emissions from fossil-fuel electricity generation – it takes great effort, much time and high costs to work against the dynamics of system development and shift it to a different trajectory. Though some sophisticated strategies are being developed to counteract these rigidities and to induce and modulate system innovations or regime shifts systematically, the prospects for success remain uncertain. For some problems, long lead times of as much as 50 years may simply be too long to motivate change. This underscores the importance of shaping new technologies, social practices and institutional arrangements at an early stage of their development while they are still malleable. Later they may become stabilised through manifold interconnections within their contexts. It remains a dilemma that at this early stage impacts are not known yet and cannot always be predicted (Collingridge 1980). However, some alternative paths of future development and possible impacts can be anticipated using methods such as scenario forecasting.

Sustainable development therefore requires careful anticipation of the long-term systemic effects of ongoing actions and developments and assessment of the resulting paths. Due to the complex dynamics of socio-ecological transformation, development paths cannot be predicted with certainty. Rather, anticipation refers to an explorative evaluation of alternative development paths that may be spurred by the actions that are taken today. Such actions should take into account various possible future developments. The general aim is to explore future opportunities for which a portfolio of options should be kept open and to avoid lock-in to trajectories that forestall the achievement of sustainable development. Such processes can, for example, be based on scenario construction, participatory modelling or policy exercises (Godet 1987; Elzen et al. 2002).

**Goal Formulation and the Ambiguity of Sustainable Development**

Sustainable development is often referred to as a normative orientation. Generically, however, it refers to a functional condition – a process that can be sustained over time without eroding its own foundations. From this perspective, the concept of sustainable development is normative only to the extent that it implies a value decision to sustain societal development on earth rather than to annihilate it. It can hence be rephrased as the long-term viability of socio-ecological systems. On this level of abstraction, not surprisingly, there is overwhelming consensus. But the crucial question is: how can societal development be sustained? Which kinds of practices or production and consumption structures are needed to sustain societal development? A prerequisite to answering this question would be to know and assess the full systemic consequences of alternative practices and the steps that would need to be taken to get there. This would require the ability to produce certain knowledge about complex social and ecological systems, the ways in which they are coupled, the dynamics of their development and the factors that influence that development. Viewed in this way, sustainable development is a cognitive, analytical question, not an evaluative, normative one. It could therefore be argued that the definition of targets for sustainability is not a matter of ethical discourse or politics, but of science.

In spite of the functional condition at the heart of the concept of sustainable development, however, other problem features, such as those elaborated in the paragraphs above, impede an 'objective' scientific clarification. The fundamental limitations to predicting socio-ecological system development mean that there can be no certain knowledge about the dynamics and thresholds critical to the resilience of societal systems and ecosystems, such as the concentration of greenhouse gases in the atmosphere or the unequal distribution of wealth in societies. It may be possible to determine parameters within which stable system behaviour can be expected with satisfying probability. These may be used to define 'corridors of sustainability' within which dangerous system change can be avoided by, for example, using indicators for emissions and living standards. In practice, however, sustainability assessment almost always deals with parameter values at the fringe of so-called sustainability corridors. For these issues uncertainty is high, thus the evaluation of risk becomes decisive. Risk assessment, however, is highly value- and world-view dependent. Evaluations of what is an acceptable risk differ greatly between actors and contexts. Several values come into play and may need to be traded off against each other. Such questions cannot be decided scientifically.

People hold different values. This also means that if they evaluate options, they make different decisions. Even if everybody agreed about what is good and what is bad, there would be differences in how certain values are ranked. This is especially relevant for sustainability assessment since equally legitimate goals – such as social justice, the reduction of environmental risk or economic viability – can only seldom be achieved simultaneously and to the same extent. Sustainability problems concern many differentiated social contexts – such as everyday family life, technology development laboratories and global business – in which particular value structures are dominant. Value trade-offs are therefore a common characteristic in the daily practice of dealing with sustainability and they effectively feed social disputes about what is sustainable and what is not. These disputes, however, can only partially be resolved scientifically, but also need to be addressed with social discourse or political decision.

Taken together, this means that sustainable development necessarily remains a contested concept. Its substantial content – a definition of the structure and the parameters of socio-ecological systems that can sustain their development – cannot be scientifically determined as 'objective knowledge' but will always incorporate normative valuations that only become ascertained in the process of social interaction. Sustainability as an orientation for societal development therefore delivers ambiguous goals. It may not be possible to eliminate the inherent discrepancies that exist between different goals or to define a clear ranking order by way of rational argumentation and empirical evidence. Social conflicts are inherent in the concept and need to be carried out with it.

Another aspect is that sustainability goals cannot be determined once and for all. Because substantial notions of sustainability are built on the basis of uncertain knowledge and social evaluation, they must be expected to change over time. Knowledge about socio-ecological system dynamics changes with scientific progress and with it the public articulation of everyday experiences of societal change. Moreover, value changes are endogenous to the process of socio-ecological transformation. They may lose importance precisely because they are being followed successfully. And there is no way to know what the needs of future generations will be.

Sustainability is thus an ambiguous and moving target that can only be ascertained and followed through processes of iterative, participatory goal formulation. In principle, sustainability goals and assessments cannot be determined permanently, but only through participatory processes that

need to be carried out for specific assessment situations. The broad participation of affected societal actors in the process of goal formulation is
necessary, because their values and respective perception of problems constitutes a basic condition of sustainable social development.

**Strategy Development and Distributed Influence**

A third feature of shaping sustainable transformation is related to the
implementation of strategies. Even if certain knowledge about socio-
ecological systems, clear goals and defined conditions for sustainability
could be taken as given, specific difficulties with implementation must still
be addressed. These refer to the distribution of capacities to influence the
direction of socio-ecological transformation. Those capacities are at the disposal of a broad range of actors. Societal development is not steered from
a single point, but from the interaction of state actors and interest groups,
producers and consumers, scientists and the media, just to name a few. To
influence long-term societal change, it is necessary to coordinate the actions
of various actors at different places along the lines of collective strategies.
  The fact that influence is dispersed is a general characteristic of governance in modern societies rather than an exclusive property of sustainability problems. There is a growing awareness of this, which is evident in the
shift, with regard to societal management, from government to governance
(Kooiman 1993; Rhodes 1996). The capacity to influence societal change is
distributed between different governance levels, for example, the nation
state and the EU, different functional domains – such as production, consumption and political regulation – and between different actors within
these domains (Schneider and Kenis 1996; Mayntz 1998; Kohler-Koch and
Eising 1999). Public officials are only one type of actors among several,
although they are equipped with democratic legitimacy as a special source
of power. Moreover, the competencies of the state are fragmented into disparate bodies such as governmental departments, regulatory agencies,
political parties and so on that often have different positions on issues concerning sustainable development. These conditions have to be taken as a
starting point for strategy formulation and implementation. Of course,
differences among governance situations do exist with respect to the extent
to which resources for control are dispersed and whether one actor, such
as the head of government, or a small coalition of actors, hold sufficient
power to make other actors follow a collective strategy. Generally, however,
the coordination of different actors' strategies cannot be taken for granted,
but it needs to be asserted anew for each specific problem.
  Control capacities regarding problems of sustainable development are,
in general, particularly widely distributed because they touch upon the

fundamental institutional and technological structures of modern society. Structural innovations are highly contingent upon a multitude of factors in the hands of many different actors – more so than governance processes that take place within established structural frameworks.

There are no established, overarching competencies and procedures for shaping structural, 'governance of governance' change. Transformation thus appears to happen uncontrolled as a result of daily interactions between consumers, producers, policy makers, researchers, journalists and various other actors. Actors involved in shaping socio-ecological transformation follow their own vital interests, partly in cooperation and partly in conflict. And they each have power over specific resources to enforce their strategies. Transformation, ultimately, results from the intended and unintended effects of these fuzzy interactions. In contrast to 'normal' policy arenas such as health or energy, the governance of transformation is not institutionalised. This is also the case for informal policy networks in which all important actors work towards a collective strategy for sustainable development.

Distributed control capacities thus have to be taken into account when devising strategies for sustainable development. In shaping socio-ecological transformation, it is necessary to coordinate heterogeneous actors. Such coordination cannot rely on institutionalised hierarchies, but must take place in networks in which the perception of problems, the interests and the practical knowledge of the various stakeholders become linked together in processes of interactive strategy development.

## STRATEGY ELEMENTS OF REFLEXIVE GOVERNANCE

The basic problems of shaping sustainable development have been outlined in the preceding paragraphs. From that discussion of the resulting difficulties for system analysis, goal formulation and strategy implementation, we have derived and briefly discussed particular requirements for strategies of reflexive governance. Compiled into a strategic framework, those requirements can be taken as a reference for discussing governance innovations needed for sustainable development. Table 1.1 gives an overview.

### Integrated (Transdisciplinary) Knowledge Production

Sustainability problems require integrated concepts. Since the problem of sustainable development is one of unintended side-effects, different perspectives that specialise in particular aspects of the world such as economics, politics, culture, technology and ecology need to work together to

*Table 1.1   Strategy elements of reflexive governance*

| Aspect of problem treatment | System analysis | | Goal formulation | | Strategy implementation |
|---|---|---|---|---|---|
| Specific problem features | Co-evolution of heterogenous elements across multiple scales (society, technology, ecology) | Uncertainty and ignorance about transformation dynamics and effects of intervention | Path-dependency of structural change, high societal impact | Sustainability goals involve value trade-offs, are endogenous to transformation | Capacities to influence transformation are distributed among actors |
| Strategy requirement | Trans-disciplinary knowledge production | Experiments and adaptivity of strategies and institutions | Anticipation of long-term systemic effects of measures | Iterative participatory goal formulation | Interactive strategy development |

define problems and perform analysis without exclusions. This refers to both the involvement of different scientific disciplines and the participation of actors from other subsystems of society. Problem definition and analysis for promoting sustainable development must be based on integrated knowledge produced in relation to the relevant perspectives.

**Adaptivity of Strategies and Institutions**

Because it is impossible to predict socio-ecological transformation accurately and because underlying values may change, solutions to the sustainable development problem cannot be defined *ex ante*. Particular strategies, even if they appear to be the best solution from the perspective of current problem definitions, must therefore be seen as hypotheses that are to be probed in practical interaction with the world. This requires that the effects are thoroughly monitored and that strategies, policy programmes and the respective institutions can be adapted according to experience and learning. Responsiveness and adaptability of social and technical structures can therefore serve as procedural criteria for sustainable development.

**Anticipation of the Long-term Systemic Effects of Action Strategies**

Within socio-ecological system dynamics, effects may appear detached from their causes. The repercussions of action strategies often occur at different places – in different social subsystems or in other parts of the world – and appear long after the triggering event took place. If system boundaries of space and time are drawn restrictively, problem analysis and the assessment of action strategies are likely to ignore important effects. Positive feedback dynamics that may lead to increasing self-stabilisation of undesired development paths, or 'lock-in' are particularly important with respect to socio-technical development (Arthur 1997; Pierson 2000). Lock-in can be avoided through the construction of explorative scenarios that integrate the perceptions and expectations of various actors. Such scenarios raise awareness of a range of interdependent factors that feed into the process of societal development and can highlight the structural dynamics that may be triggered by seemingly minor decisions. Governance for sustainable development should therefore pursue the systematic and interactive anticipation of indirect effects and long-term dynamics linked to present actions.

**Iterative Participatory Goal Formulation**

Sustainability goals cannot be defined objectively once and for all. This would require ascertainment of the necessary conditions for the long-term viability of socio-ecological systems. Involved risk assessments and trade-offs of values cannot be decided scientifically but only through social discourse or political decisions. Moreover, values may change in the course of transformation processes. Sustainability goals thus constitute ambiguous and moving targets. This needs to be taken into account in participatory processes for formulating sustainability goals. Goals need to be revised regularly to adapt to changing values and perceptions of problems in the course of transformation.

**Interactive Strategy Development**

Socio-ecological transformation is an outcome of social interactions. These interactions cut across institutionalised policy fields and functional domains such as production, consumption, regulation, research or the media. A broad range of heterogeneous actors is involved who follow their own interests and have control over specific resources of influence. Government and other public actors are only one type of actor among many, although they are equipped with political legitimacy as a special source of influence. To shape transformation processes, diverse actions have to be aligned in a collective strategy. Strategies therefore have to be developed in interaction with relevant stakeholders to integrate their know-how and resources and assure support for implementation.

## REFLEXIVE GOVERNANCE IN DISCUSSION – OVERVIEW OF THE CHAPTERS

At the beginning of this chapter, we claimed that reflexive governance provides a framework that can connect various concepts and practices of governance for sustainable development. We also stated the hypothesis that many recent governance innovations, which can be described and analysed with respect to the framework of reflexive governance, are related to the discourse of sustainable development and can be considered a practical consequence of the concept itself. The following chapters of this volume present evidence for these assertions. They provide theoretical reflections on the concept of reflexive governance and in-depth analyses of governance processes in various applied fields of societal problem handling, from research management to global politics. The chapters are organised so that they lead from general and abstract treatment of reflexive governance to more concrete empirically-grounded analyses of governance practice.

In Part One, Ulrich Beck, John Grin and Arie Rip take this introduction as a starting point for reflections on the concept of reflexive governance.

In so doing, they establish linkages between reflexive governance and other strands of theoretical discourse such as transnationalisation of governance, policy analysis, co-evolution and risk assessment. They also work out some critical aspects and articulate further conceptual questions about reflexive governance.

Ulrich Beck elaborates on aspects of how reflexive modernisation affects the very categories in which politics is conceived and discussed. He recaptures the theory of second modernity with an emphasis on ambiguity, uncertainty and unpredictability and the resulting demands for a new logic of political action. Sustainable development plays a role in this context as it eclipses 'old shared self-evidences of politics'. Beck frames reflexive governance as a new political theory, based on the critique of 'methodological nationalism' that evolves around the idea of negatively motivated processes of global social integration arising from the handling of risks ('global risk communities'). Against the background of an outline of elements of such a theory, he sketches the dynamics of 'rule-altering politics' linked to it and articulates a plea for 'cosmopolitan realism' as a guiding vision for the self-transformation of the state under conditions of reflexive governance.

In the next chapter, John Grin explores reflexive modernisation as a governance issue. He elaborates on a governance approach with which reflexive modernisation can be promoted in practice – against existing structures of simple modernity that 'fight back'. His argument is based on empirical studies of Dutch agriculture, where he sees sustainable development as a form of reflexive modernisation, focusing on risks and side-effects that concern ecological, animal welfare and human health aspects. He proposes an approach where sustainable development is defined through a combination of broad principles set by the institutions of representative democracy and concrete practices developed by those who are involved locally. To orchestrate diverse efforts at innovation, he proposes the organisation of trial-and-error learning complemented by visions of attainable futures that can serve as a functional equivalent to institutions while existing ones undergo transformation.

Arie Rip introduces a perspective on reflexive governance rooted in a co-evolutionary understanding of societal and technological development. He emphasizes *de facto* governance in the form of cognitive and institutional patterns that are the unintended outcomes of interactions that have dynamics of their own. He argues that steering actors are inside and part of changing *de facto* governance patterns, not outside. For illustration, he refers to regime shifts in science policy. With this insight he outlines a 'modulation' approach that embraces repair work, opening-up of learning spaces, macro-alignment of actors and anticipation-in-action. The latter core aspect is about enabling future-oriented interactions between actors who constitute each other's selection environment and supporting them to create narratives about unintended consequences, which then shape action. Rip emphasises maintaining diversity – in the form of grey zones and interstices within existing orders or actors who irritate, contest or are mischievous – as an important component of reflexive governance, since this is where the possibility for renewal lies. He concludes his chapter by reflecting on the possibility of strategies that take into account their own, partly unknown effects, which leads him to propose the articulation of ironies rather than strategies to guide attempts at shaping societal development.

Part Two comprises four chapters that introduce governance concepts responding specifically to uncertainty, ambiguity and limited control. In addition to theoretical discussion and programmatic conceptualisation, these chapters also report on practical experience with implementation. They can therefore be taken as empirical instances of reflexive governance, showing that quite radical changes in governance are actually occurring in connection with sustainable development. Moreover, they represent empirical examples in which the concept of reflexive governance can be probed and from which one can learn about the conditions of implementation in practice.

René Kemp and Derk Loorbach introduce the concept of transition management, which has been adopted by Dutch policy makers to work towards sustainability. They start from a discussion of the complex dynamics of change and propose transition management as a reflexive approach to organising the evolutionary processes that give rise to those dynamics. The approach relies on a model that views transitions as a multi-level system change based on interaction between innovations and on a two-pronged strategy that combines vision-constructing exercises with learning through experiments. The establishment of a transition arena for change-oriented stakeholder interaction is at the heart of practical arrangements for transition management. Kemp and Loorbach go on to discuss the concept of transition management with respect to the strategy elements of reflexive governance and with respect to practical transition policies in the Dutch energy sector.

Jan Sendzimir, Piotr Magnuszewski, Peter Balogh and Anna Vári elaborate on the approach of adaptive management and its application to the re-naturalisation of the Tisza River Basin in Hungary. They analyse flooding brought on by hydro-engineering and industrial agriculture as a major second-order problem for which no technical solution has proven feasible. The authors propose adaptive management as a framework for handling re-naturalisation. This builds on the recognition of uncertainty by organising management as a learning cycle that includes assessing what is known, developing policies as hypotheses, implementing management action as tests of hypotheses and monitoring and evaluating the results. They put special emphasis on the use of models and indicators in the context of reflexive governance.

Jan-Peter Voß, Bernhard Truffer, and Kornelia Konrad introduce sustainability foresight as a method for shaping socio-technical transformation and they document its application in the German utility sector. The method recognises that problem-solving approaches based on prediction and control cannot succeed because of uncertainty about system dynamics, ambiguity of sustainability assessment and fragmentation of the capacity to influence structural change. Instead, the authors turn towards feedback between expectations and action as an entry point for shaping transformation. They describe a three-step procedure that combines explorative scenario construction, mapping of values and modulation of innovation processes as a way to employ foresight as 'self-reflecting prophecy'. They conclude with a discussion of practical experience and lessons for reflexive governance.

Matthias Weber elaborates on an approach and methodology he terms adaptive foresight. He reviews recent developments in foresight methodology and strategic planning and illustrates them with examples from several areas of technology policy. The adaptive foresight approach is characterised by a sequence of steps including innovations system analysis, explorative scenario construction and assessment, and multiple backcasting and portfolio analysis. A key element is the development of a portfolio of real options, including technologies and policies, that are robust under evolving conditions or that can be adapted to them. Weber concludes with a critical discussion of unresolved questions within the framework of reflexive governance.

Part Three focuses on the dimensions of knowledge production and goal formulation and assessment. The three chapters gathered here deal with distinct but complementary issues. They provide an in-depth treatment of the epistemological issues involved in producing knowledge and assessing options regarding sustainable transformation. They also scrutinise practices and methods at the research programme level and interactions at the project level.

Andrew Stirling approaches the subject of reflexive governance with a focus on assessment problems. His chapter takes a specific definition of the terms 'unreflectiveness', 'reflection' and 'reflexivity' as its background. Unreflectiveness refers to conceptions and interventions that are restricted to the most obvious, instrumental attributes of an option. Reflection is when this narrow focus is widened to take account of the full range of attributes and all possible consequences of an option, including unforeseen consequences. Reflexivity is when attention is shifted to include also attributes of the actors who do the assessment as a constitutive element of appraisal. These attributes may include, for example, disciplinary perspectives, institutional interests, cultural values or economic priorities. Within this framework, Stirling conducts a critical discussion of conventional risk assessment and the uses of the precautionary principle in governance practice that leads him to the formulation of 'grounded perspectivism' as an understanding of the role of science in governance for sustainability that is both reflected and reflexive. He concludes with a discussion of practical strategies for precautionary foresight.

Katy Whitelegg compares research programmes for sustainable development in several European countries. She begins with a description of the general form of such research programmes: they combine different disciplines and types of knowledge, they are oriented towards the creation of social innovation networks and they assign to research the role of an active player in facilitating and defining societal change. Differentiating between general programme features, criteria for selecting projects and learning processes in project administration, she identifies elements of reflexive governance in research policy and highlights the influence of established structures of national research systems.

Céline Loibl moves from the programme to the project level of sustainability research. Her chapter deals with interaction processes in heterogeneous research teams and reflexive strategies of project management. It is based on two monitoring studies of research programmes in Austria, Switzerland and Germany. She emphasises the need to deal reflexively with the different cognitive, cultural and institutional contexts of actors from different domains of academic science and practice and with the challenges that are imposed by the embedding of research processes in changing societal contexts. For this purpose, she proposes elements of strategy for the reflexive governance of transdisciplinary research processes.

In Part Four of the book, attention shifts from knowledge production and assessment to issues of technology development and policy implementation. The four chapters in this section provide in-depth analyses of the introduction of new technologies and institutional arrangements in energy, water, raw material production and agriculture and assess to what extent they represent practical instances of reflexive governance.

Adrian Smith investigates the processes in which radical, grassroots experiments with new technologies can contribute to sustainable system innovations. For this purpose he compares the concept of strategic niche management with rather different niche-based concepts articulated by the Alternative Technology Movement in the 1970s. This leads him to emphasise the problem of conflicting world views in integrated knowledge production, the constraining effect of context conditions on carrying out experiments and the need for learning in niche developments to be complemented by top-down policy changes if experiments are to lead to system changes.

Bas van Vliet uses the concept of reflexive governance to evaluate two cases in which new sanitation systems were tested for implementation in the Netherlands. He finds that differences in outcomes can be related to the inclusion of social and infrastructural aspects in knowledge production, the extension of experimentation to include social arrangements, the adoption of a broad socio-technical systems perspective in anticipation, the development of goals by users and providers and the organisation of strategy development as an interactive process.

Philipp Spaeth, Harald Rohracher, Matthias Weber and Ines Oehme undertake the evaluation, from a reflexive governance perspective, of a project in Austria supporting socio-technical change in materials production. Basing their analysis on a detailed description of the process derived from a participatory scenario building with stakeholders involved in diverse R&D projects, they identify important prerequisites and pitfalls of reflexive governance in application. These findings highlight the nature of motivational and institutional constraints on stakeholders engaging in participatory governance, the need for coordination and adequate framework conditions in carrying out experiments and the need for institutional backing for initiators and moderators of reflexive governance processes.

Franziska Wolff scrutinises global policies for agrobiodiversity in terms of reflexive governance. She identifies various instances of reflexive strategies in institutional arrangements such as the 'ecosystems approach' under the Convention of Biological Diversity, participatory breeding, farmers' rights in the International Seed Treaty, farmers' field schools, and so on. As a general assessment, however, she concludes that many provisions for reflexive governance lack implementation and have limited effect, which she explains results from conflicting beliefs and adverse constellations of interest and power. Wolff identifies inherent flaws of participatory governance and stresses the need to consider conflict regulation rather than problem-handling as lessons for reflexive governance.

In the concluding chapter, Jan-Peter Voß, René Kemp and Dierk Bauknecht undertake a reassessment of the concept of reflexive governance in the light of the findings and discussion throughout the chapters of the book. They provide a discussion of critical points that have been raised with respect to the concept as formulated in the introduction and revise the concept accordingly. Four issues are addressed in depth: (1) The relationship between reflexive modernisation, reflexive governance and sustainable development is worked out more precisely: sustainable development is posited as a *chiffre* by which reflexive modernisation is politically negotiated.

(2) The concept of reflexive governance is extended by a differentiation of governance levels: shifting boundaries of governance systems and multi-level interaction. (3) Criteria for evaluating reflexive governance are introduced: process-based criteria to monitor the symmetry of interaction. Finally, (4) the focus of reflexive governance on exploration and opening up with respect to complexity, ambiguous goals and multiple options is critically, but constructively, taken up in a typology of different ways to combine it with procedures for exploitation and closing down: balancing reflexive appraisal with action-oriented reduction of complexity.

## REFERENCES

Arthur, W.B. (1997), *Increasing Returns and Path Dependence in the Economy*, Ann Arbor, MI: University of Michigan Press.

Bechmann, G. and Frederichs, G. (1996), 'Problemorientierte forschung: zwischen politik und wissenschaft', in G. Bechmann (ed.), *Praxisfelder der Technikfolgenforschung: Konzepte, Methoden, Optionen*, Frankfurt am Main/New York: Campus, pp. 1–21.

Beck, U. (1993), *Die Erfindung des Politischen*, Frankfurt am Main: Suhrkamp.

Beck, U. (1994), 'The reinvention of politics: towards a theory of reflexive modernization', in U. Beck, A. Giddens and S. Lash (eds), *Reflexive Modernization*, Cambridge: Polity Press, pp. 1–55.

Beck, U., W. Bonss and C. Lau (2003), 'The theory of reflexive modernization: problematic, hypotheses and research programme', *Theory, Culture & Society*, **20**, 1–33.

Bergmann, M. (2003), 'Indikatoren für eine diskursive evaluation transdisziplinärer forschung', *Technikfolgenabschätzung – Theorie und Praxis*, **12** (1), 65–75.

Böhret, C. (1990), *Folgen: Entwurf für eine aktive Politik gegen schleichende Katastrophen*, Opladen: Leske + Budrich.

Byrne, D. (1998), *Complexity Theory and the Social Sciences: An Introduction*, London/New York: Routledge.

Collingridge, D. (1980), *The Social Control of Technology*, London: Frances Pinter.

Conrad, J. (1997), 'Nachhaltige entwicklung: ein ökologisch modernisiertes modell der moderne?', in K.-W. Brand (ed.), *Nachhaltige Entwicklung: Eine Herausforderung an die Soziologie*, Opladen: Leske+Budrich.

Dobuzinskis, L. (1992), 'Modernist and postmodernist metaphors of the policy process: control and stability vs. chaos and reflexive understanding', *Policy Sciences*, **25**, 355–80.

Dörner, D. (1989), *Die Logik des Misslingens: Strategisches Denken in komplexen Situationen*, Reinbek bei Hamburg: Rowohlt Verlag.

Elzen, B., F. Geels, P. Hofman and K. Green (2002), 'Socio-technical scenarios as a tool for transition policy: an example from the traffic and transport domain', paper presented at the workshop *Transitions to Sustainability through System Innovations*, University of Twente, Enschede 29 October.

Funtowicz, S., J.R. Ravetz and M. O'Connor (1998), 'Challenges in the use of science for sustainable development', *International Journal of Sustainable Development*, **1** (1), 99–107.

Gallopín, G.C., S. Funtowicz, M. O'Connor and J.R. Ravetz (2001), 'Science for the 21st century: from social contract to the scientific core', *International Journal of Social Science*, **168**, 219–29.

Gladwell, Malcolm (2000), *The Tipping Point: How Little Things Can Make a Difference*, Boston, New York, London: Little, Brown and Company.

Gleick, J. (1998), *Chaos: Making a New Science*, London: Vintage.

Godet, M. (1987), *Scenarios and Strategic Management*, London: Butterworth.

Hirsch Hadorn, G. (2003), *Unity of Knowledge in Transdisciplinary Research for Sustainability*, retrieved from http://greenplanet.eolss.net on 20.09.2003.

Jahn, T. and P. Wehling (1998), 'Gesellschaftliche Naturverhältnisse: Konturen eines theoretischen Konzepts', in K.-W. Brand (ed.), *Soziologie und Natur: Theoretische Perspektiven*, Opladen: Leske+Budrich, pp. 75–95.

Kemp, R. (1994), 'Technology and the transition to environmental sustainability: the problem of technological regime shifts', *Futures*, **26**, 1023–46.

Kohler-Koch, B. and R. Eising (eds) (1999), *The Transformation of Governance in the European Union*, London: Routledge.

Kooiman, J. (1993), *Modern Governance: New Government-Society Interactions*, London: Sage.

Luhmann, N. (1990), *Ökologische Kommunikation: Kann die moderne Gesellschaft sich auf ökologische Gefährdungen einstellen?*, Opladen: Westdeutscher Verlag.

Matthes, F. (2002), 'Nachhaltigkeit als politisches Konzept', *Gaia*, **11** (2), 91–5.

Mayntz, R. (1998), 'New challenges to governance theory', European University Institute, Jean Monnet Chair Paper RSC, No. 98/50, Florence: European University Institute

Mayntz, R. (1999), 'Funktionelle Teilsysteme in der Theorie sozialer Differenzierung', in R. Mayntz (ed.), *Soziale Dynamik und politische Steuerung: Theoretische und methodologische Überlegungen*, Frankfurt am Main/New York: Campus, pp. 38–69.

Nowotny, H., P. Scott and M. Gibbons (2001), *Re-thinking Science: Knowledge and the Public in an Age of Uncertainty*, Cambridge: Polity Press.

Pierson, P. (2000), 'Increasing returns, path dependence, and the study of politics', *American Political Science Review*, **94** (2), 251–67.

Rhodes, R.A.W. (1996), 'The new governance: governing without government', *Political Studies Association*, 1996 (XLIV), 652–67.

Rip, A. (1998), 'The dancer and the dance: steering in/of science and technology', in A. Rip (ed.), *Steering and Effectiveness in a Developing Knowledge Society*, Utrecht: Uitgeverij Lemma BV, pp. 27–50.

Rip, A. and R. Kemp (1998), 'Technological Change', in S. Rayner and E.L. Malone (eds), *Human Choice and Climate Change*, Columbus, OH: Batelle Press, pp. 327–99.

Schimank, U. (1988), 'Gesellschaftliche teilsysteme als akteurfiktionen', *Kölner Zeitschrift für Soziologie und Sozialpsychologie*, **40** (3), 619–39.

Schimank, U. (1996), *Theorien Gesellschaftlicher Differenzierung*, Opladen: Leske+Budrich.

Schneider, V. and P. Kenis (1996), 'Verteilte kontrolle: institutionelle steuerung in modernen gesellschaften', in P. Kenis and V. Schneider (eds) *Organisation und Netzwerk*, FrankFurtam Main and New York: Campus, pp. 7–43.

Stacey, R.D. (1996), 'Management and Science of Complexity', *Research-Technology Management*, **39** (3), 8–10.

Thompson Klein, J., W. Grossenbacher-Mansuy, R. Häberli, A. Bill, R.W. Scholz and M. Welti (2001), *Transdisciplinarity: Joint Problem Solving among Science, Technology, and Society: An Effective Way for Managing Complexity*, Basel/Boston/Berlin: Birkhäuser.

Walker, W.E., A.S. Rahman and J. Cave (2001), 'Adaptive Policies, Policy Analysis, and Policy-Making', *European Journal of Operational Research*, **128**, 282–9.

WCED (1987), *Our Common Future: Report of the UN World Commission on Environment and Development*, Oxford: Oxford University Press.

UNCED (1992), Agenda 21: *Report of the United Nations Conference on Environment and Development*, United Nations.

# Reflections on reflexive governance

# 2.   Reflexive governance: politics in the global risk society

**Ulrich Beck**

## INTRODUCTION

The question raised by this contribution to the present volume is that of an alteration, at the beginning of the twenty-first century, to the very foundations of politics. Its thesis is the following: we are witnessing today a meta-transformation of the political. In other words, the change we see is neither a change occurring within an established system of politics nor a change from one such system to another. Rather, the change is one that affects the very language in which 'politics' is conceived and discussed. We require new, exploratory ideas and schemata, for example, 'reflexive governance', in order to describe, understand, observe and explain the shifts now occurring in the very foundations of political action.

States alone no longer constitute the arena of collective action. In other words, political actors are no longer assigned and prescribed, in and by their respective state, the space and the 'rules of the game' – including the indispensable social institutions for decision and for the execution of decisions – of their actions. Rather, a question is raised both in practice and in reality as to the degree in which this meta-transformation of the political is becoming reflexive, or self-confronting. That is, to what extent are the foundations of state power and of state-based politics themselves becoming subject to global–political and global–economic metamorphosis? The scenario whereby nation states, and the system of international relations between such states, determine the space of collective political action is presently falling apart under both internal and external pressures. This collapsing system is being partially covered up by and has actually already been, to some extent, replaced by a more complex system. This new system, which is transgressing former borders and boundaries, is altering the rules governing political power and the handling of political problems; this is the rule-system of 'reflexive governance'.

What does this actually mean? I shall elucidate this in three stages. First, I will give a general sketch of the theory of a 'second modernity'. I will then apply this theory specifically to political action in order to end up at the concept of 'reflexive governance'. Finally, using hypothetical prognoses, I shall present certain conclusions relative to a 'cosmopolitan realism'.

## THEORY OF A 'SECOND MODERNITY'

For purely pragmatic and methodological reasons – that is, without any intent to hypostatize the terms in question into categories of ontological status and significance – I make a distinction in this essay between a 'first' and a 'second' modernity. The present context does not permit a full description of the premises from which I proceed in making this distinction, let alone all the fields in which and topics to which this distinction finds application. In fact, the 'second' modernity can be traced from the sphere of science and technology, through that of social inequality, lifestyles and forms of biography, the organization of work, forms of the interrelation of capital and enterprise, up to the state and politics in both national and transnational contexts (Beck and Bonß 2001; Beck and Lau 2004). Here, I shall consider only some elements of the theory which are important for the concept of 'reflexive governance'.

Speaking very generally, the theory of a second modernity can be divided into three related complexes: the theorem of the global risk society, the theorem of forced individualization and the theorem of pluridimensional globalization. All three theorems represent developments of the same line of argument such that each interprets and reinforces, and is interpreted and reinforced by, the others. 'Global risk society', 'individualization' and 'globalization' (or, alternatively, 'cosmopolitization') are conceptionalized as radicalized forms of a dynamic of modernization. As the twentieth century gives way to the twenty-first century, this dynamic, which is turning back reflexively – in the sense of a kind of 'self-confrontation' – upon itself, is now dissolving the familiar formulae of simple modernity.

The 'first' – the 'classical' or 'high' – modernity, which is specifically associated with industrial society, was characterized by a logic of organization and action, which is only now, at a time when its practical relevance is diminishing, becoming clearly recognizable as such. This logic involved establishing of extremely fine divisions between categories of people, things and activities and making distinctions between spheres of action and forms of life such as facilitating an unambiguous, institutional ascription of competence, responsibility and jurisdiction. Today, the limitations of this logic of fine division and unambiguousness are becoming ever more evident. It is proving increasingly difficult to justify and substantiate, and in some areas it has completely collapsed. This logic of unambiguousness – one might speak here, metaphorically, of a 'Newtonian' social and political theory of the first modernity – is now being replaced by logic of ambiguity – which one might envisage, to extend the metaphor, in terms of a new 'Heisenbergian fuzziness' of the social and the political.

For the institutions of advanced Western societies, the transition to a 'second' – a reflexive, in the sense of a self-confronting – modernity means the challenge of developing a new logic of action and decision, which no longer finds its orientation in the principle 'either this or that' but rather in the principle 'this and that both'. In various spheres – from science and technology through the state and the economy, individualized life-worlds and social structures, up to the level of the present debates and confrontations regarding the new ordering of global politics – one thing is becoming more and more apparent: that great body of distinctions, standardizations, norms and role-systems essential to the very institutions of the first modernity can no longer be treated as valid; these elements describe the current normal condition of societies, states and inter-state relations less and less adequately. The reality we face today is rather that of a (more or less) acknowledged plurality in respect of forms of work, family life, lifestyle, political sovereignty and politics in general. We see the fusion of formerly strictly separated spheres – as, for example, in the area of genetic engineering and the new risks attached to technology – and the growing obsolescence of old boundaries and divisions also in such areas as the organization of enterprises, movements in civil society, the legal systems of nation states and cultural identity (Beck 1993; Beck and Lau 2004). Consequently, it is quite generally true that spaces of action and experience have ceased to be exclusive. To return to a metaphor already up-to-date in the social sciences, we live in the 'era of flows': capital flow, cultural flow, flows of human beings, information and risks (the risk of terrorism being only the latest in the evolution of the global risk society).

We recognize the nature and extent of this fundamental transformation in noting how new key concepts – new semantics of conflict – are currently in the process of eclipsing, subverting and rendering open to new political possibilities the old shared languages and shared manifestations of the politics of the nation state. One of these universal 'magic words' is 'sustainable development'. Noteworthy here is how the demand for 'sustainability' has eclipsed or entirely displaced both the discourse of technical–economic 'progress' and that of 'Nature' and 'the destruction of Nature'. This talk of 'sustainable development', accusatory, exhortatory and ever more omnipresent, is an indication not only that the old shared manifestations regarding 'economic growth' and 'technological progress' have ceased to be perfect and immediate, but also that their proponents now find themselves very much on the defensive, forced to argue in favour of these erstwhile axioms and against alternatives to them, at every level of the process of industrial modernization.

Moreover, the heat of the debate about what 'sustainable development' actually is – or what it should be, what it implies and what it does not imply – is evidence of the degree to which so-called environmental problems have in fact long ceased to be seen and treated merely as problems of the 'world around' us and have become integrated into the social world itself, emerging in almost all social institutions (from traffic systems to architecture to the system of consumption), as political (ethical, economic, legal) conflicts. This is all the more the case as the very phrase 'sustainable development' harbours a potentially litigious contradiction: sustention and development, which is to say, development and non-development. Which of these two mutually exclusive demands actually imposes itself (or which of the two imposes itself to the greater, which to the lesser, degree) remains – as we are taught by a fundamental theorem of sociology – qua institutionalized contradiction a question to be decided in the arena of political power.

## On the Distinction Between the 'Reflection' and the 'Reflexivity' of Modernity

I speak, then, of a second, a reflexive modernization where modernization finds itself ever more occupied with the mastering of problems arising from the process of modernization itself. Here, it encounters certain limits of established problem-solving procedures: specifically, the limits to the possibility of applying the process of modernization to the side-effects of this very process. This is not without consequences for modernity's own self-understanding, which finds to an ever diminishing degree its foundation in simple formulae of control and supervision, of progress and of human welfare. It is a contention of the theory of a second modernity, however, that this reflexivity is not to be confused with reflection; rather, reflexivity tends to undermine the foundations of modern self-descriptions. It becomes a problem for reflection.[1]

The sociological theory of modernity stresses, still today, two forms of self-reference above all others as typical of this epoch of social development: namely, reflection and reflexivity. Often, these two forms of self-referentiality are treated as if they were identical, a practice which has led, particularly in the English-speaking world, to misunderstandings in the reception of the theory of a second, reflexive or self-confronting modernity (Giddens 1997). The transition, however, from the first – or industrial – modernity to the second modernity – the epoch of risk – is one which occurs unintentionally, imperceptibly and obligatorily, in the course of a process of modernization which, in accordance with a logic of latent side-effects, acquires its own independent dynamic. One might almost say that the social configurations characteristic of the global risk society arise as a consequence of the actual thought and action of human beings and institutions coming to prevail over the assumed manifestations of industrial society (the consensus regarding 'progress'; the abstraction from ecological consequences and perils; the optimism with respect to the limits of control and supervision). The global risk society is no option which might have, or might still be, chosen or rejected in a process of political debate. This societal form is rather one which arises due to the autonomous dynamic of processes of modernization which have acquired an impetus of their own and which are quite blind to consequences and quite deaf to warnings of danger. These processes, indeed, tend, taken as a whole, to latently engender various self-imperilments which go to delete, to transform and to politicize the foundations of that first modernity associated with industrial society.

## On the Distinction Between 'Second Modernity' and 'Post-Modernity'

What distinguishes a second modernity, so described, from post-modernity? Now, there are surely as many different kinds of post-modernism as there are post-modernists. The theory of a second modernity presupposes, indeed, and proceeds upon post-modernism's critique of a certain (namely, the 'first') modernity. On the other hand, a theory which conceives of itself specifically as a theory of the 'post-modern' tells us only what is not the case, not what is the case. My main criticism of the various forms of post-modernism, then, is the following: that the proponents of these theories have got deconstruction down to a fine art – without, however, taking the least care as to reconstruction; in other words, that they forget that the social sciences, no less than individual social actors, require, if they are really to understand and overcome the mischievous uncertainties and ambivalences arising in the present age, new, informative ideas of proven empirical validity. Measured by this requirement, the post-modern idea proves inadequate. It explains, indeed, why the old ways of perceiving modernity are no longer valid; but it does not even pose the question as to what concepts we need in order to describe, to analyse and to make ourselves masters of the new realities which are gradually being imposed.

It is, moreover, by no means the actual case that – as the theorists of post-modernity typically maintain, often in tones of celebration – all borders, boundaries and dualities are currently in the process of melting into air. On the contrary – and the insight into this truth is another feature which distinguishes the theory of a second modernity from theories of post-modernity – the collapse of the old boundaries and dualisms rather compels to a decision between alternatives. The fewer the number of boundaries and dualities, which confront the social actor as 'givens', the greater the obligation to take decisions, the greater the necessity to establish provisional moral constructions in the form of provisional divisions and distinctions. This is what is meant by 'politics of the boundary' (Beck et al. 2004).

All social actors – governments and political parties, international organizations, labour and capital, rich and poor, people of different religions and races – need to find, in this transnational field of forces, new positions for themselves, a necessity which cannot but result in profound fractures and conflicts. Financial and other burdens must be redistributed, goals redefined, new paths discovered, new alliances formed and visions developed of a future co-existence in a shared and single world. A key question, then, for our second modernity is: how, in a modern age characterized by the collapse of fixed and given boundaries, 'politics of the boundary' is to be defined, reconstructed and developed? Modernity, as I have said, gives rise, while undermining the institutionalized conventions which once formed the fixed foundations for social decisions, precisely thereby to pressures which oblige social actors to take decisions. The conflicts and confusions, which ensue from such dilemmas on all levels and in all contexts of social action, form and will continue to form the key problem of our second modernity and the central theme also of this second modernity's investigation by the social sciences.

**The Production of Uncertainty and the Acknowledgement of Ambivalence**

Returning to the distinction between reflexivity and reflection, it must be understood that, given the mere fact that the structures typical of classical, industrial modernity have been subverted and transformed, it by no means follows automatically that the society emerging from this subversion and transformation will be one which consciously reflects upon the changes which have produced it. Whether or not the dissolution of the structures of industrial society and their replacement by other structures will eventuate in a public and scientific reflection on how these changes affect us and this reflection in turn eventuate in a transformation of politics – whether, in other words, such changes will become an abiding topic for the mass media and mass political parties, a subject of public controversies or an issue in elections and reform programmes – this question is subject in the end to no confirmation or disconfirmation except an empirical one. Only time will provide an answer to it, depending as this answer does on many factors and conditions which cannot be predicted by any theory. Far, though, certainly from the self-dissolution and self-transformation of the first modernity's automatically and inevitably eventuating in modernity's reflection on itself, it is quite possible that these developments might issue rather in movements of a directly anti-modernizing nature.

The analytical core of the theory does not aim at raising sanguine hopes for the future but consists rather in a contention entirely morally neutral: namely, that reflexive – in the sense merely of blindly self-confronting – modernization has led to a shaking of the foundations of our social world which can eventuate either in an animus against modernity per se which will add grist to the mill of neo-nationalism or, should things happen to turn out quite differently, in the development of new capacities for reflection and in a refoundation and reinvention of the political, apt, at least in principle, to mitigate or even entirely to solve, in continuing by new means the gradual process of social rationalization, the problems thrown up by moderni-zation. There thus emerges at the very cutting edge of modernity, and as a consequence of the modernization process itself, the challenge: how am I, how are we, to deal with the uncertainty and unpredictability which is pro-duced as a result of societal rationalization precisely in its most advanced stage?

This question is of vital political importance because, in the risk society, it is precisely by the guardians of law, order, prosperity and freedom that these latter values have come to be most endangered. It is of vital existen-tial importance because this endangerment is one which extends into the deepest privacy of the private individual, placing in question his manner of life and indeed his life tout court. Thus, the transformation of the over-looked side-effects of industrial production into ecological crisis-breeders of global import is anything but a problem of 'the environment', of 'the world around us' alone, rather, it is a profound institutional crisis of indus-trial modernity, and of its typical political form of the nation state itself. So long as we persist in the attempt to grasp these developments in terms of the conceptual apparatus provided by the first modernity they will seem no more than regrettable side-effects of an apparently funda-mentally responsible and calculable human action, and their actual propen-sity to bring, through their consequences, the whole system of industrial modernity to collapse will remain unrecognized. It is only when seen and grasped from the perspective of the global risk society that their real and central significance shows forth, and shows a new self-definition and self-determination to be imperative for our society in the face specifically of the condition of modernity's self-confronting reflexivity.

In the phase of global risk society, the acknowledgement of the incalcu-lable nature of the perils unleashed by technical–industrial development compels to reflection upon the foundations of the social whole and to re-examination of accepted conventions and of shared criteria of rationa-lity. Society becomes, where it begins to understand itself as a risk society, *reflective* (in the narrower sense of the word). That is to say, society itself becomes, for itself, a theme and a problem. What, at bottom, tends to disturb here might be called 'the return of uncertainty into society'. By this is meant, in the first instance, that ever more social conflicts are treated not, as hitherto, as problems of social ordering but rather as problems of social risk. The defining quality of such risk-problems is that they are not susceptible of univocal solutions but are rather distinguished by an essential ambivalence which may indeed be, in most cases, theoretically grasped by recourse to calculations of probability but cannot, by such calculations, be eliminated. It is in this inherent ambivalence that there consists the difference between risk-problems and problems of social ordering, the latter being per definitionem oriented toward unambiguousness and decidability. So that 'the return of uncertainty into society' implies in the second instance also an almost inevitable dwindling, in the face of the multiplication of ambiguities or of problems susceptible of being handled only in terms of the logic of 'this and that both', of faith in the project of the technical construction and ordering of the social.

Risks not only presuppose decisions but also promote them – in individual cases as on the level of general principle. Questions of risk cannot be 'translated' into terms which will render them questions of social ordering, because these latter questions tend as it were to 'choke' on the pluralism immanent in questions of risk and to metamorphose ultimately, unavowedly and despite whatever pseudo-objective statistical façades might be erected in the attempt to hide the fact, into questions of power and questions of subjective moral decision. In other words, questions of risk compel – or, put more cautiously, incite – to the 'recognition of ambivalence' (Zygmunt Bauman).

## THE POLITICAL THEORY OF A SECOND MODERNITY: REFLEXIVE GOVERNANCE

Not least in importance among the factors contributing to this dynamic of global risk society is the transformation in the nature of science itself. There was a time when science was something which took place in a laboratory – a spatially and temporally limited form of the process of scientific investigation. This equation of science with laboratory experiment has been rendered obsolete, however, by nuclear energy and the new systems of weaponry. Suddenly, the whole earth has become a laboratory – the risks are now as it were mobile, fluid, flowing over and under national and other boundaries. Genetically modified wheat, for instance, exemplifies, in its extreme mobility, these new difficulties. Modern science tends more and more to treat the whole world as its laboratory, thus spreading risks across the globe.

## The Critique of Methodological Nationalism

This point about the collapse of boundaries and the new mobility of risks has fundamental implications for the social sciences inasmuch as it helps us to the insight that sociology (as well as historiography, political science, jurisprudence, and so on) remain bogged down in a 'methodological nationalism'. What is this 'methodological nationalism', and why is it a problem?

Methodological nationalism rests on the assumption that 'modern society' and 'modern politics' are synonymous with a society and a politics organized in terms of nation states. The state is understood as creator, supervisor and guarantor of society. Societies (the number of which is equal to the number of nation states) are understood as mere containers, arising and subsisting in a space defined by the power of the state. This way of thinking, which equates societies with national societies and conceives of the former as by their nature territorially limited, is deeply ingrained in all that the social sciences understand by concepts and perspectives, by gathering and comparing data and conducting empirical research. It is, one may say, constitutive of the sociological imagination (Beck 2004).

We need, indeed, to distinguish clearly between two aspects of this problem. Where such dogmas are manifest in the words and attitudes of individual social actors, I speak of a 'national point of view'; where they prove to be implicit in the third-person-language and third-person-perspective of the social sciences, I speak of 'methodological nationalism'. This distinction between the perspective of subjects acting in society and the perspective of the social scientist is an important one because there is no logical connection between the two. The correspondence here is to be traced back merely to the similarity in the conditions of their historical emergence. The rise of the social sciences coincided with the rise of the nation-state, of the system of international politics and of nationalism. It is this specific historical involvement which alone accounts for the methodologically nationalist axioms upon which the social sciences proceed and which dictate that nation, state and society constitute the 'natural' social and political forms of the modern world.

At some point in the not too distant past (say, around the 1960s) there occurred a qualitative transformation in the perception of social order. This order ceased, at this time, to be understood primarily as a conflict centered on the production and distribution of goods; from then on, the primary issue became the contradiction between the production and distribution of bads and the claims to control raised by the established institutions of the nation states. This shift in the categories of self-perception threw modern societies' manner of organizing their own institutions and functions into a crisis of global interdependence which has expressed itself in phenomena of widely divergent political value and significance – climate change, global poverty, transnational terrorism, the BSE crisis, AIDS, and so on. This crisis of global interdependence I call the 'global risk society'. Also thrown into crisis by this shift are that social science and that political theory which, combining Karl Marx with Max Weber, attempt to understand modern society in terms of the categories 'capitalism' and 'rationalization'. It is this unleashing of perils and uncertainties engendered by the civilizing process itself and characterized above all by a global interdependence, as well as the dominance of a public, mass-media-dominated perception of risk, which constitutes a transition from one epoch into another.

**The Political Theory of Global Risk Society**

What distinguishes new risks from old risks and dangers and why must the dynamics of conflict typical of the global risk society be understood as a second, reflexive phase of radicalized modernization? These questions I intend to answer by means of ten theorems or characterizing clarifications:

1.  Global risks as social construction: one must clearly distinguish between, on the one hand, the (physical) event of the catastrophe (or ongoing process of destruction) and, on the other, the global risk as the increasingly boundless expectation of such catastrophes. Whether a possible destructive event counts as a global risk or not does not here depend only on the number of the dead and injured or the extent of the actual damage done to nature but is rather the expression of a career of social recognition. Concern for environmental issues, for example, was perceived for a long time as a quirk of the Germans; this is no longer the case since the Rio de Janeiro Conference of 1992. In other words, the ongoing process of destruction and the career of recognition which falls to the lot of a global risk are in no sense to be conceived of in terms of a cause–effect relationship; rather, process and risk have their places in opposite contexts and systems of meaning and must, as regards their actual causes and effects, be examined and understood quite separately from one another.

2.  Global risk as reflexive globality: global risks are a form of expression of global interdependence and they force, in turn, its pace of development. Sociologically speaking, this means an alteration in spatial and temporal relations; what was far away draws near, in the dimension

of time as well as space. In contrast to global chains of commodity or food production, which need not become objects of perception or awareness, the physical explosiveness of global risks and their attendant propensity to shatter all political boundaries ensures that they break as a rule into public awareness. One of their peculiarities consists in the combination they present of global interdependence and actual consciousness of global interdependence, that is, in their 'reflexive globality'.

3. The production of uncertainty: global risks possess a potential for destruction equal to, or possibly even greater than, that of wars (as is verified by the projections made of the consequences of gradual catastrophic climate change).

The paradigm of threats to national security characteristic of the Cold War has not indeed, since the end of this latter, become entirely obsolete; there still exist states which compete for territory and resources and pose military threats to one another. Nevertheless, the dangers which, since the end of the East–West conflict, are pressing ever more strongly into public perception are dangers of quite another sort. These dangers often involve no concretely definable perpetrator, no hostile intention, nor need any role be played in them by any military potential. The danger is not direct, intentional or certain, but rather indirect, unintentional and uncertain. In short, it is a question not of threats but of risks . . . We may say, then, that a risk to security is distinguished from a threat to security by the lack, in the former case, of any certainty of expectation, such certainty falling out of the equation wherever one or more of the quantities making up the classical security calculation – agent, intention, potential – becomes an unknown. Where this occurs, the simple threat triangle becomes an indefinite plurality of risk factors and the number of possible dangers increases exponentially. (Daase 2002: 15f)

An essential difference between the international system of the first modernity and that system of the second modernity which is less exactly to be described as 'international' consists in the fact that the old system was, in principle, calculable and predictable, since the states which composed it held each other in check, whereas the new system is in principle incalculable and unpredictable. This inasmuch as it not only happens to be the case that we do not know if and when some suicide bomber will fly an aircraft into an atomic power station and set off a reactor catastrophe, or if and when climate change will give rise to floods in this region or the devastation of landmasses in that; far more than this, we cannot ever possibly know such things, because here there can be no recourse even to calculations of probability. We are dealing here with 'unknown unknowns' (Beck 1996; Wehling 2001). In this respect, the international system of our second modernity is subject to transnational imperilments which are under-mining the stability of that state system which gradually emerged during the era of a first modernity.

4.  Uncertainty lends power to perception: the more obvious it becomes that global risks are insusceptible to being calculated or precisely predicted by scientific method, the more influence accrues to the per-ception of risk. The distinction diminishes and gradually vanishes between real risks and the perception of risk (Douglas and Wildavsky 1983). More important than all the ingenious probability scenarios of the experts becomes the question of who believes there to be a risk, and why. In other words: central importance accrues to the social–scientific investigation of cultural risk perception.

5.  Unclear lines of conflict: global risks mean the start of a meta-power-game involving the deconstruction and reconstruction of boundaries, rules, responsibilities, 'them-and-us' identities, spaces of action and action priorities. Paradoxical in all this is the fact that the ruling uncertainty, the indeterminability of the risk, also goes to create new certainties – for example, the clear conscience of those who being in possession of the global risk, while the risk-consciousness of the others is plainly paranoid, irrational, highly questionable and mis-leading as to their own real interests. The choice between different risks is also a choice between different visions of the world. Essentially involved in it are the grander questions of who is guilty and who inno-cent, whose star is in the ascendant and whose in decline – military force or human rights, the logic of war or the logic of peaceful accord. Adapting the famous phrase of Samuel P. Huntington, we might say that we are concerned, in the recent trans-Atlantic political disagree-ments, with a clash of risk cultures: the USA accuses Europe of suffering from ecological hysteria, while Europe accuses the USA of having succumbed to a hysterical fear of terrorism.

6.  The failure of national and international rule-systems: the phrase global risk 'society' must be understood in a specifically post-social sense, since there exist neither in national nor in international politics and society rules and institutions that can provide fixed procedures for dealing with these risks, for ranking them in terms of urgency or for developing political and military strategies to counter them. To this extent, there tends to be played out, in each specific conflict between different perceptions of risk, also a meta-power-game con-cerning what rules must be adopted in future with regard to such inde-terminate and illimitable risks.

7.  A new politics of uncertainty: global risks compel to a new politics of uncertainty. They make imperative a distinction between things which

lie by their nature beyond all possible control and things which happen in fact presently not to be under control. 'Dangers' in the pre-modern sense these are not, because they rest on decisions and therefore raise questions regarding the attribution of responsibility and the just distribution of blame and of costs. Political counter-measures are in every case seen to be imperative. Neither national nor international political authorities – and multi-national companies are often today in the same case – can point to the fatal uncontrollability of the modern world to absolve themselves of the obligation to take action; rather, they are placed by the discourse of risk conducted throughout the global public sphere under an absolutely irrecusable pressure to justify themselves by action. They are damned to counter-measures. This intense expectation of counter-action alone suffices to lend life to the contrafactual hypothesis of controllability, even when all available models of response prove inadequate. Not to take action in the face of recognized risks is politically out of the question – regardless of whether the measures taken do in fact minimize the risk, increase it or have no effect at all.

8. The politics of risk construction and the politics of risk minimization: here we must distinguish between two forms of 'risk politics', namely (A) the politics of risk construction (the social construction of risks) and (B) the politics of risk minimization (provision, prevention, minimization and appropriate cross-border intervention). (B) presupposes (A), while (A) helps to define (B)'s sphere of action. Both represent forms of the definition of reality: (A) on the cognitive level, (B) on the level of an actual moulding and remoulding of this reality by political action; (A) is a defining characteristic of sociological constructivism, (B) rather one of political–scientific realism.

9. Consequences for the social sciences: the global risk society poses new challenges not only to the politician and the man in the street but also to the practitioner of the social sciences. Not only must these sciences recognize that social interaction is no longer so clearly spatially and temporally defined as it was assumed to be in the old nation-state paradigm (critique of methodological nationalism). Global risk society also introduces them to a model of global socialization which is at odds with the traditional picture of positive social integration on the basis of shared norms and values, resting as it does upon the conflict around *negative* values (risks, crises, dangers of annihilation). Here, the issue is not so much the multiplication of uncontrollable risks of a sort apt to generate a global interdependence as the freeing of these risks from all formerly decisive boundaries – and this at once on the spatial, temporal and social plane.

On the spatial plane, we find ourselves confronted with risks which pay no regard to the borders of nation states or other political entities. Climate change, air pollution and holes in the ozone layer are matters that concern everybody (albeit in different ways). The same holds true on the temporal plane. Given the long latency period involved for problems such as the removal of nuclear waste or the effects of genetically manipulated foodstuffs these issues cannot be handled in the same manner as earlier industrial perils. Likewise on the social plane, a problem has emerged as regards the ascription of potential endangerment, and therefore also of ultimate liability. It is hard to establish who has been, in a legally relevant sense, the 'cause' of environmental pollution (or of a financial crisis), since such phenomena arise out of the confluence of the actions of many individuals. These dangers to civilization arising out of civilization present themselves as in large measure de-territorialized, and thereby difficult to trace back to 'guilty parties' and to check and control within the framework of an individual nation-state.

We must distinguish at least three different axes of conflict in the global risk society. The first turns on risks apt to generate a global interdependence and *ecological* in nature; these tend immediately and by their very nature to set a global dynamic in motion. The second turns on risks with a similar aptitude but economic in nature; these are at least initially susceptible of being individualized and dealt with within a national framework; thirdly, we have an axis turning on interdependence-generating risks of a specifically terrorist nature (Beck and Grande 2004). For all the differences between them, these three types of risk have one essential characteristic in common: they cannot be classified as external risks in the sense of risks arising solely from the world around humankind – the environment – but must rather be understood as consequences, deeds and uncertainties which, for all their posing threats to civilization, are clearly products of the human civilizing process itself. To this extent, such risks affecting civilization – in the double sense of risks to civilization arising from the process of civilization – have the potential to render keener a globally-shared consciousness of norms, to help establish a global public sphere and to facilitate the emergence of a 'cosmopolitan point of view' (Beck 2004). In the global risk society – such is my thesis – questions as to the causes of, and as to the persons or groups responsible for, global endangerments tend to spark new political conflicts, which tend in turn to promote, in and through the ensuing struggle over definitions and responsibilities, the emergence of an institutionalized cosmopolitanism.

Conflicts over civilization risks in the sense just described emerge, for example, where opinions diverge as to how far the industrialized countries have a right to demand that developing countries protect such important global resources as the rainforests, given that the former countries arrogate to themselves the lion's share of energy resources. A certain reasoning sees, indeed, in precisely such differences of opinion a reason not to speak here of a form of global socialization. But to reason so is to make the mistake of equating 'society' with 'consensus'. In fact, such conflicts themselves already have an integrative function, inasmuch as they make it clear that the solutions found will have to be cosmopolitan ones. Such solutions are hardly imaginable, however, except on the basis of new global institutions and parameters – and thereby also of a closing, to some degree, of the gap between industrial and developing worlds. Just that, indeed, is a key distinguishing feature of the idea of reflexive governance. The long-term consequences – transgressive by their nature of all borders and boundaries – of that constitutively unexpected to which, nonetheless, there can be no possible response but the development of uncertain expectations, can provide the spark and the fundament for transnational risk communities – Folgen-Öffentlichkeiten, or public spheres emerging from and sustained by the necessity to deal with commonly suffered consequences – which might in their turn lead to an (indeed involuntary) politicization and thus, should the circumstances be right, to a reinvention of politics on a transnational or global level.

The development referred to here – that whereby the space of everyday experience becomes a space of cosmopolitan interdependence – is not to be conceived of as a kind of universal 'love-in'. The condition evoked is one arising and subsisting in and through the perceived emergency of situations of global imperilment. The risks which make up this imperilment give rise to a pressure for cooperation which cannot be ignored. With the social construction and general social acceptance of the idea of a cosmopolitan dimension of imperilment, there is created, in disregard of national borders and their attendant enmities, a space of common responsibility and common action which, analogously to the space formed by the territory of a nation, can (although it need not) provide an impulse for subjects without prior bond with one another to engage in common political action. This potential is realized where the socially acknowledged dimension of imperilment leads to cosmopolitan norms and agreements – in other words, to an institutionalized cosmopolitanism.

Research done to date, however, into the emergence of the supra- and trans-national forms of organization which would correspond to such an institutionalized cosmopolitanism and actually embody reflexive governance has shown how difficult it is to make the transition from a determination of the fact of imperilment to a determination as to action. Constant communication regarding various imperilments forms an important component of the informal cosmopolitan development of shared norms. It does not suffice, in order to grasp adequately the character of global risk society, to conceive of its potential as just the potential to create new and not yet existing institutions of successful global governance. Already prior to all cosmopolitan institutionalization, global norms take form as a spontaneously emerging outrage over certain situations perceived as situations simply intolerable. That is, these norms characteristic of reflexive governance can emerge also there where no conscious effort of 'positive' norm-establishment has been made, but rather a certain as it were 'negative' consensus has established itself with regard to the evaluation of global crises and dangers. This is shown by the fact alone that, where conflicts emerge, the lines of confrontation are not susceptible of representation in simple regional terms. Rather, we see new lines of confrontation (for example, that between First and Third World) which do not coincide with geographical distinctions.

This means that cosmopolitanism has ceased to be what it was in the understanding of one of its earliest influential modern proponents: a Kantian 'Idea of Reason', and even as such a controversial Idea, and has descended – whatever the price, in terms of distortion, of this descent – out of the philosophical empyrean into concrete reality. More than this: it has become the characteristic of our second modernity, in which the boundaries and distinctions between the nation states are dissolving and being, in a process we might call a politics of politics, renegotiated. If we are to grasp, in this newly cosmopolitan world, the social and political realities in which we live and act, we urgently need a new observational viewpoint: in terms of the social agent the 'cosmopolitan point of view'; in terms of the third-person-language of the social sciences a 'methodological cosmopolitanism'.

The cosmopolitan point of view (or methodological cosmopolitanism) makes possible a non-nostalgic critique of the category of the national – of the law of nations, of international institutions, of the turn toward new wars which becomes a threatening possibility as the guiding dualism: 'national' and 'international' fade and decline – in the spirit of a cosmopolitan critical theory (Beck 2002).

10. The global public sphere as a secondary consequence of secondary consequences: a further central characteristic of reflexive governance is the law of the secondary consequence. The self-imperilling process

of civilization produces secondary consequences of the first order – risks and uncertainties which tend to be ever less rather than ever more calculable – and these give rise in their turn, as a secondary consequence of the second power, to public spheres stretching across borders and boundaries. This thesis, as an element of the theory of the global risk society, casts into question, and itself steps into the shaken position of, a basic premise of political theory: what calls public spheres into vital existence is less the practice of decision-making than the consequences of decisions, insofar as these are perceived to be problematical, to be dangerous. Decisions as such are a matter of indifference and even tend to render social subjects indifferent. What tears these subjects out of their indifference and their egoism – first by annoying them and dismaying them, but, in so doing, also animating them and making them concerned – is perception of the problematical consequences of decisions and communication to one another of such perceptions, so that in this way there is gradually established the commonality and the community of a trans- and post-national public space of action. In other words, dangers are not just dangers, and the difference between them with regard to their social and political 'logic' – that is, with regard to their construction in terms of economic, ecological or terrorist conflict – is not the only significant difference between them. Rather, constructions of risk have for their own part secondary consequences: they establish a public sphere, and this public sphere does not extend so far as the mass consciousness staged by the mass media. Here we have a further aspect of reflexive governance: one of the effects of global risks which we can reliably expect to follow from them as an unintended consequence is their contributory role in regard to the public and political aspect of modern existence. In a risk-sensitive global public sphere, it is particularly the recognized unimaginability of possible consequences that raises the question as to power. There where we had once seen national and universal integration on the basis of shared values, we see, with the advent of a globality of risks reflected in a global public sphere, a new kind of dialectic of cross-border conflict and cooperation. It is only in this way, and on pain of total destruction, that there can and must be invented and negotiated, in the context of reflexive governance, formulae of consensus for international action and international institutions. Naturally, it remains an open question whether such formulae will in fact be successfully developed.

Interestingly, it is not, or at least not exclusively, social movements – let alone revolutionary coups d'état – but rather the catastrophic intensification of the global risks themselves which 'involuntarily' and 'imperceptibly' bring into being the global public sphere (under certain conditions): the more omnipresent the threat in the mass media, the greater the political force of risk-perception in breaking down borders. And in this sense risks can be understood as negative media of communication. Almost all involved want to hide and hush them up. In distinction from the positive media of communication, money, truth and power, risks establish unintended structures of action across national and systemic boundaries, forcing into existence a communication where communication is not wished for and a public sphere where all attempts were being made to hinder its emergence. They allocate obligations and costs to those who reject such allocation (and often in this have the law of the day on their side). In other words, risks shatter the self-referentiality of the systems and of the national and international agendas of politics, overthrow their priorities and establish structures of action between parties and camps which of themselves tend to ignore and to clash with one another.

**The Metamorphosis of the Political, New Global Actors and Strategies**

I quote from *The Reinvention of Politics* (Beck 1993):

> This return of politics after the East–West conflict and after the old certainties of the industrial epoch compels and justifies a further distinction, which runs traversely to that above, that is, the distinction between rule-directed and rule-altering politics. The former type can certainly be creative and nonconformist, but it operates within the rule system of industrial and welfare state society in the nation state (or, in our terms simple modernity). Rule-altering politics, on the other hand, aims at a 'politics of politics' in the sense of altering the rules of the game themselves . . .
>
> Even inside simple politics, the bridge game, there are a number of individual variants of a more or less sophisticated type which one can play with various degrees of skill and mixed success. A completely different situation arises, however, if the rules of the game themselves are altered or switched. The height of confusion is attained when one plays both at once, bridge and the game of switching its rules. People play with swapped rule systems in order to change the rule systems themselves. Some continue to play bridge and are outraged as others attempt to invent and implement new displaced rules of the game during the bridge game. We face precisely this kind of normality and absurdity everywhere today.
>
> The game of classical industrial society, the antagonisms of labour and capital, of left and right, of the conflicting interests of the groups and the political parties, continues. At the same time, many demand and actually begin to turn the rule system itself inside out . . . Rule-directed and rule-altering politics overlap, mingle and interfere with one another . . . The distinction between official politics and sub-politics, which is oriented to the systemic structure of society, must therefore be contrasted with the distinction between simple

(rule-directed) and reflexive (rule-altering) politics . . . The phrase 'politics of politics', or 'reinvention of politics', which aims at this need not be meant normatively by any means . . . Ever since the end of the Cold War, we have been speaking in linguistic ruins in which, behind the shiny façades of words, new realities are nesting everywhere, breeding and being set up . . . Strictly speaking, this is a façadism in politics which is made possible by the collapse of the East–West order. Drastic as it may sound at first, the image from architecture is completely apt. The Biedermeier façades of the old western republic are preserved and at the same time, below the threshold of visibility or criticism, the walls and floors behind those façades are being replaced by new ones. One could say that not a single brick or principle remains in its accustomed place.

Take military policy as an example. The Bundeswehr is still the Bundeswehr (NATO is still NATO and so on). At the same time, the old domestic Bundeswehr is being transformed into a new global Bundeswehr. The Bundeswehr is being 'gutted'. Its Biedermeier appearance remains, but otherwise it bears only a distant resemblance to the military organization of the same name.

Foreign policy is another example. In the East–West constellation, the principle of non-intervention in the affairs of other countries was an iron-clad rule. Anyone who demanded military interventions was suspected and accused of war-mongering, on both sides of the Iron Curtain. Now the opposing principle applies or seems to apply: intervention for humanitarian and moral/political reasons under the aegis of the United Nations, a kind of positive Brezhnev doctrine of the former West. The latter denounces itself as weak and cowardly whenever it does not defend human rights in other countries, no matter where or when or on the basis of what independent verdict. Such a defence, however, implies the invasion of a foreign country, that is, attacking and war-making. It must therefore be permissible to inquire how this axial shift of politics and the global political constellation became possible, how it is justified and how it should be handled in a violent world. (Beck 1993: 206–13)

The neo-liberal agenda is the attempt to give enduring institutional form to the momentary historical gains of globally politically mobile capital. The perspective of capital, thought through radically to its logical conclusion, posits itself as an autonomous absolute and thus unfolds classical economics' strategic space of power and possibility as a sub-political, but also global-political, power-oriented mode of action. In these terms, what is good for capital is best for everyone. Everyone – so runs the promise – will get richer, and in the end even the poor will profit. The seductive power of this neo-liberal ideology does not, then, lie in the unleashing of egoism or in the maximization of competition but rather in the promise of global justice. The insinuated message is: in the end, the maximization of the power of capital is the better way to socialism.

The neo-liberal agenda insists, indeed, also on a second point: namely, that capital, in the meta-power-game, has disposition over two 'counters' and two 'moves', while all other players dispose, now as heretofore, over just one 'counter' and just one 'move'. The power of neo-liberalism, then, rests on a radical inequality in the matter of who is permitted to break the rules and who is not. The changing of the rules is and remains the revolutionary privilege of capital. All other actors are damned to conform to them. The national point of view in politics (and methodological nationalism in political and social theory) cements this power-advantage of capital, which has broken the bounds of the specifically national power-game and which continues to enjoy the power-advantage that it does enjoy essentially because the states have not made this boundary-breaking move along with it – because politics, for its part, continues to conform to the old rules and to tie itself up in the old structures of the state as nation-state.

**The Counter-Force of a Global Civil Society**

The role of counter-force with respect to the rule-altering force of capital falls, in public consciousness, not to the states but to global civil society and to the plurality of agents who make it up. The counter-force constituted by the social movements rests on the figure of the political consumer, whose power consists in the fact that he can, always and everywhere, refuse to buy. This 'no-sale weapon' is subject to no limitation, be it geographical, temporal or substantial. It is indeed dependent upon certain conditions – for example, that some money is there to be disposed of, or that the supply of products and services to some degree exceeds demand. Precisely, however, where these conditions – namely, the plurality of opportunities to buy and to consume – cease to apply, there cease also to be any subjective costs attached to penalizing this product of this company by means of an organized refusal to buy. For every act of buying can be transformed into a voting slip casting a vote for or against a company policy without any disadvantage accruing thereby to the buyer.

It is fatal to the interests of capital that there should exist no counter-strategy against the growing oppositional force of the consumer. Not even all-powerful multi-nationals can dismiss their consumers as they can their workers. Unlike workers, consumers neither have nor aspire to the status of members. Nor can the consumer be blackmailed by the threat to shift production to other countries, where the consumers are better behaved and swallow whatever is dished up to them. In the first place, the consumer is already globalized (and this precisely as a consequence of the globalization strategies of the enterprises) and, as such, indispensable if the companies are to make profits. In the second place, to respond to consumer protests in one country by marching off into another one would mean, for the companies, a maiming of themselves. Nor is it feasible, as it had been in the case of states, to play off against one another the national solidarities of consumers. In other words, all of that, which workers were and are, consumers are not. And it is this which makes the counter-force represented by the consumer – a counter-force which has as yet barely begun to exert itself – so dangerous for the force of capital.

## The Transformation of the State

In the last analysis, however, there can be no getting around the problem of how to redefine politics specifically qua science and practice centred on the instance of the state. No question, indeed, but that the advocates and agents of global civil society play an indispensable role in the global play of force and counter-force, and in particular in the process of the establishment of global norms and values, or, in other words, of reflexive governance. We should never, however, so far over-estimate this role as to think that the contradictions, crises and indirect consequences of our second modernity could ever possibly be entirely, and on a global scale, 'civilized away' by the forces embodying this merely civil-societal form of political commitment. Whoever thinks in this way revives and repeats the old, old error of the man who would prefer to steer clear of politics.

In the face of this error, it must be insisted upon that the global–political meta power–game cannot be restructured as a system of reflexive governance – cannot, that is to say, be turned from a lose–lose into a win–win situation – except through the transformation of politics qua politics of the state (along with, concomitantly, state theory and political theory). The key question, then, is: how can and must the concept and the form of organization of the state be opened up and reconstructed in the face of the challenges posed by the global risk society? How can a cosmopolitan self-transformation of the state be made possible?

If we can safely dismiss, as a discredited shibboleth dear to those who think themselves 'above politics', the idea that the existence of global civil society renders the renewal of state-oriented politics superfluous, the same does not hold of the new and as yet untested idea that civil society might itself as it were seize power. Indeed, such a symbiosis of civil society and inter-state cooperation constitutes the very nature of reflexive governance. The key question is: how can the ideas, theories and traditions of the state be freed from their national limitations and opened up to the challenges posed by a cosmopolitan interdependence? In order, in this connection, to avoid altogether entering into a pointless discussion of the falsely-stated alternative (state-centered politics or a politics of civil society), it is necessary clearly to distinguish between centeredness on the state and centredness on the nation state. One proceeds rightly, indeed, in abandoning political theory's erstwhile fixation on the nation state, since this latter is today no longer the actor in international politics but only one actor among many; anybody who extends, however, his critique of the nation state fixated point of view so far as to exclude, both on the analytical and the political plane, the very possibility of a continued effective activity and a self-transformation of the system of state relations, is throwing out the baby with the bath-water. Reflexive governance means, then, that states too must be understood and investigated as entities contingent and politically transformable – or, where they are not already so, must be made so. The question thus posed is: how is the transnationalization of states to become possible?

There is such a thing as the law of the decline of the power of the nation state: he who plays the national card in the global meta-power-game must lose. What is required, then, is a reversal of this perspective. That is to say, the principle also holds that the counter-force represented by states becomes really active and effective where these latter undergo a process of transnationalization and cosmopolitization. Only if the states succeed in keeping step with mobile capital and in redefining and reorganizing their power-positions and their moves in the game will it prove possible to put a halt, internationally, to the process of the collapse of state power and authority, and even to reverse this process.

We thus see posed a whole series of questions answers to which would amount to a veritable reinvention of politics: who is it, in fact, who has the authority and the right to take decisions and to create institutions such as will be able to manage the currents of international finance? What sort of consensus is necessary, and who must be involved, in order that an appropriate response emerges to the worldwide climate catastrophe? Can the decision to struggle against AIDS (or alternatively to neglect or forego such a struggle) really be a decision legitimately taken in the private space of an alleged non-attributability since it is one on which turn the lives of millions of human beings? And what sort of political agents or political institutions might ideally be proposed as appropriate to handle this problem, on what level and with what sort of mandate? In what manner are global, transnational, national and local authorizations of decisions related to one another and at the same time distinct and separate from one another? Who is it in fact who imposes, over the heads of the nation states, norms and rulings which are nonetheless binding on said nation states, and which norms and rulings do they impose, and what legitimates their doing so?

The insight is gaining ground that new, global institutions are required in order to address such themes as global environmental damage, weapons control, world financial order, currents of migration, poverty and justice and respect for human rights; no such institution, however, nor any measure taken by such an institution, should be permitted to overlook the fact that these global problems have also a regional – that is to say a national and local – side to them. Who, then, should control these agencies? To whom should they be responsible? Only to the national states? To which parliaments, which public sphere? To the United Nations? To the NGOs?

If we are to escape, in our thought and our action, the trap of nationality, the drawing of a distinction between sovereignty and autonomy is essential. (Methodological) nationalism rests upon the equation of the former with the latter. Seen from this perspective, such things as economic dependence, cultural diversification and military, legal and technical cooperation between states automatically lead also to a loss of sovereignty, inasmuch as they imply a loss of autonomy. However where one takes as one's criterion of sovereignty the power to structure social existence politically – or, in other words, the success of a state in increasing the prosperity of its population and in bringing closer to a solution such urgent national problems as unemployment, protection of the environment, crime and social and military security – then that loss of autonomy implied by increasing interdependence and cooperation is seen to result, in fact, in a substantial gain in sovereignty. The capacity of governments actually to guide and steer political developments becomes ever greater, the closer the cooperation and integration of states with one another and the greater the political advantage accruing from this closeness. In short, then: the division of sovereignty and its reconcentration into a new nexus situated on some other plane than that of the individual state proves not, in fact, to be tantamount to a reduction in the sovereignty of this latter but rather to its expansion.

## PROSPECTS FOR THE FUTURE: COSMOPOLITAN REALISM

In the light of all this, we may say that there lies at the basis of reflexive governance a 'cosmopolitan realism', a brief outline of which I want now, by way of conclusion and in the form of five theses opening prospects for the future, to sketch (Beck 2004; Beck and Grande 2004):

Firstly: the emergence of the global risk society has ensured that, at this point in history, a new logic has become key to the operation of all other social logics, according to which no nation can deal with its problems alone. This is no longer an idealistic principle of utopian internationalism or a philosophy of the social sciences thought up in some ivory tower. It is, on the contrary, an insight, and one gained, moreover, on the basis of the most sober *Realpolitik*. It is the fundamental law of cosmopolitan realism.

Secondly: global problems create transnational common concerns. He who plays the national card, loses. He alone will survive who understands and practises national politics in a cosmopolitan spirit and from a cosmopolitan point of view. National states – be they weak or strong – are no longer the primary entities as regards the solution of national problems. Interdependency, far from being a scourge of humanity, is rather the precondition of humanity's survival. Cooperation is no longer a means to an end, but rather the end itself. States act, for the most part, at the same time unilaterally and multilaterally, depending on which issues concern them and which spheres they are operating in. The more recognized and conscious the condition of globalism becomes – the more cultures, countries, governments, regions and religions come to be affected by it – the less effective – the less realistic – does unilateral action become, since, in a world where both efficacy and legitimacy have become functions of cooperation between states, he who acts unilaterally is correspondingly more likely to fail.

Thirdly: international organizations are more than just the continuation of national politics by other means. They draw national interests into new nexuses in such a way as actually to transform these interests. The emergence of such organizations means the beginning of a positive-sum game between the participant states which can replace the negative-sum game of national autonomy. The (neo-)realism of nation-state oriented thinking says: international organizations serve above all national, not international interests. Cosmopolitan realism says: international organizations serve interests which are neither (in the old sense) national nor primarily international; rather, they alter, maximize and expand national interests into transnational interests and thereby open new transnational spaces of power and restructuration for global–political actors of the most various kinds, states among them.

Who or what sustains this cosmopolitan integration of states? Certainly (as the political–scientific realists maintain) the calculation, by the participant states and governments, of their 'national' interests – but precisely with the addition of a cosmopolitan bonus which has undergone an essential alteration. In the end, everyone profits from this, since it is only in such an expanded national political area that those global problems which are also national problems can be, if not solved, then at least reined in. The creation of international organizations presupposes the USA's readiness to itself place limits on its own power, be it only as a strategy for said power's legitimation and for its cooperative expansion. Something else emerges, something new, when states asymmetrical in power decide, in the face of global threats, to work together under conditions of law and of democratic values.

Fourthly: this is the reason why two institutions closely related to one another in aim and intention – the European Union and the United Nations – are so important for the efficacy and the legitimacy of global risk politics. That certain European states as well as the UN Security Council refused to play the role of rubber stamp for solo military adventures on the part of the US government has not, as many commentators supposed it would, led to a loss of power by the European Union and the UN. On the contrary, both bodies have, on the global scale, gained in credibility thereby. The legitimacy of reflexive governance is founded in essence in a global division of powers between the force of military disposition on the one hand and the force, on the other, of a consensus gradually achieved through the medium of a worldwide public sphere. If the unipolar military force that is the USA is to achieve at all the legitimacy it needs to achieve, it can do so only by virtue of the proven autonomy, in the face of this force, of the European Union and the UN.

Fifthly: unilateralism is uneconomical. Cosmopolitan realism, on the other hand, is also economic realism. It reduces costs and also redistributes them. It reduces them not only because actual military costs are in any case far, far higher than would be the costs of a political strategy to render said military costs unnecessary, but also because a nation's loss of political legitimacy brings with it an exponential increase in costs of all sorts. It redistributes them because the opposite principle also applies: a shared responsibility, a shared sovereignty also means shared costs. Solo adventures on the part of individual nations close off the possibility of such courses of action, which are characteristic rather of a transnational politics. In other words: cooperation between individual states on the one hand and between states and social movements on the other – and it is such cooperation that goes, in no small part, to constitute the attitude of cosmopolitan realism – is good business.

## NOTE

1.  The problem described here is by no means restricted to the theory of a second modernity. Similar diagnoses might be formulated on the basis of Luhmann's 'systems theory' and of various theories of action. These theories too work with models of reflexive processes which are not self-stabilizing but lead rather to contradictions, ruptures or 'dialectical suicides' (Beck and Holzer 2004) of entire systems.

## REFERENCES

Bauman, Zygmunt (1995), *Moderne und Ambivalenz: das Ende der Eindentigkeit*, Hamburg: Junis.
Beck, Ulrich (1993), *Die Erfindung des Politischen*, Frankfurt a.M.: Suhrkamp.
Beck, Ulrich (1996), 'Wissen oder NichtWissen? Zwei Perspektiven, reflexiver Modernisierung', in Ulrich Beck, Anthony Giddens and Scott Lash (1996), *Reflexive Modernisierung, Eine Kontroverse*, Frankfurt a.M.: Suhrkamp, pp. 289–315. [*World Risk Society*, Cambridge: Polity Press]

Beck, Ulrich (2002), *Macht und Gegenmacht im globalen Zeitalter*, Frankfurt a.M.: Suhrkamp. [*Power in the Global Age*, Cambridge: Polity Press, 2005]

Beck, Ulrich (2004), *Der kosmopolitische Blick*, Frankfurt a.M.: Suhrkamp. [*The Cosmopolitan Vision*, Cambridge: Polity Press, 2005]

Beck, Ulrich and Wolfgang Bonß (eds) (2001), *Die Modernisierung der Moderne*, Frankfurt a.M.: Suhrkamp.

Beck, Ulrich, Wolfgang Bonß and Christoph Lau (eds) (2004), *Entgrenzung und Entscheidung*, Frankfurt a.M.: Suhrkamp. ['Second modernity as a research agenda: theoretical and empirical explorations in the "meta-change" of modern society', *British Journal of Sociology*, 2005]

Beck, Ulrich and Edgar Grande (2004), *Kosmopolitisches Europa*, Frankfurt a.M.: Suhrkamp. [*Cosmopolitan Europe*, Cambridge: Polity Press, forthcoming]

Beck, Ulrich and Boris Holzer (2004), 'Reflexivität und Reflexion: Ulrich Beck and Christoph Lau', *Entgrenzung und Entscheidung*, Frankfurt a.M.: Suhrkamp, pp. 165–93.

Beck, Ulrich and Christoph Lau (2004), *Entgrenzung und Entscheidung*, Frankfurt a.M.: Suhrkamp.

Daase, Christopher (2002), 'Internationale Politik', in Christopher Daase, Susanne Freske and Ingo Peters (eds) *Internationale Risikopolitik*, Baden-Baden: Nomos, pp. 9–36.

Douglas, Mary and Aron Wildavsky (1983), *Risk and Culture*, Berkeley, CA: University Press.

Giddens, Anthony (1955), *Beyond Left and Right: The Future of Radical Politics*, Cambridge: Polity Press.

Wehling, Peter (2001), 'Jenseits des Wissens?', in *Zeitschrift für Soziologie 30*, pp. 465–84.

# 3. Reflexive modernisation as a governance issue, or: designing and shaping *re*-structuration

**John Grin**

## INTRODUCTION

In this chapter, I will assume (cf. Grin, 2005) that the concept of 'reflexive modernisation', which I will more accurately circumscribe below, provides a sensible orientation for socio-technological development in a variety of domains as they find themselves in late modernity. My purpose is to present a view on reflexive modernisation as a governance issue. What does it mean to consider reflexive modernisation as a governance issue? A quick and basic answer is easy to give. Whatever definition of governance we take, it centres on the idea of what we may loosely indicate as 'shaping the market and society [and science – J.G.] into a desired form.' (Pierre and Peters, 2000: 1) This basic definition implies that the two basic questions on reflexive modernisation as a governance issue are: (1) how to determine the 'reflexively modern' shape that society and the market should take? and (2) how to effectively shape society and the market? And, indeed, it is these two questions on which this chapter will focus.

Yet, in order to deal with these questions in any fruitful way, we have to gain a deeper understanding of what it means to consider reflexive modernisation as a governance issue. As we will see, such understanding implies a re-formulation of these questions in more specific and subtle terms. Why is this necessary? One point here is that governance and reflexive modernisation are referring both to concepts (and elaborations of these concepts into theory) about phenomena, and to these phenomena themselves. A second point is that both, as concepts, explicitly consider the institutions of state, market, science and society and their relations (and the ways in which they are conceived) not as givens, but as objects of more or less considerable scrutiny and change. Thus the expression 'reflexive modernisation as a governance issue' is essentially non-trivial.

Therefore, in the next section I will discuss the concept of governance in light of the concept of reflexive modernisation. Then follows a brief review of a recent conversation on reflexive modernisation theory so as to identify more precisely what should be the unit of analysis when we employ governance theory to discuss the phenomenon of reflexive modernisation as a challenge for governance practices. It is in light of the considerations raised in these two sections that I will then discuss the above basic questions of governance.

The fact that the concepts brought together here are associated with a reconceptualisation of politics, the market, science and society and their boundaries, also implies that we must fundamentally review not only basic concepts in sociology, political science and other social sciences, but also the boundaries between these disciplines. In addition to all the usual warnings, this implies a fundamental reason for considering the view presented in this chapter as a rather tentative one – more than anything else, it sketches a programme for the social sciences, which they must necessarily undertake in close association with practice.[1]

## GOVERNANCE IN LIGHT OF REFLEXIVE MODERNISATION

'Governance' must be understood here in a more precise sense than the currently fashionable, casual use of the term for designating any kind of social regulation. We will deal with the concept as one that refers to new modes of governing, of 'shaping the market and society into a desired direction', that differ from classical–modernist government. A range of factors are mentioned in literature as the rationale for the shift from government to governance (for example, Rhodes, 1997; Pierre and Peters, 2000; Kooiman, 2003). While authors differ concerning the meaning of and the mutual relations between these factors, it is probably fair to say that most lists include: the changing (views on) the capacity of states to shape society and the market; the deterioration of the state's self-evident authority vis-à-vis increasingly fragmented societies; the relative 'autonomy' of economic and societal developments that challenge that nation state and its relations with the market and society; and globalisation processes that imply another challenge to a nation state's sovereignty. The quintessence of the difference between government and governance is, in line with this rationale, often described by saying that practices of governance (that is to say, of 'shaping the market and society') can neither be located exclusively in nor be solely directed by political–administrative institutions (as the government concept presumes) but essentially involves interactions between state, market and society.

This depiction is problematic not in the way it portrays governance, but in the way in which it considers classical–modernist government. Underlying that conception is a presumption that goes back to the received view that, in the course of modernity, the state, market, society and science have become separate realms. To be sure, it is not difficult to see that functional differentiation between these institutional realms has indeed occurred. Yet, if we take this received view as an adequate description of modernity, we have – to paraphrase Latour (1993) – never been modern. The received view is too simple in one crucial respect: it neglects the fact that the development of these institutional realms – in ways that vary between nation states and societal domains – can best be described as a process of co-evolution, guided by a common orientation. That orientation may be summarised in two dogmas, which belong to the core of the Enlightenment project. The first one is that it is possible to know 'Truth' on the basis of universal knowledge, grounded in some Archimedal point. The second dogma is that it is possible to control reality on that basis, and that this will yield social progress by freeing humans from fate.

These two dogmas received widespread adherence in the course of the sixteenth and seventeenth centuries (Kumar, 1995: 78–80), as a response to what Richard Bernstein (1983) has called the Cartesian Anxiety: the quest for certain, universal, grounded knowledge to deal with the widely felt threat of chaos. While the notion of progress through control was, in the path of the work of Galileo, Newton and other natural scientists, initially primarily related to nature, it soon evolved into a worldview that also included the idea of a controllable social reality. From the early eighteenth century onwards, this view has guided the development of nation states.[2] Views on the cosmos and on the polity melted into a 'Cosmopolis' (Toulmin, 1990), and rational knowledge became the basis on which nation states relied to ensure the legitimacy of their actions and the success of their attempts to promote social progress for the people within their territories. In addition, especially since the Industrial Revolution, it was this vision that provided orientation to a process of fine-tuning between nation states, societies, the market and science. (Kumar, 1995: 81–2; Gill, 2003: 115–48) As a consequence, these different realms have co-evolved as parts of the same project. In modern nation states, domains like healthcare, agriculture, water management, transportation and so on have grown into systems of efficient and carefully interrelated institutions that are tailored to nurture knowledge-driven development that was supposed to – and in many respects actually did – yield social–economic progress.

The concept of reflexive modernization theory starts from the recognition that these 'simple modernization processes' of 'first modernity' (Beck, 1997) have now been recognized to bring with them risks and side effects that society does not tolerate, or no longer tolerates. This is because modern institutions, which have emerged around this development towards progress through control, have developed blind spots for risks and side effects and lack capacities for designing and pursuing strategies which are able to deal with them effectively. This is partly due to the fact that modernisation processes have brought about a 'logic of homogenisation and virtual elimination of local knowledge' or, with an Aristotelean notion, of mētis – the craft to take contextual conditions into account (Scott, 1998: 302; 309–41). This disdain for and the associated undermining of mētis has reduced society's capacity to compensate for these blind spots.

The idea behind the concept of reflexive modernisation is the idea (Beck, 1992) that the very processes that were designed to – and did – yield progress, also produced side effects and risks. The same institutions that nurtured progress have developed blind spots for the negative effects that come with it. A re-orientation of modernisation is therefore necessary towards the vision of a 'radicalised modernity' or 'second modernity' (Beck, 1997): the vision that we may and must eventually realise the 'demand of the Enlightenment'. The normative dimension of this concept of reflexive modernisation is especially clear from the way in which Beck contrasts it with the 'arbitrariness' which he finds with some post-modern thinkers, and which he rejects because, in his view, it amounts to throwing away the child (the 'demand of Modernity': using rationality to improve the human condition) with the bathwater (side-effects and risks) (ibid., p. 14). Such a re-orientation, he further assumes, is possible and is occurring (see also Beck et al., 2003). It presumes and brings with it[3] a process of institutional transformation to remedy the limited sight of existing institutions.

It is precisely in this respect that the concept of reflexive modernisation qualifies the concept of governance. There is a tendency in literature, and even more so in practice, to focus governance on the transformation of the ways in which government and societal and market actors are dealing with each other. Governance then gets elaborated through such notions as 'network management' (Kickert et al., 1997), 'public participation' (Newman, 2001) or 'promoting self-organisation' (Rhodes, 1997). To be sure, each of these (and other) notions provides a range of opportunities to organise governance beyond the modernist 'control' fashion. This is, however, not a sufficient condition for using these concepts as ingredients for a governance concept for reflexive modernisation. The reason is that, without further measures, practices of network management, public participation, self-organisation and so on will reflect many of the assumptions of first modernity, and reproduce the patterns of action typical for it. Governance practices based on these concepts may help to promote reflexive modernisation as a phenomenon – if, and only if, these concepts and practices are designed from the perspective of reflexive modernisation as a concept, a Vision of bringing about a radicalised modernity through not only other modes of action, but also a profound institutional transformation.

This has two important implications. The first is that these processes of transformation from a particular substantial perspective (dealing with 'risks' and 'side effects' in relation to 'progress') need in concreto be underpinned by a substantive understanding. More precisely, they presuppose an understanding, for that concrete context, of the substance of the specific transformation of societal development sought, of the associated institutional transformation and of the precise relations between them. Given that the substance and praxis of policy analysis appears to be influenced by its institutional embedment (Hoppe and Grin, 2000), this presents a challenge which policy analysts normally do not have to meet, and therefore requires the development of rather new types of policy analytical practice. We will return to this subject in the final section of this chapter on the basis of an example.

The second implication is that the locus of governance, the polity, cannot be found in any of the current institutions, or in any well-defined location in between them. Over the past decades, a rather complex institutional landscape has developed, which combines important modernist institutions with a variety of institutional arrangements that have emerged more recently (Van Tatenhove et al., 2000). Governance is thus facing what Hajer (2003) has called an 'institutional void', a lack of fixed and generically usable institutional arrangements in which it can effectively take place. As a consequence, the polity itself has become discursive. Where we might look for contextually suitable polities is a question we can only deal with after we have taken up a question that needs be answered first: (why) is it meaningful to consider reflexive modernisation as a governance issue?

## (WHY) IS IT MEANINGFUL TO CONSIDER REFLEXIVE MODERNISATION AS A GOVERNANCE ISSUE?

A good starting point for discussing this question is provided by a recent exchange in *Theory, Culture and Society* between, amongst others, Bruno Latour and Ulrich Beck. The conversation focuses, in Latour's paper (2003: 42) framing, on their 'common undertaking' in understanding how 'modernity has progressed in the last 20 years'. Latour characterises their difference as one of analytical focus: while Beck deals with the substance of the phenomena studied, Latour is interested in the collective interpretation given to these phenomena. He argues (ibid. 38–41) that this distinction is relevant both concerning the question whether first modernity has actually ended, and to the question whether reflexive modernisation is actually occurring.

Latour then continues by admittedly playing the role of devil's advocate through listing a set of questions for empirical inquiry that could provide evidence whether processes of what he prefers to call '*re*-modernisation' are actually occurring. He suggests that it will be difficult to 'prove' this, and then concludes (2003: 45–6) by noting that reflexive modernisation 'might not describe what has already happened, but it can offer a powerful lever to make new things happen', by – in the language of section 2 – offering guidance to societal development from the perspective of a radicalised modernity.

Beck et al., in their account (2003), argue that the idea that 'the paradigm of modern society reproduces itself through a flux of continuous self-renewal' reflects the presumption of 'a particular hierarchy of history, namely the dominance of the past and history over the future'. Reflexive modernisation is the attempt to leave this assumption of the hierarchy of time in favour of a more radical modernity.

Beck et al. assert that we should not ignore an actual 'dynamics of second modern society', quickly adding that '[o]f course, one must take into account the resistance to this overthrowing of the categories of time' (Beck et al. 2003: 12–3). They then develop an argument on 'meta-change resulting from the unintended consequences of simple modernisation', that is, structural adaptations that are created by the politicisation of side-effects (2003: 14–5). In these processes of meta-change, modern institutions lose their taken-for-granted character, and are being considered and treated as objects that may be transformed. At the core of meta-change is a different view of rationality: from universal, grounded, certain knowledge to contextual wisdom. In outlining different modes of meta-change, Beck is referring to practices in which development processes are politicised and institutional arrangements are actually being transformed so as to facilitate reflexive modernisation (such as radically new legislation following a veterinary crisis).

Reviewing this exchange, we may first observe that it seems fair to acknowledge that Beck and his collaborators are correct to point to 'existing dynamics of reflexive modernisation,' which are all too quickly neglected by Latour's deliberate irony; in the next section we will add an example to the ones given by Beck et al. The problem is that their discussion proceeds on the basis of examples concerning isolated practices, while reflexive modernisation, as we have seen in section 2, involves the entire range of interrelated governmental, market, scientific and societal practices in a particular domain. Unless different practices are being created and made to respond to each other, guided by the vision of a radical modernity, there is a significant risk that the isolated institutional changes created by such individual practices are hardly effective: the processes of reflexive modernisation they are designed to promote may easily fly into the face of the modernist institutions otherwise surrounding them – a risk further increased by the lack of other practices with which they might ally to counter that threat and produce reflexive modernisation. A better understanding – beyond the mere recognition of potential 'resistance' – is needed of how these practices may reach out to each other in such a way that they may start to reinforce each other and together contribute to a process of increasingly comprehensive transformation, both substantively and institutionally.

The second observation to be made here relates to that point. Unless the sort of understanding just mentioned is developed, a focus on practices that create significant institutional change may leave us vulnerable to the classical mistake of structuralist approaches (to which, to be sure, they do not subscribe): a focus on structural transformation as determinant of transformation of action, without considering ways in which the existing structure may 'fight back'. Latour's attention to the role of collective interpretation and his related lever metaphor are interesting and highly relevant ingredients for an approach that does more justice to the duality of structure (Giddens, 1984). It offers opportunities for elaborating the general prescription that Fox and Miller (1996: 91) derive from structuration theory: to transform normally 'recursive practices' through 'discursive will formation'. Discursive will formation, though far from trivial, may help both to act beyond existing structures and to transform these structures. This possibility is implied by structuration theory – as well as all other recent social theory. As a range of authors from very different backgrounds – including Law (1992), Joas (1993), Leydesdorff (2001) and Archer (2003) – have observed, these theories share the idea that structures operate through an acting agent, who in principle may exhibit reflexivity – as Law nicely puts it, 'structure is a verb'.

However, in order to provide guidance to such moments of discursive will formation, Latour's proposal for attributing to reflexive modernisation primarily a critical–reflective role needs to be complemented with an elaboration of how this might help to transform practices and identify and create new opportunities for these practices to connect with each other, and contribute to a more comprehensive process of what I like to call '*re*-structuration': the interrelated transformation of structure and action through structuration processes guided by the deliberate 're-orientation' which Latour holds to be *re*-modernisation's primary meaning.

These two observations imply that we may consider reflexive modernisation not only as a concept but also as a phenomenon, provided that this concept gets defined in a contextually meaningful way for particular practices; provided that it 'gets a chance' to provide direction to these practices; and provided that these practices are made to connect with each other in some more or less 'orchestrated' way, just as occurred throughout simple modernisation processes, as illustrated below in the case of agricultural modernisation. To consider reflexive modernisation as a governance issue is to focus attention on the implications of this conclusion.

It is in this light that we must consider the two basic questions of governance presented in the introduction. Who is to decide more precisely what constitutes a contextually meaningful elaboration of the concept of reflexive modernisation for a particular practice, and how many meaningful elaborations may be expected? And how can governance effectively deal with a multitude of practices, surrounded both by the still powerful remains of modernist institutions? As these questions remain rather abstract without further specifications of these practices and their institutional surroundings, we will now discuss one domain in which reflexive modernisation is starting to take place. This will illustrate some of the basic notions in the preceding two sections as well as provide an empirical referent, which will add precision to our treatment of these questions in the final sections of this chapter.

## MODERNISATION AND REFLEXIVE MODERNISATION: THE EXAMPLE OF DUTCH AGRICULTURE

An appropriate illustration is the agricultural domain in the Netherlands. Following the late nineteenth century's agricultural crisis, a process of modernisation, typical of first modernity, was deliberately set in motion to improve the country's competitiveness in the primary sector vis-à-vis France, Denmark, Schleswig-Holstein and the United States. During this crisis, farmers started to organize themselves. An Agricultural Commission was established in 1886 to advise the government, and in 1896 it was decided to turn agriculture – hitherto left to the free forces of the market – into an object of governmental policy making. A crucial part of policy making concerned the establishment of a knowledge infrastructure: higher and lower forms of education, as well as a variety of research and development institutes. In the earliest decades, the efforts undertaken in this fresh knowledge infrastructure focused on enhancing competitiveness through product improvements and land saving (Bieleman, 2000).

After the Second World War, which ended with a traumatic 'Hunger Winter,' this knowledge infrastructure – then part of the Ministry of Agriculture and covering all levels of agricultural education, extension services and research institutes and experimenting stations – was rapidly extended, eventually comprising some 7000 academic professionals. The pace of modernisation further increased; its objective shifted to ensuring domestic food production at affordable prices (eventually without the product subsidies introduced early after the war) and freeing the labour force for industry.

This change initiated a very rapid pace of rationalization (Bieleman, 2000). The primary sector's share in the labour force decreased from 19 per cent in 1947 to 5 per cent in 1990; land use for the primary sector diminished to some 30 per cent; and the amount of capital goods (machines; cattle; buildings) increased by 80 per cent. A main focus was on exporting animal produce. Domestic production of food in the Netherlands increased from typically 15–20 per cent of the domestic demand in 1945, up to typically 200–300 per cent half a century later. Simultaneously, the high quality of Dutch food specialties on the one hand, and the competitive prices of intensively produced bulk goods on the other hand significantly improved the economic potential of the sector. Progress was based on increasing control over nature: new generations of cows were 'designed' to yield 1.5 per cent more milk every year; their udders were shaped to be milked by machines; grain was designed to be harvested more easily by giving it uniform length and shape; diseases were controlled through vaccination of animals and the use of pesticides in crop production.

This successful 'simple modernisation' has been significantly facilitated by its embedment in smoothly functioning institutional provisions. Of particular importance were two institutional triangles. The first is the so-called 'OVO triad' (OVO being the Dutch acronym for research, information and education), which generated knowledge and technology through innovative agricultural research and disseminated it to agricultural practice through information services to practising farmers as well as through agricultural schools where new generations were educated. The dominant, mutually recognised task division of farmers and researchers remained such that researchers generated knowledge and technology, which farmers were supposed to apply. By basing their work on experience with farming (many agricultural researchers come from farming families) as well as imposing an understanding of farming as a knowledge-intensive, rationalised enterprise, the utilisation of knowledge and technology, guided by the activities of the OVO triad, occurred relatively smoothly (Bieleman, 2000; Van der Ploeg, 1999).

The second triangle was the 'iron triangle' of the Agricultural Ministry, agricultural branch organisations and agricultural specialists in parliament (Bekke et al., 1994; Wisserhof, 2000). It was based on a strong consensus – partly maintained through personal commitments and unions of different kinds – on the policy objectives that were already mentioned. The consensus also pertained to the strategy for realising them: stimulating further knowledge and technology development, financial measures, land redistribution to enable concentration and specialisation, improvements in water management to increase the carrying capacity required by increasing cattle density and the use of machinery. Not co-incidentally, Dutch agricultural policy and the Common Agricultural Policy (CAP) of the European Economic Community developed a significant synergy.[4]

Modernisation also led to and was facilitated by profound institutional changes in the market. While the number of animals stayed the same and their individual productivity increased over time, the number of farms dramatically decreased (Bieleman, 2000: 21). This was accompanied by considerable specialisation. Within decades, virtually no 'mixed farms', which had both animal and crop production, were left; and, a further specialisation developed towards farms that only breed or fatten pigs, or keep cows or chickens – the latter two even split into meat production on the one hand and dairy products on the other. In addition, economic chains in the agrofood market became longer and more differentiated. Farms increasingly focused on the function of actual animal holding or crop cultivation, as other tasks became the domain of other players, specialised in (knowledge intensive, advanced) activities that produced input to the farm or processing and distributing its products (Bieleman, 2000; Priester, 2000).

This tightly woven system – that can well serve to illustrate how modernisation processes involve, as we put it in section 2, 'fine-tuning' between institutions of state, market, society and science on the basis of a common orientation – was, for a long time, widely appreciated for its many successes. Social support began to diminish in the late 1970s and mid 1980s, however, when concerns were raised on overproduction, animal welfare and environmental emissions, especially from manure and pesticides. Like the progress, these side-effects were rooted, to a significant degree, in the modernisation process and the institutions which nurtured it. Together with an increase of productivity through rationalisation, product subsidies, both national and European, led to over-production. Animal welfare concerns were associated with the 'controlling nature' paradigm that was central to the modernisation process. Productivity altogether also implied a high 'density' of pollution. Pollution itself was associated with the use of pesticides to control diseases as well as with the fact that increasing specialisation and differentiation of food production chains had reduced opportunities for closing cycles of manure substances in ways that had been normal practice in earlier times when 'mixed' farms combined animal and crop production.

Although some actors were well aware of the degree of embeddedness of concerns in the practices of the agricultural system at the time, and pleaded for a radically different agriculture, these calls for reflexive modernisation were far from being generally shared. Policy responses in the 1980s did not fundamentally call these practices into question. Measures mainly focused on environmental regulation to reduce the environmental burden of existing practices; as well as financial stimuli and voluntary agreements that, together with the announcement of further regulation and governmental funding of incremental innovation programmes, were to stimulate incremental adaptations in agricultural production.

The classical institutional arrangements (the OVO triad and the iron triangle) were opened up under the pressure of outside actors (non-governmental actors, citizens; their echoes in parliament) and successful attempts by the Ministry of Spatial Planning, Housing and the Environment to achieve a place at the table of agricultural decision making. In addition, new institutional arrangements, especially ones for strengthening market operation, were emerging (Wisserhof, 2000).

These institutional transformations may have paved the way for more extensive policies a decade later, following the different epidemics that swept agriculture throughout Europe: classical swine fever, BSE, foot and mouth disease and so on. In addition, developments in the World Trade Organisation talks as well as the burden of the CAP on the EU budget created pressure for reform (Ackrill, 2000; Hennis, 2001; Bekke and de Vries, 2001). As a consequence, the policies that had emerged in the 1980s were supplemented by programmes that aimed to stimulate the development of a different kind of agricultural practice. New institutional arrangements emerged from these programmes. One example was the transformation of the Agricultural Research Advisory Board, earlier an important part of the OVO triad, into an organisation that was to induce, at arm's length distance from the Ministry, projects for reflexive modernisation (De Wilt, 2004). Similar practices occur in a range of programmes in the agricultural research complex, commissioned by the Ministry and undertaken in deliberative arrangements among researchers, farmers, societal organisations (such as environmental groups and animal welfare organisations), industry and other stakeholders (Bos and Grin, forthcoming).

Some of these practices are explicitly aimed at innovations that go beyond the rules implied by existing institutions. These may be seen as interesting, pioneering work towards the reflexive modernisation of agriculture. At the same time, it is also becoming clear that they are facing the sort of resistance indicated at the end of section 3. One frequently encountered difficulty is that new production systems, which are to close energy and substance cycles through integral designs that relate different elements of agrofood production chains (for example, using the manure and heat produced by pigs as inputs for crop production and 'waste' from the latter as inputs for the first), appear to be at odds with the highly differentiated economic chains that have developed around simple modernisation processes. Further development of such projects will depend on the ability to realise and connect with new types of market arrangements. Another example is that new practices in animal production, designed around animal welfare as the central concern, run into existing food safety regulations, which, in addition to product criteria, also include demands on the production process, which is tailored to existing intensive agriculture. Government officials frequently find it difficult to be responsive to such problems, partly because national regulation is embedded in European legislation, partly because exceptions are difficult to realise within the existing legal framework, with principles like equality before the law, firmly anchored in the *Rechtsstaat*.

## HOW TO DEFINE REFLEXIVE MODERNISATION AS A GUIDING AMBITION?

Let us now turn to the first basic question of governance: how to determine the 'reflexively modern' shape that society and the market should take? Taking together the conclusions reached in sections 2 and 3, we need an answer to the question of where political judgement must take place: in the classical bodies of the nation state; in the variety of practices now characterising many policy domains (as we have seen in the example of Dutch agricultural policy), each of which may make claims to elaborate reflexive modernisation meaningfully; or in between these loci?

While the nation state can still claim democratic legitimacy to a larger extent than all kinds of more or less ad hoc institutional arrangements, it is a crucial point of departure of governance literature that it simultaneously faces tough problems in defining what constitutes meaningful elaborations for societal and economic actors. How does one define a direction for societal development that may expect sufficiently wide support if the authority of expertise is no longer self-evident, if globalisation and individualisation challenge existing delineations and identities and if societies are thus increasingly normatively fragmented? And how can government judge whether this direction will actually be realised in practices in which at least some sub-set of society participates? The simple answer that such judgement be left to these practices is too simple, not only because of the legitimacy aspect, but also because, as we saw at the end of section 3, such practices cannot be left to themselves.

In answering these questions, one fruitful point of departure is the recognition that reflexive modernisation should not be seen as an unambiguous objective, but rather as an 'essentially contestable' or open-textured concept that may be elaborated into societal practices that represent a variety of interpretations of the concept. Consider, for instance, the ambition of a 'transition to a sustainable agriculture'. If understood in the more radical sense indicated above, sustainable development can be seen as a form of reflexive modernisation, which focuses on risks and side-effects concerning ecological, animal welfare and human health aspects. Compared to the intensive agriculture that resulted from twentieth-century modernisation processes, practices in which such forms of sustainable agriculture are being designed are much less exclusively oriented to productivity increases. Each of the criteria considered central in these practices (concerning emissions, animal welfare, and so on) may be fulfilled in a variety of ways. For instance, emissions may be prevented by traditional organic farming methods, but also by employing advanced technology to close substance cycles by using the remains of one production process as inputs for another one. Similarly, animal welfare may be promoted by traditional, small-scale organic farming, but also by designing cow housing systems in a way that allows a farmer to follow rather than control the animals' natural behaviour. If each of the criteria can be fulfilled in various ways, optimising agricultural practices in terms of all these criteria can also be done in a variety of ways.

This can be easily generalised to other practices of reflexive modernisation, which by definition assume a multi-dimensional problem as a point of departure.[5] It is important to point out here that this is not a relativistic viewpoint. While it recognises that there is no universally valid, single best option for each of the dimensions of sustainable development – let alone concerning their integration into a valid elaboration of sustainable agricultural practice – it does not claim that 'anything might go' under that heading. Denying the existence of a 'single truth' does not preclude the possibility of identifying particular options as 'nonsense'.

In more formal terms, the underlying epistemological position is that all knowledge is situated (Haraway, 1991). This is true for the instrumental rationality that is typical for simple modernisation processes; but it is no less true for critique of that rationality. Privileging one form of critique – and the elaboration of a practice tailored to meet that particular critique – denies this situatedness as much as taking the validity of instrumental rationality beyond critique. Similarly, in commenting on the debate on post-modernity, Bernstein (1993) has reminded us that the hermeneutic turn in epistemology has taught us that the legitimacy of critique must not be sought in its objective foundations, but in the assertion in whose or what's name critique is being exercised. Critique is thus a matter, not of neutral observers, but of involved participants, which is located in a particular context and reflects a specific viewpoint. Plural societies are characterised by a diversity of contexts and viewpoints. As a corollary, any elaboration of reflexive modernisation, as a social transformation that attempts to take critique on side effects and risks as seriously as the need to fulfil human needs (Beck, 1997: 23), is necessarily situated.

A second point of departure is the recognition that practices have to be organised around a pragmatically sensible elaboration of reflexive modernisation. In our example, this idea focuses on an agricultural practice that is optimised in terms of ecology, animal welfare and so on, in a way that is deemed practical and attractive by a particular category of farmers; the products of which can be processed by a particular category of processing firms, whose products are preferred by a particular category of consumers and so on. Such an elaboration thus corresponds to a form of action-oriented agreement that we have elsewhere called congruency (Grin and van de Graaf, 1996a and 1996b). Congruency does not rely on normative consensus. Rather, it is based on the understanding that collective action is possible if (1) the various individual contributions are considered sensible by those who are supposed to co-produce them and (2) it is deemed acceptable by those having a stake in the problematics. Congruency also does not imply a form of 'grey' consensus. Congruency is to be achieved in processes of political judgement, in the sense of phronèsis (Flyvbjerg, 2001; Bernstein, 1983), in which new opportunities for collective action are identified by creatively employing the tension between what can be made feasible and what is deemed desirable. (Loeber, 2004: 54–77, 297–8)

Taken together, these two points of departure imply that the ambition of reflexive modernisation may be defined on two different levels. On the one hand, the political community as a whole may, through its democratically legitimised institutions, decide that reflexive modernisation in a particular domain is desired without specifying it: 'we should move away from dominant existing agriculture, and elaborate sustainable agriculture.' On the other hand, this still very open-textured concept may be elaborated more specifically in a variety of practices. This way of dealing with judgement on reflexive modernisation comes close to Seyla Benhabib's (2002) 'dual track democracy,' which is rooted in the epistemic position just discussed (and developed in an interesting way in Benhabib, 1992). This notion is her answer to the need of multicultural societies both to have some common principles and to allow for a variety of social practices: while it is important for a society to agree on the notion of freedom, women may differ amongst each other on the question whether a headscarf is or is not an expression of, or compatible with, freedom. The latter cannot be determined by a majority, but primarily needs reflection and debate with regard to different social practices and between these practices and the political community as a whole. The possibility should a priori be included that this question be answered in plural.

Obviously, this answer to our first question needs considerable elaboration in terms of a variety of important questions. What sort of fora may be established in between parliament and social practices so as to determine what practices may and which ones may not be seen as valid elaborations of the general ambition of reflexive modernisation? What rules could guide the relations between parliaments, such in-between fora and social practices? What are adequate heuristics for arriving at a number of elaborations that are large enough to offer something to a significant part of normatively fragmented societies and small enough to prevent the need for an impractical variety of R&D programmes, hallmarks with which to communicate them to consumers, regulations to ensure food safety, machinery for the associated agricultural practices and so on?

Interesting and promising answers to these questions may be (and are being) given and tried in practice. Examples of the diversity of practices can be found in the different programmes in which reflexive modernisation of Dutch agriculture is now being waged. For the first time ever on 17 February 2004, the Agricultural Commission of the Dutch Parliament met outside the parliamentary sessions in a joint session with farmers and others from the rural areas in the north of the country. There is discussion between market parties on the legitimacy and practical implications of the existing variety of hallmarks for sustainably produced foodstuffs. These exemplary practices raise new questions (including the question of how they relate and might be related to each other) and thus need more attention than can be given here and more reflected answers than can be given now. Asking these questions are expressions of what it means to consider governance from the concept of reflexive modernisation; developing and testing answers is part of considering reflexive modernisation as a governance issue.

## HOW TO SHAPE SOCIETY AND THE MARKET EFFECTIVELY?

In section 2, we have seen that, from the conceptual perspective of reflexive modernisation, the traditional concept of government is to be characterised not only by referring to its plan-and-control mode of governing (relying on reason), but also by its assumption of a neat separation between government and the society/economy/science it is governing. Thus, governance must be understood as a concept, which fundamentally differs from government in, first, going beyond rational planning and its neglect of the autonomy of societal and economic practices; and, second, in critically opening up, making discursive, the existing shapes and mutual alignment of the institutions of state, society, market and science, which have been tailored to the vision of simple modernisation. Next, in section 3, I have argued that reflexive modernisation does require governance, in the sense of a deliberate influencing of societal and economic practices so as to re-orient these practices to the idea of radical modernity, as well as to bring about alignment and reinforcement between these practices. In this section, I will try and take up the challenge implied by these findings and indicate the contours of a governance concept for reflexive modernisation.

**Good Old Planning Theory**

Considering our search for non-control based strategies with which to influence a variety of practices, it is useful to start with the recognition that, for a long time already, several authors have elaborated planning theories that depart from an explicit acknowledgement of the principal limitations of planning: that information used as a basis for planning can never be complete; that rationality is bounded rather than comprehensive; and that the practices to be 'steered' face and also respond to other circumstances and developments than policy interventions, in ways that depend on the interpretations of the actors that perform these practices. Already during the heydays of planning, this was recognised in work by authors like Charles Lindblom (1959; 1965; 1979) and Sir Geoffrey Vickers (1965 [1995]). Later, when significant discrepancies started to be discerned between expectations and realities concerning governmental intervention in advanced welfare societies, work by such authors as Herman van Gunsteren (1975), Aaron Wildavsky (1973; 1979) and David Collingridge (1980) provided important and early insights.

In a thought-provoking essay, James Meadowcroft (1999) has argued that the basic features of such planning theories actually meet many of the reservations of some notorious critics of planning. Referring to the work of Friedrich Hayek (1960), he stresses how firmly Hayek was committed to the ideal of human progress. That Hayek nevertheless rejected planning reflects more than his deep mistrust in planning economies. It also reflects, first, his view that progress cannot be planned, because it essentially is a voyage in the unknown, to which not-planning is a better recommendation than planning. Contrary to this, as Meadowcroft (1999: 25–7) observes, one can propose that Hayek's scepticism is more defensible against long-range planning for progress than against deliberately pursuing more limited practices for improvement; and that in many cases, improvement has been achieved in deliberate actions, based on the expectation of improvement. (What Meadowcroft fails to point out here, is that this, in many cases, is contingent upon the fact that even supposedly 'free' interactions have been embedded in the carefully fine-tuned institutions for modernity – an issue we shall return to later.) Both the planning and non-planning of such practices are facing major uncertainties. However, rather than asserting that inaction would be best, we should conclude that practices have to be planned by organising trial-and-error learning.

Hayek's rejection of planning also reflects his solid faith that human beings, if left to their own resolve, will bring about progress; deliberate interventions in institutional conditions for such practices may influence them. Meadowcroft (ibid.) points out, ironically, that Hayek thus implicitly recognises that planning through adaptation of the institutional conditions that govern practices is possible, provided that it focuses on limited practices and includes processes of learning.

Let us consider the work by Charles Lindblom as one important example of how these lessons may be taken into account in planning theory. In 'A century of planning', Lindblom (1999) claims that the most successful cases of planning have been those in which government has subtly shaped the market, not only through regulative interventions, but also through creating the societal conditions under which the market might operate. After listing a range of examples – including taxation, economic mobilisation for the Second World War, research and development and city planning – he notes that they imply four lessons, identified in his earlier works (Lindblom, 1959; 1979):

- Do not plan in order to organise but plan to alter the existing social mechanisms, whether market or not, that govern $x$.
- Show some modesty: focus on just a well-defined segment of life, specialised, even narrow, rather than vast, synoptic and broad. That is [J.G.], it should be focused on specific practices.
- Planning rarely succeeds through a big step; rather it should aim at 'an endless succession of short and fairly rapid steps' in a process of 'trial-and-error' learning or 'serial adjustment'.
- Fourth: 'There may be – we do not yet know enough – big differences between a succession of short rapid steps that is influenced by a long term perspective, and one that is not, the former probably being the more successful form of planning and decision-making.' (Lindblom, 1999: 47–8)

It should also be embedded in a process of 'mutual adjustment': since policy choice cannot be based on reason alone, but essentially involves power and imposition. Since rationality of each single actor is bounded, processes of choice should be a matter of learning and contestation between a variation of practices (Lindblom 1965; 1999: 60 ff), and ultimately on some process of choice.

This view of planning is fundamentally compatible with what we noted, in the previous section, on political judgement. First, planning is to be located at the same spots where we located, in the previous section, political judgement: in the institutional arrangements of the political community as a whole; in 'socio-economic-scientific' practices; and 'in between'. And, second, this account of planning reinforces and presupposes the notion of taking a plurality of practices as a point of departure – a notion that has appeal both from the perspective of the problem of 'homogenisation and elimination of practice', which we have seen (in section 2) to be associated with simple modernisation, and from the perspective of the approach to democratic decision-making proposed in the previous section.

**Introducing Discursive Moments in Recursive Practices**

However, one crucial difficulty still remains to be solved. As indicated, Meadowcroft ignores the degree to which social practices are embedded in institutions that have been fine-tuned on the basis of the vision of modernity that is elaborated in domain-specific visions. Similarly, Lindblom's careful words about the role of long-range perspectives seem to reflect an underestimation of the degree to which such visions do actually play a role, even if implicitly. We need to take into account through what mechanisms specific expressions of the guiding vision of first modernity may inhibit practices for reflexive modernisation, as well as to understand better the nature of the institutional adaptations needed to counter them. How does, as we put it in section 3, the existing structure fight back, and what does this imply for the structural transformation needed? Subsequently, on the basis of the answers to these questions, we have to answer two other crucial questions: can the latter be done in a way compatible with Lindblom's pledge for modesty, through limited institutional adaptations? And how may these limited adaptations 'add up' to the larger project of reflexive modernisation?

Evaluations of projects for reflexive modernisation of agriculture in the Netherlands may provide valuable insights on both the mechanisms through which institutionalised features may enter such practices, and the nature of the institutional adaptations needed to successfully pursue such projects[6] (Grin et al., 2004). A first mechanism is that participants in these projects often 'import' such features into the projects in the form of self-evident routines of thought. For instance, in projects for sustainable livestock systems, the problem is often raised that improving animal welfare through giving animals more freedom of living will lead to increased susceptibility to pathogen organisms, and thus to disease. This claim reflects established veterinary thinking – which developed throughout the process of agricultural modernisation – in which the keeping of animals is seen as a matter of control. It is important to recognise that different views on animal health exist in literature, though far less researched than this established view of 'directive control': the paradigm of recursive control, in which animal health maintenance is based on the animal's natural behaviour and natural interaction with the environment (Bos et al., 2003). The implication is that, while some 'small steps' may already be made, in order to proceed to a bigger change in parallel programmes for paradigmatically new knowledge generation will need to be started to prepare the groundwork for later steps that truly lead to the road of reflexive modernisation. Such programmes by themselves are an example of reflexive modernisation: they may be expected to presuppose and bring about changes in the institutions of science, viz. of the distinctions between and within scientific disciplines. In addition, they enable development of non-control based agricultural practices, which, moreover, create a need for different food safety regulations (because these usually include not only prescriptions on product quality, but also on the production process).

Second, features embedded in modern institutions may creep into practices of reflexive modernisation through the anticipations of participants on the way in which the designs achieved in these practices will, eventually, 'travel' into the 'real world' and be able to live and survive there. One example was encountered in a project for a pigsty, in which substance cycles were to be closed by considering pig raising (and crop cultivation elsewhere) in an integral way, the outputs of one activity considered as the input for another one, rather than as waste (Bos and Grin, 2003). It appeared that such an integral design would run into two problems. The first was the tradition – embedded in investment patterns between banks and farmers – that farmers would not procure an entire sty at once, but rather buy a new component every now and then to connect it themselves to the other components. The second was that no 'integral pigsty producers' seemed to exist; rather, a range of highly specialised firms existed that might each produce a highly sophisticated component. Both factors reflected the differentiated, specialised product chains that had emerged in the agrofood sector throughout agricultural modernisation. Pursuing the project would require some institutional adaptations in the market.

These two mechanisms – importation of assumptions and anticipations of the 'real world' – may come together. In the project just mentioned, it was calculated that the costs per kilogram of meat would be €1.42 compared with €1.37 for a more traditional pig house. This was considered prohibitive in the market, as it was assumed to be a 'law of economics' that this €0.05 price increase would imply that consumers would pay an additional €0.50 in the store, and because it was anticipated that this would be entirely unacceptable to consumers. Upon closer scrutiny, however, it appeared that both the assumption and the anticipation were contingent on the existing power relations in the long and differentiated economic chains. More specifically, the assumed 'law' reflects the usual practice that all players 'downstream' obtain some additional added value from the price increase of the primary product. The anticipation that consumers will not be prepared to pay an additional price neglects consumption patterns that have recently emerged ('grazing'; increased reliance on prepared food rather than primary products – Van Otterloo, 2000), which rely on products in which players in the centre of the food chain put significantly more added value on primary products. Here again, institutional adaptations are needed to be able to go beyond this 'multiplication law' and to somehow accept relatively small price increases of the primary product in the significant value added by the processing industry.

What do these examples teach us in terms of the first question above? They indicate that the devil is in the detail, that seemingly self-evident assumptions and anticipations need to be put under critical scrutiny in moments of 'discursive will formation'. They also indicate that the difficulties implied may be dealt with through a combination of initial small steps 'beyond the rules' of existing institutions and longer term institutional transformations. In the case of the first example, one short-term step might be to start an experimental project in which results of a transdisciplinary study on novel ways to maintain animal health in that project are tried out. Another simultaneous step might be the start of a more comprehensive programme (involving both scientists and practitioners, contributing their mētis) for developing the 'recursive control' paradigm in veterinary sciences, as well as its consequences for other areas of the animal sciences (housing, breeding, feeding, and so on). Next steps might involve improvement and extension of the experimental project on the basis of the experiences gained, as well as on the insights gained from the programme on recursive control. Ultimately in the longer term, new distinctions may emerge surrounding this programme: between 'science' and 'practice' (Grin, 2005) and within and between scientific disciplines. A similar strategy of step-by-step transformation may be followed to deal with difficulties due to market features.

Against this background, let us now turn to the final two questions raised in the introduction to this section. Reflexive modernisation on a more encompassing level may emerge from these practices, provided synergy is realised between them. Such synergy may result from actions by planners who 'make smart connections' (Grin et al., 2003), but also from these practices reaching out to each other. It is in this way that what I called above 're-structuration' may be induced. To elaborate this further into a governance concept, two additional insights may prove particularly helpful.

The first relates to the fact that recent social theory has shifted the analytical viewpoint from the chicken-or-egg question of structure and action ('does S determine A, or is it the other way around?') towards practices in which they shape each other. This theorem of the duality of structure is of course the core of Giddens's structuration theory; but it is also central to for example Bourdieu's (1977) notion of the habitus as well as to the way in which Leydesdorff (2001) has elaborated Luhmann's theory. Common to all these approaches is the fact that the mutual shaping of structure and action takes place through the work done by acting subjects – structure, in a phrase of John Law, has become a verb.

The implication of the preceding is the insight that governance should focus on providing central actors in a variety of practices[7] with the strategic insight to induce a succession of steps in which structure and action interact with each other towards a radical modernity. Meta-theoretical insights from the theories mentioned may be enriched and made more operational by empirical studies of earlier processes of 'regime change' (Geels, 2002) and by different bodies of middle-range theory, including methods of regime analysis that are based on complex system theory (Rotmans et al., 2000; 2001); and insights from the field of science and technology studies concerning the interdynamics of niches, regime change and trends of change in the wider environment (Rip and Kemp, 1998; Roep et al., 2003; as well as Kemp and Loorbach, Chapter 5 in this volume, Rip, Chapter 4 in this volume).

The second insight that may be of use here concerns the importance of guiding visions. Relying on a wide range of empirical and theoretical literature from science and society studies, Dierkes et al. (1995) have argued that successful processes of socio-technological change derive their success, to a significant extent, from guiding visions. These visions have a dual function that is well expressed in the German term *Leitbild*: they serve as a mental image of an attainable future shared by a collection of actors and they guide the actions of and interactions between those actors. An attainable future here is one that offers a perspective of going beyond established assumptions and anticipations. A vision with such characteristics can serve, as the authors put it, the 'functional equivalent' of institutional arrangements, in those cases where existing arrangements are object of transformation and therefore cannot be taken as guidance. Developing the vision of radical modernity into context-specific visions (in plural) may therefore contribute to joint action for reflexive modernisation.

These two insights may enhance each other: visions which portray a world in which 'we can do better' (Roep et al., 2003: 206) can help identify – in ways suggested by the above examples – the concrete strategies needed on the niche and regime level. Conversely, trends that have been discovered to yield strategic opportunities for regime transformation may be integrated into visions. Together, they may give 'flesh and blood' to Latour's metaphorical 'lever' effect.

The examples also suggest that this is far from a trivial task. Development of new approaches to policy analysis, which are tailored to support a variety of actors in this task, is an additional topic for elaborating a governance concept for reflexive modernisation. Such a topic deserves much more attention than it has been given both here and in literature more generally (but see Forester, 1999 and Fischer, 2003).

## NOTES

1. In fact, the insights presented here will be further developed in the context of the Dutch Knowledge Network on System Innovations, of which the author is co-director and in which scientists from a wide variety of areas (complex system theory and integrated analysis, the social history of technology, innovation studies and the policy sciences) cooperate with each other and with practitioners (Rotmans et al., 2003).
2. In processes that have been far from uniform between nation states.
3. This dual expression reflects the duality of structure (Giddens, 1984).
4. Countries like Germany and France had basically similar policies, and the first European Commissioner of Agriculture was Mansholt, the first post-war Dutch minister of agriculture. See Ackrill (2000).
5. The risks and side-effects, together with more established criteria as economic viability, are taken as the dimensions.
6. For similar examples in the area of health care, see Grin (2004).
7. In line with what I argued on the loci for both political judgement and planning, this includes actors on the level of the political community as a whole; in 'socio-economic-scientific' practices; and 'in between'.

## REFERENCES

Ackrill, Robert (2000), *The Common Agricultural Policy*, Sheffield: Sheffield Academic Press.
Archer, Margaret S. (2003), *Structure, Agency and the Internal Conversation*, Cambridge: Cambridge University Press.
Beck, Ulrich (1992), *Risk Society. Towards a New Modernity*, London: Sage.
Beck, Ulrich (1997), *The re-invention of politics. Rethinking Modernity in the Global Social Order*, Cambridge: Polity Press.
Beck, Ulrich, Wolfgang Bonns and Christoph Lau (2003), 'The theory of reflexive modernisation. Problematic, hypotheses and research programme', *Theory, Culture and Society*, **20** (2), 1–33.
Bekke, Hans, Jouke de Vries and Geert Neelen (1994), *De Salto Mortale van het Ministerie van Landbouw, Natuurbeheer en Visserij. Beleid, Organisatie en Management op een Breukvlak*, Alphen aan den Rijn: Samson H.D. Tjeenk Willink.
Bekke, Hans and Jouke de Vries (2001), *De Ontpoldering van de Nederlandse Landbouw. Het Ministerie van Landbouw, Natuurbeheer en Visserij, 1994–2000*, Leuven/Apeldoorn: Garant.
Benhabib, Seyla (1992), *Situating the Self. Gender, Community and Post-modernity in Contemporary Ethics*, New York: Routledge.

Benhabib, Seyla (2002), *The Claims of Culture. Equality and Diversity in the Global Era*, Princeton, NJ and Oxford: Princeton University Press.

Bernstein, Richard J. (1983), *Beyond objectivism and relativism. Science, Hermeneutics and Praxis*, Philadelphia: University of Pennsylvania Press.

Bernstein, Richard J. (1993), *The New Constellation. The Ethical–Political Horizons of Modernity/Postmodernity*, Cambridge, MA: MIT Press.

Bieleman, J. (2000), 'Landbouw', Deel I (p. 11–233) in: *Techniek in Nederland in de Twintigste Eeuw: Landbouw and Voeding*, Zutphen: Walburg Pers.

Bos, Bram, Peter Groot Koerkamp and Karin Groenestein (2003), 'A novel design approach for livestock housing based on recursive control – with examples to reduce environmental pollution', *Livestock Production Science*, **84**, 157–70.

Bos, Bram and John Grin (forthcoming), 'The Hercules effect of dealing with risks within modern institutions: lessons from a project on sustainable husbandry', *Science, Technology and Human Values*.

Bourdieu, Pierre (1977), *Outline of a Theory of Practice*, Cambridge: Cambridge University Press.

Collingridge, David (1980), *The Social Control of Technology*, London: Macmillan.

De Wilt, J.G. (2004), Paper prepared for a meeting at the Centre for Prospective Technology Studies, Joint Research Center at Sevilla.

Dierkes, M, U. Hoffmann and L. Marz (1995), *Visions of Technology. Social and Institutional Factors Shaping the Development of New Technologies*, Frankfurt and New York: Campus Verlag/St. Martin's Press.

Fischer, Frank (2003), *Reframing Public Policy: Discursive Politics and Deliberative Practices*. Oxford: Oxford University Press.

Flyvbjerg, Bent (2001), *Making Social Science Matter. Why Social Inquiry Fails and How it can Succeed Again*, Cambridge: Cambridge University Press.

Forester, John (1999), *The Deliberative Practitioner*, Cambridge, MA: MIT Press.

Fox, Charles J. and Hugh T. Miller (1996), *Postmodern Public Administration. Toward Discourse*, London: SAGE.

Geels, Frank W. (2002), *Understanding the Dynamics of Technological Transitions: A Co-evolutionary and Socio-technical Analysis*, Enschede: Twente University Press.

Giddens, A. (1984), *The Constitution of Society. Outline of the Theory of Structuration*, Cambridge: Polity Press.

Giddens, Anthony (1991), *Modernity and Self-Identity. Self and Society in the Late Modern Age*, Cambridge: Polity Press.

Gill, Graeme (2003), *The Nature and Development of the Modern State*, Houndmills and New York, NY: Palgrave Macmillan.

Grin, John and Henk van de Graaf (1996a), 'Technology assessment as learning', *Science, Technology and Human Values*, **20** (1), 72–99.

Grin, John and Henk van de Graaf (1996b), 'Implementation as communicative action. An interpretive understanding of interactions between policy actors and target groups', *Policy Sciences*, **29** (4), 291–319.

Grin, John, Henk van de Graaf and Philip Vergragt (2003), 'Een derde generatie milieubeleid: Een sociologisch perspectief en een beleidswetenschappelijk programma', *Beleidswetenschap*, **17** (1), 51–72.

Grin, John, Francisca Felix, Bram Bos and Sierk Spoelstra (2004), 'Practices for reflexive design: lessons from a Dutch programme on sustainable agriculture', *International Journal of Foresight and Innovation Policy*, **1** (1–2), 146–69.

Grin, John (2005), 'Knowledge society: old wine in new bottles, or a new contract between science and society?', to be published in Joske Bunders ed. (2005): Sharing Knowledge? Exploring the Interfaces Between Science and Society, Amsterdam: Boom.

Hajer, Maarten A. (2003), 'Policy without polity: policy analysis and the institutional void', *Policy Sciences*, **36** (2), 175–95.

Haraway, Donna J. (1991), *Simians, Cyborgs and Women: The Reinvention of Nature*, New York: Routledge.

Hayek, Friedrich (1960), *The Constitution of Liberty*, London: Routledge & Kegan Paul.

Hennis, Marjoleine (2001), 'Europeanization and globalization: the missing link', *Journal of Common Market Studies*, **39** (5), 829–50.

Hoppe, Rob and John Grin (2000), 'Traffic goes through the TA machine: A culturalist comparison', in Norman J. Vig and Herbert Passchen (eds), *Parliaments and Technology: the Development of Technology Assessment in Europe*, New York: SUNY Press, pp. 273–324.

Joas, Hans (1993), *Pragmatism and Social Theory*, Chicago and London: Chicago University Press.

Kickert, Walter J.M., Erik-Hans Klijn and Joop F.M. Koppenjan (eds) (1997), *Managing Complex Networks: Strategies for the Public Sector*, London: Sage.

Kooiman, Jan (2003), *Governing as Governance*, London: Sage.

Kumar, Krishan (1995), *From Post-Industrial to Post-Modern Society. New Theories of the Contemporary World*, Oxford and Malden, MA: Blackwell.

Latour, Bruno (2003), 'Is re-modernization occurring – and if so, how to prove it?', *Theory, Culture and Society*, **20** (2), 35–48.

Law, John (1992), 'Notes on the theory of the actor-network: ordering, strategy and heterogeneity', *Systems Practice*, **5**, 179–393.

Leydesdorff, Loet (2001), *A Sociological Theory of Communication. The Self-Organization of the Knowledge-Based Society*, Universal Publishers.

Lindblom, Charles E. (1959), 'The science of "muddling through"', *Public Administration Review*, **39**, 79–88.

Lindblom, Charles E. (1965), *The Intelligence of Democracy*, New York: Prentice Hall.

Lindblom, Charles E. (1979), 'Still muddling, not yet through', *Public Administration Review*, **59**, 517–26.

Lindblom, Charles E. (1999), 'A century of planning', in Michael Kenny and James Meadowcroft (eds), *Planning Sustainability*, London and New York: Routledge, pp. 39–65.

Loeber, Anne (2004), 'Practical wisdom in the risk society. Methods and practice of interpretive analysis on questions of sustainable development', Amsterdam: University of Amsterdam (PhD thesis).

Meadowcroft, James (1999), 'Planning for sustainable development: what can we learn from the critics?', in Michael Kenny and James Meadowcroft (eds), *Planning Sustainability*, London and New York: Routledge.

Newman, Janet (2001), *Modernising Governance: New Labour, Policy and Society*, London: Sage.

Pierre, J. and B. Guy Peters (2002), *Governance, Politics and the State*, Basingstoke: Macmillan.

Priester, P.R. (2000), 'Landbouw', part Ib in: *Techniek in Nederland in de twintigste eeuw: Landbouw and Voeding*. Zutphen: Walburg Pers, pp. 65–125.

Rip, Arie and René Kemp (1998), 'Technological change', in Steve Rayner and Elizabeth L. Malone (eds), *Human Choice and Climate Change*, Columbus, OH: Batelle Press, pp. 327–99.

Roep, D., J.D. van der Ploeg and J.S.C. Wiskerke (2003), 'Managing technical–intitutional design processes: some strategic lessons from environmental co-operatives in the Netherlands', *Netherlands Journal of Agrarian Studies*, **51** (1–2), pp. 195–217.

Rotmans, J., R. Kemp, M.B.A. van Asselt, F.W. Geels, G. Verbong and K. Molendijk (2000), *Transitions and Transition Management*, Maastricht: ICIS.

Rotmans, J., R. Kemp and M.B.A. van Asselt (2001), 'More evolution than revolution: transition management in public policy', *Foresight*, **3** (1), pp. 15–31.

Rotmans, Jan, John Grin, Johan Schot and Ruud Smits (2003), 'A multidisciplinary research programme on transitions and system innovations', presented at the Open Science Meeting of the International Human Dimensions Programme, Montreal, 18–20 October.

Scott, James (1998), *Seeing like a State*, New Haven, CT: Yale University Press.

Toulmin, Stephen (1990), *Cosmopolis. The Hidden Agenda of Modernity*, Chicago: University of Chicago Press.

Van der Ploeg, Jan-Douwe (1999), *De virtuele boer*, Assen: Van Gorcum.

Van Gunsteren (1975), *The Quest for Control*, New York: John Wiley.

Van Otterloo, Anneke H. (ed.) (2000), 'Part II (voeding)', in *Techniek in Nederland in de twintigste eeuw: Landbouw en voeding*, Zutphen: Walberg pers.

Van Tatenhove, Jan, Bas Arts, Pieter Leroy (eds) 2000, *Political Modernisation and the Environment. The Renewal of Environmental Policy Arrangements*, Dordrecht: Kluwer Academic Publishers.

Vickers, Geoffrey (1995 [1965]), *The Art of Judgment. A Study of Policy Making* centenary edition in the Advances in Public Administration series, London: Sage.

Wildavsky, A. (1973), 'If planning is everything, maybe it's nothing', *Policy Sciences*, **4**, pp. 137–53.

Wildavsky, A. (1979), *The Art and Craft of Policy Analysis*, London: Macmillan.

Wisserhof, Johan (2000), 'Agricultural policy making in the Netherlands: beyond corporatist policy arrangements?', in Jan van Tatenhove, Bas Arts and Pieter Leroy (eds), *Political Modernisation and the Environment. The Renewal of Environmental Policy Arrangements*, Dordrecht: Kluwer Academic Publishers, pp. 175–98.

# 4. A co-evolutionary approach to reflexive governance – and its ironies

## Arie Rip

In the Introduction to this book, sustainability is characterized as open-ended, complex and uncertain, and governance approaches are identified to cope with such a challenge, in particular, to overcome the limitations of simplistic modernist approaches. Reflexive governance for reflexive modernity is the aim. In this chapter, I will add to this undertaking by developing reflexive governance independent of the particular requirements introduced by sustainability. There is complexity of governance independent of the complexity of the object of governance, sustainability. The strategies for sustainability identified in the Introduction are important, but they tend to be strategies for governance of reflexive modernity, rather than strategies in and thus part of reflexive modernity.

Why do I create the contrast between governance *of* reflexive modernity and governance *in* reflexive modernity? The Introduction already provides arguments about the endogenous nature of steering and other attempts at governance. Still, political actors, and more generally, actors with a governance responsibility, will see themselves as somehow outside the system that they have to govern. This is almost unavoidable: to articulate a strategy, one has (so it appears) to diagnose a situation 'out there' and formulate a response. In addition, governance actors will be held accountable for what they set in motion, and for that reason they will be positioned (and will position themselves) as independent of the system that is being governed. The effects of their strategies, however, are determined by ongoing dynamics outside their influence, and by the response of other actors to the strategies of the governance actors.

Implementation studies have addressed this by emphasizing the importance of 'bottom-up' processes (Hanf and Toonen 1985, see also Pressman and Wildavsky (1984) on mutual adaptation between policy making and what happens 'on the ground') and turned it into advice for modest policy making, or better, policy making that takes implementability into account. On the other hand, even modest policy making needs to make a difference, not just follow what is happening anyway – and occasionally grasp

*82*

an opportunity. This is a well-known debate, and has been analysed by Lindblom and Woodhouse (1993) in terms of (enlightened) incrementalism. I want to broaden this debate by including de facto governance, as it emerges and might be modulated by governance actors who are part of this process. In other words, they have to work from the inside.

In general, constraining and enabling patterns and structures evolve. This constitutes de facto governance, in that they guide the actions and interactions of actors and can be appreciated in terms of embedded goals and actual outcomes. Reflexive governance can then have two forms. In its enlightened modernist version, de facto governance embedded in patterns is seen as a challenge, as something to be overcome in order to reach a better situation (even if it is still open as to what will be 'better'). In its non-modernist version,[1] the governance actor recognizes that being part of the evolving patterns, s/he can at best modulate them – just as all the other actors are modulating the patterns through their actions and interactions, intentionally or unintentionally.

Of course, being part of evolving patterns is the basic situation, whether this is recognized or not. Also enlightened modernist governance actors recognize this, and act accordingly. But they see such actions as a necessary detour and would continue to see themselves and their goals as outside the system. Non-modernist governance actors see governance as part of the overall evolution, and will draw other lessons from failures, for example by accommodating to the (evolving) situation, somewhat like Donald Schön's professional and his 'conversation with the situation' (Schön 1984).

Thus, reflexive governance, in both forms, must be predicated on a diagnosis of ongoing patterns and their constraints, how to act in their context and perhaps improve on them. Such a diagnosis has to start with the insight that in a sense, society hangs together through unintended effects, both positive and negative (Portes 2000). There is overlap with Beck's diagnosis of reflexive modernity as modernity confronted with its own, more or less unintended effects.[2] Or as Rip and Groen (2001: 21) suggest: 'Unintended and often unexpected effects occur because actors do not take the overall [sociotechnical] dynamics into account.' Thus, while society continues to be scattered by unintended effects, there can also be 'institutional anticipation', which hopefully mitigates the negative consequences.[3]

To develop the notion of reflexive governance further, I will articulate a co-evolutionary perspective. There is an instrumental argument to do so: because co-evolution happens, take that into account, accommodate, anticipate, and create nexuses (Van den Belt and Rip 1987, Schot and Rip 1997). There is a normative argument as well: variety is important, and while lock-ins occur, they may have to be broken up again, so lateral, disturbing actions must be welcomed. I will build on my analysis of co-evolution of science, technology and society (Rip 2002a, 2002b), but the thrust of the argument is not limited to science and technology and their reflexive governance. The phenomena of emerging path-dependencies and possible lock-ins which I will identify are not unique to science, technology and society, nor are the attendant limitations on the scope of steering.

## A CO-EVOLUTIONARY PERSPECTIVE

Let me start with evolutionary theories and then add mutual translations or mutual 'selections' which can add up to patterns.[4] This route is definitely plausible for scientific and technological change, but can be taken to apply to social change and social order more generally, even if it may be difficult to develop specific theories. As a perspective, it can still be used to draw attention to certain phenomena.

There is an abundance of evolutionary theories about technological change, and some evolutionary theories about science and its institutions.[5] There are good reasons for such theories, because central to modern science and technology is the introduction of novelties, which like biological mutations will at first be tentative and uncertain 'hopeful monstrosities' (Mokyr 1990, Stoelhorst 1997), but can grow and modify, and become accepted. Evolutionary theories in biology often emphasize that variation as well as selection are blind so that there is no guarantee of the quality of the outcomes other than that they will fit the contingencies of the selection environment. For science and technology, and for social life generally, the selection environment is not blind, and when variations, that is, novelties, are produced, there is anticipation on eventual selection up to attempts to change the selection environment so as to increase the chances for the variation to survive. Van den Belt and Rip (1987) showed (using the label of quasi-evolutionary theory) that nexuses between variation and selection emerge (with test laboratories for new products as an example) and positioned the existence of paradigms in science and technology as a temporary, but forceful stabilization of selection and thus continuity in variation leading to a trajectory or path of further development.

In the co-evolution of science, technology and society, patterns at the institutional and societal level also emerge and stabilize (and open up again). For example, there is a diffuse social contract between science and society visible in expectations about science, its mandate and division of responsibilities, and the institutional arrangements. The phrase 'Science, The Endless Frontier' (after Vannevar Bush's report to the US President in 1945) is often used to characterize the post-Second World War social contract, with its dual character of funding open-ended basic research on the one hand that would somehow deliver great things to society, and on the other hand, having big public laboratories, for example, for defence, nuclear energy, new materials (Guston and Kenniston 1994). The quasi-autonomous dynamics of science appear to be so strong that governance actors cannot do much more than try to modulate what is going on anyway.[6] In fact, during most of the twentieth century, science policy was defined as the support of science. It is only recently that more interventionist measures are considered and implemented – which then lead to concerns that emphasis on short-term relevance could undermine the quality of science, or at the very least introduce 'epistemic drift' (Elzinga 1985). Science policy actors now experience the tension between accommodating to ongoing dynamics, and assuming a political responsibility which implies some intervention.[7]

In other words, the earlier diffuse social contract has started to break down. By now, a new regime of 'Strategic Science', that focuses on wealth creation and support for decision making and quality of life, is emerging. This includes a more distributed character of knowledge production, which is visible in the way new fields in ICT, genomics and nanotechnology are organized (Rip 2002a).

The patterns of such regimes enable productive work and interactions, while at the same time constraining them. This can be welcomed as well as criticized. The evolutionary perspective does not offer immediate entrance points for normative evaluation – that is, as it were, delegated to the selection environment – but a second-order normativity can be drawn on: the importance of allowing for further evolution. Specifically, stabilization of patterns and of emerging irreversibilities more generally could create a lock-in that is difficult to escape. In the case of recent changes in and around science, I have argued that the regime of Strategic Science might be closing in upon itself too soon, because of strong economic and decision-making pressures to deliver, and to exclude alternative, or just different approaches, like community-oriented research and indigenous knowledges. Without necessarily pronouncing on the value of these approaches per se, I argue that they play a role in maintaining heterogeneity (Rip 2000).

Another feature where second-order normativity can be articulated is the increasing reflexivity of the co-evolution of science, technology and society. The rise of explicit science policy making (since the Sputnik shock of 1957) is a first indicator. Technology assessment, debated expertise, and participation are recent phenomena, and have become accepted as a necessary element (Rip 2002c). Such reflexivity is not just a matter of discourse and debate, even if that is part of it. It is about institutionalized feedback relations, which handle – in this case – interactions between science, technology and society. In other words, the de facto governance arrangements become reflexive. This can be welcomed as a desirable development, somewhat independent of the nature of the actual arrangements and the outcomes.

I have developed the co-evolutionary perspective discussing science and technology in society. The existence of co-evolutionary dynamics appeared to be predicated on the partial autonomy of the developments in science and in technology with respect to developments in (other parts of) society. Such relative autonomy is itself a historical phenomenon, coming into its own in the nineteenth century. Formally, co-evolution is the linked evolution of two (or more) dynamics, each of which can be conceptualized in terms of variations and selections (and retentions), but can also be used more informally.[8] The linkages give rise to patterns with dynamics of their own, like paradigms and regimes. The term has been used by Nelson (1994) for technology, firms and institutions, by Leydesdorff (2000) for science, government and industry, and by Rip and Kemp (1998) for technology and society. Other studies not using the term still address such questions, for example in the analysis of historical path dependency of national economies (North 1990). The further claim now is that co-evolutionary dynamics occur generally, because there are always emergent irreversibilities and patterns with some dynamics of their own which will interact.

Such an approach is not unlike emergent systems approaches and actor-centred institutionalism (for example, Schimank 1988, 1992). Complexity theory has a different starting point, but arrives at similar insights about governance.[9] The extra feature here is the evolution-theoretical claim that variation and selection are basic phenomena. The introduction and nurturing of novelties is not unique to science and technology: the occurrence of variations is a general phenomenon of social life, and agency can be positioned as variation rather than intentional action. Such novelties may not always be visible, because the variations are often transformed back into the regular (cf. 'repair work' as studied in symbolic interactionism) or excluded or otherwise made invisible. Whether variations remain visible and have effects depends on the constellation in which they occur: selective co-evolution, now in the small.

An interesting example of such variation-in-context is how on 1 December 1955 Rosa Parks, a black lady from Montgomery (Alabama), sat down in the bus on a place reserved for whites. She was forced to get off the bus, and this sparked off the bus protest movement. Hundreds or thousands of black persons had had this experience previously without anything much happening. Now, the circumstances were right, and other actors in the situation, notably in the nascent civil rights movement in Alabama (and later more widely) who could use Rosa Parks as a case for their cause, co-produced the effect.[10] As Beck et al. (2003: 26) phrase it, 'the subject becomes part of a self-selected network which allows connections and communication, but also makes it the object of the choices and decisions of others'.

Thus, there are good reasons to continue with a co-evolutionary approach, broadly speaking: its basic assumptions apply in the small, and its implications are important in the large. What does this imply for the role of actors? They are definitely not the lone individuals of rational choice analysis, where rules and institutions appear purely as constraints on their freedom (the second-order normativity of rational choice theory is visible here). Rational choice analysis can offer interesting insights, but only for cases where preferences can be considered as given, and anticipation and interaction are shaped according to strategic games with known rules.

For our actors, there is the experience of effects of co-evolution in terms of constraints, uncertainties, and multi-actor, multi-level dynamics: mutual interdependencies, the force of path dependency, anticipation of selection, as well as, even more precariously, anticipation of emerging patterns (the struggle for an industry standard is an obvious example). Intentional and strategic action does contribute to the co-evolution and the patterns which structure action, but the resulting patterns may not be desired by any of the actors. These emerge 'behind their backs', as it were. Using the well-known boat-shaped diagram of Coleman, where individual actions add up to patterns at the collective level (Coleman 1990), this can be phrased as: actors jostling in the bow of Coleman's boat, and so moving it ahead and creating structures larger than themselves in that movement.

While path dependencies are unavoidable (in fact, can be productive), some paths will turn out to be better than others. Actors would want to anticipate, and then do something about the paths that emerge, and the regimes and lock-ins that limit the scope of intervention for change. In the emergent phase, the direction of the path will be unclear, but intervention is relatively easy, and its effect when taken up in the path or regime will continue. (see Rip and Schot 2002 on loci for modulation of technological development.)

Furthermore, when actors, through a better understanding of their selection environments and the dynamics of co-evolution, try to achieve desired outcomes, other actors will react, and the enlightened strategies cannot be stable. Analysis of such processes should therefore endogenize (as economists would say) all steering attempts, including those of the principal or other focal actor, as elements of the overall process. The actor's attempt at endogenizing himself, at least in the analysis, may show up in a different action (further variation) and contribute to overall reflexivity.

These are basic elements (and foundational issues) of a first-round diagnosis of the complexities of governance. It shifts the role of governance actors:

> Instead of the heroism of the policy actor vis-à-vis the system, there is a variety of actors and roles, and a 'distributed coherence' which is self-organized. Some actors may contribute more to the self-organization than others, but there is no

general rule. Or better, there are lots of rules, dominant positions etc., but these are contingent and cannot be taken for granted. Instead of steering, there is reflective (and reflexive) intervention: mutual translations (that's what happens anyway) are now seen as the basic process. (Rip 2002)

This is more than the well-known criticism of rational planning and control approaches and reference to interactive approaches, policy networks, self-regulation and so on. Distributed coherence is now the effect of reflexive co-evolution, and a variety of agents are involved who all contribute to governance. Among this variety, these are reflexive agents like Constructive TA agents described in Schot and Rip (1977): ideally, all actors could take up that role. The present book implies, already in the way the editors and authors view their task, that there are sustainability agents who can profit from their analysis. Lindblom's 'disjointed incrementalism' is not only practical advice to a governance actor with limited power and limited insight, but also a way to advance what he calls 'intelligent democracy', where all citizens would be reflexive-governance agents. Lindblom advocates a political position. Schot and Rip are more ironical, and recognize the struggles between opponents of various kinds that are necessary to have incentives to act and learn.

## NON-MODERN STEERING AND ANTICIPATION-IN-ACTION

How to develop the first-round diagnosis further and translate it into strategies for reflexive governance? Basically, it must be steering from within the co-evolutionary process (what I have called 'modulation'), possibly also referring to second-order normative notions of variety, reflexivity and distributed coherence. The notion of 'steering', with its implication of an agent faced with an 'object' to be steered, is of course misleading since the steering agent is part of an evolving system including the 'object' and himself. To keep the tensions visible, I will use the term non-modern steering, a *contradictio in terminis*, as a programmatic concept. The enlightened modernist version of reflexive governance then becomes a specific version of non-modern steering, where anticipation-in-action takes the co-evolution into account, but primarily in order to better achieve one's goals.

My approach in this section is to collect possible instances of non-modern steering, and draw out insights in 'how to do' steering-from-within and what the problems and some of the paradoxes are. Let me start again with science and science policy.

The co-evolution of science, technology and society cannot be steered in a simplistic interventionist way – other than for short periods of time and/or in special circumstances. For science policy agents this is clear, for example, in the way they depend on the aggregation of views and insights in the scientific community to set priorities, even if they can make a difference by deciding on the funding. But even there, they are subject to credibility pressures; for example, which science policy agent can nowadays refuse to support genomics and nanotechnology? Further analysis is possible, in particular in terms of multi-level development with mutual dependencies between a policy and governing decision level, an intermediary level (for example, funding agencies) and the level of research performing actors (Rip 1998). This framework can be used to understand overall developments in research systems (Rip and Van der Meulen 1996), but also to understand how actor strategies emerge and interact (Morris 2004).

Important for the general idea of non-modern steering is the opportunity the framework offers to include the effect of context on policy instruments. In contrast to a major (even if now being criticized) thrust in the policy literature, policy instruments should not be discussed in isolation. They do not work because of their intrinsic characteristics but because of the context in which they are applied, and in particular, the amount of repair work that is done at other levels. This helps to articulate the global notion of steering from-the-inside and adds the possibility that success derives from repair work elsewhere in the overall system.

Such repair work happens all the time, and unavoidably so, but it tends not to be recognized because of the modernist illusion. I have argued a number of times that the apparent effectiveness of some modernist policies (in science policy, in risk regulation) derives from the repair work done during implementation and ongoingly in local practices. Thus, acceptance of local 'repair work' in order to keep things going is necessary, and one component of non-modern steering is to ensure its quality rather than try to control it from a distance. In other words, as Bruno Latour (1991) claims, we have never been modern, and the 'hybrid monsters' backgrounded by modernist ideologies actually continue to do their work and thus ensure that the modernist venture carries on, in spite of the ideologies.[11] 'Non-modern' then does not negate modernism, but draws attention to its actual practices.

There are instances of non-modern steering. Opening up learning spaces, as emphasized in the Introduction to this book, can be seen as non-modern steering. The orientation then is less towards solving problems (of sustainability), but towards creating and maintaining spaces for working towards solutions. This might include increasing reflexivity as an institutional capacity. In a co-evolutionary perspective, reflexivity and attendant learning is located in the processes and at the system level, not in the heads of individuals.[12]

A dedicated approach 'from the inside' is the setting up of what I have called 'macro-alignment actors' (Rip 1995): since successful development and embedding in society of a novelty (for example a new technological option or promising product) requires socio-technical alignment, also at the macro-level, various actors to be involved in such alignment can be brought together to work actively towards it, and can attempt to shape co-evolution together.[13] Because further articulation is necessary as well, such platforms are also spaces for learning: new ventures are discussed and negotiated, while participants select from the various tidbits they have heard about actual and possible developments. In a sense, while such a platform may avail itself of analytical support, what happens is social reduction of uncertainty, through coordination, supported by articulating a repertoire of arguments and assurance. Pro-active efforts at alignment occur also in the battle for a 'dominant design' or 'an industry standard'. Sometimes platforms or committees are formed, but even while actors recognize that a collective good has to be produced, it is only under special circumstances that there is a collaborative effort (Deuten 2003).

However important alignment is for development and success, there is also the issue of too rapid alignment, possibly in a less desirable direction, or in any case so soon that not enough learning has occurred. For science and technology policy, policy actors, because of their distance (thus, loose coupling) from performing actors, may have a governance task here. They are in a position to consider whether ongoing developments threaten to get locked-in into what might well be an unproductive path, and then actively create incentives to avoid the lock-in.[14]

A recurrent issue is how to understand the dynamics of development of which one is a part (in general, and in the particular case) so as to be able to anticipate the process to some extent.[15] This practical concern can be linked to the co-evolutionary perspective: future-oriented interactions have to be enabled between actors who constitute each other's selection environment,[16] and such arrangements must be supported by some understanding of overall dynamics so that the eventual alignment will be informed by this understanding. Such understanding is more than action-oriented knowledge; it is often embedded in and articulated through action.

Donald Schön (1984) showed how professionals and other practitioners work on the basis of 'reflection in action'. Some components of reflection-in-action he identified, like 'naming' (seeing the present situation as an instance of what happened before) and 'framing' (addressing the present situation from a perspective that has worked before), are anticipation-in-action and might well be relevant for our question which focuses on the general issue of anticipation-in-action. A third component in Schön's analysis is also important: conversation with the situation. This can directly be linked with interactive approaches of governance actors, but has a learning aspect as well.[17]

Anticipation-in-action can be functionally defined as part of reflexive modernity, embedded in feedback loops, so it is part of second-order reflexivity.[18] Knowledge is involved, but anticipation is action-orientated supported by attitudes (for instance, precautionary or risk-embracing), intelligence about what might happen (including not only monitoring and learning, but also early warning and early signalling in general), and structured knowledge about patterns and dynamics.

Such action-oriented anticipatory knowledge is increasingly visible in our societies, up to institutionalized anticipation arrangements. These include approaches to compensate for uncertainty, like risk assessment, prudence (in general, and via precautionary principle). There is a massive amount of technical work, but this should be located in terms of overall changes.[19]

There cannot be simple instrumental use of anticipatory knowledge. This is particularly clear in the case of early warnings, but the point is general: actors will respond to the availability of anticipatory knowledge, and the eventual uptake will depend on their reactions.[20] If anticipation is taken as a separate cognitive task, how to guesstimate the future, it is modernist venture.[21]

Apart from the cognitive problems of recognizing and ascertaining patterns in the dynamics so as to be able to anticipate, there are self-fulfilling and self-negating anticipations, and mutual anticipation in strategic games which reinforce (as with Moore's Law[22]) or shift the dynamics (as with some science policy interventions) depending on the nature of the strategic game.

Thus, actors should not only anticipate on future developments including strategic action from their colleagues, competitors and other actors in the system, but also anticipate on the patterns that might evolve. A sort of sociological enlightenment, including the paradox that such insights when shared will lead to further strategic actions which will shift the pattern and thus undermine the value of the insights. For example, actors have been learning about the way industry standards emerge, and try to get their standard dominant by exploiting this insight – as all the other actors will do. This will shift the dynamics and make the original insight inappropriate.

A further complexity is the contested nature of anticipatory claims, taken up in various forms of societal debate, but often inconclusively (which is perhaps what should be the case!). This can be further linked with the trend of producing anticipatory knowledge that is not limited to controlled circumstances as in a laboratory (the traditional precondition for prediction), in particular through (simulation) modelling. The models of global climate change are a case (and a contested case) in point. Models have in fact become regular decision support tools, for example in water management or traffic management. They can, but need not, push the complexity of governance issues out of sight (Nooteboom and Teisman 2003).

Clearly, anticipation-in-action has governance effects. One can actually see it as an example of non-modern steering: there will be responses, but not exclusively from a centre. And uptake and 'implementation' occur in a variety of ways, and are distributed across a range of actors.

What one sees are multi-authored narratives about unintended consequences and the need for prudence; narratives about the nature of such consequences, and about general strategies to address them. These are linked to (often implicit) narratives about how people behave, and how society evolves. Such narratives, especially when they reflect ongoing stories and storylines which constrain and enable, can be powerful in shaping action.[23] Thus, and necessarily, reflexive governance is predicated on the stories that circulate – and the circulation can be modulated.

Reflexive governance is also about enabling the learning that occurs, including the need to avoid lock-ins which would limit further learning. One should recognize, though, that learning does not occur by itself. Actors will invest in learning only when they are forced to do so, to ensure their survival and/or to meet contestation.[24]

Even with the benefit of initial understanding and further learning, an 'eternal tension' will remain between the need to fix an approach in order to do something here and now and perhaps make a difference, and the still insufficient understanding of what might happen which makes it difficult to 'fix' the appropriate approach. For new product development, for example, one might want to remain flexible as long as possible, but then run the risk of never realizing a new product, an anticipation/flexibility dilemma (Verganti 1999). For reflexive governance, with its multi-actor and multi-level characteristics, such tensions and dilemmas of anticipation-in-action are even more problematic. On the other hand, recognizing these tensions for what they are is the first step to handling them more productively.

## CONCLUSIONS AND REFLECTIONS

Anticipatory knowledge (in action) is not just a locus of reflexive governance, but it is also a key element in co-evolution. In my co-evolutionary perspective on reflexive governance, the two should of course go together. In a distantiated view, modernist, enlightened modernist and non-modern steering are just possible cross-sections of co-evolution. Anticipation can be used instrumentally by the modernist, and interactively by the non-modernist. One approach need not be better than another.

Still, I have put up non-modern steering as the preferred approach. I offer three kinds of argument. First, because non-modern steering (through 'hybrid monsters') is what happens anyway, and modernist steering is an overlay, and not necessarily effective, even in its own terms. Second, because modernist steering in a risk society increases risks since unintended effects will proliferate. This is Beck's argument, but the further point is that modernists, when positioning themselves outside their object, will also bracket their goals as given, protect them by claims about good intentions or working towards a public good, and follow a concentric approach in realizing them. The attendant myopia has been signalled before (Deuten et al. 1997, Van Gunsteren 1976). Third, because non-modern steering in principle allows variety and lateral movement, which is important to avoid lock-ins (cf. also the second-order normativity of the evolutionary perspective).

While stabilization of patterns and paths is unavoidable, it should not become complete. This is not an automatic consequence of non-modern steering, however. One should take a hard look at the actual practices of non-modern steering and the good intentions of the reflexive-governance agent. In any case, it will be important to have 'grey zones' and interstices within existing orders. And actors who create difficulties for existing orders, because they irritate, contest, or like tricksters, are just mischievous. A further component of reflexive governance is then to entertain such contesting, or merely lateral, actions, also when they might obstruct a particular reflexive governance approach as originally envisaged by the agent. In this respect, constructive disequilibrium is an interesting characterization as its two components are contrasts and invite negotiations and trade-offs.

There is another reason to take a hard look, and perhaps even go for a Machiavellian version of reflexive governance.[25] Adaptivity and experimentation, strategies identified in the Introduction to this book, are important in their own terms, but what are the conditions necessary to make such strategies possible? Adaptivity assumes a willingness to accommodate but this may not exist, and learning need not occur unless there are incentives. The Machiavellian approach is then to neglect some of the desirable features in order to realize a minimal version. Again, this becomes a trade-off, now between conditions necessary for realizing a desirable goal, which then introduce undesirable features as well.[26]

Another consideration which suggests that further reflection is necessary about positioning reflexive governance as the solution to problems, for example of sustainability, is how in spite of myopic actors (or better, myopic action) in the private as well as the public sector, and thus only limited reflexive governance, some good outcomes are still realized. Rip and Groen (2001) raise this question and offer a complex analysis emphasizing mutual translations and credibility pressures but do not offer a real answer.

One entrance point, at the level of actors, is the phenomenon of productive illusion of agency (Deuten and Rip 2000). The illusion of the modernist actor is to just go for agency (that is, making a difference), and fail or be successful, not because of the strength of his agency, but depending on circumstances out of his control. Even so, such illusions are productive because they motivate action and repair work, and thus something (whatever) is achieved. The distantiated, ironical stance of the non-modernist actor is the stance of an observer, and thus risks giving up on action altogether. To avoid the irony of ironies, which lead to suspension of action, non-modernism should develop something like irony-in-practice.

In the sixteenth century, William the Silent, Prince of Orange (supposedly) said: *'Point n'est besoin d'espérer pour entreprendre, ni de réussir pour persévérer'*. This aphorism about being prepared to persevere even if there is no hope of realizing one's goals is widely quoted.[27] If acted upon, this would imply that irony need not stifle action. This would save non-modern steering from evaporating into reflexivity.

While this would be a fitting conclusion, a further touch of Machiavellianism is in order. Take this sentence: 'Revolution is good, because it lets the oppressed become tyrants'. I encountered it written in big capitals on a wall in a shopping centre in Rotterdam, not as a grafitti, but as a decoration put up by 'those responsible' for the shopping centre.[28] How about phrasing the final lesson of this chapter as: 'Reflexive governance is good, because it maintains the illusion of governance'?

## ACKNOWLEDGEMENT

Without the encouragement and comments of Jan-Peter Voß, this chapter could not have been written. His contributions have been substantial, and this is only partially visible in the text.

## NOTES

1.  I have used the term 'post-modernist' to characterize this second approach (Rip 2002), because of its connotation with a variety of 'small' stories rather than one 'big' story, as Lyotard (1984 [1979]) characterized the contrast. See also Visscher and Rip 2003, who identify different types of business consultants: enlightened modernists, ironists and post-modernists.
2.  Beck contrasts reflexive with reflective, the latter indicating reflection on what is happening. If such reflection is part of further action and interaction, it would enhance reflexivity. Jan-Peter Voß adds to this (personal communication, 2004): 'There is first-order reflexivity, the self-shaping or self-constituting nature of a societal arrangement via feedback from its own action in and on the world. But then also (in late modernity),

second-order-reflexivity. Society adapts to this constellation, knowingly and unknowingly, it is shaped by its experience of unintended feedback. This is visible in how forms of knowledge production, technology development, governance etc. are developed, which reflects the need to deal with (the possibility) of such feedbacks.'

3. I owe this phrase to Jan-Peter Voß (personal communication, 2004).

4. The concept of mutual translation derives from actor-network theory (Callon et al. 1986), and is most often used in case studies to describe specific interactions and as a building block of analysis of co-production and co-construction (Jasanoff 2004). It is also applicable to the set of interactions adding up to precarious social orders (Rip and Groen 2001), and then refers to the same phenomenon that evolutionary theorists like Leydesdorff (2001) refer to as mutual selection.

5. For technological change there is Basalla on artefacts, Henderson on technological 'species', Nelson and Winter (1997, 1984) on innovative firms, Dosi (1984) on technological trajectories, Metcalfe on populations of firms, Van den Belt and Rip (1987) on heuristics and exemplars, Freeman on techno-economic paradigms. See also Ziman 2000. For science, see Nowotny et al. (2001) and Rip (2000, 2002a), and the approaches of evolutionary epistemology (Donald Campbell, Stephen Toulmin).

6. Science, its quality control, and its (re-)contextualisation in society (Nowotny et al. 2001), is shaped in many ways, also cognitively (Rip 2002a), but is difficult to shape intentionally.

7. Similar tensions can be found at other levels in the science system. An interesting example is how universities have to adjust to the requirements of ongoing developments in science and scholarship, as conveyed by their scientific staff, but also have an institutional responsibility to profile themselves at a national and international level and manage their contacts with relevant government ministries and agencies. Deans acutely feel the pressures from below (scientific staff) and above (university board), and seize opportunities to realize at least some of their goals, rather than implement a strategy.

8. Co-evolution is often used as a broad characterisation of co-development and mutual shaping, without specific reference to evolutionary theory. In the ESRC report on genomics and society, business and economics are 'shaping and being shaped by genomics', while the next page has 'co-evolution of laws and legal structures and genomics' (IAF/CRIC 2002, Report 1, pp. 8, 9). Such terminology carries a message (and an important message): things hang together and linear cause–effect relationships are the exception rather than the rule. Similarly, Nowotny et al. (2001) emphasize the co-evolution of science and society, not as a theory, but as a diagnosis, and a plea for more interaction between science and society. 'Co-evolution denotes an open, and certainly more integrated, system of science-society interaction which enhances the generation of variety, whether in the choice of scientific problems, colleagues or institutional designs, on the one hand, or the selective retention of certain choices, modes or solutions on the other hand.' (Nowotny et al. 2001, p. 248).

9. There is a burgeoning amount of literature that applies ideas about complex evolving systems to questions of organisation and governance. Ralph Stacey and Eve Mittleton-Kelly represent two key authors in this area. There is reference to co-evolution, in terms of organisms adapting and thus changing the fitness landscape for other organisms, and to emerging path-dependencies.

10. The common storyline here is that of an individual act of courage that triggers collective display of defiance. Schuyt (1972) already emphasized the incidental character of the action itself, noting that Rosa Parks had no intention to protest, she was just too tired to remain standing. Whatever the intentions, a 'lateral action' occurred, across rather than against the existing order. Lovell (2003) adds that Rosa Parks did have a history in human rights activities, and then shows that she, rather than other blacks who suffered this treatment, was selected as a 'standard bearer' because she was working class and respectable.

11. Cf. Latour (2003: 36) ' "reflexive" means, in my reading of it, that the unintended consequences of action reverberate throughout the whole of society in such a way that they have become intractable. Thus "reflexive" does not signal an increase in mastery and consciousness, but only a heightened awareness that mastery is impossible and that control

over actions is now seen as a complete modernist fiction. (. . .) We do not run more dangers than before, but (. . .) we are now entangled, whereas the modernist dream was to disentangle us from the past.'

12. Rip (2000d), a similar point about repertoire learning already in Rip (1986).

13. The European Commission is now establishing what they call 'Technology Platforms' for that same purpose.

14. An example is the way that attempts to stimulate the use of local knowledge in rural agriculture in KwaZulu-Natal (South Africa) get locked into supplying organic food at premium prices (if the volume and transport problems can be solved). See Rip (2003).

15. A variety of tools and approaches to anticipate so as to improve the actor's own position are available. Learning curves, product life cycles, trajectories – all presume continuation of the past into the future. Actors must still decide whether to 'fit' and thus reinforce existing dynamics, or to 'stretch' and modify the environment so as to accommodate their new venture.

16. I am indebted to Jan-Peter Voß for this turn of phrase and the underlying thought.

17. Interestingly, there is now a movement towards decentred, open-ended environmental management in which, in practice, restoration strategies do not orchestrate the return to a specified earlier stage of an ecosystem, but engage practically with the physical environment and learn what is possible and desirable (Castree 2001). Conversation occurs with the ecosystem (and with relevant human actors).

18. See note 2.

19. Cf. Beck (1992), pp. 171 ff.

20. The title of a report of the European Environmental Agency, 'Late lessons from early warning' (Harremoës, 2001) together with the existence of such an agency and their writing such reports, is indicative. As the reference to 'early warning' indicates, such anticipatory knowledge is part of actors' strategies and reactions, and its fate, i.e. uptake, is determined by existing and emerging overlapping strategic games. An example of overlapping strategic games determining uptake is the story of fluorochlorocarbons and the ozone layer from the mid-1970s onwards. An early warning from Molina, uncertainty exploited by industry to argue against regulation, the first phase of checking and expanding knowledge: while some regulatory agencies started to regulate anyway because they wanted to protect their 'turf' or extend their scope before other agencies step in (Rip 1992).

21. The emergence of forecasting in the 1950s and 1960s, and the way it was taken up in some policy making is a clear example. Of course, forecasting activities (now also foresight) can be part of anticipation-in-action.

22. For its regularity over the last four decades, Moore's Law of regular increases in the density of units on a 'chip' (an integrated circuit) and the speed of micro-processors, depends on the continuity of the strategic game among the chip producers and their government and R&D allies, using Moore's Law as a reference.

23. For examples from product development see Deuten and Rip (2000), in societal debate on acid rain, Hajer (1995). See also my analysis of social science and evidence-based policy making (Rip 2001). The narrative approach has further implications, for example how it can carry the past into the future.

24. Cf. Rip 2002d on Max Miller, and Rip 1986 on collective learning in controversies shaped by 'forceful foci'. Deuten (2003) showed that technological learning, for example about reinforced concrete, occurred only because of demanding customers.

25. I use the common-sense version of Machiavellian here, which refers to *The Prince* not to Machiavelli who wrote *The Republic*.

26. Donald Campbell has made a similar suggestion about the tribal norms necessary for scientific communities in order to produce good science (Campbell 1979). I have taken up this point in my discussion of scientific expertise, regulation and the precautionary principle (Rip 2001a).

27. In French stylistic guidelines, the quote appears again and again, and is sometimes followed by a reverse version: '*Il n'est pas nécessaire d'entreprendre pour espérer ni de persévérer pout réussir.*' (http://www.courtois.cc/citations/travail.html, visited 13 November, 2004).

28. In the same vein, the city of Rotterdam features a line from the painter and poet, Lucebert, in big letters on top of a prominent building: *'Alles van waarde is weerloos'* (everything of value is defenceless). See also proliferation of the sentence on buildings and placards, 'Trust me. I am you'. Modern societies are reflexive!

# REFERENCES

Beck, Ulrich (1992), *Risk Society. Towards a New Modernity*, London: Sage.

Beck, Ulrich, Wolfgang Boriss and Christoph Lan (2003), 'The theory of reflexive modernization: problematic, hypotheses and research programme', *Theory, Culture & Society*, **20**, 1–33.

Callon, Michel, John Law and Arie Rip (1986), *Mapping the Dynamics of Science and Technology. Sociology of Science in the Real World*, London: Macmillan Press.

Campbell, Donald T. (1979), 'A tribal model of the social system vehicle carrying scientific knowledge', *Knowledge, 1* (December), 181–201.

Castree, Noel (ed.) (2001), *Social Nature: Theory, Practice and Politics*, Oxford: Blackwell Publishers.

Coleman, James S. (1990), *Foundations of Social Theory*, Cambridge, MA: Harvard University Press.

Deuten, J. Jasper (2003), 'Cosmopolitanizing technology: studies of four emerging technological regimes', PhD Thesis, University of Twente.

Deuten, J. Jasper and Arie Rip (2000), 'Narrative Infrastructure in Product Creation Processes', *Organization*, **7**, 67–91.

Deuten, J. Jasper, Arie Rip and Jaap Jelsma (1997), 'Societal embedment and product creation management', *Technology Analysis and Strategic Management*, **9**, 219–36.

Elzinga, Aant (1985), 'Research, bureaucracy and the drift of Epistemic criteria', in Björn Wittrock and Aant Elzinga (eds), *The University Research System. The Public Policies of the Home of Scientists*, Stockholm: Almqvist and Wiksell International, pp. 191–220.

Guston, David H. and Kenneth Kenniston (eds) (1994), *The Fragile Contract. University Science and the Federal Government*, Cambridge, MA: MIT Press.

Hajer, Maarten A. (1995), *The Politics of Environmental Discourse. Ecological Modernization and the Policy Process*, Oxford: Clarendon Press.

Hanf, Kenneth, and Theo A.J. Toonen (eds) (1985), *Policy Implementation in Federal and Unitary Systems*, Dordrecht: Martinus Nijhoff Publishers.

IAF and CRIC (2002), ESRC Project on Genomics and Society. Six reports, available from http://les1.man.ac.uk/cric/genomics

Jasanoff, Sheila (ed.) (2004), *States of Knowledge. The co-production of science and social order*, London: Routledge.

Latour, Bruno (1991), 'Nous n'avons jamais été modernes. Essai d'anthropologie symétrique', Paris: La Découverte.

Latour, Bruno (2003), 'Is re-modernization occurring – and if so, how to prove it? a commentary on Ulrich Beck', *Theory, Culture and Society*, **20**, 35–48.

Leydesdorff, L. (2000), 'The triple helix: An evolutionary model of innovations', *Research Policy*, **29**, 243–55.

Leydesdorff, Loet (2001), *A Sociological Theory of Communication. The Self-Organisation of the Knowledge-Based Society*, Universal Publishers.

Lindblom, Charles E. and Edward J. Woodhouse (1993), *The Policy-Making Process*, 3rd edn, Englewood Cliffs, NJ: Prentice Hall.

Lovell, Terry (2003), 'Resisting with authority: historical specificity, agency and the performative self', *Theory, Culture and Society*, **20**, 1–17.

Lyotard, J.F. (1984), *The Postmodern Condition: A Report on Knowledge*, Minneapolis: University of Minnesota Press. Translation of *La Condition Postmoderne*, 1979.

Mokyr, J. (1990), *The Lever of Riches*, New York: Oxford University Press.

Morris, Norma (2004), 'Biomedical research in changing contexts: an analysis of the agents', PhD Thesis, University of Twente.

Nelson, R.R. (1994), 'The co-evolution of technology, industrial structure, and supporting institutions', *Industrial and Corporate Change*, **3** (1), 47–63.

Nooteboom, S. and G. Teisman (2003), 'Sustainable development: impact assessment in the age of networking', *Journal of Environmental Policy and Planning*, **5**, 285–308.

North, Douglass C. (1990), *Institutions, Institutional Change and Economic Performance*, Cambridge: Cambridge University Press.

Nowotny, Helga, Peter Scott and Michael Gibbons (2001), *Re-Thinking Science. Knowledge and the Public in an Age of Uncertainty*, Cambridge: Polity Press.

Portes, Alejandro (2000), 'The hidden abode: Sociology as analysis of the unexpected', *American Sociological Review*, **65**, 1–18.

Pressman, J.L. and A. Wildavsky (1984), *Implementation. How Great Expectations in Washington Are Dashed in Oakland*, Berkeley, CA: University of California Press, 3rd expanded edition.

Rip, Arie (1986), 'Controversies as informal technology assessment', *Knowledge*, **8** (2), 349–71.

Rip, Arie (1992), 'Expert advice and pragmatic rationality', in Nico Stehr and Richard V. Ericson (eds), *The Culture and Power of Knowledge*, Berlin and New York: De Gruyter, 357–73.

Rip, Arie (1995), 'Introduction of new technology: making use of recent insights from sociology and economics of technology', *Technology Analysis and Strategic Management*, **7** (4), 417–31.

Rip, Arie (1998), 'The dancer and the dance: steering in/of science and technology', in Arie Rip (ed.), *Steering and Effectiveness in a Developing Knowledge Society*, Utrecht: Uitgeverij Lemma, pp. 27–49.

Rip, Arie (2000), 'Fashions, lock-ins, and the heterogeneity of knowledge production', in Merle Jacob and Thomas Hellström (eds), *The Future of Knowledge Production in the Academy*, Buckingham: Open University Press, pp. 28–39.

Rip, Arie (2001), 'In praise of speculation', Ch. 8 in OECD, *Proceedings, Social Sciences for Knowledge and Decision Making*, Paris: OECD, pp. 95–103.

Rip, Arie (2001a), 'Contributions from Social Studies of Science and Constructive Technology Assessment', in Andrew Stirling (ed.), *On Science and Precaution in the Management of Technological Risk, Volume II: Case Studies*, Sevilla: Institute for Prospective Technology Studies (European Commission Joint Research Centre), November, pp. 94–122.

Rip, Arie (2002), 'Postmodern Science and Technology Policy', invited paper to the NISTEP International Symposium 2002, on New Articulation of Science and Technology Systems, Tokyo, 28 February and 1 March 2002.

Rip, Arie (2002a), 'Science for the 21st Century', in Peter Tindemans, Alexander Verrijn-Stuart and Rob Visser (eds), *The Future of the Sciences and Humanities.*

*Four analytical essays and a critical debate on the future of scholastic endeavour*, Amsterdam: Amsterdam University Press, pp. 99–148.

Rip, Arie (2002b), 'Co-Evolution of Science, Technology and Society', expert review for the Bundesministerium Bildung and Forschung's Förderinitiative 'Politik, Wissenschaft und Gesellschaft' (Science Policy Studies), managed by the Berlin–Brandenburgische Akademie der Wissenschaften, Enschede: University of Twente, 7 June.

Rip, Arie (2002c), 'A co-evolutionary perspective on ELSI, CTA and other attempts at re-contextualisation of science and technology in society', paper presented to the meeting of the European Association for the Study of Science and Technology, York, 31 July–3 August 2002.

Rip, Arie (2002d), 'Systematic learning – without systems? Commentary on Max Miller', *Sozialer Sinn*, Heft 3, 435–43.

Rip, Arie (2003), 'Technological innovation – in context', invited keynote speech at the meeting of the Lowlands Innovation Research Network, Louvain (Belgium), 14 January 2003.

Rip, Arie and Aard Groen, (2001), 'Many visible hands', in Rod Coombs, Ken Green, Vivien Walsh and Albert Richards (eds), *Technology and the Market. Demands, Users and Innovation*, Cheltenham, UK and Northampton, MA, USA: Edward Elgar, pp. 12–37.

Rip, Arie and Rene Kemp (1998), 'Technological change,' in S. Rayner and E.L. Malone (eds), *Human Choice and Climate Change*, Columbus, OH: Battelle Press, 1998. Volume 2, Ch. 6, pp. 327–99.

Rip, Arie, and Barend J.R. van der Meulen (1996), 'The post-modern research system', *Science and Public Policy*, **23**, 343–52.

Schimank, Uwe (1988), 'Gesellschaftliche Teilsysteme als Akteurfiktionen', *Kölner Zeitschrift für Soziologie und Sozialpsychologie*, **40**, 619–39.

Schimank, Uwe (1992), 'Spezifische Interessenkonsense trotz generellen Orientierungsdissens. Ein Integrationsmechanismus polyzentrischer Gesellschaften', in Giegel, Hans-Joachim (Hrsg) Kommunikation und Konsens in moderne Gesellschaften, Frankfurt: Suhrkamp.

Schön, Donald (1984), *The Reflective Practitioner: How Professionals Think in Action*, New York: Basic Books.

Schot, Johan and Arie Rip (1997), 'The past and future of constructive technology assessment', *Technological Forecasting and Social Change*, **54**, 251–68.

Schuyt, C.J.M. (1972), 'Recht, orde en burgerlijke ongehoorzaamheid', Rotterdam: Universitaire Pers Rotterdam.

Stoelhorst, J.W. (1997), 'In search of a dynamic theory of the firm. An evolutionary perspective on competition under conditions of technological change, with an application to the semi-conductor industry', Enschede: University of Twente.

Van den Belt, H. and A. Rip (1987), 'The Nelson-Winter–Dosi model and synthetic dye chemistry', in W.E. Bijker, T.P. Hughes and T. Pinch (eds), *The Social Construction of Technological Systems: New Directions in the Sociology and History of Technology*, Cambridge, MA: MIT Press, 135–58.

Van Gunsteren Herman R. (1976), '*The Quest for Control. A critique of the rational-central-rule approach in public affairs*', London and New York: John Wiley.

Verganti, Roberto (1999), 'Planned flexibility: linking anticipation and reaction in product development projects', *Journal of Product Innovation Management*, **16**, 363–76.

Visscher, Klaasjan and Arie Rip (2003), 'Coping with chaos in change processes', *Creativity and Innovation Management*, **12** (2), (June) 121–8.
Ziman, John (ed.) (2000), *Technological Innovation as an Evolutionary Process*, Cambridge: Cambridge University Press.

# Strategies for sustainable system transformation

# 5. Transition management: a reflexive governance approach

## René Kemp and Derk Loorbach[1]

## INTRODUCTION

This chapter discusses the concept of transition management that has been adopted by Dutch policy makers for working towards sustainability. Transition management can be described as forward-looking, adaptive, multi-actor governance aimed at long-term transformation processes that offer sustainability benefits. Transition management relies on each of the strategies of reflexive governance delineated in the introduction of the book: knowledge integration, anticipation of long-term systemic effects, adaptivity of strategies and institutions, iterative participatory goal formulation and interactive strategy development. It helps to influence and organize evolutionary processes of societal change in a reflexive manner.

Transition management could be viewed as 'evolutionary governance' as it is concerned with the functioning of the variation–selection–reproduction process at the societal level: creating variety informed by visions of and experiments for sustainability, shaping new pathways and reflexively adapting existing institutional frameworks and regimes. It is a model for escaping lock-in and moving towards solutions that offer multiple benefits, not just for users but also for society as a whole. It is not an attempt to control the future but an attempt to incorporate normative goals into evolutionary processes in a reflexive manner. Learning, maintaining variety (through portfolio management) and institutional change are important policy aims. In this chapter we outline the model of transition management and describe Dutch transition policies in the energy sector.

## A CHANGING WORLD

Our society is always changing. Over the past decades, however, driven by transnational trends such as internationalization, informatization and individualization (Schnabel, 2000), the process of social change has become increasingly complex. Choices at a societal level are the outcomes of interaction between the individual actions and strategies of a large number of actors that have different perspectives and goals. Increasingly, policy-makers are for example forced to take into account the issues of societal actors and social partners in the process of policy-making (Mayntz, 1994; Kooiman, 1993). This happens at different levels in parallel, generating complex multi-level governance structure (Scharpf, 1994; Kohler-Koch, 1999). Coordination within this structure seems absent since the overall picture is that of a battlefield with numerous competing networks and actors that all try to realize their own agenda, at the expense of other ones.

The liberal approach towards business and the individual, which has been dominant since the 1980s, has fostered this development that allowed for varied individual choices and stimulated competition. Although economic growth and technological progress have resulted from this approach, environmental and social benefits have not. This becomes clear in a number of societal sectors and systems that now face major revisions since they were previously based on 'old' solutions which are not sustainable: the energy-supply system, the health-care system, mobility and transport, agriculture and urban development. In all these sectors, symptomatic problems like power shortages, traffic jams or cattle diseases (to name a few problems) lead policy-makers to react with force to such incidents, while ignoring the complexity of the problems. These 'sustainability problems', also called 'wicked' problems, are so complex because they are related to economic, social as well as spatial and ecological issues. The problems are manifested at different levels, involve many actors (not just business actors) and they require a very long time to manage effectively.

The need to develop our society in a sustainable direction has been acknowledged at different levels, both at the local as well as at international levels (for example: UN, Agenda 21). Implementing sustainable development however is a cumbersome process since the notion itself is inherently ambiguous and subjective (Kasemir and Van Asselt, 1999). This does not mean however that it cannot be operationalized (Rotmans, 1998). To do so, sustainable development must be related to a specific context: something is developed sustainably. This can be for example the sustainable development not only of a region or city, but also of a utility system like energy provision or the mobility system. But what sustainable development means in such a specific context is again open to debate, since different actors with different values at different levels of society will try to put forward their definitions and goals. It is thus something highly subjective and the meaning of it will change over time. It is a continuing quest that involves both learning about solutions to problems and learning about needs. Finding sustainability thus becomes a learning-by-doing exercise; experimenting with partnerships, new institutions, new technologies and new regulations within the ecological limits defined.

Taking such a comprehensive approach towards sustainable development requires a redefinition of policy-making in this context; a more evolutionary and adaptive strategy is needed that allows for self-organization within certain limits, both ecological limits as well as social limits (often set by government, but they can include social norms as well). The central focus of such a strategy should be to realize long-term and large-scale innovations or transitions towards more environmentally and socially benign societal systems (such as agriculture or energy supply). Since realizing long-term, diffuse sustainability goals should be the aim of such policies, an emphasis on interaction, experiment and learning is crucial. In this chapter we will first address the concept of transition as a 'systems' way to view societal change. Secondly, we will present the approach of transition management as a new form of governance for sustainability and will focus on the reflexive elements in the strategy.

## WHAT IS MEANT BY TRANSITION AND TRANSITION MANAGEMENT?

The basic underlying assumption of transition theory is that society changes in a rather evolutionary and organic way, to a certain extent comparable to the behaviour and development of ecosystems (for example, Gunderson and Holling, 2002), and is therefore inherently complex. On a societal level, we can recognize patterns of variation and selection (of new technologies, but also of new fashions, ideas, politicians and so on) and of co-evolution (between politics and economy for example). Although drawing straightforward parallels between ecosystems and societal systems is not possible at this point, transition theory tries to make instrumental use of insights from disciplines such as ecology, complexity and systems science.[2] Systems-thinking in terms of causal relations, feedback mechanisms, resilience and thresholds is central to the transition concept and essential for transition management.

A key notion is transition. Before we can go into transition management, it is necessary first to define the notion of transition. According to the fourth Dutch national Environmental Policy Plan (NMP-4 2000) and the ICIS-MERIT report that provided the scientific background to the NMP-4, 'a transition is a gradual process of societal change in which society or an important subsystem of society structurally changes' (Rotmans et al. 2000, p. 19). A transition is the result of the interplay of developments that sustain and reinforce each other. Transitions are not caused by single variables – a price change, policy act or a new technology – but are the result of developments in various domains which sustain each other: technology, economy, institutions, behaviour, culture, ecology and images/paradigms (p. 20). The process of transition is non-linear; slow change is followed by rapid change when things reinforce each other, which again is followed by slow change in the stabilization stage.

Although transitions are characterized by non-linear behaviour, the process itself is a gradual one, typically spanning one or two generations (25–50 years).[3] The nature and speed of change differ in each of the transition stages:

- In the predevelopment phase there is very little visible change on the societal level but there is a lot of experimentation.
- In the take-off phase the process of change gets under way and the state of the system begins to shift.
- In the breakthrough phase structural changes take place in a visible way through an accumulation of socio-cultural, economic, ecological[4] and institutional changes that react to each other; during this phase, there are collective learning processes, diffusion and embedding processes.[5]
- In the stabilization phase the speed of societal change decreases and a new dynamic equilibrium is reached.

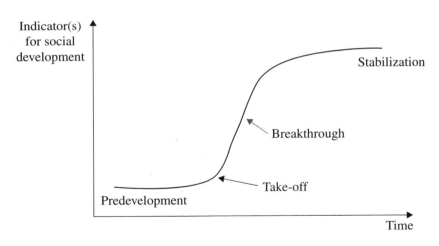

*Source:*  Rotmans et al., 2000 and 2001

*Figure 5.1   Four phases of transition*

Transitions require a number of interacting system innovations (see also Figure 5.2): organization-exceeding, qualitative innovations which are realized by a variety of participants within the system, and which fundamentally change both the structure of the system and the relations between the participants.[6] System innovations transcend the level of an individual, an individual firm or individual organization, but take place at the level of, for instance, a sector, a branch, city or region (Dirven et al., 2002). This involves innovation of production and consumption processes, technological innovation, institutional innovation and political–governmental innovation. Within these system innovations in turn, innovations occur at the individual level, in terms of product, process and project innovations. An example is a possible future energy transition to biomass, which will necessarily involve interacting system innovations in transport (bio fuels), electricity generation (co-combustion, gasification of biomass), agriculture (bio crops), as well as in policy (integral biomass policy regarding energy, biodiversity, space use, agriculture and transport) and culture (to surmount barriers among the public against alternative energy carriers).[7] To achieve these system innovations, experiments and innovations are needed for example with regard to technologies (new engines, new infrastructures, and new production facilities), behaviour (in use and production of energy) and regulation (subsidies, market conditions, legal regulations). Transitions can thus be seen as a cascade of innovations at different levels and at different speeds.

Transitions are interesting from the viewpoint of sustainability, because they offer the prospect of a magnitude of environmental benefits, alongside wider social benefits through the development of systems that are inherently more environmentally benign. However, transitions of course also

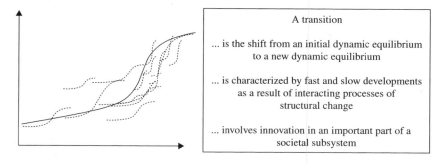

| A transition |
| --- |
| ... is the shift from an initial dynamic equilibrium to a new dynamic equilibrium |
| ... is characterized by fast and slow developments as a result of interacting processes of structural change |
| ... involves innovation in an important part of a societal subsystem |

*Source:* Butter et al., 2002

*Figure 5.2   A transition is the result of system innovations and other innovations and changes*

offer the perspective of breaking down existing systems, infrastructures and institutions, which will mean the loss of investments and thus opposition. Examples of system innovation are: a biomass energy supply, industrial ecology and customized mobility.

A second concept that is used to describe transitions is the multi-level model originating from innovation studies (Rip and Kemp, 1998 and Geels, 2000 and 2002a), which is being used in the TIN-20 project (Technology in the Netherlands in the 20th century) to describe the contextual history of technology in the Netherlands. This model differentiates three levels of socio-technical systems: macro-landscape, meso-regimes and micro-niches. In the context of transitions, these levels can be interpreted in terms of (1) societal landscape, (2) dominant-actor networks and institutions (regimes) and (3) micro-behaviour. The societal landscape is something that surrounds us and consists of the macro economy, political culture, demography, natural environment and worldviews. The term landscape refers to the socio-technical surface structure of the land with its gradients, which makes certain advances easier to accomplish. The landscape is rather autonomous and changes relatively slowly. The second, arguably most important, level for functional systems is the meso-level of regimes: the dominant infra-structures and technologies in combination with the rules, roles and belief systems that underlie strategies of companies, organizations and institutions and policies of political institutions. Regimes give stability and guide decision-making but (because of that) also have a high level of inertia and tend to reproduce rather than innovate. In this sense, regimes often tend to block change. At the micro level (niche level) there are those individual actors, technologies and local practices that present or develop alternatives to the dominant regime. At this level, variations to and deviations from the status quo can occur as a result of new ideas and new initiatives, such as new techniques, alternative technologies and social practices.

A transition is the result of interaction between changes and innovations at these different levels; slowly changing trends lead to new ways of thinking (paradigms) that lead to innovation and vice versa. Giving these interdependencies, a transition can be accelerated by one-time events, such as a war or large accident (for example, Chernobyl) or a crisis (such as the oil crisis) but not be caused by such events. Transitions are the result of endogenous and exogenous developments: autonomous trends and changes influence transitions as well as innovations and changes that emerge from within the systems. Technical change interacts with other changes, social change and economic change, which means that one should look for process explanations (multiple causalities rather than individual causal patterns).

Attempts at steering are done by actors who are part of transitions. Policy-making or rather governance, is thus situated in a context of socio-technical systems that offer functional services and disservices, housing interests and organizations with capabilities and mental models, who function in a world of beliefs, values, capital goods, prices, settlements, lifestyles and novelties. By definition, complex systems are highly chaotic and impossible to steer in the sense of command-and-control because of numerous feedback loops, inert institutions and unpredictable developments. Rather than focusing on individual components of these systems, governance for sustainable development should try to find governance strategies at a systemic level and try to change the 'condition' of the system for the better. This idea has been accepted by the model of transition management of Rotmans and others (Rotmans et al., 2000; Kemp and Rotmans, 2001, 2002; Loorbach and Rotmans, 2002). Through transition management one tries to influence the direction and speed of transitions by coordinating and enabling the processes that occur at different levels in a more systemic and evolutionary way, which leaves room for variation and selection mechanisms and innovation. This can be done in many different ways, through various types of steering mechanisms, none of which incidentally can be prescribed or even repeated in detail.

In the following pages we will give a description of our model of transition management accepting that there are other models. When we speak of transition management we mean the ICIS-MERIT model of transition management in whose development we were involved ourselves. It is an attempt at goal-oriented modulation, not an attempt to achieve predefined outcomes through planning and control. Transition management works with dynamics not against them. Ongoing developments are exploited strategically. Transition management for sustainability tries to orient dynamics to sustainability goals. The goals are chosen by society through the political process: the systems to satisfy these goals are worked towards in an adaptive, forward-looking manner. The goals and policies for furthering the goals are constantly assessed and periodically adjusted in development rounds. Policies will differ across the different transition phases. In early phases, policy should be concerned with the formulation of transition goals and engage in the formulation of sustainability visions (quality images), which are re-assessed during later phases. The attention to innovation will be a continued feature of all phases; it is not just something for the early phases.

A schematic view of transition management is given in Figure 5.3.

Policy actions are evaluated against two types of criteria: (1) the immediate contribution to policy goals (for example in terms of kilotons of $CO_2$ reduction and reduced vulnerability through climate change adaptation measures), and (2) the contribution of the policies to the overall transition process. This means that under transition management, policies have

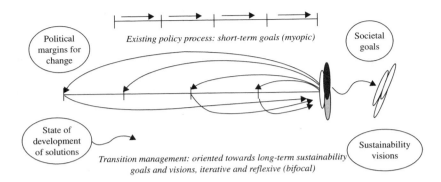

*Figure 5.3    Current policy versus transition management*

a content goal and a process goal. Learning, maintaining variety and institutional change, are important policy aims, and policy goals are used as means for change. The evaluation and adaptation of policies (strategies, involved actors, progress and so on) in development rounds brings flexibility to the process without losing a long-term focus.

Transition management is thus bifocal and based on a two-pronged strategy of simultaneously stimulating system improvement and system innovation. No choice is made between system improvement and system innovation, but special attention is given to system innovation (representing a new trajectory of development or transformation), given the many barriers to this type of change. Through its open-endedness, transition management breaks with the old planning-and-implementation model aimed at achieving particular outcomes and is based on a different, more process-oriented philosophy. This helps to deal with complexity and uncertainty in a constructive way. Transition management is a form of process management against a set of goals chosen by society. Societies' problem-solving capabilities are mobilized and translated into transition programmes, which are legitimized through the political process.

Key elements of transition management are:

- systems-thinking in terms of more than one domain (multi-domain) and different actors (multi-actor) at different scale levels (multi-level); how developments in one domain or level gel with developments in other domains or levels; trying to change the strategic orientation of regime actors;
- long-term thinking (at least 25 years) as a framework for shaping short-term policy;

- back-casting and forecasting: the setting of short-term and longer term-goals based on long-term sustainability visions, scenario studies, trend analyses and short-term possibilities;
- a focus on learning and the use of a special learning philosophy of learning-by-doing and doing-by-learning which includes carrying out experiments to develop required knowledge and the other way around;
- an orientation towards system innovation and experimentation;
- learning about a variety of options (which requires a wide playing field);
- participation by and interaction between stakeholders.

## TRANSITION MANAGEMENT: HOW?

The foremost reason for engaging in transition management is that we are locked into trajectories driven by short-term benefits instead of longer-term optimality (Kemp and Soete, 1992). Uncertainty, short-term costs, the need for change at various levels and vested interests all create barriers to system innovation. Some concerted action is needed but public policy is highly fragmented and oriented towards short-term goals. Transition management is supposed to deal with these problems. In the past section we described the basic idea behind transition management. We will now discuss the basic steps or elements. Before we do this it is important to note that transition management is not an instrumental activity. The actual policies are the outcome of political negotiations and the processes of co-evolution, which inform further steps.

The process of transition management consists of a number of activities, which can only be defined in general terms, because they are largely dependent on the nature of the transition problem at hand and, because of the interactive nature of transition management, on the actors involved. As such, transition management is an approach rather than a method; it has to be adapted and individualized for every specific context or problem.

### Transition Arenas and Multi-actor Governance

The transition arena as a new institution for interaction can be considered a meta-instrument for transition management and facilitates interaction, knowledge exchange and learning between the actors. The transition arena is an open and dynamic network in which different perspectives, different expectations and different agendas are confronted, discussed and aligned where possible. In its first phase, the transition arena is a relatively small network of innovators and strategic thinkers from different backgrounds that discusses the transition problem integrally and outlines the transition goals. In this phase, it is important to come up with creative, inspiring and integrating goals and ideas. Further on in the process, the network will expand to include less strategically oriented actors (such as local authorities and people with practical knowledge about processes of change) in order to develop transition paths and link these to existing (not only governmental) policies. Finally, short-term experiments and actions are derived from the goals and paths and more operationally oriented organizations and actors will be involved.

The establishment and organization of a transition arena forms the basis of the transition management process. The selection of participants for this transition arena is of vital importance; they need to reflect the complexity of the transition at hand. These participants need to have some basic competences at their disposal: they need to be visionaries, forerunners, have to be able to look beyond their own domain or working area and be open-minded. They must function quite autonomously within their organizations but also have the ability to convey the developed vision(s) and initiate it within their organizations. Apart from this, they need to be willing to invest a substantial amount of time and energy into playing an active role in the transition arena process. Often, only a handful of such people exist within specific societal networks and they are easily identified because of their standing, function or networks. It is nevertheless important to specify explicitly the criteria based upon which the participants of the transition arena are selected and to document these criteria.

**Problem Definition**

The starting point for transition management for sustainability is the persistent problems of existing functional systems. Because of the system-inherent nature of the problems they do not have a single 'owner'. Rather than looking for a villain to blame, one looks for a common problem definition in which all problems are considered, not just those problems that can be dealt with relatively easily. Transition management is targeted at widely acknowledged problems that require a response for which no ready-made solution is (or will be) available. Often these are not single problems but a range of problems. For energy for example, the problems are dependence on scarce (non-renewable) resources (oil, natural gas), emissions of greenhouse gases stemming from the combustion of fossil fuels that cause climatic change, price volatility from shortfalls in supply often as a result of wars, and the military conflict over oil resources and oil power. By developing a shared problem perception based on the input of different actors,[8] those actors involved will adjust their own problem definitions and perceptions because of a better understanding of the nature of the problem and the perspectives held by other actors and accordingly their behaviour (that is, second-order learning). This however will only come about if enough time and energy is invested in these discussions. A problem here is that each solution to these problems has its own disadvantages. In the short term there are all kinds of tradeoffs. The aim of transition management is to provide an environment in which these trade offs are made visible and can be negotiated. This will be a collective task for which one needs transition goals that reflect societal aspirations.

**Transition Visions and Transition Goals**

A long-term vision of sustainability can function as a guide for formulating programmes and policies and the setting of short-term and long-term objectives. To adumbrate transitional pathways, such a vision must be appealing and imaginative so as to be supported by a broad range of actors. An inspiring final vision is useful for mobilizing social actors, although they should also be realistic about innovation levels within the functional subsystem in question. The overall vision helps to set qualitative standards or goals for the system as a whole. There is also a role for quantitative standards based on the boundaries within which we want our development to take place. For example, a sustainable energy supply system has been defined in the Netherlands as reliable, cost-effective, and carbon-low with the official goal of a reduction of 30 per cent in $CO_2$ emissions by 2020.[9]

The inspiring, imaginative and innovative vision is translated into transition images at a sub-system or thematic level, for example biomass or clean gas. (What would energy production and consumption look like?) Rather than considering transition images as optimal societal blueprints, we consider them as integral target images, which evolve over time and are dependent on the required insights and learning effects. The transition images embrace transition goals, which are qualitative rather than quantitative, multi-dimensional, and should not be defined in a narrowly technological sense, but should represent the three dimensions of sustainability: economic, ecological and socio-cultural. Ideally the images should be democratically chosen and based on integrated risk analysis, but this does not imply a consensus on these goals since a number of (even contradicting) images and goals can be chosen.

The transition images could be thematic or sectoral, but have to present an inspiring future state of that specific sector or theme. This means that the starting points of the overall vision are translated into the institutional, economic, ecologic and socio-cultural aspects associated with that specific final image. The images should be adjusted as a result of what has been learned by the actors in the various transition experiments. The participatory transition process is thus a goal-seeking process, where the transition images change over time (the transition goals are likely to remain the same). This differs from so-called 'blueprint' thinking, which operates from a fixed notion of final goals and corresponding visions.

**Transition Paths and Interim Objectives**

Transition paths are possible routes towards the final images. The images do not necessarily have to be consistent (only with the vision) and multiple paths can be developed for one image (see Figure 5.4). It is important to incorporate interim goals and objectives in the transition paths that become more concrete the closer they are to the present. The transition paths however also have to reflect the necessary trend breaks and behavioural and institutional changes, the uncertainties associated with the pathway and the barriers and chances for implementation. Finally, practical experiments (programmes) are planned, which are targeted at exploring the transition paths derived from the analysis and developed strategy.

The vision, in combination with the images, the transition paths and the experiments, forms the joint transition agenda at the tactical level. This is where coalitions come together around specific options or expectations, for example specific technologies or new institutions. For example, one could think of developing new consumption patterns for sustainable agriculture; a coalition to develop this idea and explore it further would include local

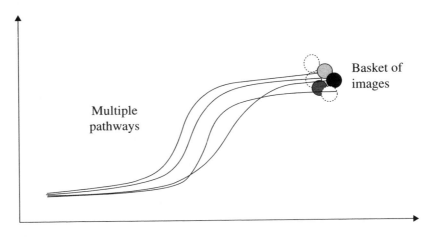

*Figure 5.4   Transition visions: images and pathways*

and national government, agriculture, business, NGOs and knowledge institutes. A transition path towards a sustainable energy supply could be via the use of biomass; a coalition there would include biomass producers, factories, the transport sector, national and local government, NGOs, and so on. These coalitions can develop experiments to test their ideas and to provide input for the overall transition programme. The development of transition paths is aimed at both comprehending in a more integral way the possible routes that specific innovations can go within a specific transition context as well as 'translating' the visionary and long-term goals at the strategic level to everyday practice at the operational level.

**Programmes for System Innovation**

Another important element of transition management includes programmes for system innovation for exploring visions of sustainability. An example is a programme for integrated mobility, identified by Kemp and Rotmans (2002) as suitable by combining user benefits with sustainability benefits. An integral part of such programmes is the real use of new technologies in society to learn from practice and facilitate processes of mutual adaptation and institution building. Experiments with new solutions and instruments are an important element of transition management. The experiments should be based on the images and should also inform them. For instance one could think of a series of consecutive experiments with electric mobility or integrated mobility. They should be undertaken as part of programmes for system innovation. They should be designed for specific learning purposes and not be undertaken in the ad hoc manner of today's experiments with sustainable technologies.

Such support programmes should be time-limited and flexible so as to prevent the creation of 'white elephants'. The choice of the programmes should be based on assessments of sustainability benefits and user benefits.

**Evaluating and Learning**

Transition management involves monitoring and evaluation as a regular activity and the use of so-called 'development rounds', where what has been achieved in terms of content, process dynamics and knowledge is evaluated.

The interim objectives are the first aspect of evaluation: have the objectives been achieved, and if not, why? Have there been any unexpected social developments or external factors that were not taken into account? Have the actors involved not complied with the agreements that were made? The second aspect of the evaluation concerns the transition management process itself. The set-up and implementation of the transition process is scrutinized. How do the actors concerned experience the participation process? Is it dominated by certain parties (vested interests)? Is it too consensual (too cosy), or is there too little commitment? Are there other actors who should be involved in the transition process? Are there other forms of participation that must be tried out?

The final issue for evaluation is the amount of learning or 'enrichment' that has taken place in the previous period. A special point of attention is what has been learned from the experiments carried out to stimulate the transition. What have been the most important learning moments and experiences? Have these led to new knowledge and new circumstances? And what does this mean for future policies? Monitoring and evaluation (of experience but also goals and visions) are key elements of transition management. In our model of transition management, learning is a policy goal in its own right.

### Creating Public Support and Broadening the Coalition

A continuing concern is the creation and maintenance of public support. This is important for continuing the process and preventing a backlash, which may occur when quick results do not materialize and setbacks are encountered. One route to follow is through participatory decision-making and the societal choice of goals, by engaging for example in experiments with technologies in areas in which there is local support for them. The experience may take away fears elsewhere and give proponents a weapon. With time, solutions may be found for the problems that limit wider application. Education can also allay fears but real experience is probably a more effective strategy. In niches new instruments (such as road pricing) may be tried.

The interactions between actors will change within the context of transition management. First and foremost the wider public is involved in policy-making, through the choice of transition goals and discussions about the future, and there is a greater orientation to innovators who are encouraged to come up with imaginative solutions. The innovators may be incumbent companies or outsiders. The latter group is more likely to come up with radical solutions. Transition management thus involves a change in governance, that is, the ways in which the plurality of interests is transformed into coordinated action, through deliberation, responsibilities and roles (Eising and Kohler-Koch, 1999, p. 5). There is still a great deal of deliberation as in the Dutch polder model and other models of interactive governance, but transition management is directed strongly to innovators and not the actors with large vested interests and is only consensual with regard to the overall ambition (or urgency) of sustainable development and the overall qualitative vision.

# TRANSITION MANAGEMENT AS REFLEXIVE GOVERNANCE

Transition management, as formulated by Rotmans and us, is a form of reflexive governance. It aims at dealing with real and perceived problems of forms of modernization and tries to avoid – or at least deal proactively – with risks and negative side effects of solutions. Each of the five elements of reflexive governance is addressed in transition management, even if it was developed prior to the theoretical framework of reflexive governance. It was informed largely by insights from innovation literature and systems theory. This section will describe in what ways each of the five elements is part of transition management.

## Knowledge Integration

Transition management can be best described as a process of learning-by-doing and doing-by-learning. Sustainability as such is not a fixed goal that can be worked towards but rather a journey of discovery. In order to explore new solutions and strategies, transition management relies on the involvement of a diverse number of actors in the transition arena. Not only will the different actors bring in different competencies, roles and networks, they will each provide a different kind of knowledge. Within the transition arena, in-depth discussions amongst the different participants will lead to confronting their different perspectives and to developing shared perceptions of the problem[10] besides the development (integration) of new knowledge and the identification of gaps in knowledge.

This way, different elements of knowledge are integrated into a common understanding of the complex problems and processes at hand. These elements of knowledge are by definition very diverse (ranging from technical knowledge about regulation, codes, or procedures to 'soft' or 'tacit' knowledge about behaviour, institutions or other practical issues) so that a lot of energy has to be invested in the process in order to develop a general level of understanding amongst the participants. By trying to discover 'sustainability' in the form of new goals and solutions, also the lack of relevant knowledge in certain areas will become clear. New questions will be posed, which in turn will generate development of new knowledge. This process of (re)combining different knowledge elements is referred to as coproduction of knowledge in which scientific knowledge is often only one part (Gibbons et al., 1994).

A further goal of transition management is of course to diffuse the new knowledge (ideas, goals and solutions, innovations, alliances, competences, etc.) into larger networks rather than to keep it within the transition arena per se. Transition management therefore is a network strategy that also tries to use the networks of the participants in the transition arena to spread the thoughts developed there. The discussions with other actors (about the (complex) system, its problems and dynamics, but about strategies as well), will have to be extensive and confrontational enough to lead to second-order learning amongst the participants. In practice, this means that the participants will reflect on their own dispositions, their own practices and their own roles within the larger context. They will supposedly take home such new insights as well as the new ideas on cooperation, solutions, and so on. By creating within their own organizations new 'arenas' that address more specific elements of the common approach and strategy, they will contribute to realizing a structure of arenas and thus knowledge and experiences can be shared and exchanged between these arenas. If actively pursued, such an elaborated structure could be seen as an instrument for knowledge production, knowledge diffusion and knowledge integration (McElroy, 2003).

**Anticipation of Long-term Systemic Effects**

Especially in the programmes for system innovation there is anticipation of long-term systemic effects through the use of scenario-analyses and trend-analyses, back-casting and forecasting exercises and identification (and selection) of innovations. Insights from innovation studies about self-reinforcement are used for creating paths while at the same time one is careful not to get locked into sub-optimal solutions by opting for a flexible, adaptive approach and by engaging in portfolio management. In this way the antici-pation and control dilemma of Collingridge (1980) – with control possibil-ities being largest when you know the least about the problem – is dealt with. It is still possible that side effects become apparent at a later time, when the technologies are in use, but the chances of this happening are reduced. Transition management combines elements of push and control, which is one of its advantages.

Transition management does not aim to control the future (to use Wildavsky's term) by engaging in comprehensive planning (based on blue-prints). It relies heavily on market forces for the delivery of functional services for the obvious reason that no authority can plan for the efficient delivery of specialized services. Yet transition management does not blankly rely on market forces, but is concerned with the conditions under which market forces operate, by engaging in 'context control' so as to orient market dynamics towards societal goals. The context control consists of regulations, economic instruments (the use of taxes, subsidies and emission trading), the use of policy goals and covenants and specific types of plan-ning (such as land use planning). It consists of the government's acting to secure circumstances that will maximize the possibilities for progressive social development by promoting innovation and mitigating negative effects (Meadowcroft, 1997, p. 27).[11]

Anticipative strategies help to deal with three problems of intelligent change: (1) ignorance: uncertainties about the future and the causal structure of experience, (2) conflict: inconsistencies in preferences and interests, (3) ambiguity: lack of clarity, instability and endogeneity in preferences and interests: (March and Olsen, 1995).[12] Like Lindblom, March and Olsen are very negative about the use of expert intelligence, saying that 'the history of efforts to act intelligently in democracies is a history of mistakes'. They are especially critical about political change based on anticipatory rationality, based on backward reasoning from anticipated consequences:[13]

> Too many atrocities of stupidity and immorality have been based on anticipatory rationality, and too many efforts to improve human action through importing technologies of decision engineering have been disappointing. (March and Olsen, 1995: 198–9)

This clearly shows the limitation of the use of anticipatory outcomes but is probably too negative with regard to anticipation. In transition management, experiences inform next steps more than grand visions do.

**Adaptivity of Strategies and Institutions**

Making adaptive steps forward is also a key element of transition management. Transition management opts for a step-by-step process, which is also characteristic of incrementalism. A step-by-step approach has three advantages: first, it is feasible because it is not disruptive from the viewpoint of special interests; second, the costs of a certain step being a mistake are kept low; third, it allows one to change course (one gets less locked into particular solutions)[14] and fourth, useful lessons may be learned informing further steps. Even though it is generally seen as slow it may bring change faster than more dirigistic approaches. Charles Lindblom powerfully states the case for incremental politics:

> Abstractly considered, incremental politics looks very good. It is intelligently exploratory when linked with sequences of trial and error. It reduces the stakes in each political controversy, thus encouraging losers to bear their losses without disrupting the political system. It helps maintain the vague general consensus on basic values (because no specific policy issue ever centrally poses a challenge to them) that many people believe is necessary for widespread voluntary acceptance of democratic government. Moreover, incrementalism in politics is not in principle slow moving. It is not necessarily, therefore, a tactic of conservatism. A fast-moving sequence of small changes can more speedily accomplish a drastic

alteration of the status quo than can a mere infrequent major policy change. (Lindblom, 1979: 520)[15]

Transition management is an incrementalist strategy for changing societal systems.[16] The reason for this is that with new technology systems, as with politics, you can't get it right the first time. There are too many variables; one has to opt for small steps in what is generally perceived as 'the right direction' by trying different solutions (cf. Lee, 1993). By means of this process in an iterative way, the 'right direction' will be redefined, as will the associated goals. Like politics, technologies are not born perfect (Latour, 1991; Rosenberg, 1976) but require adaptation before they constitute a good solution. It is often insufficiently realized that the efficiency of markets rests on the weeding out of suboptimal designs of products and technologies through market competition. Evolutionary change, founded on trial and error, while wasteful in the short term, is often the most intelligent approach in the long run. This view has greatly influenced the vision of transition management.

Transition management does not argue for blind incrementalism and takes into account criticisms levelled against incrementalism such as lack of orientation, conservatism, and negative stance against analysis (Weiss and Woodhouse, 1992). Analysis plays a role in the choice of incremental steps (doing by learning). Analysis also has an important role to play in the determination of goals, the identification of visions of sustainability for meeting such goals, and the determination of steps (policy steps and technology steps) to learn about the visions and make a contribution to them. This is not so easy. According to Weiss and Woodhouse (1992; 260) incrementalism whilst intellectually appealing has never been very helpful to practitioners, as it has failed to set forth a strategy for making fairer, more intelligent, or otherwise better social choices. Transition management is believed to be more helpful in making a number of concrete proposals, one of which is to develop the long-term vision and intermediate goals to inform incremental action. Whether this leads to better decisions is still an open issue, but practice has already shown at least that novel and alternative steps are identified.

### Iterative Participatory Goal Formulation

Transition management relies on iterative participatory goal formulation within transition arenas (as we discussed at length in section 5). Goals chosen by and in society are continuously re-assessed, together with policies to move closer to those goals. One of the crucial elements in transition management is its own evaluation, both in terms of process as well as

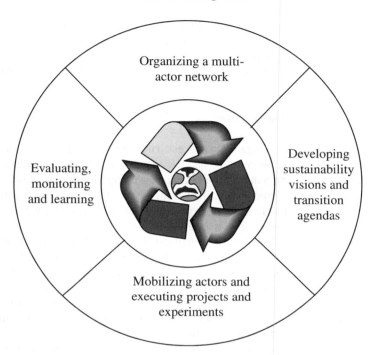

*Figure 5.5    Activity clusters in transition management*

content. By organising evaluation systematically, formulated goals, experiments and policy approaches can be adapted, which leads to a new round of learning-by-doing. The cyclical and iterative element of transition management is portrayed in Figure 5.5.

Experiential learning plays an important role in this. A real problem here of course is that you not only want to learn about a singular solution but about system innovation, and to facilitate processes of change. To learn about system innovation one should do strategic experiments as part of programmes for system innovation. Results from evaluation should feed into the projects and the overall programme; it should inform decisions at the operational and strategic level. Lessons learned depend on how experiments are designed and the types of experiments that are being undertaken. Having a good portfolio of experiments is therefore important. Experiments not only help provide information about technology and instruments but also help actors to learn about goals. It is important to engage in higher-level learning about both goals and approaches.

The participatory nature of transition management also allows for iterative problem-formulating and goal-formulating processes between different types of actors. For example the interaction between scientific knowledge, practical experience from practitioners and the regulatory context can lead to new insights into problems, complementarities, innovation and uncertainties. Through a systemic evaluation and adaptation of the programmes the process moves forward.

**Interactive Strategy Development**

Interactive strategy development is necessarily a part of transition management. In the Netherlands over the last decade, a standard practice has been to involve societal actors in policy-making, searching for agreement on environmental and economic issues. The famous or infamous Dutch polder model is a clear example of this involvement of stakeholders, which was based on negotiations to reach consensus between the vested interests (actors in the regime). The goal of transition management is to facilitate and organize outsiders, trying to empower them to be able to develop and implement alternatives. Through transition management, outsiders, especially innovators, are given room and listened to. The transition arena is created for this. Through transition management citizens and citizens' organizations including NGOs are involved in policy-formulation as well as business interests. They are involved in the setting of goals and in discussions of possible futures. Participation is not merely used to generate public support although this has some important advantages, noted by Coenen (2002). Citizen involvement enhances the legitimacy of policy, helps to reduce the risk of conflict and offers an additional source of ideas and information. Through their involvement people and organizations learn about problems and solutions. Citizen involvement is not a substitute for government; a clear role is expected of and needed from the government (Coenen, 2002).

The question thus is how to organize participation and interaction while maintaining effective governance. The solution offered by transition management is to place the process in the centre and rely on mutual adaptation against a set of collectively chosen long-term goals. When organized properly, transition management thus enables self-coordination and steering among actors without controlling the process in the classical top-down control mode. This mechanism has been described on a broader level by Lindblom (1965, 1997) as partisan mutual adjustment: in a generally understood environment of moral rules, norms, conventions, and mores, interdependent actors modify their own behaviour just enough to accommodate the differing purposes of others, but not so much that the mutual adjusters lose sight of collective goals.

For transition management, this implies organising and facilitating interaction, while not influencing the content of the process, since the outcomes are the result of the interaction itself and not of individual choices or demands. By co-developing visions and agendas and collectively carrying out practical projects and experiments, the mutual adjustment of these perspectives and expectations takes shape.

## TRANSITION POLICIES FOR ENERGY

Transition management as developed by Rotmans and others is not a theoretical fancy. The Dutch government uses the model of transition management to manage four transitions: the transitions to sustainable energy, sustainable mobility, sustainable agriculture, and the biodiversity and natural resource transition. This section will describe how this abstract model is translated into policy in the energy area. The ministry responsible for this transition is the Ministry of Economic Affairs (responsible for industry and energy). This ministry has been very active since 2001 in developing transition policies for the transition to a sustainable energy-supply system by 2050 (see www.energietransitie.nl). In 2001, the Ministry of Economic Affairs started consulting various stakeholders (companies, researchers, NGOs) to assess whether they saw possibilities for the transition to take place, and if so, what the chances were. Based on these conversations and an intensive scenario-study (LTVE), they selected five 'robust elements' or subprojects in the transition to a sustainable energy system, with a time horizon of 2030:

- Biomass International;
- New Gas Services;
- Sustainable Industrial Production;
- Toward a Sustainable Rijnmond (an industrial ecology project);
- Policy Renewal.

In 2002, the Ministry started Project Implementation Transition management (PIT), which was meant to investigate whether the selected subprojects would meet enough support, enthusiasm and commitment from the relevant stakeholders to create a climate in which they would be willing and able to work together. The project was initially financed with 35 million euros and supported by an eight-person staff. The main conclusions from this phase were that the transition approach proved to be appealing to the majority of the stakeholders and they would be willing to invest (time and money) and commit themselves to such a process under the condition that the transition management approach would be made more concrete, that more explicit visions for the future would be developed, and that the

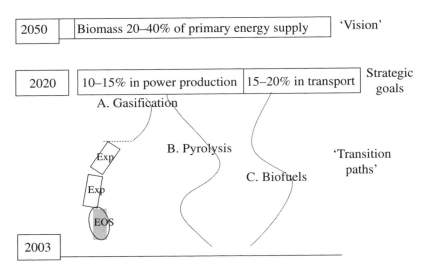

*Note:*   Exp = experiments; EOS = R&D

*Source:*   presentation of Hugo Brouwer from Ministry of Economic Affairs in the Netherlands at final BLUEPRINT workshop in Brussels in 2003

*Figure 5.6    The Dutch vision for biomass*

government would support the transition endeavour both financially as well as process-wise.

Based on these findings, the green light was given for the implementation of phase 2 in 2003. The objectives of this phase were to develop a long-term vision on energy in general and for each of the sub-projects supported by all relevant actors, to have these actors committed to the process, to map possible paths, barriers and necessary preconditions for the transition, to set up plans for knowledge development and knowledge sharing and communication, to chart international developments and finally to develop transition experiments. For biomass this resulted in the following vision[17] which is to be adapted with time.

Different options are explored. A portfolio approach is used also with respect to research. So-called 'Spearhead' projects were selected as part of the new energy research strategy on the basis of two criteria: knowledge position of the Netherlands and contribution to a sustainable energy system. The two criteria resulted in the following categorization of projects: 'spearhead projects', 'knowledge export projects', 'knowledge import projects' and 'irrelevant' (for those projects that scored low on both accounts). The portfolio approach used in finance to hedge risks fits with transition management.

Following these developments, 35 million euros were made available in 2004 for strategic experiments. In the 'Policy Renewal' project the Ministry is reconsidering its instruments and interactions with society. They are opting for a more participatory and interactive type of governance. An example of this is the establishment on 21 January 2004 of an 'intervision group for the energy transition', an independent think tank composed mostly of non-energy experts and independent people.

Different ministries are now using the model of transition management and applying it in their own way. It is too early to evaluate outcomes, but what already seems apparent is that the approach leads to integration of activities across the spectrum. The first successes, in terms of agreements, projects, subsidies, inspiring images and so forth, serve as a flywheel and attract an increasing number of actors to the process. However, organizing the process, especially within the context of the existing institutional frameworks, has proven to be difficult because of the tension between the existing interests and institutionalized routines and the innovation promoted by the transition network. Through engaging in transition management activities, the barriers to innovation become clear and conflicting interests are identified. This leads to tension, negative feedback, irritation and sometimes conflict, but these are necessary to achieve the intended changes. The exploitation of win–win options does not get you far. So far also little progress has been made in involving citizens in the transition process in a direct way. The goals of 20–40 per cent biomass for example have been chosen by business interests. The selected transition goals of reliability, cost efficiency and reductions in carbon dioxide emissions were chosen by the government.

## CONCLUSIONS

In this chapter we outlined the concept of transition management that is currently used in the Netherlands for managing the transition to sustainable energy, sustainable mobility, sustainable agriculture, and the biodiversity and natural resource transition, and delineated the reflexive governance characteristics. Transition management for sustainable development consists of deliberate attempts to work toward social, economic and ecological objectives in a gradual, forward-looking manner in full recognition of system dynamics and windows of opportunity to effect change. Transition management is concerned with the normative orientation of socio-economic processes and seeks to overcome the conflict between long-term imperatives and short-term concerns. Because of its focus on the evolutionary dynamics of socio-technological innovation processes, transition management pays particular attention to learning, maintaining a variety of options (through portfolio management, see also Chapter 8 by Weber in this book) and institutional change – to avoid becoming locked into 'evolutionary traps' and to escape existing ones.

Transition management employs an integrative and multi-scale framework for policy deliberation, choice of instruments, and actions by individuals, private and public organizations, and society at large. Transition management is inclusive and calls for setting long-term and intermediate goals, alignment of short-term and long-term policies and strategic experimentation in addition to traditional policies. Because it aims for long-term change through relatively small steps, the risk of getting locked into suboptimal solutions is limited.

In this chapter we explained why transition management de facto is a form of reflexive governance, even though it was developed independently of theories of reflexive modernization (Beck, 1997) and reflexive governance. Transition management is based on each of the strategies of reflexive governance delineated in the Introduction to this book: knowledge integration, anticipation of long-term systemic effects, adaptivity of strategies and institutions, iterative participatory goal formulation and interactive strategy development. Alternative labels are evolutionary governance, directed incrementalism (Grunwald, 2000) and goal-oriented modulation (Kemp and Rotmans, 2001).[18]

It should be clear from what we said that transition management is not a megalomaniac attempt to control the future but an attempt to orient dynamics to sustainability goals in a reflexive manner. Policy is concerned with the dynamics of variation, selection and reproduction, not just with obtaining predefined policy outcomes. By opting for relatively small steps transition management seems feasible, and by implementing it not only the knowledge problem but also the governability problem (Mayntz, 1994) can be addressed. Whilst the idea of managing variation-selection processes sounds very abstract, the model of transition management offers practical suggestions for how to do it, in terms of institutions and instruments. It is not an instrument as such, but a new perspective for decision-making and governance.

# NOTES

1. We thank Bernhard Truffer, Jan-Peter Voß and Dierk Bauknecht for comments on an earlier version of the chapter.
2. Senge (1990) has also underlined the importance of systems-thinking for enabling interaction, learning and cooperation. More recently, Midgley (2000) has synthesized most recent work on systems thinking under the heading 'critical systems thinking', a looser way to apply systems properties and use systems language. For transition management,

systems-thinking is not a straitjacket, but rather a way to identify main drivers, be aware of side effects and develop more integrated strategies.

3. The time span is not a defining characteristic but a result.

4. Because of changes in human activity, technologies and production processes used, the ecological impact of the activities changes.

5. In Rotmans et al. (2000 and 2001) this phase is called the 'acceleration phase'.

6. Transitions can be seen as system innovation at the highest level of societal systems. These societal systems can be broken down into sub-systems (for example the regulatory, the technological or the user sub-system) at which level system innovations take place. Within these sub-systems, simple or singular innovations occur.

7. Other examples of system innovation are: biomass-based chemistry, multiple sustainable land use (the integration of the agricultural function with other functions in rural areas) and flexible, modular manufactured construction (Ashford et al., 2001).

8. Discussions within the transition arena have to be based on a systems approach, which allows for a more comprehensive and integrated analysis of the problem. The focus has to be on the issue of what the structural origins of all the individual (symptomatic) problems of the different actors are.

9. See also section 7. The website www.energietransitie.nl gives an overview of the result of discussions amongst Dutch actors related to energy, which resulted in the vision, images and transition experiments.

10. The discussions are based on a participative systems analysis in which the different participants contribute specific knowledge about specific parts of the system so that they together develop an integrated image of the systems at hand and the main causal relations and dynamics within this system.

11. Context control may be viewed as a form of planning (see Meadowcroft 1997, p.27).

12. A nice discussion of adaptive policy with operational elements is Walker et al.'s paper (2001).

13. The criticism of anticipatory rationality should probably not be taken as criticism of anticipation or a call for short-sightedness but as a criticism of a particular method for dealing with the future: strategic planning. According to Club of Rome member Mesarovic (2001), sustainability requires anticipatory democracy.

14. We take the view that path dependencies cannot altogether be prevented, each act will influence future acts in ways that are not entirely clear. Incrementalism, portfolio management and the stimulation by policy of robust solutions help to circumvent but not altogether prevent the problem of suboptimal solutions. Lindblom (1997) proposes relying on the 'intelligence of interaction' by relying on partisan mutual adjustment.

15. Of course there is a danger of conservatism but forces of conservatism (in the form of special interests, veto powers, and timid/unimaginative thinking) always play out themselves, at any time and place, as noted by Lindblom in a defence to his critics.

16. Not just incremental steps are taken. From a contemporary point of view, we have discontinuous policies and steps.

17. What is referred to here is what we described in section 5 as a basket of images. From all scenario studies, it was concluded that biomass will play a significant role in any future energy supply system. The form in which biomass will be used however is uncertain. Within the context of the overall vision for a sustainable energy supply, different images have been developed (gasification, pyrolysis and biofuels), linked to different transition-paths, which together must lead to the overall ambition.

18. Similarly, transition management could also be considered an example of a 'mixed scanning approach', a hierarchical mode of decision-making that combines higher-order, fundamental decision-making with lower-order incremental decisions that work out and/or prepare for the higher order ones (Etzioni, 1986). The fundamental choices are the long-term goals, the creation or abandoning of programmes for system innovation, reliance on certain ways of decision-making. The fact that we can use different labels for transition management shows that the ideas behind it are not new; what is new is the operationalization of these ideas.

# REFERENCES

Ashford, Nicholas, Wim Hafkamp, Frits Prakke and Philip Vergragt (2001), *Pathways to Sustainable Industrial Transformation: Cooptimising Competitiveness, Employment and Environment*, Cambridge, MA: Ashford Associates.

Beck, Ulrich (1997), *The Reinvention of Politics: Rethinking Modernity in the Global Social Order*, Cambridge, UK: Polity Press.

Butter, Maurits (2002), Een handreiking voor transitiebeleid, Delft: TNO-STB.

Coenen, Frans (2002), 'The role of stakeholders in changing consumption and production patterns', expert report for OECD seminar 'Improving Governance for Sustainable Development', held 22–3 November 2001, available at http://www.oecd.org/dataoecd/50/21/1940033.pdf.

Collingridge, David (1980), *The Social Control of Technology*, London: Pinter.

Dirven, Jan, Jan Rotmans and Arie-Pieter Verkaik (2002), 'Samenleving in Transitie. Een vernieuwend gezichtspunt', LNV, ICIS en Innovatienetwerk Groene Ruimte in Agrocluster, April.

Eising, Rainer, and Beate Kohler-Koch (1999), 'Introduction: network governance in the European Union', in Rainer Eising and Beate Kohler-Koch (eds.) *The Transformation of EU Governance*, London: Routledge.

Etzioni, Amitai (1986), 'Mixed scanning revisited', *Public Administration Review*, January/February, 8–14.

Geels, F.W. (2002a), 'Technological transitions as evolutionary reconfiguration processes: a multi-level perspective and a case-study', *Research Policy*, **31**(8/9), 1257–74.

Geels, F.W. (2002b), 'Understanding the dynamics of technological transitions, a co-evolutionary and socio-technical analysis', PhD thesis, Enschede: Twente University Press.

Gibbons, M., H. Nowotny, C. Limoges, M. Trow, S. Schwartzman and P. Scott (1994), *The new production of knowledge: the Dynamics of Science and Research in Contemporary Societies*, Thousand Oaks, CA: Sage.

Grunwald, Armin (2000), 'Technology policy between long-term planning requirements and short-ranged acceptance problems. New challenges for technology assessment', in John Grin and Armin Grunwald (eds), *Vision Assessment: Shaping Technology in the 21st Century Society. Towards a Repertoire for Technology Assessment*, Berlin and Heidelberg: Springer.

Gunderson, L.H. and B. Holling (2002), *Panarchy: Understanding Transformations in Human and Natural Systems*, Washington DC: Island Press.

Kasemir, B. and M. Van Asselt (1999), 'Integrated assessment: multiple perspectives in interaction', *International Journal of Environment and Pollution*, **11** (4), 407–25.

Kemp, René, and Luc Soete (1992), 'The greening of technological progress: an evolutionary perspective', *Futures*, **24** (5), 437–57.

Kemp, René and Jan Rotmans (2001), 'The management of the co-evolution of technical, environmental and social systems', paper for international conference 'Towards Environmental Innovation Systems', September 27–9 2001, Garmisch Partenkirchen, Germany' forthcoming in Matthias Weber and Jens Hemmelskamp (eds) *Towards Environmental Innovation Systems*, Springer Verlag.

Kemp, René and Jan Rotmans (2002), 'Managing the transition to sustainable mobility', paper for international workshop 'Transitions to Sustainability through System Innovations', University of Twente, 4–6 July; published in Boelie

Elzen, Frank Geels and Ken Green (eds), *System Innovation and the Transition to Sustainability: Theory, Evidence and Policy*, Cheltenham UK and Northampton, MA, Edward Elgar, pp. 137–67.

Kemp, R. and J. Rotmans (2005), 'The management of the co-evolution of technical, environmental and social systems', in M. Weber and J. Hemmelskamp (eds), *Towards Environmental Innovation Systems*, Heidelberg/New York: Springer Verlag, pp. 33–55.

Kohler-Koch, Beate (1999), 'The evolution and transformation of European governance', in Rainer Eising and Beate Kohler-Koch (eds), *The Transformation of EU Governance*, London: Routledge, pp. 14–35.

Kooiman, Jan (1993), 'Governance and governability: using complexity, dynamics and diversity', in Jan Kooiman (ed.), *Modern Governance. New Government–Society Interactions*, London: Sage, pp. 35–48.

Latour, B. (1991), 'Technology is society made durable' in J. Law (ed), *A Sociology of Monsters: Essays on Power, Technology and Domination*, Routledge: London, pp. 103–31.

Lee, Kai N. (1993), *Compass and Gyroscope. Integrating Science and Politics for the Environment*, Washington DC: Island Press.

Lindblom, Charles (1965), *The Intelligence of Democracy*, New York: Free Press.

Lindblom, Charles E. (1979), 'Still muddling, not yet through', *Public Administration Review*, November/December, 517–26.

Lindblom, Charles (1997), 'A Century of Planning', in Michael Kenny and James Meadowcroft (eds) *Planning Sustainability*, London and New York: Routledge, 39–65.

Loorbach, Derk, and Jan Rotmans (2002), 'Society in technology and technology in society', paper presented at the international conference 'Engineering Education for Sustainable Development' (EESD), 24/25 October, Delft, The Netherlands.

March, J.G. and J.P. Olsen (1995), *Democratic Governance*, New York: The Free Press.

Mayntz, Renate (1994), 'Governing failures and the problem of governability: some comments on a theoretical paradigm', in Jan Kooiman (ed.), *Modern Governance. New Government–Society Interactions*, London: Sage, 9–20.

McElroy, M. (2003), *The New Knowledge Management: complexity, learning and sustainable innovation*, Burlington: Butterworth–Heinemann.

Meadowcroft, James (1997), 'Planning for sustainable development: what can be learned from the critics?', in Michael Kenny and James Meadowcroft (eds) *Planning Sustainability*, London and New York: Routledge, 12–38.

Mesarovic, Mihaljo (2001), 'Evolution of sustainability concept', mimeo.

Midgley, G. (2000), *Systemic Intervention: Philosophy, Methodology and Practice*, Dordrecht: Kluwer Academic Publishers.

NMP-4 (2000), 'Een wereld en een wil. Werken aan duurzaamheid', ('A world and a will. Working on sustainability'), The Hague.

NRLO (1999), 'Innovating with ambition, opportunities for agribusiness, rural areas and the fishing industry', The Hague.

Rip, A. and R. Kemp (1998), 'Technological change', in S. Rayner and E.L. Malone (eds), *Human Choice and Climate Change*, Volume 2, Columbus, OH: Battelle Press, 327–99.

Rosenberg, N. (1976), 'The direction of technological change: inducement mechanisms and focusing devices', in Nathan Rosenberg, *Perspectives on Technology*, Cambridge: Cambridge University Press.

Rotmans, J. (1998), 'Methods for IA: the challenges and opportunities ahead', *Environmental Modelling and Assessment*, **3** (3), 155–79.

Rotmans, Jan, René Kemp, Marjolein van Asselt, Frank Geels, Geert Verbong and Kirsten Molendijk (2000), 'Transities en Transitiemanagement. De casus van een emissiearme energievoorziening'. Final report of study 'Transitions and transition management' for the 4th National Environmental Policy Plan (NMP-4) of the Netherlands, October 2000, Maastricht: ICIS and MERIT.

Rotmans, Jan, René Kemp and Marjolein van Asselt (2001), 'More evolution than revolution. Transition management in public policy', *Foresight* **3** (1): 15–31.

Scharpf, F. (1994), 'Community and autonomy. Multi-level policy making in the EU', *Journal of European Public Policy*, **1**, 219–42.

Schnabel, P. (2000), SCP presentation, The Hague.

Senge, Peter (1990), *The Fifth Discipline. The Art and Practices of the Learning Organization*, New York: Currency Doubleday.

Walker, Warren E., S. Adnan Rahman and Jonathan Cave (2001), 'Adaptive policies, policy analysis, and policy-making', *European Journal of Operational Research*, **128**, 282–89.

WCED (1987), *Our Common Future*, Oxford: Oxford University Press.

Weiss, Andrew and Edward Woodhouse (1992), 'Reforming incrementalism: a constructive response to the critics, *Policy Sciences*, **25**(3), 255–73.

# 6.  Adaptive management to restore ecological and economic resilience in the Tisza river basin

## Jan Sendzimir, Piotr Magnuszewski, Peter Balogh and Anna Vári

## INTRODUCTION

While many of the chapters in this volume deal with the governance of socio-technical systems to make them more sustainable, the management of complexity has been an important issue in the area of socio-ecological systems for quite some time. Adaptive management (AM) has been developed as a structured learning process to deal with uncertainty of socio-ecological development in natural park management, fisheries and so forth.

These approaches can be viewed as instances of reflexive governance since they acknowledge the impossibility of planning and control in a complex and changing world. They anticipate unintended effects of management strategies and actually build on them in an understanding of 'management as learning'.

This chapter discusses the set-up of an Adaptive Management process for renaturalisation in the Tisza River Basin (TRB) in Hungary where it has been applied in order to deal with increasing flood risks which represent a 'second-order problem' of modern hydro-engineering and industrial agricultural practice. River basins rarely gain our attention except in the context of great floods, but their future revolves around far more than pulses of water. Their integrity and development also depend on how their communities interact with flows of people, commerce, and ideas. Sustainable progress in the evolution of these regional socio-ecological systems (*sensu*, Walker et al. 2000) depends on the resilience and dynamism of their heritage, in all its ecological, economic and social dimensions. Over the past century, regional decline, and even collapse, of the heritage of major river basins on every continent signal our failure to understand or manage all the intertwined processes that drive these complex systems.

To answer this challenge, it is neither science nor policy but their integration in a learning cycle along with local knowledge and practice, that will help us adapt to the uncertainty and surprise of complex, large-scale systems like river basins, coasts, continental plains and mountain ranges. None of the perspectives along the way can be neglected, and small steps seldom taken address how we steer the process of learning and managing as we integrate these views, reflect and experiment. Adaptive management is an on-going experiment for developing such a steering process (Gunderson et al. 1995, Gunderson and Holling 2002, Sendzimir et al. 1999, 2003).

Adaptive management is an example of a reflexive governance (RG) approach, starting from some of the same premises and pursuing some of the same methods as those described in the Introduction to this volume. AM begins from the assumption that surprise is inevitable in complex evolving systems and will confound and ultimately defeat efforts to control and eliminate uncertainty through science, policy, or practice. If the uncertainty inherent in natural and social evolution is compounded by inflexible attempts to control ambient variability, then management only increases uncertainty. However, the effect is further amplified because it often emerges after a period of initial success lulls society into complacent dependence on short-sighted methods. Delays are potent sources of destabilizing surprise in evolving systems (Sterman 2000). The adaptive label is partly an attempt to recast management in the wider role as a nimble experimenter, with the patience to consider long-term consequences. As such, management takes place in a learning cycle as the driver and implementer of the experiments proposed by science to probe how the world is changing and by what means we can adapt to that change.

RG and AM jointly advocate and pursue a number of adaptive strategies (see Table 1.1 in the Introduction). For example, both apply 'transdisciplinary knowledge production' as a means to address co-evolutionary relations between different dimensions (ecological, economic or social) across multiple scales. AM invokes modelling techniques (conceptual and formal) to integrate the insights of multiple perspectives across these scales. Likewise, as mentioned above, AM embraces uncertainty through a cycle that links hypothesis with policy with implementation with monitoring. In this way we can adapt how we understand and how we react to the shifting re-alignments of inter-relations within socio-ecological systems. The RG goal of facing the dangers of path dependence and technological lock-in (Arthur 1983) through anticipation of long-term systemic effects is often addressed by looking at long-term system dynamics and sensitivities through the use of formal models in AM exercises. AM processes are fundamentally iterative and participatory and have been aimed at RG strategy element 4, 'iterative participatory goal formulation' (Sendzimir et al. 2003) as well as goal 5, 'interactive strategy development'.

This chapter describes how AM can be applied in the Tisza River Basin (TRB) to address a key RG target – 'second-order' problems, unintended and unanticipated consequences that are more severe than the initial challenges that provoked the original management intervention. The Tisza River flows from the Trans-Carpathian region of the Ukraine, and, fed by numerous tributaries from Romania and Slovakia, cuts across the Great Hungarian Plain (Alföld), the largest sedimentary basin in Europe (Juhász 1987, Sümegi 1999). While the length and breadth of the Tisza River Basin (TRB) are not imposing in size (see Figure 6.1), the vast differential between them and the far larger four-nation area it drains (more than 150 000 square kilometers in parts of Ukraine, Romania, Slovakia and Hungary) give the Tisza some of the most dramatic flow fluctuations in Europe (Kovács 2003). Loosely hemmed in by the bowl shape of the Alföld,

*Figure 6.1*    *The Tisza river basin with tributaries in catchments in the Carpathian mountain range across portions of five different national territories (Romania, the Ukraine, Slovakia, the Federation of Serbia and Montenegro, and Hungary)*

these fluctuations spread like flood waves over vast areas of floodplain, suspended there for considerable periods by thick, impermeable sediments. Pre-industrial societies managed to develop cultures that could utilize and thrive on massive, periodic flooding, by building fisheries and fruit enterprises that made them one of the richest regions of Hungary before 1850 (Andrásfalvy 1973, Molnár 2003, Paget 1850, Tóth 2002). How could such a self-sufficient region collapse to its present state of economic and social poverty, and be threatened increasingly by the very floods on which it used to thrive?

This chapter examines some of the sources of uncertainty from both human and environmental sources that have combined to produce such surprising regional collapses. It then considers adaptive management (AM) as a reflexive governance approach, which has proven useful in addressing uncertainty in river basins and describes its implementation in the Tisza River Basin.

## RISING UNCERTAINTY IN SOCIO-ECOLOGICAL SYSTEMS

Confidence in human capacity to manage Nature surged with the dramatic scientific and engineering advances that drove the Industrial Revolution (Davies 1996), which increased society's throughput of energy and materials by several orders of magnitude (Odum 1996). That confidence faded, beginning with a series of surprising, catastrophic collapses of regional fisheries, agriculture and forestry in the twentieth century (Gunderson et al. 1995, Holling 1986, Walters 1986). As variability has increased at macro scales (for example with climate change and globalization), uncertainty increasingly replaces confidence as a central attitude driving the search for policy. The 'stubborn' refusal of many such crises to respond to any remedy (the decline of rural society and 'mad cow' disease to name but two prominent cases in the past 20 years) has earned them a reputation as 'wicked' problems (Rittel and Webber 1973). In many cases, policies that initially 'cured' problems have suddenly foundered on 'policy resistance', the counter-intuitive, often delayed, emergence of new challenges that would reverse initial success (Sterman 2002).

The degree and quality of uncertainty inherent in the dynamics of ecological, social and economic change can be classified as statistical uncertainty, model uncertainty, or fundamental uncertainty (Hilborn 1987). Discourse about change in the popular media may acknowledge the shallowest level of uncertainty, namely statistical uncertainty, wherein one may not know the condition of a variable at any one point, but the overall chances of its occurrence (probability distribution) are known. An example of this might be the chances of being struck by lightning.

More profound kinds of uncertainty are currently encountered at the frontiers of science and practice. For example, the depth of surprises that occur in natural and human systems are forcing us to re-examine our most basic ideas about how variables are connected in a model (model uncertainty) or whether we can conceive of any model at all that applies (fundamental uncertainty) (Peterson et al. 1997). In the case of model uncertainty one still can predict the impacts of outcomes but have no idea of their likelihood. For instance, evidence from periodic drops in Europe's temperatures is best explained at present by the switching off of a deep ocean current, the Atlantic Conveyor, yet we have little idea what processes combine to toggle these systems on and off and less idea of their likelihood (Broecker 1996). Fundamental uncertainty applies to situations so novel that no current model applies. The discovery of the atmospheric ozone hole exemplified such profound novelty; at that time we couldn't even conceive of a cast of characters let alone a set of relationships between them.

One begins to appreciate the complexity of systems when one realizes that, as our Earth is increasingly connected by ecological and human processes, all three levels of uncertainty can apply at any one place. Uncertainty, therefore, arises from sources both external and internal to society. We consider two of the most prominent sources of uncertainty currently confronting river basins: climate (primarily external with respect to river basins, though over-development within the basin may trigger larger flood pulses (Ripl 1995), and our history of river basin engineering (internal).

## Uncertainty in Nature

Climate change (CC) is anticipated to increase uncertainty in river management through short-term direct effects on temperature and precipitation that may generate medium- to long-term indirect effects on the rates and functioning of ecosystem processes and the interactions between them (IPCC 2001, Walther et al. 2002, Parmesan and Yohe 2003, Sendzimir et al. in review). CC impacts can complicate flood management by increasing the variability of river inputs from melt water, groundwater and precipitation. Rising temperatures and shorter winters should diminish both ice and snow volumes thereby decreasing melt water contributions and increasing the dominance of rainwater inputs to river flow.

Over the past 50 years rising atmospheric temperatures have already decreased alpine glacier ice volumes by 50 per cent and should completely melt all glaciers that feed the Rhine river by 2070 (source: www. waterandclimate.org, accessed June 2004) and consequently decrease steady melt water inputs by 15 per cent in summer. CC impacts are expected to drive increases in rainwater fluctuations, such as a 20 per cent increase in winter precipitation. Rising temperatures can drive higher throughput of the hydrological cycle with higher rates of evapotranspiration (water flux through plants and the soil back to the atmosphere) and precipitation (IPCC 2001). Higher precipitation rates will probably lead to increased spatial heterogeneity of precipitation, concentrating rainfall into tighter patterns of more intense rain and thereby increasing the likelihood of flooding.

Such intensification of the volume and spatial pattern of rainfall is likely to be amplified by human conversion of floodplain land cover from wetlands to agriculture or habitation. This lowers contributions of wetland functions that buffer fluctuations in gases, particulates, nutrients, toxics, water, temperature and kinetic energy (for example wave and wind). For example, wetland productivity contributes to carbon sequestration and evapotranspiration fluxes that moderate air and water temperature variability. As a result, cooler micro-climates over river valleys and marsh plains sustain higher rates of smaller, local rainfall events, thus buffering the basin from more intense rain upstream that generates more extreme flood events (Pokorny et al. 1998, Ripl 1995). The combined decline of steady base inflows and increase in rain-driven input variability should increase flood volumes and peak levels substantially. Along the Rhine river, flood peaks should rise 20 per cent higher than previously experienced (source: www.waterandclimate.org, accessed June 2004).

**Uncertainty in Society**

The sources of surprise and uncertainty in the TRB emerge not only from the complexity of Nature but also from the ways that human intervention has lowered the basin's resilience to change. We consider here the ways that the basin's structure and function have been altered through shifts in land use and basin morphometry (shape in three dimensions, such as elevation, area of floodplain) by hydro-engineering.

By the nineteenth century the promise and power of the ideas of the Enlightenment began to shake and reconfigure commerce and society in Europe. As Davies (1996) notes: 'There is a dynamism about nineteenth-century Europe that far exceeds anything previously known. Europe vibrated with power as never before: with technical power, economic power, cultural power, intercontinental power.' A rising tide of energy, raw materials and people converged on growing urban agglomerations that became regional manufacturing centres for new products and economic opportunity, which in turn drew yet more people and resources from the countryside. Nations grew following the new, 'modern' industrial model, swelling every index of growth, including urban populations and the demand for food.

This demand was seen as a new opportunity by the major landholders on the TRB. The Habsburg nobility, including the Emperor, as well as Hungarian aristocrats and nobility, to some extent, began to convert the agricultural land of the floodplain from a diverse polyculture of fruits, nuts and maize to larger fields with monocultures of wheat (Kovács 2003). There was far more profit in providing a durable grain for the main staple of urban populations, bread, than in handling the enormous variety of perishable fruits, which were far more daunting items to store and ship. Within a few decades Hungary would become the first wheat-exporting nation in Europe, earning large profits in the short run but at a far higher price in the long run than originally imagined.

Agricultural transformation immediately raised two challenges. First, no variety of wheat known then could withstand flooding or even high groundwater levels for any length of time, so the Tisza had to be tamed to keep its surges off the floodplain. Second, the twisting meanders of the Tisza across the Great Plain had to be straightened to shorten shipping distances and make export profitable. Changing the shape and content of the fields led to the Herculean task of reshaping the entire floodplain and the river channel itself, officially conceived and implemented by the Austro-Hungarian Empire as the Vásárhelyi Plan. Such radical surgery on the landscape was an affront to tradition and sparked great controversy (see Vay 2002), but eventually the Plan was pushed through in 1870 and the wood and coal-fired power of the nineteenth century began to sculpt the Tisza River valley with the clean and smooth lines of an engineer's ruler (Figure 6.2).

To grow, protect and export wheat the Tisza floodplain was modified for flood defence, and the river was straightened and deepened. Wheat export became possible when the flow of the Tisza was concentrated in a single, deeper channel that cut a smoothed arc through the maze of twists and turns of a braided river's floodplain. Overall the Tisza's length was shortened by more than 400 km (Botári and Károlyi 1971). In addition, the original Vásárhelyi Plan began a process that over a century eventually protected 97 per cent of the basin at risk from flooding with over 4500 km of primary and secondary dikes along the Tisza and its tributaries. Overall, the dike defence system lowered the floodplain area by more than an order of magnitude, from 38 500 km$^2$ to 1800 km$^2$ (Horváth et al. 2001).

Simply mentioning that a major Tisza flood could inundate 17 per cent of Hungary (Váradi 2001) made the threat so palpable that it locked up

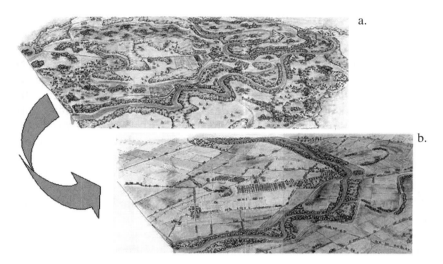

*Figure 6.2    An artist's interpretation of different landscape mosaic
              patterns in the Tisza river floodplain both before (a) and after
              (b) the execution of the original Vásárhelyi river engineering
              plan in 1871*

most funding in dike defence. Water authorities are driven by enormous
political pressure in the event of any loss of life or injury following dike
failure in a flood (Linerooth-Bayer and Vári 2003). However, the prodi-
gious engineering of the dike defense system failed repeatedly under the
mounting pressure of floods with higher crests and volumes. More and
larger floods created a race to raise and reinforce the dikes higher than the
next major flood, but the history of dike failures shows how re-engineering
the defense system could never catch up.

The TRB has known large floods for more than a millennium of recorded
history and undoubtedly over the eons of geological time since the rise of
the Carpathian range. Tisza floods are events of European stature, with
volumes (4000 cubic meters a second) that approach half that of the far
larger Danube River at flood stage. The Tisza may be moderate in dimensions, but the forces moving through it are considerable. Such extreme
floods are currently estimated to occur on average every ten to twelve years
in the Tisza River Basin (Wu 2000), but the last century has seen rising
trends in all facets of flooding: flood crest or peak height, flood volume, and
flooding frequency. Since the average minimal flow has declined, the
difference between flood and drought extremes is increasing. The interval
between extreme floods has declined sharply from once every 18 years

(between 1877 and 1933) to once every three to four years (between 1934 and 1964) to almost every other year over the last decade. An engineering race to raise the dikes started after each flood, as each subsequent flood exceeded the previous one in height (Fetivizig 2000).

Practically in step with mounting flood statistics, regional development has also climbed since the mid-nineteenth century, and the clash between these two rising trends has created ever larger losses. The infrastructure of towns and row crop farms burgeoned and spread into the flood danger zone, the TRB floodplain, with reassurance from the apparent security of a dike and canal flood defense system. The security promised by hydro-engineering might hold for a decade or two, but ever-larger floods breached these defenses, and as a result devastated homes, roads and crop fields. Damage to built capital and commerce from one major flood event could reach as high as approximately 25 per cent of the riverine basin GDP or 7–9 per cent of the national GDP (Halcrow Group 1999). The most vulnerable groups, such as low income farmers, are often hit hardest, depleting their scarce reserves and pushing them to the brink of bankruptcy (Linerooth-Bayer and Vári 2003). The force of major floods perennially rises to surpass expensive efforts to engineer, reinforce and defend the dike system. Without a very quick, competent and heroic capability to react to floods in crisis, the failures of hydro-engineering would be even more apparent (ibid.).

## Entangled Dynamics that Give Rise to 'Wicked' Problems

The TRB faces a complex of related problems that are so entangled as to defy understanding or remedy. The subset of challenges underlying such 'wicked' problems includes ecology (loss of biodiversity, habitat, rising intensity and frequency of floods), economy (farms and related businesses disappearing, loss of fisheries, fruit, nut and timber industries) and society (disappearance of schools, communities, children uninterested in history and culture). These problems have been compounded by a series of profound interventions to re-engineer the river basin's morphometry and to replace completely local agricultural methods with dryland wheat production. In ways paradoxical to the modern sense of progress, investments in technology have increased, rather than diminished, the uncertainty that faces the inhabitants of the TRB. Periodic disasters increase in intensity while the ecological, economic and social bases of resilience erode slowly. Clearly, future actions must rely on wider disciplinary foundations than the narrow engineering and economic concepts that have been applied so far.

## ADAPTIVE MANAGEMENT: LEARNING WHILE MANAGING

Uncertainty challenges more than our need to understand, because the responsibility to manage systems of humans and nature creates tension between two needs: for useful simplifications to communicate and probe with (theory) and for effective action (practice). This tension increases as nature's uncertainty is compounded by society's attempts to learn and manage. Both natural and human systems constantly change and evolve, sometimes in synchrony and sometimes not. If our appreciation of uncertainty forces us to admit that there are no 'truths' which persist, and that no person or group is the guardian of such truths, then we can recognize the importance of discussion between a variety of competing ideas. In other words, coping with novelty and surprise requires the sustained capacity to learn and to manage flexibly. For more than thirty years a decision making process has been evolving to address the twin challenges of learning and management. This process, 'adaptive environmental assessment and management' (AEAM), also known as adaptive management (AM), has been refined in a series of on-the-ground applications in problems of forestry, fisheries, national parks, and river systems (Holling 1978, Walters 1986, Gunderson et al. 1995, Gunderson and Holling 2002, Sendzimir et al. 1999, 2003).

The driving assumption underlying AM is that uncertainty is inevitable, because the behaviour of complex systems is only partly knowable. Therefore, as ecosystems and societies evolve, humans must adapt and conform as systems change. However, the challenges presented by the degrading condition of Nature and society require action. Historically, understanding has often proven shallow and of limited use when developed in isolation from the discipline of managing a changing system. Therefore, AM is not about learning before one can manage; rather it is learning while one manages (Gunderson et al. 1995). Structured learning in an iterative cycle (see Figure 6.3) is the way that uncertainty is winnowed. Surprise is never eliminated, but by embracing uncertainty we may reduce the consequences of the way our understanding lags behind evolving systems. That embrace includes deepening understanding and adaptively responding to system changes. Adaptive responses and management actions must meet social objectives, such as protecting people or resources, but learning must continue as policies are modified to adapt to surprises. Therefore, a second function of management is to probe the system, perturbing it slightly to provoke some minimal, safe response that gives an indication of the working and true structure of the system (Walters, 1986). AM has taken many different pathways as its implementation responded to local needs,

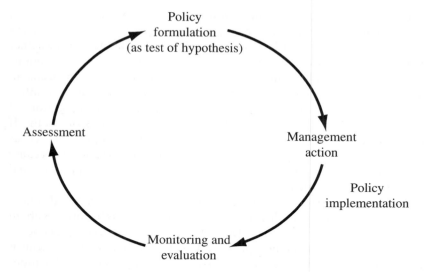

*Figure 6.3* *The adaptive management process as a structured learning
cycle that iteratively links four phases: assessment,
formulation, implementation and monitoring*

but the following four phases offer a template of activities that integrate
research, management and practice in a cycle (see Figure 6.3).

**Phase 1 – Assessing the Known and the Uncertain**

The assessment phase simultaneously engages two apparent opposites,
integrated understanding and uncertainty, and counter-poses them in ways
that are revealing to both. Rather than dodging uncertainty with simplifying assumptions or rationalizations, the AM process focuses on uncertainty
from the very beginning, utilizing disagreements to reveal and highlight
gaps in understanding and other sources of uncertainty. The adaptive
process identifies new bases for sharing understanding when gaps or uncertainties are recognized as common to all the different disciplines, sectors,
occupations, trainings and experiences represented in the discussion.

The common gaps and links in understanding can bridge the various
backgrounds present and establish a foundation of trust that may eventually
unlock information and experiences that were previously unshared. This
trust is one way in which the AM process addresses the refusal to share information, a frequent source of gridlock in environmental decision processes.
Another way is to select representatives of various backgrounds based on

competence, respect within their group and the willingness to cooperate. Participants are given to understand, that a great potential for communication can emerge only if each person 'leaves his/her gun at the door', whether that gun is an opinion, a philosophy or a mandate from one's organization.

The assessment phase aims to initiate and foster discussion by using an informal workshop setting and computer models. Care is taken to introduce and use computer models simply as translators and integrators of people's understanding, not as technically superior vehicles of 'truth'. If dialogue begins where there was none before, then the computer model has succeeded. If people begin to reassess their assumptions seriously because model output based on their ideas seems questionable, then important and novel insights are possible.

The goal of the assessment phase is to integrate understanding and ponder uncertainties to the point that they can be clearly stated as hypotheses about how the system works and what effects interventions (management or uncontrolled human actions) might produce. Complexity in adaptive systems is partly the result of the diversity of causes, and the alternative explanations that address these causes can become the basis for policy in the next phase.

**Phase 2 – Policies as Hypotheses**

Policies are one means to constrain or encourage various kinds of human behaviour. They fit within a society's collection of social institutions that range from the formal (government acts, laws, administrative codes, and legal contracts) to the informal (understandings and shared views among groups). But policies are more than the governing plan. AM casts them as the question set based on experience that sets the stage for further action. Instead of pursuing the 'correct' policy as a solution to problems, AM differs from traditional engines of policy by seeking policy sets that strike a balance between the need to learn in the face of uncertainty and other social objectives, such as minimizing vulnerability to change (Gunderson and Pritchard, 2002). In this light, policies are not magic bullets that address the right mix of objectives to solve a problem; rather they are astute hypotheses about how the world works or 'questions masquerading as answers' in the words of Steve Light (Gunderson et al., 1995). AM embraces uncertainty by trying to find the best questions, and thereby tries to dodge the trap of rallying around solutions based on assumptions of certainty.

**Phase 3 – Management Actions as Tests**

Many environmental problems stem from administrative pathologies, such as those that narrow the focus of policy and research to achieve efficiency at the expense of awareness about where the system is going. For example, if initial policies achieve high production and profit levels, one could bank on maximizing the profit of such success by cutting research costs, but only if one was sure of where the system is going. The AM process strives to avoid this pathology by broadening implementation to mean the testing and evaluating of hypotheses (policies). This prevents the intent of policy from being changed during implementation, and shifts the search for efficiency from cost reduction to checking whether management actions were executed as anticipated (Gunderson, 1998). This gives implementation a disciplinary rigor of consistency in execution, because otherwise the test of the policy becomes meaningless, and one loses the power to gain new information about the system.

For example, in the mid-1990s when the Canadian government re-opened the Newfoundland cod fishery primarily for political reasons (unemployment), it severely endangered the scientific process of selecting criteria by which to measure the recovery of the cod population and thereby set policy about when to open or close the fishery. The policy disconnected permission to fish from the dynamics of the fish population, making it impossible to test ideas based on evidence. An AM process would have posed policies as tests of what action (or lack of action) can re-establish the resilience and carrying capacity of the fishery.

## Phase 4 – Monitoring and Evaluation

One of the more fundamental weaknesses of modern policy processes is the failure to recognize the constant need to monitor and evaluate the impacts of policy implementation. This weakness is evident in failures to fund the manpower, time and equipment adequately to establish baseline (pre-implementation) and policy (post-implementation) databases and to analyse them for trends. For example, up until the 1990s environmental regulatory agencies in Florida usually received funding to oversee and police the process of obtaining permission to develop land but nothing for follow-up to see how the development proceeds. The authors' personal experience is that it was often only the rare personal commitment of agency officers that led them to revisit development sites on their own unpaid time that revealed inadequacies in the execution of the project. The policy process sets up a high wall of restrictions at the beginning, but once permission is obtained the process is often blind to the effects.

The AM process explicitly targets these weaknesses and tries to increase the breadth of learning across society by including all stakeholders as part of the monitoring process. Effective participation in policy processes addressing the complexity of socio-ecosystems requires deep knowledge of what is meaningful and useful in terms of data, analysis and conjecture. Such knowledge comes mostly from direct experience, and as policy makers and concerned citizens gain this knowledge their capacity to introduce their unique experience to the policy process increases. For example, the multi-year experiment to reintroduce meanders in the Kissimmee River involved close collaboration between scientists, policy makers and the public in the evaluation of the pilot projects that tested ideas about how to re-naturalize a river. With time and experience scientists, in their efforts to design next generation pilot experiments, increasingly recognized the input of concerned citizens as valuable (Light and Blann 2000).

### Integrative Learning – A Summary

Amassing information does little to help anticipate surprise and uncertainty. Projections based on previous system behaviour have limited utility in the face of true novelty. Integration of the information gained in policy probes has little to do with data quantity and everything to do with quality. To what extent have we winnowed uncertainty and closed the gap on these elusive and dynamic systems? How is this put into action? First, it integrates across multiple disciplines and backgrounds. Second, the focus group, and the community at large, learns by doing. In this way understanding deepens by probing the workings of ecosystems and society and by considered and thoughtful sharing of new ideas and previous experiences. Such inquiry is structured by expert facilitation of discussion, summing up new insights and consolidating gains before reformulating the questions at hand. Finally, this understanding often builds from ground made more fertile by complete re-inspection of assumptions and conceptual frameworks (Gunderson et al. 1995).

Enhancing understanding through integrated learning is a second loop type of learning (Sterman 2000, Light and Blann 2000, Magnuszewski et al. 2005) that is fundamental to adaptive management in several ways. Whereas 'single-loop' learning tries to improve the cycle of learning directly from experience, 'double-loop' learning tries to establish a second loop that links the first loop with the ways in which our underlying assumptions and world views influence how we see and interpret the world. When both loops are invoked effectively, we have a transparent process in which we can consciously change how we assess and understand, formulate policy, act, monitor, analyse, and, finally, how we frame the world with our assumptions. Any phase can interact with any other phase.

AM has developed the use of modelling far beyond the reflexive governance conception (as described in this book's Introduction) of modelling as part of 'rationalist problem-solving' tools. Within the AM learning cycle, especially the assessment phase, modelling is not used to 'blend away' the messy entanglements of relations to distil them down to one rational vision of a system. Distillation and simplification are possible, but within a far wider context that can also generate a diversity of views at the end.

First, the modelling phase often addresses in parallel not one but many different hypotheses about how a system operates to create the problem of concern to stakeholders. Thus, stakeholders may consider not one but many models that emerge from different world views, trainings and experiences. The pressure to distil these many visions further stems from the urgency for the group to move on from assessment and formulate policy. Thus a small subset (perhaps one or two) of the full set of hypotheses (and perhaps different models) are chosen as the basis for policy recommendations. That subset has not been elevated to the 'rationalist truth' but has been selected as the most compelling sub-set of questions for the project to test. This selection is done with full awareness of the fact that when the cycle of management implementation of policy, monitoring and evaluation again returns to the assessment phase, other hypotheses and models may now appear to be the most compelling. Therefore, we do not end with one model and one explanation. Rather, the full set of models is retained while the current favourites are tested in policy implementations. Furthermore, as opposed to rationalist conclusions, modelling is used to dig down to a 'less rational' sub-terrain to reveal to stakeholders the implications of their assumptions. The models are pictures of a world that is based on their assumptions. Modelling exercises are opportunities for stakeholders to bore beneath the official façade of conventional explanations to encounter what their, often not very rational but profoundly powerful, sub-conscious assumptions are. Profound questioning of one's assumptions is a major step to honestly and earnestly examining the world through other assumptions, through the eyes and hearts of others. As such, it offers a key to grid-lock and confrontation that opens the door to compromise. Such compromise is facilitated by the AM atmosphere of experimentation. If every next step is not a proof but a test, then we are less likely to become stuck on one position, but will continue to experiment and revise how we see the world and how we do things.

Adaptive management is not unique. It is similar to an entire family of approaches used to understand and manage uncertainty in ecosystems and society (see Walker et al. (2002) for a current survey). It reflects the theoretical and methodological training in ecology and modelling that the professionals used as they developed AM as a framework to deal with regional environmental crises. It represents ecologists' attempts to communicate and work with a variety of disciplines as well as the governance and business sectors of society. It continues to evolve and mature as theory and methods of economics and the social sciences are incorporated in its application. For example, the study of institutions has gained equal status with that of natural sciences and economics in the articulation and bounding of the question at hand and in formulating hypotheses and policies (see Ostrom (1999) and Andersson and Jansson (2004) as examples of the growing influence of institutional analysis in AM).

AM has not always succeeded. It has been stymied by failure to reach a conclusion or to produce meaningful and concrete results, because participants can indulge in endless discussion and modelling if they are not vigilant or are incompetently guided by facilitators. Some applications of AM have been criticized as 'too theoretical' and therefore impractical to act as a framework for people without advanced education or sophisticated means of discussing complexity. This latter point may depend on the complexity of the system and the questions at hand, as well as on the skill and patience with which AM is applied. However, AM still represents the best opportunity to create truly multi-disciplinary, multi-sectoral cooperation that can unite research, policy and praxis in a learning cycle.

For practitioners interested in applying AM the daunting reality is that a scientific, transparent participatory process is not enough by itself. Success in engaging the uncertainty of complex, evolving systems requires a vast array of factors (Gunderson et al. 1995, Light and Blann 2000) that many people might sweep into one broad category: luck. Experience in the Odra river valley in Poland (Sendzimir et al. 2003) suggests that little can be accomplished without one critical factor: a foundation of trust built over years of fruitful collaboration between actors (government, NGOs, scientists) and stakeholders. If this trust can be carefully and respectfully expanded to embrace novel ideas and methods (such as AM, modelling and even the scientific method) then real innovation in participatory science and management may be possible. However, dozens of factors can potentially derail this innovation (see Figure 1.12 in Sterman 2000). It often founders simply because funding horizons are too short to sustain research, community dialogue, policy implementation and monitoring long enough for real learning to occur and to respond to long-term change.

## RENATURALIZATION OF THE TISZA FLOODPLAIN IN HUNGARY

Government, academia and NGOs in Hungary are coming to the same conclusion as the Dutch (Van Stokkom et al. 2002, van der Molen et al. 2002) about flood security: hydro-engineering cannot, by itself, maintain flood safety and stop the degradation of the biological and cultural heritage of the Tisza River Basin (TRB). The prospect of yet another round of massive investment in dikes after failure of the defence infrastructure during the last major flood in 2001 brought about a fundamental re-examination of alternatives. Several years of discussion produced a new flood protection initiative in the TRB, the new Vásárhelyi Plan. This initiative is named after the engineer who fathered the original reshaping of the Tisza in the nineteenth century, as an official façade to maintain some solidarity with past engineering traditions. However, for the first time a response to the flood crisis does not recommend raising and reinforcing dikes. Instead, the potential to remove the dikes and use certain areas of the original floodplain is being developed. This was never an easy consideration for water engineers in Hungary, because dike failure leading to loss of life was the fastest way to lose one's job and even end up in jail. But the series of dike failures over the past century pointed only to ongoing failure as climate change and other factors increased flood frequency and intensity.

By utilizing the floodplain for flood control, the new Vásárhelyi Plan raises a new set of questions. Should the floodplain only be used for flood control? What are the opportunities to re-establish the traditional roles of flooding to store water on a dry landscape and to sustain biodiversity as well as fish productivity? And where and how should people live and earn a living if they must move off the flooded parts of the plain?

Beginning in 2002 a new research initiative (Kovács 2000), sponsored and coordinated in part by WWF Hungary, set out to answer some of these questions in the middle reaches of the Tisza around the village of Nagykörü. It aims to explore questions related to ecology, agriculture and fisheries as part of a comprehensive assessment of the impacts of re-connecting the floodplain with the Tisza river channel. We now consider some of the key elements of this programme within the context of proposing how adaptive management could serve as a framework for linking these research projects with management interventions and efforts to start local floodplain-based enterprises.

**Nagykörü – Study Area**

The village of Nagykörü is located in the middle reaches of the Tisza River (see Figure 6.1). The village of some 10 000 people is situated on a ridge of high ground that extends along an east–west axis to within a few hundred meters of the Tisza river as it swings in a wide arc from north to west. The village ridge is surrounded by low areas that, prior to hydro-engineering, were flooded relatively frequently (almost annually). The spatial heterogeneity of depressions of different depths in the floodplain offered a wide variety of water storage options. Local people developed a culture that used this dynamic water storage potential to sustain a mosaic of a rich and diverse landscape that supported a variety of uses: orchards, grazing meadows and fish ponds.

People today would scarcely recognize the TRB landscape and culture that existed before the industrial revolution. Far from its current depressed appearance, the economy of the TRB was thriving, self-sufficient and rich enough to export fruits, vegetables, timber and fish (Dr Veres Nandor, Mayor, village of Nagykörü, personal communication). Our modern sense of diversity, tuned to the three or four varieties of any domestic fruit a supermarket might offer, would be amazed to find the hundreds of varieties of fruit and nuts traditionally grown in the TRB.

Such extreme variety in agricultural produce is neither an extravagant gesture nor some slavish adherence to tradition. This ancient tradition has flourished for centuries in the TRB (Andrásfalvy 1973, Molnár 2003, Paget 1850, Tóth 2002). It represents a strategic response by which people have adapted to the variability in nature in every region of the globe since the Neolithic era (McNeely and Scherr 2003). Plants and people must contend with severe fluctuations in water within the TRB, from sudden and intense flooding that lasts for weeks over hundreds of square kilometres, to droughts that may last for years over the entire basin. These sudden flows and slow ebbs produced a huge variety of flooding durations over the different elevations on the floodplain, and the web of sluices connects the many depressions in the landscape with the river channel, which links fish nursery areas with the river.

A diversity of capabilities has been the traditional answer to the uncertainty inherent in such extreme fluctuations from wet to dry in river valleys. Farmers along the Tisza developed fruits that were differentially adapted to variable durations and intensities of flooding and drought. They also developed a local corn variety so well adapted to a short growing season that one could plant it after the annual spring floods and still harvest a mature plant by autumn. In comparison to the pesticides and fertilizers required by the relatively few global varieties that consumers from the UK to Austria recognize, these local TRB varieties have proven far more robust against insect pests and diseases, and did not require as much pruning or intensive care (Siposs and Kis 2002). However, continental and global varieties are rapidly replacing them.

### Science Initiative to Re-establish Sustainable River Basin Culture

Decades of scientific research have examined the natural and social history of the Tisza basin. This scientific legacy offers a wealth of information, but many local people are offended by how few concrete results all this scientific research has yielded on the ground. Some stakeholders threaten not to cooperate with scientists in the future, saying that the scientists only stay long enough to get the information they need to further their careers but never engage in the long-term struggle to convert new insights into policies or structures that improve peoples' lives. The WWF research initiative attempts to address this admonition by working in parallel on both the ecological and economic potential created by reconnecting the floodplain to the Tisza River channel. This potential includes traditional fruit orchards, fishponds, and wet meadow grazing by ancient breeds of cattle.

The challenge to any science policy initiative is that our present understanding is insufficient to re-establish a functioning society, agriculture and ecosystem in a naturalized Tisza river basin. Research has given us an incomplete view of what ecological services and functions existed and what humans did to exploit those opportunities sustainably. However, even if we had a complete view, the past cannot simply be resurrected (Light and Blann 2000). The context never remains the same. The landscape and its human and animal communities evolve and co-evolve. Efforts to try to freeze the landscape context in some arbitrary vision of the past are doomed to failure, because new species and new arrangements must learn to survive in a context that has shifted from the past. The landscape may not be very different from what was, but it will be different. In brief, simple reverse engineering futilely aims to resurrect a system that no longer exists. And since society is changing far more rapidly than the ecosystem, we need a framework to integrate our research, policies and practices to adapt to the evolving context of changing society and ecosystems.

Adaptive management (AM) offers such a flexible framework. It can be modified to increase public participation and engage all local stakeholders, even those who feel exploited by professional scientists and policy makers. One way to open the process and make it more transparent is to use it to provide tools to measure progress. AM does this first and foremost by offering structure. It provides a set of activities in an iterative cycle. The pause for each activity signals how far the community discussion has gone. AM has worked well in defining issues and problems and formulating policies to test hypotheses as to why the problem exists. However, how can the community be involved in measuring the performance of these policies? Participants gain a sense of progress in the AM process in a number of ways. One is the structure of the learning process itself, where movement from one phase to another, while not always serial (the process may jump back and forth to address issues that suddenly arise), can give a sense of progress. Similarly, progress can be apparent in how discussion and the sense of understanding matures with advancement in formulation of hypotheses, development of models to examine hypotheses, elaboration of goals, policies to achieve those goals (and test hypotheses) and interventions to assess the impact of policies. Measuring progress can be addressed directly by explicitly formulating indicators of progress or change in variables considered key to achieving a project's goals.

To this latter end we propose an AM approach below that allows participants to derive and use a variety of tools for developing graphic maps of the whole system, key variables, goals, policies to achieve those goals and indicators of successful performance of policies. Experience in applying AM in the Odra river valley (Sendzimir et al. 2003) shows that we can use the scoping exercises at the beginning in ways different from the 'classic' AM previously described (see Figure 6.3). Following that example, we can begin with problem articulation and identify the key variables and their interactions that are involved in the problem(s) of concern to stakeholders. Stakeholder-driven discussion can help connect the variables into a graphic map of the interactions that are the skeleton or structure of the system (mental model map).

While the Odra river valley AM process continues, reflection on our experience to date suggests the following structure for an AM framework (AMF) to help people identify and use sustainability indicators (see Figure 6.4). This more elaborate learning cycle still employs modelling to articulate hypotheses and to organize a mental map that incorporates inputs from all stakeholders into an overview of the problem. However, such maps do not replace a common vision. The vision of where a community wants to be is the overarching goal against which all actions and ideas can be measured. This AM framework mandates that directly after mapping the system such a vision be pursued as part of setting objectives. This clarifies the identification of indicators, because key variables for which we determined indicators are considered important only in relation to objectives. Therefore, making objectives explicit accelerates the identification of indicators that clearly relate to the community's vision and goals, not merely to variables that are prominent and easy to measure.

## APPLYING THE AM FRAMEWORK IN THE TISZA RIVER BASIN

The capacity to adapt and innovate is at a low tide in the TRB. Among local stakeholders, little trust remains in central government, outside experts or between the people themselves to solve their dilemma. This results from a combination of prolonged and recurrent flood defence failures, degradation of natural and social heritage, economic decline and the lack of democratic traditions in a centralized political system. No sustainable future can be built without re-establishing a foundation of trust, first within the community and then as a bridge to people and agencies working at regional, national and international levels.

Trust arises as a sense of deeper understanding, commitment and accomplishment shared across the broader community through participation in cycles of learning and doing that continue over long time periods. The AM framework establishes a base of trust in developing a shared vision, and that trust is extended as all participants work together in proposing different policies and action plans to test the vision and how to attain it. In this way, AM allows all participants recurring chances to correct the paradigms, hypotheses, policies, action plans, and measuring tools (such as indicators) in a transparent and cyclic process.

Achieving a sustainable river basin culture requires a framework like the AMF to allow scientists and stakeholders to collaborate in research and in revising policy and local practices. In a social context such as the TRB that is suspicious and sometimes antagonistic to outside academics, the AM

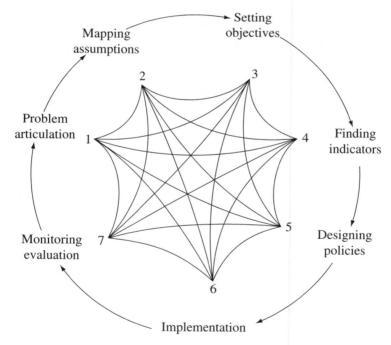

*Figure 6.4    Adaptive management framework revised according to system dynamics modelling approaches of Sterman (2000) to incorporate performance indicators explicitly*

process should offer the means for collaboration across the community to investigate, intervene and act, and measure progress. We propose that the AM experience of the Odra and Barycz Rivers (Sendzimir et al. 2003), while preliminary, still suggests that local stakeholders will provide solid experience and support if they become engaged in all phases of a transparent process, especially monitoring of indicators of policy performance. For example, an AM dialogue about the challenges of establishing a landscape park along the Odra River revealed the key indicator of successful implementation as the frustration level of the foresters who were left by default to make a similar plan work along the river some years before. As higher governmental levels mandated a park without any extra resources (funding, personnel or equipment) to support its establishment or execution, foresters were forced to divide their resources between normal duties and supporting the park. Failure to work with all stakeholders to design the park programme or to fund it eventually led to the park's collapse into disuse as the foresters could no longer manage two jobs. Subsequently, these same foresters came to stand against any similar new plan.

Local stakeholder experience can prove vital to experiments that explore how to establish an economically viable culture on a re-naturalized floodplain in the TRB. Key research tasks include: testing what varieties of fruit and nut trees can withstand extremes of flooding and drought, what sluice and channel morphologies establish hydroperiods that support productive fisheries, what breeds of cattle can thrive on floodplain wet meadows. Such questions will provide stakeholders and policy makers with the most compelling evidence of the potential offered by denaturalizing rivers. As local stakeholders become confident, through their participation, that economic (and hence social) development is well addressed in the AM process, they are more likely to support the expansion of inquiry into the ecological impacts of re-establishing river floodplain hydroperiods some of which are complex and difficult to communicate to non-scientists. However, AM also offers the opportunity for such questions to become more understandable when a wider portion of the community has participated in the framing of the questions and the field monitoring of the experiments.

We have adapted the general adaptive management framework to suit the needs of the project (see Figure 6.4). The modified framework consists of a series of steps (see Magnuszewski et al. 2005 for details) that begins with a vital step whose imposing delicacy and complexity make its proper implementation and practical description rare: forming the group of participating stakeholders and actors. This step may seem simple, either because it seems straightforward to attempt to include every viewpoint or if one anticipates that one has to accept whoever is available, since few people can afford to attend or want to participate. However, including people who refuse to learn, cooperate or compromise or who actively try to sabotage such processes can destroy such an AM process and hinder future efforts to create such an initiative. Thus mistakes made here can doom the entire process to bitter stalemate.

We recommend that part of identifying where to establish a learning cycle process includes locating places where some trust and understanding exists through participation in local activities, often with the help of insightful government or NGO facilitators. In such an atmosphere, the chances increase of finding people with the rare combination of integrity (such that their decision and opinion will be respected by the group they represent after the AM process makes a determination of policy) and willingness to compromise. Often, collaboration with local government and NGOs can be initiated in a preliminary set of meetings that address ways to deal with the key local problems. AM is just one candidate to be considered at these meetings during which the most productive and suitable local partners can be identified and qualified through closer discussions.

The capacity to adapt requires that the learning process has no absolute end point(s) or beginning point(s). The point of entry depends greatly on the context created by evolution of society and Nature. Sufficient trust and understanding may have developed over time to make rapid entry and progress in an AM process possible from the outset. However, when the social atmosphere is dominated by profound distrust and acrimony, it may require years of patient mediation and then education about possible learning paths before an AM process can openly commence. And while AM has been criticized for sometimes failing to escape endless discussion and take concrete steps forward, fundamentally there is no end to learning. The process may appear to stop while certain steps take time to carry out. However, true adaptation may require leaps forward, backward or across to other points on the cycle (as suggested by the arrows in Figure 6.4). In summary, the learning cycles may appear as a linear series for initial clarity, but implementation may require weaving a far more complex path.

**Visualizing and Measuring Change with Models and Indicators**

As an extension of the WWF science initiative we plan to use conceptual modelling to develop a river basin model to identify the most important variables (see Figure 6.5 for the results of an anticipatory modelling effort) and then derive and apply sustainability indicators using the following steps: identify key variables, derive indicators for each variable, develop criteria to measure the usefulness of indicators, use the criteria to select a practical, small sub-set of the best indicators, collaborate with the participating stakeholder group in monitoring the indicators. While many projects

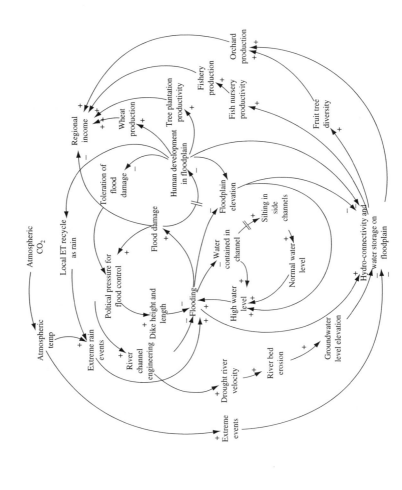

*Figure 6.5    Conceptual model (mental model map) of key variables and causal loops that interact to affect Tisza river floodplain resilience to climate related hydro-dynamic variability*

may terminate by successful nomination of an impressive slate of indicators, the purpose of an AM process is to sustain learning over time periods long enough to adapt to change at all levels in socio-ecological systems, even long term change like climate. Therefore, the true test of an AMF is whether it catalyses broad participation in using the indicators, analysing the indicator data over time, and revising indicators when they no longer track factors that are critical to the sustainability of the system. Indicators are not the goal; sustained learning is. They are simply one more tool that allows stakeholders to revise their assumptions, world-views, goals, models, policies, interventions and activities.

Following the AM approach used in the Odra river valley in Southwest Poland (Sendzimir et al. 2003, Magnuszewski et al. 2005), NGO stakeholders and systems science researchers in the TRB initiative will meet in an initial series of scoping sessions to establish a common language. Variables and links between the variables are the basic elements of this language, which will be used to develop mutual understanding shared by all participants and join diverse experiences and backgrounds of the participants into a common model. First a list of potential variables will be elicited. The scoping process then proceeds to winnow the list of key variables down to a practical range (fewer than 25) and uses causal loop diagramming (Sterman 2000) as a discussion guide in linking variables and slowly developing a graphic image of the system structure. Experience in using recursive, learning processes that develop and refine performance indices in businesses – the Balanced Scorecard approach (Kaplan and Norton 1996), but see Rydzak et al. 2004 for a dynamic interpretation – provided a target range for a reasonable number of indicators that the participants can keep in mind and use. The AM process must also examine broader issues than local ecology and economy, however, since it is not yet determined whether local production should support local consumption or must also generate income from export. Such questions expand the range of inquiry to include institutions, markets, and ecological processes that operate on a scale larger than the village of Nagykörü. For example, defining the scope (including mental mapping) of factors that influence sustainability in the Nagykörü area of the Tisza river basin, should address institutions such as EU, national and provincial regulations, markets and distribution networks at different scales, and the potential impacts of climate change on regional precipitation and river dynamics.

For the TRB initiative sustainability indicators will be developed using the soft approach following Bell and Morse (1999), Sendzimir et al. (2003) and Magnuszewski et al. 2005. Accordingly we will try to avoid or mitigate its weaknesses in two ways. We will use a structured learning process within an adaptive management framework to identify and address errors transparently. The same framework will allow us to integrate different phases tightly, using them to challenge and reinforce one another. For example, we can mesh the phases of bounding and then measuring the problem by linking the results of the conceptual modelling phase with the process of defining indicators. As conceptual modelling provides the 'big picture' of the problem and helps to overcome human information processing limitations, it also makes the process of indicator selection more rigorous and leads to more comprehensive results.

Causal loop diagramming will therefore be used as a discussion guide in linking variables and slowly developing a graphic image of the system structure. As the web of relations takes shape, certain sections become more understandable as identification of reinforcing and balancing feedback loops reveals the macrostructure of the system. In this way the vast and dense 'thicket' of links is reduced to a smaller set of clusters of variables that tend to interact with each other. The group's desire to focus on specific parts of the model often generates sub-model diagrams that clarify some of the causal details underlying the more aggregate variables and relations in the general model.

Causal loop diagrams can been used to elicit from the participants their underlying assumptions and mental models and to express it graphically in the form of a 'map' that contains key factors and processes in the region. While a range of exercises for participating individuals and groups can be used to define underlying paradigms, assumptions or world-views before scoping and modelling begins (Hare and Pahl-Wostl 2002), the give-and-take of discussion in defining the models can also help to reveal the mental frameworks participants rely on to judge and predict. Fundamental world views present great opportunity and great risk. Because they lie so close to a participant's emotional core, their revelation can open profound trust and cooperation, breaking political stalemates. On the other hand, exposure, or even the possibility of exposure, can also provoke hostility and resistance. Such revelations are often best left to emerge on their own from a well run AM process that makes it natural and obvious to explore all influences on the problem, even how we think and construct the world in our minds. However, some very skilled facilitators may try consciously to assess the paradigms that participants bring to the AM process.

The mental map functions as the knowledge container, open and easily modifiable as new facts or ideas are provided or revealed during the process. Graphic tools such as diagrams and mental maps open the discussion of complex systems to include people who find verbal descriptions too complicated or too long and involved. Often a single map replaces pages of text required to describe all the variables and their interactions. In every discussion a map (or maps) on the wall or in the computer will plainly show the complex relations between nature and society in the Tisza landscape.

Using the map will provide discipline for the group discussions in a positive sense as follows: (1) differences (and agreements) in opinions will be articulated much more precisely; (2) gaps in understanding will be discovered more efficiently.

Figure 6.5 illustrates an exercise in advance modelling in preparation for the TRB initiative. Building from the centre outward, the model evolved by addressing key issues as clusters of interactions and described derivative or spin-off issues by attaching new clusters to the emerging core structure. The evolution of model structure also recapitulates the chronology of events. As the web of relations takes shape, certain sections become more understandable as identification of reinforcing and balancing feedback loops reveals the system macro-structure. The group's desire to focus on specific parts of the model often generates sub-model diagrams that clarify some of the causal details underlying the more aggregate variables and relations in the general model. While model evolution is impossible to predict, we may anticipate that a model of TRB factors and interactions will likely examine some of the following areas. Provided that it does not create a new set of biases for a discussion facilitator or a modeler, modelling a system in advance of stakeholder participation can help prepare him/her by challenging assumptions and exploring different interpretations of variables and model structure. Such preliminary exercises can deepen one's intuition about how to avoid conceptual traps when exploring system structure and dynamics.

## CONCLUSIONS

No system of analysis, policy, or practice will ever eliminate surprise and uncertainty. Innovation and novelty as well as wicked problems incessantly emerge from evolving systems of nature and humanity, and will continue to do so. Our understanding of complexity suggests that 'control' and 'certainty' are romantic notions born on the rising tide of the optimism of the early Enlightenment. Radical and profound change from climate and technology (genetic engineering), to name only a few sources, will certainly surpass our current imagination of how the environment and society can be reconfigured in unprecedented ways over the next few decades. Our responsibility to address the impacts of evolution through new ways of learning, managing, and discussion must engage uncertainty as a stimulus to explore innovations and not as a basis of apprehension and apathy.

Adaptive management offers a framework to meet that challenge by addressing, among other things, the five strategic requirements of reflexive governance. It creates trans-disciplinary knowledge production (Strategy 1) and anticipation of long-term systemic effects of action (Strategy 3) through an interactive discussion framework within which modelling tools (conceptual and formal) can integrate the perspectives not only of different disciplines but those of different sectors of society by integrating research, policy and practice. The learning process at the heart of the AM approach challenges assembled stakeholders and actors to bound and define a problem and develop a vision and goals (iterative participatory goal formulation – Strategy 4) once they have defined the problem. The process iterates so as to link dynamically the group's formulation of hypotheses and resultant policies (ibid.) with subsequent efforts to implement, monitor and evaluate these policy experiments (Strategy 2 – experiments and adaptivity of strategies and institutions).

Proponents of reflexive governance may find it quite useful to experiment with modelling in the wider sense pioneered within AM projects. Modelling can be a source of multiple visions of causation, not the tool with which to distil complexity down to one rationalist perspective. As the AM learning cycle iterates, a suite of models that reflect a diversity of perspectives can be tested, either in sequence or in parallel. Systems analysis and modelling can be paths for stakeholders to work together to clarify 'messy' entanglements of assumptions, biases and habitual thought patterns that underlie ways in which we filter information and construct reality. Such exercises in 'double-loop learning' help us integrate our messy world views with the logical decision-making processes that command the political high ground at present.

AM is not a panacea. It can falter for lack of generating concrete results while endlessly processing and discussing. Its evolutionary character is threatening to people who favour clear and simple rules and answers as distinct paths through uncertainty. But through all these applications AM still offers a window into how democratic action might operate in a technologically complex society, allowing people from all relevant philosophies, backgrounds, political classes, and organizations to share experience, learn together, and devise the policies and practices that allow socio-ecological systems to adapt better to change. Applications of AM in river basins such as the Tisza should generate the experimental evidence needed to found new forms of agriculture, fisheries as well as a new understanding of river ecology. When executed with a high degree of scientific rigor and cross-society collaboration, an AM process can generate the trust and understanding that will drive full implementation of useful but unrecognized innovations. The authority of good science broadly understood and supported across society is essential for taking risks with new ideas in an age of increasing uncertainty.

# REFERENCES

Andersson, X. and M. Jansson (2004), 'Institutional innovation and adaptive management: learning from Bolivia's decentralization experiment S. Light, (ed.), *The Role of Biodiversity Conservation in the Transition to Rural Sustainability*, NATO ARW Series.

Andrásfalvy, B. (1973), 'A sarkoz osi arteri gazdalkodasa', *Vizugyi Torteneti Fuzetek*, Budapest, pp. 52–3.

Arthur, B. (1983), 'On competing technologies and historical small events: the dynamics of choice under increasing returns', IIASA interim report wp-83–90, International Institute for Applied Systems Analysis, Laxenburg, Austria.

Bell, S. and S. Morse (1999), *Sustainability Indicators: Measuring the Immeasurable*, Earthscan: London.

Botári I. and Z. Károlyi (1971), 'A Tisza szabályozása 2. Rész,' (1846–1879) The regulation of River Tisza: Phase 2. (1846–79), Budapest, Hungary.

Broecker, W.S. (1996), 'Thermohaline circulation, the Achilles heel of our climate system: will man-made $CO_2$ upset the current balance?' *Science*, **278**, 1582–8.

Davies, N. (1996), *Europe: A History*, New York: HarperPerrenial.

Fetivizig (2000), 'Report on flood protection in Szabolcs-Szatmár-Bereg Cannty', Upper Tisza Water Management Authority, Nyíregyháza, Hungary.

Gunderson, L.H. and C.S. Holling (2002), *Panarchy: Understanding Transformations in Systems of Humans and Nature*, Washington, DC: Island Press.

Gunderson, L.H., C.S. Holling and S.S. Light (eds) (1995), *Barriers and Bridges to the Renewal of Ecosystems and Institutions*, New York: Columbia University Press.

Gunderson, L.H. and L. Pritchard (eds) (2002), *Resilience and the Behavior of Large-Scale Ecosystems*, Washington, DC: Island Press.

Halcrow Water (1999), 'Flood control development in Hungary: feasibility study', final report, Halcrow Group Ltd.

Hare, M. and C. Pahl-Wostl (2002), 'Stakeholder categorization in participatory integrated assessment processes', *Integrated Assessment*, **3**(1), 50–62.

Hilborn, R. (1987), 'Living with uncertainty in resource management', *North American Journal of Fisheries Management*, **7**, 1–5.

Holling, C.S. (ed.) (1978), *Adaptive Environmental Assessment and Management*, New York: John Wiley & Sons.

Holling, C.S. (1986), 'The resilience of terrestrial ecosystems: local surprise and global change', in W.C. Clark and R.E. Munn (eds) *Sustainable Development of the Biosphere*, IIASA and Cambridge, UK: Cambridge University Press.

Horváth, Gábor, Sándor Kisgyörgy, Jan Sendzimir and Anna Vári (2001), 'The 1998 Upper Tisza Flood, Hungary: case study report', draft report, International Institute of Applied Systems Analysis, Austria.

IPPC (2001), 'Third Assessment Report: Climate Change 2000: The science of climate change', J.J. McCarthy, O.F. Canziani, N.A. Leary, D.J. Dokken and K.S. White (eds), Cambridge, UK: Cambridge University Press.

Juhász, Á. (1987), *Évmilliók emlékei. Magyarország földtörténete és ásványi kincsei*, (History of the last million years. Mineralogy and geological history of Hungary), Gondolat Kiadó, Budapest, p. 532.

Kovács, Z.C. (2000), 'Revitalisation project of the ancient flood-plain agriculture of the Tisza river', Local government of Nagykoru, Budapest, p. 13.

Kovács, Z.C. (2003), *Sustainability Along the Tisza River*, Oxford: Oxford Brookes University, p. 88.

Light, S. and K. Blann (2000), 'Adaptive Management and the Kissimmee River Restoration Project', Collaborative Adaptive Management Network, accession date: 2004. Website address: http://www.iatp.org/AEAM/.

Linerooth-Bayer, J. and A. Vári (forthcoming), 'Floods and loss sharing: A clumsy solution from Hungary'.

Magnuszewski, P., J. Sendzimir and J. Kronenberg (2005), 'Conceptual modeling for adaptive environmental assessment and management in the Barycz Valley', Lower Silesia, Poland, *International Journal of Environmental Research and Public Health*, **2**(2), 194–203.

McNeely, J.A. and S.J. Scherr (2003), *Ecoagriculture: strategies to save the world and save wild Biodiversity*, London: Island Press.

Molnár, G. (2003), 'Arteri gazdalkodas Magyarorszagon', proceedings of Szovetseg II evfolyam 2 szam, 17 January, p. 6.

Odum, H.T. (1996), *Environmental Accounting: Emergy and Environmental Decision Making*, New York: John Wiley, pp. 370.

Ostrom, E. (1999), 'Coping with tragedies of the commons', *Annual Review Political Science*, **2**, 493–535.

Paget, J. (1850), *Hungary and Transylvania with Remarks on their Condition, Social, Political, and Economical*, New York: Arno Press.

Parmesan, C. and G. Yohe (2003), 'A globally coherent fingerprint of climate change impacts across natural systems', *Nature*, **421**, 37–42.

Peterson, G., G.A. De Leo, J.J. Hellmann, M.A. Janssen, A. Kinzig, J.R. Malcolm, K.L. O'Brien, S.E. Pope, D.S. Rothman, E. Shevliakova and R.R.T. Tinch (1997), 'Uncertainty, Climate Change, and Adaptive Management', *Conservation Ecology* [online] **1**(2), p. 4. available at http://www.consecol.org/vol1/iss 2/art4.

Pokorný, J., W. Ripl and M. Eiseltová (1998), 'Impacts of deforestation and drainage on climate: landscape management and policy implications', report on proceedings of WaterTech (conference promoting technology, science and business in the water industry), Brisbane, Australia pp. 1–12.

Ripl, W. (1995), 'Management of water cycle and energy flow for ecosystem control – the energy–transport-reaction (ETR) model', *Ecological Modelling*, **78**, 61–76.

Rittel, H. and M. Webber (1973), 'Dilemmas in a General Theory of Planning', *Policy Sciences*, **4**, 155–9.

Rydzak, F., P. Magnuszewski, P. Pietruszewski, J. Sendzimir and E. Chlebus (2004), 'Teaching the Dynamic Balanced Scorecard', Proceedings of the 22nd international conference of the System Dynamics Society, 25–9 July 2004, Keble College, University of Oxford, Oxford, UK.

Sendzimir, J., H. Gottgens and J. Pokorn' (in review). 'Assessing multiple scales of climate change impacts on northern-hemisphere freshwater wetlands', *Climatic Change*.

Sendzimir, J., S. Light and K. Szymanowska (1999), 'Adaptive Understanding and Management for Floods', *Environments*, **27**(1), 115–36.

Sendzimir, J., P. Magnuszewski and J. Kronenberg (2003), 'A scientific based framework for sustainability indicators', World Wide Fund for Nature Report – contract number DBU AZ 18902, Berlin: WWF.

Siposs, V. and F. Kis (2002), 'Living with the river: LIFE–Nature project in the Tisza floodplain', Budapest: WWF Hungary, p. 24.

Sterman, J. (2000), *Business Dynamics*, New York: Irwin/McGraw Hill.
Sterman, J. (2002). 'All models are wrong', *System Dynamics Review*, **18**, 501–31.
Sümegi, P. (1999), 'Reconstruction of flora, soil and landscape evolution, and human impact on the Bereg Plain from late-glacial up to the present, based on palaeoecological analysis' in J. Hamar and A. Sárkány-Kiss (eds) *The Upper Tisa Valley – Preparatory proposal for Ramsar site designation and an ecological background*, Tisza Klub for Environment and Nature, Szolnok, Hungary.
Toth, J. (ed) (2002), *A Tiszai Cianszennyeezes: Rednszerszemleletu Elemzes*, Szeged.
Van der Molen, D.T., A.D. Buijse, L.H. Jans, H.E.J. Simons and M. Platteeuw (2002), Ecologisch rendement van herstel – en inrichtingsmaatregelen. Voor het traject van Lobith tot de Noordzee. No. 2002.032, RIZA (Rijksinstituut voor Intergraal Zoetwaterbeheer en Afvalwaterbehandeling), Lelystad.
Van Stokkom, H.T.C. and A.J.M. Smits (2002), 'Flood defense in the Netherlands: a new era, a new approach', in F. Wu et al. (eds) *Flood Defence*, New York: Science Press, pp. 34–47.
Váradi, J. (2001), 'How to proceed after floods and before new floods? Development of the Vásárhelyi Plan', Budapest: Hungarian Ministry of Transportation and Water Management.
Vári, A., J. Linnerooth-Bayer and Z. Ferencz (2003), 'Stakeholder views on flood risk management in Hungary's Upper Tisza Basin', *Risk Analysis*, **23**(3).
Vay, A. Baron (2002), 'Észrevételek a Tisza és mellékfolyóinak szabályozásáról, Guelmino János (eds) Tisza-parti jegyzetek, Vége nincs Tisza-szabályozás. http://www.zetna.org.yu/zek/konyvek/48/b9.html, Budapest.
Walker, B., S. Carpenter, J. Anderies, N. Abel, G. Cumming, M. Janssen, L. Lebel, J. Norberg, G.D. Peterson and R. Pritchard (2002), 'Resilience management in social-ecological systems: a working hypothesis for a participatory approach', *Conservation Ecology* [online] at http://www.consecol.org/vol6/iss1/art14, **5**(1), 14.
Walters, C.J. (1986), *Adaptive Management of Renewable Resources*, McGraw Hill, New York.
Walther, G.-R, E. Post, P. Convey, A. Menzel, C. Parmesan, T.J.C. Beebee, J-M. Fromentin, O. Hoegh-Guldberg and F. Bairlein (2002), 'Ecological responses to recent climate change', *Nature*, **416**, 389–95.
Wu, F. (2000), 'The Tisza river crises: integrating stakeholder views for policy decisions', YSSP working paper, report no. IIASA, Laxenburg, Austria, p. 29.
WWF (2002), 'Ecological effects of mining spills in the Tisza river system in 2000', World Wide Fund for Nature, Danube Carpathian Office, Vienna.

# 7. Sustainability foresight: reflexive governance in the transformation of utility systems

## Jan-Peter Voß, Bernhard Truffer and Kornelia Konrad

## INTRODUCTION

Utility systems play a key role in a broader project of transforming industrial society for sustainable development. At the same time, these sectors are particularly resistant to change. This is due to strong interlinkages between technological systems, natural resources, institutions and value orientations which stabilise consumption, production and governance patterns and constitute a so-called socio-technical regime (Kemp 1994; Rip and Kemp 1998). The interconnectedness of the elements mentioned and the dependency of modern societies on the provision of utility services make it hard to introduce radically new production and consumption patterns – such as energy provision based on renewable sources, recycling of drinking water or provision contracts based on demand-side management. The high complexity implies that it is difficult to predict the consequences from exchanging parts of the prevailing socio-technical regime.

The large scale introduction of intermittent renewable energy sources such as offshore wind energy in electricity systems is a case in point. As a consequence, incumbent interests may profit from such uncertainties by emphasising risks to the security of supply in order to prevent changes which could endanger their established position. Political power based on the existence of asymmetrical information therefore plays a crucial role in stabilising regimes of utility provision. Some research work and political effort has been put into strategies to transform prevailing socio-technical regimes (Kemp et al. 1998; Summerton 1992; Mayntz and Schneider 1995).

Utility systems have often been chosen as a field of application (Voß 2000; Kubicek 1994; Schneider 2001; Mez 1997; Arentsen and Künnecke 2003). Utility regimes are currently undergoing accelerated and fundamental changes linked to liberalisation and privatisation policies which started in the 1990s. These comprise corporate organisations, political institutions, technology, cultural values and theoretical concepts of utility provision.

The current phase of transformation succeeds a long period of structural stability which has persisted starting from the Second World War until the beginning of the 1990s. During this phase utility systems were characterised by a socio-technical regime that consisted of public or semi-public monopolies and was organised around the principle of central control of large-scale generation and integrated distribution networks. During the 1970s and 1980s, pressures on the regime had built up. They included, for example, the reduced effectiveness of rate-of-return regulation of monopolies to a point where great investments for the extension of network infrastructures were not needed anymore because domestic markets were saturated; a growing perception of environmental problems connected with the established regime structure; and the advance of new technologies which would create opportunities for more decentralised and competitive modes of service provision.

In combination with neo-liberal ideas these changes culminated in the adoption of liberalisation and privatisation policies in the 1990s (Midttun 1997; Arentsen and Künnecke 2003; Schneider 2001). In parallel and supported by some of these changes, a shift towards decentralised technology could be observed in most industrialised countries (Patterson 1999). Furthermore, a new understanding and evaluation of utility system performance began to take shape over the past couple of years. The society-wide shared goal of 'public service' is fading, giving way to values like efficiency, entrepreneurial spirit and consumer sovereignty. These changes trigger further adaptive changes that build up momentum, thus opening spaces for a spectrum of new socio-technical configurations ranging from highly decentralised generation of electricity, heat and water in the context of 'intelligent' buildings, to centralised renewable electricity generation in areas of concentrated energy flows such as off-shore wind fields or solar plants in deserts. The future structure of utility provision is being shaped by a myriad of individual actions and decisions: companies sketching market or investment strategies, consumers purchasing appliances or signing up for supply contracts, policy makers negotiating subsidies or drafting rules for network access.

Shaping these ongoing changes with the aim of a sustainable transformation of utility systems is linked to some fundamental problems. As illustrated above, the transformation process comprises complex non-linear interactions between many very heterogeneous factors. We find that co-evolutionary concepts of development make good sense of the contingent and open-ended character of socio-technical transformation (Rip and Kemp 1998; Norgaard 1994). In such a context, straightforward steering is not an option. Co-evolutionary dynamics have no single control centre where information and power are concentrated. Moreover, the ambiguity of the sustainability concept impedes the application of standard modes of 'rational problem-solving' as it presupposes a clear definition of goals, which are independent of the process of problem-solving. The dilemma can be demonstrated by confronting the presumptions of conventional problem-solving approaches with the conditions given for the shaping of sustainable transformation in utility systems. Whereas conventional problem-solving requires the following:

- $(A_{conv})$ system analysis for the prediction of consequences of alternative actions,
- $(B_{conv})$ a clear definition of goals in order to rank alternatives, and
- $(C_{conv})$ a powerful steering centre able to implement specific instruments,

we face different conditions in all three points in the case of complex problems such as the long-term transformation of utility systems.

- $(A_{complex})$ Potential transformation paths and effects of intervention are highly uncertain, because they are a result of complex interactions between social, technical and ecological processes which cannot be fully analysed and predicted.
- $(B_{complex})$ Sustainability goals remain ambivalent, because they are endogenous to transformation itself. Conflicts between objectives cannot be resolved scientifically or politically, once and for all.
- $(C_{complex})$ The power to shape transformation is distributed among many autonomous, yet interdependent actors without anyone having the power to control all others.

But how can such co-evolutionary developments across the boundary of society, technology and nature be shaped in order to assure sustainability, that is, the long-term viability of society? In the following pages we present and discuss an approach to deal with the specific challenges that are linked to the shaping of ongoing socio-technical transformation. The approach is called 'sustainability foresight' and comprises the following three steps:

1.  Exploring transformation dynamics: constructing alternative paths of transformation in participatory scenario workshops, and identifying highly dynamic fields of innovation.
2.  Sustainability assessment: eliciting evaluation criteria held by different stakeholders and discursive assessment of transformation paths with respect to sustainability impacts.

3. Developing strategies: analysing options and constraints for actors to shape transformation, developing measures to modulate innovation processes with respect to sustainability.

The sustainability foresight method was developed and is currently being tested in German utility systems (provision of electricity, natural gas, water and telecommunications).[1] Building on and extending established foresight methodology, this approach aims at providing a platform for collective, future-oriented learning across the four utility sectors and the action domains of production, consumption and regulation.

Using the sustainability foresight method, we want to explore alternatives to conventional problem-solving with a view to assessing their practical potential for implementing reflexive governance for sustainability. We expect sustainability foresight to work complementarily to conventional problem-solving by increasing the reflexivity in 'wicked' problem areas which do not lend themselves to straightforward problem-solving (Hisschemöller and Hoppe 2001). As such it can play a mediating role in shaping sustainable transformation. Sustainability foresight provides for emerging structural patterns to be shaped not only by the interference of 'external effects' of specialised rationalities and narrowly defined strategies but also by the anticipation of long-term consequences on a system level and prior mutual adaptation of strategies.

We first explain the conceptual background behind the method. We then give a more detailed description of the sustainability foresight approach with examples from the application in the German utility system. This will be the basis for discussing the results which are hitherto available and putting the approach in relation to the concept of reflexive governance as formulated in the Introduction. In a concluding section we reflect on the practical potential of reflexive governance in general and sustainability foresight in particular to shape processes of socio-ecological transformation in a sustainable way.

**Shaping Transformation Through Foresight**

Since the 1960s both the business and public policy sectors have systematically employed foresight methods to explore the embedding of strategies in dynamic contexts (Godet 1987; Ringland 1998). The approach has become popular through the Shell oil company which used it to deal with the uncertainties of their business environment that cropped up with the oil crises in the 1970s.

Foresight is about anticipating possible future developments in a focal area. It differs from forecasting, however, because it recognises the impossibility of predicting the future due to the complex dynamics that are involved in bringing it about. Foresight conceptualises the future as open, not determined by natural necessities, but contingent and influenced by human action. The future is therefore seen as malleable and apt to strategic shaping, not to fatalistic adaptation. 'Foresight is not a process of forecasting the future but rather an attempt to explore the space for human actions and interventions to shape the future. Foresight is aimed at producing orientations rather than predictions; it provides guidance to all actors and reduces uncertainty' (Renn 2002, cited in Borup 2003, p. 3).

Foresight is not about finding out about one most probable path of development, but rather it entails the construction of a range of different, equally plausible paths of future development. Such paths are derived from the partly contingent interaction of various factors of influence. Foresight is also referred to as a 'scenario approach' to system analysis (Gallopín 2002; Berkhout and Hertin 2002). It is qualitative and explorative and does not aim at numerical predictions. As such it does not focus on exactitude but on a comprehensive account of the diversity of factors from society, technology and nature that work together in shaping transformations in the real world. For this purpose foresight exercises seek to make use of the distributed knowledge, expectations and understanding which are contained in the diverse perspectives of present-day actors on developments of common concern.

By putting these expectations in the form of scenarios, they have an effect on present-day actions and thus feed back on the development itself. The actual results of foresight activities are therefore not the more or less probable stories about alternative futures on their own, but the repercussions they have in social interaction processes in the present (Truffer et al. 2003). This may be that expected opportunities enhance actions, which in turn support developments that spur their actual realisation (self-fulfilling prophecy) or, vice versa, that expected risks call for preventive action, which makes them less likely to occur (self-defeating prophecy). Foresight processes thus potentially shape the developments they set out to explore. As such they become a strategic device in shaping socio-technical transformation.

How foresight, which yields alternative futures, affects present actions, however, differs remarkably from the effect of forecasting, which yields one most probable future. Beyond self-fulfilling or self-defeating effects, the 'pluralistic vision' which is constituted by the alternative scenarios that are the outcome of foresight exercises has a self-reflecting effect. The variety of future developments across the scenarios calls the inevitability of each single scenario into question and points out the indeterminacy of long-term transformation. As such foresight can prepare decision makers for alternative courses of development and prevent premature lock-in to specific trajectories. In this respect foresight relates to reflexive governance as out-lined in the Introduction to this volume. It is a method for systematically embedding decision making into contingent contextual developments. A closer examination of the similarities is provided towards the end of this chapter.

Variants of foresight methods exist for different purposes. The sustain-ability foresight approach has been developed for the task of shaping processes of socio-technical transformation. It is designed to integrate a broad range of interacting factors from heterogeneous domains. Moreover, it includes two steps beyond explorative scenario building. This is a partici-patory procedure for assessing threats and opportunities that are connected to the scenarios and the development of measures to shape innovation processes, which appear critical for sustainable development. A more detailed description of these phases and how they are linked is given in the next section.

If we try to specify the role of sustainability foresight for the transfor-mation of utility systems, it seems clear that it cannot easily be assigned to knowledge production, innovation, or governance. Instead, it appears to be a hybrid process which combines elements from each of these domains of social practice. It generates knowledge about utility transformation and factors that drive it, coordinates interaction processes between interdepen-dent stakeholders who shape the transformation process, and plays a role in technological and social innovation processes by providing a specific form of strategic guidance.

In doing this, sustainability foresight reflects a number of lessons from recent literature on knowledge production, governance and innovation. In the science studies literature, knowledge production is claimed to transcend disciplinary scientific boundaries increasingly and to take place in networks of scientists from different disciplines and societal stakeholders (Nowotny et al. 2001). Governance studies diagnose that policy networks of public and private actors, which span several institutionalised policy fields and different levels of societal organisations, overcome the limitations of conventional institutions of national democratic government (Mayntz 1998). Innovation studies ultimately claim that innovation processes increasingly take place in networks of heterogeneous actors and become linked with broader social and environmental developments through intensified and interaction-based technology assessment and strategic R&D policy (Rammert 1997).

Against this background the sustainability foresight method can be seen to provide a platform for these developments, which is open to heteroge-neous actors, institutions and purposes. As a consequence, it can be expected to fulfil an important integrative function in an otherwise highly differentiated modern society. The need for arrangements to transcend the established institutional separation between functional domains is repeatedly stressed in analyses of modern society and sustainable development (Beck 1993; Mayntz 1999; Minsch et al. 1998; Brand 2002).

Another approach to conceptualising the working of the sustainability foresight method is from a co-evolutionary understanding of societal change (Norgaard 1994; Rip 2002). In this perspective, transformation in the utility system is conceptualised as the outcome of interacting developments in technology, the economy, politics, culture, science and so on. For any one of these developments to unfold it is crucial that it fits the context which is constituted by all the other developments. Their interaction may work as selection when, say 'performance contracting' as a new business model is being tested and does not survive in the market. However, it may also work as mutual adaptation when market conditions are anticipated in the development of business models (and vice versa, the emergence of new business models is anticipated in the development of market regulations and user practices).

In the co-evolutionary study of technological development, specific social arrangements have been identified that serve to facilitate mutual adaptation by linking developments at an early stage when they are still adaptable (that is, when form and function of an artefact are not irreversibly fixed and when users have not yet developed stable attitudes towards that technology). These arrangements have been termed 'nexus' (van den Belt and Rip 1987). As far as nexus arrangements give actors the opportunity to probe strategies before they make large investments at the risk of failure, the actors involved have a substantial benefit. By promoting the alignment of ongoing developments in technology, policy, culture and so on, the working of nexus arrangements also provides social benefits in avoiding unexpected side effects, irreconcilable developments and social conflict.[2] Sustainability foresight can thus be conceptualised as a 'macro-nexus' for the interaction of actors which bring about sectoral transformation. By collectively going through a process of exploring and assessing the aggregate outcome of their actions and drawing conclusions for their own particular strategies, actors fulfil a necessary precondition for alignment. The articulation of mutual dependencies and potential interference in the collective anticipation of system dynamics makes distributed innovation processes more reflexive, that is, they become strategically embedded in their respective context.

In the following pages we give an overview on the concrete procedural set-up of sustainability foresight as it is currently applied in German utility systems.

# THE SUSTAINABILITY FORESIGHT PROCESS

Sustainability foresight comprises a three-step process in which a selection of diverse actors from the utility systems addresses the problem of sustainable transformation. The challenges of system analysis, goal formulation and strategy development are dealt with in sequence.[3] The specific methods which have been devised for each step take account of the inherent complexity and ambivalence:

1. uncertainties of system dynamics are taken up in explorative scenario analysis,
2. ambiguity of sustainability goals is taken up in a discursive sustainability assessment procedure, and
3. distributed control capacities are reflected in strategies to shape critical innovation processes.

The process is described in detail in the remainder of this chapter. (For an overview of the phases, process steps and actors involved see Tables 7.1 and 7.2).

The intended effect of the process can be found in two directions. First, integrated knowledge about system dynamics, sustainability goals and strategy options is produced in interaction of various stakeholders who contribute practical insight and expertise. This knowledge can provide a robust basis for political action. Direct involvement of stakeholders is likely to raise issues and achieve encompassing strategies which would not be obtainable from classical expert policy analysis (Fischer 1993). Second, the process itself has an effect on the actors involved. They are actively participating in shaping the transformation of utility systems through their daily activities. If they learn about the interdependency of their particular strategies and how they are embedded in broader system contexts, they are able to adapt their strategies accordingly. Moreover, new cooperative relationships between stakeholders may become established and this in turn increases their capacity for collective action.

In an important initial step of sustainability foresight, the general method is thoroughly adapted to a specific field of application. This includes an empirical study of the structure and dynamics and future expectations that are put forward by actors. As a starting point we chose to take expectations on future developments of the utility system which are discussed in the practice of electricity, gas, water and telecommunications provision. These expectations are not articulated in the form of full-fledged scenarios but rather appear more often as expectations about prices, technologies, market structure and so on. If carefully analysed, however, they do link up to form

*Table 7.1    Overview of the sustainability foresight process*

| Phase | Process steps | Actors |
|---|---|---|
| Adaptation to problem area | Scanning of future discourse and visions discussed in problem area | Project team |
| | Development of heuristic conceptual framework of the transformation process | Project team |
| Phase I: Explorative scenarios | Collection of factors which influence transformation | Stakeholders |
| | Selection by uncertainty and impact, elaboration of alternative projections for 30 factors | Stakeholders |
| | Cross-impact analysis, construction of scenarios as combinations of factor projections, composition of narrative storylines for selected scenarios | Stakeholders |
| Phase II: Discursive Sustainability Assessment | Elicitation of criteria for sustainability assessment held by stakeholders | Stakeholders |
| | Development of impact profile of scenarios with respect to identified criteria | Experts |
| | Discursive assessment of risks and opportunities connected to scenarios | Stakeholders and experts |
| Phase III: Shaping innovation processes | Identification of critical innovation processes (contingent across scenarios and high sustainability impact) | Project team |
| | In-depth analyses of actor networks and context conditions of critical innovations, identification of 'loci of influence' | Project team and stakeholders |
| | Development of integrated strategy for shaping interdependent institutional, cultural and technological innovation | Project team and stakeholders |

a more encompassing picture. In our case we identified three central features of the future utility system which frequently came up in expert discussions:

1.  System structures are going to be more decentralised than today (for example, renewable energy, fuel cells, biogas, membrane technology for drinking water processing and mobile telecommunications).
2.  Utility provision will be oriented towards services, not commodities, with the boundary between supply and demand dissolving (for

*Table 7.2   Participants in scenario workshops*

| | |
|---|---|
| MVV Energie AG | small integrated utility company |
| RWE AG | large integrated utility company |
| Vaillant GmbH | heating appliance manufacturer |
| VIK e.V. | association of industrial energy users |
| Gelsenwasser AG | water company |
| Enervision | energy management appliances manufacturer |
| Deutsche Telekom AG | telecommunications company |
| Alcatel SEL AG | control appliance manufacturer |
| BUND LV Berlin | environmental NGO |
| Ver.di LV NRW | trade union |
| Verbraucherzentrale NRW | consumer protection agency |
| Uni Essen | power plant engineering |
| DIW | energy economics |
| Fraunhofer ISI | innovation studies in water and sewage |
| RegPT | regulator for telecommunications |
| BMWA | federal ministry for economic affairs, energy department |
| Umweltministerium Bayern | regional state ministry for the environment, telecommunications department |

   example, customer generation in small combined heat and power units, contracting, facility management).
3.   Organisational and technical linkages between electricity, gas, water and telecommunications will become more intensive (for example, integrated service contracts, intelligent networking of infrastructure and appliances in smart buildings).

These three 'dimensions of change', as they are referred to in the project, provide an exploration space in which 'integrated microsystems of supply' is a hypothetical extreme scenario in which decentralisation, service orientation and the interlinkage between sectors is fully developed. This vision serves as a background foil for contrasting alternative possible developments.

   If not systematically reflected, implicit visions may translate into agendas for action, and eventually socio-technical structures, without being consciously assessed with regard to their actual conditions of realisation including wider impacts. Through the sustainability foresight process, however, they are critically scrutinised and discussed from diverse viewpoints like those of large utility companies, equipment manufacturers, consumer groups, environmental associations, trade unions and public administration (see Grin and Grunwald 2000). The long-term perspective adopted for the process helps to strengthen a communicative orientation of involved actors to prevail over strategic orientations.[4] In terms of actually influencing transformation processes, sustainability foresight focuses on innovation processes as the breeding grounds of future structures. Integrating radical alternatives into established utility structures is less conflict intensive at an early stage in the lifecycle of socio-technical configurations. Fostering innovation is more likely to gain broad societal support than attacking the given set-up right away. At the same time it can have strong and long lasting effects, if sustainability considerations already become incorporated into the design and performance specifications of a new system architecture. They do not have to be asserted against the rationality and inner dynamics of the utility system then, but rather they have to work for themselves (Rip and Schot 1999). In light of uncertainty and ambivalence associated with sustainability assessments of emerging utility structures, however, a crucial task is to find ways to shape new structures constructively and at the same time keep up structural adaptability for adequate responses to new knowledge, evaluations and experiences of unexpected effects.

A second step for problem structuring, besides the empirical study of future expectations of actors, is the development of a heuristic concept for the particular transformation process under study. This is necessary to guide the detailed set-up of the sustainability foresight process. The concept will provide a comprehensive account of the action arenas and types of factors of influence which are important for the course of transformation and its impacts. Such a heuristic approach is useful in order to ask the right questions, include the right actors and not 'overlook' any influential processes.

For the utility systems we have differentiated the following categories which we considered important to give a comprehensive image of transformation. Most of them may also be relevant for other areas of transformation. In principle, however, important categories should be derived from an empirical study of the specific transformation which is in focus of sustainability foresight:

- multiple sectors for provision of electricity, natural gas, water and telecommunications, which undergo transformation in parallel;
- action fields of production, consumption and political regulation whose inherent dynamics as well as their interaction drive transformation;
- structural dimensions of values, knowledge, institutions, technology and ecology which in combination enable and constrain patterns of utility provision;
- levels of socio-technical organisation like sectoral regimes, niche developments within the regime and changes in the socio-technical landscape in which regimes are embedded.

We use co-evolution as a general concept to understand the interaction of patterns within and across these different overlapping categories (Konrad et al. 2003; Voß 2004).

The conceptual framework is useful for systematically structuring issues and selecting stakeholders. Especially the latter is important since the participants have a very strong role in defining the substantial contents and results of sustainability foresight, whereas the organisers (in our case an interdisciplinary research team) act to a large extent as facilitators, moderators and service providers in gathering and structuring information. Problem structuring thus includes the development of a participation concept which should clearly define the functions of stakeholders within specific steps in the procedure and derive respective criteria with respect to recruitment. We distinguished between 'diversity of perspectives', 'affectedness' and 'influence on transformation' as specific recruitment criteria for the process steps of scenario analysis, sustainability assessment and strategy development, respectively. These criteria have been translated into respective quota for groups of stakeholders to be part of the process.

**Phase I: Explorative Scenarios**

The objective of the first phase of the process is to re-construct alternative visions of future utility systems out of the specific expectations held by different stakeholder groups. This has been carried out in a series of scenario workshops with 20 participants. The participants represented the variety of perspectives from production, consumption and political regulation in the four sectors (see Table 7.2).

In a first step various factors which influence the transformation of utility systems were collected. This took place in the form of a moderated process, initiated by the following question: 'What does the future of utility provision (electricity, gas, water, and telecommunications) look like (. . .) and on which factors does it depend?'. The first rather large sample of factors was clustered and selected according to the uncertainty of their future value and their potential impact in shaping future structures of utility provision. For a selection of the 30 most relevant factors, detailed descriptions were formulated which provided alternative projections of their value at the end of the exploration period (2025 in our case). Different combinations of factor values formed different scenario frameworks. These were based on a cross-impact analysis supported by a software tool. Consistent and particularly interesting scenario frameworks with respect to the three features of decentralisation, service orientation and sector integration were selected and fleshed out with narrative storylines.

This first phase resulted in four elaborated scenarios that represent alternative future structures of utility provision as well as a set of detailed descriptions of highly relevant factors influencing the transformation process. Both developed from the interaction of heterogeneous perspectives on utility provision. By means of this procedure it is possible to overcome some limitations often set by particular institutional perspectives like, for example, the one of technology development, business or consumer protection. This yields a trans-disciplinary and trans-professional view of the system in which processes become central that are – under everyday conditions – often externalised (such as societal acceptance for new technologies).

Another effect of the collective scenario construction is the 'creative destruction' of expectations and visions of future development which were taken for granted by participants. Routine thinking about how things unfold and what will come next could be replaced with a fan of contingent alternatives which would each require specific strategic responses. This pluralisation of the future can work as a particular kind of 'steering through visions' (Canzler and Dierkes 2001; Brand 2002). In this case it is not the coordinating force of visions which become embraced as commonly held expectations and translated into agendas (van Lente 1993; Konrad 2004), but the ambiguity of multiple expectations that may influence general action orientations towards experimenting, adaptivity and cooperation.

**Phase II: Discursive Sustainability Assessment**

The second phase moves from exploration to assessment. The focus is on the production of knowledge about goals, that is, the criteria for sustainable utility development and respective opportunities and threats in ongoing developments.

It is not possible to determine sustainability criteria objectively. We do not know the exact conditions for the long-term viability of coupled societal and ecological systems. Trade-offs between goals rest on differences in normative values and cannot be resolved scientifically. Moreover, values are endogenous to transformation and may change over its course. Sustainability goals will therefore always remain ambivalent. What counts is to keep the balance between equally legitimate but potentially conflicting values and to develop problem-specific practical judgements (Loeber 2003: 20). This can only be achieved in societal discourse among those who 'own' these values (see Stirling and Zwanenberg 2002). Such discourses may change the views of actors and allow for consensus or help to identify areas of irresolvable conflict which need careful political attention.

The sustainability foresight method envisages a systematically structured process in which stakeholders articulate their values, experts assess possible future developments with respect to their effect on these values and a broad range of affected actors engages in a discursive assessment of opportunities and threats which have to be taken special care of in future transformations.[5]

The result of the assessment phase is the explication of threats and opportunities of transformation from the perspective of the various actors who are potentially affected by them. In this way critical aspects can be identified, which form starting points for the development of adequate strategies. Such an open-ended approach to sustainability assessment allows for a concretisation of the abstract notion of sustainability without passing over inherent ambiguities. It yields a map of the societal value landscape with respect to the transformation of electricity, gas, water and telecommunications provision. Societal goal formulation can be supported by differentiating between facts and values and making them accessible for differentiated modes of conflict resolution such as discourse about problem framing and bargaining over distributional aspects (see Saretzki 1996).

## Phase III: Shaping Innovation Processes

The third phase focuses on the development of strategies. It addresses 'critical innovation processes' to shape broader transformation patterns. Critical innovations are identified on the basis of the foregoing scenario analysis and sustainability assessment: factors which have a central role in the transformation of utility systems as a whole and are linked to outstanding threats, opportunities or areas of conflict with respect to sustainability are candidates for a closer investigation into the innovation processes that determine future characteristics of this factor. If, for example, 'service orientation', 'demand-side management' and 'market development for smart building technology' are identified as important factors, and discursive assessment shows consensus on the desirability of user involvement in the utility systems, but at the same time divergent evaluations with respect to smart building technology, the latter would qualify as a critical innovation process and should be given special attention in strategies for sustainably shaping utility transformation.

Critical innovation processes thus refer to the emergence of new technological, institutional or cultural patterns in utility provision. Institutional innovations related to economic, political or cultural contexts are treated symmetrically with technological innovations in this context. In addition to smart building technology or small combined heat and power generation, network regulation, performance contracting schemes or cultural practices to switch providers or engage in self-supply of utility services could also receive special attention as critical innovations processes.

Since it is impossible actually to steer co-evolutionary processes, shaping strategies need to rely on 'modulation', that is, influencing innovation processes, while knowing that it is impossible to understand and control their outcome completely (Rip 1998, and Chapter 4, this volume). Influence can be exercised by various means of 'context steering' such as extending innovation networks to comprise users, affected or critical actors, empowering weak actors, providing information, moderating cooperative problem solving and so on. Such approaches can be effective in opening up opportunities or making undesired developments less likely, but they cannot determine final outcomes (such as what smart building technologies will actually look like, what they will be used for, etc.). Such a modest approach with respect to the steering of transformation is not only due to the distribution of power and resulting limitations for central control. It is also due to uncertainty and ambiguity in assessing the sustainability of innovations. These conditions make it necessary to create possibilities for social learning rather than implementing 'best solutions' in a straightforward way.

The core of this approach is to create connections between actors and processes which are otherwise institutionally separated. Even though they are separated with respect to strategy and internal dynamics, there can be strong interference in implementation and outcomes. Such is the case for example with departmental policies on energy and the environment, with science dynamics and societal problems, with technology development and user practices and with political regulation and business strategies. This can show up in two ways:

- Strategies which are developed in isolation from their contexts fail when they are confronted with their selection environments, because they did not adequately anticipate conditions of fit with their environment (for example in their technologies, policies, business strategies).
- If successful, the interaction of strategies with unanticipated context developments has unintended consequences ('external effects') for society as a whole and – in the form of indirect and delayed feedback – also for the strategy itself. Problems which are related to sustainable development are indeed mostly linked to such repercussions (such as the side effects of industrial agriculture, climate change, poverty induced migration, nuclear risk).

The strategic approach of the third phase of sustainability foresight thus is to foster the contextualisation of critical innovation processes. This happens on two levels. On the level of the interactions that are relevant for critical innovations, new arrangements are created which bring together the rationalities of developers, investors, users, interest groups, regulators and other stakeholders who represent the socio-ecological context in which innovations are to take effect. Such arrangements can take the form of R&D consortia, focused impact assessments, collective experiments and so on. On the level of expectations of changing sector structures, new visions are constructed which can serve to orient the search for sustainable transformation paths. Such visions are based on the scenarios and evaluation of sustainability impacts.

Concrete arrangements for the contextualisation of innovation processes need to be based on in-depth empirical analysis. This is oriented towards specific actor constellations and relevant context conditions which have historically contributed to shaping the innovation path and those which are likely to play a role in future development. On this basis possible courses of the 'innovation journey' are mapped in relation to contingent actor strategies and context developments. Turning points can be anticipated which represent windows of opportunity for influence.

New visions of sectoral transformation need to be based on discussion among stakeholders which take into account both (1) the breadth of possible developments and contingency of factor interactions and (2) the ambiguities in assessing these developments with respect to sustainable development. It is against this background that reflexive visions can be constructed, which are based on the diverse expectations of stakeholders. These visions reflect the interaction of multiple factors and pluralistic viewpoints in utility transformation. Moreover, they can orientate experimentation and shaping strategies to search for sustainable transformation paths.

## SUSTAINABILITY FORESIGHT AS REFLEXIVE GOVERNANCE

So far we have given a brief account of the sustainability foresight method. The method was developed based on general considerations about the role of foresight for the shaping of socio-technical transformation. A project in which sustainability foresight is applied in the German utility system and which provides the empirical experience for this chapter has, by this time, been implemented half way. It is therefore too early for a concluding evaluation. Nevertheless, it is possible to discuss initial results and articulate some linkages between our case and the more encompassing concept of reflexive governance as outlined in the Introduction to this book.

The scenario workshops brought up four different scenarios which represent alternative future structures of utility systems and which chart a spectrum of possible developments until 2025 (see Table 7.3). One interesting

*Table 7.3   Overview of scenarios of utility transformation*

| Scenario A 'Technological competition in a cooperative society' | Scenario B 'Development along the lines of "conservative ecology"' | Scenario C 'Broadening technology mix by competition of transnational corporations' | Scenario D 'The old Rome' |
|---|---|---|---|
| Decentral technology Low market concentration Utility sectors tightly coupled Visions generated in societal discourse become decentrally implemented State as moderator Competition stimulates technology development | Central technology Low market concentration Utility sectors separated Active innovation policy (R&D) State regulates utility markets and technology development | Centralised and decentralised technology High market concentration (international oligopoly) Utility sectors separated Innovation policy concentrated on national champions Strong market regulation | Central technology High market concentration Utility sectors separated Economic stagnation No active innovation policy Weak market regulation |

aspect, to mention only one example, is the scope of alternative developments in terms of decentralisation of technologies and concentration of markets. Here, the four scenarios represent all possible combinations, including technological decentralisation combined with high market concentration.

The scenarios tell stories which make one think in new ways and draw attention to factors and their ways of interacting that go beyond the expected paths of future discourse in the utility system. Apart from these substantial results, the process by which the scenarios were created also proved effective in itself. Participants affirmed that they learned about the utility system as a whole, about long-term dynamics, interdependencies and about the different perspectives and capacities of other actors. Many of them particularly emphasised the special opportunity to stand aside, take some time to reflect and look at the larger picture of sectoral transformation – a quality of thinking and communicating which they miss in their daily work.

When one examines sustainability foresight from a governance perspective, that is, concerned with patterns of social regulation, it is important not to misinterpret its intention. Sustainability foresight is not a steering approach or a policy instrument in the classical sense. We have already mentioned its hybrid character between knowledge production, innovation and governance. It does not shape utility production, technological innovation, consumption behaviour or the regulatory process in any direct manner. Accordingly, it is also not oriented towards the achievement of any specific output goals such as a determined amount of money spent on R&D, technologies to be applied in households, or greenhouse gas emissions linked to utility services. The goal of sustainability foresight is to shape the processes by which any of these outputs are generated. It could rather be called 'second-order governance' which is complementary to other modes of policy making. The central orientation in this respect is to bridge the gaps between distributed activities which exert influence on the transformation process in an uncoordinated way. The black box of large-scale and long-term transformation will be opened a little to allow for anticipatory adaptation of strategies according to their embedding in larger processes of change.

As such, the concept of reflexive governance described in the Introduction to this book works well in understanding sustainability foresight. It is not a process to steer transformation, but to modulate it by establishing linkages between its various sub-processes. As such, it 'reflects, orients and supervises diverse specialised problem-solving processes' (Voß and Kemp in the Introduction to this volume). The following paragraphs give an overview on how elements of the sustainability foresight method can be related to the strategy elements of reflexive governance.

Integrated knowledge production: in order to combine distributed knowledge for the understanding of transformation in utility systems, their assessment and a development of action strategies, a great variety of stakeholders is involved in the different stages of the sustainability foresight process. They bring knowledge from production, consumption and political regulation in four different utility sectors into the process (see Table 7.2). Scientific expertise in the project team is interdisciplinary, comprising physics, engineering, geography, economics, political science, sociology and psychology. These different types of knowledge are integrated by various methods which make particular use of the diversity of perspectives such as scenario workshops, value analysis, discursive assessment, and interactive strategy workshops.

Adaptivity of strategies and institutions: the exploration of four quite different futures for the utility system and the contingencies which have been encountered in the process of scenario construction emphasise the need to be prepared for adaptation when things turn out to be different than expected. This is what sustainability foresight 'teaches' its participants as well as the users of its products such as the scenarios, 'value landscape' and the integrated strategy for shaping innovation processes. Especially the latter takes due account of uncertainty about system dynamics as well as ambiguity of sustainability assessments and therefore follows a procedural and experimental approach by facilitating interactive learning instead of pushing particular best solutions, be it technologies, policy instruments or behavioural patterns. Strategies aim to open innovation processes to integrate diverse perspectives and to remain open for the revision of guiding visions and design principles.[6]

Anticipation of long-term systemic effects: anticipation is the general idea behind any kind of foresight process. The approach of sustainability foresight in particular is to draw the system boundaries in a very broad manner in order to become aware of distant side effects and long feedback loops which are linked to certain strategies (for example, the four utility sectors, action domains production, consumption and regulation, interactions across the dimensions of society, technology and nature). Anticipation is not done with impact assessment by experts but in the context of moderated interaction of stakeholders from various parts of the system under investigation. It is important to note that this approach to anticipation does not aim to make correct projections, but to collectively explore plausible futures by actors who themselves shape this future by their daily interactions. The process may as such help to create an alignment of strategic orientations and is therefore more about bringing about and shaping developments than predicting them.

Iterative participatory goal formulation: the discursive sustainability assessment which serves to identify risks and opportunities of transformation acknowledges that sustainability goals must become established and weighed against each other in broader social processes, not by scientific experts or politicians alone. It builds on the participation of the spectrum of different social actors who are affected by utility transformation in order to lay bare the ambivalence involved in sustainability assessment and prepare the ground for the deliberation of pragmatic judgements. Iteration is not part of the process itself, if it is only conducted once. By proposing the method, however, we envision that successive sustainability foresight processes are performed in order to keep track of the changes in knowledge and values that are part of the transformation process and adapt goals and assessments accordingly.

Interactive strategy development: the strategy recommendations which are elaborated in the course of the sustainability foresight process are interaction oriented in two ways. First, they are developed in interaction with the stakeholders who are the ones to implement them or are affected by them. This happens in the course of group interviews linked to the in-depth analysis of critical innovation processes and in the form of a strategy workshop for drawing conclusions from these analyses. A second aspect of iterative strategy development is linked to the kind of strategies which are developed in the sustainability foresight process. Their procedural orientation actually puts interactions between actors who are involved in and affected by critical innovation processes at the core of the shaping approach. Thus, strategies and measures which result from sustainability foresight are indeed aimed at moderating the self-organisation of actors who play a part in the transformation process. Distributed capacities to influence the course of transformation are utilised by this means without the need to exert central control.

## CONCLUSIONS AND REFLECTIONS ON REFLEXIVE GOVERNANCE

In the preceding section we have shown how sustainability foresight relates to the concept of reflexive governance. We have established that it actually represents an illustrative case of interactive anticipation and analysis which fits very well into the five criteria for reflexive governance for sustainable development. In this concluding section, we emphasise the lessons learned from this approach for refinement of the reflexive governance concept.

Sustainability foresight can be seen as an example of the existence of reflexive governance in practice. As stated in the Introduction it represents a new form of governance, or societal problem treatment more generally, which developed out of learning experiences in a concrete area of practice. In the case of sustainability foresight it is the elaboration of technology assessment methods which moved from single technologies towards socio-technical systems as the object of study and from expert assessments to citizen participation and stakeholder interaction as the ways of producing knowledge and evaluative judgements. The concept of sustainable development played an important role for this process in demanding to take into account long-term effects of technologies in larger socio-ecological system contexts (that is, including social impacts and global effects) and to face for assessment diverse criteria that are not easily reconcilable (such as social, ecological and economic) (Grunwald 2002).

In this respect the concept of sustainable development has effectively induced changes in social practice. Up to now, one cannot speak of a full regime change which has taken place in technology assessment, but it is clearly visible that new and more reflexive forms of governing technological change are developing and becoming institutionalised (Simonis 2001). A separate question which cannot be answered here is about the conditions of these governance innovations to develop further and diffuse to actually become established as part of a new governance regime. In order to assess the potential for reflexive governance adequately in technology assessment and possibly elsewhere, however, we can offer some reflections on our experiences with the operation of sustainability foresight in practice.

We had to learn that interactive research involving a diverse set of heterogeneous actors is a precarious endeavour. It opens the research process towards ongoing dynamics in the field of study, and makes it more vulnerable to the influence of interests and conflicts. This requires a high level of attention to current political processes, relations between actors, and possible tensions which will have repercussions within the process. A great deal of flexibility in the management of the process is necessary in order to navigate through the currents of the real world stream of action. The sustainability foresight method, as described here, should thus not be understood as a toolkit for straightforward application, but rather as an ideal-type process arrangement which may inspire similar processes elsewhere. This may also be extended to reflexive governance in general. Rather than providing a specified toolkit, it may serve as a 'regulative idea' which orients the problem-specific design of process arrangements.

This means that the project team, that is, researchers, public officials, or whoever else is initiating and conducting sustainability foresight, has strong influence on the process and indirectly on its results. A clear example is the selection of stakeholders which is an important factor in shaping the processes of problem analysis, goal formulation and strategy development. Yet, there is no standard method available by which relevant stakeholders for a particular problem can be identified. The project team therefore has important discretionary powers which go beyond the role of a facilitator of stakeholder interaction. Also the specific set-up and moderation do, of course, shape the results of sustainability foresight. This central role of the project team should be reflected by providing good documentation of the specific process set-up and the reasoning behind it. It also underlines the importance of having interdisciplinary competences and process management skills represented in the project team.

Another proviso with respect to the capabilities of reflexive governance to bring about sustainable development is the basic dilemma of (critical) discursive communication about problem-solving on the one hand and (affirmative) realism towards interests and power in actual institutional contexts on the other hand. Although it is necessary to promote an argumentative orientation of the participating stakeholders in order to produce integrated problem definitions and cooperative strategies, it is questionable if knowledge and strategies which were produced under these conditions will actually prove to be robust in real world policy processes where institutional inertia, competitive struggle and opportunistic behaviour are prevalent. It is necessary to strike a balance between detached observation and strategic role playing.

Sustainability foresight cannot overcome this dilemma; it can only help to find a good way to deal with it. This means that the social processes that take place when working with the method are not free from particular interests, asymmetrical power relations and strategic interaction. It is also not guaranteed that the results which are produced in the 'laboratory' of sustainability foresight can and will be implemented in the real world contexts to which they refer, because the specific institutional embedding constrains what actors think, value and what they can do. In this respect, sustainability foresight, and perhaps reflexive governance more generally, cannot be regarded as a solution to the problems which are linked to established institutional patterns in modern societies. In providing space for collective, problem-oriented learning it can be regarded as a means to create opportunities for making use of institutional slack to establish more adequate practices for dealing with uncertainty and ambivalence in the shaping of sustainable transformation.

In this context it is important to note that sustainability foresight, as other reflexive governance approaches, cannot, in our understanding, be a complete substitute for more conventional problem-solving methods in policy making and management which are based on a positivistic conception of rationality (such as model-based forecasting, cost–benefit analysis and mobilisation of powers for political control). One reason is that taking uncertainty and ambivalence seriously makes one careful to make final decisions though this is necessary for taking (collective) action. Another reason is that the emergence of strategies from stakeholder deliberations – which sustainability foresight seeks to facilitate – does not allow for assignment of responsibility. Legitimising by democratic control through those who are not themselves part of the deliberation is therefore not applicable.

Here is another dilemma which cannot be overcome. Where positivist problem-solving works productively it does so by constructing an 'illusion of agency' on the grounds of a simplified conception of system dynamics, goal definition and steering capacity. The illusion of agency is effective and indeed necessary for mobilising (collective) action. At the same time, however, it is bound to induce uncontrollable side effects and 'second-order problems' precisely with respect to those aspects which are neglected for the sake of constructing decisiveness. While productive in stimulating action, conventional governance forms based on a rationalistic problem-solving orientation are therefore prone to shift problems rather than solve them. Reflexive governance arrangements, on the other hand, face limits in reaching decisions which are necessary for action – as long as they keep up reflexivity and do not evade to pragmatic simplifications. Sustainability foresight and other reflexive governance arrangements therefore have to be conceived as being complementary to conventional problem-solving. Their particular value is to buffer the side effects of routine problem-solving by opening up narrow problem conceptions and recontextualising specialised operations with the perspectives of interdependent and affected stakeholders. It is in this respect that the effect of sustainability foresight should be valued and evaluated. How the balance of reflexive and positivistic approaches to sustainable development can be evaluated and how they can be productively combined are questions which lead us beyond the scope of this chapter. A first step that we have attempted to take is to contribute to a better understanding of the specific quality of reflexive governance by discussing sustainability foresight as a specific case.

## ACKNOWLEDGEMENTS

We thank Dierk Bauknecht, Bas van Vliet and René Kemp for comments on an earlier version and Arie Rip for the discussion of background concepts which shaped our ideas beyond what is visible in the references.

## NOTES

1. We appreciate funding through the programme on socio-ecological research by the German Federal Ministry for Education and Research (www.sozial-oekologische-forschung.org) under the project title 'Integrierte Mikrosysteme der Versorgung. Dynamik, Nachhaltigkeit und Gestaltung von Transformationsprozessen in netzgebundenen Versorgungssystemen' (www.mikrosysteme.org).
2. With the concept of 'Constructive technology assessment', the social phenomenon of nexus arrangements has been turned into a programmatic approach to overcome the 'control dilemma' in technology assessment which refers to the discrepancy between a lack of knowledge about the effects of technological developments at an early stage and a lack of opportunity to influence its course at a later stage (Collingridge 1980). For a more encompassing elaboration of the concept which has also played a role in the development of the sustainability foresight method see Rip et al. 1995; Rip 2002; Simonis 2001.
3. The three steps are related to the distinction of system knowledge, knowledge about goals and transformation knowledge as elements of sustainability research (see Mogalle 2001).
4. Looking at long-term developments, the uncertainty about one's own position increases. As a result, a 'veil of indifference' (Rawls 1999) with respect to the distribution of benefits and burdens to particular actor groups may increase the probability of future knowledge which is less biased with respect to individual interests.

5.  The procedure resembles the method of participatory policy analysis developed by Ortwin Renn et al. (1993).
6.  Here we touch on a fundamental problem which has to do with the dilemma of exploration and exploitation as elaborated nicely by March (1991). While it is necessary, especially in the face of uncertainty and ambivalence, to have many options ready and keep up flexibility to adapt, it is also necessary to choose certain paths for concentrated investment of resources and accumulation of learning effects in order to allow for the development of momentum for new structures. By focusing on exploration and opening up, which we think is important in the current state of utility development, though, we leave the task of developing appropriate approaches to select paths for exploitation to processes beyond the method of sustainability foresight as it is presented here.

# REFERENCES

Arentsen, M. and R.W. Künnecke (eds) (2003), *National Reforms in European Gas*, Amsterdam, Boston, Heidelberg et al.: Elsevier.

Beck, U. (1993), *Die Erfindung des Politischen*, Frankfurt am Main: Suhrkamp.

Berkhout, F. and J. Hertin (2002), 'Foresight futures scenarios. Developing and applying a participative strategic planning tool', *Greener Management International*, **37** (Spring), 37–52.

Borup, M. (2003), 'Green Technology Foresight as Instrument in Governance for Sustainability', presented at the conference 'Governance for Industrial Transformation', organised by AK Umweltpolitik und Global Change, Deutsche Vereinigung für Politikwissenschaft, Berlin.

Brand, K.-W. (2002), 'Politik der Nachhaltigkeit. Voraussetzungen, Probleme, Chancen – eine kritische Diskussion', Berlin: Edition Sigma.

Canzler, W. and M. Dierkes (2001), 'Informationelle Techniksteuerung: öffentliche Diskurse und Leitbildentwicklungen', in G. Simonis, R. Martinsen and Saretzki (eds), PVS Politik und Technik. Analysen zum Verhältnis von Technologischem, politischem und staatlichen Wandel am Anfang des 21. Jahrhunderts. Sonderheft 31/2000, Wiesbaden: Westdeutscher Verlag, pp. 457–75.

Collingridge, D. (1980), The Social Control of Technology, London: Frances Pinter.

Fischer, F. (1993), 'Bürger, Experten und Politik nach dem "Nimby"-Prinzip: Ein Plädoyer für die partizipatorische Poilcy-Analyse', in A. Héritier (ed.), PVS Policy-Analyse Sonderheft 24/1993. Kritik und Neuorientierung, Opladen: Westdeutscher Verlag, pp. 451–70.

Gallopín, G.C. (2002), 'Planning for resilience: scenarios, surprises, and branch points', in L.H. Gunderson and C.S. Holling (eds), *Panarchy. Understanding Transformations in Human and Natural Systems*, Washington, DC: Island Press, pp. 361–94.

Godet, M. (1987), *Scenarios and Strategic Management*, London: Butterworth.

Grin, J. and A. Grunwald (2000), Vision Assessment: Shaping Technology in 21st Century Society. Towards a Repertoire for Technology Assessment, Berlin, Heidelberg and New York: Springer Verlag.

Grunwald, A. (ed.) (2002), *Technikgestaltung für eine nachhaltige Entwicklung. Von der Konzeption zur Umsetzung*, Berlin: Edition Sigma.

Hisschemöller, M. and R. Hoppe (2001), 'Coping with intractable controversies: the case for problem structuring in policy design and analysis', in M. Hisschemöller et al. (eds), *Knowledge, Power, and Participation in Environmental Policy Analysis*, New Brunswick, NJ and London: Transaction Publishers.

Kemp, R. (1994), 'Technology and the transition to environmental sustainability. The problem of technological regime shifts', *Futures*, **26**, 1023–46.

Kemp, R., J.P. Schot and R. Hoogma (1998), 'Regime shifts to sustainability through processes of niche formation: the approach of strategic niche management', *Technology Analysis and Strategic Management*, **10** (2), 175–95.

Konrad, K. (2004), *Prägende Erwartungen*, Berlin: Edition Sigma.

Konrad, K., J.-P. Voß and B. Truffer (2003), 'Transformation dynamics in utility systems. An integrated approach to the analysis of transformation processes drawing on transition theory', presented at the conference 'Governance for Industrial Transformation', Berlin.

Kubicek, H. (1994), 'Steuerung in die Nichtsteuerbarkeit. Paradoxien in der Entwicklung der Telekommunikation in Deutschland', in I. Braun and B. Joerges (eds), *Technik ohne Grenzen*, Frankfurt am Main: Suhrkamp, pp. 107–65.

Loeber, A. (2003), *Practical Wisdom in the Risk Society. Methods and Practice of Interpretive Analysis on Questions of Sustainable Development*, Amsterdam: University of Amsterdam.

March, J.G. (1991), 'Exploration and exploitation in organizational learning', *Organization Science*, **2** (1), 71–87.

Mayntz, R. (1998), 'New challenges to governance theory', European University Institute, Jean Monnet Chair Paper RSC, No. 98/50.

Mayntz, R. (1999), 'Funktionelle Teilsysteme in der Theorie sozialer Differenzierung', in R. Mayntz (ed.), Soziale Dynamik und politische Steuerung: theoretische und methodologische Überlegungen, Frankfurt am Main and New York: Campus, pp. 38–69.

Mayntz, R. and V. Schneider (1995), 'Die Entwicklung technischer Infrastruktursysteme zwischen Steuerung und Selbstorganisation', in R. Mayntz and F.W. Scharpf (eds), Gesellschaftliche Selbstregelung und politische Steuerung, Frankfurt am Main and New York: Campus, pp. 73–100.

Mez, L. (1997), 'The German electricity reform attempts: reforming co-optive networks', in A. Midttun (ed.), *European Electricity Systems in Transition. A Comparative Analysis of Policy and Regulation in Western Europe*, Amsterdam: Elsevier.

Midttun, A. (1997), *European Electricity Systems in Transition. A Comparative Analysis of Policy and Regulation in Western Europe*, Amsterdam: Elsevier.

Minsch, J., P.-H. Feindt, H.-P. Meister, U. Schneidewind and T. Schulz (1998), *Institutionelle Reformen für eine Politik der Nachhaltigkeit*, Berlin, Heidelberg and New York: Springer.

Mogalle, M. (2001), *Management transdisziplinärer Forschungsprozesse*, Basel, Boston and Berlin: Birkhäuser.

Norgaard, R.B. (1994), *Development Betrayed. The End of Progress and a Coevolutionary Revisioning of the Future*, London: Routledge.

Nowotny, H., P. Scott and M. Gibbons (2001), *Re-thinking Science. Knowledge and the Public in an Age of Uncertainty*, Cambridge: Polity Press.

Patterson, W. (1999), *Transforming Electricity. The Coming Generation of Change*, London: Earthscan.

Rammert, W. (1997), 'Innovation im Netz. Neue Zeiten für technische Innovationen: heterogen verteilt und interaktiv', *Soziale Welt*, **4**, 396–415.

Rawls, John (1999), *A Theory of Justice*, (revised edn.), Cambridge, MA: Belknap Press.

Renn, O. (2002), 'Foresight and multi-level governance', presented at the conference 'Role of Foresight in the Selection of Research Policy Priorities', organised by IPTS Seville.

Ringland, G. (1998), *Scenario Planning: Managing for the Future*, Chichester: John Wiley.

Rip, A. (1998), 'The dancer and the dance: steering in/of science and technology', in A. Rip (ed.), *Steering and Effectiveness in a Developing Knowledge Society*, Utrecht: Uitgeverij Lemma BV, pp. 27–50.

Rip, A. (2002), 'A co-evolutionary perspective on ELSI, CTA and other attempts at re-contextualisation of science and technology in society', presented at the conference 'Responsibility under Uncertainty', organised by European Association for the Study of Science and Technology, York, UK.

Rip, A. and R. Kemp (1998), 'Technological change', in S. Rayner and E.L. Malone (eds), *Human Choice and Climate Change*, Columbus, OH: Batelle Press, pp. 327–99.

Rip, A., T.J. Misa and J.P. Schot (eds) (1995), *Managing Technology in Society. The Approach of Constructive Technology Assessment*, London: Pinter.

Rip, A. and J.P., Schot, (1999), 'Anticipating on contextualization – loci for influencing the dynamics of technological development', in D. Sauer and C. Lang (eds), *Paradoxien der Innovation. Perspektiven sozialwissenschaftlicher Innovationsforschung*, Frankfurt and New York: Campus, pp. 129–48.

Saretzki, T. (1996), 'Wie unterscheiden sich Argumentieren und Verhandeln?', in Prittwitz, V.v. (ed.), *Verhandeln und Argumentieren*, Opladen: Leske und Budrich, pp. 19–39.

Schneider, V. (2001), *Die Transformation der Telekommunikation Vom Staatsmonopol zum globalen Markt (1800–2000)*, Schriften des MPIfG, Frankfurt: Campus.

Simonis, G. (2001), 'Die TA-Landschaft in Deutschland – Potenziale reflexiver Techniksteuerung', in G. Simonis, R. Martinsen and T. Saretzki (eds), *PVS Politik und Technik. Analysen zum Verhältnis von Technologischem, politischem und staatlichen Wandel am Anfang des 21 Jahrhunderts*. Sonderheft 31/2000, Wiesbaden: Westdeutscher Verlag, pp. 425–56.

Stirling, A. and P.v. Zwanenberg (2002), 'Precaution in the European Union: from principle to process', paper presented at the EASST 2002 Conference on Responsibility under Uncertainty, York: 31 July–3 August.

Summerton, J. (ed.) (1992), Changing Large Technical Systems, Boulder, CO: Westview.

Truffer, B., A. Metzner and R. Hoogma (2003), 'The coupling of viewing and doing. Strategic niche management and the electrification of individual transport', *Greener Management International* **37**, 111–24.

van den Belt, H. and A. Rip (1987), 'The Nelson-Winter–Dosi model and synthetic dye industry', in W.E. Bijker, T.P. Hughes and T.J. Pinch (eds), *The Social Construction of Technological Systems*, Cambridge, MA: MIT Press, pp. 135–58.

van Lente, H. (1993), 'Promising technology, the dynamics of expectations in technological development', PhD Thesis, Enschede: University of Twente.

Voß, J.-P. (2000), 'Institutionelle Arrangements zwischen Zukunfts- und Gegenwartsfähigkeit: Verfahren der Netzregelung im liberalisierten deutschen

Stromsektor', in V.v. Prittwitz (ed.), *Institutionelle Arrangements in der Umweltpolitik. Zukunftsfähigkeit durch innovative Verfahrenskombination?*, Opladen: Leske und Budrich, pp. 227–54.

Voß, J.-P. (2004), 'Ko-Evolution und reflexive Gestaltung', in Querschnittsarbeitsgruppe Steuerung und Transformation (ed.), 'Überblick über theoretische Konzepte in den Projekten der sozial-ökologischen Forschung', Disskussionpapier 1, Berlin.

# 8. Foresight and adaptive planning as complementary elements in anticipatory policy-making: a conceptual and methodological approach

## K. Matthias Weber[1]

## INTRODUCTION

Requirements with respect to science, technology and innovation policy have been changing over the past years. First of all, processes of innovation have become more interactive, distributed and complex, thus broadening the range of potential inroads for policy far beyond the realm of science and technology (Kuhlmann 2001). Secondly, confidence in S&T policy has declined in parallel to the decline of confidence in science and technology in general. This has resulted in demand for more transparency, accountability and participation in related policy decisions (EC 2001). Thirdly, policy increasingly requires a more strategic and forward-looking approach in order to cope with the aforementioned societal risks, uncertainties and dynamics of multi-level innovation systems (for example, Tübke et al. 2001).

These new requirements are particularly pressing in the context of policies that address the issue of sustainable development. Several attempts have been made in recent years to understand better the emerging challenges as well as to develop approaches for coping with them. As recognised by Gibbons et al. (1994) and Funtowicz and Ravetz (1993), knowledge production needs to take place in different ways than it previously did when dealing with future risks and uncertainties. The long-term impacts that current knowledge production can have, require comprehensive approaches to the management of equally long-term transformation processes (Rotmans et al. 2001, Kemp and Rotmans 2005). Such approaches, however, raise questions of structural change and second-order reflexivity. In the introduction to this volume, Voß and Kemp have translated these new requirements into a set of basic guidelines of what they call reflexive governance: integration of knowledge, adaptivity, anticipation, iterative and participatory goal formulation and interactive strategy development.

In spite of much progress in conceptual terms, the implementation of these approaches is still confronted with many barriers. In policy practice, it is very difficult to strike a balance between the demands for greater accountability, transparency and participation on the one hand and the need to manage potential risks and uncertainties of socio-technical innovation strategically on the other. The reasons for this tension are manifold. On the one hand, opening up political decision processes to criticism can put into question their legitimacy as well as the coalitions of interest that are associated with them. On the other hand, coalitions and alliances are crucial for successfully implementing strategies for dealing with risks and uncertainties. Moreover, processes of political agenda-setting tend to be driven by short-term concerns that can be addressed in the course of the electoral cycle rather than by long-term concerns. In spite of these rather detrimental framework conditions, initial changes towards a more reflexive and long-term approach to policy making can be observed. In many European countries, forward-looking and participatory processes have been initiated under the heading 'Foresight' (see Gavigan 2002), and technology assessment has increasingly embraced interactive elements to complement conventional analytical approaches (Joss and Bellucci 2002). Principles of transdisciplinary research have increasingly gained recognition in policy as well as in parts of the academic community (Balzer and Wächter 2002, Thompson Klein et al. 2001). However, the processes of policy development and design still tend to rely predominantly on conventional retrospective learning and intuition, and they lack a clear systematic and strategic foundation.

The contribution of this chapter is set in this context. It aims to develop an approach and methodology in support of policy development and design that reflects the principles of reflexive governance. More specifically, it combines insights from recent developments in foresight, strategic planning and policy portfolio analysis in order to develop a heuristics and process that can be used as a guideline for developing more reflexive policy strategies.

In this chapter, first a brief look will be taken at the new emerging requirements for policy-making and the implications for the roles and strategies of government over the policy and innovation cycle. The next section focuses on recent developments in foresight and strategic planning, highlighting in particular the complementarities between these two lines of work. This analysis will be further specified in terms of a methodological approach to guide processes of forward-looking, adaptive and portfolio-oriented strategy development in policy-making and then illustrated by some examples where this 'adaptive foresight' methodology has already been applied. Finally, some conclusions will be drawn on the experiences with and the perspectives of further application of this approach and methodology.

# NEW REQUIREMENTS FOR THE GOVERNANCE OF SUSTAINABILITY-ORIENTED INNOVATION SYSTEMS

## Key Functions of Innovation Systems

The changing nature of innovation processes in connection with the normative implications of an orientation towards sustainable development and the decline in confidence in government policy raises a number of new requirements with respect to the functions that innovation systems ought to fulfil (and that related policies should thus support):[2]

- Transformation: as an overarching function, innovation systems are supposed to enable processes of innovation and socio-technical change in society. Moreover, the framework conditions and incentive structures should ensure that the innovations that are produced contribute to a process of sustainable socio-technical change. In a wider sense, this transformation function also comprises the ability of self-transformation of the innovation system itself, that is, the ability to change the structural and organisational settings as well as the incentive structures for innovation in line with new insights about the requirements of sustainable development and the mechanisms determining innovations. Managing such long-term processes of transformation and structural change – both in society at large and within the innovation system – requires the political ability to realise major reform projects and to make intelligent use of self-reinforcing mechanisms.
- Anticipation: one of the pre-conditions for transformation is the ability to anticipate alternative future directions of socio-technical change under conditions of uncertainty, complexity and ambiguity (Renn 2002). This requires from society a highly developed ability to explore future scenarios and develop decision options as a foundation for strategic policy-making. New analytical (for example, benchmarking, evaluation) as well as interactive (for example, foresight, scenario development) methods are needed to provide strategic input to policy.[3]
- Goal-orientation: another pre-condition for transformation must be seen in the ability to deliver orientations for the future, for instance by means of vision-building and pro-active agenda-setting. Government

can play a key role not only in both respects, but also by defining incentives and incentive structures that are compatible with the visions and agendas, for instance in R&D policy by striking a balance between generic support measures for R&D and other, thematically oriented RTD programmes.

- Co-ordination: orientation by visions is a powerful means of supporting processes of co-ordination between different actors, but in particular with respect to horizontal policy matters such as sustainability, the coordination between different policy areas and levels needs to be reinforced, for instance by joint action plans and harmonised regulations. Similarly, the coordination between policy actors and other stakeholders requires active measures, which in most cases will rely on some kind of participation process in the early phases of the policy cycle.

- Experimentation: underinvestment in research and development under market conditions has been one of the main arguments for legitimising RTD policy measures since its early days. This argument holds even more in the face of interactive, interdisciplinary and transdisciplinary research practices that require the involvement of a wider range of disciplines, stakeholders and practitioners. Enabling bottom-up experimentation (and subsequent learning about the experiences with and the desirability of innovations) is thus another important role for research and technology policy.

- Adaptation: in an increasingly globalised economy and society, the ability to adapt to new emerging challenges (for example, environmental, migratory) or unpredictable events becomes an essential asset. It implies that simple goal orientation is not sufficient any more in view of the fact that the evolution of societies depends to a large extent on decisions made elsewhere. Experimentation and variety-creation are prerequisites for maintaining adaptability, but adaptation also requires being able to change structural characteristics of multi-level systems. However, adaptability needs to be balanced with stabilising characteristics such as goal orientation.

- First-order and second-order learning: learning is crucial for being able to strike the right balances, for instance between adaptation and goal orientation, or between generic and directed research policy measures. In the case of sustainability, both first-order learning about past experiences with policy measures (for example, by means of evaluations) and second-order learning (that is, reflexivity) about the cross-cutting governance implications of experiences in different specialised policy areas are needed (c.f. Voß and Kemp, in the Introduction to this volume). Second-order learning implies the ability to change the role of politics and policy (and thus also of other actors) in the course of the innovation process and the system transformation.

- Participation: beyond being a means to enhance the legitimacy of policy decisions, participation also enhances the integration of technological, economic, political and institutional sources of knowledge. This is particularly important in the case of sustainability where underlying conflicts about values and risk perception related to innovation and new technologies make it essential to involve a wide range of stakeholders in policy decisions about these new technologies. Ensuring the participation of an appropriate range of actors and stakeholders in network-based processes of preparing policy decisions is thus another functional requirement of sustainability-oriented innovation systems of which government should take care.

## Implications for the Roles and Strategies of Government

Assuming that these observations represent an accurate description of the new functions of innovation systems and the requirements they raise for policy, the main role of government can be seen in ensuring that these functions are fulfilled. In some instances, this may imply a very active role for government, in others a less interventionist one than often adopted in the past. In any case, they imply a number of obvious departures from the current interpretation of the role and the strategic behaviour of governments.

First of all, the self-understanding of government actors is likely to change. They should not regard themselves as external to innovation or other socio-technical systems but rather as an integral part of them. This implies that policy-makers are just one type of actor among others who contribute to processes of system change. One may nevertheless argue that public policy-making has a special role to play because it is expected to guarantee certain key functions that are necessary to enable structural transformations of innovation systems towards sustainability (see the previous section).

As a consequence of positioning government agents this way, they can no longer assume a steering role but rather a moderating and modulating function with respect to the different relevant actors (Kuhlmann 1998). For instance, most foresight initiatives tend to stress the importance of the ability to shape the future, and the same tends to hold true for most strategy-oriented approaches to research and technology policy (Elzen et al. 2001, Rip et al. 1995, Hoogma et al. 2002, Kemp and Rotmans 2004). Participatory initiatives for anticipating future developments and using them as an orientation for decision-making make the expectations, goals and preferences of the actors involved explicit and are thus supposed to help make their collective and individual decisions more coherent. The shaping power of governments may be important, but their main function is not to determine the results of such processes, but rather to make sure that they take place in a constructive way. Collective learning processes are thus considered crucial for ensuring the development of better and more 'coherent' public and private policies (OECD 2005). Such a moderating and modulating role also entails the responsibility to engage the most suitable range of actors in the process. This is particularly important when assuming that successful innovation in society is increasingly dependent on the distributed intelligence of the actors involved (Kuhlmann 2001).

From this perspective, foresight – or more generally speaking the management of expectations – has an important role to play as a soft coordination mechanism for shaping the future, on top of its forward-looking, anticipatory nature. However, several limitations to the political and social shaping of future developments are often neglected but are particularly pertinent with respect to sustainability. These limitations have severe implications for the role that government can play, and in particular with respect to the balance between adaptive and pro-active elements of policy strategies.

Eriksson (2003) makes this point very cogently by opposing two basic policy strategies in this respect: strategic opportunism vs. strategic commitment. The former emphasises the adaptive qualities of policy and the latter the willingness to steer and shape the future. There are many reasons why the strategic commitment is likely to fail, and why a better balance thus needs to be found between adaptation and flexibility on the one hand, and goal-oriented steering on the other. This need for a more adaptive approach to policy-making can be traced back to at least four reasons:

- Adaptation to external developments and unexpected events: this is the 'classical' example of adaptation, aiming to take precautions against major external events.
- Adaptation to other actors: in a governance context, in which other actors' decisions and value positions constrain the possibilities of governments and where key decisions are increasingly taken by a range of actors collectively rather than centrally by a single actor, the adaptations of one's own strategies to those of the other actors becomes imperative.
- Adaptation to a multi-level policy context: being almost a special case of the preceding point, there is a growing need for adaptation to other levels of policy making. National policy-making is embedded in European and international politics and often frames regional processes. The division of labour between these levels is often unclear.[4]

- Adaptation over time, that is, over the policy and the innovation cycles: policy roles may also change over time. As shown in Table 8.1 for the case of transport technology policy, the appropriate role for EU policy changes in the course of the innovation process, and key policy functions may move down to lower policy levels or altogether out of the policy realm. Moreover, time is also a critical factor from the perspective of the complex innovation systems because of the necessity to exploit time windows of opportunity. Similar arguments can be made with respect to the policy cycle and the resulting changes in policy roles over time.

These arguments in favour of adaptive policy strategies point to a need to reassess the balance between pro-active and reactive elements in policy strategy development. Maintaining the ability to adapt flexibly to changing circumstances seems to become increasingly important. Within such a framework, a moderating role for government becomes crucial to enhance the coherence of decisions taken by different actors. More specific policy roles can still be played in a flexible manner, that is, adapted to the specific innovation phases and using a variety of instruments and policies.

In addition to conventional policy instruments (such as regulation, finance, S&T policy, infrastructure investment), a moderating role also requires the use of new instruments, such as the stimulation of processes of networking and knowledge exchange, the initiation of processes of vision-building and foresight in order to anticipate future developments and generate orienting knowledge for the actors involved.

In other words, foresight can be interpreted as a valuable instrument that promises to help make policy-making and governance more reflexive. However, the significance for policy depends on its embedding in a flexible and forward-looking approach to policy strategy development. This could be achieved by tightening the linkages between foresight on the one hand, and modern strategic planning-type approaches to policy-making on the other. The recent developments in both strands of work as well as the methodological conclusions that can be drawn from them will be addressed in the subsequent sections.

## FORESIGHT AND ADAPTIVE PLANNING AS BUILDING BLOCKS OF AN APPROACH FOR REFLEXIVE POLICY STRATEGY DEVELOPMENT

In the preceding sections, a number of requirements for sustainability-oriented policy-making have been identified. They point to the need to

*Table 8.1  Possible roles of EU transport technology policy over the innovation cycle*

| | Neutral | Monitoring | R&D agent | Regulator | Innovation agent | Implementer | Developer |
|---|---|---|---|---|---|---|---|
| Invention | + | + | ++ | – | – – | – – | + |
| Test | □ | + | + | □ | + | + | + |
| First application | □ | + | – | + | ++ | ++ | + |
| Market introduction | □ | □ | – | ++ | ++ | ++ | – |
| Matureness | + | + | – – | + | – | – | – – |
| Decline | □ | + | – – | + | – – | – – | – – |
| Replacement | + | + | + | + | □ | + | + |

*Notes:*
– – role has conflict with innovation phase
–   role does not match innovation phase
□   combination of role and innovation phase is possible
+   role fits phase
++ role is required in this phase

*Source:*  van Zuylen and Weber (2002)

translate findings of foresight exercises into inputs for formulating policy strategies, and as a basis for reflexive policy-making.

In order to address this challenge, an attempt will be made to combine foresight approaches with elements from strategic planning. Foresight emphasises the forward-looking and participatory element of policy-making that allows taking into account the future perspectives of a wide range of actors and stakeholders. Strategic planning has particular strengths to offer in terms of strategy formulation for dealing with future risks and opportunities, in particular when using the concept of adaptivity as a basis for developing a flexible and forward-looking policy strategy (Eriksson 2003).

The purpose of this approach is to help improve the relevance and impact of the results of forward-looking activities with respect to policy strategy development and to take into account the roles and requirements outlined above. At the same time, the frequently stated optimism regarding the shaping power of foresight is put into question, and instead a more cautious interpretation of its findings for forward-looking policy-making is suggested.

## Foresight – Recent Developments and Deficits

Over the last ten to fifteen years, forward-looking approaches under the headline of 'foresight' have acquired a prominent role in policy-making, in particular not only in science and technology policy (Gavigan 2002, Tübke et al. 2001), but also in relation to sustainability and other long-term, risk-prone issues. In the early years of foresight, mainly Delphi methods were applied to assess the development potential and the competitive positions in different areas of science and technology. In recent years, participatory and panel-based approaches have become more common, not the least to better capture the social and economic aspects related to future changes in science and technology (see Georghiou 2001). Generally speaking, foresight processes represent a mechanism with which to deal systematically with future risks, opportunities and options by drawing on a broad range of future expectations and by involving an equally broad range of actors in a participatory process. It is applied with respect to emerging developments in science and technology or socio-economic developments likely to exert an impact and 'pull' on scientific–technological research and development. In some countries, foresight has become a widely used tool to support S&T policy-making, leading to the establishment of a forward-looking political and governance culture (Gavigan 2001).

There are several different types of foresight, each aiming at different purposes. A first basic distinction refers to the exploratory or normative nature of forward-looking activities. Exploratory approaches tend to be used to identify new emerging developments and resulting risks and opportunities that open up new issues and agendas for action. They start from the present and 'explore' the range of possible development paths. In contrast to forecasting, however, exploratory foresight emphasises the multitude of possible development paths resulting from the interaction between society and scientific–technological opportunities.

Normative approaches start with one or several images of the future in order to assess them along different dimensions and to identify the steps and requirements to realise them. Often, a desirable image of the future is developed and taken as a starting point, but also 'doomsday' scenarios can be found, which are confronted with more desirable futures. As such, normative foresight processes serve to negotiate societal goals and visions related to science, technology and society.

In practice, most foresight processes that have been realised over the past years combine both exploratory and normative elements, using a range of more or less formalised methodologies (Gavigan et al. 2001).

In spite of the variety of possibilities, a number of general trends in foresight can be observed.

- First of all, it has moved away from a pure focus on science and technology that dominated the scene until the early to mid-1990s to an incorporation of first market and then also increasingly social considerations. Broadening the scope of foresight in this way can be interpreted as a reflection of the abandonment of linear models of technological change and the adoption of a systemic understanding of socio-technical change.
- Secondly, foresight has become an increasingly participatory activity. Initially, foresight activities were mainly based on S&T expert opinion, but in line with broadening the scope of foresight, the notion of expert has undergone a re-definition. With respect to participation, one can observe similar developments in technology assessment where the growing prominence of social, economic, environmental and ethical concerns related to scientific and technological developments has led to a strengthening of participatory and constructive approaches (Decker and Ladikas 2004, Joss and Bellucci 2002). Here, the aim is to negotiate consensus on risks and opportunities or at least achieve transparency about conflicting viewpoints to contribute to a normative debate on desirable future development paths.
- Thirdly, we can see today a strong emphasis on and belief in the contribution of foresight activities to shaping rather than predicting the future. The initial Delphi exercises were still strongly influenced by the

linear idea that the consensus achieved in Delphi could serve as a forecast and thus as a foundation for taking preparatory actions. Today, by bringing together in a foresight process not only experts, but in particular also decision-makers from research, industry, policy-making and society, a shared understanding of current problems, goals and emerging development options is expected to emerge among those actors that have an important role to play in shaping the future. This converging understanding of the issues at play is expected to contribute to improving implicitly the coherence of the distributed decisions of these actors, in line with the shared mental framework developed. In other words, the future is shaped by aligning expectations and thus creating a self-fulfilling prophecy. These so-called 'process outputs' are in the meantime often regarded as more important than the actual 'substantive outputs' like reports and websites.[5]

In this sense, foresight processes provide a mechanism for collecting and focusing vague future expectations, and for developing shared views of individual and collective actions to take. Moreover, they also serve as a means in fact to realise the expectations on which they build by influencing agenda-setting and decision-making. However, although only very few impact assessments of foresight exercises have been conducted so far, their actual and traceable influence on decision-making seems to vary to a great extent. In some cases (such as the UK Foresight Mark I), the influence was quite significant because priority-setting in RTD policy was directly influenced by its results, but in hindsight this must be regarded as a rather blunt impact. In many other cases, the impact chains are difficult to trace, because the influence on participants' mindsets and decisions is hard to observe, as well as the influence on the wider public debates.

Foresight, as it is practised today, also shows a number of shortcomings that need to be mentioned:

- While the optimism as regards the shaping power of foresight exercises is at least founded in some qualitative evidence, there are serious doubts about whether the influence of foresight really contributes to moving in a more sustainable direction. Several critical questions can be raised with respect to the biases brought in by the foresight process itself: can we really trust our expectations, or the expectations raised in a foresight exercise? How can individual actors and policy-makers in particular protect themselves against the fallacies of false promises and over-optimistic expectations expressed and brought to the fore in a foresight exercise? Should we not be more precautionary when aiming at seemingly desirable scenarios? It is commonly known that socio-technical change is tied to a wide range of uncertainties and ambiguities that can not be anticipated. While on the one hand (over-) optimistic expectations may be important to increase the momentum of a topic in public or political discourse, a naïve belief in these expectations may lead to a misallocation of resources and create deep disappointments at a later stage.

- A second main shortcoming of foresight relates to the 'impressionistic' nature of many foresight exercises, where workshops and expert panels are taken as the main source of information for constructing scenarios. The findings run the risk of being insufficiently rooted in a scientific base, where first the best available and often diverging sources of knowledge ought to be brought together in an explicit way. Consolidated integration of retrospective and prospective scientific methods (such as modelling) and participatory processes and interactions would probably help enhance the scientific credibility of foresight results.

- Thirdly, foresight is increasingly used as a basis on which to build coherent and co-ordinated strategic agendas for action, both in the public and the private sector. Whereas foresight processes have developed into quite sophisticated and well thought-through activities, the subsequent processes of strategy development still lack a similar level of sophistication, for instance in terms of deriving basic strategies for dealing with the opportunities, risks and unexpected changes that have been identified in the context of foresight exercises.

Both the first and the third shortcoming could be addressed by building on insights from strategic planning. This is in particular the case as regards the dilemma between the need to keep future options open in order to be able to adapt swiftly to changing circumstances on the one hand (adaptive strategies) and the willingness to actively shape the future on the other (proactive strategies).

**Adaptive Planning – Moving Towards Exploratory Scenarios and Policy Portfolios**

Strategic planning has a history as long as foresight. Moreover, both Delphi approaches and strategic planning have a common root in military strategic analysis. However, over the past twenty years the interactions between these two schools of thought have been rather weak. Similar to foresight, strategic planning has undergone significant changes over the past years. The often criticised top-down planning paradigm has given way to a perspective that stresses the notion of adaptivity ('adaptive planning') (Walker et al. 2001).

The basic philosophy behind adaptive planning consists of deferring actions and choices as long as possible, that is, until more knowledge is available, in order to cope with uncertainty. Keeping options open obviously comes with a cost, namely to continue developing alternative options (for instance technologies) in parallel until a choice between them is effectively made.

Adaptive planning can be interpreted as an attempt to circumvent the Collingridge dilemma (Collingridge 1980): making choices about the directions of new emerging technological options is very difficult in the early stages of development, because we know too little about their advantages and disadvantages, costs, opportunities and risks. However, once we know enough about them to make informed choices, they have already become so entrenched that effective choices are no longer possible. Adaptive planning aims to devise strategies to keep open and advance options but without making definitive choices that would entail too early and uninformed entrenchment. In theory, these choices should only be made once more is known about the technology itself or about the context in its likely context of use. Proponents of science and technology studies (STS) tend to be sceptical about adaptive planning, because – as they would argue – the actual implementation of technology in its final context of use is vital to understanding modes of usage and impacts. As a consequence, adaptive planning is regarded at best as a partial solution to the Collingridge dilemma. Still, experimental and learning approaches (such as strategic niche management see Hoogma et al. 2002 and Weber et al. 1999) have been suggested within STS that should help one learn about and shape technology in an adaptive manner.

The classical approach to adaptive planning is based on a staged development process with key decision points to confirm or reject a development trajectory depending on the progress made and the changes in context. More recently, adaptive planning approaches have emphasised the need to combine scenario development to capture a wide range of possible future contexts with the maintenance of a set or portfolio of real options.[6] It has thus developed into a much more flexible tool for supporting strategic decision-making, by applying principles of continuous monitoring and decision-making (Eriksson 2003). The portfolio-based approach is particularly well-suited for dealing with contexts that are in themselves characterised by adaptive strategies of other actors.[7]

Socio-technical scenarios are thus a first important building block for operationalising the principles of adaptive planning. They serve to capture the range of possible futures in which the addressee might be operating and which he can partly influence. In other words, scenario development serves in the first instance to make different possible future contexts for action explicit, in scientific–technological and economic as well as in socio-political and cultural terms. For the purposes of adaptive planning, socio-technical scenarios should be neither purely exploratory nor purely normative. In fact, it is important that they represent a mixture of desirable and undesirable elements in order to be able to derive non-trivial conclusions.

Usually exploratory scenarios are taken as a starting point for adaptive planning exercises. However, from a policy perspective, exploratory scenarios alone are not sufficient as a basis for policy strategies. Different exploratory scenarios just describe how different future worlds might look. While for instance a national government may be able to exert an influence on the course of future events, it is by no means in any position to determine what the future will look like. It only has rather limited power to shape the future; its room for manoeuvre is restricted by the extent to which the exploratory scenarios developed are driven by exogenous factors. The normative dimension comes into play when assessing and selecting different decision options that would allow these – largely exogenously driven – exploratory scenarios to be influenced in a direction that could be regarded as desirable, even if the actual influence of these decisions may be rather limited. Thus, the exploratory scenario approach needs to be combined with a normative element in order to realise future oriented policy strategies that are in line with major societal objectives (such as sustainable development).

The notion of portfolios of real options is the second main building block considered here. Initially the notion of portfolios of options was introduced in finance and described a set of financial options that allows the investor to minimise (or hedge) financial risks. Sophisticated models have been developed to deal with portfolio optimisation. In the world of research and innovation, modelling approaches are also tested but real options cannot be easily captured in financial terms (Schauer 2005).

The key argument behind maintaining a portfolio of real options can be best explained by a simple question: 'What preparatory and precautionary actions can be taken today to make sure that an actor can adapt to unexpected adverse conditions and exploit unexpected upcoming opportunities tomorrow?' This approach admits that our possibilities to shape the future are constrained to a large extent by developments outside of our scope, and that we must be able to adapt to these. It implies that a good portfolio of real options is characterised by two main features. First of all, there are options that are helpful under the conditions of all scenarios considered. These 'robust' options represent the quick gains from a portfolio-oriented scenario analysis. In other words, robust policies are those that do well under the conditions of all scenarios considered. Secondly, policy options exist that enable adaptivity, that is, they are meant to maintain the ability to exploit upcoming opportunities rapidly or to cope swiftly with major unexpected risks. This can be achieved by maintaining an appropriate portfolio of options and by developing options that are flexible and adapt on their own.

The notion of a robust and adaptive portfolio of options can be applied to both technologies and policies. Looking first at technologies, the approach suggests maintaining two types of options, namely (1) options that would be beneficial under all circumstances in the different scenarios ('robust technologies'), and (2) options that would allow us to react swiftly to unexpected events or different courses of development than we had initially expected ('adaptive technologies'). In concrete terms, for instance, this approach is compatible with policy recommendations to develop competencies in generic technologies that are likely to be applied in a wide range of sectors. The relative importance of these sectors may differ across scenarios. Obviously, although generic technologies are characterised by a certain degree of robustness and adaptivity, they are usually not sufficient to ensure the level of adaptivity needed. Advancing additional technological options may thus be necessary. The history of renewable and energy-saving technologies can serve as an example of the benefits of an adaptive technology portfolio. After the first oil crisis the introduction of alternative and efficient energy technologies was promoted, but it took several years to make some of the options in question (such as heat pumps, combined heat and power generation, solar collectors, and so on) technologically and economically viable. In those countries where these technologies had already been developed early on, their uptake took place much faster and thus facilitated the adaptation to the scarcity and high price of fossil fuels.

In terms of research and technology policy, adaptivity can be achieved by keeping a fairly broad range of research programmes and activities in order to be able to build on the acquired competencies if a research field turns out to 'take off' or if changing circumstances require adapting and changing course rather swiftly. Rather than focusing on a very restricted set of research and technology priorities (which is currently the dominant argument in the context of competitiveness policies), a portfolio-based and risk-averse research and technology policy strategy would aim at advancing a broader set of options in a kind of 'waitstate' and support technologies that are inherently adaptive. Obviously, as it is not possible to keep all options open, it is still necessary to prioritize,[8] but the notion of portfolios of real options should be taken into account as an additional building block for designing strategies to cope with the uncertainties, risks and opportunities inherent in different future scenarios.

The timing of exerting policy options is an important aspect of a portfolio-based policy approach because of the criticality of the timing for the impact of a decision. We know from evolutionary and sociological S&T policy studies that there are 'windows of opportunity' when exerting an option (for instance starting a major R&D programme to give a new emerging technology area a boost) can have a particularly strong impact because it allows self-reinforcing processes of change to operate effectively and thus makes a policy strategy effective with minimum resources (Erdmann 2005). Portfolio analysis is not a purely analytical task, but needs to refer to the goals and objectives of the addressee(s). Real options are assessed in terms of the impact they are likely to have on these objectives and under the conditions of the different scenarios. Portfolio thinking is useful when there is widespread agreement on the objectives to pursue because it allows discussing the options for moving as closely as possible to the desired state of the future, even if the course of events makes it very unlikely that it will ever be reached. A normative vision of the future may then still serve as an orientation for choosing options of a portfolio that is meant to cope reasonably well with a range of different possible future scenarios. However, there is not necessarily consensus on what the desirable direction of change is. At this point, value judgements and related conflicts regarding the objectives of different actors come into play, and the analysis of the potential impacts of real options under the conditions of different scenarios provides a rational basis for discussing the underlying objectives and values. In both cases, the incorporation of a process of 'iterative goal formulation' in scenario and policy portfolio development is helpful to enhance the reflexivity of decision-making (Voß and Kemp, Introduction to this volume).

The approach of adaptive planning, when using exploratory scenarios in combination with policy portfolios, facilitates striking a reasonable balance between our capabilities and limitations to anticipate the future, our wish to steer in a desirable direction, and the need to adapt to the occurrence of events that we can neither predict nor influence.

**Moving Towards Policy Strategies**

The preceding overview of recent developments and characteristics of foresight and of adaptive planning has shown that these two conceptual tools have the potential to contribute to enhancing the reflexivity of policy-making processes in at least three respects:

- they strengthen the rational basis by capturing often implicit assumptions, expectations and underlying values about the future explicitly in different scenario images and corresponding pathways;
- they make policy strategies more realistic by emphasising the limitations to actively shaping the future, as reflected in the notion of adaptivity and path-dependence in the context of scenario development;
- they support strategic thinking about portfolios of options across different scenarios and during different phases of the policy cycle.

In this sense, foresight and adaptive planning are instruments that facilitate exceeding first-order learning about the impacts of individual instruments (for example by means of conventional evaluation) and enable second-order learning.

# ADAPTIVE FORESIGHT – A METHODOLOGY FOR SCENARIO AND POLICY PORTFOLIO DEVELOPMENT

## Theoretical and Methodological Foundations

The new requirements for policy-making described above underline that more is expected today from policy research than retrospectively analysing and generalising hypotheses as inputs to policy-making. Instead, more attention needs to be paid to devising transparent and constructive methodologies in support of forward-looking policy strategy development. While Voß and Kemp (in this volume) have elaborated on some of the specific requirements with respect to a more reflexive approach to governance, focusing in particular on the issue of sustainable development, the next step needed consists of formulating operational methodologies for putting these principles into practice.

In this section, such a methodology will be presented under the headline of 'adaptive foresight'. It is based on insights from past experiences with foresight methods and socio-technical scenarios, but also reflects principles of adaptive planning and reflexive governance.[9] When geared specifically to the needs of policy-making, these and other tools are often referred to as strategic policy intelligence (SPI, see Box 1). SPI has previously been rather weak in terms of explicitly addressing tasks of systematic policy strategy development. The methodology outlined below aims to fill this gap, and it is illustrated by a few examples where it has already been employed in practice.

Conceptually, the adaptive foresight methodology builds on findings from system approaches in innovation research and from science and technology studies that emphasise the importance of complex mechanisms for the explanation of innovation dynamics. Such a 'complex innovation systems' perspective provides the main elements to be addressed by the methodology (Weber 2005). The most recent developments in innovation research stress the importance of multi-level analysis, covering levels from that of individual actors and networks to the macro-level of national, sectoral or functional innovation systems. Providing an explicit theoretical foundation of the methodology has several advantages: it facilitates the interaction process with the participants of scenario workshops, it allows an explicit interpretation of the findings of the process, and thus contributes to the overall understanding of potential future innovation dynamics and the role of policy interventions in these.

---

BOX 8.1    STRATEGIC POLICY INTELLIGENCE
                 FOR TECHNOLOGY AND INNOVATION
                 POLICY

Over the past twenty years, one could observe a major change in policy-making as well as in policy research, emphasising the need for more strategically oriented inputs as a foundation for policy. Several different approaches that had been employed thus far in a rather isolated way have been brought together under the heading 'strategic policy intelligence' (Tübke et al. 2001). They comprise, for instance, forecasting, foresight, technology assessment, scenario development and other forward-looking approaches. In particular scenario techniques have proven a powerful tool to integrate elements from the aforementioned approaches into consistent visions of and pathways towards the future. Also methodologies to enhance policy learning from past experiences fall under the headline of strategic policy intelligence, for instance by way of systematically evaluating policy programmes, initiatives and institutions or by comparing national practices ('benchmarking'). Strategic policy intelligence is thus expected to support policy-making over the entire policy cycle from agenda-setting to policy learning.

The strategic turn in policy-making implies a major shift in terms of governance, and it raises new requirements with respect to the strategic competencies of policy-makers vis-à-vis other actors in the system. First of all, we are increasingly confronted with a situation, in which the necessary knowledge, competencies and intelligence is distributed across society (Kuhlmann 2001), thus calling for a higher degree of participation in policy decision in order to draw on this distributed intelligence. Therefore, strategic policy intelligence methods tend to employ interactive methods such as expert panels, scenario workshops, citizen conferences and so on, in order to complement conventional analytical methods. In other words, strategic policy intelligence also needs to devise ways of drawing on these distributed competencies.

Secondly, there is a clear need to devise systematic methods to exploit prospective findings for the purposes of policy strategy development. Although strategic policy intelligence is increasingly recognised as important support for policy-making, also with respect to enhancing participation in political decision making, it has not been able to provide the necessary systematic approaches to strategy development thus far. It is in this respect that adaptive foresight is supposed to deliver new insights.

## Looking Back: Problem Definition, System Delimitation and Analysis

Before looking ahead as part of a policy strategy development process, it is necessary to conduct a solid retrospective analysis of the field of investigation, that is, of recent and current developments along the lines of the conceptual framework of complex innovation systems. And even before starting such analytical work, two initial clarifications need to be achieved. First of all, one has to be clear what the focal issue of the strategy development exercise is, that is, the main question or problem that the addressee of an exercise would like to have tackled. In government-led exercises, these focal issues are usually related to societal goals and the (policy) strategies to pursue in order to achieve them. They can be at highly aggregate levels (how can we achieve an overarching transition towards a more sustainable energy supply system?) or more specific to individual sectors and policies (what innovation and technology policy strategies should be pursued in order to contribute to the joint objectives of sustainable mobility and enhancement of the competitiveness of domestic transport technology industries?).

Secondly, the analytical boundaries of the innovation system that determines the evolution of the focal issue need to be clarified. This implies making a distinction between the inside and outside of the system under study, that is, the distinction between the aspects that can be influenced by, for instance, national policy, and those that are outside its scope and thus to be regarded as exogenous factors. This delimitation of the innovation system will be further refined in the course of the scenario-building exercise.

There are several typical elements and aspects that need to be addressed in the course of an innovation system analysis:

- Actors, that is, the entities that exert an influence on processes of innovation, either directly or indirectly. These entities do not necessarily have to be individuals or organisations, but can also be based on looser forms of coordinated behaviour like networks. The set of actors that makes up an innovation system can obviously change over the course of time.

- Decision-making processes and interactions, that is, the objectives, rationales and behaviour of the actors identified, and the processes of interaction by which these decisions are influenced.
- Structures, that is, an analysis of the structural characteristics of the system and their transformation. This includes institutional and organisational changes like, for instance, not only a liberalisation of relevant markets or a financial crisis, but also major technological developments, patterns of networking or changes of socio-technical regime.
- Socio-technical knowledge base, that is, the entirety of the distributed knowledge that is available to the different actors. Apart from describing the capabilities and competencies that exist in an innovation system, the knowledge-base also comprises information about the performance and the potential of new technologies and innovations. Moreover, it may be used to anticipate impacts and generate future visions and *Leitbilder*.

Apart from describing these changing patterns in actors, interactions, structures and knowledge of an innovation system, it is also important to understand the underlying system dynamics in terms of interdependencies between the different levels of analysis (for example, between actors and structures). Currently, mechanisms from complex systems research are increasingly tested to capture basic principles of innovation system dynamics (Fischer and Fröhlich 2001), but one must admit that this is an area in which much research work still has to be done.

In methodological terms, this first phase is usually based on a combination of analytical desk research to collect important background information and interactive workshops to define the focal issue and interpret them with respect to key mechanisms determining system change.

**Looking Ahead: Combining Exploratory and Normative Elements**

The forward-looking step consists of three main parts, namely an exploratory part, a specification part and a normative part. The exploratory part aims to define different possible future scenarios which serve as frames for further specification and also for adjusting the scenarios according to the normative objectives and goals.

Both endogenous and exogenous developments (that is, the ones from within the system and from outside) are taken into account as possible factors of influence that are likely to shape the future evolution of the system under study.[10]

After collecting the range of factors of influence, an analysis of current trends and possible trend breaks can be performed in order to differentiate between factors that are likely to be stable and others that are still open to evolve in qualitatively new ways. Especially the latter ones are useful to differentiate one scenario from another. Such trends and trend breaks can be of a technological as well as of a socio-economic nature.

Trends and trend breaks are the basic material from which to develop scenarios. Here, a variety of methods is available, ranging from 'bottom-up' methods of constructing and clustering storylines into scenarios to 'top-down' methods that concentrate on selected dominant factors of influence, possibly supported by cross-impact analysis, Delphi methods or simulations to strengthen the credibility of results. However, most of these methods rely in the end on expert or stakeholder judgement, thus reflecting these actors' implicit theories about impact chains.

What is essential for these scenarios is that they are plausible, multifaceted and challenging. They must be regarded as tools to stimulate thinking about potential future developments rather than as predictions of the future. Moreover, the distinction between endogenous and exogenous factors of influence helps identify where the opportunities and limitations for action are for the main actors addressed, that is, for instance a national government. Trends and trend breaks also point implicitly to important decision options of the different actors, that is, the strategic moves they can make. Games (*Planspiele*) are a tool by which these implicit strategic options can be made explicit.

When the basic scenarios are defined, they represent different frameworks that still leave much room for further specification. In fact, they define a corridor of actions that needs to be refined and related to the focal issue under investigation. As guidance for how to describe such framework scenarios, the main types of factors of influence can be taken as a starting point. Typically, categories such as technologies, producers, users, policy and so on, are defined by the participants, that is, categories that can easily be related to actors' strategies.

The normative dimension is addressed in the subsequent stage. At this point, goals and values of the different actors come into play (see also Box 2). A possible starting point is therefore a debate on visions related to the focal issue of the exercise. This is useful in order to clarify shared (or diverging) policy and/or societal goals, ambitions and underlying values of the actors and stakeholders involved. A second element is related to the potential future risks and opportunities tied to the focal issue of the exercise.

Both elements serve in the end to agree on the dimensions along which the exploratory scenarios are to be assessed. In many current cases, sustainable development is taken as a guiding vision that needs to be operationalised in terms of different assessment dimensions, for instance along the lines of

---

**BOX 8.2    THE FUTURE OF FREIGHT TRANSPORT IN AUSTRIA: OVERCOMING BARRIERS BETWEEN POLITICAL ADMINISTRATIONS**

In a project that deals with the future of freight transport in Austria, several different, and sometimes even contradictory, policy objectives had to be taken into account to derive insights into opportunities for defining the future strategy for transport technology and innovation policy. Transport policy objectives as well as environmental and industrial policy considerations had to be brought to bear for the conceptualisation of future policy initiatives and strategies. Although, for instance, transport and technology policy were hosted in the same ministry, the level of cooperation between the respective Directorates General was only weak. Clarifying these objectives was thus crucial for incorporating them in suggestions for new technology policy initiatives as well as for the success of the entire exercise (Whitelegg 2005, Weber et al. 2002).

---

the pattern developed by the German Helmholtz Society (Coenen and Grunwald 2003).

When assessing the scenarios along these main dimensions, it would be unrealistic to expect clear-cut statements on which is the better or the worse scenario from the perspective of sustainable development. First of all, the scenarios are designed in a way so as to avoid scenarios that are simply 'good' or 'bad'; on the contrary, multi-faceted scenarios are regarded as most productive. Moreover, in most cases the level of uncertainty of impacts is such that it will at best allow identifying 'critical issues' that require the attention of policy-makers or could potentially have significant impacts on the focal issue (Weber et al. 2004b). These tend to be issues which require additional research to understand potential impacts in the future better. In other words, the assessment serves to identify potential but uncertain levers for shaping future development in a more desirable direction.

The basic argument behind this approach is that, to a large extent, the framework scenarios determine the future evolution of the focal issue. However, within a corridor they define, there is still room for manoeuvre and adjustment in a direction that converges with the negotiated goals and objectives.

The assessment and subsequent identification of critical issues opens up the opportunity to modify the scenarios developed towards best possible variants (what could be best achieved within each of the framework scenarios?), but it is not a necessary condition for the subsequent backcasting and portfolio analysis.

Methodologically, this step is largely based on interactive and creative methods, but can at least in principle be supported by computer tools, forecasts and modelling.

### Pathways Towards the Future: Multiple Backcasting

Conventional backcasting approaches take a single and desirable image of the future as their starting point (for example, Vergragt 2000). While this is a valid method for clarifying necessary steps towards a desirable future, it underrates the limitations imposed on the ability to shape a desired future, and in particular the dependence on decisions outside of one's own control. In order to make use of backcasting in a more realistic, strategy-oriented manner, its application to each of the scenarios developed is regarded as more helpful ('multiple backcasting').

In essence, backcasting looks at the steps necessary to achieve a specific scenario. This requires analysing barriers and incompatibilities with which the realisation of a scenario may be confronted over the course of time. Key decisions and bifurcations need to be identified, and the compatibility of, for instance, technologies, values and actors' interests need to be assessed as a first consistency check.

By staging the pathways that lead to the realisation of different scenarios, it is possible to identify needs for action and intervention that can serve as important inputs to the subsequent portfolio analysis. In principle, backcasting the scenario pathways in stages also allows for discussion of the appropriate timing of policy and other measures, for instance, in terms of 'windows of opportunity' for introducing a new technology or starting a policy initiative. By developing consistent pathways, the backcasting exercise represents a second level of testing the credibility of a scenario.

Methodologically, backcasting tends to rely on qualitative methods in order to capture the full range of aspects that can potentially come into play in the course of a scenario pathway. However, in particular, quantitative tools can also support consistency checks.

### Portfolio Analysis: Robust and Adaptive Policy Options

So far, individual scenarios were developed, refined and analysed. Each of the scenarios and pathways can be characterised in terms of technologies

---

**BOX 8.3  WOOD–PLASTIC COMPOSITES, FIBRE COMPOSITES AND BIOPOLYMERS FROM RENEWABLE RESOURCES – SCENARIO DEVELOPMENT OF ADAPTIVE POLICIES**

In order to support the medium- to long-term strategy development of a research programme on 'The Factory of Tomorrow' (see also Späth et al., Chapter 14 in this volume), a scenario-building exercise has been implemented for the area of wood–plastic composites, fibre composites and biopolymers from renewable resources (see Weber et al. 2004b). The emphasis was put on the policy options on the basis of which Austrian technology and innovation policy could influence the future evolution of this transition field towards more sustainable production systems. As the ability to shape the evolution of this field from within a rather small policy area in a small country like Austria are comparatively limited, policy options were explored within the context of different framework scenarios that were largely driven by developments outside of the reach of Austrian technology and innovation policy. By using this approach, the limits to the political shaping of the future were explicitly taken into account, and the emphasis was rather put on the need to adapt to and prepare for scenarios that are driven by external factors, and not the least also international and European developments.

---

and policies that have been realised. The options delivered by the scenarios have also been assessed with respect to our focal issue.

From today's perspective, portfolio analysis then looks across different scenarios to assess and select those technology options and corresponding policies that promise to be either robust or adaptive (or both). In other words, robust options are fairly easy to identify, because they are positively assessed in all or most scenarios. Adaptive options have been identified as part of a normative stage of scenario development when possibilities are sought to move the basic scenario in a more desirable direction. They are thus either crucial for avoiding major negative impacts or for exploiting specific opportunities in a single scenario. These kinds of insights should then serve as input for today's policy-makers to prioritize, for instance, emerging technologies and design policies correspondingly.

Of particular interest are technologies that embody characteristics of both robustness and adaptivity, that is, in general terms they are beneficial in all scenarios, but their specific shape depends on the conditions of the respective scenarios. In fact, many technologies tend to have a double-edged character, because they can be beneficial under certain circumstances and detrimental under others. What kind of impact they will have depends on the context of use and often on politically defined framework conditions. Embedded systems, to take an example from the information and telecommunication technologies, are expected to have a very positive impact within an optimistic information society scenario. The same technology, however, can be abused in a 'big brother' type of scenario when used for invading the privacy of individuals.

The matter is further complicated by the fact that policy options can have an impact at different levels. For instance, they can refer to the promotion of individual technologies (for example an R&D programme) as well as to the structural settings of the innovation systems (such as the liberalisation of energy supply). Moreover, the impact of policies depends on their time of implementation.

These examples show that the analysis of portfolios of real options is far from easy and that technological options and policy options are closely intertwined. However, the basic principle still holds that promising technology and policy portfolios are composed of options that promise to have at least the potential to help improve the focal issue in all scenarios (robust options) and either avoid major problems or help exploit opportunities in some selected scenarios (adaptive options).

Methodologically, interactive methods can be used to discuss different options from a range of viewpoints. In order to come up with new and fresh ideas for policy options, comparative analysis of other countries' practices can be instructive. Finally, while they are by far less sophisticated than in financial portfolio analysis, modelling tools are being developed that promise to be applicable also to real options in quantitative terms, for instance for analysing research and technology portfolios (Schauer 2005).

## Policy Implementation and Learning: Monitoring, Shaping and Adjusting to the Future

Suggesting policy options and portfolios is just an input to actual policy design and implementation. In other words, so far we have been mainly discussing the early phases of the policy process. The implementation of policies, as well as the learning processes that take place between design and implementation, represent the wider framework in which adaptive foresight processes are situated. Moreover, emphasis has been on the strategy level, where the basic orientations and guidelines for policy are defined to trigger and frame more specific initiatives. In practice, however, policy design and implementation rely on concrete actions and initiatives, often even at local level.

If the principles behind adaptive foresight are to be effective, they need to be closely tied not only to policy design, but also to policy implementation and learning, at the strategic as well as at the local level. More specifically, the experiences made in the course of local implementation need to be monitored and fed back to strategy development.

In other words, adaptive foresight should be interpreted as part of a broader continuous learning process that comprises the implementation and evaluation of specific policy measures as well as monitoring relevant developments in policy at large.

Strategy development, policy design, implementation and learning should thus not be understood as distinctly separate phases but rather as a continuous process of mutual adjustment. This adjustment refers to goals and objectives, to the identification of new socio-technical options, to the growing knowledge and understanding of their impacts, to the design of new types of policy options and to their integration into portfolios.

Within such a comprehensive setting, the impact of guiding policy strategies should nevertheless not be underestimated, in particular because public policy strategies fulfil an orienting function for many private actors as well, and in the best case play an implicit coordinating function in their decision-making.

One of the main difficulties of this continuous process consists of the fact that all actors involved can recur to strategic and adaptive (and thus interdependent) behaviour. This is why issues of policy coordination – both between different policy areas and between public and private actors – have started to play such an important role in policy-making.

In practice, processes of scenario developments and portfolio analysis will nevertheless hardly be conducted on a continuous basis but rather be repeated every few years, for instance in line with an update of the overall technology and innovation policy strategy. The practical tools and methods are available based on many years of experience with foresight, adaptive planning, evaluation and monitoring; what is still missing is the integration of these methods in a continuous and long-term strategy development process.

## CONCLUSIONS: A (SELF-)CRITICAL ASSESSMENT

The purpose of this chapter has been to introduce an operational methodological proposal of how reflexive governance principles can be implemented

---

BOX 8.4   THE IMPACT OF ICT ON TRANSPORT
AND MOBILITY – DEVELOPING
A PORTFOLIO OF ROBUST AND
ADAPTIVE POLICY OPTIONS

The impact of ICT on transport and mobility (ICTRANS) is a scenario development exercise that aims to explore in a qualitative
way policy options at the European level to enhance the impact
that the use of ICTs could have on the volume, modal choices and
efficiency of mobility service provision in the realms of living,
working and producing (Wagner et al. 2004). As the potential
impacts of ICT on mobility are subject to a high degree of uncertainty and dependent on the future of the information society in
general, the scenarios developed had to span a wide spectrum of
possible futures. Moreover, potential impact chains of ICT use on
transport and mobility had to be identified before the actual exploration of future impacts could be implemented. The role of different
policy options for shifting impacts in a more sustainable direction
could then be explored under the conditions of the different scenarios. Some options clearly turned out to be 'robust' in the sense
of being helpful in all scenarios, while others could be identified as
being 'adaptive' in the sense of being necessary to prevent negative impacts in one specific scenario or to maintain the ability to
exploit upcoming opportunities specific to that scenario.

---

at the level of policy strategy development. Adaptive foresight, as suggested
here, is based on a combination of participatory foresight processes, socio-
technical scenario building and policy portfolio development. More
specifically, the approach is geared towards policy strategy development in
the area of research, technology and innovation policy. To assess whether
this objective has been met, the five main requirements of reflexive governance as formulated by Voß and Kemp (in this volume) will be used to discuss
the pros and cons of the approach presented.

**Integrated Trans-disciplinary Knowledge Production**

Based on a participatory process, the methodology is designed to allow for
the incorporation of a variety of perspectives and attitudes of experts and
stakeholders, and as such enables inter-disciplinary and trans-disciplinary
knowledge production. This also holds true with respect to expectations,

goals and values, due to the incorporation of normative elements in the methodology.

A systems language is employed in order to integrate the diversity of theoretical and practical insights. The weakness of the systems language, which is often criticised for having little theoretical value in itself, thus turns out to be a major advantage by providing a platform for knowledge integration across disciplinary boundaries as well as between research and practice.

In the context of policy-making, additional boundaries between domains of knowledge production need to be taken into account. One of the main barriers to developing interdisciplinary and trans-disciplinary solutions consists of the lack of policy coordination between different policy departments. Also in this respect, the methodology suggested can serve as a tool for facilitating cross-departmental knowledge production.

### Anticipation of Long-term Systems Effects of Action Strategies

In general terms, the adaptive foresight methodology can be applied for different time horizons. It is certainly possible to use it for anticipating long-term system changes as part of the scenario and policy portfolio development process. Impact assessments, especially of long-term impacts, can in principle be conducted within the context of each individual scenario, but the high degree of uncertainty associated with these assessments calls for a very cautious interpretation. This observation underlines the importance of a portfolio-based approach, which aims to avoid structural lock-ins, maintain a range of options and ensure a high degree of flexibility to react to unexpected developments and impacts.

A major difficulty with respect to anticipation of long-term effects must be seen in the impossibility to anticipate the strategic behaviour of other actors that – in principle – would have to be taken into account in order to define one's own strategy. While this sounds straightforward in theory, it is extremely difficult to achieve in practice. The methodology proposed does not claim to meet this requirement fully, but at least acknowledges the strategic behaviour of other actors. Potentially, current developments in agent-based simulation will open up new possibilities to take into account the strategic behaviour of several actors simultaneously.

### Adaptivity of Strategies and Institutions

Adaptivity is one of the key concepts underlying the proposed methodology. The notions of robust and adaptive policies and of policy portfolios interrelate conventional scenario development and policy strategy development. Policy decisions of an individual actor may play an important role in shaping future scenarios in a particular field, but it is by no means the only or most decisive force. It is often necessary to adapt to developments brought about by exogenous events, by other actors' strategies, by new technological opportunities and in particular by international developments. A continuous policy learning process is vital for monitoring such exogenous developments, as well as the impacts of any policy measures taken. Adaptive foresight processes as part of such a learning process are thus a means to enable decision-makers to think through strategies and options that are both adaptive and proactive.

Adaptivity is not just a matter of specific policy measures and portfolios, but also of institutional and structural settings. Therefore, the notion of 'policy measures' as employed here should be interpreted as also comprising measures that have a structural and institutional impact, for example by creating new organisations or introducing major structural reforms.

### Iterative Participatory Goal Formulation

Adaptive foresight is meant in the first instance as a support to policy, but in line with the current perception that participation is increasingly important for effective governance of long-term and uncertain issues. This support relies on the involvement of a broad range of stakeholders. Wide participation is even crucial for long-term, sustainability-oriented issues, not the least in order to ensure public support for issues beyond the short-term agendas. The normative phase of the methodology facilitates addressing the goals and values of the participants. The claim for making this process a continuous or at least iterative activity would then ensure that these goals are recurrently put into question, based on the new scientific and policy insights gained in the meantime. Access to reliable quality information and the existence of an effective monitoring system thus turn out to be crucial for this dimension of reflexivity as well. The participants in such a process may then serve as a sounding board and quality check for the monitoring results to adjust policies as well as goals. The methodology can thus be regarded as a participatory learning space that brings together experiences from several different areas, ranging from individual impacts of past policies via external and technological developments to new scientific insights on impacts and societal goals.

### Interactive Strategy Development

The existence of a joint space where different actors come together to discuss scenarios, goals and policy options can be regarded as a soft co-ordination mechanism of their heterogeneous strategies. By debating problem perceptions, long-term expectations, scenarios and pathways, a transparent, though sometimes diverging view on different futures is reached that serves as a basis for discussing strategic needs and activities. This does not necessarily lead to consensus about well-orchestrated joint strategies, but the individual strategies get embedded in wider pictures that comprise a consolidated understanding of other actors' strategies. At best, coalitions are built that can move joint agendas forward. A major benefit could be achieved if adaptive foresight processes were also used beyond the reach of individual policy areas and would thus contribute to a better coordination between them, for instance as an important stepping stone towards making sustainability a guiding principle across policy areas

## NOTES

1. The author would also like to thank Dierk Bauknecht and Jan-Peter Voß for constructive comments on draft versions of this contribution.
2. For more details see the article by Jacobsson and Johnson (2000) on functional innovation systems. More specifically, the conceptual framework that underlies the arguments raised here is elaborated in Weber (2005) under the heading 'complex innovation systems'. It specifies the interactions between policy-making processes on the one hand and innovation processes on the other, as well as the resulting dynamics.
3. See Tübke et al. (2001) for a review.
4. See also Renn (2002) who argues with respect to foresight processes that mainly 'epistemological' discourses, that is, debates about 'potential opportunities and risks based on a common vision and the likely developments that we can foresee without relying on pure speculation', should be conducted at the EU level, whereas debates about assessments of trade-offs and values require stronger participation from the bottom up and taking local specificities into consideration. However, we should also be aware that this argument may have to be differentiated with respect to different problem areas, because in a highly internationalised or Europeanised field (such as climate change or aeronautics, genetic technology), the appropriate level for assessment and value discourses may well be at these higher levels.
5. Obviously, there are also certain types of foresight exercises that have a less pro-active intention by concentrating only on the identification of future challenges and issues rather than aiming at solutions.
6. The term 'real options' is used to stress their difference from financial options in which portfolio management has become a standard practice.
7. The concept of real options is usually applied with respect to a specific actor or addressee who has the choice between different options. It is important to be very clear about the addressee of an adaptive planning activity and about the scope of his or her decision options because this determines what is to be regarded as an endogenous or an exogenous variable, that is, as a factor he/she can or cannot influence. In most policy-oriented exercises, this addressee can be society at large, but in more operational terms it is usually a public agent like a ministry or a regional government.
8. Priority-setting in research and technology policy has become a major issue in most European countries, both due to concerns about global competitiveness and in response to the realisation of the European Research Area. Transparent processes, heuristics and rationales for setting priorities are still widely absent from the policy debates, but building blocks are currently being developed (Weber et al. 2004a).
9. See also Elzen et al. (2005) on socio-technical scenarios and their application to the evo-

lution of different large technical systems. However, they mainly applied the scenario method for purely experimental purposes and did not link them up with actual policy-making processes.
10. The boundaries between the inside and the outside of a system do not need to be stable but can change in the course of a scenario, thus also influencing the range and the scope of options for the actors considered.

# REFERENCES

Balzer, I. and M. Wächter, (eds.) (2002), *Sozialökologische Forschung. Ergebnisse der Sondierungsprojekte aus dem BMBF-Förderschwerpunk*, München: Ökom.
Coenen, R. and A. Grunwald, (eds) (2003), *Nachhaltigkeitsprobleme in Deutschland. Analyse und Strategien*, Berlin: Sigma.
Collingridge, D. (1980), *The Social Control of Technology*, London: Pinter.
Decker, M. and M. Ladikas, (eds) (2004), *Bridges between Science, Society and Policy Technology Assessment – Methods and Impacts*, Berlin: Springer.
Elzen, B., U. Jørgensen, K.H. Sørensen and O. Thomassen (2001), 'Towards an interactive technology policy – implications from the social shaping of mobility and transport policies for a new technology policy paradigm', final report to the European Commission from the INTEPOL Project (SOE1-CT97-1057), Enschede: University of Twente.
Elzen, B., F. Geels, P. Hofman and K. Green (2005), 'Socio-technical scenarios as a tool for transition policy: an example from the traffic and transport domain', in B. Elzen, F. Geels and K. Green (eds), *System Innovation and the Transition to Sustainability: Theory, Evidence and Policy*, Cheltenham UK and Northampton, MA, USA: Edward Elgar.
Erdmann, G. (2005), 'Innovation, Time and Sustainability', in K.M. Weber and J. Hemmelskamp (eds) (2005), *Towards Environmental Innovation Systems*, Heidelberg: Springer/Physica, pp. 193–204.
Eriksson, E.A. (2003), 'Scenario-based methodologies for strategy development and management of change', in M.-O. Olsson and G. Sjöstedt (eds), *Systems Approaches and Their Application: Examples from Sweden*, Dordrecht: Kluwer.
EC (2001), 'European governance. A White Paper', COM(2001) 428 final, Brussels: European Commission.
Fischer, M.M. and J. Fröhlich (eds) (2001), *Knowledge, Complexity and Innovation Systems*, Berlin: Springer.
Funtowicz, S. and J. Ravetz (1993), 'Science for the post-normal age', *Futures*, **25**, 735–55.
Gavigan, J. (2001), 'Panorama de la Prospective en Europa. Principios y Visión General por Países', *Economia Industrial*, **341**, 107–18.
Gavigan, J. (ed) (2002), 'The role of foresight in the selection of research policy priorities', conference proceedings, EUR 20406, IPTS: Sevilla.
Gavigan, J.P., F. Scapolo, M. Keenan, I. Miles, F. Farhi, D. Lecoq, D. Capriati and T. Di Bartolomeo (2001), 'A Practical Guide to Regional Foresight', final report of the FOREN Project, EUR 20128 EN, Sevilla: IPTS.
Georghiou, L. (2001), 'Third generation foresight: integrating the socio-economic dimension', in 'Technology Foresight – the approach to and potential for New Technology Foresight', conference proceedings, NISTEP research material 77.

Gibbons, M., C. Limoges, H. Nowotny, S. Schwartzman, P. Scott and M.P. Trow (1994), *The New Production of Knowledge. The Dynamics of Science and Research in Contemporary Societies*, London: Sage.

Hoogma, R., R. Kemp, J. Schot and B. Truffer (2002), *Experimenting for Sustainable Transport. The Approach of Strategic Niche Management*, London: Spon Press.

Jacobsson, S. and A. Johnson (2000), 'The diffusion of renewable energy technology: an analytical framework and issues for research', *Energy Policy*, **28**, 625–40.

Joss, S. and S. Bellucci (eds) (2002), *Participatory Technology Assessment. European Perspectives*, London: CSD.

Kemp, R. and J. Rotmans (2005), 'The management of the co-evolution of technical, environmental and social systems', in K.M. Weber and J. Hemmelskamp (eds) (2005), *Towards Environmental Innovation Systems*, Heidelberg: Springer/Physica, pp. 33–54.

Kuhlmann, S. (1998), 'Moderation of policy-making? Science and technology policy evaluation beyond impact measurement: the case of Germany', *Evaluation*, **4** (2), 130–48.

Kuhlmann, S. (2001), *Management of Innovation Systems. The Role of Distributed Intelligence*, Antwerp: Maklu-Uitgevers.

OECD (2005), 'Governance of innovation systems', Volume 1: Synthesis Report, Paris: OECD.

Renn, O. (2002), 'Foresight and Multi-Level Governance', paper for the conference 'The role of foresight in the selection of research policy priorities', Sevilla, 13–14 May.

Rip, A., T. Misa and J. Schot (eds) (1995), *Managing Technology in Society: the Approach of Constructive Technology Assessment*, London: Pinter.

Rotmans, J., R. Kemp and M. van Asselt (2001), 'More evolution than revolution: transition management in public policy', *Foresight*, **3** (1), 15–31.

Schauer, B. (2005), 'R&D project selection under risk using real option and utility theory', PhD Thesis, Vienna University of Economics/ARC systems research.

Thompson Klein, J., W. Grossenbacher-Mansuy, R. Häberli, A. Bill, R.W. Scholz and M. Welti (eds) (2001), 'Transdisciplinarity: Joint problem solving among science, technology, and society: an effective way for managing complexity', Basel: Birkhauser Verlag.

Tübke, A., K. Ducatel, J.P. Gavigan and P. Moncada-Paternò-Castello (2001), 'Strategic policy intelligence: current trends, the state of play and perspectives – S&T intelligence for policy-making processes', research report, IPTS/ESTO: Sevilla.

Van Zuylen, H. and K.M. Weber (2002), 'Opportunities and limitations of European innovation policy in transport', *Technological Forecasting and Social Change*, **69**, 929–51.

Vergragt, P.J. (2000), 'Strategies towards the sustainable household', final report of the EU SusHouse project, Delft University of Technology.

Wagner, P., D. Banister, K. Dreborg, E.A. Eriksson, D. Stead and K.M. Weber (2004), 'Impact of ICT on Transport (ICTRANS)', an ESTO research report, EUR 21058, Sevilla/Seibersdorf: IPTS/ARC systems research.

Walker, W.E., A.S. Rahman and J. Cave (2001), 'Adaptive policies, policy analysis, and policy making', *European Journal of Operational Research*, **128**, 282–9.

Weber, K.M. (2005), 'What role for politics in the governance of complex innovation systems? New concepts, requirements and processes of an interactive technology policy for sustainability', in J.N. Rosenau, E.U. von Weizsäcker and U. Petschow (eds), *Governance and Sustainability. Exploring the roadmap to sustainability after Johannesburg*, Sheffield: Greenleaf (forthcoming).

Weber, K.M., H. Gassler, W. Polt, B. Dachs and G. Streicher (2004a), Ansätze und Befunde zur Schwerpunktsetzung in der österreichischen Forschungs- und Technologiepolitik, *Wirtschaftspolitische Blätter*, **51** (3), 405–18.

Weber, K.M., K. Kubeczko, K.-H. Leitner, K. Whitelegg, P. Späth, H. Rohracher and I. Oehme (2004b), *Transition zu nachhaltigen Produktionssystemen. 2. Zwischenbericht*, Seibersdorf/Graz: ARC systems research/IFZ.

Weber, K.M., R. Hoogma, B. Lane and J. Schot (1999), *Experimenting with Sustainable Transport Technologies: A Workbook for Strategic Niche Management*, Enschede/Sevilla: University of Twente/IPTS.

Weber, K.M., A. Geyer, D. Schartinger and P. Wagner (2002), 'Zukunft der Mobilität in Österreich. Konsequenzen für die Technologiepolitik', Jahresbericht 2001, Forschungsbericht ARC-S-0185, December.

Whitelegg, K. (2005), 'Patchwork policy making – linking innovation and transport policy in Austria', in *OECD: Governance of Innovation Systems Vol. 3: Case Studies in Cross-sectoral Policy*, Paris: OECD (forthcoming).

# Knowledge production and assessment

# 9. Precaution, foresight and sustainability: reflection and reflexivity in the governance of science and technology

**Andy Stirling**

## REFLECTION, REFLEXIVITY AND THE GOVERNANCE OF SUSTAINABILITY

The introductory chapter to this volume demonstrates how the advent of the 'sustainability agenda' holds crucial significance for the prospects of more reflexive governance. (Voß and Kemp, this volume). Nowhere is this truer than in the governance of science and technology. Discourses on sustainability are dominated by understandings and possibilities mediated by science. They are pervaded by the aims and potentialities associated with different forms of technology. It is also the experience of the unfolding implications of twentieth-century science and technology that forms the principal reference point in Giddens's (1990) and Beck's (1992) seminal applications of the concept of reflexivity to modernity and which continue to feature prominently in the subsequent literature on this theme. (Giddens, 1994; Beck et al., 1994; Lash et al., 1996; Adam et al., 2000). However, social scientific discourses on reflexivity are also notorious for the questions that they beg, as well for those that they raise, illuminate or resolve. It is against this background that the present chapter will seek to examine some of the key issues that arise when considering the prospects for establishing more deliberately reflexive governance for sustainable science and technology.

As also hinted at in the Introduction to this book (Voß and Kemp, this volume), one key question that emerges right at the outset concerns the extent to which sustainability and reflexivity can necessarily always be assumed to hold convergent, or even consistent, governance implications. Wynne has observed, for instance, that questions might be raised about the degree of reflexivity embodied in increasing preoccupations with policy agendas framed in terms of 'environment' and 'risk' (Wynne, 2002). Given that these are key constitutive themes of sustainability, similar concerns might be raised on this somewhat broader canvas. Certainly, where such thematic labels encourage the 'objectification' and compartmentalization of different governance domains, or where they are appropriated instrumentally to legitimate particular favoured interventions, then they may actually militate against reflexivity in wider governance processes. I return to this theme in the next section. For the moment, it suffices to note that this kind of compartmentalization (Weale, 2000) and instrumental legitimation (Stirling, 2004) are all too often a feature of the relationship between sustainability and wider areas of governance.

It is with this type of question about the precise nature of the relationship between reflexivity and sustainability in governance discourses, with which this chapter might most usefully begin. A key initial point in this regard concerns the proliferating understandings of exactly what is meant by the term 'reflexivity' in various contexts bearing on this theme (Gouldner, 1970; Giddens, 1976; Steier, 1991; Bourdieu and Wacquant, 1992; Alvesson and Skoldberg, 2000; Woolgar, 1988). In particular, questions arise about distinctions between normative and descriptive usages, and about the role of intentionality (Lash, 2001). For purposes of clarity in the present account, it may therefore be useful to begin with a clear working distinction between three key concepts on which this analysis will rest: 'unreflectiveness', 'reflection' and 'reflexivity'. This is not intended as an effort at general synthesis, but simply as a consistent and transparent point of departure for the present discussion. Accordingly, each term will be addressed in relation to modes of representation, understanding and intervention in the governance of science and technology. Schematic pictures of key elements in these working definitions are provided in Figure 9.1.

Unreflectiveness is, in these terms, a governance situation in which representations, understandings and interventions are effectively restricted to whatever are held to be the most obvious, operational, or instrumentally pertinent attributes of the object under attention. Here (and in Figure 9.1), the 'subject' is the governance system itself. The 'object', in this context, might be a resource allocation across contending scientific research programmes, a choice among alternative technological trajectories or a decision concerning wider regulatory or technology policy commitments. In the context of discussion over sustainability, these might hypothetically be exemplified by the way in which the governance system relates to the development of a family of novel chemicals. Here, representations take the form of different forms and styles of regulatory appraisal – including risk assessment, cost–benefit analysis, expert advisory committees, stakeholder negotiations and wider political discourses over the nature and scale of contending interests. Options for governance intervention might include: mandatory requirements on production processes, emission controls, product-specific standards, voluntary agreements, labeling provisions, liability rules, life cycle management protocols, phase-out targets and negotiated moratoria or legislation for bans.

In a case like this, the governance situation might be one in which the main 'selection pressure' (Nelson and Winter, 1982) exerted by an innovation system focuses primarily on operational efficacy: 'Do the chemicals work?' This kind of relatively unreflective representation provides only a circumscribed basis for tightly bounded forms of governance intervention. For instance, it ignores the possibility that attributes of the chemicals in question that are not seen as relevant to operational efficacy, might be relevant in some other way – perhaps through causing unintended environmental or health consequences. In other words, this suggests systematic neglect of what Voß and Kemp (this volume) term the 'second-order problems' associated with sustainability. In current governance debates, this equates quite closely with influential laissez-faire normative positions over the appropriate style for risk regulation and technology policy (Morris, 2000).

Reflection (or reflectiveness), by contrast, refers to a mode of representation, understanding and intervention by governance systems in which attention extends to a 'full range' of whatever are held to be broadly salient attributes of the object in question. Relevant dictionary definitions yield colloquial senses like 'deep serious consideration' (OED, 1989). By analogy with a mirror, this entails faithful reflection of all that lies in the field of view. In the case of the novel chemicals already mentioned, this might involve the application of a comprehensive technology assessment, including symmetrical attention to alternatives, as part of the innovation or regulatory process (O'Brien, 2000). In economic appraisal, this implies attention to a full range of 'externalities' (Hanley and Spash, 1993). Likewise, there are formulations of the 'precautionary principle' (discussed later in this chapter), which hold that complete account should be taken of all possible environmental or human health consequences before any commitments be made in governance (Martuzzi and Tickner, 2004). It is by such means, that we may hope to minimise the scope for adverse 'unintended consequences' from any given governance intervention (Voß and Kemp, this volume).

Reflexivity (or reflexiveness) goes beyond the 'deep serious consideration' of reflection. Dictionary definitions here yield the sense that attention 'turns back on itself' (OED, 1989). According to the mirror analogy, reflexivity involves recognition that 'the subject itself forms a large part of the object' – as a matter of 'self-awareness' (Giddens, 1976:17) or 'self reflection' (Bohmann, 1996). Reflexivity thus requires attention not just to the 'representation' of the object to the subject, but also to the way in which the attributes of the subject help condition the representations of the object and how these representations themselves can help recondition the subject.

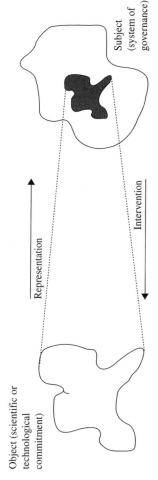

*Unreflectiveness:* Attention focuses only on most obvious or instrumentally pertinent attributes of object (restricted representation, circumscribed basis and focus for intervention), *e.g. 'the chemicals work so let's use them'.*

Object (scientific or technological commitment)

Representation

Intervention

Subject (system of governance)

*Reflection:* 'deep, serious consideration' extends to all salient aspects of the object of attention (full representation, aspiration to 'objective synoptic' basis and focus for intervention), *e.g. 'let's take account of all possible consequences before using the chemicals'.*

Object (scientific or technological commitment)

Representation

Intervention

Subject (system of governance)

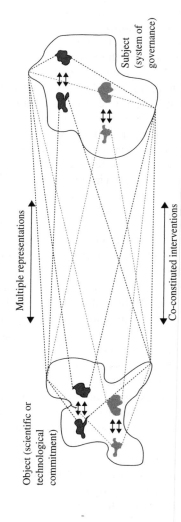

*Reflexivity:* Attention simultaneously encompasses and helps constitute both subject and object (recursive mutual contingency of subjective representations and interventions),
e.g. *'the consequences depend on our point of view and our expectations of use'.*

Object (scientific or technological commitment)

Multiple representations

Co-constituted interventions

Subject (system of governance)

*Figure 9.1   Working definitions for 'unreflectiveness', 'reflection' and 'reflexivity' for the present chapter*

In other words, we face a recursive loop, in which it is recognized that representations are contingent on a multiplicity of subjective perspectives, and that these subjective perspectives are themselves reconstituted by processes of representation. As a result, any associated interventions are also simultaneously contingent on and help condition a series of divergent but equally valid potential subjective representations.

In the present illustrative example of a family of novel chemicals, reflexivity is distinct from reflection in that it requires an appreciation of the way in which any representation of the purposes, conditions or consequences associated with use of these chemicals must necessarily be socially contingent (Wynne, 1992). Different disciplinary perspectives, institutional interests, cultural values and economic priorities will typically influence the interpretation of evidence and analysis in different ways (Stirling, 2004). Contrasting social commitments will thus yield divergent prescriptive bases for governance interventions. In this way, reflexivity implies a recursive nesting of representations of 'science/technology in governance' and 'governance in science/technology'. An intentionally reflexive system of governance therefore involves explicit recognition that policy appraisals are contingent and constructed, in part by commitments to the interventions that they ostensibly inform.

Right at the outset, these working understandings raise a number of key issues for the relationship between reflexivity and sustainability in governance. First, there is the question of whether we are principally concerned with reflexivity or reflectiveness in the particular senses distinguished here (cf: Beck, 1994:6; Chapter 2, this volume). Different areas of the literature highlight one or the other meaning in different ways and to varying extents. For instance, a framing of 'reflexive governance' largely in terms of responsiveness to 'unintended consequences' (Voß and Kemp, this volume) focuses at least as much on reflectiveness as it does on reflexivity. This is the case, because unintended or unpredicted consequences are as likely to be due to a lack of reflection as reflexivity. For many purposes, this distinction is of only secondary importance. But there may be occasions when reflection and reflexivity hold different governance implications. For instance, where reflection implies an aim of constructing representations that are as fully comprehensive as possible, then it may encourage rather unreflexive, synoptic ambitions for appraisal (Wynne, 1975; Collingridge, 1980; Stirling, 2004). This idea contrasts strongly with the pluralism and humility prompted by recognitions of the intrinsic indeterminacies of appraisal under a reflexive approach (Wynne, 1992; Stirling, 2003). The ensuing sections of this chapter will focus on a number of different practical consequences of this working distinction between reflection and reflexivity in sustainable governance.

The second key issue concerns the role of intentionality in governance (Lash, 2001). Both 'sustainability' and 'reflexivity' may, in principle, vary in the extent to which they result from the premeditated exercise of agency in the governance system. Sustainability and reflexivity may each arise as a result of deliberate action or design. On the other hand, they might, to varying degrees, arguably simply be incidental, spontaneous or contingent features of the system. In the case of sustainability in governance, the degree of intentionality makes little difference to the 'first order' analytic use of this term. Yet for reflexivity in governance, an incipient paradox emerges if the term is used of an unpremeditated 'reflex', or 'blind self-confrontation' (Beck, Chapter 2, this volume). This is because any unre-flexive governance system will, by definition, be prompted to respond to the realization of unpredicted consequences – as a 'reflex'. Yet if unintentional 'reflexes' are included within the meaning of the term 'reflexive', then the inevitable fact of such an eventual response would make the system both reflexive, as well as unreflexive! In other words, given a terminology that includes unintentional or 'blind' reflexes alongside (or instead of) deliber-ate reflexivity, it is difficult to imagine how any governance system could be viewed as anything other than 'reflexive'. The usage of the adjective 'reflex-ive' to include unintentional action thus seems in this context not so much a description of a form of governance, as a declaration of a general epis-temic commitment under which all governance systems are seen as reflex-ive. Among other things, this would render difficult any attempt to discriminate general relationships between reflexivity and sustainability in governance. It is for this reason that the present discussion takes the term 'reflexive governance' to imply the exercise ex ante of deliberate agency, rather than to describe ex post unintentional reflexes in the face of unpre-dicted consequences.

With these broad questions in mind, the next section will begin on a wide canvas, with a review of the significance of the sustainability discourse for persistently influential deterministic notions of 'technological progress'. Despite the serious ambiguities, it will be argued that the broad normative scope of the sustainability agenda significantly enhances the pressure for more reflective technology appraisal. Perhaps more importantly, it also presages a move towards greater reflexivity over the plural nature and potentialities of 'progress' and the sensitivity of scientific and technologi-cal trajectories to being shaped by patterns of governance.

Building on this, the discussion then moves on to review the specific implications of the sustainability agenda for the development of discourses on technological risk. It is shown how newly enriched appreciations of the depth and diversity of different forms of incertitude are posing a formid-able challenge to the dominant role in governance of conventional 'risk assessment' techniques. It will be shown that a disparate array of alternative approaches exists by means of which more reflective and reflexive appraisal for the sustainable governance of science and technology can be achieved. This leads to a particular illustration of one way in which we can distinguish and build on some of the practical implications of imperatives to reflectiveness and reflexivity over the role of science.

Attention then turns to the manner in which these themes are currently being integrated in governance discourses under the rubric of the 'precautionary principle'. Again, it is shown that we can usefully distinguish the implications of reflectiveness and reflexivity. For all their value as an impulse to greater reflection in the governance of technology, it is shown that conventional representations of precaution as a putative 'decision rule' are often little more reflexive than reliance on current risk-based approaches. The resolution of this issue is argued to lie in a move towards a more process-based understanding of precaution. It is on this basis that precaution might more readily be articulated with existing 'foresight' procedures into more integrated and reflexive forms of governance for sustainability.

Finally, drawing on the five 'adequate strategies for reflexive governance' developed by Voß and Kemp (this volume), the chapter will close with a review of some practical implications of the integration of strategies for precaution and foresight for the more reflexive governance of sustainability. It will be concluded that the full importance for sustainability of imperatives to more reflexive governance cannot be realized simply by reference to improved processes of ex ante technology appraisal – such as those embodied in discourses of foresight and precaution. In the end, it is by 'opening up' the institutions and procedures of technology choice, and by deliberately encouraging greater diversity in their outcomes that we may hope better to fulfill the potentials for reflectiveness, reflexivity and sustainability alike.

## SUSTAINABILITY, PROGRESS AND REFLEXIVITY

For many generations, Enlightenment notions of progress have dominated 'western' governance discourses on science and technology (Mokyr, 1992). Although accompanied by persistent pockets of dissent, general ideas of scientific and technological progress have attained something of a hegemonic status (Smith and Marx, 1994). Indeed, scientific and technological progress continue to be viewed as normative ends in their own right. The substantive indicators of such progress amount to little more than the emergent consequences of incumbent patterns of research and innovation. The result is an unreflexive 'normative teleology', in which the manifest unfolding of certain scientific or technological trajectories is itself taken as the principal evidence of their intrinsic social merit.

This circular character to the rhetoric of progress is endemic in high-level governance debates (Blair, 2000; CEC, 2000) as much as in wider cultural discourse. (Smith and Marx, 1994; Morris, 2000) It is common to hear scepticism about some specific technology, labelled by defendants of the incumbent order as being generally 'anti-technology' or 'anti-innovation' in sentiment (CST, 2000). This is the case even in the institutional heart-lands of the sustainability debate (UNDP, 2000). Likewise, the direction of particular innovation pathways is frequently justified by official and indus-try bodies, simply by reference to a general 'pro innovation' position (Brown, 2004). Policy documentation continues to treat technological innovation (both in principle, and as realized in practice) as a self-evident good in its own right, without reference to wider contextual or evaluative discussion (HMT, 2004).

Of course, the specific outcomes of scientific and technological progress are vociferously contested in numerous particular arenas. The urban auto-mobile, intensive agriculture, hazardous chemicals, fossil fuels, nuclear power, compulsory vaccinations, supersonic transport, public surveillance, processed food, genetic modification and reproductive cloning all provide examples of energetic but ultimately isolated challenges to the way that incumbent interests are conditioning the unfolding of particular scientific or technological pathways. Indeed, there are even episodes – as arguably with nuclear power in OECD countries, federal stem cell research in the USA or agricultural biotechnology in Europe – in which the resulting con-flicts show signs of exerting a substantive influence on the momentum or direction of particular established trajectories.

Yet, even where criticism is successful, the salient themes nonetheless tend to be treated as 'risk' issues that are subject to relatively circumscribed, unreflective, 'regulatory' debate. As a result, governance discourses on science and technology tend to be mediated by – and constrained to – wran-gles over expert-led analyses of the magnitude, likelihood or distribution of benefits or harm. What is missing are general arenas to enable uncon-strained discourse about the orientation of scientific and technological choices. In short, we lack a truly reflective (let alone reflexive) 'politics of technology'. Indeed, the hegemony of Enlightenment vocabularies of progress is so entrenched that we lack even the language to appreciate fully the magnitude of this gaping void in contemporary governance discourses.

It is against this background (and at a similar discursive level to the theme of 'progress') that we are now seeing the ascendancy of 'sustainabil-ity' as a 'generally accepted normative orientation' (Voß and Kemp, this volume). Sustainability discourses certainly do embody a remarkable array of explicitly normative commitments. These can take a series of ostensibly highly substantive and even measurable forms, including improved resource efficiency, lower environmental impact, reduced health effects, enhanced welfare and increased social equity (UNCED, 1987). Notions of 'sustainable technology' subsume a range of specific means to achieve these normative ends, including 'clean technology' (Stone, 1990), 'cleaner production' (Markman, 1997) and 'environmental technology' (Boyce, 1996). These encompass a series of concrete practices and disciplines such as industrial ecology in bulk chemicals (Graedel and Allenby, 2002), integrated pest management in agriculture (Norris et al., 2002) and energy efficiency in buildings and appliances (Sorrell et al., 2004). Taken together, there can be little doubt that 'sustainable technology' discourses call for the adoption of a broad range of challenging normative objectives, such as high-level 'architectural' design principles, at an early stage in the innovation process.

At face value, this represents an impressive contrast with the essential normative vacuum associated with mainstream discourses on technological progress. However, in other ways concepts of sustainability are hardly less normatively ambiguous than is the unqualified notion of progress itself. Indeed, as with other 'boundary objects' (Jasanoff, 1990), a certain level of interpretive flexibility (Bijker, 1995) is an essential element in the burgeoning discursive success of concept(s) of sustainability. As a result, there is often ample latitude for divergent interpretations of the concrete implications of 'sustainability' for crucial choices between real technologies. For instance, take the example of competing (and in large part contradictory) claims to 'sustainability' on the part of nuclear and renewable energy technologies as a basis for carbon reduction strategies in electricity supply. Likewise, genetic modification and organic farming present contending and (as presently constituted) mutually exclusive means to reducing pesticide use in agriculture. Indeed, it is sometimes the case that the object of the 'sustaining' is not only ambiguous, but can amount to little more than the status quo. For example, in current debates within the UK Department of Environment, Food and Rural Affairs (DEFRA), the term 'sustainable science' is sometimes used to include support for activities associated with the general innovation and dissemination of pesticides (DEFRA, 2002). Yet this conflicts with the well-established normative commitment under sustainability agendas to a reduction in pesticide use. Indeed, just such a commitment is acknowledged elsewhere in DEFRA's own 'sustainability indicators' (DEFRA, 2004). Where 'sustainability' is used in this way, simply to mean 'sustaining' existing practice, it embodies essentially the same 'normative teleology' to that displayed by discourses on 'technological progress'. Either way, it is clear that 'sustainability' can readily be invoked on opposite sides of the argument even in highly specific cases of technology choice.

These kinds of mismatch may sometimes reflect the scope for genuinely divergent views on the detailed implications of authentic, normative commitments to sustainability. In other cases, we might interpret such disjuncture as instances of what Wynne (2002) identifies as 'legitimatory discourse'. In the terms discussed in the introduction to this chapter, this involves the appropriation of the language of sustainability, in order to justify different normative, or instrumental ends. Wynne makes a persuasive case that this kind of legitimation can often indicate a lack of reflexivity in governance. Moreover, there is no doubt about the important (and often invisible) role that this kind of strategic engagement plays (Rowell, 1996). Yet, where such appropriations themselves are informed by understandings of the interpretive flexibility and social contingency in the notion of sustainability, they might actually be considered on occasion to embody an element of reflexivity, rather than its absence.

Indeed, it is possible that the reflexivity in this kind of legitimatory appropriation can work two ways. This might be the case, for instance, with incorporation of the environmentally focused 'sustainability' agenda itself, into the more mainstream economist language of 'sustainable development'. In one sense, this represents an appropriation of the radical thrust of this environmental agenda, resulting in a dilution of efforts to this end (Rowell, 1996). In another sense, this might be seen as the reverse appropriation, using economist discourse to legitimate and thus help foster the more radical agenda. The correct interpretation in any given context will remain a matter of perspective, and probably time scale. Either way, the key point is that the discursive relationship between sustainability and reflexivity is not necessarily one of straightforward synergy and positive reinforcement, but can be quite complex, multivalent and even conflicting. Whichever way the process works, it is reflexivity that drives the articulation of different representations of sustainability in constituting the associated interventions.

Whilst they may be significant for any understanding of the relationship between sustainability and reflexivity, these kinds of rather abstract considerations may seem less obviously important to the practical promotion of sustainability itself. In this case the dominant picture is that the efficacy of governance interventions routinely falls far short of the professed ambitions. Even where there is agreement on the specific normative commitments and clarity about the implications for real technology choices, Voß and Kemp (this volume) are correct to observe that the results are all too often 'disappointing'. This is manifestly the case, for instance, with curbs on EC fossil fuel emissions, reductions in urban automobile use and the achievement of step changes in energy efficiency. Whether this reflects 'legitimation', or the sheer inertia in technological and governance systems, the effect is essentially the same.

Yet, just as we appreciate the daunting scale of this mismatch between the aspirations and actuality of sustainability, we also encounter a further important, neglected, but more hopeful implication of governance. This relates not to the normative orientation or substantive character of whatever might be deemed to constitute a 'sustainable technology' in any given instance. Rather, it concerns the way in which sustainability discourses involve the emphatic introduction of the normative dimension itself. Even where we may be unsure or disagree about the precise meanings of sustainability, it is clear that with this term, we are invoking at least some kind of transcendent evaluative framework. In itself, this constitutes a serious blow for the hegemonic status of the established Enlightenment notions of progress. No longer can the mere existence of a particular scientific or technological potentiality be taken as a self-evident indication of normatively desirable 'progress'. In this sense, the very existence of 'legitimation discourses' as a subset of wider discourses on sustainability is a positive indication of some transcendent substance to the concept of sustainability. In this respect, it contrasts strongly with a concept of 'progress' under which it seems that legitimation *is* the substance. Even where the detail of the substantive implications are in doubt, the ascent of the sustainability agenda into the most rarefied arenas of governance raises the prospect of an unprecedented transformation in discourses on science and technology. For the first time, we catch a glimpse of the potential for a move away from isolated 'risk controversies' and circumscribed 'regulatory debates' towards a more truly reflective and reflexive general 'politics of technology'.[1]

The importance of this political trend in governance debates is all the more notable, because it is reinforced by parallel epistemic developments. Here, the abandonment of teleological ideas in biological evolution (Dennett, 1996; Dyson, 1998) signals an independent pressure for the demise of derivative but more durable understandings in technological evolution. This takes the form of a growing recognition across a variety of disciplines of the crucial role played by context, agency and path dependency in the forms and directions taken by scientific and technological trajectories. Despite the different specialist vocabularies, understandings of science–society–technology relationships that arise in philosophy, economics, history and social studies paint a remarkably common picture (Williams and Edge, 1996). In each of these specialist arenas, early linear, deterministic notions of technological 'progress' are giving way to a more complex and dynamic picture of contingency (Mokyr, 1992), autopoeisis (Luhmann, 2000); homeostasis (Sahal, 1985); network interactions (Callon et al., 1986), social-shaping (Bijker, 1995), co-construction (Misa et al., 2003), paradigms and trajectories (Dosi, 1982), path dependency (David, 1985), momentum (Hughes, 1983), lock-in (Arthur, 1989), autonomy (Winner, 1977), regime-building (Kemp et al., 1998) and entrapment (Walker, 2000). Accordingly, the form and direction taken by our science and technology are no longer seen as inevitable and unitary and awaiting 'discovery' in nature. Instead they are increasingly recognized as open to being shaped by individual creativity, collective ingenuity, economic priorities, cultural values, institutional interests, stakeholder negotiation and the exercise of power. In other words, these different emerging conceptualizations signal further enhanced reflexivity over the way in which scientific and technological commitments are both conditioned by, and help reconstitute, encompassing systems of governance.

In this sense, a reflective governance of science and technology seeks to anticipate and understand the complete range of implications associated with a contending array of scientific trajectories or technological choices, including a wider array of normative considerations than those conventionally applied by incumbent institutions and markets. This is the domain of many invaluable procedures for technology assessment (Loveridge, 1996), options appraisal (O'Brien, 2000) precautionary regulation (Raffensberger and Tickner, 1999) and participatory deliberation (Joss and Durant, 1995; Renn et al., 1995). Beyond this, the reflexive governance of science and technology seeks to appreciate the contingencies on, and conditioning by, its own representations and interventions in the processes of social choice. It is to this end that we see emerging experiments mentioned by Voß and Kemp in the Introduction to this book: 'constructive technology assessment' (Schot and Rip, 1997), 'transition management' (Rotmans et al., 2001), 'social intelligence' (Grove-White et al., 2000) and 'upstream engagement' (Europta, 2000; Wilsdon and Willis, 2004; Stirling, 2005). Ensuing sections of this chapter explore some of the specific ways in which these opportunities for greater reflection and reflexivity relate to each other and challenge established procedures in the governance of science and technology.

## RISK, UNCERTAINTY AND REFLECTIVE APPRAISAL

A second conceptual product of the Enlightenment, that has closely accompanied the notion of 'progress' through the past few centuries, is its notorious alter ego, 'risk' (Beck, 1992). Socially conditioned through successive cultural and institutional developments such as fashions for games of chance (Bernstein, 1996), the historical advent of stock and insurance markets (Hacking, 1975), the growth of financial annuities and statistically based administration (Weatherford, 1982) and the emergence of engineering-focused risk analysis (Starr, 1969), the classical formulation of the concept of risk envisages a determinate set of 'outcomes', each with an associated 'magnitude' and 'likelihood'.

Although it is often based on qualitative judgments, the idiom of this 'risk assessment' approach is overwhelmingly quantitative. Whether literally or metaphorically, both likelihoods and outcomes are typically considered reducible – at least in principle – to some simple cardinal scale. For the likelihoods, this is a probability. For the magnitudes, there is a multiplicity of metrics depending on the context, with leading contenders being mortality, morbidity, utility or monetary value (Stirling, 2003). In this way, even where it is partly qualitative, this 'risk assessment' approach typically involves reduction under individual metrics and aggregation across different metrics.

So deeply ingrained is this 'reductive aggregative' understanding of risk, that it is typically viewed as being essentially synonymous with the application of 'rationality' to 'science-based' decision-making under circumstances of incomplete knowledge (Berlinski, 1976; Byrd and Cothern, 2000; USDA, 2000; Morris, 2000; Lloyd, 2000). Different variants of this reductive aggregative style have emerged to address different empirical and institutional contexts. Decision theory (Hogwood and Gunn, 1984), life cycle analysis (van den Berg et al., 1995), technology assessment (Loveridge, 1996), risk assessment (von Winterfeldt and Edwards, 1986; Suter, 1990), multi-criteria evaluation (Janssen, 1994; Clemen, 1996; Dodgson et al., 2001) and cost–benefit analysis (Pearce and Turner, 1990; Hanley and Spash, 1993) all compete at the margins of jealously guarded disciplinary niches. Yet all share the common application of this same kind of reductive aggregative framework. In short, they all aspire to convert by this means the indeterminate and contested socio-political problems of incomplete knowledge into precisely defined and relatively tractable 'decisionistic' puzzles (Kuhn, 1970; Funtowicz and Ravetz, 1989; 1990; Wynne, 1997).

Perhaps the best recognized challenge to this elegant and ambitious, but relatively unreflective, analytic programme, lies in the difficulties with definitive substantiation of the key concept of probability (Hacking, 1975; Weatherford, 1982). Although obscured by sometimes acrimonious disputes between 'frequentist' and 'Bayesian' understandings (Collingridge, 1982; Jaynes, 1986; Wallsten, 1986) and variously allied epistemological perspectives (Szekely, 1986; Klir, 1989; Watson, 1994; Porter, 1995), the difficulties here are essentially quite simple. How might we distinguish between circumstances under which there exist greater or lesser grounds for confidence in the probabilities that may be assigned to different outcomes? The classical formulations of 'risk', constructed entirely in terms of probabilities and

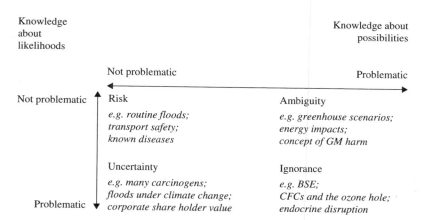

*Figure 9.2*    *'Risk', 'uncertainty', 'ambiguity' and 'ignorance' as 'degrees of incertitude' (with examples)*

magnitude, simply do not allow for this dimension of 'incertitude' to be addressed, or even represented (Stirling, 2003).

It was for this reason that early work in economics (Knight, 1921; Keynes, 1921), which was repeatedly endorsed and reinforced in other disciplines (Luce and Raiffa, 1957; Morgan, et al., 1990; Rowe, 1994), developed a canonical distinction between concepts of 'risk' and 'uncertainty'. In short, risk is a condition in which it is considered possible to derive confidently probabilities for a range of discrete outcomes (or for increments on a continuous magnitude scale). The condition of 'uncertainty' (in this same strict sense) refers to a situation in which it is possible to define a finite set of discrete outcomes (or a single definitive continuous magnitude scale), but where it is acknowledged that no single basis exists for the confident assignment of corresponding probability distributions. For heuristic purposes, the resulting definitions for contrasting 'states of incertitude' may be represented in graphical form as Weberian 'ideal types' as shown in Figure 9.2, together with some corresponding examples (Stirling, 1998; 2003).

Although uncontroversial from most disciplinary perspectives, this distinction between risk and uncertainty is hotly contested – and often denied – under a reductive aggregative 'risk-based' approach (Lumby, 1984; McKenna, 1986; Brealey and Myers, 1988). This is of crucial importance to the governance of science, technology and sustainability, because it is this 'risk-based' approach that typically dominates mainstream regulatory discourses. Essentially, the grounds for dispute might be seen to arise from varying degrees of reflectiveness over the extent to which differing conditions of incomplete knowledge about likelihood can be confidently captured in probabilities. Where empirical data are held (or asserted) to be applicable and complete, analytic models robust and sufficient, or expert opinions adequate and credible, there is little problem with the application of elegant and sophisticated methods of risk analysis. However, where further reflection admits the possibility that these conditions may not hold, the reductive aggregations of risk assessment are of more limited value. Under such circumstances, it is significant that the celebrated probability theorist, de Finetti, reflected that 'probability does not exist' (De Finetti, 1974 quoted in Morgan et al., 1990:49).

This is not to say that some of the more versatile 'risk-based' methods – such as Bayesian, 'conditional', or 'imprecise' probabilities – might not still be deployed in relatively more or less reflective fashions. If they are aimed simply at scoping or exploring the various salient subjectivities and contingencies, then – cautiously handled – they may offer significant heuristic value. But where such techniques are used to aggregate a single ostensibly 'definitive' picture, then they represent a highly unreflective denial of the real nature of uncertainty. In the words used in his Nobel acceptance speech by the economist Hayek, this represents little more than 'pretence at knowledge' (Hayek, 1978:23).

Such persistent adherence to narrow reductive aggregative methods is in any case unnecessary in an analytical sense, because a wealth of alternative approaches exists that do not require the treatment of uncertainty in a reductive, aggregative fashion, as if it were mere risk. These include various forms of scenario (Werner, 2004), sensitivity (Saltelli, 2001) and interval analysis (Jaulin et al., 2001), as well as a range of different 'decision heuristics' (Forster, 1999). The specific value of some of these methods will be reviewed in a little more detail in the final section of this chapter. For the moment, the central point is more general. The tendency for regulatory procedures to remain fixated with conventional probabilistic techniques and an associated reductive aggregative idiom typically leaves the full potential of these more 'reflective' approaches greatly under-fulfilled. Following the structure adopted in Figure 9.2, Figure 9.3 shows the wide variety of alternatives that exist to risk-based approaches. As with Figure 9.2, it is important to recall that this is a matrix of concept definitions that are represented as Weberian 'ideal types'. There is no necessary implication that there will be any one-to-one mapping with circumstances as they prevail in the real world, which will almost always constitute a combination of these conditions. However, what is clear from this picture, is that the disciplinary controversies involved in distinguishing 'uncertainty' from 'risk' are unfortunately just the most obvious and tractable 'tip'

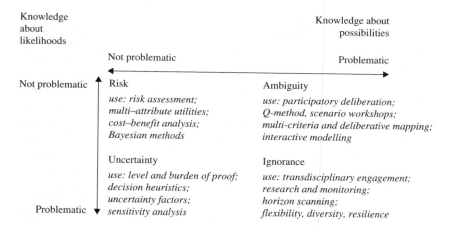

*Figure 9.3*   *Contrasting methodological responses appropriate under different degrees of incertitude*

of an epistemic and ontological 'iceberg'. Attention will now turn to the further challenges highlighted in the right hand column of the matrix.

## AMBIGUITY, IGNORANCE AND REFLEXIVE SCIENCE

As shown in the right hand column of Figures 9.2 and 9.3, the accepted twofold formal definition of risk also implies, beyond 'uncertainty', two further equally coherent and complementary, but still more seriously neglected states of knowledge. These are the conditions of 'ambiguity' and 'ignorance'. Ambiguity describes a state of knowledge in which the problem lies not in the basis for determining the likelihood of each of a variety of different 'outcomes', but in coming to a common understanding of how to select, partition, characterize, prioritize, bound or interpret the meanings of these outcomes (Wynne, 1992, 2002; Rosenberg, 1996; Stirling, 1998). Ambiguity is thus about the 'framing' of the appraisal process – the questions that are posed, the perspectives that are engaged, the methods that are adopted, the assumptions that are made and the mode of representing any findings in wider governance discourses (Wynne, 1992, 2002; Stirling, 2004).

Although often intimately intertwined with uncertainty, the condition of ambiguity is thus conceptually quite distinct. Examples of this kind of dilemma might be seen in the definition of 'harm' in the regulation of genetically modified crops (Grove-White et al., 1997; Levidow et al., 1998; Stirling and Mayer, 1999), the understandings of institutional motivations and practice in the regulation of food safety (van Zwanenberg and Millstone, 2004), the framing of comparative assessments of impacts from different energy technologies (Keepin and Wynne, 1982; Stirling, 1997; Sundqvist et al., 2004), divergent disciplinary, sectoral or regional inter-pretations of global climate change temperature scenarios (Shackley and Wynne, 1996) and the inclusion and exclusion of different categories and permutations of conditions, vectors and end-points in chemical risk assess-ment (Amendola et al., 1992; EEA, 2000; Saltelli, 2001). Under ambiguity, the 'answers' that arise in appraisal of scientific and technological pathways are thus highly contingent on disciplinary approaches, social perspectives, cultural values, economic constraints, institutional interests and political priorities. Instead of uncertainty, ambiguity involves 'contradictory cer-tainties' (Thompson and Warburton, 1985).

What is interesting about this challenge of ambiguity is that (in different terminology) it forms the focus of some of the most elegant classical theo-retical work in the field of rational choice (Kelly, 1978; MacKay, 1980; Collingridge, 1982; Bonner, 1986). Here, it is well established axiomatically that there can be no effective analytic means to compare rigorously the intensities of subjective preference displayed by different social agents (Bezembinder, 1989). Indeed, even where social choices are addressed simply in ordinal terms – as a matter of relative rankings – the economist Arrow went a long way toward earning his own Nobel Prize by demonstrat-ing formally that it is impossible under the rational choice paradigm itself to guarantee any definitive aggregation of preference orderings in a plural society (Arrow, 1963). Although variously nuanced and qualified by refer-ence to frameworks outside the reductive aggregative rational choice pro-gramme (Sen, 1970; Jaeger et al., 2001), the central elegant tenets of this work have not been refuted within this paradigm, which underlies the 'sound science' rhetoric of risk assessment. Yet, these crucial findings remain virtu-ally ignored in the practical implementation and representation of the resulting approaches in policy analysis and technology appraisal (Stirling, 1997).

What is especially important about this result is that it is based on prin-ciples of rationality which themselves underpin reductive aggregative approaches to risk assessment. In this sense, it is an admirable example of reflexivity on the part of what might otherwise be argued to be a relatively unreflexive paradigm. For all the rhetoric, such reflexivity is rarely achieved with such specificity elsewhere in the social sciences. The irony then, is twofold. First, the 'impossibility' finding is itself an example of reflexivity, yet indicates a crucial lack of reflexivity on the part of the same disciplines under circumstances where this finding is ignored. Second, the 'impossibility' finding is a 'sound scientific' result in social choice theory that refutes the general applicability of 'sound science' in social choice. Aspirations (still more, claims) to 'science based' prescriptions on risk are thus not just unrealistic, unreflective and unreflexive. In a plural society, they are a fundamental contradiction in terms (Stirling, 2003). 'Sound scientific decision making' is an oxymoron.

As with uncertainty, no shortage of practical responses exists to this condition of ambiguity. Yet, as before, these remain unduly neglected by the tendency to over-apply the 'risk-based' understanding of incertitude. As summarized in Figure 9.3, the portfolio of approaches includes some quantitative techniques, such as the relatively narrow (restrictively dualistic) procedures of fuzzy logic (Klir and Folger, 1988; Dubois et al., 1988; Zadeh and Kacprzyk, 1992), Q-methodology (McKeown and Thomas, 1988) and various forms of interactive modelling (de Marchi et al., 1998) and 'open' forms of multi-criteria appraisal (Stirling, 2005). Beyond (and potentially encompassing) this, a well-documented diversity of qualitative frameworks exists for specialist deliberation, stakeholder negotiation and citizen participation (Fischer, 1990; Irwin, 1995; Sclove, 1995). These include citizens' panels (Renn et al., 1995), consensus conferences (Joss and Durant, 1995), scenario workshops (Berkhout et al., 2001) and deliberative mapping (Davies et al., 2003). In addition to the contending, normative, democratic and instrumental institutional imperatives (Stirling, 2004), all these approaches offer concrete means to be more explicit, rigorous and truly reflexive about the framing and conduct of appraisal.

The heuristic 'mapping' of the neglected dimensions in risk-based understandings of incertitude that is schematized in Figures 9.2 and 9.3, prompts one further imperative to reflectiveness and reflexivity in the governance of science and technology. This concerns the final condition of 'ignorance', which occupies the lower right-hand corner of this definitional matrix. This is a state of knowledge under which we are *neither* able to quantify likelihoods entirely *nor* to characterize, partition or commensurate all the possible attributes for characterizing outcomes definitively. Although they are even more subject to neglect and denial than the strict understanding of 'uncertainty', both the concept and the term 'ignorance' have long been recognized in economics and wider decision analytic and social study of incertitude (Keynes, 1921; Shackle, 1968; Loasby, 1976; Collingridge, 1980, 1982; Ford, 1983; Ravetz, 1986; Smithson, 1989; Wynne, 1992; Faber and Proops, 1994; Stirling, 2003).

Put at its simplest, ignorance is a reflection of the degree to which 'we don't know what we don't know' (Wynne, 1992). Approached variously as 'epistemological' or 'ontological' in character (Winkler, 1986; von Winterfeldt and

Edwards, 1986; Rosa, 1998), ignorance represents our uncertainty about our uncertainty (Cyranski, 1986). It is an acknowledgement of the importance of the element of 'surprise' (Brooks, 1986; Rosenberg, 1996). This emerges not just from the actuality of unexpected events, but from their very possibility (Dosi and Egidi, 1987). It is a predicament that intensifies directly in relation to the social and political stakes that bear on a particular decision (Funtowicz and Ravetz, 1990). It emerges especially in complex and dynamic environments in which social agents and their cognitive and institutional commitments may recursively influence supposedly exogenous 'events' (Dosi and Egidi, 1987). Indeed, it is due to this reflexive relationship between environmental learning and social commitments, that Wynne has seminally emphasized that ignorance entails even more intractable forms of what he terms 'indeterminacy' (Wynne, 1992, 2000).[2]

The relevance of the predicament of ignorance to the governance of sustainability is obvious. Many of the most pressing specific challenges that have arisen in this field were, at their inception, not so much matters of inaccurate attributions of probability to anticipated outcomes, as they were of intrinsically unexpected outcomes. This was the case, for instance, with recognition of halogenated hydrocarbons as key agents in stratospheric ozone depletion (Farman, 2001), endocrine disruption as a novel mechanism of harm in chemical regulation (Thornton, 2000) and the resilience to processing and interspecies transmissibility of certain spongiform encephalopathies (van Zwanenberg and Millstone, 2001).

Of course, the specific locus of ignorance within the governance process can vary from case to case and over time. Ignorance can be a property of a particular institutional context for decision-making as well as a pervasive societal condition (Stirling, 2003; EEA, 2001). The former is addressed by processes of communication, engagement and organizational learning. The latter is mitigated by processes for baseline monitoring, scientific research and wider social learning. Wherever they apply, such procedures might together be referred to as 'precautionary' approaches to the appraisal of scientific, technological and wider policy choices in sustainable governance. Some examples are indicated in Figure 9.3, alongside the parallel responses in appraisal to risk, uncertainty and ambiguity. The implications will be further explored in the following sections.

Before turning in more detail to these 'precautionary' approaches, however, it is worth considering the complex way in which considerations of reflection and reflexivity emerge from the contrasting approaches summarised in Figure 9.3. It is not simply the case that those methods that are restricted to application under risk are necessarily uniformly less reflective or reflexive than those that are more appropriate under uncertainty, ambiguity or ignorance. Under each idealized 'state of incertitude', the array of available and applicable approaches enables and embodies contrasting degrees of reflection and reflexivity. Indeed, judgements on this question are likely to be determined more by the detailed manner and context of implementation than by any generic structural features of the method.

This said, however, it is possible to discern some broad tendencies within – as well as between – the four different groupings of approaches in Figure 9.3. For instance, it is arguable that multi-attribute techniques offer more reflective approaches to risk than do conventional reductive probabilistic risk assessment or cost–benefit analysis. This is because the accommodation of a variety of different metrics (nominal and ordinal as well as cardinal), permits greater flexibility and scope. They might also be considered to enable greater reflexivity, by virtue of the more deliberate and explicit attention to contending modes of aggregation. Likewise, the case may be made that the interactive element in participatory deliberation makes these approaches generally more reflexive towards ambiguity than is the case for the highly structured, uni-directional form of communication in attitudinal surveys (Spash et al., 1998). Similarly, participatory deliberation may allow greater reflexivity than more structured interactive modelling methods. Yet the extent to which this may also indicate greater reflectiveness will depend further on the particular range and quality of information that is taken into account in either case. Where interactive modelling involves greater scope or deeper scrutiny, it may achieve enhanced levels of reflectiveness, despite an arguably lower level of reflexivity than many less structured approaches to participatory deliberation.

The purpose of the preceding discussion is tentative and indicative rather than definitive. Any confident conclusions would require much more detailed and empirically grounded treatment. The aim is simply to illustrate the way in which considerations of reflectiveness and reflexivity, in the senses defined for the purposes of this chapter, might reasonably be decoupled. What does seem to emerge quite clearly from this account, however, is an injunction to caution over the automatic assumption that greater reflexivity will always accompany greater reflectiveness, and vice versa.

It is on this point that one final implication of the contrasting significance of reflection and reflexivity for emerging understandings of uncertainty, ignorance and ambiguity arises. This concerns the status and role of science in the governance of sustainability. Here, it is important to be clear that the critical tone of the preceding discussion should not be taken as a general denigration of the value of science – or even of risk-based methods in particular. This is far from the intention. Figure 9.2 shows that there are many circumstances where the dominant condition in governance might justifiably be identified as one of 'risk' in the strict sense. Where such conditions are held to prevail, even the narrowest of risk-based methods may be both applicable and useful. Beyond this, there is nothing in this analysis that denies the essential role that science plays in the wider appraisal of uncertainty, ambiguity and ignorance. The key point is not that 'risk science' is always problematic. It is that science offers a necessary, rather than sufficient, basis for the governance of sustainability.

The question then arises as to exactly how we should think about the role and value of science in the 'reflexive governance of sustainability'? This raises a series of deep epistemic and ontological issues concerning the multiple natures (respectively) of 'knowing' and 'being' (Leach et al., 2005). Without presuming to attempt a synthesis of the rich, complex and open-ended character of these discourses, Figure 9.4 provides a schematic 'snapshot' of some key implications of the present discussion of reflection and reflexivity. For this purpose, the role of science is conceived as a means to determine and represent the 'truth' value associated with different possible ontologies ('ways of being in the world') and epistemologies ('ways of knowing the world').[3] The initial point that immediately arises is that even the slightest element of reflection or reflexivity refutes what might be termed the 'naïve realist' position, to the effect that science provides precise representations of whatever might be held to be either epistemic or ontological 'truth'.

Yet the invocation of reflexivity raises its own challenges. Discussion can quickly descend into animated fears over the spectre of a caricature relativist conclusion that 'anything goes' (Feyerabend, 1975, 1978). As a paradigmatic example of reflexivity, the adoption of a social constructivist 'principle of symmetry' over contending representations of scientific knowledge provides a highly rigorous framework for analytical understandings of the social dynamics behind these representations (Barnes and Edge, 1982; Woolgar, 1988). But this does not necessarily mean that this can be applied equally robustly as a normative principle in governance, for the purpose of arbitrating between contending scientific and other types of knowledge. Indeed, such an extension from analytic to normative usage would risk being unreflective in a similar fashion to the over-application of risk assessment. Just as risk assessment fails to address differing grounds for confidence in the 'framing' of analysis, so would unqualified normative use of a principle of symmetry fail to address the manifest 'social fact' of the existence of differing degrees of plausibility and (self-recognised) self-consistency attached to different knowledge claims about sustainability. For instance, such 'caricature relativism' would not only fail to adjudicate the contending positions on global climate change. It would compel equal attention to any representations of 'the science' – no matter how ill-conceived, inconsistent or fanciful. At the extreme, it would neglect any particular role for specialist expertise, empirical grounding, analytical rigour, or technical discipline.

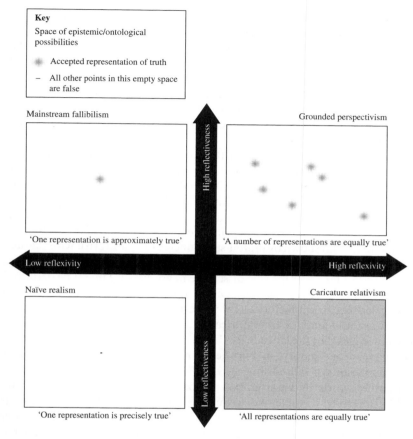

*Figure 9.4    Implications of reflection and reflexivity for the role of science in sustainable governance*

This would effectively deny the relevance of error and leave no operational means by which governance discourses might address crucial issues of quality or strategic bias in the wider conditioning of knowledge by circumstance and power.

In the mainstream governance of sustainability, the conventional resolution to the dilemma represented schematically in the lower half of Figure 9.4, lies in recourse to various forms of what might be summarized as Popperian 'fallibilist' perspectives (Popper, 1963). [4] Here, it is acknowledged that the more bullish 'realist' claims sometimes made on the part of science are naïve and potentially misleading as a basis for policy making. In particular, fallibilism is more reflective than 'naïve realism' about the nature of uncertainty and error. It recognizes that science is only rarely able to justify the provision of unitary, precisely formulated prescriptive representations – for instance concerning sustainability. Accordingly, this mainstream fallibilist perspective holds that science should be viewed rather as offering only approximate representations. Yet the persistent adherence in fallibilism to a generally 'unitary prescriptive' understanding of the normative role of science in governance still justifies a continued (if more modest) use of the language of 'science based' and 'sound scientific' decisions (Byrd and Cothern, 2000) in sustainability discourses.

This is where the importance of the implications of reflection and reflexivity begin to become clear (as shown in the top right hand corner of Figure 9.4). For there are other possible understandings of the role of science in the governance of sustainability, that lie beyond the conventional dichotomy between fallibilism and relativism as alternatives to realism. Indeed, there seems no reason in principle why we may not combine the high level of reflection shown by fallibilism to uncertainty and error with the deep degree of reflexivity shown by relativism towards ambiguity. This fourth type of understanding over the role of science in governance might be described as a kind of 'grounded perspectivism'[5] (Hales and Welshon, 2000). It is 'grounded' because it includes a role for criteria of self-consistency, societal robustness and analytic or empirical quality. It is 'perspectivist' because it acknowledges that the latitude for divergent framings of such 'consistency', 'robustness' or 'quality' in knowledge extends beyond the monocentric approximations of fallibilism.

In other words, under grounded perspectivism, it is acknowledged (with fallibilism) to be possible to discriminate between different representations of 'the science' on the basis of their plausibility or self consistency under any particular set of framing conditions. Accordingly, unlike caricature relativism, there is reflection over uncertainty and the possibilities of bias or error. Yet grounded perspectivism also displays reflexivity over the plurality of possible socially contingent and institutionally conditioned framings of science, each of which will yield different criteria of plausibility and self-consistency. It thereby refrains from the unreflexive assumption that there will always be a unitary (if approximate) coherent scientifically founded basis for governance commitments. Instead, grounded perspectivism entertains the possibility that multiple, equally scientifically valid, representations may prescribe radically different governance interventions.

The practical implications of this grounded perspectivist position for the governance of sustainability are obvious. Even the most authoritative expertise, the most detailed bodies of evidence and the most rigorous modes of analysis typically admit a number of equally valid but mutually inconsistent interpretations. Yet, just because a number of representations may be equally true, does not mean that many are not false (Rosa, 1998; Stirling, 2003). The key challenge is thus presented as one of combining reflection over uncertainty and error with reflexivity over ambiguity and ignorance. Rather than aspiring to derive a single uniquely 'science based' representation, this requires reflexive procedures for exploring and arbitrating among a limited number of equally self-consistent, plausible and scientifically founded – but mutually incoherent – alternatives. By definition, this is not a matter on which science alone can play a lead role. In order truly to realize the implications of both reflection and reflexivity in governance of sustainability, the bottom line is an emphatic paraphrase of the Churchillian injunction that 'science should be on tap, not on top' (Lindsay, 1995).

## PRECAUTION, FORESIGHT AND REFLEXIVITY

It was argued in the last section that twin imperatives for reflection and reflexivity compel more broad-based and pluralistic understandings of the role of science in the governance of sustainability. Conventional reductive aggregative 'risk-based' techniques are of only limited applicability. A variety of alternative but neglected responses to uncertainty, ambiguity and ignorance were identified, which offered varying degrees of reflectiveness and reflexivity. This raises the obvious question as to how we might articulate these disparate approaches alongside risk-based techniques in a coherent operational fashion, and how we might in practice apply them as part of more reflective and reflexive institutions for the governance of sustainability.

Perhaps the most useful and prominent arena for critical discussion on this theme, lies in heated policy discourses over the 'precautionary principle'. Arising repeatedly in different guises since the 1972 Stockholm Environment Conference (O'Riordan and Cameron, 1994), the precautionary principle found its first coherent formal shape in the *Vorsorgeprinzip* in German environmental policy (Boehmer-Christiansen, 1994). Since then, initially through the campaigning and lobbying efforts of international environmental organisations, precaution has moved from the field of marine pollution (Hey, 1992) into diverse areas such as climate change, biodiversity, genetic modification, chemicals regulation, food safety, public health and trade policy (Sand, 2000). As a result, the precautionary principle has become a potent and pervasive element in contemporary risk and environment policy (O'Riordan and Cameron, 1994; Fisher and Harding, 1999; Raffensberger and Tickner, 1999; O'Riordan and Jordan, 2001). Precaution forms a key intrinsic element of sustainability – the classic and most globally influential exposition being Principle 15 of the 1992 Rio Declaration on Environment and Development. Here, the crucial operational passage holds that: '. . . Where there are threats of serious or irreversible damage, lack of full scientific certainty shall not be used as a reason for postponing cost-effective measures to prevent environmental degradation' (UNCED, 1992).

This language provides an elegant synthesis of a highly complex set of ideas. It addresses many practical issues. Indeed, for some a number of quite direct implications follow. In chemicals policy, for instance, the consequence of 'triggering' the precautionary principle might be that regulation takes place on the basis of 'hazard' (anticipated outcomes) rather than 'risk' (degrees of likelihood) (MacGarvin, 1995; Johnston et al., 1998; CEC, 2001b). Essentially, this involves greater reflectiveness over the nature of incertitude. It achieves this by approaching decision-making in terms of outcome-based criteria of 'seriousness' and 'irreversibility' (using properties like carcinogenicity, bio-accumulativity or persistence), rather than on an attempt to determine precise probability distributions of the kind that are formally inapplicable under uncertainty (Jackson and Taylor, 1992).

However, the more reflective status of these interventions remains hotly contested (Morris, 2000). Indeed, this forms the focus of repeated intensive high profile diplomatic disputes between the USA and Europe, adjudicated under the auspices of the World Trade Organisation (Vogel, 2000). Here, the various formulaic statements of the 'Precautionary Principle' are found themselves to be vague, circumscribed and underdetermining (Morris, 2000). Under the statement of precaution cited above, for instance, what implicit threshold of likelihood is embodied in the notion of a 'threat'? How 'serious' is 'serious'? How are we to define 'irreversibility'? By what means and under what authority can the degree of 'scientific certainty' be judged? What is the most appropriate metric of 'cost', and to whom? With respect to what end are we to measure 'effectiveness'? In short, these kinds of questions appear simply to reproduce many of the same issues that qualify and limit the straightforward applicability of reductive aggregative risk-based approaches – to which challenges, precaution is ostensibly a response. Were the critics of precaution inclined to use this kind of social scientific language, they might find the persistence of these ambiguities as an indication of a comparable lack of reflexivity, to that with which risk assessment itself stands charged. In terms of the present discussion (summarized in Figure 9.4), such understandings of precaution are of a relatively unreflexive, 'fallibilist' form and in tension with the more pluralistic 'grounded perspectivism' that is argued to form the best basis for achieving both reflectiveness and reflexivity in the governance of sustainability.

It is in recognition of this dilemma that the influence of more reflexive social scientific understandings, though often tacit, are beginning to be positively felt in discourses on precaution in sustainable governance. This becomes most evident in considering the question of what might be called 'precautionary appraisal' – the means by which precaution informs wider processes of social learning and decision-making (Stirling, 1999; 2003; Stirling and van Zwanenberg, 2003; van Zwanenberg and Stirling, 2004). Here attention turns away from attempts to characterize the substance of an intrinsically intractable problem definitively. Instead, the focus lies more pluralistically in the process of responding to this problem (Hunt, 1994; Fisher and Harding, 1999). When precaution is understood as a social process, rather than as a formulaic decision rule, a number of analytic, institutional, juridical, commercial and regulatory implications begin to grow clear (O'Riordan and Cameron, 1994; Raffensberger and Tickner, 1999; Fisher and Harding, 1999; O'Riordan and Jordan, 2001). Some of these will be addressed in the final section of this chapter. For the moment, what is significant is that this shift from 'closed decision rule' to 'open process' represents a potentially major step towards enabling greater reflexivity in the application of precaution (Stirling, 2005). In addition, it reveals some striking synergies between precaution and the principal governance discourse with which it is often seen to be in tension: that over 'foresight' for technological competitiveness.

In many ways, 'foresight' is the normative counterpoint to the precaution discourse. Here, the great challenge of governance lies in anticipating those scientific or technological trajectories that offer the greatest opportunities and in developing the most competitive means to learning and exploitation. The dangers lie not in the unanticipated adverse 'external effects' of the precaution agenda, but in the failure to realize the potential benefits of a given technology – either through the imposition of undue constraints and burdens, or through the making of premature commitments to what turn out to be relatively uncompetitive innovation trajectories.

As such, there are obvious and persistent contrasts between precaution and foresight. Whereas precaution tends to highlight pessimistic perspectives on technological innovation, foresight embodies more up-beat sentiments. Precaution addresses the restrictive aspects of social ambiguity and the dangers of ignorance. Foresight highlights the creative propensities of social diversity and the positive potentialities of incertitude. Although well established in a range of forms (and under a variety of names) in government and corporate settings, and subject to strong debates over the efficacy of different specific approaches, the activity of foresight as a whole tends also to be significantly less high profile and controversial than precaution. That this is so may be seen as a further indication of the persistent hegemonic status of deterministic notions of technological progress. Where 'optimal' technological pathways are essentially predetermined, efforts to promote competitiveness by successfully anticipating their orientation are effectively the only legitimate or reasonable basis for wider social engagement in innovation, and therefore brook little dissent, or even discussion.

Until recently, the particular procedures embodied in foresight have – like risk assessment – been of a rather reductive, aggregative and expert-centered nature. They have tended to construe the competitiveness of organizational or national innovation systems in a rather narrow, corporate-oriented fashion (Irvine and Martin, 1984; Martin and Irvine, 1989; Martin, 1995). However, these activities have, over the past decade, been subject to a variety of broad, social scientific influences (Martin and Johnston, 1999; Grupp and Linstone, 1999; Hansen and Clausen, 2000). Emerging cross-disciplinary understandings of the contingent and socially constructed nature of the innovation process were discussed earlier in this chapter and have exerted an important impulse towards greater reflexivity (Winner, 1977; Hughes, 1983; Arthur, 1989; Kemp et al., 1998). Likewise, specific new insights have emerged concerning the benefits of cross-sectoral processes for knowledge production (Nowotny et al., 1995). Appreciation for the importance of transdisciplinary alignments and institutional heterogeneity in fostering innovation has grown (Callon et al., 1986). Moreover, on a broader canvas, intimations of a key role are emerging that institutional diversity and cultural pluralism play in fostering more productive innovations (Grabher and Stark, 1997; Stirling, 1998).

Taken together, these converging themes have begun to exert strong pressures towards the development of more reflective and reflexive discourses on foresight. In many ways, these influences reproduce many of the key features of the incipient development of precaution, from principle towards process. For all the differences, both precaution and foresight are concerned with intrinsic indeterminacy, social contingency and path dependency in the governance of science and technology. Both display similar trends towards methodological pluralism and political engagement. In particular, there is the recurrent refrain that governance procedures should be augmented and extended in a number of concrete ways. First, they should go beyond the reductive, aggregative, specialist analysis and extend to more qualitative, heuristic processes of social learning. Second, these procedures should be conducted in a more open, inclusive and accessible fashion, providing for engagement of a wider range of disciplines, a greater variety of institutions, a more diverse body of stakeholders and the more representative array of public constituencies. Although not explicitly formulated in terms of the encompassing concepts of precaution and foresight, we have begun to see the advent of new, more expansive, integrated understandings of this discourse in transcendent terms like 'strategic intelligence' (Kuhlman, 1999), 'post-modern steering' (Rip, 1998), 'constructive technology assessment' (Schwarz and Thompson, 1990; Rip, 1995; Rip et al., 1996; Schot and Rip,

1997; Grin et al., 1997; Schot, 2001), 'transition management' (Rotmans et al., 2001) and 'upstream engagement' (Europta, 2000; Wilsdon and Willis, 2004; Stirling, 2005).

Though many features of these more broad-based architectures have yet to be instituted in practice, they do suggest (at least in principle) provision for significantly greater reflectiveness – and to some extent reflexivity – in processes of science and technology governance. Yet, for all their undoubted value and potential, it is clear that the wealth of emerging, more reflective, frameworks for the governance of science and technology still have some way to go before they might truly claim to fulfil the integrated promise of a truly reflexive integration of precaution and foresight.

For instance, for all their breadth, notions of 'strategic intelligence' generally presume (implicitly or explicitly) an over-arching instrumental agenda, thereby marginalizing normative deliberation over the framing of this agenda. In this way, they risk leaning towards relatively unreflexive adoption of whatever happen to be the interests of those incumbent institutions that shape this agenda. Likewise, there is a slight tendency in the 'transition management' literature to neglect the provenance and nature of the formative deliberations that underlie the development of the 'guiding vision' (Berkhout et al., 2004). Where this is the case, it may foster a certain lack of reflexivity over the implications of those contending candidate 'guiding visions' that are not adopted. For its part, by contrast, the burgeoning literature on 'upstream engagement' seems to sidestep slightly the reflexive character of the relationship between scientific and technological systems and their encompassing governance processes. Indeed, the very term 'upstream engagement' suggests in the linear metaphor of a stream flow precisely the monolithic deterministic notion of 'progress' that more reflexive understandings have come to refute (Stirling, 2005).

For all their shortcomings, these emerging approaches offer real opportunities to enhance reflection and reflexivity in governance systems towards more sustainable science and technology. In a field of academic discourse, which sometimes seems to revel in endless deconstruction, complication and elaboration of practical implications, what is even more remarkable about these approaches is that they offer an unusually elegant and parsimonious opportunity for practical integration. Together, they embody an emerging acknowledgement that if governance is to make a success of either precaution or foresight individually, it must effectively do both together. The real question is how might we harness this practical opportunity and build more reflexive governance institutions for realizing this integrated process of 'precautionary foresight'?

# PRACTICAL STRATEGIES FOR 'PRECAUTIONARY FORESIGHT'

This chapter began by noting the fact that prevailing discourses of techno-logical progress suppress a general 'politics of technology'. Given this back-ground, the institutional integration of precaution and foresight discourses constitutes a key element in the development of more reflective and reflexive governance for sustainability. In short, 'precautionary foresight' involves the adoption of more long-term, holistic, integrated and inclusive social processes for the exercise of explicit and deliberate social choice among contending scientific and technological trajectories (Stirling, 2003; 2004). In particular, this entails a series of concrete elements that are well documented and increasingly the subject of parallel methodological and institutional experimentation in the individual fields of precaution and fore-sight. In drawing some final practical conclusions for policy making, it is interesting to note how closely these specific emerging and converging fea-tures of 'precautionary foresight' relate to each of the five 'adequate strate-gies for reflexive governance' that are developed in the Introduction of this book by Voß and Kemp. To illustrate this fact, each strategy may be taken in turn.

## Anticipation of Long-term Systemic Effects of Action Strategies

It is with the aim of achieving greater breadth and depth of reflectiveness in the anticipation of possible positive and negative effects of governance inter-ventions, that the integration of foresight and precaution, itself, represents the principal strategy. Voß and Kemp rightly identify the rich variety of practical frameworks under which this might be pursued. These include 'strategic intelligence' (Kuhlman, 1999), 'post-modern steering' (Rip, 1998), 'constructive technology assessment' (Schwarz and Thompson, 1990; Rip, 1995; Rip et al., 1996; Schot and Rip, 1997; Grin et al., 1997; Schot, 2001), 'transition management' (Rotmans et al., 2002) and 'upstream engagement' (Europta, 2002; Wilsdon and Willis, 2004; Stirling, 2005). Although each embodies important means towards greater reflection and reflexivity in the senses defined at the beginning of this chapter, the preceding section outlined a series of specific difficulties and residual challenges. And it is these difficulties and challenges that are addressed by the complementary strate-gies for the reflexive governance of sustainable science and technology dis-cussed below.

## Iterative Participatory Goal Formulation

'Iterative participatory goal formulation' includes, but goes beyond, the emphasis on the potential volatility of changing social values and interests mentioned by Voß and Kemp (this volume). It also involves a high degree of reflexivity concerning the constructed and partly contingent character of scientific knowledge in the process of social appraisal (Wynne, 1992; Fisher and Harding, 1999; Stirling, 2003). Crucially, it highlights the multifaceted nature of social priorities and interests (and associated knowledges) at any given point in the governance process. Under the associated 'grounded perspectivism' developed earlier in this chapter, we see that the crucial property of 'independence' in risk regulation or scientific research systems increasingly rests on pluralistic engagement, rather than claims to unitary transcendent notions of 'scientific objectivity', 'institutional legitimacy' or 'expert or moral authority'. A move from 'independence through objectivity', to 'independence through pluralism', is thus a key feature of more reflexive approaches to 'iterative participatory goal formulation' in the governance of sustainability.

One particular necessary feature of such an approach involves the adoption of greater humility on the part of analytical methods, scientific disciplines and expert institutions involved in the governance process (Dovers and Handmer, 1992; Mayer, 1994; ESTO, 1999). In practice, this can be achieved by the greater use of 'heuristic' tools in appraisal, such as those indicated in Figure 9.3. For instance, although rarely used in this way, even something as straightforward as sensitivity analysis (Saltelli, 2001) can (depending on the chosen parameters) reveal some of the contingency under divergent framings of any quantitative method. A similar role is played by provision for explicit deliberation over the use of different 'decision heuristics' (Forster, 1999) under uncertainty – such as maximizing minimum benefits, minimizing maximum impacts or focusing on 'regrets'. Likewise, attention may extend to the contending implications of different ways of setting 'levels of proof' or assigning alternative 'burdens of persuasion' in the interpretation of scientific data (ESTO, 1999; EEA, 2001). This involves a greater degree of reflexivity over the weighting in social appraisal of the perspectives of those who stand to be affected by a scientific or technological commitment, in relation to those proposing it (O'Riordan and Cameron, 1994; Wynne, 1996). At a more general level, the simple expedient of a shift from 'unitary and prescriptive' to 'plural and conditional' policy recommendations (Stirling, 2003) can enable even relatively narrowly constituted forms of scientific advisory bodies to make real contributions towards more reflexive governance.

## Integrated (transdisciplinary) Knowledge Production

Beyond the integration of precaution and foresight, both as fields and cultures of interest, there are three somewhat more specific ways in which we may envisage more integrated frameworks of knowledge production for the sustainable governance of science and technology. The first is that attention should extend across an array of contending technology and policy options, rather than restricting attention to the 'opportunities', 'competitiveness', 'acceptability', 'tolerability' or 'safety' of a single option taken in isolation (Johnston et al., 1998; O'Brien, 2000). This resists outcomes under which the governance process is driven in a path-dependent fashion by those interests and perspectives that happen to be most privileged in the framing of the initial problem formulation, research question or regulatory issue.

The second aspect of additional reflection, concerns the extension of the scope of social appraisal to address production systems taken as a whole (including full resource chains and life cycles), rather than a single product, process or technology viewed simply in terms of the 'use' phase (Jackson and Taylor, 1992; MacGarvin, 1995; Tickner, 1999). This holds out a significant role for more broad-based analytical tools, such as life cycle assessment, and energy input–output analysis as well as more wide-ranging discursive processes.

The third area for integration involves attending to the 'pros' (benefits, justifications and purposes) as much as the 'cons' (costs, risks and wider impacts) (Jackson and Taylor, 1992; MacGarvin, 1995). It is interesting that – in different ways – this resonates with all sides in a typical technology governance controversy. Proponents are often concerned by what they hold to be a dearth of attention to the claimed benefits of their favoured technologies. For their part, sceptics are typically frustrated by the lack of scrutiny of these claims, when compared with the exhaustive regulatory demands to substantiate any suspected disadvantages. It is a rare opportunity indeed to meet both concerns simultaneously.

## Adaptivity of Strategies and Institutions

Together, emerging precaution and foresight discourses point to two principal means by which reflexive governance might seek to achieve the crucial properties of 'responsiveness' and 'adaptivity' highlighted by Voß and Kemp (this volume). The first involves a particular implication for the regulatory field, of their highlighting the general role of monitoring. At present, the regulation of science and technology – for instance in the fields of chemicals or biotechnology – is based to a large extent on laboratory experimentation and theoretical models (Jackson and Taylor, 1992; Tickner, 1999; EEA,

2001). It is a key implication of the greater humility of precautionary approaches towards ignorance (mentioned above) that significantly greater emphasis should be placed on scientific baseline studies and the systematic and comprehensive monitoring of environment and human health. The history of risk regulation repeatedly highlights how the neglect of basic monitoring – and associated avenues for scientific research – has significantly impeded the rate at which society comes to learn of what are later recognized to be serious problems (EEA, 2001).

A second means to foster adaptive responsiveness in governance involves a variety of strategies for enhancing the resilience of scientific and technological trajectories in the face of residual ignorance of a kind that can never be reduced through monitoring or research (Stirling, 1999). For instance, the deliberate pursuit of a diversity of technology or policy options avoids 'putting all the eggs in one basket' (Stirling, 1998). Intriguingly, diversification also offers an under-recognized strategy for accommodating the divergent interests and perspectives associated with the condition of ambiguity. Where we are unable to identify a single optimal course of action (satisfying all points of view), a judicious mix of actions may prove much more effective. It is generally much more practical to focus on constituting portfolios of options than it is to 'pick a winner' or 'engineer a consensus' through definitive analysis or deliberation over all possible benefits, impacts and scenarios.

Beyond this, there exists a series of further attributes of resilience. Options may differ in their agility in the face of particular possible developments (Clark and Bradshaw, 2004), involving the degree to which they might be reconfigured to adapt to a range of alternative scenarios (Holling, 1994; Killick, 1995; Farber, 1995). Flexibility concerns the ease with which commitments may be withdrawn from a particular option should it prove to be the object of adverse surprise (Collingridge, 1983). Likewise, there are issues around the robustness with which the strengths and weaknesses of a portfolio of options complement one another, such as to address the full range of potential developments or stakeholder concerns (Stirling, 1999). All these offer a basis for dynamic, adaptive system strategies, offering concrete ways to enhance the reflexivity of the governance process in the face of intractable challenges of ignorance and ambiguity.

**Interactive Strategy Development**

The promotion of productive interactions between different constituencies and networks of social actors, links at a more strategic level with the themes of transdisciplinarity and participation in appraisal already addressed above in relation to Voß and Kemp's strategy of 'iterative participatory goal formulation'. The key common challenge faced here lies in finding practical ways to articulate complex forms of integrated 'transdisciplinary' appraisal with deeper and more inclusive forms of stakeholder engagement and citizen deliberation – this time in strategy implementation. For its part, the theme of 'interactive assessment' of contending strategic options is a well-established and highly topical governance discourse in its own right (Grin et al., 1997; de Marchi et al., 1998). Divergent rationales for interactive engagement here extend well beyond precaution and foresight to include general discourses on democratic governance. Even with respect to highly specific operational matters of 'strategy development', they raise a range of profound normative, substantive and instrumental issues.

Under many normative democratic points of view, for instance, more inclusive forms of interactive engagement are quite simply 'the right thing to do', irrespective of the outcomes. Under more instrumental understandings, interactive engagement is justified on the grounds that it may help secure greater confidence or trust in existing institutions and procedures (Fiorino, 1989; NRC, 1996) or 'support' for particular decisions (Voß and Kemp, this volume) or 'social intelligence' for the purpose of managing residual adverse reactions (Grove-White et al., 2000). Here, the aim may be to provide legitimation for particular outcomes. The specific argument for interactive engagement highlighted in the precaution and foresight discourses, however, invokes a third rationale, which we may call substantive. Here, the aim is one of establishing a broader knowledge base and more effective social learning in order to achieve 'better outcomes' in the implementation of strategy (Stirling, 2005).

It is important to distinguish between these three (normative, instrumental and substantive) rationales and orientations for interactive engagement in strategy development. This is so, not least, because each approach embodies significantly different forms of reflexivity with respect to the prevailing distribution of political, institutional and economic power (Stirling, 2004). This is relevant, for instance, with respect to Voß and Kemp's (this volume) identification of the importance of the 'alignment' of such interaction towards a single 'collective strategic goal'. This kind of hegemonic ambition is consistent with an instrumental, but less with normative or substantive approaches to inclusive engagement. Returning to issues raised at the beginning of this chapter in relation to 'legitimation discourses' over sustainability, the presumption of an orientation towards 'alignment' may foster a certain vulnerability to the justificatory exercise of power (Collingridge, 1980; Wynne, 2002).

It is perhaps in the achievement of greater reflexivity over the role of power in the framing of interaction in strategy development, that the aspiration to more reflexive governance faces what is arguably its greatest challenge. One possible means to help enhance this particular form of reflexivity, may lie in deliberate initiatives to complement existing preoccupations with 'alignment', 'aggregation' and 'closure' in social appraisal with more deliberate attention to the 'opening up' of a full range of expectations, implications and possibilities (Stirling, 2004).[6] As it stands, there tends to be a presumption that effective inclusive engagement (by means such as consensus conferences and citizens' juries) is effectively synonymous with an aspiration to consensus or common ground. Yet there is increasing recognition, both in precaution and foresight discourses (Pellizzoni, 2001; Dryzek, 2000; Dryzek and Niemeyer, 2003; Stirling, 2004), of the positive role that persistent scepticism, divergence and dissent may play.

Just as there is a variety of concrete 'heuristic' tools to facilitate more pluralistic forms of 'iterative participatory goal formation' (discussed above), a range of more radical institutional means is also available for achieving greater reflexivity through the 'opening up' of what are presently relatively 'closed' processes of strategy development. 'Scenario workshops' (Werner, 2004) offer ways to develop and explore a number of alternative and mutually inconsistent strategies, perspectives and possibilities, and explore their permutations, without requiring their final aggregation. Various forms of interactive modelling (for example, de Marchi et al., 1998) show how participatory approaches can be articulated with even the most complex forms of quantitative specialist analysis. Q-methodology (McKeown and Thomas, 1988) offers a unique means to reflect on the social contingency of the qualitative frameworks that underlie any exercises in quantification, but itself uses quantitative methods in an open-ended fashion to illuminate interrelationships between contending (sometimes implicit) social discourses. Multi-criteria mapping (Stirling and Mayer, 2000) adapts decision analytic techniques to a more heuristic purpose, as a means to elicit and explore the implications of divergent social framings, providing a transparent basis for informing deliberation over areas of convergence as well as divergence. Deliberative mapping (Davies et al., 2003) builds on this approach to enable symmetrical engagement between divergent citizen – as well as specialist and stakeholder – perspectives, without compartmentalizing the contribution of each or emphasizing facilitated closure.

Although challenging and radical in some of their implications, the adoption of these kinds of 'opening up' approaches need not be intrinsically inconsistent with established institutions, procedures or even individual methods. What all these approaches have in common is the fact that they offer concrete ways to build greater reflexivity over the role of power in 'closing down' wider governance discourses.

## 'Opening up' in the Reflexive Governance of Sustainability

If we are to weave these various threads of discussion into a single normative chord, then this final theme on 'opening up' discourses on science and
technology arguably introduces the single most important practical implication of reflexivity for the governance for sustainability (Stirling, 2004).
The present chapter has shown a number of ways in which such 'opening up'
goes beyond the requirement simply for greater reflection in social appraisal
– important though this is. For sure, the 'precautionary' extension of attention to a wider variety of options, complexities, perspectives and possibilities, offers crucial means to mitigate exposure to the inevitable 'unintended
consequences' of science and technology. Yet, though necessary, this aspiration to greater depth and completeness in social appraisal is, in itself,
insufficient as a basis for more reflexive governance. Indeed, hubristic aspirations to this kind of synoptic reflection may even militate against reflexivity. They do this by neglecting the intrinsically subjective and contingent
nature of appraisal. Rigorous assessment – no matter how deeply reflective
or broad in scope – is thus essential, but not enough.

Likewise, this chapter has tried to show how a reflexive 'opening up' of
science and technology choice, also goes beyond the currently much-
discussed shift away from expert risk assessment and towards more inclusive 'upstream' processes of participatory deliberation. It is here that we
witness the potentially fruitful conjunction between 'precaution' and 'foresight'. Yet, where the reductive aggregations of risk assessment or the consensus orientations of deliberation are aimed at 'unitary prescriptive'
representations to policy making, they both fail a further criterion of reflexive governance. This is especially the case where such reflexivity includes
consideration of the effects of political and institutional power. Powerful
instrumental pressures towards institutional legitimation and decision
justification serve to privilege consensus in participatory deliberation just
as they demand aggregation in risk assessment. Either way, power exerts
familiar pressures towards an unreflexive 'closing down' of wider discourses and possibilities in science and technology choice.

The essence of reflexive governance, which is aimed at more sustainable
science and technology, certainly includes these kinds of deeper, broader
reflections and engagements. However, it goes beyond them by addressing
the inherently 'plural and conditional' natures, both of scientific understandings and of technological potentialities. Here, it has been further
argued that we must transcend the stylized dichotomy between the mainstream fallibilism of 'science-based decision-making' and an 'anything goes'
caricature relativism on the role of science in governance. Neither option
captures the multiplicity of contending, equally scientifically-founded

representations typically sustained by uncertainty, ambiguity and igno-rance. Instead, reflectiveness (over bias and error) and reflexivity (over diver-gent 'framings') can be reconciled by what might be called a 'grounded perspectivist' understanding. In this way, it is possible to achieve reflexivity over the plurality of legitimate interpretations of science without requiring an unreflective neglect of scientific discipline itself.

Likewise, the multiplicity of contending orientations for 'sustainable technology' is also 'plural and conditional'. They are plural in that a mul-tiplicity of divergent but equally dynamically-viable trajectories typically exists. They are conditional in that these disparate technological pathways are themselves contingent on (and themselves reconstitute) different forms of governance intervention. The 'opening up' of discourses on sustainable governance simply recognises this intrinsically 'plural and conditional' nature of both science and technology.

We may therefore conclude that the reflexive governance of sustainable science and technology requires explicit, deliberate attention to this multi-plicity of challenges. We have seen in the last section of the chapter how there is is no shortage of practical methodological tools or institutional processes by which to help foster the requisite 'opening up' of the social appraisal of science and technology and the delivery of 'plural and conditional' repre-sentations to wider discourses on sustainable governance. These can surely assist by catalyzing, nurturing and guiding more reflective and reflexive insti-tutions and procedures. However, in drawing this argument to its conclusion, we might recall the observations made at the outset over the implications for governance of persistently monolithic notions of scientific and technologi-cal 'progress'. No amount of methodological, institutional or discursive 'procedure' can negate the central normative imperative of reflexive gover-nance. In the end, this lies not in unified policy architectures or deliberate procedural design – but in the flowering of a spontaneous, vibrant, unruly general politics of technology.

## ACKNOWLEDGEMENTS

Thanks are due to René Kemp and Jan-Peter Voß for the initial stimulus, subsequent patience and invaluable advice, to Brian Wynne for longstand-ing inspiration and to Adrian Smith, Erik Millstone and Melissa Leach for some extremely helpful comments. This chapter builds on a number of earlier discussions, especially Stirling (2003) – a great debt is also owed to commentators on these preceding incarnations. The usual disclaimer applies to the more embarrassing passages.

# NOTES

1. This may represent one specific element in Beck's observation (Chapter 2, this volume) of a current 'meta-transformation of the political'.
2. The relationship between Wynne's (1992) seminal concept of 'indeterminacy' and that of ambiguity (Stirling, 1999) is briefly discussed in Stirling (2003). 'Indeterminacy' can be interpreted relatively unreflexively as a physical feature of quantum or nonlinear systems (Faber and Proops, 1994; Ruelle, 1991), separable from subjective social processes (Harremoes, 2000). As such, unlike 'uncertainty', 'ambiguity' and 'ignorance', it suggests an 'objective' property of an observed system, rather than a 'state of knowledge' that is co-constituted by the subjective conditions of the observer. In any event, Wynne himself also later uses the present term 'ambiguity' in an essentially similar sense (2002).
3. I am extremely grateful to Melissa Leach for reminding me of the potential for treating contending ontologies, as well as epistemologies, in these terms (see Leach et al., 2004). This is reflected in Figure 9.4. But – with gratitude for enlightening conversations with Erik Millstone – I believe that the basic point here applies in principle to a variety of understandings of the relationship between ontology and epistemology (see Quine, 1961; Wittgenstein, 1953).
4. I also owe to Erik Millstone a valuable clarification over the correct terminology on this point.
5. I use the present term in a sense which broadly resonates at a societal level with the more individualistic 'Nietzschean' concept of 'weak perspectivism' (Nietzsche, 1968; Hales and Welshon, 2000). This stands independently of any subsequent political baggage (Ortega Y Gasset, 1980), and usefully transcends an alternative term like 'epistemological pluralism', in suggesting an engagement not only with 'epistemic' issues, but also with ontology and power.
6. This normative call for enhanced balance between processes of 'closing down' and 'opening up' in the social appraisal of scientific understandings and technological potentialities displays interesting resonances with Beck's programme of 'cosmopolitan interdependence' (Chapter 2 this volume).

# REFERENCES

Adam, B., U. Beck and J. van Loon (2000), *The Risk Society and Beyond: critical issues for social theory*, London: Sage.

Alvesson, M. and K. Skoldberg (2000), *Reflexive Methodology*, London: Sage.

Amendola, A., S. Contini and I. Ziomas (1992), 'Uncertainties in chemical risk assessment: results of a European benchmark exercise', *Journal of Hazardous Materials*, **29**, 347–63.

Arrow, K. (1963), *Social Choice and Individual Values*, New Haven, CT: Yale University Press.

Arthur, W. (1989), 'Competing technologies, increasing returns, and lock-in by historical events', *Economic Journal*, **99**.

Barnes, B. and D. Edge (1982), *Science in Context: readings in the sociology of science*, Milton Keynes: Open University Press.

Beck, U. (1992), *Risk Society: towards a new modernity*, London: Sage.

Beck, U. (1994), 'The reinvention of politics: towards a theory of reflexive modernization', in U. Beck, A. Giddens and S. Lash (eds), *Reflexive Modernisation: politics, tradition and aesthetics in the modern social order*, Cambridge: Polity Press.

Beck, U., A. Giddens and S. Lash (1994), *Reflexive Modernisation: politics, tradition and aesthetics in the modern social order*, Cambridge: Polity Press.

Berkhout, F., J. Hertin and A. Jordan (2001), 'Socio-economic futures in climate change impact assessment: using scenarios as learning machines', Tyndall Centre Working Paper No. 3, Norwich: Tyndall Centre for Climate Change Research.

Berkhout, F., A. Smith and A. Stirling (2004), 'Socio-technological regimes and transition contexts' in B. Elzen, F. Geels and K. Green (eds), *System Innovation and the Transition to Sustainability: theory, evidence and policy*, Cheltenham, UK and Northampton, MA, USA: Edward Elgar.

Berlinski, D. (1976), *On Systems Analysis: An essay concerning the limitations of same mathematical models in the social, political, biological sciences*, Cambridge: MIT Press.

Bernstein, P. (1996), 'Against the Gods: the remarkable story of risk', London: Wiley.

Bezembinder, T. (1989), 'Social choice theory and practice', in C. Vlek and D. Cvetkovitch, *Social Decision Methodology for Technical Projects*, Dordrecht: Kluwer.

Bijker, W. (1995), *Of Bicycles, Bakelite and Bulbs: toward a theory of sociotechnical change*, Cambridge, MA: MIT Press.

Blair, T. (2000), T. Blair, speech delivered by the UK Prime Minister to The European Bioscience Conference, London, Monday, 20 November, available at: http://www.monsanto.co.uk/news/ukshowlib.phtml?uid=4104.

Boehmer-Christiansen, S. (1994), 'The precautionary principle in Germany: enabling government', in T. O'Riordan and J. Cameron (eds), *Interpreting the Precautionary Principle*, London: Cameron May.

Bohmann, J. (1996), *Public Deliberation: pluralism, complexity and democracy*, Cambridge, MA: MIT Press.

Bonner, J. (1986), *Politics, Economics and Welfare: an elementary introduction to social choice*, Brighton: Harvester Press.

Bourdieu, P. and L. Wacquant (1992), *An Invitation to Reflexive Sociology*, Cambridge: Polity Press.

Boyce, A. (1996), *Environment Technology: preserving the legacy*, Chichester: Wiley.

Brealey, R. and S. Myers (1988), *Principles of Corporate Finance*, 3rd edn, New York: McGraw Hill.

Brooks, H. (1986), 'The typology of surprises in technology, institutions and development', in W.C. Clark and R.E. Munn (eds) (1986), *Sustainable Development of the Biosphere*, Cambridge: Cambridge University Press.

Brown, G. (2004), speech delivered by the UK Chancellor to UK Government Conference on Advancing Enterprise, London, 26 January, available at: http://www.hm-treasury.gov.uk/newsroom_and_speeches/speeches/chancellorexchequer/speech_chex_260104.cfm.

Byrd, D. and C. Cothern (2000), 'Introduction to Risk Analysis: a systematic approach to science-based decision making', Government Institutes, Rockville Maryland.

Callon, M., J. Law and A. Rip (1986), *Mapping the Dynamics of Science and Technology: sociology of science in the real world*, Basingstoke: Macmillan.

CEC, (2000), 'Towards a European Research Area', Communication from the Commission to the Council, COM(2000)6, Brussels: Commission of the European Communities, January.

Clark, W. and T. Bradshaw (2004), *Agile Energy Systems*, London: Elsevier.

Clemen, R. (1996), *Making Hard Decisions*, 2nd edn., Belmont: Duxbury.

Collingridge, D. (1980), *The Social Control of Technology*, Milton Keynes: Open University Press.

Collingridge, D. (1982), *Critical Decision Making: a new theory of social choice*, London: Pinter.

Collingridge, D. (1983), *Technology in the Policy Process: controlling nuclear power*, London: Pinter.

CST, UK Council for Science and Technology (2000), 'Technology Matters: report on the exploitation of science and technology by UK business', London: HMSO, February.

Cyranski, J. (1986), 'The probability of a probability', in L. Justice (ed), *Maximum Entropy and Bayesian Methods*, Cambridge: Cambridge University Press.

David, P. (1985), 'Clio and the Economics of QWERTY', *American Economic Review*, **75**, 332–7.

Davies, G., J. Burgess, M. Eames, S. Mayer, K. Staley, A. Stirling and S. Williamson (2003), 'Deliberative mapping: appraising options for addressing "the Kidney Gap"', final report to Wellcome Trust, June, available at: http://www.deliberative-mapping.org/.

De Finetti, N. (1974), *Theory of Probability*, New York: Wiley.

De Marchi, B., S. Funtowicz, C. Gough A. Guimaraes Pereira and E. Rota (1998), 'The Ulysses voyage', ULYSSES at JRC, EUR 17760EN Ispra: Joint Research Centre – EC, available at: http://zit1.zit.tu-darmstadt.de/ulysses/tutor-ial.htm.

DEFRA, L. Cornish and C. Porro (2002), 'Science for Sustainability' DEFRA Agency Review, UK Department for Environment and Rural Affairs, London, December.

DEFRA, (2004), 'Sustainable development indicators in your pocket', London: HMSO, at: http://www.sustainable-development.gov.uk/indicators/sdiyp/sdiyp 04a4.pdf.

Dennett, D. (1996), *Darwin's Dangerous Idea: Evolution and the Meanings of Life*, London: Penguin.

Dodgson, J., M. Spackman, A. Pearman and I. Phillips (2001), *Multicriteria analysis: a manual*, London: Department for Transport, Local Government and the Regions, HMSO.

Dosi, G. (1982), 'Technological paradigms and technological trajectories', *Research Policy*, **11**.

Dosi, G. and M. Egidi (1987), 'Substantive and procedural uncertainty, an exploration of economic behaviours in complex and changing environments', SPRU DRC discussion paper no. 46, 1987, SPRU, Sussex.

Dovers, S. and J. Handmer (1992), 'Ignorance, the precautionary principle and sustainability', *Ambio*, **24** (2), 92–7.

Dryzek, J. (2000), *Deliberative Democracy and Beyond: liberals, critics, contestations*, Oxford: Oxford University Press.

Dryzek, J. and S. Niemeyer (2003), 'Pluralism and consensus in political deliberation', paper presented to the 2003 Annual Meeting of the American Political Science Association, Philadelphia, 28–31 August.

Dubois, D., H. Prade and H. Farreny (1988), *Possibility Theory: an approach to computerised processing of uncertainty*, New York: Plenum.

Dyson, G. (1998), *Darwin among the Machines: the Evolution of Global Intelligence*, London: Penguin.

EEA (2000), 'Chemicals in the European Environment: Low Doses, High Stakes?', Copenhagen: European Environment Agency.

EEA (D. Gee, P. Harremoes, J. Keys, M. MacGarvin, A. Stirling, S. Vaz and B. Wynne 2001), *Late Lesson from Early Warnings: the precautionary principle 1898–2000*, Copenhagen: European Environment Agency.

European Science and Technology Observatory (1999), 'On "science" and "precaution" in The Management of technological risk', volume I: synthesis study report to the EU Forward Studies Unit by European Science and Technology Observatory (ESTO), IPTS, Sevilla, EUR19056 EN, available at: ftp://ftp.jrc.es/pub/EURdoc/eur19056IIen.pdf.

Europta, L. Kluver et al. (2002), 'European participatory technology assessment: participatory methods in technology assessment and technology decision-making', Danish Board of Technology, Copenhagen, available at: http://www.tekno.dk/pdf/projekter/europta_Report.pdf.

Faber, M. and J. Proops (1994), *Evolution, Time, Production and the Environment*, Berlin: Springer.

Farber, S. (1995), 'Economic resilience and economic policy', *Ecological Economics*, **15**, 105–7.

Farman, J. (2001), 'Halocarbons, the ozone layer and the precautionary principle', in EEA, 2001.

Feyerabend, P. (1975), *Against Method*, London: Verso.

Feyerabend, P. (1978), *Science in a Free Society*, London: Verso.

Fiorino, D. (1989), 'Environmental risk and democratic process: a critical review', *Columbia Journal of Environmental Law*, **14**, 501.

Fischer, F. (1990), *Technocracy and the Politics of Expertise*, Newbury Park, CA: Sage.

Fischoff, Baruch (1995), 'Risk Perception and Communication Unplugged: Twenty Years of Progress', *Risk Analysis*, **15** (2), 137–45.

Fisher, E. and R. Harding (eds) (1999), *Perspectives on the Precautionary Principle*, Sydney: Federation Press.

Ford, J. (1983), *Choice, Expectation and Uncertainty: an appraisal of G.L.S. Shackles Theory*, Totowa, NJ: Barnes and Noble.

Forster, M. (1999), 'How do simple rules "fit to reality" in a complex world?', *Minds and Machines*, **9**, 543–64.

Funtowicz, S. and J. Ravetz, (1989), 'Managing the Uncertainties of Statistical Information', in J. Brown (ed.), *Environmental Threats*, London: Pinter, pp. 95–117.

Funtowicz, S. and J. Ravetz (1990), S. Funtowicz, J. Ravetz, *Uncertainty and Quality in Science for Policy*, Amsterdam: Kluwer.

Giddens, A. (1976), *The New Rules of Sociological Method*, London: Hutchinson.

Giddens, A. (1990), *The Consequences of Modernity*, Stanford, CA: Stanford University Press.

Gouldner, A. (1970), *The Coming Crisis of Western Sociology*, London: Heinemann.

Grabher, G. and D. Stark (1997), 'Organizing diversity: evolutionary theory, network analysis and postsocialism', *Regional Studies*, **31** (5), 533–44.

Graedel, T. and B. Allenby (2002), *Industrial Ecology*, 2nd edn, New Jersey: Prentice Hall.

Grin J., H. van de Graaf, and R. Hoppe (1997), *Technology Assessment through Interaction: a guide*, The Hague: Rathenau Institute.

Grove-White, R., P. Macnaghten, S. Mayer and B. Wynne (1997), 'Uncertain world.

Genetically modified organisms, food and public attitudes in Britain', Centre for the Study of Environmental Change, Lancaster University.

Grove-White, R., P. Macnaghten and B. Wynne (2000), 'Wising up: the public and new technologies', Centre for the Study of Environmental Change, Lancaster University.

Grupp, H. and Linstone H. (1999), 'National technology foresight activities around the globe: resurrection and new paradigms', *Technological Forecasting and Social Change*, **60**, 85–94.

Hacking, I. (1975), *The Emergence of Probability: a philosophical study of early ideas about probability induction and statistical inference*, Cambridge: Cambridge University Press.

Hanley, N. and C. Spash (1993), *Cost–Benefit Analysis and the Environment*, Cheltenham, UK and Northampton, MA, USA: Edward Elgar.

Hales, S. and R. Welshon (2000), *Nietzsche's Perspectivism*, Illinois University Press.

Hansen, A. and C. Clausen (2000), 'From participative TA to TA as participant in the social shaping of technology', *TA Datenbank Nachrichten*, **3** (9), October.

Harremoes, P. (2000), 'Methods for integrated assessment', paper to International Workshop on Information for Sustainable Water Management, Nunspeet, The Netherlands, 25–28 September.

Hayek, F. von (1978), *New Studies in Philosophy, Politics, Economics and the History of Ideas*, Chicago University Press.

Hey, E. (1992), *The Precautionary Principle and the LDC*, Erasmus University.

HMT (2004), 'Science and innovation investment framework', 2004–2014, London: HM Treasury, July, available at: http://www.hm-treasury.gov.uk/spending_review/spend_sr04/associated_documents/spending_sr04_science.cfm.

Hogwood, B. and L. Gunn (1984), *Policy Analysis for the Real World*, Oxford: Oxford University Press.

Holling, C. (1994), 'Simplifying the complex: the paradigms of ecological function and structure', Futures, **26** (6), 598–609.

Hughes, T. (1983): Networks of Power: electrification in western society 1880–1930, Baltimore, MD: Johns Hopkins University Press.

Hunt, J. (1994), 'The social construction of precaution', in T. O'Riordan and J. Cameron *Interpreting the Precautionary Principle*, London: Earthscan.

Irvine, J. and B. Martin (1984), *Foresight in Science: Picking the Winners*, London: Pinter.

Irwin, A. (1995), *Citizen Science: A Study of People, Expertise and Sustainable Development*, London: Routledge.

Jackson, T. and P. Taylor (1992), 'The precautionary principle and the prevention of marine pollution', *Chemistry and Ecology*, **7**, 123–34.

Jaeger, C., O. Renn, E. Rosa and T. Webler (2001), *Risk: uncertainty and rational action*, London: Earthscan.

Janssen, R. (1994), *Multiobjective Decision Support for Environmental Management*, Dordrecht: Kluwer.

Jasanoff, S. (1990), *The Fifth Branch: Science Advisers as Policymakers*, Cambridge MA: Harvard University Press.

Jaulin, L., M. Kieffer, O. Didrit and É. Walter (2001), *Applied Interval Analysis*, London: Springer Verlag.

Jaynes, E. (1986), 'Bayesian methods: general background', in L. Justice (ed),

*Maximum Entropy and Bayesian Methods*, Cambridge: Cambridge University Press.

Johnston, P., D. Santillo and R. Stringer (1998), 'Risk assessment and reality: recognizing the limitations', working paper, Exeter University.

Jordan, A. and T. O'Riordan (1998), 'The precautionary principle in contemporary environmental policy and politics', paper delivered to conference on 'Putting the Precautionary Principle into Practice: how to make "good" environmental decisions under uncertainty', London Resource Centre, April.

Joss, S. and J. Durant (1995), *Public Participation in Science: the Role of Consensus Conferences in Europe*, London: Science Museum.

Keepin, B. and B. Wynne (1982), 'Technical Analysis of IIASA Energy Scenarios', *Nature*, **312**.

Kelly, J. (1978), *Arrow Impossibility Theorems*, New York: Academic Press.

Kemp, R., J. Schot and R. Hoogma (1998), 'Regime shifts to sustainability through processes of niche formation: the approach of strategic niche management.' *Technology Analysis and Strategic Management*, **10** (2), 175–95.

Keynes, J. (1921), *A Treatise on Probability*, London: Macmillan.

Killick, T. (1995), 'Flexibility and economic progress', *World Development*, **23** (5), 721–34.

Klir, G. (1989), 'Is there more to uncertainty than some probability theorists might have us believe?', *International Journal of General Systems*, **15**, 347–78.

Klir, G. and T. Folger (1988), *Fuzzy Sets, Uncertainty and Information*, New Jersey: Prentice Hall.

Kluver, L. et al. (2002), *European Participatory Technology Assessment: participatory methods in technology assessment and technology decision-making*, Danish Board of Technology: Copenhagen, available (April 2005) at http://www.tekno.dk/pdf/projecktor/ehropta_Report.pdf.

Knight, F. (1921), *Risk, Uncertainty and Profit*, Boston: Houghton Mifflin.

Kuhn, T. (1970), *The Structure of Scientific Revolutions*, Chicago: Chicago University Press.

Kuhlmann, S. (1999), 'Distributed intelligence: combining evolution, foresight and technology assessment', *IPTS Report*, **40**, 16–22.

Lash, S., B. Swerszynski and B. Wynne (eds) (1996), *Risk, Environment and Modernity: towards a new ecology*, London: Sage.

Lash, S. (2001), 'Technological forms of life', *Theory, Culture and Society*, **18** (1), 105–20.

Leach, M., I. Scoones and B. Wynne (eds) (2005), *Science, Citizenship and Globalization*, London: Zed.

Levidow, L., S. Carr, R. Schomberg and D. Wield (1998), 'European biotechnology regulation: framing the risk assessment of a herbicide-tolerant crop', *Science, Technology and Human Values*, **22** (4), 472–505.

Lindsay, R. (1995), 'Galloping Gertie and the precautionary principle: how is environmental impact assessment assessed?', in T. Wakeford and N. Walters, *Science for the Earth*, London: Wiley.

Lloyd, L. (2000), 'The tyranny of the L-shape curve', *Science and Public Affairs*, February.

Loasby, B. (1976), *Choice, Complexity and Ignorance: an inquiry into economic theory and the practice of decision making*, Cambridge: Cambridge University Press.

Loveridge, D. (ed.) (1996), Special issue on Technology Assessment, *International Journal of Technology Management*, **11** (5/6).

Luce, R. and H. Raiffa (1957), 'An axiomatic treatment of utility', in R. Luce and H. Raiffa (eds), *Games and Decisions: introduction and critical survey*, New York: Wiley.

Luhmann, N. (2000), *The Reality of the Mass Media*, Stanford, CA: Stanford University Press.

Lumby, S. (1984), *Investment Appraisal*, 2nd edn. London: Van Nostrand.

MacGarvin, M. (1995), 'The implications of the precautionary principle for biological monitoring', *Helgolander Meeresuntersuchunge*, **49**, 647–62.

MacKay, A. (1980), *Arrow's Theorem: the paradox of social choice – a case study in the philosophy of economics*, New Haven, CT: Yale University Press.

Markman, H. (ed.) (1997), *Environmental Management Systems and Cleaner Production*, Chichester: Wiley.

Martin, B. (1995), 'A review of recent overseas programmes', *Technology Foresight*, **6**, Office of Science and Technology, London.

Martin, B. and J. Irvine, (1989), *Research Foresight: priority-setting in science*, London: Pinter.

Martin, B. and R. Johnston (1999), 'Technology foresight for wiring up the national innovation system', *Technological Forecasting and Social Change*, **60** (1), 37–54.

Martuzzi, M. and J. Tickner (eds) (2004), 'The precautionary principle: protecting public health and the environment and the future of our children', World Health Organisation Europe, Geneva, 2004.

McKenna, C. (1986), *The Economics of Uncertainty*, Brighton: Wheatsheaf-Harvester.

McKeown, B. and D. Thomas (1988), *Q Methodology*, Newbury Park: Sage.

Misa, T. and P. Brey (eds) (2003), *Modernity and Technology*, Cambridge, MA: MIT Press.

Mokyr, J. (1992), *The Lever of Riches: technological creativity and economic progress*, Oxford: Oxford University Press.

Morgan, M., M. Henrion and M. Small (1990), *Uncertainty: a guide to dealing with uncertainty in quantitative risk and policy analysis*, Cambridge: Cambridge University Press.

Morris, J. (ed.) (2000), *Rethinking Risk and the Precautionary Principle*, London: Butterworth Heinemann.

Myers, S. (1984), 'Finance theory and financial strategy', *Interfaces*, **14**.

Nelson, R. and S. Winter (1982), *An Evolutionary Theory of Economic Change*, Cambridge: Belknap.

Nietzsche, F. (1968), 'On truth and lies in an extra-moral sense', in W. Kaufmann (trans.), *The Portable Nietzsche*, New York: Viking Press.

Norris, R., E. Caswwell-Chen and M. Kogan (2002), *Concepts in Integrated Pest Management*, New Jersey: Prentice Hall.

Nowotny, H., P. Scott and M. Gibbons (1995), *Re-Thinking Science: Knowledge and the Public in an Age of Uncertainty*, Cambridge: Polity Press.

NRC (United States National Research Council), H. Fineberg (1996), 'Understanding risk: informing decisions in a democratic society', National Research Council Committee on Risk Characterization, Washington: National Academy Press.

O'Brien, M. (2000), *Making Better Environmental Decisions: an alternative to risk assessment*, Cambridge MA: MIT Press.

O'Riordan, T. and J. Cameron (1994), *Interpreting the Precautionary Principle*, London: Earthscan.

O'Riordan, T. and A. Jordan (2001), *Reinterpreting the Precautionary Principle*, London: Cameron May.

Ortega Y Gasset, J. (1980), *The Origin of Philosophy*, New York: W. Norton.

OED (1989), J. Simpson and E. Weiner, *The Oxford English Dictionary*, 2nd edn, Oxford: Oxford University Press.

Pellizzoni, L. (2001), 'The myth of the best argument: power deliberation and reason', *British Journal of Sociology*, **52** (1), 59–86.

Popper, K. (1963), *Conjectures and Refutations*, London: Routledge and Kegan Paul.

Porter, T. (1995), *Trust in Numbers*, Princeton, NJ: Princeton University Press.

Quine, A. (1961), *From a Logical Point of View*, Harper and Rowe.

Raffensberger, C. and J. Tickner (eds) (1999), *Protecting Public Health and the Environment: Implementing the Precautionary Principle*, Washington: Island Press.

Ravetz, J. (1986), 'Usable Knowledge, usable ignorance: incomplete science with policy implications', in W.C. Clark and R.E. Munn (eds), *Sustainable Development of the Biosphere*, Cambridge: Cambridge University Press.

Renn, O., T. Webler and P. Wiedemann (1995), *Fairness and Competence in Citizen Participation: evaluating models for environmental discourse*, Dordrecht: Kluwer.

Rip, A. (1995), 'Introduction of new technology: making use of recent insights from sociology and economics of technology', *Technology Analysis and Strategic Management*, **7** (4), 417–31.

Rip, A. (ed.) (1998), 'Steering and effectiveness in a developing knowledge society', proceedings of a workshop at the University of Twente, Utrecht: Uitgeverij Lemma.

Rip, A., T. Misa and J. Schot (1996), *Managing Technology in Society*, London: Pinter.

Rosa, E. (1998), 'Metatheoretical foundations for post-normal risk', *Journal of Risk Research*, **1** (1), 15–44.

Rosenberg, N. (1996), 'Uncertainty and technological change', in R. Landau, T. Taylor and G. Wright (eds), *The Mosaic of Economic Growth*, Stanford, CA: Stanford University Press.

Rotmans, J., R. Kemp and M. van Asselt (2001), 'More evolution than revolution: transition management in public policy'. *Foresight*, **3** (1), 15–31.

Rowell, A. (1996), *Green Backlash: Global Subversion of the Environment Movement*, London: Routledge.

Rowe, W. (1994), 'Understanding uncertainty', *Risk Analysis*, **14** (5), 743–50.

Ruelle, D. (1991), *Chance and Chaos*, London: Penguin.

Sorrell, S., E. Malley, J. Schleich and S. Scott (2004), *The Economics of Energy Efficiency: barriers to cost-effective investment*, Cheltenham, UK and Northampton, MA, USA: Edward Elgar.

Sahal, D. (1985), 'Technological guideposts and innovation avenues', *Research Policy*, **14**, 61–82.

Saltelli, A. (2001), 'Sensitivity analysis for importance assessment', EC Joint Research Centre, Ispra, available at: http://www.ce.ncsu.edu/risk/pdf/saltelli.pdf, (December).

Sand, P. (2000), 'The precautionary principle: a European perspective', *Human and Ecological Risk Assessment*, **6** (3), 445–58.

Schot, J. and A. Rip (1997), 'The past and future of constructive technology assessment', *Technological Forecasting and Social Change*, **54**, 251–68.

Schot, J. (2001), 'Towards new forms of participatory technology development', *Technology Analysis and Strategic Management*, **13** (1), 39–52.

Schwarz, M. and M. Thompson (1990), *Divided We Stand: redefining politics, technology and social choice*, New York: Harvester Wheatsheaf.

Sclove, R. (1995), *Democracy and Technology*, New York: Guilford Press.

Sen, A. (1970), *Collective Choice and Social Welfare*, North Holland.

Shackle, G. (1968), *Uncertainty in Economics and Other Reflections*, Cambridge: Cambridge University Press.

Shackley, S. and B. Wynne (1996), 'Representing uncertainty in global climate change science and policy: boundary-ordering devices and authority', *Science, Technology and Human Values*, **21**, 275–302.

Smith, M. and L. Marx (eds) (1994), *Does Technology Drive History: the dilemma of technological determinism*, Cambridge, MA: MIT Press.

Smithson, M. (1989), *Ignorance and Uncertainty: emerging paradigms*, New York: Springer.

Spash, C., A. Holland and J. O'Neill (1998), 'Environmental values and wetland ecosystems, CVM, ethics and attitudes, research report by Cambridge Research for the Environment, Cambridge University, August.

Starr, C. (1969), 'Social Benefit versus Technological Risk: what is our society willing to pay for safety?', *Science*, **165**, 1232–8.

Steier, F. (1991), *Research and Reflexivity*, London: Sage.

Stirling, A. (1997) 'Limits to the Value of External Costs', *Energy Policy*, **25** (5), 517–40.

Stirling, A. (1998), 'On the economics and analysis of diversity', SPRU electronic working paper no. 28, October, available at: http://www.sussex.ac.uk/spru/publications/imprint/sewps/sewp28/sewp228.html.

Stirling, A. (1999), 'On "Science" and "Precaution" in the management of technological risk', report to the EU Forward Studies Unit, IPTS, Sevilla, EUR19056 EN.

Stirling, A. (2003), 'Risk, uncertainty and precaution: some instrumental implications from the social sciences', in F. Berkhout, M. Leach and I. Scoones (eds), *Negotiating Change*, Cheltenham, UK and Northampton, MA, USA: Edward Elgar.

Stirling, A. (2004), 'Opening up or closing down: analysis, participation and power in the social appraisal of technology', in M. Leach, I. Scoones and B. Wynne (eds), *Science, Citizenship and Globalisation*, London: Zed.

Stirling, A. (2005), 'Opening up or closing down: analysis, participation and power in the social appraisal of technology' in M. Leach, I. Scoones and B. Wynne (eds), *Science and Citizens: globalization and the challenge of engagement*, London: Zed, pp. 218–31.

Stirling, A. and S. Mayer (1999), 'Rethinking risk: a pilot multi-criteria mapping of a genetically modified crop in agricultural systems in the UK', SPRU, University of Sussex.

Stirling, A. and S. Mayer (2000), 'Precautionary approaches to the appraisal of risk: a case study of a GM crop', *International Journal of Occupational and Environmental Health*, **6** (3), October–December.

Stirling, A. and P. van Zwanenberg (2001), 'Background report on the implementation of precaution in the European Union', interim report to PRECAUPRI project, SPRU, Sussex University, December.

Stirling, A. and P. van Zwanenberg (2003), 'A general model for the precautionary regulation of risk', section B in the final report of EU STRATA project on 'Regulatory strategies and research needs to compose and specify a European policy on the application of the precautionary principle' (PrecauPri), Centre for Technology Assessment, Stuttgart, April, available at: http://www.sussex.ac.uk/sprn/environment/precaupripdfs.html

Stone, K. (ed.) (1990), *Environmental Challenge of the 1990s: pollution prevention, clean technologies and clean production*, US Government Printing Office, Washington, DC.

Sundgvist, T., P. Soderholm and A. Stirling (2004), 'Electric power generation: valuation of environmental costs', in C.J. Cleveland (ed.), *Encyclopedia of Energy*, San Diego: Academic Press.

Suter, G. (1990), 'Uncertainty in environmental risk assessment', in G. von Furstenberg (ed.), *Acting under Uncertainty*, Dordrecht: Kluwer.

Szekely, G. (1986), *Paradoxes in Probability Theory and Mathematical Statistics*, Dordrecht: Reidel.

Thompson, M. and M. Warburton (1985), 'Decision making under contradictory certainties: how to save the Himalayas when you can't find what's wrong with them', *Journal of Applied Systems Analysis*, **12**.

Thornton, J. (2000), 'Pandora's poison: on chlorine, health and a new environmental strategy', Cambridge, MA: MIT.

Tickner, J. (1999), 'A map towards precautionary decision-making', in C. Rattensberger and J. Tickner (eds), *Protecting Public Health and the Environment: Implementing the Precautionary Principle*, Washington DC: Island Press.

UNCED (1987), G. Brundtland, 'Our common future: report of the United Nations Commission on Environment and Development', Oxford: Oxford University Press.

UNCED (1992), Final Declaration of the UN Conference on Environment and Development, Rio de Janeiro.

UNDP (2000), M. Malloch Brown, Head United Nations Development Programme (UNDP), statement reported on UNDP website available at: http://www.undp.org/hdr2001/clips/newsweek1.pdf

USDA (2000), C. Woteki, 'The role of precaution in food safety decisions', remarks prepared for Under Secretary for Food Safety, Food Safety and Inspection Service, US Department of Agriculture, Washington, DC, March.

Van den Berg, N., C. Dutilh and G. Huppes (1995), *Beginning LCA: a Guide to Environmental Life Cycle Assessment* Rotterdam: CML.

Van Zwanenberg, P. and E. Millstone, (2001), 'Mad cow disease' – 1980s–2000: how reassurances undermined precaution', in EEA 2001.

Van Zwanenberg, P. and A. Stirling (2004), 'Risk and precaution in the US and Europe', *Yearbook of European Environmental Law*, **3**, 43–57.

Vlek, C. and D. Cvetkovitch (1989), *Social Decision Methodology for Technological Projects*, Kluwer, Dordrecht.

Vogel, D. (2000), 'The WTO vote: the wrong whipping boy', *The American Prospect* **11** (14), 5 June.

Von Winterfeldt, D. and W. Edwards (eds) (1986), *Decision Analysis and Behavioural Research*, Cambridge: Cambridge University Press.

Walker, W. (2000), 'Entrapment in large technical systems: institutional commitment and power relations', *Research Policy*, **29** (7–8), 833–46.

Wallsten, T. (1986), 'Measuring vague uncertainties and understanding their use in decision making', in von Winterfeldt and Edwards, 1986.

Watson, S. (1994), 'The meaning of probability in probabilistic safety analysis', *Reliability Engineering and System Safety*, **45**, 261–9.

Weale, A. (2000), *Environmental Governance in Europe: an ever closer ecological union*, Oxford: Oxford University Press.

Weatherford, R. (1982), *Philosophical Foundations of Probability Theory*, London: Routledge and Kegan Paul.

Werner, R. (2004), *Designing Strategy: Scenario analysis and the art of making business strategy*, New Jersey: Praeger.

Williams R. and D. Edge (1996), 'The social shaping of technology', *Research Policy*, **25**, 865–99.

Wilsdon, J. and R. Willis (2004), *See-through Science: why public engagement needs to move upstream*, London: Demos, available at http://www.demos.co.uk/catalogue/paddlingupstream/.

Winkler, G. (1986), 'Necessity, chance and freedom', in von Winterfeldt and Edwards (eds), *Decision Analysis and Behavioural Research*, Cambridge: Cambridge University Press.

Winner, L. (1977), *Autonomous Technology: technics out of control as a theme in political thought*, Cambridge, MA: MIT Press.

Wittgenstein, L. (1953), *Philosophical Investigations*, (trans.), G. Anscombe, Oxford: Blackwell.

Woolgar, S. (ed.) (1988), *Knowledge and Reflexivity: new frontiers in the sociology of knowledge*, London: Sage.

Wynne, B. (1975), 'The rhetoric of consensus politics: a critical review of technology assessment', *Research Policy*, **4**.

Wynne, B. (1987), 'Risk perception, decision analysis and the public acceptance problem', in B. Wynne (ed.), *Risk Management and Hazardous Waste: implementation and the dialectics of credibility*, Berlin: Springer.

Wynne, B. (1992), 'Uncertainty and environmental learning: reconceiving science and policy in the preventive paradigm', *Global Environmental Change*, 111–27.

Wynne, B. (1996), 'May the sheep safely graze?' in S. Lash, B. Szerszynski and B.Wynne (eds), *Risk Environment and Modernity: toward a new ecology*, London: Sage, pp. 44–83.

Wynne, B. (1997), 'Methodology and institutions: value as seen from the risk field', J. Foster (ed.), *Valuing Nature: economics, ethics and environment*, London: Routledge.

Wynne, B. (2002), 'Risk and environment as legitimatory discourses of technology: reflexivity inside out?', *Current Sociology*, **50** (30), 459–77.

Zadeh, L. and J. Kacprzyk (1992), *Fuzzy Logic for the Management of Uncertainty*, New York: Wiley.

# 10. The (re)search for solutions: research programmes for sustainable development[1]

## Katy Whitelegg

## INTRODUCTION

The more accepted the concept of sustainability becomes, the more obvious are the shortcomings of current forms of policy making and knowledge production. The departmentalisation of policy making and the isolation of research disciplines cannot provide the integrated solutions needed to pursue sustainable development. Implementing sustainable development depends on the integration of different areas of policy making and conflicting goals with research and practical experience. However, attempts at integrating and co-ordinating policy areas, research disciplines and praxis have been increasing over recent years. Not only are there more mechanisms and initiatives to increase the coherence and co-ordination of policy fields to support sustainable development, but also in research policy the design of programmes has begun to reflect the need for greater integration.

Research activities have always been valued for their contribution to furthering the aims of sustainable development both through activities on understanding the natural environment and through analysing the impact human activities can have. Such research activities have led to the development of a wealth of instruments for defining what sustainable development means in concrete areas and measuring the current distance from it. More recently, however, the demands on the research system have been changing and expanding. Research is no longer seen as the mere provider of information on the basis of which policy decisions can be taken and targets determined. Research is now expected to be a more active player in facilitating and defining change. It should play a role in moving from the provision of information to the development of integrated solutions. Research on goals and indicators for sustainable development can be brought together with the problem of finding context-specific solutions. In this way abstract goals can be confronted with looking at the expectations, values and behavioural patterns of the actors involved.

The integrated and context-specific approach to the role of research has gained strength over the last decade. Research programmes have been established with the specific objective of facilitating research activities that provide problem orientated context-specific solutions, programmes that require a combination of expertise from different disciplines together with praxis relevant knowledge.

This chapter looks at research programmes that focus on sustainable development and asks to what extent they can be seen as an example of reflexive governance. In the introduction five elements of reflexive governance are suggested that are important for the development and implementation of policies and initiatives that are sustainable.

At first sight it would seem as though all research programmes that support sustainable development are organised along the lines of the five principles. However, closer observation shows that this is not the case and that there are considerable differences between the ways in which the programmes address the five principles.

The focus on programmes and not on the project level is a deliberate one. Much work has been done on transdisplinarity on the project level. Less emphasis has been placed on how programmes for sustainable development work and especially on comparing the different approaches European programmes take to defining and implementing programmes for sustainable development.

The chapter starts by defining the object of observation. It asks what a research programme for sustainable development is. It then develops a framework for assessing the programmes. This framework works along slightly different lines to the five principles outlined in the introduction as it was developed specifically to capture the characteristics of research programmes. The framework breaks the programmes down into a series of interacting levels. The programmes are then assessed along the levels in the framework, but also drawing on the five elements of reflexive governance in order to discuss the extent to which the levels in the programmes can be called examples of reflexive governance. The conclusion draws together the assessments of the different levels and suggests key characteristics that enable research programmes to be reflexive.

## WHAT ARE RESEARCH PROGRAMMES FOR SUSTAINABLE DEVELOPMENT?

Over the past two decades most European countries have designed and established research programmes that specifically focus on sustainable development. Putting sustainability as the main goal of the programmes has meant thinking about the implications of translating the concept of sustainable development into concrete research activities and defining the role that research should play.

The concept of sustainable development entails combining environmental, economic and social goals. On a relatively abstract level there is general consensus that the current development model is unsustainable and that we should be moving towards a more sustainable model that is able to integrate different aims and not trade one off against the other. Trying to define the concept on a more concrete level, however, automatically leads to disputes. There is no one vision of what sustainable development means and different players have their own interests and ideas. One of the main questions asked of researchers is what exactly these aims could mean on a concrete level and how to achieve the transition. Research on sustainable development should not only define aims, goals and visions and translate them into strategies and indicators, but should also look at how to embed sustainable development institutionally. Supporting policy goals, which are integrative in terms of its policy aims, time scales, spatial dimensions and actors, challenges the current research system to provide equally integrative answers.

The expectations of sustainable development programmes are high and the methods to meet them diverse. The focus here is on programmes that define themselves as being research programmes that support sustainable development. This is an inductive approach and the programmes presented here have not been selected by any external criteria or evaluation process. These programmes are organised differently than conventional research programmes are in that they combine different disciplines and different types of knowledge. Many of the research programmes do not just attempt to create new knowledge but aim to form new networks around themes and to change the way in which issues are perceived. Although the term research programme is used here, the activities within the programmes go beyond what is commonly understood as a research programme.

This chapter draws on an analysis of the sustainable development research programmes in seven European countries.[2] These programmes do not represent a comprehensive review of research programmes in support of sustainable development in Europe. However, they include a broad selection of different approaches and methods for organising research for sustainable development. The focus here on research programmes also cannot provide a representative sample of research activities on the national level as they make up only a small proportion of overall research funding in each country. Research funding is channelled through a variety of different methods including institutional funding, general university funds and more generic funds. However, this research has shown that in many cases programmes are important ways for the policy-making process to introduce and direct new areas of research.

## BARRIERS IN NATIONAL RESEARCH SYSTEMS

Problem-orientated sustainability research questions cannot be adequately answered by one disciplinary perspective alone, but instead require a variety of disciplines (both from the social and natural sciences) and view points in order to understand the problem fully. However, conventional research methods and practices are generally not supportive towards this type of inter-disciplinarity and trans-disciplinarity research questions.

On a practical and organisational level this type of research is difficult to perform due to the fact that research systems are organised according to discipline-based rules. There are barriers to performing inter-disciplinary and trans-disciplinary research on many levels. This can be observed from their funding mechanisms, to their networks to their career possibilities whether at postgraduate or professorial level. However, it is not just the organisational set-up, but also the logic that underlies current research methods that favour disciplinary research. A research process that is based on the collection of data on the basis of a particular hypothesis, the search for correlation and causalities, and objectivity is of limited use for non-discipline-based, problem-orientated and highly complex questions (Frederichs 2001).

## RESEARCH PROGRAMMES FOR SUSTAINABLE DEVELOPMENT AS AN EXAMPLE OF REFLEXIVE GOVERNANCE

The aim of this book is to analyse to what extent existing policies already contain elements of reflexive governance. Such an analysis can be conducted by assessing the five strategy implications outlined: transdisciplinary knowledge production, adaptivity of strategies and institutions, anticipation of long-term effects, participatory goal formulation and interactive strategy development. These five elements can be applied to the way in which research programmes are designed and established. However, before the programmes can be analysed it is necessary to develop a framework to assess the programmes.

# FRAMEWORK FOR ANALYSING THE PROGRAMMES

Analysing programmes that aim to support sustainable development requires an analytical framework that allows for a pragmatic comparison across a number of diverse programmes with considerably different aims, frameworks and national characteristics. It has to be a framework that captures the similarities whilst maintaining an eye on the detail so as not to remain on a superficial level. It also has to be a framework that takes both the concept of sustainable development and the characteristics of the research system into account.

The first step of most national sustainable development programmes are faced with when designing new programmes is how to incorporate these new requirements into the design and implementation of a research programme. Policy makers face issues concerning the translation of the concept of sustainability into concrete research activities and also the level on which sustainable development should be incorporated or whether all levels from the programme to the project level should be able to prove their relevance to supporting sustainable development. Also what elements should a sustainable programme or project be comprised of and how do project and programme levels fit together? The framework used here includes four elements that incorporate the different levels of programme design and development to analyse how programmes for sustainable development are structured. These are defining the role of sustainability research, creating programmes lines, selecting projects and learning within the programmes. These four elements should not be seen as separate entities, but as a continuum from the strategic programme level to the practical implementation on the project level. They are not fixed parts of individual programmes, but are designed to support the analysis.

# DEFINING THE ROLE OF SUSTAINABILITY RESEARCH

There is no such thing as a definitive role for research that supports sustainable development. Defining the role research should play in the transition process takes place separately in each country on the national level. The reason for starting with this meta-level approach to analysing the programmes is that it provides an important contextual background for understanding the design and development of the individual programmes. Analysing the definition sets the framework within which the programmes are established and implemented. Defining the role that research can play in supporting sustainable development is one of the main elements that supports the process of developing successful programmes. A precise definition and clear vision of the role that research can play provides a stable framework within which the development of research areas and individual projects can take place.

### Creating Programme Lines

Following the definition of the role that research can play for sustainable development, comes the need to create specific thematic programme lines. In many cases, the overlying definition given to the research activities plays a large role in creating the thematic content of the programmes by influencing the methods used to define the content. The methods can range from linking the thematic content to national sustainable development plans to using methods such as foresight and backcasting to identify long term goals and measures to achieve them. However, although the programmes use different methods to define the content, there are similarities in the approaches taken, as programmes that support sustainable development tend to take a broader and systemic approach to defining the thematic content of the programmes. The focus is on systems or on chains and thus allows a problem to be examined and analysed from a holistic point of view and to understand the causes and not just the effects of the problem. A regional focus (either rural or urban) to such programmes is a common way of defining such a system. Others approaches to define the borders of the system under analysis include innovation processes, consumption and production processes and health issues. The six most common programme categories that can be identified are:

- behaviour, organisation and structures;
- consumption, nutrition or health;
- region, city or a spatially defined eco-system;
- sustainable technologies and sustainable innovation systems;
- sustainable economic development;
- global change and sustainable development.

The above list gives an idea of the systems approach that research programmes in support of sustainable development take. However, although many of the overall thematic topics appear to be similar, it would be misleading to believe that the implementation and the detailed definition of the programmes within the specific national contexts is the same in each category. There are considerable thematic differences between the programmes in the different countries as the thematic approach is often determined by national cultural specificities and problems.

**Selecting Projects**

Once the thematic content of the programmes is in place, the next level to be defined is the selection of individual projects within the programmes. This concerns the issue of how to ensure that the individual projects comply with the overall thematic and programme goals and to guarantee that the project level also fulfils criteria related to sustainable development. Many programmes have developed methodologies for implementing research for sustainable development and have defined sets of criteria (see below) for ensuring that each individual project contributes to further the aims of sustainable development. This has been important to ensure quality assurance in projects that do not adhere to formal current research methods and practices.

Since the first sustainable development programmes were established in the Netherlands, the body of literature on designing research for sustainable development has been growing. There is considerable consensus that research for sustainable development differs from more conventional types of programmes and that the design of such research activities needs to adapt to integrate both inter-disciplinary and trans-disciplinary research activities. Using conventional research organisation methods in such circumstances would not achieve the desired results. Some programmes have put the process design element first, ahead of thematic goals, claiming that achieving the right process will have a significant effect on the thematic content.

Some of the criteria used for selecting projects are now relatively well understood whereas the inclusion of others in the design of research programmes has not yet been fully operationalised. In many cases this is due to the fact that these concepts are not easily introduced, but entail a complete restructuring of the research process. The most commonly used elements for designing programmes include interdisciplinarity, stakeholder involvement, inclusion of different time frames and geographical areas and an emphasis on the dissemination of the results.

Inter-disciplinarity, or the integration of different academic disciplines in a research project is often defined as a prerequisite for problem-solving research activities and the majority of the SD targeted programmes define the inclusion of different disciplines as a core element of the research activities. Equally, stakeholder involvement (trans-disciplinary research) or the involvement of non-academic stakeholders has been defined as one of the main criteria for selecting projects for sustainable development research. Stakeholders not only have a different understanding of the problem, they are also able to implement change. Other criteria for selecting are not as well understood. These include the inclusion of different time frames, geographical areas and dissemination despite being considered important.

Combining short-term and long-term goals as well as local, regional and national perspectives is proving more challenging.

Dissemination and networking are an important part of the overall design of programmes for sustainable development. As the results of the projects are often specific to a certain context, learning between projects has to be supported through other means. Setting up horizontal or support programmes can significantly assist the establishment and the development of this type of research. They can encourage the transfer of knowledge from one programme or project to another. They can also develop methods that allow an easier transfer of knowledge from one discipline to another, or they can support the formation of new networks across traditional disciplinary boundaries. All these go beyond the individual programme and are aimed at the longer term development of research activities and communities.

**Learning**

Learning plays a central role in the development, design and implementation of research programmes for sustainable development. This does not just apply to the development of the programme level and the integration of sustainability into research aims. It also applies to the way in which actors within the programme interact with each other. As one of the key aims of programmes in support of sustainable development is to bring together different actor constellations in order to define more sustainable ways of organising processes, learning from one another is at the centre of the research activities. One of the main ways in which the programmes have attempted to increase the learning on both levels is to create programme management structures that facilitate learning. These structures see their role as broader than the organisation of calls and administration of research activities. In many cases they see their role as increasing the acceptance and embedding research in support of sustainable development in national research contexts and increasing know-how concerning the establishment and implementation of such programmes. Programmes with these types of long-term programme management structures and clear structured programmes are often referred to as 'umbrella programmes'.

## ANALYSIS OF SELECTED PROGRAMMES FOR SUSTAINABLE DEVELOPMENT

Concentrating on the four elements described above (defining the role of sustainability research, creating programmes lines, selecting projects and learning within the programmes), the following analysis illustrates the approaches taken by different programmes in defining and implementing research programmes in support of sustainable development. Table 10.1 provides an overview of the programmes analysed. The left hand column indicates the type of organisation (to be detailed below), whereas the right hand column lists the individual programmes or, in the case of umbrella programmes, the sub-programme level.

*Table 10.1   Overview of targeted SD programmes*

| Country | Programme |
| --- | --- |
| *Austria* (individual programmes) | Austrian Landscape Research<br>Austrian Programme on Technology for Sustainable Development<br>PFEIL 05 Programme for Research and Development in Agriculture, Forestry, Environment and Water Management |
| *Belgium* (umbrella programmes and sub-programmes) | Scientific Support Plan for a Sustainable Development Policy 1 (Sustainable management of the North Sea, Global Change and Sustainable Development, Antarctica 4, Sustainable Mobility, Norms for Food Products, Telsat 4, Levers for a Sustainable Development Policy and Supporting actions)<br>Scientific Support Plan for a Sustainable Development Policy 2 (Sustainable Modes of Production and Consumption, Global Change, Eco Systems and Bio-diversity, Supporting Actions and Mixed Actions)<br>Scientific Support to an Integration of Notions of Quality and Security of the Production Environments, Processes and Goods in a Context of Sustainable Development |
| *Germany* (umbrella programme and sub-programmes) | Research on the Environment<br>Research on Sustainable Economic Management, Regional Sustainability, Research on Global Change, Socio-Ecological Research) |
| *The Netherlands* (umbrella programme with structured and coordinated individual programmes) | Economy, Ecology and Technology (EET)<br>Dutch Initiative for Sustainable Development (NIDO)<br>HABIFORM (Expertise Network – Multiple Use of Space) |

*Table 10.1*    (continued)

| Country | Programme |
| --- | --- |
| *Sweden*<br>(individual<br>programmes) | Urban and Regional Planing<br>Infrasystems for Sustainable Cities<br>The Sustainable City<br>Economics for Sustainable Development<br>Sustainable Forestry in Southern Sweden<br>Sustainable Food Production<br>Sustainable Coastal Zone<br>Sustainable Management of the Mountain Region<br>Paths to Sustainable Development – Behaviour, Organisations, Structures (Ways Ahead)<br>Innovation Systems Supporting a Sustainable Growth |
| *UK*[3]<br>(individual<br>programmes) | Environmental Strategy Research Programme<br>Towards a Sustainable Urban Environment<br>EPSRC Infrastructure and Environment Programme<br>Environment Agency Sustainable Development R&D Programme<br>Sustainable Development Commission<br>Sustainable Technologies Initiative – LINK Programme |

*Source:*    Whitelegg et al. 2002

## Defining the Role of Research for Sustainable Development

The definition of research for sustainable development behind the programmes has a profound effect on the way they are designed and implemented. The debate on the definition of research for sustainable development has been prominent in many European countries since the middle of the 1980s. Initially, the Dutch experience dominated the discussion. More recently, however, the German approach to organising research for sustainable development has taken centre stage in the debate. Both these countries have highly structured programmes that clearly define the role that research for sustainable development should play and its different approach to current research methods and practices. In contrast, research policy in Belgium, Sweden and the UK reveal different approaches. Whereas Sweden and the UK have both made attempts to establish new types of research on a smaller scale and with a stronger thematic delineation, Belgium has taken a more science-policy approach to organising the research process.

The Dutch sustainable development research policy debate began in the late 1980s and concentrated on the development of indicators. Part of this definition process was orientated towards assessing the scale of the challenge of sustainable development. The results concluded that resource productivity would have to be improved by a factor of 10 to 20 over the period up until 2050 in order to secure economic growth, environmental protection and greater global equity. This was understood as a clear message to integrate sustainable development into research policy. The main motivation was that current productivity improvement rates were unlikely to achieve the levels aspired to. It was clear that there was a need for innovation in the innovation process itself that would create a shift towards a new development paradigm in which economic, social and environmental policy aims can be achieved simultaneously (Weaver and Jansen 2002). The result was an Inter-Ministerial Sustainable Technology Development Programme (DTO/STD) (1992–7).

The DTO/STD programme was an attempt to integrate sustainability policy and technology policy. The programme's approach was to view innovation as a social process where social networks play a key role in creating and stabilising new technologies. It integrated a series of tools that ensured the basic principles of stakeholder participation, adaptive management and 'learning-by-doing' were implemented. These included 'backcasting', 'whole chain' approaches, 'constructive technology assessment' and 'social niche' management. An important element of the programme was the identification of three different time tracks: short, medium and long term. The assumption behind the three-track approach is the long lead time for developing and securing sustainable technologies. Work on the medium term of five to twenty years needs to start now. This runs in parallel to short-term environmental protection aims and longer-term system renewal aims.

The experiences of the DTO/STD programme have had a significant impact on the development of subsequent research programmes in support of sustainable development in the Netherlands. The methods developed for encouraging innovation in the innovation process are being further developed in the NIDO[4] programme. Several of the innovation lines are being developed in the EET[5] and ICES-KIS[6] impulse projects.

In Germany, the Scientific Council came to the conclusion in 1994 that the 'human science research activities investigating the relations between society and environment [. . . .] are up to now little developed elements of environmental research' (Wissenschaftsrat 1994, quoted in Coenen and Krings 2002). The first step taken to integrate the social sciences with environmental research was the funding priority, Urban Ecology. It was, however, the establishment of the German 'Research on the Environment' programme in 1997 that marked the move from problem-orientated research to sustainability-orientated research with regard to the integration of environmental, economic and social aspects of sustainable development (Willms-Herget and Balzer 2000, quoted in Coenen and Krings 2002).

The programme Research on the Environment is comprised of four funding priorities, Sustainable Economic Management, Regional Sustainability, Research on Global Change and Socio-Ecological Research. Each funding priority consists of four to five thematic priorities. The strength of the programme lies in the fact that it combines thematic dimensions with a strong new methodological element aimed at the integration of the three pillars of sustainable development. The central features of the approach are inter-disciplinarity and the integration of field actors into the research process.

The new research process has been named 'search processes' as the research also includes projects which aim to explore the potential of such research. The funding priority Socio-Ecological Research is such an example. The approach described here is, however, not rigidly applied throughout the programme and each funding and thematic priority adapts it to suit its own needs and actors. It is more important to communicate and establish this type of research than it is to impose particular individual elements.

In the Socio-Ecological Research programme this is also achieved through the three central goals of project funding, structural funding and training the next generation of researchers. These three are specifically aimed at including small, non-university and non-governmental research institutes in the research process and through the establishment of a new generation of academics who are qualified to do trans-disciplinary work.

The Dutch and the German programmes have in common the fact that they have both defined what research activities can do to support sustainable development. Both programmes have large involvement of non-academic participants and aim to use research as a driver of change towards a sustainable transition.

Although there are similarities between the two programmes described previously (Dutch and German) and the Belgium programme, the basic understanding of the role of research for sustainable development differs fundamentally. The similarity lies in the fact that the Belgian programme is also highly structured. However, the Belgian approach to organising research for sustainable development does not place the same emphasis on the research process and the inclusion of different types of actors that can be found in the Dutch and German programmes.

The Belgian Scientific Support Plan for a Sustainable Development Policy does precisely what it states and focuses on research that will support the policy-making process. The first support plan was conceived in 1996 and moved into its second phase in 2000. The plan is closely linked to the Belgian Federal Plan for Sustainable Development. Although the aim of the programme is to support an integrated approach of both policy areas and scientific disciplines, it does not display the same level of methodological development that forms the basis of the German and Dutch programmes.

The final two national programmes described in this section, Sweden and the UK, have had significantly higher barriers to overcome in their respective research systems. This has influenced their ability to define research for sustainable development. The funding structures of both countries are fragmented and consist of individual research councils who bear the main responsibility for defining research activities in their own fields. The co-ordination barriers to defining research policy for sustainable development are considerably higher than in the three countries described previously. In Sweden and in the UK there are many more smaller and less co-ordinated research programmes that thematically fit into the competencies of one of the funding bodies. This does not mean that the individual research activities are not interesting and well developed, but that the approach taken towards research for sustainable development is neither as methodologically nor as thematically developed as in the Dutch or German case.

The UK has taken several steps in recent years to rectify the lack of co-ordination and strategy regarding research policy for sustainable development. It has established a research network for sustainable development. The network aims to become a clearing house for research that addresses sustainable development. Research for sustainable development is defined as research that combines environmental research with either the economic or social dimension, or the one-plus-one criterion (Eames and Policy Studies Institute 2001).

## From Definitions to Creating Thematic Priorities

The type of research and the role of research for sustainable development identified by national research policy define to a certain extent the framework for the thematic content. This can be seen in the case of the Dutch programme described above and its focus on innovation processes. However, the focus in the Netherlands is equally formed by the specific Dutch geographical, economic, social and environmental situation. The thematic focus is closely linked to immediate environmental problems. The Netherlands has a particular geographical situation that consists of a high water table and slow drainage. On the other hand, the country generates high levels of waste due to its processing activities mainly from its strong refining and petrochemicals sector. The Dutch economy is heavily dependent on adding value to imports and exporting final products. Approximately 70 per cent of GDP is derived from imported eco-capacity (Weaver et al. 2000).

The context in the Netherlands goes some way to explaining the sustainable development research policy's focus on de-coupling economic growth from sustainable development. The same context-specific approach to programme definition can be observed in Austria. Although there are several separate programmes that focus on sustainable development in Austria, the programme with the broadest thematic approach to sustainable development is the Austrian Landscape Research Programme. It focuses on the sustainable utilisation of landscapes in Austria. Austria's dependency on tourism also goes some way to explaining the need to focus research on integrating different economic and environmental policy goals with regard to safeguarding its landscapes.

The national, political, cultural and environmental setting thus shapes the context in which the programmes are developed. Within these contexts, however, a variety of concepts are used to define the individual programme goals. In Germany and Austria, the definition process is considered to be an integral part of the research programme. The German funding priority Socio-Ecological Research was not launched as a call for proposals but rather as an initial programme phase of 25 explorative projects that aimed to develop the aims of the programme and to mobilise researchers to get involved in inter-disciplinary projects (GSF 2002). The thematic focus of the first call for tenders is based on the results of the first phase. These themes include nutrition and health, policy strategies, infrastructure of public utilities and regional sustainability.

Other national programmes have also developed considerably different methods for designing the thematic goals of the research programmes. Of particular interest are the Belgium Scientific Support Plan for a Sustainable Development and the Dutch back-casting methodology used to help formulate the DTO/STD programme.

The Belgium national sustainable development programme aims to support the Federal Plan for Sustainable Development.[7] The plan is developed by an interdepartmental committee and follows the Agenda 21 guidelines. The research activities are designed to provide advice to the policy makers who are responsible for the Federal Plan. The specific programme themes thus concentrate on those in the Federal Plan. The research concentrates on the integration of the three pillars of sustainable development and the implications for the policy-making process.

Dutch sustainability research works on three different levels based on sustainability targets with horizons of 30 to 50 years. Activities are designed to address the different levels. The structured nature of the activities in the Netherlands entails good coverage of issues and also consists of formal reviews that are able to identify important gaps, also through foresight studies. This is by far the most sophisticated method for defining short, medium- and long-term goals in research programmes.

## Selecting Projects through Process Criteria

Research into sustainable development and the generation of context specific knowledge presents challenges not just with regard to the definition of research programmes but also concerning the implementation of such research activities. The goals and objectives of sustainable development research differ from those of conventional research practices. This also means that the implementation of such programmes has to differ. These programmes require the development of ways to include concepts such as trans-disciplinarity, inter-disciplinarity, multiple time frames and different spatial levels into research activities.

The development of concepts and methodologies for the implementation of research for sustainable development is more advanced in those programmes that have defined a role for sustainable development such as Germany and Holland. National programmes in Sweden and the UK are interesting from a thematic point of view, but the programme methodology is not as developed.

The UK has interesting thematic programmes, and the Engineering and Physical Sciences Research Council (EPSRC) has developed new programmes to support sustainable development. The Infrastructure and Environment Programme is of particular relevance. This programme aims to set up a series of multi-disciplinary consortia who will work closely with the users of the research. Another EPSRC programme is the programme 'Towards a Sustainable Urban Environment'. It has also been designed to carry out inter-disciplinary and trans-disciplinary projects concerning the future development of the urban environment. There is, however, less understanding in these projects of the difficulties of inter-disciplinary and trans-disciplinary research activities and less support for the consortia, despite the fact that the UK research councils are aware of the difficulties faced by such research activities (Joint Research Councils 2000).

Two examples from the German Research on the Environment programme give interesting examples of how trans-disciplinarity can be used as a key element to promote sustainable research activities at the project level. The objective of the Regional Approaches funding measure of the Regional Sustainability priority area is to create social processes. Scientific knowledge is combined with different perspectives including social and interest groups from the region. The goal of the projects is to combine theory with practice and to initiate social change through developing new models and options for acting. Experiences so far have highlighted the difficulties of integrating the social dimension. Addressing all three dimensions of sustainable development together can cause conflicts. However, valuable lessons have been learned concerning the involvement of non-scientific actors. Such actors have to be included in the project at an early stage and kept involved throughout. They should not just be handed the finished project.

Another example is the funding measure, Framework for Innovations Towards a Sustainable Economic Behaviour. This sub-programme aims to expand on the achievements made in technical efficiency by including the social dimension. It looks at three central questions: the role of the State, the development of indicators for sustainable development, and the integration of political institutions such as the Federal Environment Office, the Ministry of the Environment and the Ministry of Trade and Commerce into the research process, as these institutions are responsible for the framework conditions for innovation. One of the interesting aspects of the Socio-Ecological Research Programme is the continuous development of the research methodology. An example is the project Evalunet, an 'infrastructure project', which is aimed at developing assessment methods and criteria for trans-disciplinary research.

The Belgian approach is different again as its current Scientific Support Plan for a Sustainable Development Policy (SPSD II) consists of two parts that are linked by separate projects. The first part has a greater social science focus on issues such as energy, agro-food and transport, and the second part has a greater environmental focus on climate and ecosystems. These two parts do not attempt to integrate disciplines. This is left up to the mixed actions that aim to draw on the results of both parts. The selection criteria for these projects are based on the precautionary principle, vertical and horizontal policy integration and social equity to name just a few (Verbeiren 2002). The Belgium programme is very focused on the requirements of the policy process. It does not include actors other than those from the policy-making process.

Developing selection and assessment criteria that are sensitive to research for sustainable development is also important. The German Socio-Ecological Programme has taken steps in this direction and assesses a project's ability to formulate the problem field clearly. Projects are furthermore assessed as to their relevance to three cross-cutting central topics: theoretical development of methods and instruments, the relationship between theory and practice, and the relationship between gender and environment.

## Learning

The comparison of the programmes of seven countries has shown that some individual countries have established highly developed programmes and have recognised the necessity to restructure the research process by redefining each of the four key elements of programme design. In the majority of the cases, this has meant developing a concept of sustainability research and giving the programmes a high national profile. In Belgium, Germany and the Netherlands, sustainability research does not take place on the level of the individual programme, but rather is organised into a structured 'umbrella programme' that defines the focus of each sub-programme and places this within the framework of the whole programme.

There are many benefits to organising sustainable development research under one programme and not in separate programmes focused on thematic themes. Firstly, synergies can be used through the development of process and organisational aspects of programme design. In umbrella programmes research on the research process plays an important part in the development, of the programme. The development of concepts and methods to deal with inter-disciplinarity and trans-disciplinarity and other concepts described above is vital for the development of the programme. These are supported as a separate element that feeds its results into the other sub-programme and projects and is continually fed with results from their experiences.

Equally important is the continuity that umbrella programmes provide. Research for sustainable development aims to establish a research community that is able to perform inter-disciplinary and trans-disciplinary research. This can be facilitated through umbrella programmes that are able to run long-term programmes and have the visibility to attract actors who would not otherwise have been involved. It takes time to build up a network of researchers who can perform such research. Individual research programmes that are run by one ministry or research council find it more difficult to establish a research community. This is especially the case when the programme ends and the networks that have been established are, to a certain extent, lost if there is no follow up programme or resources available for inter-disciplinary and trans-disciplinary research.

A final benefit can be seen in the ability of the umbrella programme to co-ordinate research activities. It is able to identify gaps and see synergies in the themes and subjects that are addressed. Such programmes also have the opportunity to set aside a proportion of the resources for definition at a later date. That is, they are able to take stock of the results and define the allocation of the second stage based on the results of the first stage. The study on which this chapter is based gave the impression that individual programmes tended to be more rigid in their planning and have less room for change.

# CONCLUSIONS – COMMON GOALS AND LOCAL SPECIFICITIES

A comparison of such complex programmes that cover a wide range of subjects and use a variety of methods can easily get lost in describing the benefits of each individual programme in its own context. However, the purpose of this analysis was to identify key elements (defining the role of sustainability research, creating programme lines, selecting projects and learning within the programmes) and analyse the different ways they are dealt with in the various national contexts.

The comparison shows that in many countries the establishment of programmes that specifically focus on sustainable development is well developed. Inter-disciplinary and trans-disciplinary research activities are becoming more accepted as a way of understanding the interaction between the human and physical environments and as a way of finding solutions. The national and context-specific focus of sustainable development programmes is also evidence of the way in which programmes attempt to bridge the gap between the abstract goals of sustainability and the operational level of finding concrete solutions. In this way, research activities play an important role in ensuring that sustainable development is more than a logo and that the concept is broken down into concrete solutions.

The specific and local nature of the results of programmes for sustainable development often makes the research results difficult to translate to another circumstance. This does not mean to say that these types of programmes and projects cannot learn from each other. They can learn about the process and can reflect on the barriers and the success stories of designing and implementing these types of research activities. Conceptually and methodologically there are many areas where greater contact would be beneficial especially concerning the institutionalisation of such forms of knowledge production.

Programmes that support sustainable development also carry problems with them. There is the danger that research for sustainable development becomes ghettoised with the result that other programmes do not consider it their responsibility to integrate sustainability concepts into their own research. There is also the issue of authenticity. Not everything that claims to be sustainable is sustainable, and this also applies to research programmes. Inter-disciplinary and trans-disciplinary research activities are more difficult to carry out than mainstream activities. This presents a danger that individual projects will quickly revert back to disciplinary methods unless there are mechanisms in place to prevent this from happening. Hence, more exchange and interaction is needed on how this kind of research works.

# REFLEXIVITY IN RESEARCH PROGRAMMES FOR SUSTAINABLE DEVELOPMENT

The introduction of this book discussed five strategy implications for reflexive governance (transdisciplinary knowledge production, adaptivity of strategies and institutions, anticipation of long-term effects, participatory goal formulation and interactive strategy development). To a large extent these issues are addressed in the content of the programmes and especially within the individual projects. It is more interesting, however, to ask whether the programmes themselves as individual policy initiatives are organised according to the five strategy implications.

All the programmes analysed consider trans-disciplinarity to be an important part of research for sustainable development. Combining different academic disciplines and sources of knowledge is the key to producing knowledge that can cope with complex situations. As has been mentioned above, some programmes (German and Dutch) are more thorough in putting the concept of transdisciplinarity into practice than others where it is mentioned, but not practised.

Adaptivity is a more difficult concept to apply to research programmes. On the one hand, programmes that address sustainable development need to be flexible and need to take into account the problem-orientated nature of this kind of research. On the other hand, the need for legitimisation requires the programmes to have clear goals and for the projects within the programme to work towards these goals. Too much adaptivity within the main goals of the programme would be counterproductive. One way in which the Dutch and German programmes have been able to solve the issue of adaptivity has been to run parallel funding strands within the programmes. These can either address different time horizons or can be left more flexible so as to include short-term changes.

The inclusion of long-term effects is one aspect of research programmes for sustainable development that is less understood than others (such as trans-disciplinarity) in terms of how to translate it into the research programme concept. Only some of the Dutch programmes seem to have taken the long-term perspective into account systematically and applied a backcasting method to the design of their programmes. On the other hand, it is important to consider on which level concepts such as long-term effects and transdisciplinarity should be taken into account in a research programme. In many cases (especially the Belgian), not every part of the programme and every project have to be organised along these lines. There needs to be a careful combination of different types of research in one programme.

The participatory nature of the definition of goals within research programmes is less of an issue. The definition of the programmes is usually undertaken by the relevant ministries together with the research community. Participation with a wider range of actors is usually left to the project level. The same can be said for interactive strategy development. The involvement of heterogeneous actors is very important on the project level and also for building up a community of researchers and practitioners for sustainable development. They are, however, also not usually involved in the definition of the programme itself.

Research programmes for sustainable development are very strong examples of reflexive governance. The specific context of research programmes and the national research contexts, however, entails that some programmes are more reflexive than others. This book emphasises the process approach to governance for sustainable development. Some of the programmes (especially the German programme) subscribe to this approach to organising research for sustainable development. Other programmes take a different approach to research for sustainable development and focus on other goals such as policy support or technological development. This does not mean to say that such programmes are not reflexive in their approach, but that they define reflexivity in a slightly different way.

## NOTES

1. This chapter is based on the paper 'Organising Research for Sustainable Development: An assessment of National Research Programmes' first presented at the Conference on the Human Dimensions of Global Environmental Change 'Knowledge for the Sustainability Transition: The Challenge for Social Science', 6–7 December 2002 in Berlin.
2. The paper is based on the results of the study 'Identifying and assessing national research activities on sustainable development' set up through the ESTO network in February 2001. The study identified and assessed the national SD research programmes of seven European countries: Austria, Belgium, Germany, The Netherlands, Portugal, Sweden and the UK. One hundred and two programmes were assessed using both a set of thematic and process-orientated criteria.
3. To be able to compare the programmes across the seven countries, not all UK programmes identified in the country report as addressing SD have been included in this table.
4. NIDO – Nederlands Initiatief voor Duurzame Ontwickkeling (Dutch Initiative for Sustainable Development).
5. EET – Economics, Ecology and Technology Programme.
6. ICES-KIS is the Inter-ministerial working group that advises on strengthening the knowledge infrastructure. It advises on the spending of a budget drawn from natural gas revenues. This budget funds the programmes HABIFORM – Expertise Network 'Multiple Use of Space', CONNEKT – transport congestion programme, NIDO – Economics, Ecology and Technology Programme and SKB – Soil Quality Management.
7. It should be noted that Belgium (together with the Netherlands) is one of the only countries that specifically links its sustainable development programme to its federal sustainable development plan. In other countries the responsibilities are divided among different ministries or research councils.

# REFERENCES

Brand, K.-W. (ed.) (2000), *Nachhaltige Entwicklung und Transdisziplinarität*, Berlin.

Coenen, Reinhard and Bettina-Johanna Krings (2002), 'Country report Germany – national research activities and sustainable development', [online], available at: ftp://ftp.jrc.es/pub/EURdoc/20389-Annexes.pdf.

Eames Malcolm and Policy Studies Institute (2001), Sustainable development research network, 1st Annual Report (November 2000–April 2001) London: PSI.

Frederichs, G. (2001), ITAS-Projekt 'Umweltforschung zwischen Wissen und Handeln', *TA-Datenbank-Nachrichten*, **2**, 10. Jg, S. 105–11.

GSF (Forschungszentrum für Umwelt und Gesundheit GmbH), (2002), *Zukunft gewinnen – Der Beitrag für der sozial–ökologischen Forschung*, Bonn: Bundes Ministerium für Bildung und Forschung.

Joint Research Councils (2002), 'Promoting interdisciplinary research and training – report of the Joint Research Council visits to 13 UK universities', [online], available at: http://www.epsrc.ac.uk/WebSite/default.aspx?ZoneID=3&MenuID=752.

Verbeiren, Sara (2002), 'Country report Belgium – national research activities and sustainable development', [online], available at: ftp://ftp.jrc.es/pub/EURdoc/20389-Annexes.pdf.

Weaver, Paul and Leo Jansen (2002), 'Country report, the Netherlands – national research activities and sustainable development', [online], available at: ftp://ftp.jrc.es/pub/EURdoc/20389-Annexes.pdf.

Weaver, Paul, Leo Jansen, Geert van Grootfeld, Egbert van Spiegel and Philip Vergragt (2000), *Sustainable Technological Development*, Sheffield: Greenleaf Publishing.

Whitelegg, Katy, Matthias Weber and Fabio Leone (2002), 'National research activities and sustainable development', research report EUR 20389 EN. Vienna/Seville: ARC/JRC-IPTS, available at: http://www.jrc.es/cfapp/reports/details.cfm?ID=1017.

Wilms-Herget, A. and I. Balzer (2000), 'Auf dem Weg zu einer Nachhaltigkeitsforschung', in K.-W. Brand (ed.) (2000), *Nachhaltige Entwicklung und Transdisziplinarität*, Berlin, pp. 197–208.

# 11. Integrating perspectives in the practice of transdisciplinary research

## Marie Céline Loibl

## INTRODUCTION

This chapter deals with the integrated production of knowledge within heterogeneous research teams, namely the challenge of facilitating such knowledge production via productive communication within the team. While integrated knowledge production is one of the elements of reflexive governance, it can only be achieved, if the process of knowledge production itself is based on reflexivity, that is, is marked by professional observation and analysis of problem perceptions, interpretations and argumentation. Designing and steering such team processes demands a high degree of self-reflexivity also from team-leaders. They have to be very attentive to tensions within their teams, to the multitude of possible reasons behind such tensions and to the effects of their own interventions into team dynamics and into the process of knowledge production.

Conflicts within teams are very natural, when different disciplines, institutions and professions work together. They have to cope with a plurality of problem views, solution strategies and quality norms. Thus in order to use the full variety of team competencies, such teams need reflexive, internal communication and management strategies for converting this heterogeneity from a source of friction into a source of understanding.

## FROM INTERDISCIPLINARITY TO TRANSDISCIPLINARITY

The introduction to this publication refers to the disappointment prevailing in the public discourse about sustainability (Voß and Kemp, this volume). In fact interdisciplinary and transdisciplinary research co-operations have been very much promoted throughout these last years for being innovative and effective models of sustainable knowledge production (Gibbons, Limoges and Nowotny 1994, Häberli and Grossenbacher-Mansuy 1998, Nowotny, Scott and Gibbons 2003, Bammé 2004). But at the same time they have caused intense and still ongoing discussions as to their proportional empirical relevance within science as a whole and as to their practical relevance for real world policy implementation (Krott 1996, Weingart 1997, Krücken 2001, Weingart 2001).

The reproach of poor outcome as compared to the rhetoric boom, the concept set off after the end of the twentieth century, was, in fact, accompanied by frustration of many researchers who personally had been involved in interdisciplinary sustainability research initiatives. Disappointment was not only perceived amongst the addressees of sustainability research who had hoped for particularly innovative research results with clearly higher social and political impacts. It also affected many teams who had started off their co-operation with great enthusiasm and ambition to overcome the barriers and blinders of traditional disciplinary science.

Having assumed the responsibility for a long-term methodological monitoring project within a large Austrian sustainability research programme from 1995 to 2001,[1] the author had the opportunity to observe this development closely. She was also able to observe cases of personal frustration and resignation as well as learning processes and the implementation of new adequate working methods and adapted team models.

The solution of forming working groups that bring together all the disciplines necessary to analyse the complexity of interlinked problems of ecological, economical and social developments had seemed very promising. However when working together on a practical level and when trying to link theoretical backgrounds and methods and to integrate findings, the researchers found that good will and a common vision in no way guarantee the successful integration of competencies. The experiences with interdisciplinarity revealed that, in deciding upon questions of data relevance, criteria weighting and product development, the pragmatic pressure to define common quality standards caused very tricky problems.

The cooperation of sciences and humanities especially turned out to be a complex challenge. On the one hand, egalitarian and democratic team models assuring equal importance to all the disciplines involved promised a maximum of multidimensional insights to the problem fields that were to be analysed. It had seemed reasonable at first glance that the more complete the number of relevant quality standards, the more representative the results would be. The possibility of producing scientifically robust knowledge, which would provide a solid base for holistic sustainability strategies, had also seemed feasible. However, disappointment set in when it became obvious that in many cases paradigms and background theories turned out not to be compatible and that it was nearly impossible to accumulate concepts of excellence without an external frame that would help in weighting criteria and values. In many cases these values turned out to be not only incompatible but contradictory and as there existed no common cognitive structure or external value system that would allow deciding these difficult questions of relevance and scientific reliability consensually, results would either remain disintegrated or would be selected rather then integrated. In fact, in many projects such questions of relevance and of quality standards were not decided by scientific discourse but by formal and informal power relations within the research teams.

With regard to the output of the projects, many of the researchers who worked in interdisciplinary projects had to face the fact that ultimately their results were not considered very innovative by the addressed scientific communities. The mixture of disciplines did not at all automatically increase the probability of producing outstanding findings that would provide a scientific reputation for individual career-strategies of the team members. Even publishing results was definitely more difficult because they were not strictly linked to actual disciplinary discourses. Furthermore, it was a disappointing experience to discover that the results were also no more practical for implementation than the findings of disciplinary research. The multitude of different scientific terms was even harder to understand for professionals and users. Moreover, the multidimensionality of disciplinary perspectives turned out to be more of an increased burden than a surplus of comprehensibility and attractiveness.

Thus the next step within the development of sustainability research was to try and cooperate much more closely with practitioners, decision makers, consumers and citizens in order to handle these challenges of defining a common reference frame for relevance discussions and priority setting. Transdisciplinarity research approaches that already involve non-scientific partners throughout the phase of project development should assure the identification of the most urgent problem areas in which it would be most reasonable to invest public research funding. Also, for the transfer of the working results and for the design of all kinds of products out of the research process, it seemed to be a good idea to involve the addressees. The integration of addressees should help find out how to communicate the findings of the projects in a most understandable way and how to connect them with the specific priorities of the addressed target groups. Participatory and impact-oriented research promised not only to contribute innovative ideas for sustainable transformation strategies but also to produce practicable and effective implementation concepts.

What can we learn from these projects today? Were they successful and was it easier to handle the dilemma of different but equally valid disciplinary relevance scales simply by raising the heterogeneity in involving non-scientific partners? What are the specific challenges that such transdisciplinary project teams have to cope with, and did the teams develop efficient strategies to cope with these challenges?

# CHALLENGES IN TRANSDISCIPLINARY RESEARCH

As described above, transdisciplinary models of knowledge production are becoming more and more common in the context of sustainability research because of their potential to cope with the complexity of problem settings to be worked on. Especially in fields in which not only knowledge production as such is demanded, but – more than that – the production of knowledge that will answer the urgent needs of society, non-scientific actors are being involved or consulted in order to form transdisciplinary working groups for knowledge generation. Due to the resulting internal heterogeneity of paradigms and cultures, such teams are inevitably confronted with problems that are caused by incompatible rationales and competing obligations towards background institutions. Amongst these problems arising from different institutional function and success criteria (as to theories of social differentiation see Schimank 1996), two key challenges can be identified, the successful handling of which turned out to be a crucial precondition for the success of transdisciplinary research projects. The first challenge is to develop strategies of integrated knowledge production (cognitive dimension of transdisciplinarity). The second challenge is to develop new approaches to reflexive project steering (social and operational dimension of transdisciplinarity).

**Focusing on Diversity**

Sustainability research that seeks to emphasize the interlinkages of ecological, economical and social problems and that seeks to reflect long-term and indirect effects of solution strategies must delve deeply into the differences of rationales of the involved interest groups. Transdisciplinary projects that integrate selected actors into their research process can make use of the value conflicts that occur within the team for exploring the dynamics of problem-relevant societal interests and driving forces outside. Such intentions to explore the frictions of value systems and problem sights amongst the team members seem, however, to endanger the delicate coherence of heterogeneous teams that are not held together by institutional forces but that are only linked by temporary agreements. Will not disintegration rather than integration be the consequence of focusing on the differences instead of the common visions within the team?

In order to turn the identification of incompatibilities from a source of disintegration into a strategy of integration, it is necessary to create a counterbalance of centripetal forces that holds together the teams and to develop an alternative working base that somehow replaces the tempting illusion of common grounds in perceptions and interests. The question is which technical approaches and cognitive shifts can provide such a stabilizing compensation to the team members and an inspiring kick to the research process.

**Steering Flexibility**

The introductory chapter to this book refers to the need for new strategies of coping with the complexity of interlinked social, technological and ecological development – claiming that reflexive governance modes should be based on processes for continued learning and modulation of ongoing developments, rather than on complete knowledge and maximization of control (Voß and Kemp, this volume). Could this reflexive approach for dealing with complexity possibly be efficient not only for organizing transition processes in society but equally productive within the process of transdisciplinary knowledge production and value balancing itself?

Frequent painful experiences with unpleasant instabilities of agreements and a general lack of control and predictability in transdisciplinary research have revealed the striking similarities between steering problems in society and steering problems in complex research settings.

The mix of disciplinary and professional project partners in transdisciplinary teams is not only a strategy to maximize the knowledge base of a project but also a strategy to reproduce the heterogeneity of competing real world interests and rationales. It consequently results in a multitude of uncertainties and unforeseeable team dynamics. Far from fulfilling classic standards of traditional disciplinary research, such transdisciplinary projects seem to systematically undergo radical relaunches concerning research objectives, methodological strategies, time planning and product development. In consequence, the projects are often confronted with reproaches that concern insufficient quality management ('muddling through') and reduced scientific consistency of the results due to the multitude of adaptations in research plans.

That is the reason why there is – in addition to knowledge integration – a second key challenge in transdisciplinary research: the implementation of flexible but nonetheless stable steering processes and decision models that derive efficiency not from fixed targets and criteria but from uttermost reflexivity and transparency. This increased reflexivity must compensate for the loss of control and certainty that is characteristic in transdisciplinary research processes. The profit of transdisciplinarity consists in stimulating a considerable surplus of insights on hidden driving forces within the problem system by transforming tacit knowledge of involved actors into manifest contributions to the joint research process. The identification and integration of such precious but unpredictable outcomes is an important product of transdisciplinary research. At the same time, the realization of this added value is very demanding in terms of providing a set of stable reference factors and frames to allow transparent adaptivity and prevent arbitrariness.

## SURVEY ON TRANSDISCIPLINARY TEAM PERFORMANCE

In watching and analysing the special team dynamics, which are being set off by priorily focusing differences within a team instead of common denominators, a surprising impression could be experienced throughout two long-term monitoring studies for an extensive Austrian research programme on sustainable regional development.[2] Within the monitoring study experiences of researchers have been analysed with different team models, working methods and integration strategies implemented in 11 interdisciplinary and transdisciplinary projects of this large research programme. These teams had up to 20 members, including a multitude of disciplines and many non-scientific partners.

It was one of the most interesting and useful outcomes of this study, that team performance is not necessarily combined with a high degree of accordance amongst team members but that it rather seems closely connected to the conscious handling of team heterogeneity and to a very open and down-to-earth analysis of divergences. A most striking result of the monitoring study was the observation that a number of projects that had been merged by the programme management and that consequently passed through an extremely difficult start phase of team building, performed very well in the end: these merged teams soon enjoyed and cultivated the very direct style of discussion they had developed during the hot kick-off periods of the projects, and they felt more satisfied with their scientific results than other teams, that had started off in harmony and that later on had great difficulties in establishing a culture of open confrontation of contradictory views. What was it, that enabled these merged projects to perform successfully after having passed an extremely difficult start, marked by experiences of open disunity and heavy conflicts? These teams had done something in the beginning, that is unusual amongst new teams that generally want to establish quickly a solid team coherence and a good working atmosphere: instead of investing their energy directly into team coherence, the members of the merged project teams had bluntly confronted their different analytical and theoretical views, their competing research interests and their incompatible backgrounds. The only common denominator in the beginning of the co-operation was the annoyance towards the programme management and an overall consent of deep dissent.

In collecting the multiple reasons for the impossibility of properly joining their teams and their research approaches they broke the taboo of going into the details of the organizational pressures and constraints they were exposed to and that would – apparently – make it impossible to integrate their different working objectives. Instead of producing common perceptions as to the research problem, they jointly measured the abysses separating their research interests and their theoretical backgrounds. In the start phase of the co-operation the members of these teams had very little motivation to seek common denominators and much more commitment to constructing an arrangement that would allow them to keep as much distance as possible within these enforced mergers. There were no illusions set up with respect to common views and values.

Only at first glance, it seemed a paradoxical effect that putting the emphasis on differences of perceptions and values could nonetheless produce coherence instead of increased distance. In fact the open confrontation of interests and constraints did not only establish, as has been described, a scientifically very productive culture of open and critical discussion; it also very effectively trained the team competencies in reflecting institutional driving forces and limited action scopes, which are key factors in the context of sustainability research.

Teams – to the contrary – that had cultivated a rather harmonic and consensual style of discourse from the very beginning of their cooperation and that unexpectedly came across incompatible paradigms and methodologies in the middle of their working processes, were often deeply irritated by these incompatibilities and further knowledge integration was blocked considerably; blocked not only by cognitive barriers (not having realized the existence, the nature and the backgrounds of different perceptions and values in the team) and by communicative barriers (not having established an atmosphere of critical confrontation and discussion) but also by heavy emotional disturbances: the unintended and sudden dissolution of a consent that had been considered stable and reliable, caused frustration and inner withdrawal. It turned out extremely disappointing to go through such processes of late and spontaneous team disintegration. In many cases such delayed and 'accidental' exposures of divergent team interests and quality concepts ended up in heavy de-motivation of the team members, partly experienced as proper project disasters. However, other than such unexpectedly-popping-up team dissonances, well-directed and intended efforts of identifying internal resonance effects to external disciplinary and institutional heterogeneity proved to be powerful integrative experiences. This observation seemed contradictory at first sight, but was well understandable, after taking a closer look at the characteristic strategies of successful transdisciplinary research.

# STRATEGIES OF TRANSDISCIPLINARY RESEARCH

## Identification of Different Rationales

Understanding the reasons and the functional logics behind differences and incompatible positions in transdisciplinary project teams, which serve as 'labs of society', builds new meta-levels for understanding and comparing the involved functional rationales. The first step is to analyse the reasons behind diversity amongst the team members and their backgrounds. The next step is to do the same for the problem fields and the institutional interests, which the project is addressing. Transdisciplinary teams should – through their heterogeneity – develop the competence to reflect the 'real world' dynamics by investigating their resonance effects within the team (Hollaender et al. 2003). Interest conflicts amongst team members can then be instrumentalized as indicators for institutional and societal interest conflicts behind sustainability problems. It is a very effective strategy of knowledge integration to combine the variety of team competencies for uncovering the hidden complementarities of different rationales, and – even more important for developing sustainability strategies – to identify the blind spots of policies and market dynamics that are not covered efficiently by any of these rationales.

## Adaptive Management of the Research Process

To handle the challenges of transdisciplinary research in practical application, a three-level steering approach for facilitating the process of knowledge integration in transdisciplinary research can be recommended. This three-level approach has been developed from both the results of the Austrian monitoring study mentioned above, and from the results of an international survey[3] following that study. The survey analysed team experiences on an expanded quantitative base of four research programmes in Austria, Switzerland and Germany, which involved all 650 researchers working in the interdisciplinary and transdisciplinary projects of these four programmes (Loibl 2003). The three-level steering approach has been derived by integrating the findings of the preceding Austrian monitoring study and the following international survey. It has been successfully tested in different contexts like project meetings, team coaching and quality circles. Its objective is to connect project development and team building by training group capacities in reflecting different functional rationales, as well as different individual relevance filters and success criteria. The steering model is based on the experience that a fruitful solution to the problems caused by team diversity is to use a self-reflexive learning approach by frequently and systematically changing between three dimensions:

1.  The first dimension reflects the 'real-world problems' upon which the research project focuses: transdisciplinarity strives to produce innovative insights into the dynamics behind the examined problems and to create sustainable solutions by better integrating and balancing the diversity of societal interests, institutional structures and sector policies (external heterogeneity).
2.  The second dimension constitutes the operative working process within the research project: it is this second analytical dimension that reflects the plurality of disciplinary knowledge, of practical expertise and of working methods, forming the 'joint knowledge base' of transdisciplinary project teams: the diversity of various techniques of problem analyses and data interpretation and the different cultures of communication and project management (internal heterogeneity).
3.  It is the third dimension, which represents the meta-level of building a common understanding for patterns and functionality of heterogeneity itself, which stimulates the crucial process of knowledge-integration within transdisciplinary teams. For the societal 'project' of sustainability, it is of increased importance to discover the dynamics behind the formation of different value systems and relevance perceptions in society. Moreover, it is just as important for the success of heterogeneous teams to find out which relevance criteria are of higher importance to specific team members than to others and to understand why it is these very criteria and not others. Relevance scales and success criteria employed within the research team are obviously not strictly identical to those of the actors in the problem field, but they will correspond if the transdisciplinary team is well composed. The third dimension of analysis focuses on effects of societal and institutional plurality within the microsystems of transdisciplinary research teams.

A frequent problem that occurs when teams want to work with this three-dimensional approach is that the very special competencies which are necessary to analyse differences of disciplinary paradigms, organizational logics and institutional forces, are rarely represented within the team and certainly are not familiar to all of the team members. A robust and simple approach is needed for identifying patterns of heterogeneity and for producing integrated knowledge on interrelations between research problems (external interest conflicts) and research team problems (internal interest conflicts). Due to the fact that the internalized experience of institutional pressures is rather part of the tacit knowledge than of disciplinary skills, these paradigmatic blinkers can be revealed best by joint efforts of a mixed team providing mutual cognitive assistance (Loibl 2005, pp. 132–54).

## Joint Analysis of Institutional Backgrounds

It is a comprehensible and very productive approach to reveal such different functional logics through analysing the professional environments of the team members (project level) as well as the institutional structures relevant to the research questions (problem level) by using the following set of additional analytical perspectives.

The first perspective, which is useful to reflect the plurality of involved rationales, focuses on the conditions of admission to a specific discipline, organization or institution. Formulating such criteria of affiliation helps one to better understand the diversity of career pressures and quality criteria within the team and amongst the addressees of a project. Making such pressures explicit helps to consider adequately the scope for action for team members as well as for 'real world actors' and to remain realistic in designing research concepts as well as in developing action programmes and strategies of sustainable transformation.

The second perspective focuses on hierarchical structures and on *vertical differentiation* within the organizational and institutional environments of the project as well as on strategies by which these structures of power distribution are safeguarded. It is by understanding such different modes of power regulation, structural stabilization and innovation control that integrated knowledge for reflexive governance can be produced and sustainable transformation can be successfully stimulated. In public as well as in private research institutions, in enterprises, administrations, political parties and NGOs it is a most important success criteria for individual career planning, to link personal working objectives with 'survival interests' of background institutions and organizations. The special challenge of constructing interinstitutional win-win coalitions of individual and organizational survival interests can only be handled successfully by transdisciplinary working teams if the diversity of involved power structures and regulation mechanisms is thoroughly examined and well considered.

The third perspective focuses on *horizontal differentiation* of the organizations, which are involved in the research activities and of the institutional actors, which are involved in the problem area. In complex organizational systems, competencies are generally divided and separated into different departments and such 'territories of competence' defend vigorously their boundaries of influence if recommendations out of a research project undermine their importance by disregarding decision structures and threatening sectorial power. The same effect can be observed on the project level: for the implementation of an effective project management and for the development of feasible research approaches, the members of transdisciplinary teams need to understand mutually how wide individual competence territories can be extended without provoking reproaches and resistance in the background institutions, which are caused by territorial defensiveness.

The challenge of integrated knowledge production, therefore, is not reducible to the micro system of the research team on the one hand or to the directly addressed target groups on the other hand. Side effects due to power balancing counter-reactions within addressees as well as within the background institutions of team members are extremely effective resisters. High team performance and successful implementation of results are linked with integrated analytical efforts to anticipate such counter-reactions. Transdisciplinary knowledge production must strive not only to produce integrated knowledge but also to interlink this process of knowledge production with the environments that are affected by the process of knowledge production as well as by the process of real-world transformation. Integrated knowledge could also be understood as a special category of knowledge, including profound consideration of institutional forces and preconditions that are relevant for its implementation.

The fourth perspective focuses on *central and peripheral differentiation* within the involved social systems. The identification and differentiation of the various criteria of centrality, which are relevant within a discipline as well as within an interest group or an enterprise, help to analyse the specific way in which communication flows and knowledge management are organized and which product and communication strategy is adequate in order to achieve a maximum of attention and acceptance for the results of the research.

Last but definitely not least, it is crucial for the process of knowledge integration in transdisciplinary projects to discuss by which criteria *orthodox and reformist positions* can be differentiated within project environments, organizations of team members and addressees of the project. Very often it happens that more reform-oriented actors of an administration or enterprise get involved in transdisciplinary cooperations and that at first they feel extremely comfortable and empowered by the backing of such 'avant-garde' task forces. The dominant orthodox strategies and majority positions within their background systems get out of sight or are considered outdated at best. This might work very well until the reform-oriented results begin to cause irritation amongst the more conservative colleagues or superiors of the department and at this moment many transdisciplinary projects encounter heavy turbulence – sometimes so heavy that the projects have to undergo complete relaunches or to live with the fact that their results will have very little impact because of system resistance. In order to optimize the output (products) as well as the outcome (policy implementation) of transdisciplinary sustainability research, it is of predominant importance to understand the various dynamics of system stabilization and reformation.

## Double-loop Learning Through Team Reflection

Knowledge integration and double-loop learning can be achieved by reflecting alternatingly on the research problems as such and on the meta-level of team heterogeneity. The frequent and intended change of perspectives between problem level and project level reveals similarities between the two of them. Discussing these interrelations between research problems and project environments on the one hand and disciplinary and institutional socialization of team members on the other hand is a process of mutually explicating internal knowledge. Systemic techniques of group reflection and supervision are helpful to support such efforts of comparing rationales and relevance filters and to apply the results in team management and knowledge integration. Successful knowledge co-production amongst scientists and actors is linked to the systematic transformation of societal expertise and tacit knowledge into explicit insights and positions.

## Iterative Goal Formulation and Participatory Decision Making

Transdisciplinary research projects need to develop and implement flexible modes of project steering and risk management. However, the high degree of team diversity that results from multiple research interests, working styles and quality concepts causes a lot of problems in realizing this concept of flexibility. One of the most accentuated results of the empirical surveys was the conclusion that successful reflexive project steering is only manageable if a team invests a considerable share of analytical attention and operational energy in the steering process as such. Careful progress monitoring and documentation is an essential precondition for successfully carrying out steps of joint team reflection and self-evaluation. The project teams need clearly defined check points and milestones in order to decide whether changes of the research plan are necessary, because the risk of continuing as planned would be higher than the risk of change for the final success of the project. But in order to take such decisions after having reflected on interim findings and team experiences, it is necessary to monitor constantly the progress of a project and to oblige explicitly all team members to keep an eye on the question of whether the research path, the instruments and products still correspond to the increased and integrated knowledge base the project has reached at that time.

The possible range of research questions and corresponding team compositions in sustainability research make it extremely difficult to define a set of general success criteria of project progress to be observed for self-monitoring. The effort of discussing and agreeing on a set of contextualized success criteria for the progress of the specific project is considered a crucial element for reflexive project steering, because it is mostly through this effort that tacit knowledge bases of the team members can be made explicit and available for the entire team.

Constantly monitoring and analysing the performance of social systems (be this a research team, an enterprise, a community or society as a whole) and systematically opening up the complexity of competing – but interlinked – interests is essential for promoting sustainable development. But in order to manage transdisciplinary research (and reflexive governance) successfully in practice, a complementary challenge of closing down again this process of unfolding the multiplicity of heterogeneous interests and action strategies must be mastered (Voß, Kemp and Bauknecht, Chapter 16, this volume). After the phase widening up the analytical approach to a maximum, it is necessary to narrow the focus again and to reduce the complexity of perceptible system dynamics for developing a manageable portfolio of research products and action strategies. In order to master this challenge, a reliable model of final decision-making must be formally agreed in the beginning of a transdisciplinary research project. It is indispensable though, to integrate strong participatory elements in this decision model because disciplinary as well as functional differentiation needs the element of participation for reintegrating partial problem perceptions and identifying externalities and blind spots. Team members should not only participate in designing the research plan and in defining the rules for team co-operation, they should in particular participate in decisions on methodological question, criteria weighting and interpretating results.

**Integrated Knowledge Production**

In order to produce coherent project results and not just a sample of multidisciplinary problem views and solution approaches, transdisciplinary teams need to integrate working steps and interim findings throughout the whole length of the project. The integration of academic knowledge with knowledge from practical actors has special relevance, because problem definition, goal formulation and the development of strategies include normative assessments. In heterogeneous teams this integration cannot be easily achieved by referring to common paradigms and value scales, because many paradigms and value scales tend to be inconsistent or even contradictory. Integration is only possible on the basis of common meta-criteria developed by the team in discussing the evolution of the different interests and value scales occurring amongst the team members. Identifying and discussing the functional logics behind these different values leads the team to common explanations for the inner heterogeneity of relevance conceptions and quality norms.

In constructing explanations for this diversity of their own research interests, the team members create the very set of meta-criteria that will allow the joint analysis of various societal interests behind the sustainability problems the project is dealing with. Though the specific range of such criteria depends on individual research problems and team constellations, there is one common element that seems to be of fundamental importance for transdisciplinary research: it is through better understanding not only the achievements, but especially the problematic consequences of functional differentiation in society, that the members of transdisciplinary research teams can establish common value frames for the confusing diversity of involved methodological standards and quality norms. The specific contribution of their research findings to identifying (and transcending) inadequate institutional structures and to designing (and implementing) new modes of reflexive governance can serve as the foremost meta-criteria for the quality of transdisciplinary research findings and the long-term relevance of working results.

The joint efforts of developing common success criteria can be facilitated by focusing the analytical view of the team rather on the question of how to identify and to balance the original human needs beyond the specific research problems then on the question of how to maximize the satisfaction of involved societal interests. It is in transgressing the limited analytical horizons of institutionalized problem perceptions, that transdisciplinarity can help to create sustainable solutions for re-integrating ecological and societal aspects that have so far been externalized and neglected.

## CONCLUSIONS

This chapter has examined the specific aspects of integrated knowledge production in transdisciplinary research projects. It has shown how the heterogeneity of research teams can be dealt with as both a vital ingredient for integrated knowledge production and a major challenge. It has actually shown how diverging interests and viewpoints, which could potentially hamper the research process, can be turned into important assets.

This chapter has especially highlighted the nested character of reflexive process management on the micro-level of transdisciplinarity as on the macro-level of governance. 'Reflexive governance' of transdisciplinary research is based on a set of specific strategies for integrated knowledge production: the identification of different rationales, adaptive management of the research process, joint analysis of institutional backgrounds, double-loop learning through team reflection as well as iterative goal formulation and participatory decision-making.

Reflexive governance models cannot be implemented without installing numerous feedback loops to assure the consideration of potential side effects or without constant meta-analysis of process effectiveness. Goals and agendas have to be re-evaluated and redesigned regularly due to the particularly high degree of uncertainty concerning the feasibility and the effectiveness of solutions. It is only possible to react adequately to unforeseen interim results and their implications by combining stable models for participatory decision-making and flexible procedures of goal adjustment. Therefore, it is a major success factor for transdisciplinary research, to provide a flexible frame for project adjustments by installing self-reflecting 'learning teams' (corresponding to the 'learning organizations' described by Senge et al., 1997), that 'walk the talk' of reflexive governance in realizing participatory models of knowledge production and self-evaluation.

## NOTES

1. 'Translation of complex sustainability strategies into regional environmental management'; duration 1995–2001; Austrian Institute for Applied Ecology for the Austrian Federal Ministry for Education, Science and Culture research programme: 'Austrian Landscape Research'.
2. Reseach programme: 'Austrian Landscape Research 1995–2003' (www.klf.at) Monitoring projects: 'Translation of complex sustainability strategies into regional environmental management'; duration 1995–2001; Austrian Institute for Applied Ecology for the Austrian Federal Ministry for Education, Science and Culture and 'D-A-CH – Co-operation on inter- and transdisciplinary environmental research' 1998–2000; Austrian Institute for Applied Ecology for the Austrian Federal Ministry for Education, Science and Culture.
3. 'D-A-CH – Co-operation on inter- and transdisciplinary environmental research'; duration 1998–2000; Austrian Institute for Applied Ecology for the Austrian Federal Ministry for Education, Science and Culture; research programme: 'Austrian Landscape Research'.

# REFERENCES

Bammé, A. (2004), *Science Wars. Von der akademischen zur postakademischen Wissenschaft*, Frankfurt and New York: Campus Verlag.

Gibbons, M., C. Limoges and H. Nowotny (1994), *The New Production of Knowledge. The Dynamics of Science and Research in Contemporary Societies*, London: Sage Publications.

Häberli, R. and W. Grossenbacher-Mansuy (1998), 'Transdisziplinarität zwischen Förderung und Überforderung', in *Gaia*, **7** (3), 196–213.

Hollaender, K., M.C. Loibl and A. Wilts (2003), 'Management of Transdisciplinary Research', in Gertrude Hirsch-Hadorn (ed.), *Unity of Knowledge in Transdisciplinary Research for Sustainability*, in *Encyclopedia of Life Support Systems*, Oxford: Eolss Publishers.

Krott, M. (1996), 'Interdisziplinarität im Netz der Disziplinen', in P.L. Balsiger, R. Defila and A. Di Giulio (eds), *Ökologie und Interdisziplinarität – eine Beziehung mit Zukunft? Wissenschaftsforschung zur Verbesserung der fachübergreifenden Zusammenarbeit*, Birkhäuser Verlag Basel/Schweiz.

Krücken, G. (2001), 'Wissenschaft im wandel? Gegenwart und zukunft der forschung an deutschen hochschulen', in Erhard Stölting and Uwe Schimanks (eds), *Die Krise der Universitäten Lenathan Sonderheft 20*, Opladen: Westdentscher Verlag, pp. 326–45.

Loibl, M.C. (2003), Spannungen in heterogenen Forschungsteams. Prioritätenkonflikte nach Wissenschaftskulturen, institutionellen Zugehörigkeiten und Gender, in Kooperation im Niemandsland. Neue Perspektiven auf Zusammenarbeit in J. Gläser, M. Meister, I. Schulz-Schaeffer, J. Strübing (eds), *Wissenschaft und Technik*, Opladen: Leske und Budrich und Westdt. V.

Loibl, M.C. (2005), Spannungen in Forschungsteams – Hintergründe und Methoden zum konstruktiven Abbau von Konflikten in inter- und transdisziplinären Projekten. Verlag für Systemische Forschung (VSF) im Carl-Auer Verlag, Heidelberg (forthcoming).

Nowotny, H., P. Scott and M. Gibbons (2003), 'Re-Thinking Science: Mode 2 in Societal Context', in Minerrd R. MacLeod (ed.), *Technology, Innovation and Knowledge*, Management Book Series, Vol. 2, *Knowledge Creation, Diffusion and Use in Innovation Networks and Clusters: A Comparative Systems Approach Across the U.S., Europe and Asia*, USA: Greenwood Publishing Group, Praeger Books.

Schimank, U. (1996), *Theorien gesellschaftlicher Differenzierung*, Opladen: Leske und Budrich.

Senge, P., A. Kleiner and C. Roberts (1997), *Das Fieldbook zur Fünften Disziplin. 2. Aufl.*, Stuttgart: Klett-Cotta.

Weingart, P. (1997), 'Neue Formen der Wissensproduktion: Fakt, Fiktion und Mode'. Institut für Wissenschafts- und Technologieforschung, IWT Paper 15, Bielefeld.

Weingart, P. (2001), *Die Stunde der Wahrheit? Zum Verhältnis der Wissenschaft zu Politik, Wirtschaft und Medien in der Wissensgesellschaft*, Velbrück Wissenschaft, Weilerswist.

# Development of technology and policy

# 12. Niche-based approaches to sustainable development: radical activists versus strategic managers

**Adrian Smith**

## INTRODUCTION

'Policies for science and technology must always be a mixture of realism and idealism'. (Freeman, 1991)

Recent social science research into innovation and sustainable development can be classified into two related areas of work: cleaner technology (for example, Howes et al., 1997); and systems innovation (for example, Hoogma et al., 2002). Cleaner technology research tends to analyse the development of individual technologies whose throughput of energy, materials and contamination is lower per unit of output. Questions regarding the innovation of systems tend to shift attention upwards, towards the transformation of entire 'socio-technical regimes' into more sustainable forms (Kemp et al., 2001). Cleaner technology research might, for example, look at greening individual farming techniques. Systems innovation seeks to understand the transformation of entire food production systems into more sustainable ensembles.

The concern for reflexive governance as outlined in the Introduction to this book (Voß and Kemp, this volume) can be considered, in part, to include this shift towards a systems innovation perspective. Research into sustainable technological development is feeding back recommendations for new governance processes, based on inadequacies identified in existing governance processes. System innovation recommendations arise from a belief that: (1) the diffusion of cleaner technologies is being held up by an absence of complementary changes in wider systems of production and use; and (2) that individually cleaner technologies may not deliver sufficient progress towards sustainable development (Berkhout, 2002). In short, interest in system innovation has arisen for second-order reasons, and is a response that contains elements similar to strategies given for dealing with reflexive governance.

One body of work prominent in recent systems innovation debates has been strategic niche management (SNM) (for example, discussions and papers under the auspices of the Blueprint network of systems innovation researchers).[1] SNM involves the planned creation of novel 'socio-technical' niches. Advocates argue that the knowledge created by these experimental niches can subsequently seed the transformation of the relevant incumbent socio-technical regime. As we shall see, SNM seeks to integrate knowledge production through these experiments, and recommends the subsequent pursuit of adaptive strategies on the basis of these lessons. Throughout, the leitmotif for SNM is to promote social learning through participatory and iterative experimentation. As such, SNM recommends innovations in governance along lines not too dissimilar to those argued in the Introduction to this book. It is a 'governance innovation' (Voß and Kemp, this volume) that merits analysis as a candidate strategy for coming to grips with the challenge of reflexive governance.

The key task for this chapter is to provide an analysis of that strategy. This is done by contrasting recommendations for SNM with another niche-based approach to transforming technological regimes, namely the alternative technology (AT) movement, which flourished in the 1970s.[2] Unlike SNM – in which academic research recommends an approach for technology policy-makers – the AT movement involved activists seeking out more sustainable ways to live with technology. Activists were grassroots innovators,[3] in the sense that they sought sustainable technological transformation through community-based action. This history suggests that niche-based approaches to transforming technology systems may not be as novel as is sometimes supposed. Indeed, by drawing comparisons and making contrasts between SNM and AT perhaps some more enduring and fundamental issues can be drawn about the role of niches in sustainability governance.

Both SNM and AT seek changes to the use of technology. Dunphy (1996) has suggested, in the context of change in organisations, that comparative analysis be drawn using five elements: (1) the basic metaphor for the organisation; (2) the analytical framework for understanding change processes; (3) the ideal model of an effectively functioning organisation; (4) a theory of how best to bring the organisation closer to the ideal; and (5) identifying the change agent. This useful checklist suggests that comparative analysis must consider the way a problem is understood, the change objectives, and the model of change pursued. Such comparative analysis is strengthened when we place each approach in its social and historic context. A gap of 30 years separates academic/policy-oriented SNM from activist/community-based AT. Analysts must be sensitive to such differences in circumstance. Only then can comparison begin to identify more enduring, fundamental challenges that confront niche-based approaches.

Given these methodological points, SNM and AT are compared along three common dimensions in this chapter – origins, objectives, and models of change – beginning with SNM. SNM is illustrated in the case of Danish wind energy and cites this as exemplifying how policy-makers can help nurture sustainable niches. It is relevant to this chapter because it is also an AT success story, and thus acts as a bridge between the two approaches. Comparisons between the two are discussed after a section that analyses AT. The chapter concludes by considering the implications of the analysis for niche-based approaches to sustainability.

It is stating the obvious to mention how inappropriately anachronistic it is to consider AT as a case study in strategies for reflexive governance. The AT movement emerged 30 years before such strategies had been conceptualised. SNM, which clearly seeks to draw out second-order learning, is more explicitly in tune with the ideas and strategies for reflexive governance outlined in this book (as will become apparent in the next section). Even so, SNM advocacy has led to little practical and prospective implementation to date (although developments in the Netherlands are promising – see Kemp and Loorbach, Chapter 5). Neither case can be considered an empirical study in implementing strategies for reflexive governance. Nevertheless, if drawn carefully, then it should be possible to draw lessons relevant for such strategies (cf. testing empirical cases of the strategies themselves). In this respect, the way that the history of AT informs comment upon SNM means it can also carry lessons over to strategies for reflexive governance.

## STRATEGIC NICHE MANAGEMENT

SNM has been promoted since the late 1990s (Schot et al., 1994; Kemp et al., 1998; Weber et al., 1999; Kemp et al., 2001; Hoogma et al., 2002). Work has been conducted in several areas, including transport, energy and wastewater. Many of these are ex post analyses in which an SNM interpretation is made for the success or otherwise of experiments in sustainability (success being niche growth, branching and influence upon the incumbent technology system). SNM is, however, proposed as a forward-looking policy approach. As such, it has been discussed in a Working Paper by the Science and Technology Foresight Office of the European Commission (von Schomberg, 2002). Most advanced, however, are Dutch government attempts to incorporate a version of it into its technology policy (Hoogma et al., 2002; Rotmans, 2003; VROM, 2003; Ministry of Economic Affairs, undated).

**Origins**

A number of researchers have contributed to the intellectual development of SNM. While researchers from several European countries have been involved, many of the seminal ideas for SNM came from the Netherlands (for example, Schot et al., 1994; Kemp et al., 1998; Kemp et al., 2001). Collective research experience in a number of areas was drawn upon. These areas include co-evolutionary approaches to innovation, Constructive Technology Assessment, and sociological studies of past transformations (for example, Kemp and Soete, 1992; Shot and Rip, 1997; Schot, 1998; Geels, 2002). Thus ideas about socio-technical regimes and trajectories, the value of widening participation in innovation, and the role of niches as crucibles for change are all present in SNM.

SNM injects normative purpose by conceiving niche experiments as a compass for guiding future regime transitions in sustainable directions. Given its intellectual heritage, SNM understands technology in a sociological sense. It argues that discussion of technology must include relations between the hardware/technological artefact and the software/social organisation that enables the overall 'socio-technical configuration' to be considered to 'work' successfully (Rip and Kemp, 1998). Technologies are shaped by society (the knowledge, values, skills and resources of the societies producing them); whilst, at the same time, technologies shape society (opening up new opportunities, imposing restrictions, bringing benefits, distributing risks).

The term 'socio-technical regime' captures this co-evolutionary perspective. A regime is the set of 'rules of the game' that guides the direction of technological innovations for meeting human needs, such as the fossil fuel-based regime currently dominating energy (Geels, 2002). Socio-technical regimes tend to filter expectations and constrain the realms of the realistic. Innovations consequently follow a trajectory set by the regime, which is sustained by social processes and institutions. A socio-technical regime includes, by definition, both a narrow element associated with engineering routines and knowledge (Nelson and Winter, 1982), and a wider element associated with the social context in which the technology is customarily used (Rip and Kemp, 1998). A key challenge for SNM is to integrate knowledge across these domains. Analysis of regimes should include: technology; user practices and application domains; symbolic meanings of technology; infrastructures; industry structure; policy; and knowledge (Geels, 2002; Schot, 1998).

## Objectives

The key objective for SNM is to transform regimes in accordance with a long-term sustainable development 'vision'. Transformation results in a new selection logic and innovation trajectory (for example, greater stress on environmental criteria). New incentives, social organisation and consumption patterns must interact with the innovation of technological hardware in order to make this transition (Kemp et al., 1998: 184). Strategic niches are sites where these new rules can develop. As we shall see, these broad ambitions are not too dissimilar to those of AT activists 30 years ago. There is a difference in the expected pace of change. Where SNM anticipates an evolutionary process of transformation over many years led by government and business, AT perceived the imminent ecological crisis (for example, 'Limits to Growth'; Meadows et al., 1972) as demanding revolutionary change in society.

The SNM literature does not seek a single, precise definition of what a sustainable regime will look like. It understands sustainable development in a very broad sense: concerns for intergenerational justice; trade-offs between economic growth and environmental sustainability; more equity within generations; and society, government and business working longer-term (Hoogma et al., 2002). The argument is that sustainability can be learnt as niche experiments grow, exert influence, recede, branch, or are succeeded by others. The strategy is adaptive and iterative. However, this sits a little uneasily with the SNM requirement that a guiding consensual 'vision' be the basis for building coalitions of support for niche experiments (Berkhout et al., 2004). In practice, a vision for sustainability is inevitably and implicitly present in the way the niche is configured.

## Model of change

Historically, innovative socio-technical configurations that seed regime transformations are understood to begin as novel niches, emerging at the margins of the incumbent, mainstream regime (Kemp et al., 2001). The transition from sail power to steam power in maritime shipping provides an archetypal example (Geels, 2002). This long transition process required the perfection of steam ship technologies. It also needed infrastructure change (a network of coal stores at ports suited to take the new boats), as well as new skills, and novel organisational routines (amongst other social innovations). Early steam technology could not compete with sail ships, and a niche role as tugboats proved important in developing technology use. The steamboat niche grew into other areas as the socio-technical configuration improved: mail shipments, and then into the new, higher value market of transatlantic passenger shipping. Ironically, sail ships retreated into a niche shipping coal to the global network of depots for steam ships (Grübler, 1990). Eventually the performance of steam became sufficiently attractive to compete in markets shipping lower value bulk goods (Geels, 2002).

Historical examples prompt SNM advocacy of the purposeful nurturing of niches. Whether such niche-based transformations are universal historically or not is not the point. Rather, it is the case that a niche-based model has inspired the SNM advocacy for purposive transitions in socio-technical regimes.

> The introduction of novelty has been studied in great detail. However, the adoption of novelty is decisive for society, not its introduction. Adoption is an active process, and has elements of innovation itself. Individual behaviour, organisations, and society have to rearrange themselves to adopt, and adapt to, innovation. In this sense, the introduction of a new technology is an unstructured social experiment. (Rip and Kemp, 1998: 338)

SNM is an attempt to help adoption. Lessons learnt from niches will enable sustainable socio-technical configurations to breakthrough and become mainstream practice. The literature is at pains to point out that niche experiments that fail to grow and branch nevertheless succeed in generating useful experience. Little is wasted in their probe-and-learn strategy (Hoogma et al., 2002). The central tenet in SNM is social learning. Two sets of lessons are drawn from the niches, both of which can help advocates promote niche growth and regime transitions.

## 1.  Lessons internal to the niche

The first set of lessons is internal to the niche: how can the technological artefacts, social practices, and their underlying values be improved so that the configuration works more effectively? More precisely:

- 'to learn more about the technical and economical feasibility and environmental gains of different technological options, i.e. to learn more about the social desirability of the options'; and
- 'to stimulate the further development of these technologies, to achieve cost efficiencies in mass production, to promote the development of complementary technologies and skills and to stimulate changes in social organisation that are important to the wider diffusion of the new technology'. (Kemp et al., 1998: 186)

## 2.  Lessons external to the niche

SNM recognises that top-down support can provide opportunities for niche growth. After all, it was socio-economic changes (mass migration to the Americas in the nineteenth and early twentieth century) that reinforced demand for regular passenger shipping, and sustained steam technology diffusion. The second set of lessons is consequently more outward looking: which types of institutional reforms can help niche growth? SNM advocates describe the purpose of this set of lessons as:

- 'to articulate the changes in technology and in the institutional framework that are necessary for the economic success of the new technology'; and
- 'to build a constituency behind a product – of firms, researchers, public authorities – whose semi-coordinated actions are necessary to bring about a substantial shift in interconnected technologies and practices'. (Kemp et al., 1998: 186)

Top-down intervention suggests, as a minimum, a supportive role from policy-makers and/or key economic interests is needed for SNM to succeed. The SNM literature tends to be non-prescriptive on who should actually 'manage' niche building. Wide participation is considered important. This ensures that a diverse and widely relevant set of knowledge is created through niche learning-by-using, and that this knowledge becomes widely disseminated. The inclusion of groups beyond usual policy and corporate participants in technology policy is intended to move thinking beyond the constraints of the incumbent regime. SNM is the 'collective endeavour' of 'state policy-makers, a regulatory agency, local authorities (for example, a development agency), non-governmental organizations, a citizen group, a private company, an industry organization, a special interest group or an independent individual' (Kemp et al., 1998: 188). SNM is a technology policy approach, however, so government actors would appear, implicitly at least, to hold a key position in niche management.

As we shall see from the AT analysis, some civil society actors hold views on sustainability different to those held by members of incumbent technology policy networks. So whilst government and corporate organisations may appear to hold the ring, they will also need to have carefully thought-through strategies for responding to such diversity. It must be clear to everyone just how responsive different participants are prepared or able to be in the light of lessons generated by the niche, especially the more powerful participants from government and business. There can be limits to the degree to which strategic niche managers can respond to all lessons at any one time. Indeed, the diversity of participants might mean different groups will draw different lessons entirely, let alone act differently on the same lessons. Under which circumstances might a mainstream firm search for lessons from alternative niches? How are such activities brought to their attention? How easy, and by which processes, do these lessons become translated into a form more in accordance with the logic of the existing regime? As niche lessons get adapted, or if the niche grows, what were once relatively clear distinctions between niche and mainstream may become blurred. These points, regarding action based on the social learning generated by SNM, will be picked up in the discussion and conclusion.

## AN EXAMPLE – THE DAVID VS. GOLIATH ORIGINS OF THE DANISH WIND ENERGY INDUSTRY

It is interesting that the origins of the Danish wind energy industry are interpreted positively by SNM advocates (Kemp et al., 2001). Wind energy began its international expansion in the early 1990s. The fact that Danish turbine designs could generate 70–100 per cent more electricity than competitors, owing to a robust and reliable design (Karnøe, 1996), meant the former were able to lead in the new markets. The Danish wind industry is the world leader, generates a turnover of €3 billion, and commands 50 per cent of the world market.[4] Advocates of SNM claim this success was due to the fact that Danish technology policy evolved an approach similar to their own: supporting bottom-up development in niches; in contrast to the large, technology-push R&D projects elsewhere (Kemp et al., 2001; Douthwaite, 2002).

Modern Danish wind began with AT activists who experimented with small turbines in the mid-1970s. These idealists wanted alternatives to the nuclear vision of the electricity utilities. Social networks built up, which shared experience in turbine construction and use. The Organisation for Renewable Energy held meetings and disseminated performance information about different turbines through its magazine *Naturlig Energi* (*Natural Energy*). A social innovation – a new form of community-based wind co-operative – facilitated the purchase of turbines for local use, thereby creating a market. Local agricultural machinery manufacturers noticed this niche market, and began manufacturing turbines. In both cases, the designs drew on past practical experience, and tended to be robustly made owing to the engineering skills and tools available.

The grassroots also lobbied government for support. The (pro-nuclear) electricity utilities needed persuading over the connection of community turbines to the grid. Government support to this effect eventually emerged, as did the creation of a public testing facility for turbine manufacturers at the government's Risø laboratory. This standardised practical experience. The well-tested Danish turbines consequently performed relatively well in the Californian wind-rush of 1980 to 1986. Policy support was by no means easily forthcoming, but what support there was seemed to help the niche. Indeed, learning-by-doing improved reliability and performance to such a degree that the government announced investment subsidies for turbine installations. This made it easier for wind co-operatives to purchase and install grid-connected turbines, and so helped sustain home markets through an international retrenchment in the late 1980s.

The early 20–30 kW machines do not compare with modern 1–2 MW turbines of today. The industry has come a long way from the back-yard idealists. However, analysts argue that policy support for grassroots innovation placed the Danish wind industry onto a favourable development trajectory. Policy for wind energy in other countries focused R&D around big (MW), high-tech projects and technology push. This accorded with the prevailing regime for centralised electricity generation. While these projects contributed to wind energy science, all were practical failures. None was robust and reliable. The relatively simple, extensively road-tested Danish design performed better (Jørgensen and Karnøe, 1995).

What is apparent is how (unwittingly, perhaps) policy-makers acted as strategic niche managers. Unsurprisingly, this case has been used to exemplify SNM:

> From the perspective of regime management, the Danish policy is very interesting. It confirms our model of technological transitions about the importance of the coincidence of successful niche policies against the backdrop of changing regimes. It also shows the importance of learning, the creation of new actor networks, and changes in the institutional framework. More importantly, it demonstrates some of the advantages of a flexible, sequential policy aimed at modulating the dynamics of socio-technical change into socially beneficial directions and using windows of opportunity within the evolving dominant regime. (Kemp et al., 2001: 287)

It is also a case whose roots lie in the AT movement. Here is a direct link between the two approaches. What SNM considers an exemplar is considered a success story in grassroots innovation (Douthwaite, 2002). It was AT idealists that were opposed to nuclear power who seeded the billion-euro export industry of today.

## THE ALTERNATIVE TECHNOLOGY MOVEMENT

The AT movement flourished in the 1970s. A 1979 survey by the OECD Development Centre found that 388 organisations from 79 countries were active in AT (Jéquier, 1979). A follow-up study in 1984 added 316 organisations to the list (in 90 countries) (Jéquier and Blanc, 1984). Just Faaland, President of the Development Centre, wrote how AT 'was no longer the preserve of small marginal groups but had become a major preoccupation of national science and technology policy institutions, governmental research centres and private industrial firms' (preface to Jéquier and Blanc, 1984). The surveys included organisations with a developing country focus as well as those with a developed country focus. A concern for environmentally harmonious technologies attuned to local needs, and whose control is possible in a convivial, socially-inclusive manner is common to AT in the North and South (Schumacher, 1973). However, the circumstances under which AT sought influence in developed countries contrasted considerably with the situation in developing countries, and the legacy and impacts of each has been different (Willoughby, 1990). AT in industrialised countries is relevant here, with the UK serving as the example.

**Origins**

The AT movement was the R&D department for Utopia. It combined the reality of environmental degradation with the idealism of the new left and counter-culture (Veldman, 1994). Activists were interested in technologies that would serve a society radically different to industrial capitalism (Dickson, 1974). They demanded a transformation of technology systems (and society) into forms that did not threaten ecological catastrophe, and which were much more convivial in use. AT would not be as alienating or soul-destroying to work and live with, compared to the mass production and consumption offered by the large corporations. AT was utopian in the sense that widespread expansion of the niches they created 'would be virtually impossible within the existing structure of society' (Dickson, 1974: 99). Might the same be said of SNM?

Today, apart from a visitor centre in Wales (the Centre for Alternative Technology attracts around 60 000 visitors each year), the label 'AT' is rarely used in the UK. The Alternative Technology Group at the Open University – which was home for some AT movement intellectuals – became the Energy and Environment Research Unit in 1986. What was the Urban Centre for Alternative Technology in Bristol is now the Centre for Sustainable Energy, with over 30 staff promoting community energy projects nationally. Nevertheless, alternative niches and ideas continue to be (re)created at the grassroots level. Beneath the slow evolution of government and corporate policies for sustainable technology, networks of grassroots innovators continue to create alternatives to the mainstream. Niches exist in community-supported organic food schemes, eco-housing and community energy projects. Not all participants will have heard of AT, nor SNM for that matter, and yet, in their own way, these grassroots innovators reclaim an approach last attempted by AT.

## Objectives

AT was, above all, a social movement, and consequently held a diversity of views together in a dynamic relationship. Consensus over objectives was sometimes present, and at other times not. AT activists were concerned with technology systems in so far as they would facilitate more sustainable communities. In contrast to SNM, some in the AT movement did attempt, however vaguely, to picture their ideal, sustainable vision. This tended to be based on decentralised, relatively self-sufficient communities; in which participatory democracy is widely practised in the management of steady-state economies; and in which goods and services were provided through local production, using low inputs and renewable resources in relatively closed cycles (Ecologist, 1972; Hollick, 1982). 'The tools and machines required to maintain this alternative would necessarily embody a different set of social and cultural values from those we possess at present. These tools and machines, together with the techniques by which they are used, form what is generally meant by the term alternative technology' (Dickson, 1974: 96). This vision is the antithesis of reflexive modernity. The AT vision anticipates a world where economic relations are steady-state, the pattern of society more enduring, and exploitation of the environment can be sustained. There is no room for the kind of perpetual crises and adjustments thrown up by the unanticipated side effects and second-order characteristics of modern technological societies.

Within their guiding visions of the ecological society, the practical objective for AT activists was to facilitate developments such as a switch to 'soft energy paths' (using diverse, local renewable sources) rather than the 'hard energy path' (centralised nuclear energy and fossil fuels) (Lovins, 1976). The gentle features of AT were defined in contrast to the brutish technologies perceived in industrial society: ecologically sound, not unsound; resource efficient, not materials intense; long-lasting, rather than throw away; participatory, not technocratic; supply based upon needs, not profits; using production cycles, not lines; and so on (Clarke, 1973).

Not everyone in the AT movement foresaw such fixed specifications as practicable or desirable (Harper, 1976; Willoughby, 1990). More critical advocates argued that blueprints and lists were misguided. Wind-pumps were of little improvement if they were still used, say, in the profligate over-abstraction of water resources from finite aquifers. Decentralisation without limits might be just as inappropriate as growth without limits. The smelting of ores into metals, and the production of items such as light bulbs, screws, spectacles, cement, and so on, might simply be better performed using mass production techniques (Harper, 1976). The focus on the small-scale, non-complex, and so forth 'tends to bias the outcome of the inquiry in advance' (Winner, 1979: 83).

At this point in the debate, alternative principles for technology choice, and ensuring their appropriateness for specific social and environmental circumstances, became the objective for AT (Willoughby, 1990). Indeed, it is these critical AT principles, rather than AT artefacts per se, that still strike some resonance for today. We continue to grapple with principles for economic and ecological balance and forms of socially responsible production. Questions keep being raised about received wisdom, such as 'economies of scale' and narrow conceptions of 'economic efficiency'. In this light, AT contributed to 'the awakening of a widespread realization that technology is a controllable force for human betterment, rather than an autonomous juggernaut' (Hollick, 1982: 226; see also Winner, 1979). So the common objective of the AT movement was to transform technology use into a strong form of sustainability. Precise strategies were shrouded in debates about what did and did not constitute an alternative technology, and whether AT should deliver a social blueprint or develop principles for participatory technology choice.

Such debates, reconsidered today, pose questions of relevance for the promotion of sustainable technologies and possibility for social learning, such as in SNM experiments. Can sustainable technologies be listed like artefacts, or does everything depend upon their context of use? If context is important, then how reasonable is it to expect technologies to diffuse across divergent contexts without degrading or changing their sustainability (for example, from niche to mainstream)? The fact that SNM is attempting to change the principles by which socio-technical practices are developed (cf. technologies are diffused) provides clues for answers to such questions. Nevertheless, more research is needed to work through them.

**Model of Change**

A further debate within the movement was over the purposes of AT niches in relationship to social change. Some activists foresaw the widespread diffusion of AT, but recognised that this would not be possible without a radical transformation of society. Others were primarily interested in developing the ecologically-harmonious technologies that would facilitate their retreat from the system into relatively self-sufficient communities (usually in rural locations). The idyll created by the latter might or might not be intended as a beacon for others to follow, if they so wished (Rivers, 1975).

An accommodation was reached between the social revolutionaries and the back-to-the-land folk, because they could meet around the locus of AT niches. For the first group, niches prefigured the technology systems that were needed in the more progressive, sustainable society of tomorrow. For the second group, AT provided tools for retreat from the society of today. A stream of practical initiatives emerged. Grassroots innovators experimented with organic farming techniques, solar heating systems, wind energy, recycling, low-impact housing, and so on. Whatever the philosophical differences, a unifying objective was the creation of practical, AT niches. It is the aspiration to wider transformation held by the first group that orientates their approach to technology along a broadly similar bearing to SNM.

AT networks shared their experiences in developing a wide-range of 'human centred' technologies (Boyle and Harper, 1976). Practical education was mixed with political consciousness raising in publications like *Undercurrents* magazine, which began in 1972 and served as a forum for the movement. Annual AT gatherings organised by the Comtek group in Bath attracted hundreds of activists in the 1970s. The Network for Alternative Technology and Technology Assessment (NATTA), created in 1979, continues to produce a regular newsletter to this day.[5]

Activists pursued a twin-track approach. On the one hand, they set about creating AT niches. These offered practical examples of the sustainability that could diffuse more widely and effectively under the right conditions. It was therefore important to lobby for those conditions. Here the activities of the wider environmental movement were important. Groups such as Friends of the Earth[6] and the Socialist Environmental Resources Association[7] were advocating AT-friendly policies as solutions to the environmentally destructive industries they criticised. Other political alliances were less successful. Few AT activists joined trades unionists in their campaign to avoid industrial redundancies by switching to socially-useful, AT production – such as the Lucas Plan in 1975–6 (Wainwright and Elliott, 1982). Union initiatives received positive coverage in some AT circles, but attempts at building bridges (for example, a Conference on Industry, the Community and Alternative Technology held in November 1975) became mired in political dispute (*Undercurrents*, Issue 14: 12). Back-to-the-land activists saw the unions' 'mass production' of AT as contradicting key lifestyle principles, while unions became frustrated over limited practical help from AT 'dreamers' (*New Scientist*, 20 November, 1975: 472).

Local government initiatives at alternative economic development in the early 1980s provided another opportunity for some in the AT movement. The Greater London Enterprise Board's (GLEB) technology networks included NATTA and other AT activists amongst its membership. The networks attempted to use AT in economic development plans (Mole and Elliott, 1987). However, neither local government initiatives nor trades union greening survived the rightwing Thatcher government.[8] Some niches did manage to survive political hostility and business indifference,[9] and a less hostile political climate today is encouraging grassroots initiatives to re-emerge. Often, AT niches were really experimenting with relatively straightforward or already existing technologies. The grassroots innovators were exploring how to live with AT, trying to improve performance, assessing limitations, learning-by-using:

> having realised the non-neutrality of technology, they consciously seek to design the life-style, and the technology that would go with it, as an integrated whole . . . [their] ideals are firmly placed in technological practices that, in many cases, have already been successfully developed, albeit in piecemeal and fragmented fashion. (Dickson, 1974: 100)

As with SNM, the role of AT niches was learning-by-using. The Danish wind energy industry is one example of the successful diffusion of a technology system that was initiated by grassroots innovators who were sympathetic to AT ideals. The initial turbine design was based on one used in the 1940s. The solar heating boom in Austria in the 1990s is another example that appears to fit the AT tradition. Over 100 000 Austrian homes produce hot water from the sun. A large network of do-it-yourself 'solar clubs' exists.

The movement was inspired initially by motives similar to AT (that is, a practical expression of living more ecologically). Grassroots user involvement in the testing of the different designs available, and information activities similar to the early days of wind turbines in Denmark, are attributed to the successful diffusion of solar heater technology. However, another important (and obvious) factor in this success was that this mode of diffusion helped improve technology performance for users and made it much more cost-effective for them (Ornetzeder, 2001). Thus, while the ideas and motivations that kick-started this example (as with wind energy) permits comparison with AT, it was less idealistic, more conventional factors that determined wider technological diffusion (albeit achieved in socially innovative ways, that is, co-operatives and solar clubs). Would participants label themselves AT today? Probably not: times and terms change. An interesting question for such examples is, even if they do share features with the AT tradition, might they be labelled SNM, too?

## DISCUSSION: COMPARING SNM AND AT

So far we have introduced both SNM and AT. SNM was introduced as a candidate in 'governance innovation' for dealing with reflexive governance in technology issues. The objective now is to try and draw some lessons through comparative analysis. There is a gap of 30 years between AT and

SNM. The gap is felt in the language of each approach and the ideals associated with their experiments. So what can we learn from a comparison, and with what implications for future research? Table 12.1 compares the approaches in summary form. This section discusses the issues that a comparison with AT raises for SNM.

**Niche Purposes**

The core approach for SNM and AT is to generate knowledge, learn lessons and demonstrate alternatives based around niche socio-technical configurations. Members of the AT movement were willing to learn to live with sustainable technologies, such as solar water heating, even if initial instalment was costly or performance less convenient. But participants sometimes interpreted the niches differently. Some entrepreneurs sort to sell designs on a commercial basis (for example, the firm Conservation Tools and Technology). However, given the radical roots of other activists, some were less comfortable embracing or creating markets. Niches can be nurtured for different purposes. Some in AT were developing and using technology that permitted an escape from industrial society, others saw it pre-figuring ecological socialism, and others still were green entrepreneurs. Depending upon the diversity of actors involved, SNM participants will also approach the experiments with a variety of purposes in mind. This could have concomitant influence on the degrees of adaptation each participant is willing to make. This reminds us that niches are boundary objects, in which actors come together with different motivations, perspectives and expectations; and, as a result, social learning will be plural and unlikely to be integrated automatically into a seamless, transdisciplinary knowledge that diffuses unchanged.

**Widening Participation**

Both approaches wish to open innovation to new participants. As one AT advocate put it many years ago: '[Our] approach differs from the "technology-push" approach that underlies most of today's technology promotion policies, by bringing knowledge and expertise of users and other actors into the technology development process'. In fact, this was not written by an AT pioneer. It was written about SNM in 1998 (Kemp et al., 1998: 186). The list of participants suggested for SNM experiments is not very different to those involved in the 'radical' local government initiatives supported by AT activists.

One big difference appears to be the provenance of niche initiatives. AT came from activists in civil society, who sometimes found it difficult to engage

*Table 12.1* Comparison of strategic niche management and alternative technology

| Feature | Strategic niche management | Alternative technology |
|---|---|---|
| *Origins* | Emerged in late 1990s. Takes ideas from evolutionary economics, constructive technology assessment, and sociological histories of past technology transformations. | Emerged in the early 1970s. Developed its ideas from radical science, environmentalism, counter-culture, new left and critique of technocracy. |
| *Objective* | The transition to sociotechnical regimes that meet human needs more sustainably. | Demonstrate technologies that could function in a less alienating society more in harmony with nature. |
| *Understanding of technology* | The technological and social are bound together in a co-evolutionary relationship. | Technology is not neutral. It embodies social values. |
| *Model of change* | Evolutionary. Create sociotechnical niches which generate lessons for: 1. technology and its use; 2. policies to support growth of promising niches. | Revolutionary. Create practical, bottom-up alternatives to: 1. act as beacons for others; 2. challenge mainstream intransigence. |
| *Change agents* | Strategic niche managers. Focus is on business and policy-makers. | Grassroots innovators. Focus is on civil society. |
| *Style* | Managerial. | Political. |
| *Focus* | Learning-by-doing: socio-technical diffusion as innovation. | Learning-by-doing: diffusion of alternative technologies. |
| *Impact* | Probably advocated more niches than actually created. Contributed to ideas about steering technological trajectories in a more sustainable direction. | Probably advocated more niches than actually created. Challenged faith in technological progress and contributed to critical technology assessment. |

with business and government. SNM calls for government and business to engage more with civil society in innovation. Whilst widening participation brings in wider knowledge, it also opens up the challenge of reaching consensus between diverse groups, social values and priorities. More radical niches will experience a greater gulf between advocates and mainstream participants, presenting a challenge for reflexive governance strategies.

**Political Activism, Education, and Innovation Management**

Both approaches recognise that higher-level changes are necessary in order for their niches to breakthrough into everyday practice: evolutionary institutional reform, in the terminology of SNM, a revolutionary restructuring of society for AT. AT activists saw sustainable technology as a political task: they wanted a 'radical science and people's technology' (as the *Undercurrents* slogan stated it). SNM is reformist and managerial in tone: feeding lessons into policy and business strategies, in order to 'modulate ongoing dynamics' (Hoogma et al., 2002: 198).

After 30 years it is clear the AT movement did not build their original blueprint, 'for Utopia remained persistently at the end of the rainbow' (Rivers, 1975: 34). That said, the legacy of AT merits serious consideration. Not only do grassroots innovations continue to emerge today, but some AT ideas have made an important contribution to thinking about sustainable technologies (such as the design of greener homes, the distributed use of renewables). Having cut their teeth in AT projects, some individuals have moved into the new environmental professions that AT had a hand in creating (Jamison, 2001).

Some AT activists were involved in developing the first commercial wind farms in the UK in the 1990s, and some now advise government on renewables policy. Others continue to press for change through political involvement in the green movement or in journalism. Finally, activist involvement in university teaching and research is another route that influences thinking today.[10] Indeed, some consider AT activists' critical analysis of technocracy to have paved the way for sociological understandings of technology and the development of the science–technology–society academic discipline that some of us work in today (Bijker, 1995; Darnovsky, 1991; Waks, 1993). In sum, the burst of radical activity and debate generated a residual measure of social learning.

Perhaps the most striking contribution of AT is an explicit recognition that questions of political and economic power must be a concern in regime transformations. A constituency of political support will need to push for the necessary institutional and infrastructure reforms if, say, an electric vehicle system is to breakthrough. The agitprop role that the AT activists envisaged in their alternative niches is a useful reminder to SNM of the higher-level political challenges in sustainability.

On the other hand, by grounding recommendations in evolutionary economics (cf. revolutionary) and creating more measured expectations over the pace of regime change, SNM may offer a tool for sustainable technological transformation that is palatable within the status quo. Incumbent firms may consequently become involved in niche experiments in ways they found difficult with AT activists. SNM takes on the (no less Herculean) challenge of modulating the existing dynamics of innovation, rather than building a whole different rhythm (Rip and Kemp, 1998). Consequently, the SNM literature seems to devote more attention to nurturing endogenous niche growth, compared to AT interest in wider social and political change. This comparison suggests that change will come through a combination of social learning and political power. Whilst learning can challenge power, power can filter learning. The art for innovative governance strategies will be knowing when it is appropriate to challenge and confront, and when to seek consensus and cooperate.

**Mechanisms for Purposeful Regime Transformation**

Beyond creating knowledge about alternatives, what are the precise mechanisms available for niche-based change? In SNM, niche growth generates transformations. Given its evolutionary orientation, it is unsurprising that growth is ensured through: (1) a degree of niche compatibility with the dimensions of the incumbent regime; (2) niche performance should be robust, and (3) that the niche shows development potential, for example through extension to new applications and, especially, markets (Weber et al., 1999). Thus the idealists who might initiate a niche need to be joined by more entrepreneurial 'systems builders'. The managerial challenge is to carry niche development through to the stage when it can attract the big capital needed for the niche to become a commercial prospect. The paradox is that the 'good compatibility' criteria can imply that niches at radical odds with the incumbent regime will need to offer considerable positive returns if they are to attract investment. The alternative technologies developed in GLEB networks struggled because, besides a hostile political climate, the social needs they served lacked purchasing power in markets (Mole and Elliott, 1987). In a sense, the AT movement's attachment to higher level political change recognised that their niches would never attract such capital unless investment incentives (and institutions) were altered radically through public policy.

There is another mechanism by which niche initiatives might influence mainstream change (Geels, 2002). Some aspect of the niche activity may offer a solution to problems or 'tensions' experienced in the incumbent regime. Obviously, many socio-technical regimes currently experience environmental tension, to the extent that social mechanisms (such as regulations or consumer boycotts) seek to constrain the degree to which they exploit the natural environment. The political focus of AT suggests that one way for regimes to be placed under targeted tension is political campaigning.[11] Relevant and palatable components of the niche are adapted by incumbent regime actors, and thereby modify the regime.

We can see this in the way supermarkets are including organics in their food range, in response to perceived consumer concerns. One UK supermarket is even investing in organic R&D. Organic food, however, remains a niche product range (56 per cent of which is imported (Soil Association, 2004)). Supermarkets are adapting organic farming to suit their business commitments. Some organic activists believe supermarket adaptation does nothing to deliver other sustainability principles evident in their niches: intensive farming remains dominant, imports cause polluting food miles, and local rural economies do not revive. The current growth in local food initiatives can be considered a response to continued inadequacies in the way supermarkets have co-opted organic farming into their dominant business model.

In a similar vein, the giant (2MW) wind turbines built by electricity utilities in the offshore 'wind fields' of north-western Europe do not meet activists' ideals for energy conservation and small-scale, community energy provision. Yet in both cases, the technology 'solutions' to incumbent regime problems can be traced back to niche origins. What is interesting is the way social lessons are drawn differently, and both bend and fit around existing economic structures to varying degrees.

**Niche Values and Technology**

The way the mainstream appropriates sustainable practices raises questions about values and technology. Indeed, the notion of sustainable technology becomes slippery. The supermarkets and local organic groups, and the utilities and community energy groups, each claim their initiatives as sustainable – even though each has a different socio-technical configuration, which embodies different understandings of sustainable development, and which prioritises different environmental, social and economic criteria.

Niche influence in regime shifts may relate to the degree to which the values and criteria originally forming the niche adhere to the socio-technical configuration. If values and criteria are tightly related to the socio-technical practice, will this limit the variety of contexts (values and criteria) to which the configuration can be applied without major modification? In other words, unless the mainstream buys into the values embodied in the niche, then the scaling-up of the niche will be distorted perversely or simply not happen – because adoption demands too much change to the mainstream. On the other hand, if socio-technical practices can easily be stripped of values, and adapted to suit incumbent interests and contexts, then the niche socio-technical configuration may well diffuse much more easily, but with key sustainability features becoming lost in the translation. Niche influence is wider, but less profound.

## CONCLUSIONS

This chapter has compared two niche-based approaches to systems innovation. Clearly, SNM and AT are different. Yet what they share in common is an aim to create knowledge about sustainable technology use in niches that can (hopefully) transform incumbent regimes. Considered together they raise a number of issues for research and practice of relevance to governance. Thinking about alternative technology niches and the sustainable development of mainstream society forces us to consider the following.

### 1.   Integrated Knowledge Production

AT was rooted in civil society, and was inclined toward political lobbying as well as grassroots initiative. The AT experience illustrates how innovative ideas can emerge through informed dissent beyond conventional business contexts. SNM is oriented more toward policy-makers and technology producers, and suggests how they may engage with change by including leading users and other participants. In practice, the ability to create niches with transformation potential is distributed, unevenly, across a variety of social actors. It makes sense to include technology producers, users, regulators and others with the necessary skills, money, tools, knowledge, and power to force legitimate change.

However, as AT debates illustrate, there exists flexibility over how a sustainability problem gets interpreted. Diverse solutions are favoured differently by different actors, depending upon their ideas, values and experience. Integrated knowledge production will have to navigate the (sometimes conflicting) social values attached to different knowledge claims and priorities. In short, how can world views be bridged and the energies and capabilities of political activists and business investors harnessed more effectively? Though both elements are important for progressive change, it may simply be unrealistic to expect them to co-ordinate neatly in the systematic way anticipated by some governance innovations.

## 2.  Experimentation and Adaptation

Real world change is far more messy, challenging and context-dependent than neat processes of niche growth and their bottom-up displacement of incumbent regimes (Berkhout et al., 2004). Only aspects of niche practices might breakthrough into the mainstream, for technical, institutional or ideological reasons. The mainstream appears a shade greener as a result, but darker green fundamentals remain unaddressed. More radical, challenging niches can persist or re-emerge. System building entrepreneurs in government and business can try and bridge these two worlds. This is a challenging position to be in because, on the one hand, the systems builders are trying to cajole an incumbent regime into change and, on the other hand, they are having to compromise over niche principles. System building proves to be a political task. Indeed, system building is probably the wrong term since it implies social change to be the smooth rearrangement of interacting functions. In practice, change may be subject to social forces beyond the system builders' unilateral control.

## 3.  Social Learning and Power

Further translation efforts, which enable more challenging niche ideas to cross into mainstream practice, can be facilitated through higher-level policy and institutional changes. However, there may come a point, as argued in some AT debates, when the only way to progress a radically sustainable idea is to challenge existing structures. AT faced considerable institutional rigidities and was unable to force adaptation. At some point, and in some way, technology policies for bottom-up niche creation must be augmented with top-down changes that favourably restructure the selection environment. This chapter has illustrated how the intrinsic properties of green niches alone can struggle to drive a breakthrough. They need the assistance of higher-level changes and the opportunities that these create. In multi-actor governance settings, the challenge is to get these top-down and bottom-up processes operating in relative harmony. Moreover, at this point governance has to confront questions of power. The positive lessons learnt from sustainable niche experiments may simply be too unpalatable or incompatible with the powerful interests, entrenched institutions, economic commitments, and prevailing social values that operate at the level of the incumbent regime.

As the history of AT reminds us, the grassroots provide a rich stream of niche sustainable initiatives. Some have asked how many alternative niches provide an optimum degree of diversity? Approaches to optimising diversity do exist (Stirling, 1998). However, activists are likely to be impervious to such measurements, so long as they have energy and time, they will try and lever in the resources to create their ideal niches. Governance strategies committed to sustainable development might consider how better to support this innovative zeal. This chapter has tried to argue such support must not merely be quantitative. There is a qualitative dimension in the way support transmits niche lessons to the mainstream and facilitates action for their incorporation. Indeed, new interest in niche-based approaches rekindles a challenging research and policy agenda.

## ACKNOWLEDGMENTS

This chapter draws upon research funded by the UK Economic and Social Research Council (ESRC) under their Sustainable Technologies Programme. I am grateful to all those people who have given freely of their time, conversation and insights during the course of the research. Of course, the views expressed here remain my responsibility.

## NOTES

1. http://www.blueprint-network.net/.
2. This chapter is based on an earlier version published as Smith, A. (2004) 'Alternative technology niches and sustainable development', *Innovation, Management, Policy and Practice*, 6(2), pp. 220–35, in A. Griffiths (ed.), *Corporate Sustainability: Governance, Innovation Strategy, Development and Methods* (ISBN 0975043625), eContent Management, Maleny, Queensland. I am grateful to the publishers for permission to develop it into this chapter.
3. Grassroots innovators develop bottom-up solutions to public problems. They tend to come from outside mainstream firms and operate instead in civil society arenas. They are often idealists, and experiment with social innovation as much as technological hardware. Indeed, limited access to financial and other resources can force interest to focus upon the software issues of social organisation and new rules.
4. Data supplied by the Danish Wind Industry Association.
5. The focus now is limited to sustainable energy issues, but it retains AT sensibilities with a concern for community action. See http://eeru.open.ac.uk/natta/welcome.html.
6. Amory Lovins, a high-profile 'soft energy' advocate, worked as Energy Campaigner for FoE in the 1970s.
7. Which later affiliated to the Labour Party.
8. The Conservative government introduced legislation restricting trades union activity; local government spending was brought under tighter central control; and GLEB disappeared with the abolition of the Greater London Council in 1986.
9. Community groups running home insulation schemes, for example, have evolved into regional dissemination centres, such as the Centre for Sustainable Energy mentioned earlier.
10. Such as the thousands of students who studied AT as part of courses at the Open University.
11. Of course, uncoordinated socio-economic trends and changes might also manifest 'tension' in particular socio-technical regimes, such as demographic changes and water demand. Niches may still offer solutions.

# REFERENCES

Berkhout, F. (2002), 'Technological regimes, path dependency and the environment', *Global Environmental Change*, **12** (1), 1–4.

Berkhout, F., A. Smith, and A. Stirling (2004), 'Socio-technical regimes and transition contexts', in B. Elzen, F. Geels and K. Green (eds), *System Innovation and the Transition to Sustainability: Theory, Evidence and Policy*, Cheltenham, UK and Northampton, MA, USA: Edward Elgar.

Bijker, W.E. (1995), *Of Bicycles, Bakelite and Bulbs*, Cambridge, MA: MIT Press.

Boyle, G. and P. Harper (1976), *Radical Technology*, London: Wildwood House.

Clarke, R. (1973), 'Technology for an alternative society', *New Scientist*, 11 January.

Darnovsky, M. (1991), 'Overhauling the meaning machines: an interview with Donna Haraway', *Socialist Review*, **21** (2), 65–84.

Dickson, D. (1974), *Alternative Technology*, Glasgow: Fontana/Collins.

Douthwaite, B. (2002), *Enabling Innovation*, London: Zed Books.

Dunphy, D. (1996), 'Organizational change in corporate settings', *Human Relations*, **49** (5), 541–51.

Ecologist (1972), *Blueprint for Survival*, London: Ecosystems.

Freeman, C. (1991), 'Technology, progress and the quality of life', *Science and Public Policy*, **18** (6).

Geels, F. (2002), *Understanding the Dynamics of Technological Transitions*, Enschede: Twente University Press.

Grübler, A. (1990), *The Rise and Fall of Infrastructures*, Heidelberg: Physica-Verlag.

Harper, P. (1976), 'Autonomy', in G. Boyle and P. Harper (eds), *Radical Technology*, London: Wildwood House.

Hollick, M. (1982), 'The appropriate technology movement and its literature: a retrospective', *Technology in Society*, **4**, 213–29.

Hoogma, R., R. Kemp, J. Schot and B. Truffer (2002), *Experimenting for Sustainable Transport*, London: Spon Press.

Howes, R., J. Skea and R. Wheelan (1997), *Clean and Competitive*, London: Earthscan.

Jamison, A. (2001), *The Making of Green Knowledge*, Cambridge: Cambridge University Press.

Jéquier, N. (1979), *Appropriate Technology Directory*, Paris: OECD.

Jéquier, N. and G. Blanc (1984), *Appropriate Technology Directory Volume II*, Paris: OECD.

Jørgensen, U. and P. Karnøe (1995), 'The Danish wind-turbine story: technical solutions to political visions?', in A. Rip, T.J. Misa and J. Schot (eds), *Managing Technology in Society*, London: Pinter.

Karnøe, P. (1996), 'The social process of competence building', *International Journal on Unlearning and Learning*, **11** (7/8), 770–89.

Kemp, R., A. Rip and J. Schot (2001), 'Constructing transition paths through the management of niches', in R. Garud and P. Karnøe (eds), *Path Dependence and Creation*, Mahwah, NJ: Lawrence Erlbaum.

Kemp, R., J. Schot and R. Hoogma (1998), 'Regime shifts to sustainability through processes of niche formation: the approach of strategic niche management', *Technology Analysis and Strategic Management*, **10** (2), 175–95.

Kemp, R. and L. Soete (1992), 'The greening of technological progress: an evolutionary perspective', *Futures*, **24**, 437–57.

Lovins, A. (1976), 'Energy strategy: the road not taken?', *Foreign Affairs*, **55** (1).

Meadows, D.H., D.L. Meadows, J. Randers and W.W. Behrens III (1972), *The Limits to Growth*, New York: Universe Books.

Ministry of Economic Affairs (undated), 'Energy transition: impulse for sustainability and innovation', Ministry of Economic Affairs, The Hague.

Mole, V. and D. Elliott (1987), *Enterprising innovation: an alternative approach*, London: Frances Pinter.

Nelson, R. and S.G. Winter (1982), *An Evolutionary Theory of Economic Change*, Cambridge, MA: Harvard University Press.

Ornetzeder, M. (2001), 'Old technology and social innovations: inside the Austrian success story on solar water heaters', *Technology Analysis and Strategic Management*, **13** (1), 269–78.

Rip, A. and R. Kemp (1998), 'Technological change', in S. Rayner and E.L. Malone (eds), *Human Choices and Climate Change, Volume 2 – Resources and Technology*, Columbus, OH: Battelle.

Rivers, P. (1975), *The Survivalists*, London: Methuen.

Rotmans, J. (2003), *Transitiemanagement: Sleutel voor een Duurzame Samenleving*, Assen: Koninklijke Van Gorcum.

Schot, J., R. Hoogma and B. Elzen (1994), 'Strategies for shifting technological systems: the case of the automobile system', *Futures*, **26**: 1060–76.

Schot, J. (1998), 'The usefulness of evolutionary models for explaining innovation. The case of the Netherlands in the nineteenth century', *History and Technology*, **14**, 173–200.

Schot, J. and A. Rip (1997), 'The past and future of Constructive Technology Assessment', *Technological Forecasting and Social Change*, **54**, 251–68.

Schumacher, E.F. (1973), *Small is Beautiful*, London: Blond and Briggs.

Soil Association (2004), *Food and Farming Report 2004*, Bristol: Soil Association.

Stirling, A. (1998), 'On the Economics of Diversity', SPRU electronic working paper series, available at: http://www.sussex.ac.uk/spru/1-6-1-2-1.html.

Veldman, M. (1994), 'Fantasy, the Bomb and the Greening of Britain', *Romantic Protest, 1945–1980*, Cambridge: Cambridge University Press.

Von Schomberg, R. (2002), 'The objective of sustainable development: are we coming closer?', working paper from Office of Science and Technology Foresight, DG RTD, European Commission, Brussels.

VROM, Ministry of Housing, Spatial Planning and the Environment (2003), 'Transitions progress report: making strides towards sustainability', VROM, The Hague.

Wainwright, H. and D. Elliott (1982), *The Lucas Plan. A New Trades Unionism in the Making?*, London: Allison and Busby.

Waks, L.J. (1993), 'STS as an academic field and a social movement', *Technology in Society*, **15**, 399–408.

Weber, M., R. Hoogma, B. Lane and J. Schot (1999), *Experimenting with Sustainable Transport Innovations: a Workbook for Strategic Niche Management*, Enschede: University of Twente Press.

Willoughby, K.W. (1990), *Technology Choice. A Critique of the Appropriate Technology Movement*, London: ITDG.

Winner, L. (1979), 'The political philosophy of alternative technology: historical roots and present prospects', *Technology in Society*, **1**, 75–86.

# 13. The sustainable transformation of sanitation

## Bas van Vliet

## INTRODUCTION

Probably the most sensible and most pressing environmental problem in Western cities of the nineteenth century was the accumulation and inappropriate handling of human waste. Since the discovery of the relationship between the lack of sanitation on the one hand and epidemic diseases like cholera on the other, networks of drinking water supply and sewage systems have been rolled out in almost all urban centres of the world.

Water works that were constructed during the last century largely solved the urban problems of waste accumulation, malodours and health risks. Treated water is delivered through municipal pipelines and used as drinking water. Human waste is transported out of the cities by means of huge quantities of water-flushing sewer pipelines. During the last decades most of these sewer pipe lines have been connected to waste water treatment systems before the waste water is discharged in open waters.

Yet, while having solved many public health-related and environmental problems, water works have introduced problems that relate to sustainability. The availability of a cheap and clean water supply system caused an increase of water consumption in the Netherlands from 97 litres per capita per day in 1970 up to 126 litres in 2004 (Vewin, 2004). Drinking water production depletes valuable ground water resources above its carrying capacity and causes irreversible desiccation of natural reserves, swamps and wetlands. Future water supplies in the Netherlands will therefore increasingly be based on surface water sources. Utilisation of surface water for the production of drinking water is problematic as well, as it requires reservation of space for storage basins and lots of energy and chemicals to obtain drinking water of a minimum quality. For these various economic and environmental reasons, the government, water companies and consumers have taken measures to save on water use.

Sewer systems use huge amounts of drinking water to transport human waste out of the cities. Toilet flushing alone consumes one quarter of daily personal drinking water use (Vewin, 2004). Apart from wasting high quality water, the dilution of human waste by huge amounts of water makes waste water treatment highly inefficient in terms of capacity use, energy consumption and overall treatment performance. Instead of being recovered, the nutrients from human waste are ultimately landfilled, incinerated or discharged to open waters.

An increasing number of environmental scientists and engineers (GTZ, 2003; Lens et al., 2001) argue that all of these valuable flows could and should be brought back into a closed-loop system, which recovers the nutrients from human waste and minimises the use of energy, water and material resources. Closed-loop systems differ radically from contemporary waterworks and sewer systems in both technical and social respects. To implement closed-loop systems, a strategy is needed which incorporates both technical and social changes within the practices of sanitation. Rather than an expert-driven approach, which leads to environmentally optimal technical systems, there is a need to widen the closed-loop approach to a more reflexive strategy including participatory goal definition by a wide variety of actors rather than only sanitation experts.

This chapter aims to draft the key elements of a reflexive strategy of socio-technical change in waste water systems. Firstly I elaborate in Section 2 on the kind of socio-technical changes that are (implicitly) proposed in closed-loop systems to solve the second-order sustainability problems of sewer systems. Section 3 presents two cases of experimentation with such systems in the Netherlands. The cases are selected on the premises that they differ in particular in terms of reflexive governance. This is followed by an evaluation of the cases (Section 4) based on the five process requirements for reflexive sustainable governance as presented in the Introduction of this volume. The conclusion addresses the lessons learned and the key elements of a strategy of sustainable transformation of sanitation as well as a critical assessment of its implications.

# SOCIO-TECHNICAL CHANGE IN SANITATION

## Multi-level Change

Closing the loop means that the very principles of current water works should be altered, and that large-scale physical infrastructures of water works should be abolished and replaced over time. Proponents of such closed-loop or eco-sanitation systems aim to introduce radically different house-on-site and community-on-site systems to treat human waste. These systems minimise water use to transport faeces and urine so as to obtain highly concentrated waste for efficient treatment. Urine can be separated from other wastes for efficient recovery of specific nutrients. In most systems, energy is produced during the process of digestion and treatment. The recovered nutrients can be re-used as fertiliser in agriculture (Werner et al., 2003).

The establishment of eco-sanitation systems requires more than just a next step in a well-defined trajectory of sewer technology development. It is a radical shift away from the basic principles of sewer technology. For one: it encompasses treatment of concentrated waste instead of treatment of a mix of waste water and storm water. Secondly, treatment of waste is done mostly on-site or close to waste production, while the sewer system transports waste and water to distant centralised treatment facilities. Thirdly, closed-loop systems generate energy from bio-gas that is produced, and reuse treated waste water and its nutrients, for example, in irrigation and fertilisation, while sewer systems consume energy and produce large quantities of sludge that cannot be reused (Zeeman and Lettinga, 1999).

Such major technological shifts require different rules and regulations and institutional organisation as these are now perfectly geared to manage sewer systems, not eco-sanitation systems. The changes that users, suppliers and service managers need to make in their daily practices are equally as radical. Consumer roles may change from those of passive users of sewer systems to co-managers of decentralised waste treatment. In sum: apart from a change of technological hardware, technological shifts of this magnitude encompass much more of a socio-technical change. Socio-technical change can be distinguished on three levels (adapted from Kemp et al., 1998):

- Socio-technical landscapes (macro level): a range of contextual factors that influence technological development but cannot be changed by technology actors;
- Regimes (meso level): rule sets that are built up around a dominant technology and give it stability;
- Niches: protected spaces of social learning around new technologies at the micro level.

The management of radical and long-term social-technical changes is called transition management (Rotmans et al., 2001) and is presented by Kemp and Loorbach in Chapter 5 of this volume. Transition management does not provide a clear recipe for changing network-bound systems. The approach leaves much room for changing insights, feedback and reformulation of goals during the long-term course of socio-technical change. The long-term view also complicates the issue of implementing eco-sanitation probably more than environmental engineers would have wished. However, the kinds of changes eco-sanitation inherently tries to establish can only be achieved over the long term and by built-in reflexivity as is done in transition management. In case of a transition from sewer to eco-sanitation systems, the three levels of socio-technical systems can be described as follows.

## LANDSCAPE LEVEL

The landscape metaphor refers to the structural character of its influence on technological development: technological trajectories are guided by the gradients in the landscape. Changes at this level only occur gradually and very slowly. An example of such a gradient is the robustness of socio-cultural notions and practices that have been developed around the availability of the sewer system (and the connected devices like water closets). At the beginning of the twentieth century, water closets became highly desired artefacts to have installed in modern homes. Today, in many countries and areas were there is no sewer system, the water closet is still a landmark of a modern lifestyle. Moreover, most people who have one would not consider the use of water closets and sewer systems as particularly problematic, on the contrary: they are quite happy with it. The principle of 'flush and forget' is especially appealing when it comes to the handling of human waste. An attempt to change the system radically will probably render harsh public opposition, especially when such a system would require extra effort with, or would cause a (more frequent) sight or smell of human waste.

## REGIME LEVEL

The regime level refers to the cognitive, social and technical rule-sets that are embodied in practices, artefacts and organisations. The rules are carried out by a heterogeneous network of producers, providers, users, researchers, governmental and non-governmental bodies.

The new eco-sanitation techniques require a different regime as compared to the systems in place. Sewer systems and other water works are mostly centrally managed and controlled by state-owned organisations. It has taken a whole century to construct not only a huge network of pipes, pumps and treatment facilities, but also to set up a legislative and organisational framework to govern the entire system. Eco-sanitation techniques require much more distributed control capacities compared to the centrally controlled sewer systems. In some cases, house-owners will become the managers of waste treatment; in other cases, entire new intermediaries should be put in place to manage the much more fragmented chain from human waste collection, transportation, treatment and recovery.

## MICRO (NICHE) LEVEL

Equally radical are the changes that users, suppliers and service managers need to make in their daily practices related to sanitation. Urine separation toilets require male users to sit down (!); composting toilets involve timely management and control at the household level. In general, collection, storage and discharge of human waste in eco-sanitation systems bear more resemblance to modern domestic waste management (separation in different fractions with different collecting systems) than to the current sewer system.

Earlier social scientific studies on socio-technical change revealed that a focus on the practices of providers and consumers that deal with infrastructures and the changing relations between them offers new insights in the process of infrastructural reconfiguration (see also Van Vliet, 2002; Southerton et al., 2004; Van Vliet et al., 2005). One insight is the increasing differentiation of consumer roles towards infrastructural provision. Apart from remaining captive consumers, consumers may become clients or even co-providers of the services that were formerly exclusively offered by utility companies. For this reason, I need to explore and compare not only the technical layout of eco-sanitation and sewer systems, but also the changes in social practices around the building and the use and management of these sanitation systems.

## SOCIO-TECHNICAL VARIABLES IN ECO-SANITATION SYSTEMS

This contribution is partly based on ongoing empirical research of socio-technical change in sanitation in the Netherlands.[1] In order to do case study research on the issues of niche development and changing consumer–provider relations in sanitation as elaborated above, a variable set was designed for the selection of cases. The variable set includes the scale of technology; level of consumer involvement; a central or decentralised organisation; and the separation or combination of incoming or

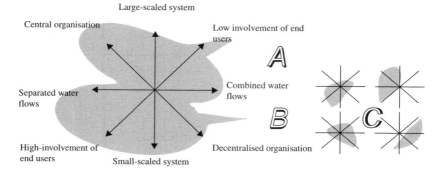

*Figure 13.1    Variables characterising sanitation technologies*

outgoing water flows. These variables can be put in a diagram as follows (see Figure 13.1):

Three main clusters of variables can be made to categorise sanitation systems: conventional systems (A), alternative systems (B) and what may be called 'modernised mixtures' (C).

A.  Conventional systems can be found in the clustering of values at the top of the diagram: central organisation, large-scaled systems and low user involvement.
B.  Alternative systems are to be found at the opposite end of the diagram: small-scale systems, responsible users, de-centralised organisation.
C.  Various combinations of social and technical variables make up for 'modernised mixtures'.

Conventional sanitation systems (A) are centralised systems designed for the treatment of single water flows. Large-scale sewer systems that collect all water flows are the extreme example of this category. The end-user involvement in these systems is low.

The category of alternative systems (B) has since the early 1970s been propagated and developed by supporters of Schumacher's 'small is beautiful' thesis (Schumacher, 1975), which encompasses consumers, technicians, philosophers and environmentalists. The idea is that not only the hardware of sanitation systems should be of a small, 'human' size, especially the social organisation around the design, implementation, use and mainte-nance should be kept as small or local as possible to secure democratic control by the users of such systems. Besides, it is believed that such small systems are the most environmentally sound. Examples within such an alternative category are 'stand-alone' systems that do not need a connection to larger infrastructures, like composting toilets or rainwater recycling systems.

The category of 'modernised mixtures' (C) encompasses various score-sets on the four variables mentioned. Examples include centrally managed vacuum systems at the scale of a residential area with a high separation of flows and low consumer involvement; or small-scale but sewer-connected water systems that are based on the dual water flows and high consumer involvement. As these empirical examples illustrate, we are dealing here not only with a mixture of 'conventional' and 'alternative' technological aspects but also with a mixture of social elements. The modernised mixtures bring together social and technical elements that used to be strictly separated and organised into ideological debates between the opponents and defenders of conventional, centralised and complex large technical systems.

Our case studies have been conducted at small and medium scaled systems in which some waste streams are treated on-site and others are transported and treated elsewhere for reasons of environmental efficiency. In such cases of modernised mixtures, the process of initiation, development and implementation of the new technology has been monitored. The views of providers (technology developers, municipalities, utilities, water managers) about possible routes of diffusion and the role of end users have been assessed. In addition, particular emphasis is placed upon the involvement of end users in design, diffusion, use and management and the consequences of these changes for current practices and standards of convenience, cleanliness, comfort (Shove, 2003) and health that people tend to uphold.

## TWO CASE STUDIES OF GOVERNING THE IMPLEMENTATION OF ECO-SANITATION

Two projects are selected to discuss reflexive governance in eco-sanitation. They were both set up to implement new ideas and technologies for the sake of sustainability, but differ greatly in the execution of these. The data are derived from the previously mentioned project that focuses on the diffusion of eco-sanitation in the Netherlands.

### Vacuum Toilets and Digestion Tanks in Newly Built Apartments

The first case that is monitored is the planned installation of a vacuum transport and anaerobe treatment system of toilet and kitchen waste in a new residential site in the city of Wageningen. After obtaining a subsidy from a ministerial programme for environmental innovation in 2001 (Programme Economy, Ecology, Technology), a project group of environmental engineers (the initiators), the municipality, the regional water supply company, project developers, and two other firms (one specialist in building anaerobe digestion installations and one in vacuum systems) was formed. It was commissioned to make a technical design for the separated collection, transport and treatment of grey water, concentrated toilet waste and kitchen waste in a new, small apartment block (six apartments) within a larger housing project that is located close to the centre of Wageningen.

The project proposal emphasised that this was a technological demonstration project: the techniques of vacuum toilets and especially anaerobe treatment systems were to be tested. It was explicitly mentioned that the reuse of digested sludge in agriculture was beyond the scope of the demonstration project. Thus, during the two-year project the sludge was to be treated in an existing waste water treatment plant. The organisation of sludge collection and transport was to be decided upon among the project members during the preparation phase.

Although most parts of the proposed system have been successfully applied in other settings (vacuum toilets in trains and aircraft, anaerobic treatment in industry), this would be the first application of such technology in a domestic urban setting in the Netherlands. The technology can be characterised as medium- to small-scale, based on a separation of wastewater flows, and on a decentralised organisation. There was no involvement of end users as they were unknown until the apartments had been built and sold. The case resembles many aspects of a technological niche-project: the installation of a deviating technology for (human) waste treatment as well as its transport system (vacuum pipes and toilets) needs protection in the form of (legal) exemptions and subsidies. Among the many legal hurdles to take is the national building regulation that states that 'the design of a biological wastewater treatment system should cater for a sufficient inflow of air to maintain an aerobe biological treatment process'.[2] Anaerobe systems as proposed in this project are not even mentioned as a possibility in such regulations. Subsidy is required for instance to build and reserve extra space in the basement of the apartment building for the installation of utilities.

Although these measures of niche protection were more or less secured in advance of the project, it was certainly not enough to get the project started. In discussing the project among the actors of the project group, it became apparent that both the municipality and the project developers claimed to be spokespersons for the still unknown end-consumers. As project developers and real estate agents are, generally speaking, the risk takers in selling the apartments, they were the first to object to experiments that may affect either the price or the attractiveness of the apartment to the potential buyer, or both. The municipality, although committed to the execution of the project, felt responsible for the well-being of its (future) citizens, as well as for the proper management of the whole system.

At the start of the project, many aspects of the experiment with vacuum toilets and anaerobe treatment systems were still unresolved – from seemingly trivial issues like the shape and colour of toilets to more crucial aspects of management and transfer of technology after the experiments came to an end. The initiators (a group of environmental engineers) tried to resolve these problems during a number of project meetings as well as bi-lateral meetings; however, there was no satisfactory result. Both the municipality and the project developers decided in 2003 to withdraw from the project and another building site had to be found to implement the proposed technology.

In hindsight, the following can be said about why the project failed in achieving its goal, which was the testing of eco-sanitation techniques in a residential area. A first lesson that can be drawn is that apart from a commitment of the municipality and a subsidy for the installations, one has to deal with many more conditions under which such anomaly in the current system can be developed. Municipalities and water boards are legally responsible for the proper handling of human waste and they want solid guarantees that alternative systems will work as well as, or even better than, the systems they are used to working with. Project developers and real estate agencies are even more reluctant to accept the risks of technical or managerial failure. As long as there are as many uncertainties as in the current project, the willingness of all these actors to co-operate is limited.

Furthermore, commitment of institutional partners was not adequately secured before the project started. Before the subsidy was granted, there was a commitment of the local city alderman to join the proposed project, as it would very much add to the municipality's green image. Once the project really started, however, the municipality was represented by the civil servants of Public Works, who did not show an equally green commitment as their political boss. Furthermore, there was a major disagreement about the character of the group of end users. The initiators of the project claimed that there are enough potential buyers in Wageningen who are committed to the environment to join such an environmental innovation project voluntarily. The builders (project developers) disputed this and claimed that any alteration in the standard sanitary system will be considered a hazard, even to 'green' consumers.

## Eco-sanitation in Lanxmeer, Culemborg

The second example case (EVA Lanxmeer, Culemborg) is in many respects different from the first case, but both cases have some principles of the (proposed) waste water treatment system in common. In both cases a separation is made between the treatment of grey water (that is, from kitchen-sink, shower and washing machine) and black water (from toilets). Black water is to be treated on-site in anaerobe digestion tanks, thus without using sewer pipes and central treatment facilities (although there is a connection in case things go wrong).

The process of implementation of these technologies in Culemborg, however, differs significantly from the Wageningen case. The initiative for the building project of about 200 homes was born in 1994 when Stichting EVA[3] was founded. Its objectives are to create a living environment in which there is room for involvement of its residents in the natural environment through making environmental issues visible and sensible. Moreover, it aims to enable environmentally sound lifestyles and to restore damaged ecosystems (Siemensma, 2000). The foundation wished to build a residential site that could fulfil these objectives. In 1996 it found a municipality (Culemborg) that was willing to realise it. A project team was established that consisted of the municipality, Stichting EVA, an association of (future) residents and a project bureau. Architects, landscape architects, energy consultants and other experts were commissioned on an ad hoc basis. The presence of future inhabitants and the enthusiastic participation of the project partners that were involved resulted in a higher level of environmental ambition than could probably be realised otherwise.

Another success factor is based on the philosophy behind the project. It encompasses a much broader vision of the outcome of the project than in the Wageningen case. It is a vision of sustainable living that links quality of life with quality of the surrounding environment, in which the use of sustainable technology is just the means to an end, not the centre of the project itself.

Half of the residential site is now completed. The reed-bed filters for grey water treatment started operation in 2003 but the biogas installation is still to be completed. Initially, the plan was to install a vacuum system for the transport of toilet waste and organic kitchen waste. The group of residents, however, successfully opposed this technology. They pointed out its higher energy consumption compared to other transport systems and expressed their concerns about hygiene and possible clogging. In the end, low-flush toilets with boosters were installed. These will be connected to the biogas installation by means of a local sewer system (Siemensma, 2000).

Due to time pressure, the level of inhabitant participation was much lower then envisaged beforehand. Although three workshops were held in which the wider group of inhabitants could ventilate their wishes, they were not able to modify their houses individually, as was planned. The professionals who were involved in the project were mainly responsible for the choice of sustainable technologies; inhabitants had no say in the choice of water-saving toilets as opposed to a vacuum system or composting toilets. Inhabitants do not seem worried about this lack of participation; they do not mind the fact that the professionals decide on the definite technology, as long as this technology meets the environmental and living standards of its users.

Two major differences between the two cases discussed here might explain the limited results to date in the first case and the initially successful course of the second case. One difference is that of the scope of the project: the first case is mainly about the implementation of a new technique. The 'hardware' was known, but problems emerged as soon as issues about the 'software' (management and maintenance issues) became apparent. The scope of the second case was much broader from the very start of the project: the technology itself was not placed in the foreground, but the implementation of a sustainable way of building and living, for which new technologies should be developed and implemented. In other words: technology is the means and not the end towards sustainable living.

The second major difference between the two projects concerns the involvement and representation of (future) inhabitants. They were not known in the first case so only general assumptions could be made about their acceptance of new routines. The mere existence of (future) end users in the second case prevented other actors from presenting themselves as their spokespeople. But this is certainly not the only success factor. Consumer participation in the design and in assessing principles of a project seems to have enhanced the willingness to change routines and to accept new responsibilities towards the use and management of new technologies.

## PROSPECTS FOR THE FUTURE GOVERNANCE OF WASTE WATER FLOWS

The two cases presented above only show a small segment of the variety of today's innovations and experimentation in eco-sanitation. Moreover, they were not deliberately set up to test a special mode of governance, rather to test technologies and new arrangements for sustainable living. However, the analysis of the two cases can provide a starting point to draft reflexive governance strategies to transform sanitation systems into a more sustainable way. Below I address the five process requirements for sustainable governance as outlined in the Introduction of this volume.

**Integrated Knowledge Production**

The solving of problems of sustainability around conventional sewage systems requires, in the first place, knowledge of technology and technological processes: microbiology of (an)aerobic waste water treatment and the technical layout of infrastructure and other hardware. This was clearly covered especially in the first case. But presenting such technical 'solutions' to a world that is (willingly or not) quite ignorant of the sustainability problems of current sewage systems is not enough. Knowledge of the socio-cultural aspects of sanitation, the institutional set-up of sanitation and waterworks in general, actor-networks around housing and building, and the local and national regulation (all of which are regime and landscape characteristics) should be produced as well. In the Wageningen case, this kind of knowledge production was totally absent in the project outline. The learning objects predominantly addressed the (combination of) technologies applied rather than the implementation of a socially and technically deviating sanitation practice within wide networks of providers and end consumers. In contrast, in the second case the application of sustainable technologies was just a means to meet the widely expressed goal of 'sustainable living' rather than a main objective. Knowledge about new technologies, building processes, all kinds of legislation around housing and building and urban water management or policies of utility companies has been generated from the start until today. However, such integrated knowledge production has mainly been done on an ad hoc basis, without systematic planning or pre-set learning goals. The case also showed the limitations to the kinds of knowledge the different actors can absorb. For instance: inhabitants did not care too much about the peculiarities of different treatment technologies for black water. Likewise, some of the experts invited to develop parts of the system were not too committed to the holistic goals of the initiators.

**Adaptivity of Strategies and Institutions**

Integrated knowledge production is only a first step. Implementing eco-sanitation also requires a renewal of institutions around sanitation, as the existing institutions (that is, all rules and regulations around waste water transport and treatment, and the responsibilities of different actors) are built around and specifically geared to large-scale sewage systems. New institutions should be developed, and they should be flexible enough to be applied in different social contexts and adaptive enough to cater for changing insights during the course of transition. For sure, this is easier said than done. In most cases of eco-sanitation, especially in developed countries, not only is a large sewage infrastructure very close by, but so are the institutions supporting it. The two cases discussed here showed that in the first place one should 'massage' existing institutions, rather than invent new ones. Only when traditional parties like water boards, municipalities and utilities are willing to cooperate, may one invent new forms of management that will fit the new socio-technical arrangements. An example of such new management might be the management of reed-bed filters by working groups of inhabitants.

The main cause of failure in the first case was that institutional changes seemed to be considered of minor importance compared to the technical installations and were to be dealt with only after the start of the whole project. The second case demonstrated new forms of management and collaboration (between municipality, future residents, architects, water boards and urban planners) that were conducive to the success of the technical implementation of eco-sanitation.

## Anticipating Long-term Effects of Measures

The Wageningen implementation project was scheduled until 2007. Within this period all technical assistance, transport of sludge and management was financially secured. It turned out to be a major impediment to the municipality that nothing was arranged for the period after 2007. Who will maintain the installations? Who is going to bear the costs of deconstruction of the installation if that turns out to be necessary? Who will be responsible for the transport and treatment of remaining sludge from the digestion tanks? These were still unanswered questions even after the project had officially started. Obviously, proper niche-management would include an anticipation of such longer term requirements. The cases showed that – ideally speaking – such anticipation should be done well in advance of a project rather than during the implementation phase. The scope of such anticipation should also be expanded to include institutional, social and ecological effects, rather than only technological and financial effects.

## Iterative Participatory Goal Formulation

The case of Culemborg showed that the project's aim was not just to experiment with new technologies, but also to reach sustainability in housing and living. The whole area was planned to fulfil the explicit overall vision of sustainable living as articulated in various workshops by the group of future residents, landscape architects, environmental engineers and sustainable housing experts. The vision embraced everything between the materials that were used in building and construction, to the communal garden growing organic vegetables and an education centre with a 'living machine' to visualise the treatment of waste water. The terms of reference for the whole urban design was based on the wishes of a group of interested future inhabitants who were assembled by the EVA foundation even before the location of Culemborg had come into sight. A series of three workshops was organised to inform the participants on the state of the art and especially to invite them to present their views on the project. A brochure was produced and offered to a project group of professionals who where commissioned to make a first urban plan. This was presented in 1997 during a so-called 'masterclass' but did not meet the high expectations. Inhabitants experienced a lack of understanding of the holistic vision and special character of the site. A new project team was formed to do the work all over again. This resulted in a year of delay, which among other things limited the number and scope of further participation meetings with future inhabitants (Kaptein, 1999).

Both positively and negatively, the two cases teach us that in the formulation of goals and means of a niche project, the character and phasing of involvement of – on the one hand – a wide network of providers (not only the technological experts responsible for the experiment, but also the water board, municipality, local technicians and plumbers, project developers, investors, toilet manufacturers and their representatives, and so on), and consumers on the other, are crucial for implementing new techniques of sanitation. The cases are recent, hence the iterative aspect of goal formulation and the ways of dealing with the moving target of sustainability could not be properly assessed during the course of these projects. There is no doubt, however, that the sustainability concept as envisaged in Culemborg will turn out to be specifically related to today's innovative sustainable building methods and technologies and today's concerns about housing and living. For this project is just like all other previously built sustainable housing projects that in hindsight appear to reflect the social and environmental considerations of the time era in which they were built.

## Interactive Strategy Development

Transformation in sanitation does change the social interactions between sanitation providers and consumers. As we have seen in other infrastructures in transformation (Van Vliet et al., 2005), consumers obtain new roles in the system of provision. Eco-sanitation may involve end users in the management and maintenance of waste treatment, as can be seen in

Culemborg and many other cases. The blurring boundaries between provision and consumption and the coming into place of new intermediaries (community associations for maintaining systems, caretakers, control systems) should go hand in hand with new, interactive strategy development of which the Culemborg case is an example. Top-down regulation and planning that is so characteristic of sewage systems should be replaced by a process of trial and error, citizen participation, discussions with experts, requests for subsidies, competition for eco-city awards and so forth. The case also showed that it is very difficult to develop niche projects like this systematically: the local geographical and institutional circumstances seem to require specific local approaches. However, there are still some general lessons to learn from the processes of both the Culemborg and Wageningen cases in terms of strategy development. These will be addressed in the following, concluding section.

## CONCLUSION

A sustainable transformation of sanitation has only recently gained attention, especially when compared to other urban infrastructures such as energy supply or waste systems. A transformation in sanitation requires considerable changes at the micro-level, regime-level and – not least – at the landscape level. Factors at the landscape level in sanitation are vested, cultural beliefs and routines that have been built up around the handling of human waste, the appealing flush-and-forget principle of conventional toilet systems and the enormous physical infrastructure of water works that have been put in place over the last century. The transition management approach seems to be appropriate here as it encompasses socio-technical niches to be developed at the micro level to change sanitation regimes and ultimately landscape factors.

Many of the innovations in sanitation technology that are now being experimented can be characterised as 'modernised mixtures', socio-technical constellations to be situated in the midst of the social-technical dichotomy between 'small-is-beautiful' and conventional large scale sewage systems. Technologies of a modernised mixture may be connected to larger grids and at the same time be small-scale, co-developed and co-managed by both users and providers.

The two case studies described the attempts to experiment with modernised mixtures of eco-sanitation rather than strategies of reflexive governance. But a further analysis of how these projects were governed clearly showed the need for reflexive governance when dealing with niche development in sanitation. A purely technology-driven approach (as in

Wageningen) appears to be a dead-end road. A more process-oriented approach (as in Culemborg), which includes only a guiding principle of sustainable living rather than aiming to put in place a pre-described technology, seems to lead to more promising results. Future experiments with respect to eco-sanitation by closing loops should therefore be set up in such a way that there is maximum room for learning processes as well as revisions of means (technologies, institutional arrangements) to meet the end goals of sustainability.

In particular, the case studies point us to the need to anticipate the future after experimentation and to involve an extended network of providers and (future) end users of the system before the start of experimentation. Interaction between providers and consumers and participatory goal formulation were indeed success factors. Reflexive governance is all the more needed to avoid unintended effects that affect the sustainability of innovations. The best one can say from the Wageningen case is that major actors (project developers and the municipality) were reflexive enough to recognise major problems in managing the system in the period beyond the time horizon of the project. Many relevant questions that relate to the sustainability of the systems were raised, but a solution was never suggested.

A reflexive strategy to govern sustainability in sanitation should therefore consist of at least the following building blocks:

- To identify and consult end users and the various providers at an early phase to build up mutual trust relations and to formulate the goals of a project jointly.
- To define goals in terms of social needs and sustainability requirements rather than defining the technical solutions to be put in place.
- Modernised mixtures call for modernised, flexible institutions. In some cases the 'old' institutions may be sufficient, but in most cases there is a need for new institutions and intermediaries. New institutions may involve more flexible legislation around water and waste recycling in urban neighbourhoods, legitimisation of the sharing of responsibility between consumers (associations), water professionals and municipalities. New intermediaries may be put in place in cases of community-on-site systems, which are too small for existing water boards and municipalities and too big for individual households to manage. Such intermediaries might be residents' associations, professional care-takers or service companies.
- 'Widening' of eco-sanitation (niche) experiments in social and institutional respects: technological experimenting should be coupled to deliberate and systematic experiments in different modes of management and use.

- 'Widening' of eco-sanitation experiments in terms of scope and time: although experiments mostly have pre-set time frames, projects should anticipate the transfer of niche experiments to the regime level. Before and during experimentation, there should be continuous feedback on the regime requirements the experiment would have if the 'protected' status of a niche should come to an end.

Closing loops take a long time, and eco-sanitation is still at a very early stage. Likewise, the suggested building blocks of an implementation strategy move a few first steps away from straightforward technological experimenting and towards more reflexive governance of a transformation to sustainable sanitation. Obviously, the proposed building blocks of a reflexive strategy require a lot more of stakeholders' time and effort than a straightforward technological approach. But if it makes the difference between eventual failure and success, it is worth the effort.

## NOTES

1. The project was funded by the Dutch Ministries of Economic Affairs and Environment and Spatial Planning and executed by a consortium of environmental engineers, municipalities, utilities and housing developers to develop, study and implement several techniques of on-site anaerobic waste water treatment in the built environment. The aim of the project is to enhance the diffusion of eco-sanitation within the Netherlands, by setting up niche projects in which researchers, municipalities, consumers and other actors can learn about the new technology.
2. Article 2, Algemene bouwvoorschriften voor zuiveringssystemen en infiltratievoorzieningen (General building regulation for treatment systems and filtration utilities), Chapter 2 of 'Uitvoeringsregeling Lozingenbesluit Bodembescherming' (Tweede Kamer der Staten Generaal, 18-12-1997, source: www.overheid.nl)
3. The Dutch abbreviation stands for 'Ecological Centre for Education, Extension and Advice'.

## REFERENCES

GTZ (2003), 'Ecosan – closing the loop', Proceedings of the 2nd international symposium on ecological sanitation, 7–11 April, Lübeck.

Kaptein, M. (1999), Eco Housing Project EVA Lanxmeer (Culemborg), 'Sustainability: a matter of people', presentation text, 26 October.

Kemp, R., J. Schot and R. Hoogma (1998), 'Regime shifts through processes of niche formation: the approach of strategic niche management', *Technology Analysis and Strategic Niche Management*, 7, 139–68.

Lens, P.N.L., G. Zeeman and G. Lettinga (2001), *Decentralised Sanitation and Reuse – Concepts, systems and implementation*, London: IWA Publishing (Integrated Environmental Technology Series).

Rotmans, J., R. Kemp and M. van Asselt (2001), 'More evolution than revolution: transition management in public', *Policy Foresight* **3** (1), 15–31.

Schumacher, E.F. (1975), *Small is Beautiful, a study of economics as if people mattered*, London: Blond Briggs.

Shove, E. (2003), *Comfort, Cleanliness and Convenience: The Social Organization of Normality*, Oxford: Berg Publishers.

Siemensma, M. (2000), 'De ontwikkeling van decentrale sanitatie en hergebruik in een woonwijk', [The development of decentralised sanitation and reuse in a residential area], MSc thesis, Wageningen: Wageningen University.

Southerton, D., H. Chappells and B. van Vliet (eds) (2004), *Sustainable Consumption: the Implications of Changing Infrastructures of Provision*, Cheltenham UK and Northampton, MA, USA: Edward Elgar.

Van Vliet, B. (2002), *Greening the Grid, The Ecological Modernisation of Network-bound Systems*, Wageningen: Wageningen University (PhD Thesis).

Van Vliet, B., H. Chappells and E. Shove (2005), *Infrastructures of Consumption. Environmental Innovation in the Utility Industries*, London: Earthscan.

Vewin (2004), Huishoudelijk waterverbruik www.vewin.nl.

Werner, C., P.A. Fall, J. Schlick and H.-P. Mang (2003), 'Reasons for and principles of ecological sanitation', paper presented at Ecosan– Closing the Loop, Proceedings of the 2nd International Symposium on Ecological Sanitation, 7–11 April, Lübeck, pp. 23–30.

Zeeman, G. and G. Lettinga (1999), 'The role of anaerobic digestion of domestic sewage in closing the water and nutrient cycle at community level', *Water, Science & Technology*, **39**, 187–94.

# 14. The transition towards sustainable production systems in Austria: a reflexive exercise?

## Philipp Späth, Harald Rohracher, K. Matthias Weber and Ines Oehme

## SUMMARY

In this chapter, we discuss the potential contribution of R&D policy to the establishment of sustainable production systems. More specifically, we look at a recent experiment in Austria with a new way of supporting socio-technical change and a related new approach to the design of public R&D policy. The innovation in question is the concept of biorefineries as a potentially important segment of a sustainable production system.

In the late 1990s, R&D actors in Austria became interested in the concept of biorefineries and made first assessments of the contribution that biorefineries could make to more sustainable production systems. Their quest for support of R&D towards an Austrian type of 'green biorefinery' using biomass from meadows fit within the framework and the goals of a new research funding programme called 'Factory of Tomorrow', which aims to support research towards sustainable production systems. Several projects within this programme explored the technical and economic potential of green biorefineries. In parallel, an accompanying strategic research project was conducted that aimed at adapting and applying the approach of transition management in support of the R&D programme 'Factory of Tomorrow'. This has been done as a pilot experiment in the research field of biorefineries.

We describe the challenges and outcomes of this accompanying project and discuss whether the intertwined process of policy and technology development with respect to biorefineries in Austria can be conceived of as a case of reflexive governance. Several elements of reflexive governance indeed were applied in the process of supporting and assessing biorefineries. For instance, a participatory methodology of scenario-building was developed and applied to anticipate long-term systemic effects. However, this

process so far has only been loosely tied to policy-making, thus predominantly staying at an experimental level and not signifying a general shift
of Austrian R&D policy towards reflexive governance. Although the
specific process described here has to be seen as a rather isolated experiment
within the Austrian context – happening in the shadow of the governmental R&D policy rather than driving it – some conclusions about the applicability and pitfalls of the concept of reflexive governance can yet be drawn.
We discuss prerequisites of a participative assessment of socio-technical
pathways especially with regard to political mandate and constraints for the
delegation of such socio-technological decision-making processes to non-
governmental actors.

## INTRODUCTION

Is Austrian Research and Development (R&D) policy an example of
reflexive governance? This is an interesting question insofar as Austria is
usually regarded as one of the more advanced countries in terms of implementing sustainability policy or introducing environmental technologies.
However, it is far from clear whether this success has been effectively
influenced by a specifically reflexive type of policy-making and what role
the respective governance settings have played.

In general, Austrian government supports objectives of sustainable
development as outlined in its sustainability strategy. These objectives
also hold for R&D policy where the 'double dividend' argument is often
applied, which says that R&D policy is supposed to contribute both to
enhancing the economic competitiveness of Austrian firms and to sustainable development (and sometimes further policy objectives). This kind of
approach is also favoured by the Austrian Council for Science and
Technology Development, an institution that has become a key actor for
determining priorities in research and technology policy since its inception
in the year 2000.

We analyse this question by looking at a specific area of R&D policy:
sustainable production–consumption systems. The interest in this area
stems first of all from the fact that it is a multi-faceted and heterogeneous
field with many technological, economic and social interdependencies.
Moreover, production–consumption systems are very complex results of
longstanding development processes, since they are embedded in and
closely interlinked with structures and processes in their societal and ecological environments, which range from the extraction of resources and
land-use practices, via long production chains right through to private consumption. They interfere with every single aspect of life. This high degree

of intertwinement implies that the area is difficult to influence in a targeted way and that only a long-term transition strategy might lead to a shift towards sustainability. As production–consumption systems depend on a wide range of actors within and outside the research community, a participatory approach to strategy development is needed to induce change.

Secondly, interest in this area is also due to the existence of a major and long-term research programme that explicitly pursues the objective of contributing to the establishment of sustainable production–consumption systems. However, the mere existence of such a programme, called Factory of Tomorrow, is not a guarantee for success. It provides a context in which the impact of policy and governance on longer-term transition processes can be studied.

With that purpose in mind, an accompanying strategic research project was set up within the programme 'Factory of Tomorrow' in order to establish a platform to reflect upon strategies to shape a transition towards sustainable production–consumption systems. The project puts particular emphasis on the contribution of R&D policy to such a transition process, but also takes into account the role of other policy areas.

In contrast to large-scale infrastructure systems like energy supply, transport or water management which until now have been the focus of attention for systemic transition processes, the field of 'production' is much more heterogeneous and more difficult to address by an overarching transition process for the production system as a whole. Therefore, the decision was made to focus on the more disaggregate level of 'transition fields', which represent clusters of closely related production technologies (Weber et al. 2003) and will be discussed in more detail later (see Voß et al. in Chapter 16 on 'finding the right place and space to tackle specific problems of sustainable development').

More specifically, the decision was made to study the case of biorefineries – plants which process biomass into several useful substances. This case is particularly interesting because right from the beginning, that is, in the early 1990s, the interest of some researchers in the subject met with the emerging agendas of sustainability-oriented R&D policy in Austria.[1]

From a technical point of view, biorefineries can be a source of chemical products, such as lactic acid, amino acids, furfural, ethanol and others – depending on the feedstock – some of which are conventionally synthesized from petroleum. In addition to its potential to substitute fossil resources, biorefineries[2] are supposed to be beneficial to rural development and the preservation of Austrian landscapes. However, it is still far from clear which broader scenarios would be compatible with and conducive for an uptake of biorefineries, what the specific conditions for a successful diffusion would be, and whether they would indeed contribute to the transformation of the production system towards sustainability. R&D policy is thus in a state of ambivalence and uncertainty with respect to the support of biorefineries, which would make a reflexive and adaptive design of the policy process advisable as well as an embedding of this issue within broader socio-technical contexts.

The question of whether biorefineries should be supported by Austrian R&D policy is thus predestined for a case study in the participatory building and assessment of socio-technical scenarios, which we consider an important step towards reflexive governance in the field of technology policy.

The key questions that this chapter sets out to address are:

- To what extent have key elements of reflexive governance been applied in Austria in the case of the research programme Factory of Tomorrow, specifically in the field of biorefineries?
- What elements of reflexive governance turned out to be effective? Why do they work in Austria (or why not)?

Hence the chapter is structured as follows. The following section elaborates on the relationship between R&D policy and sustainability policy in Austria, pointing in particular to the difficulties of integrating sustainability principles in other sectoral or thematic policies. Then, the process of the emergence of biorefineries in Austria will be briefly reconstructed. The next section will then address the core issues of this chapter by describing a reflexive exercise that was conducted in the context of the national R&D policy programme in support of sustainable production. The experiences gained in this experiment will be assessed in terms of the criteria of reflexive governance. The final section will draw some conclusions regarding the potential, the barriers and the limitations with which reflexive governance is confronted in Austria, drawing on both the experiences with the biorefinery case and the broader political settings.

## THE BACKGROUND: AUSTRIAN R&D POLICY AND SUSTAINABILITY

### R&D Policy in Austria: Context, Actors and Objectives

To gain a better understanding of the context of current R&D policies to support the transition towards sustainable production systems, we begin with some remarks on the general framework of R&D policy in Austria.

In the 1970s Austrian policy makers became aware of the deficits of a linear 'science and technology push' approach towards technology policy

(Meyer 2002). It was increasingly recognised that innovation is an interactive process of knowledge accumulation that interlinks the different phases of innovation and requires cooperation between different actors. As a consequence, new bridging institutions were established in the 1980s, for instance the so-called Christian-Doppler Research Association in 1989 and a first wave of technology transfer centres aiming to reinforce the diffusion of research results. At this time, first efforts were also made to develop targeted research programmes. In some cases, they focused on the functional characteristics of what will later be called the national innovation system (for example, science–industry relations) and in other cases had a thematic orientation (for example, programmes on transport technology).

Both lines of programmes continue to exist in Austria and have been further refined over the past years. However, all programmes tend to suffer from a major problem in the structure of the Austrian R&D policy landscape, namely the dispersion of responsibilities. In essence, four ministries are in charge of different segments of research, technology and innovation policy, three of which actively support sustainability objectives. In addition, regional policy initiatives continue to grow in importance. For instance, in some provinces very active initiatives have been implemented to foster the creation and expansion of industrial clusters. Until the end of the last century, efforts to improve coordination with sectoral ministries and among different political actors in charge of R&D policy agendas have remained patchy.[3]

In the last few years, however, the landscape has changed again. First of all, with the establishment of the Austrian Council for Science and Technology Development in the year 2000, a new actor has entered the scene whose main role is to improve coordination between different research and technology policy initiatives by formulating an overarching national research and innovation strategy (Rat für Forschung und Technologieentwicklung (RFT) 2002) as well as by formulating recommendations to the Ministry of Finance on research funding programmes that are suggested by the different ministries.

## Sustainability as an Issue of Austrian R&D Policy and the Factory of Tomorrow Programme

With the establishment of targeted research programmes, sustainability became one of several core topics of Austrian R&D. Under the heading Austrian Landscape Research, a first research programme has been established by the Ministry of Science. Thus more than 200 representatives from research and public administration have been involved in the development of the programme. The target of research projects, which have been funded by this programme since December 1995, has been to develop options for a sustainable development of Austrian landscapes and regions.

At about the same time, the National Environmental Plan (NUP) BMU: Bundesministerium für Umwelt (Detter 1995) was formulated, which obviously focused mainly on the environmental dimension of sustainability. It was followed by the Federal Sustainability Strategy in 2002, which was a reaction to changing requirements at the European and international levels.

In the late 1990s, a major research and technology initiative was started at the Federal Ministry for Transport, Innovation and Technology (BMVIT), which aimed at the development of technologies for sustainable development (*Nachhaltig Wirtschaften*). For the purpose of this chapter, one of its sub-programmes entitled 'Factory of Tomorrow'[4] is of major interest. This programme focuses on the advancement of research and technologies that are supposed to deliver a 'double dividend'; that is, they are supposed to enhance the competitiveness of Austrian industry while at the same time contribute to the establishment of a more sustainable production system.

In general, the lack of horizontal cooperation and the division of labour between ministries in matters of research, technology and innovation policy implies that major pre-conditions for reflexive governance could not be met. With BMVIT focusing on technologically-oriented R&D and technology policy initiatives, the changes to the broader policy framework and further preconditions for a structured transition towards sustainability (stakeholder inclusion, social and economic dimension of sustainability) can be achieved only with difficulty. Consequently, the programme *Nachhaltig Wirtschaften* mainly focuses on environmental technologies and demonstration projects that could serve as a visible orientation and model for adopters ('beacons' as they are called in the programme). There is not much connection to the general sustainability research of the Ministry of Science and Education (for example, focusing on ecosystems, sustainable lifestyles, transdisciplinary research or 'social dialogues' on sustainability), nor is the programme closely integrated in initiatives of the responsible departments for environment or energy.[5]

Leading industrial and academic researchers from different fields and institutions of science and engineering relevant to the scope of the programme were invited to contribute to the designing of the programme. As a consequence, the programme acquired a strong technological orientation, whereas wider contextual issues relevant to sustainable development were addressed in the aforementioned cultural landscape programme hosted by the Federal Ministry for Science, Education and Culture.

Nevertheless, the Factory of Tomorrow programme aims to support the structural shift towards eco-efficient management and a sustainable production system through research, technological development, demonstration and dissemination measures. Concepts and technologies are to be developed for the production and provision of goods and services in an economy geared towards sustainability. While not only technological but also economic, social and structural issues have been addressed in the calls, the thematic priorities mainly focus on three fields:

- sustainable technologies and innovations in production processes,
- use of renewable raw materials,
- sustainable products and services.

With respect to sustainable development, the programme is based on a number of 'guiding principles of sustainable technology design':

- orientation towards benefit and need,
- efficient use of resources,
- use of renewable resources,
- multiple use and recycling,
- flexibility and adaptability,
- fault tolerance and risk precaution,
- securing employment, income and quality of life.

The actual calls for project proposals, which identified specific problems to be solved,[6] put this rather broad framework into more concrete terms. With regards to any criteria for sustainability, the way is clear for applicants and the jury to operationalise 'sustainable production' and decide on what is promising in terms of sustainability. Furthermore the overall funding volume is comparatively small (about €10.54 million for the first three calls 2001–3).[7] Of this budget, 'production' represents a very broad research domain. As a result, the 88 projects that have been funded so far are rather diverse and only loosely integrated into joint research agendas.

These pitfalls are part of the reason why the programme funded an accompanying strategic research project, which tried to embed these technological projects in broader strategies of a transition towards sustainable development and to foster interaction and coherence. This accompanying project is seen as an experiment for further initiatives to integrate and implement research carried out in the programme. The establishment of a special advisory group, which includes representatives from different funding bodies, ministries and the Austrian Research Council, expresses the interest of these research funding organisations to find new ways to link research with implementation strategies and longer term planning. The strategic accompanying project set out to demonstrate the applicability of transition management approaches for R&D programmes by focusing on two exemplary fields of technology development: biorefineries and wood–plastic composites/biopolymers. In this chapter, we reflect on the results and experiences gained in the case study on biorefineries.

## BIOREFINERIES: WHAT THEY ARE AND HOW THEY BECAME AN ISSUE

Research issues in the area of 'green biorefineries' are addressed by several projects funded in the 'Factory of Tomorrow' programme. It is the hope of the advocates of the concept of biorefineries that these technologies and the production concepts brought together under this notion – once adopted by industry – would fundamentally transform the production process of many industrial goods. The mobilisation of scientists around the concept of biorefineries, the subsequent establishment and support of an R&D network, and the accompanying foresight exercises share some features with what is described as 'reflexive governance' in the Introduction of this book. We therefore briefly describe the concept of biorefineries and its role in Austria before we report on our experiences with sustainability assessment and scenario building.

### Expectations in the Concept of Biorefineries

Biorefineries are integrated systems that combine physical, chemical and/or biotechnological processes and plants in which biogenic raw material of different origins is processed into a whole range of industrial intermediates and/or final products.

In close analogy to other types of refineries such as fossil oil or sugar refineries, the concept of biorefineries aims to convert in integrated processes the complete biomass of whole plants into a whole portfolio of products or precursors for further product lines that are free of residues. Besides biobased materials, energy (via biogas generation) may be supplied by this technology. The concept thus puts broader and longstanding concepts such as bio-based production into concrete terms. Whole crop utilisation and sustainable land use serve as guiding principles (in the sense of Gleich et al. 2004) – and help to create a regional community of supporters of such an innovation.

With the concept of biorefineries, it seems possible to substitute an increasing share of fossil sources with material of biogenic (and potentially regional) origin and thus increase independency from scarce sources of raw material and volatile prices, and reduce $CO_2$ emissions and other negative effects on the environment. In Austria, decentralised and small-scale 'green biorefineries' especially are considered to be a promising and sustainable concept.[8]

However, despite these high hopes, it is still far from clear whether the concept is economically feasible (in which technical configuration and with which specific products and outputs of the plant), and how it will be integrated in the wider systemic contexts of energy generation, agriculture, landscape preservation and the production system. Consequently, there are still major uncertainties about the potential carrier of this development in industry and the agricultural system, and which framework conditions (regulations, subsidies and so on) would be necessary for successful implementation of this concept.

While some success in 'biorefinery systems research' was achieved in Europe as early as the 1980s (most notably in Germany and Denmark: see Kamm and Kamm 2004), it was years before the first government committed itself to concrete substitution goals. It was the US President and Congress who first declared in the year 2000 that by the year 2020 at least 25 per cent of organic industrial feedstock chemicals shall be provided on a renewable basis (US National Research Council 2003). Since then, big industrial plants have been built in the USA to produce in this way, for example, lactic acid from maize.

At the EU level, crop-derived raw materials have also entered the political agenda relatively recently, in 2000, with the establishment of a working group Renewable Raw Materials (RRM) within the European Climate Change Programme. This working group states in its report on the Current Situation and Future Prospects of EU Industry using renewable raw materials that 'EU policies and measures would be required to establish a more supportive political framework for this industry sector to prosper in the future' and respective suggestions have been made. The report (Working Group 'Renewable Raw Materials' 2002) identifies the potential for bio-based products especially in the case of surfactants, polymers, solvents and lubricants.

However, biorefineries are not seen as only instrumental for substitution strategies away from increasingly rare and expensive petrol.[9] Some scholars argue that beyond their energy and resource efficiency (due to the synergetic production and use of by-products), biorefineries will gain importance because they will provide opportunities to produce completely new products with qualities – even beyond the important quality of biodegradability – that cannot be produced on the basis of petrol. Of course, to achieve these goals specific processes and organisational structures need to be in place that comply with the characteristics of biogenic raw materials (Wimmer et al. 2003, Katter et al. 1999, Kromus 1999).

Advocates of biorefineries expect them to be beneficial especially for industries and agriculture (Danner et al. 1999, Industriewissenschaftliches

Institut 2001). Since the integrated processes involve demanding chemical and biotechnical engineering processes, it is expected that biorefinery technology will be developed first in technologically advanced regions. Therefore, establishment of biorefineries is seen as one factor that possibly countervails the shift of industrial production to countries with cheap labour.

### Biorefineries in Austria

While some research efforts were made in the late 1980s with regard to the use of green biomass for ethanol production and use of grass fibres for paper production, research with respect to the concept of green biorefinery was only intensified in the late 1990s (Narodoslawsky 1999).

Biorefineries were promoted in Austria to begin with because of their assumed positive impact on regional development by (1) stabilising the current use of green land, thus 'keeping the landscapes open and attractive' and (2) 'direct impact on the economic structure of rural regions'. Kromus et al. (2004) go on:

> The decentralized nature of the raw material generation for the Green Biorefinery calls for decentralising . . . This will generate jobs in rural areas thus considerably reinforcing the economic structure of these regions as well as raising the skills of the workforce in these regions as operating this technology needs up-to-date technical knowledge especially in the field of chemical engineering.[10]

Biorefineries are predominantly seen as a mode of income generation in rural areas:

> The exploitation of grassland might have intriguing side effects like the conservation of cultural landscapes and the improvement of the 'stay option' of farmers. Therefore interest is focused on the type of green biorefineries, using grass from meadows as feedstock . . . In contrast to the centralized Biorefinery concepts in Europe, the Austrian Green Biorefinery focuses on a decentralized system based on grass-silage . . . with lactic acid and amino acids (proteins) as key products from silage. (Kromus et al. 2004)

With their requirements for fundamental changes in production systems (complex logistics, due to seasonal and distributed harvesting, respective requirements for infrastructure, integrated production, completely new and regionally varying product portfolios), the innovation of biorefineries requires a systemic multi-dimensional approach. As we will see in the next section, the complexity of the issue indeed undermines any 'modernist problem-solving approach' (as contrasted with reflexive governance in the Introduction to this volume).

Recent years have indeed seen extensive research activities and attempts to set up pilot studies, which demonstrate the potential of green biorefineries in the region of southern Styria. Before now, industry has not been intensively involved in the funding of these research activities, though. Research has thus been limited to a number of projects within the Factory of Tomorrow programme, complemented with equity-funded activities by several research institutions. Yet a national network of researchers and institutions interested in biorefinery-related R&D has been set up and coordinates research on an informal level.

The aforementioned hopes in biorefineries, which were presented mainly by a small group of researchers, are to a large extent based on assumptions which have not yet been clarified. With respect to R&D policies the government agencies find themselves in a (common) state of ambiguity. The technologies and concepts of biorefineries might yield a high potential to solve several problems in one go (sustainable production, income generation, landscape preservation). At the same time, it has not been assessed at this early stage of technology development how the innovation would impact on the broader socio-technical context, and under which conditions this impact would be positive. So how can policy deal with promising technologies and concepts like these in an adaptive and reflexive manner and take into account the broader systemic requirements of transition processes towards sustainable socio-technical systems?

## REFLEXIVE POLICY SUPPORT FOR A TRANSITION TOWARDS BIOREFINERIES

Austrian R&D efforts to develop green biorefineries have therefore been accompanied by a strategic project, which attempts to introduce a new level of reflection (for example, on long-term systemic effects) to policy making. However, as we will see, the 'delegation' of reflexivity to accompanying research projects is not without problems and does not necessarily result in a practice of reflexive governance. In the following section we first discuss requirements for effective measures to support technological developments such as biorefineries and subsequently focus on a case study of managing the transition to biorefineries by an accompanying 'transition management' project.

### The Quest for a Multi-level, Multi-actor Learning Process

Since biorefineries are supposed to contribute positively to a change towards more sustainable production systems, and since they seem to foster regional development in Austria, there are a number of arguments why governmental actors could be interested in stimulating this technological development, both by extensively funding R&D and by initiatives in other policy areas. However, recent developments in innovation research and the analysis of technology policy have emphasised that such measures fail more often than they succeed. The reason is grounded in the fact that they underestimate the complex nature of technological innovations and resulting changes at a systemic level. The success of such change processes is highly dependent on the capacity and appropriate strategies to manage the co-evolution of technological change along with new use practices, the reconfiguration of actor networks, and institutional changes. Changes towards more sustainable production technologies, such as 'green biorefineries', can therefore be best understood as gradual transformations of socio-technical systems.

In this context, special purpose applications and niche markets often play a very important role at an early stage and later gain more and more importance on broader segments of an economy. Such processes can lead to the stabilisation of new technological 'paradigms' or 'regimes' when developments in different realms of society like institutional settings, markets, technologies, cultures, behavioural patterns and policy-making and policy mutually reinforce each other. Such 'socio-cultural transitions' are often defined as long-term processes that can span over several decades and finally result in changes in the socio-technical landscape in the wider sense.[11]

From a policy perspective, the understanding of transitions raises two questions, namely, (1) to what extent can comprehensive and goal-oriented transformation processes be influenced and guided in a desirable direction at all (that is, in the direction of sustainable development)?, and (2) what role can and should government actually play in this process?

As the case of biorefineries illustrates, uncertainty, ambiguity and complexity of future developments prevent any attempt to plan the future in a linear fashion. Consequently, policy cannot aim at central planning and realisation of future development paths. However, policy may focus on the conscious implementation of structures and on the facilitation of collective processes for the support of long-term transitions. Such policy strategies need to be adaptive and reflexive, to absorb frequent readjustments according to newly emerging knowledge and changing requirements. In order to integrate the distributed intelligence[12] required for the development of biorefineries (in research, industry, agriculture and so on), a multilevel and multi-actor learning process needs to be initiated in society. The involvement of a broad range of actors helps to improve the coordination and coherence of their behaviour. In particular, experimentation and bottom-up learning processes are required to maintain the adaptive capacity of the innovation system. An adequate approach to policy and any methodology for such processes should therefore provide for the development of shared problem perceptions, common guiding visions and overarching strategies. These elements should increase the possibilities of convergence in the decisions and actions of the different actors and thus of a successful 'transition' in terms of certain policy goals such as the development of sustainable production systems.

All these notions and prerequisites are condensed in a policy approach called 'transition management' (TM) (see Kemp and Loorbach, Chapter 5 in this volume and Rotmans et al. 2001). On the basis of this approach, a methodology has been developed, mainly in the Netherlands, which aims to provide the necessary framework conditions for such collective learning and co-ordination exercise and to stimulate processes of anticipating and formulating long-term perspectives that can serve as an orientation and focusing device for the range of actors involved (Elzen et al. 2002). Both the policy approach and the derived methodology have served as conceptual starting points and inspirations of the accompanying project on R&D policy for biorefineries described in the following section.

### Anticipating System Change: A Participative and Reflexive Foresight Exercise

To gain more direction on how to manage such transition processes and improve the strategic orientation of the Factory of Tomorrow programme, a 'strategic accompanying project' has been set up. This project, entitled 'Transition towards Sustainable Production Systems', uses scenario methodologies as a tool for supporting technological change towards sustainable production systems.

The joint development of scenarios by a multitude of actors in the form of visions and the development of transition paths aims to create a common orientation for the participants and thus to increase the coherence of the R&D efforts within and beyond the Factory of Tomorrow programme. The scenarios shall furthermore support the development of concrete policy options both for technology policy and other policy areas.

In terms of methodology, the objectives of the accompanying research project have been defined as follows:

- to experiment with new methodology of scenario-based R&D strategy development that are adequate with regard to the notion of socio-technical transitions, and
- to assess the potential of these methods to improve steering capacities of R&D policy and sustainability governance in general.

In terms of policy support, central tasks were:

- to support strategy development regarding R&D policy and its coordination with other relevant policy areas, and
- to encourage network/community building.

Such accompanying and applied research inevitably has a very hybrid character: the borderlines between scientific research, research strategy development, innovation support/capacity building and policy development are certainly blurred.[13] In other words, they tend to be transdisciplinary in nature.

It is even more important to note that the project is perceived as an experiment by the Federal Ministry for Transport, Innovation and Technology (BMVIT). Though the project formally has the same status as other research projects of the programme, the following aspects signal the high attention that the ministry pays to the project. As mentioned earlier, a board of advisers has been installed to supervise and support the advancement of the project. This board is staffed by the ministry, members of the (outsourced) programme management, members of the Austrian Research Council and an external expert who serves as an advisor to the programme and as the head of the project selection committee.

The results of the project are expected primarily to provide a methodological orientation and – by focusing on case studies such as biorefineries – explore transition paths for selected thematic fields that are potentially relevant for the future development of R&D policy in relation to sustainable production.

### The Scenario Methodology

One of the main aims of the accompanying project is to develop a level of reflection beyond the individual projects within the programme by involving programme participants (programme managers and project partners) and other stakeholders (firms and interest groups) in a scenario-building exercise. The intention is to create a context for relevant actors to develop a better understanding of the system and its interdependencies and to reflect on their role within the systemic context in a joint effort. By anticipating systemic effects of individual strategies, the process thus shall lead to increased coherence of individual actions and lay the ground for cooperative strategies and policy support.

In principle, the transition management perspective lends itself to a normative approach to scenario-building, where a single desirable scenario or vision of the future is developed (hence normative scenario). Subsequently,

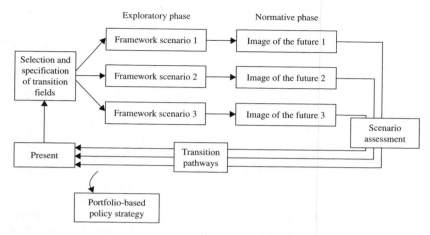

*Figure 14.1    Overview of the methodology developed for the project*

a backcasting methodology is applied to identify a promising future pathway at the levels of needs areas, transition fields and technologies. Such an approach may be useful to help clarify goal orientations and desirable future states. However, it does not sufficiently take into account the fact that the future is inherently open. The realisation of any future development path, even the most desirable one, is contingent on many other factors that are outside the influence of, for instance, a small country like Austria.

The alternative approach – constructing an exploratory scenario which takes into account various possible conditions and frameworks for future developments – would not be appropriate, either, because it does not sufficiently provide orientation with respect to sustainability objectives. These considerations show that a simple and straightforward application of a normative or an exploratory scenario-building methodology would not be appropriate to the given objectives. Instead, what is needed is a combined approach, which takes into account bottom-up exploratory elements (for instance new technology options, external driving forces) with top-down normative features implied by the sustainability-orientation of future images. Such a combination of exploratory and normative elements has been applied in the project.

In practice, the methodology can be described by the following five steps. It was implemented in the course of a series of three workshops.

1.   Definition, specification and selection of transition fields: the initial phase served to identify two transition fields to be subject to the

scenario development process (see above). The status quo and current developments within these fields have then been explored by literature and Internet research and 15–20 in-depth interviews per transition field. It is essential to have a clear understanding of the transition fields and how they can be systematically represented in terms of the three levels of analysis: (1) broad normative goal or need area, (2) transition field, and (3) individual technological experiment.

2.  Scenario development: the following scenario development process aimed to develop first a set of different possible scenarios – basically in an explorative way by asking what is likely to happen in the future rather than what actors want to happen. On a practical level, the participants of a first workshop collected important factors of impact on the future of, for example, biorefineries. These impact factors were then combined in plausible impact constellations and effects called 'storylines'. One such storyline for example read: 'The industrialisation of milk production in Austria is likely to further reduce the use of green land for grazing, resulting in the succession of woodlands'. Another read: 'High political support for biogas production and respective financial incentives are likely to narrow the biomass feedstock left for biorefineries'. These storylines were then clustered in consistent families, thus building the foundation of three different scenarios. This methodology could be called 'inductive' or 'bottom-up' scenario development as opposed to the top-down deduction of scenarios from a variation of two or three main factors. The latter approach was used to develop the well-known Shell scenarios on the future of energy consumption and others (Van der Heijden 1996). The three scenarios of two to three pages each were further elaborated and completed by the project team after the first workshop.[14] It was important to ensure that each of the scenarios could not be simply classified as 'desirable' or 'not desirable'; rather each of them should demonstrate its positive and negative aspects in order to provide a multi-faceted, plausible and at the same time challenging image of the future. The results were sent to the participants, who discussed and further specified them at the beginning of the second workshop.

3.  Sustainability assessment of scenarios: the scenarios differed of course in terms of their overall sustainability orientation. This was intended and is useful with regard to the deduction of policy perspectives, because it promotes further discussion on how to move towards sustainability even under detrimental conditions. The following 'normative phase'[15] started with the selection of the most important criteria for an assessment of the sustainability potentials of the scenarios.[16] These criteria were negotiated among the participants[17] on the basis of a

pre-selection provided by the 'technology assessment study on green biorefineries' (Schidler 2003), which itself related to the categorisation of sustainability principles suggested by the Helmholtz Society (Coenen 2002, Grunwald Armin et al. 2001). Six criteria were prioritised: (1) economic feasibility, (2) creation of value within regions, (3) intensification/extensification of agriculture, (4) overall energy consumption, (5) preservation of landscape and (6) participation of the rural population. On this basis, participants compared the three scenarios and identified positive or problematic aspects with regard to sustainability.

4. Identification of critical developments and actions: also within each of the scenarios, key terms and conditions could be identified which are critical for the future sustainability of the production system. In addition to these key issues, further needs for actions have been pointed out which seem decisive for the realisation of the scenarios and for sustainability potentials. A special focus has been put on a research agenda and adequate support and network structures.

5. Policy analysis draws on these considerations in order to identify potential intervention points with respect to which policy initiatives promise to be effective for shaping the scenario in a more sustainable direction. In addition to policy conclusions that refer to individual scenarios, it is also important to perform a cross-scenario analysis in order to identify portfolios of policy options that are both robust and adaptive, that is, they deal with different possible futures reasonably well. Robust policy options are those that would have a beneficial impact in all or most of the scenarios. On the other hand, adaptive policy options are an important element of a precautionary strategy that aims to prepare for unexpected negative impacts of single scenarios and to exploit opportunities opening up at certain development stages flexibly.

On average, between 50 and 60 people from relevant research institutions (most of which are involved in projects of 'Factory of the Future'), industry and other stakeholders such as relevant financial institutions and government bodies have been invited to the workshops. In the case of biorefineries, only 8–15 people participated, which was an initial indication of the lack of dedication of both research and industry to this issue. The group was dominated by researchers who represent the core community on biorefineries in Austria, thus reflecting that the technology is still in a comparatively early stage of development. Consequently, a major interest of the participants was the linking up with representatives of complementary fields, especially policy making and financing. The workshops, however, could fulfil the function of bridge-building between different communities only to a limited extent. However, indications suggest that the scenario process could have served much more as a catalyst if the mandate and the project budget had been larger.[18]

## Outcomes of the Scenario Process

There are three levels of outcome that we can discern:

1. the concrete scenarios as the main product,
2. effects of the scenario process on the interaction of stakeholders involved,
3. policy recommendations that were derived from the scenarios and the process.

### The main product: three scenarios

As a product of this process, images of possible future scenarios regarding biorefineries and crucial bifurcation points in such developments especially with regard to sustainability have been described and may be useful to several actors in the future.

The first scenario called 'Made in Styria' features conditions for the close cooperation of regional actors (local industry, farmers and so on) who realise a decentralised form of biorefinery adapted to regional conditions, strongly supported by active and integrated policies in favour of sustainable agriculture and substitution of fossil resources.

The second scenario named 'Big players push for biorefineries' suggests that trans-national companies could adopt the concept at a large scale: they could invest in their own R&D efforts, realise big-scale centralised plants and would probably buy standardised biomass at low prices from agriculture in the wider region as well as from the international market.

In the third scenario, 'following the rise of bioenergy', the production concept of biorefineries is realised as a consequence of developments in the energy system. Due to the widespread operation of bioenergy plants (biogas and biomass combustion) and respective infrastructures, the separation of specific biomass fractions to be processed in biorefineries for use as chemical feedstock and use of the remaining biomaterial for energy generation could be achieved at very low additional costs.

Although uncertainty about future developments remains very high, the scenarios at least document possible starting points for harnessing the sustainability potentials identified by the actors. In the future, they may serve as a joint reference system for the diverse actors involved in this issue. Furthermore, such scenarios might provide a background for research strategies towards sustainability, ranging from a broad range of exploratory and more ground-laying research projects to applied research pilot actions.

Finally, the scenarios will help the programme management of Factory of Tomorrow and the project selection jury to prioritise research fields and activities by building a conceptual bridge between highly general guiding visions and very concrete projects within the research programme. Furthermore, these scenarios will provide a background of plausible developments and crucial bifurcation points, which have been jointly identified by a range of actors.

### Effects of the Interactive Scenario Process

The actors involved in the scenario workshops modified their views on the subject during the exercise, for example, with regard to the probabilities of certain framework conditions, research priorities and strategies for the promotion of biorefineries. The scenario process stimulated new debates about long-term perspectives for the transition field of biorefineries. By giving the participants an opportunity to reflect upon the contribution and conditions required for success of their projects, the process facilitated second-order learning effects. A growing awareness for critical framework conditions and necessities for a successful development of biorefineries in Austria could be observed. The participants stated that it was the first opportunity for them to develop such detailed images of the future and assess strategic action with regard to these scenarios. Although it was a rather homogenous group of people, the scenario process was a novel opportunity to exchange views that had not been exchanged before.

As discussed above, the scenario-building process was only partly successful in enabling interaction between researchers and other actors outside the R&D programme, as only few corporate actors and actors from other policy fields participated in the workshops.

### Derived Policy Recommendations

Working out policy recommendations on the basis of the scenario process has not been completed yet. Furthermore, one has to keep in mind that the responsible ministry (BMVIT) funded the scenario development process as an experiment to assess the usefulness of such exercises for a better priority setting in R&D programmes. It still remains to be seen whether outcomes of the scenarios will actually be taken up by the research administration.

However, one can already notice that the broader picture provided by the transition scenarios has opened up new perspectives for the further development and research priorities of the Factory of Tomorrow programme, which aimed to initiate transition processes towards sustainable development from its beginning.

Many participants, however, strongly suggested that 'Factory of the Future' was perceived as too broad and unfocused for its limited size (the budget of the years 2001 to 2004 was 11 Million euros). Indeed, the perspective of transition management particularly raises the question of a minimum size and duration of R&D funding measures in order to induce a technological impulse effectively. The analysis of 'transition fields' such as the concept of biorefineries might become a useful framework for designing R&D policy strategies in the future.

What also became very obvious in the scenario process is the fact that the establishment of networks of heterogeneous actors for mutual learning exercises can be very time consuming. In order to get all crucial actors involved, such processes need to be designed in a mid to long-term perspective and require sufficiently stable framework conditions for at least five to ten years.

During the scenario development process, actors realised some interdependencies that sound banal but were not obvious before. The innovation of biorefineries and any local and national strategies aiming at their support rely heavily on (1) adequate EU policies in the fields of agriculture and the use of resources (which currently are both under fundamental revision), and (2) a supportive framework in several fields of national and international economic policy (namely policies on industrial, structural and regional development). The transition management approach provided means to define overarching transition strategies for the field of biorefineries, for example by identifying complementary policy measures needed to enable and strengthen R&D strategies to support biorefineries.

The scenarios thus made clear once again how important it is to anticipate policy developments and research activities on the EU level when designing Austrian policy and research agendas. They also showed how contingent any local development may be due to these manifold interdependencies.

Moreover, these results strongly support current attempts to reintegrate the rather fragmented Austrian science and R&D policy, which accept that research for sustainable development is a cross-cutting issue that needs to be addressed in inter-institutional cooperation (Paula et al. 2004).

## AN ASSESSMENT OF INNOVATIVE GOVERNANCE MODES FOR R&D IN AUSTRIA

We can now come back to the two guiding questions of this chapter:

● To what extent have key elements of reflexive governance been applied in Austria in the case of the research programme Factory of Tomorrow and more specifically with respect to the case of biorefineries?

- What elements of reflexive governance turned out to be effective? Why do they work in Austria (or why not)?

As the accompanying project goes beyond the established practices, approaches and institutions in Austrian technology and innovation policy, we will also look at the specific barriers that confronted these experiments in the governance context in which 'Factory of the Future' was designed and implemented.

Finally, we will reflect on possible impulses that could be derived from this application with regard to the concept of reflexive governance itself.

**Elements of Reflexive Governance in Factory of Tomorrow**

Although the design and implementation process of the Factory of Tomorrow programme certainly does not correspond to a full-fledged model of reflexive governance (as described in the Introduction to this volume), some first steps in this direction have been taken with some elements of reflexive governance. This is especially the case in the experimental project accompanying the research on biorefineries as described in this chapter. The following paragraphs will therefore be organised along the main dimensions of reflexive governance in order to assess both the programme and the project.

**a) Was integrated and trans-disciplinary knowledge production used?**
Most of the funded research projects within the Factory of Tomorrow programme do not specifically support integrated knowledge production. They tend to be very specific and of a predominantly technical, problem-solving nature. However, a strong emphasis has been put in the programme design on the cooperation of research institutions with commercial partners. Furthermore, with the call for accompanying projects, an explicit attempt has been made to add a more process-oriented meta level of reflection to the programme and to draw on insights from the social sciences. A further important step on this road would be to make a broader strategic perspective and higher standards of inter-disciplinary and trans-disciplinary cooperation a precondition for the funding of projects. In this way, R&D actors would be encouraged to integrate important stakeholders in their R&D activities more than they currently are.

The accompanying project itself went a long way to achieve trans-disciplinarity in the process of knowledge production. The scenario exercise was intended to integrate the views of all relevant actors along the product chain of bio-based production and the expectations of members of government with influence on support schemes and framework conditions by constructing a shared image of the system, its elements and interdependencies.

As previously discussed, the participation in the process was limited for several reasons. The lack of commitment on the part of government has been identified as a crucial stumbling block in this regard. However, this is also due to the set-up of the project, which – as a research project – has not been jointly developed or agreed upon by different government departments and has not been adopted (or even been recognised) at a sufficiently high policy level. The possibilities of departments or individuals within government to get involved actively in trans-disciplinary knowledge production are limited and have to be seen in the broader context of the concepts of governance, which are hegemonial within a certain government, department or political party.

However, the described scenario process had an important function as an experiment with integrated knowledge production. If the results (despite the limited participation) were meaningful to members of government, the latter could use them as a case of reference for internal lobbying in favour of more such exercises with increased government support.

### b) Was there room for experimentation and were strategies and institutions adaptive?

As mentioned before, the scenario process has been experimental with regard to new modes of governance. Also methodologically, it has explored new terrain and in a way carried on the attempt of an earlier technology assessment on the concept of biorefineries (Schidler 2003), by trying to supplement it and to overcome its limitations.

The three different scenarios have been developed to explore different variants of biorefineries and to learn about different socio-technical pathways and strategies for their diffusion. By combining exploratory and normative elements, the scenarios are predestined to underpin the formulation of robust and adaptive policy strategies, that is, of strategies that are geared towards the objective of sustainable development, but at the same time allow one to prepare for different uncertain future scenarios.

However, the project, with its integrative approach, has not been initiated by those responsible for the programme. Instead, it was initiated from outside by interested research institutes. It thus emerged behind the backs of governmental actors rather than being initiated or driven by them.

The programme as a whole supports the experimental search for sustainability potential in the form of research projects. The expectation that such experiments would build on one another, which would allow for a successive development of pilot implementations within the five-year duration of the programme (the beacon principle), was only fulfilled partially. For example, several projects handed in as follow-up activities to previous projects on biorefineries have not been approved by the jury. From the perspective of many affected parties, this calls into question the beacon principle. Supposedly, shifts of priorities existed even within the short time span of five years, which in any case might be too short for carrying out decent experiments and definitely for building up extensive networks for driving socio-technical change. In general, sustainability-oriented innovation policy is caught in a field of tension or trade-off between adaptivity and an experimental status of research priorities on the one hand and the requirements for long-term experiments and the creation of stable networks and niches on the other hand. The appropriate time frame for experiments and the optimal frequency of revision has not been codified yet. However, Factory of Tomorrow is on the shorter side of the time spectrum. Readers of the concluding chapter of this volume might recognise here a specific form of the efficacy paradox.

### c) What attention was paid to the anticipation of long-term systemic effects of measures?

The Factory of Tomorrow programme calls for proof of the long-term sustainability effects of new technologies, products and processes. The programme itself, however, has been designed for a period of just five years and even within this time span, its budget is negotiated on a yearly basis and thus is not entirely predictable for longer than one year.[19] Reflections on the long-term effects of the programme have so far been limited in scope.[20]

The accompanying project paid a lot of attention to the anticipation of long-term effects of biorefineries. The technology assessment conducted earlier by the Austrian Institute for Technology Assessment (Schidler 2003) explored the earliest point in time that an assessment of socio-economic and environmental impacts can be pursued by following a 'modelling approach' and by carrying out a hypothetical life-cycle analysis.

The scenario process, which follows a 'transition approach', made further progress towards the comparison of different scenarios, which in the form of visions and transition paths created a common orientation for the participants. This will hopefully not only increase the coherence of the R&D efforts within and beyond the Factory of the Future programme, but will furthermore inform the development of concrete policy options both for technology policy and other policy areas. Ideally, the scenarios could serve as a touchstone of policies with regard to their long-term effects on the implementation of biorefineries and sustainability goals. The developed method thus aims to provide instruments for the anticipation of path dependencies and avoidable lock-in situations, but at the same time acknowledges that the effects of all measures are highly contingent due to the complexity and intertwinement of the issues.

**d) Was goal formulation an iterative and participatory process?**
The Factory of Tomorrow programme incorporates several elements of a bottom-up approach: the guidelines that accompanied the calls for proposals have been rather open, for example with regard to the meaning of the term 'sustainable production'. Such an approach certainly helps to make use of the heterogeneous research capacities in Austria. The programme thus allows for an organic, iterative and shifting process of agenda setting and for the emergence and evolution of a heterogeneous understanding of sustainability. On the other hand, the great diversity of resulting initiatives limits the possible impulse of the dispersed capacities to act (which are limited after all) with regard to their influence on ongoing transitions. Top-down elements or mutual exercises in goal formulation, possibly resulting in greater cohesion among the R&D initiatives, might be necessary to create critical masses, especially in relatively small national innovation systems.

The applied scenario process itself met the challenge of contested concepts of sustainability by asking the participants of the scenario process to develop their own specific definition of sustainability in the form of criteria that they considered most crucial with regard to the development of biorefineries.

Participatory exercises attempting to assess scenarios with regard to sustainability goals have to find pragmatic compromises between two extremes. It might be impossible to define and select specific criteria of sustainability in a really participative, profound and innovative way, owing to limitations of resources such as time and the patience of participants. On the other hand, avoiding the invention of the wheel all over again by using any common set of sustainability criteria is of course also methodologically problematic.

**e) Was a broad range of contributors involved in strategy development?**
Factory of Tomorrow strongly promotes the cooperation of research institutions with commercial partners based on the expectation that they will jointly develop marketable 'sustainability solutions'. These two realms, however, are not sufficient from the perspective of socio-technical transitions, which also involve end users and policy makers, to name just two. The scenario-building process actually revealed two things at the same time. First, it clearly demonstrated how widely distributed the capacities are that are needed to realise concepts like biorefineries. Second, it became

clear how difficult it is to mobilise these actors towards the joint efforts of strategy development and implementation (that is, how demanding it is in terms of time, money and legitimacy). The experiences lead us to conclude that R&D policy can only exert a major impact on long-term socio-technical transitions towards sustainable production if it is implemented in the context of a broad participatory process. Compared to these requirements, the resources for the experimental project on biorefineries definitely were not sufficient to trigger anything like a transition process. Further and more substantive steps would be needed to initiate joint and coherent efforts of the different parties involved.

## CONCLUSIONS

Although the described experiment that included elements of reflexive governance was conducted in a challenging context with regard to participation and reflexivity, it has shown promising results and perspectives for further refinement of the Factory of Tomorrow programme. After all, the notions of 'socio-technical transitions' and 'transition management' have proven to be very productive for creating greater coherence among the actors representing singular research projects, industrial investment and public policy, especially in the process of participatory scenario development. It would thus be advantageous for the continuation of the Factory of Tomorrow programme if the results of the example scenario development process were convincing enough to trigger similar processes in other fields.

Furthermore, we believe that the participative development and assessment of socio-technical scenarios on such promising and yet ambiguous issues such as biorefineries could help overcome an overly technical orientation in many other research programmes which also aim at sustainable development. In general, the consideration of integrated transition strategies seems to be a very promising element of R&D programmes enabling them to create closer links between technical developments, social and organisational changes, and policy-making for sustainability.

## ACKNOWLEDGEMENT

The described accompanying project is supported by the Austrian research programme Factory of Tomorrow (an initiative of the Austrian Federal Ministry of Transport, Innovation and Technology, BMVIT), which is gratefully acknowledged.

## NOTES

1. The development of biorefineries is furthermore predestined for exemplary accompanying research (with regard to Austrian R&D policy) because of its following features: (1) a high potential for fundamental, systemic change in wide segments of the production system, (2) a relatively young phase of transition (still experimental, with potential for early pilot implementations), (3) high economic relevance (for Austria), (4) sufficient linking up of actors, (5) relevant research capacities (in Austria), (6) actors with sufficient contact with partners around Europe, (7) the existence of potential lead actors.

2. Especially green biorefineries, which use green biomass such as grass, clover and so on, as feedstock.

3. See for instance Whitelegg 2004 where the difficulties of policy coordination between transport, transport technology and innovation policy are analysed.

4. For more details see www.nachhaltigwirtschaften.at and www.fabrikderzukunft.at.

5. There is one exception, see the last footnote to the chapter and www.forne.at.

6. Again, these specifications framed the problems in a rather techno-centric way and thus encouraged the often narrowly defined and specialised character of the projects funded within the programme.

7. Further €17.2 million will be provided for four planned calls in 2004–7.

8. 'Green biorefineries' are one of three main types of biorefineries, the other ones being Lignocellulose feedstock biorefineries (using, for example, wood) and crop/wheat refineries (using e.g. maize and wheat), the latter of which is closest to economic viability.

9. Biorefineries in this sense are expected to benefit from advancements in biotechnological production, which becomes economically competitive in more and more production processes.

10. See also Soyez and Pfeffer (1999).

11. See for further details Rip and Kemp (1998) and for an extensive case study Geels (2002).

12. See Kuhlmann (2001) for an introduction to the concept of distributed intelligence.

13. However, it has to be said that such heterogenous objectives on a multitude of levels hold the danger of conflicting role models for those carrying out such projects, having to be researchers and facilitators and somehow evaluators and policy advisors at the same time.

14. All three scenarios shared the same structure in nine chapters headed as follows: (1) abstract, (2) nucleus of network development, (3) land use and resources, (4) political context and support, (5) R&D strategy and policy, (6) role of industry, (7) products and qualities, (8) technological features and scale, and (9) external factors.

15. Naturally, the explorative and normative elements of these phases cannot be completely separated, for example, *some* normative bias cannot completely be ruled out during the 'explorative phase'.

16. This was necessary, because the programme does not provide an operational definition of what is 'sustainable production' that could be applied on the scenarios (see Section 3.2 on the programme).

17. Some participants had difficulties accepting this distinctive normative approach of the project and argued from a fundamental position in favour of 'hard forms of sustainability' (will something allow mankind to survive or not?) instead of comparing scenarios against relative sustainability criteria. This might have been eased by clarification beforehand. However, the difficulties of such participatory exercises relating to the term 'sustainability' should not be underestimated.

18. Anonymously filling out a questionnaire after the third workshop, seven participants stated uniformly that they considered the format, methodology and organisation of the workshops as adequate, but that three days are too much of an investment especially for commercial parties. A refund of expenses would have at least partially eased this barrier. Also time and money for intensive networking beyond the R&D community was not available within the projects budget. Various participants mentioned that one reason they gave the workshops low priority was that they did not perceive nor expect

a strong commitment of the ministry to change governance in accordance to the project's results.

19. This means for example, that by November 2004 the budget allocation for the year 2005 has not been decided upon – and subsequently when there will be further calls for projects.

20. See the mid-term evaluation of the programme (Paula 2004, presented in detail on 12 October 2004 in Vienna), which aimed to evaluate the long-term effects of the programme, but was limited in scope.

# REFERENCES

Bundesministerium für Umwelt (1995), *Nationaler Umweltplan*, Vienna: BMU.

Coenen, Reinhard (2002), 'Sustainable development – new challenges for technology assessment', in Andrew Jamison and Harald Rohracher (eds), *Technology Studies and Sustainable Development*, Munich, Vienna: Profil Verlag GmbH, pp. 127–43.

Danner, H., B. Mazingaidzo, B. Molzbichler, M. Neureiter and R. Braun (1999), 'Austrian and European markets for products from a green biorefinery', in proceedings of the 2nd International Symposium 'The Green Biorefinery', Feldbach, Austria.

Elzen, Boelie, Frank Geels, Peter Hofman and Ken Green (2002), 'Socio-technical scenarios as a tool for transition policy – an example from the traffic and transport domain', in proceedings of the workshop 'Transitions to Sustainability through Systems Innovation', Enschede: University of Twente.

Geels, Frank W. (2002), 'Understanding the dynamics of technological transitions', PhD thesis, Enschede: University of Twente.

Gleich, A. v., R. Haum and U. Petschow (2004), 'Guiding principles for sustainability', Ökologisches Wirtschaften, (5), 29–30.

Grunwald, Armin, R., Coenen, J., Nitsch, A. Sydow and P. Wiedemann (2001), *Forschungswerkstatt Nachhaltigkeit. Wege zur Diagnose und Therapie von Nachhaltigkeitsdefiziten*, Berlin: Sigma.

Industriewissenschaftliches Institut (2001), *Stoffliche Nutzung Nachwachsender Rohstoffe in Österreich Marktanalyse und Handlungsmaßnahmen*, Studie im Auftrag des Bundesministeriums für Verkehr, Innovation und Technologie, Vienna: BMVIT.

Kamm, B. and M. Kamm (2004), 'Biorefinery – systems', *Chemical and Biochemical Engineering Quarterly*, **18** (1), 1–6.

Katter, R., H. Mackwitz, Michael Narodoslawsky, K. Payer, W. Stadlbauer, Brigitte Weiß, Robert Wimmer and M. Wörgetter (1999), *Nachwachsende Rohstoffe: Ergebnisse aus der Vorbereitungsphase für das Impulsprogramm Nachhaltig Wirtschaften*, Studie im Auftrag des Ministeriums für Wissenschaft und Verkehr, Graz.

Kromus, S., B. Wachter, W. Koschuh, M. Mandl, C. Krotscheck and M. Narodoslawsky (2004), 'The green biorefinery Austria – development of an integrated system for green biomass utilization', *Chemical and Biochemical Engineering Quarterly*, **18** (1), 7–12.

Kromus, Stefan (1999), 'Elaboration of a decentralized "green biorefinery" for the Austrian region of Feldbach: a sustainable concept?', Master of Science Thesis, Wageningen: Wageningen Agricultural University (WAU).

Kuhlmann, S. (2001), *Management of Innovation Systems. The Role of Distributed Intelligence*, Antwerp: Maklu Uitgevers.

Meyer, K. (2002), 'Running after the international trend: Keynesian power balances and the sustainable repulsion of the innovation paradigm in Austria', in Peter Biegelbauer and S. Borras (eds), *Innovation Policies in Europe and the US: The New Agenda*, Ashgate: Aldershot.

Narodoslawsky, Michael (1999), in proceedings of the The Green Biorefinery, 2nd International Symposium, Feldbach, Austria: SUSTAIN – Kornberg Institut.

Paula, Michael (2004), *Zwischenbilanz 2004, Impulsprogramm Nachhaltiges Wirtschaften*, Vienna: BMVIT.

Paula, Michael, C. Smoliner and Brigitte Tiefenthaler (2004), *FORschung für Nachhaltige Entwicklung: FORNE*, Vienna: Rahmenstrategie 2004 plus.

Rat für Forschung und Technologieentwicklung (RFT) (2002), Nationaler Forschungs- und Innovationsplan, Vienna.

Rip, Arie and René Kemp (1998), 'Technological change', in Steve Rayner and Elizabeth L. Malone (eds), *Human Choice and Climate Change: Resources and Technology, Vol. 2*, Columbus, OH: Batelle Press, 327–99.

Rotmans, J., R. Kemp and M. van Asselt (2001), 'More evolution than revolution: transition management in public policy', *Foresight*, **3** (1), 15–31.

Schidler, Susanne (2003), *Technikfolgenabschätzung der Grünen Bioraffinerie, Band 1: Endbericht*, Vienna: Institut für Technik folgen-Abschätzung der Osterreichischen Akademie der Wissenschaften.

Soyez, K. and E. Pfeffer (1999), 'The industrial implementation of the green biorefinery', discussion paper, available at http://www.gts-oekotech.de/docs/theses_biorefinery.pdf.

US National Research Council (2003), Committee on Biobased Industrial Products B. I. P., *Biobased Industrial Products – Priorities for Research and Commercialisation*, Washington DC: National Academic Press.

Van der Heijden, Kees (1996), *Scenarios: The Art of Strategic Conversation*, Chichester: John Wiley.

Weber, Matthias K., Philipp Späth, Harald Rohracher, Ines Oehme, Karl-Heinz Leitner and Katy Whitelegg (2003), 'Middle-range transitions in production-consumption systems: The role of research programmes for shaping transition processes towards sustainability', in proceedings of the Conference on the Human Dimensions of Global Environmental Change: 'Governance for Industrial Transformation', Berlin.

Whitelegg, Katy (2004), 'Patchwork policy-making – linking innovation and transport policy in Austria, case study report for the OECD NIS MONIT Project, Seibersdorf/Vienna: ARC systems research/tip.

Wimmer, Robert, Michael Narodoslawsky, Luise Janisch, Hannes Hohensinner and Manfred Drak (2003), *Stoffliche Nutzung Nachwachsender Rohstoffe. Beiträge zur forschungspolitischen Diskussion, Series: Berichte aus Energie – und Umweltforschung*, 27/2003 Ed., Vienna: BMVIT.

Working Group 'Renewable Raw Materials' (2002), Current situation and future prospects of EU industry using renewable raw materials.

# 15. The transformation of agriculture: reflexive governance for agrobiodiversity[1]

**Franziska Wolff**

## INTRODUCTION

The sustainable transformation of agriculture has become a major issue of debate in the past decades. Agriculture placed between societal expectations and the requirements of a globalising production chain, the effects of agricultural industrialisation on the environment, on rural development and society as a whole are some of the dimensions discussed here. One aspect frequently neglected is plant and animal breeding and the maintenance of biological diversity in agriculture (agrobiodiversity). These very foundations of agriculture and food production have been increasingly eroded.

To a great extent, agrobiodiversity loss is the consequence of unreflexive governance. Specifically, it can be considered an unintended feedback of an earlier problem-solving strategy – namely the post-war policy of food security that aimed at alleviating food scarcity. This strategy massively promoted the industrialisation of agriculture, first in developed nations (for example through the EC Common Agricultural Policy) and later in developing countries (in the 'Green Revolution'). A number of seemingly petty side effects lead to a far-reaching loss of agrobiodiversity: high-yielding plants and high-performing animals crowded out local crops and livestock, the spread of tractors decreased demand for traditional workhorses and for the cultivation of oats, the mechanisation of slaughtering and processing demanded 'standardised' livestock, and so on. Agrobiodiversity loss thus can be considered a 'second-order problem' (Jahn and Wehling 1998) to the extent that it is at least partly caused by efforts to solve (other) problems. These efforts are characterised by the flaws of 'modernist' governance – an unbalanced technical problem definition ('food scarcity as result of backward technologies') formed on the basis of highly specialised agro-engineering knowledge; the goals[2] of the new, centralised paradigm defined in administrative and industrial headquarters; mega-strategies[3] designed without regard for adaptability pushed through by an internationalising agroindustrial complex. The consequences were never systematically anticipated.

This chapter portrays agrobiodiversity loss as a sustainability problem and presents strategies for the reflexive governance of the conflict. According to the structural definition of sustainability problems laid out by Voß and Kemp in the Introduction to this volume, agrobiodiversity loss is a sustainability problem since first, breeding and the maintenance/use of agrobiodiversity are characterised by a tight interaction of social, technological and ecological factors. Second, the problem definition is socially contentious and introduces divergent scientific analyses and uncertainties as regards the scope as well as the exact consequences. The irreversibility of agrobiodiversity loss and path dependencies in breeding put additional pressure on the social definition of goals and strategies, which revolve around conflicting poles: strong versus weak sustainability, long-term risk avoidance versus short-term productivity increase, ex-situ conservation of genetic resources versus on-farm and production-oriented development of agrobiodiversity. Steering potential is widely distributed between different economic actors, social groups and policy fields on the national, EU and international levels.

A complex constellation like this requires reflexive governance. Some approaches to participatory and transdisciplinary research into agrobiodiversity exist. The ecosystem approach that was developed within the Convention of Biological Diversity constitutes an important political framework for the systematic integration of diverse knowledge sources in agrobiodiversity management. It also provides guidelines requiring the adaptivity of strategies and institutions in agrobiodiversity management. While to date, there are hardly any mechanisms to anticipate long-term systemic effects of action strategies, various approaches to participatory goal formulation and interactive strategy development do exist. Among these, 'Farmers' Rights' aim at farmer involvement in national policy formulation, while participatory breeding and community seed banks address decentralised and democratic control of (genetic) resources. The conclusions elaborate practical problems of reflexive governance and some of their structural causes as well as ways to overcome these.

## THE PROBLEM SETTING

The dramatic decrease in agrobiodiversity represents a constantly worsening global problem (FAO 1996, 1993). Agrobiodiversity is that part of biodiversity in the context of agriculture that contributes to nutrition (agricultural crops, productive livestock), to livelihoods (by delivering raw materials, medical plants, animals used for transport and so on) and to the maintenance of habitats. The term comprises several dimensions: the genetic diversity between and within crop varieties and livestock races/lines, the diversity of species and of agroecosystems.[4] Agrobiodiversity is the result of human interaction with nature through breeding and farming. It is also the result of (a specific mode of) governance – that is, of specific societal patterns to solve the problem of food and raw material supply. This mode is characterised by the diversity of agricultural management practices and the encompassing socio-economic organisation (Brookfield 2001; Almekinders et al. 1995).[5]

## From Riches to Risk

The loss of agrobiodiversity is an insidious problem. The majority of the world food supply today is based on only 10 cultivated plants (FAO 2000). It is estimated that the plant genetic resources (PGR) that are presently actively cultivated represent only 25 per cent of the worldwide diversity which was in use at the beginning of the twentieth century. While in the Global South a great deal more plant genetic diversity and traditional varieties are still available on-farm (GTZ 2000), in industrial nations like Germany the disappearance of species, plant varieties and gene complexes ('genetic erosion') is estimated to reach up to 90 per cent (TAB 1998). Low variability in crop rotation and a high standardisation of management practices are associated with these trends.

The situation is similar for farm animals. The FAO warns that two farm animal races are lost on average per week. Approximately half of the breeds present in Europe at the turn of the twentieth century have disappeared forever. In Germany, of at least 35 original cattle breeds only five have endured. The everyday use of almost all species is dominated by very few breeds. Just 14 out of the about 30 domesticated mammalian and bird species provide 90 per cent of human food supply from animals (FAO 2004a). Within these species in use, only a very few races and lines dominate. Holstein Frisian cattle, for example, have spread globally and on a large scale.[6] In turn, within this race only a very few top bulls dominate and 'produce' up to a million descendants.

## Social, Technological and Ecological Interlinkages

Structurally, agrobiodiversity can be seen as the result of socio-ecological transformation, that is, a process of co-evolution of social, technological and ecological structures. As opposed to 'wild' biodiversity, agrobio-diversity (for the most part) is characterised by close interaction between human action and natural 'material' systems or processes. The diversity of productive livestock and crops is the result of a century of human breeding efforts based on locally differentiated resources. It reflects the diversity of agricultural production systems, of regional nutrition habits, of even aesthetic preferences reflected in breeding[7] and of socio-cultural environments.

Agrobiodiversity is inseparably linked to the use and utilisation of crops and livestock by humans. Whereas in the case of 'wild' biodiversity, 'leaving it alone' suffices to sustain it, the maintenance of agrobiodiversity requires its active utilisation in agriculture. In short, to survive, crops and livestock need to be 'eaten up'. Furthermore, the development (and partly also the destruction) of agrobiodiversity is closely related to human knowledge of cultivation and husbandry as well as the emergence of different breeding techniques and technologies. They range from the discovery of the Mendelian laws to the development of artificial insemination, multiple ovulation, embryo transfer, hybrid breeding, gene transfer, and so on. Modern technologies often either allow for an extremely targeted selection of individuals, genotypes[8] and alleles[9] or promote their broad suprare-gional dissemination (Wetterich 1999: 45).

Another crucial factor in the shaping of agrobiodiversity is the devel-opment of food processing technologies. The industrialisation and stand-ardisation of wheat milling, chicken culling or fruit packaging, for example, have sped up the reduction of the crop and livestock diversity in agricultural use as well as the intraspecific genetic diversity of those crops and animals bred. Globalising agricultural commodity markets and the homogenisation of habitats by means of machinery, irrigation, fertilisers, pesticides and pharmaceuticals makes it superfluous in breeding to take account of different regional conditions. Native varieties and breeds are substituted with high-yielding 'universal' crops and breeds (FAO 1996: 13, FAO 1993) that no longer need to be adapted to natural conditions like climate or soil but depend strongly on external inputs. Finally, agricultural policies and legal provisions such as breeding law and intellectual prop-erty rights (IPR) regimes partly have contributed to agrobiodiversity loss (Wolff 2004a). For example, in order for a plant breeder to receive a Plant Variety Protection right, the variety needs to show a high degree of uni-formity.[10] The economic desire to identify a variety as a precondition for granting an IPR to its breeder thus promotes genetic erosion (Crucible Group 1994).

**Impacts of Agrobiodiversity Loss**

Why is agrobiodiversity loss problematic at all?

First, the loss of locally adapted, robust varieties and races has an impact on the surrounding eco-system and wild biodiversity. Their substitution by genetically homogenous high performance crops and animals (kept in high-tech sheds) necessitates unecological inputs such as fossil energy, fertilisers and pesticides, feed supplements and pharmaceuticals. Although the plants and animals frequently have lower productivity regarding specific traits, their protection is still valuable. Among other reasons, the crops and breeds frequently possess qualities that are important for low-input, sustainable agriculture.[11] Generally, agrobiodiversity loss undermines the foundations of future breeding as breeding options are narrowed down, and with them the possibility to adapt to future challenges such as climate change.

Second, agrobiodiversity loss has economic impacts. Monotony in the fields increases vulnerability, for example, to climate stress, insect pests and diseases that can devastate a uniform crop, especially on large plantations.[12] Similarly, the lack of genetic diversity among farm animals impedes adaptation to diseases, parasites, or variations in the availability and quality of food. Thus, agrobiodiversity loss increases the economic risks for farmers and the food business (Thrupp 1997).

Finally, there are substantial social impacts. Agrobiodiversity, along with soil and water, secures the existence particularly of smallholder and subsistence farmers. It is also the foundation of world food security (FAO 1996: 6).[13] Other social impacts range from the general relationship of humans with nature to the loss of knowledge connected with agrobiodiversity. Gender relations are also implicated. As breeding, animal husbandry and plant cultivation become more high-tech operations and are carried out mostly by men, traditional subsets of peasant women activity are being devalued.

# GOVERNANCE CHALLENGES RESULTING FROM AGROBIODIVERSITY LOSS

After having outlined the material dimensions of agrobiodiversity loss, in the following section I introduce the structural dimensions of agrobiodiversity loss as a governance problem. First, research on agrobiodiversity is characterised by dispersed knowledge clusters and uncertainties. Path dependencies are typical in agrobiodiversity management. In addition, severe social conflicts exist with regard to the definition of goals and means in agrobiodiversity maintenance. Finally, governance capacities are widely scattered along the production chain and within different societal subsystems, which makes it difficult to tackle the problem effectively.

## Complex Systems Dynamics

### Heterogeneity of knowledge and the need for integration
Agrobiodiversity loss implies challenges to knowledge integration on (at least) the following three levels.

The first level refers to problem identification. For a long time, the loss of agricultural biodiversity was not the focal point of biologists who dealt predominantly with 'wild' flora and fauna; from this perspective, agriculture was seen as a foe rather than as the creator of (parts of) biological diversity. Genetic erosion especially was an issue that breeding scientists and agronomists tackled rather than biologists. Apart from the need to accommodate these different general perspectives, scientific observations referring to the different levels of analysis (ecosystem, species, genetic diversity) need to be consolidated. This implies that diverse scientific approaches need to be integrated which specialise in the different levels and which have differing basic assumptions and targets of explanation: approaches of ecology, taxonomic–systematic biology and population genetics (see Hertler, 1999; Perlman and Adelson, 1997).[14] In addition to this, an integration of the more practical knowledge of breeders, farmers, veterinarians, gene bank staff and so on will widen the scope of problem identification. For example, it might highlight the constitutive role of local knowledge in adapted forms of sustainable use.

The second level of knowledge integration refers to the identification of problem causes and effects. Here, accounting for the multitude of drivers and impacts of agrobiodiversity loss requires a 'transdisciplinary' analysis: it includes scientific knowledge from different disciplines and the applied knowledge of stakeholders. The complexity of the subject matter and the multi-causality of the problem call for specialised disciplinary expertise on the one hand, and for a strong integration of disciplinary perspectives on the other hand – to account for overlaps and avoid 'blind spots'. The topic needs biological or agronomist knowledge to analyse the loss of plant and animal diversity competently, to assess causes such as breeding, farming and processing-related technologies and to anticipate ecological/agricultural effects. Economic expertise is necessary to understand the inherent incentives in reducing diversity within the innovation system (breeding), agriculture, the production chain and trade. Legal and social science know-how helps to understand the regulatory and institutional drivers of agrobiodiversity loss as well as the supporting socio-cultural practices and discursive strategies. Practitioners' knowledge is indispensable to 'ground' the sometimes theoretical disciplinary knowledge and steer it into productive directions. It is also necessary for identifying the problem perceptions and interests of stakeholders that are associated with the causes of the problem and its effects. Such comprehensive and structurally diverse knowledge is necessary to eventually make practical policy recommendations or to intervene in social/political opinion-forming.

**Uncertainty**

A core element of the agrobiodiversity problem is uncertainty and lack of reliable knowledge.

The first difficulty is to measure the exact extent of the loss. As a concomitant of the diversity of analytical levels of analysis (ecosystem, species, genetic diversity) and of scientific approaches (see above), there is a lack of widely accepted indicators.[15] Also, data availability varies depending on which level of genetic diversity is to be described. Difficulties arise even at the apparently unproblematic level of recording the numbers of species, races and varieties.[16] Assessments of the various components are conducted separately and without an integrated evaluation of agricultural biodiversity as a whole. These limits to scientific analysis imply uncertainty about the full scope of agrobiodiversity loss.[17]

The second dimension of uncertainty relates to the consequences of agrobiodiversity loss and to risk assessment. In major ignorance as to the value of agrobiodiversity (and of biodiversity in general), and partly even as to its functions,[18] interactions and causal relations, it is unclear what specific impact the decline of agroecosystem, species and genetic diversity will have (CBD 2000a: 92). This applies to ecological impacts as well as to economic costs and socio-cultural consequences. Plausible evaluations of the risks and dangers can be made (see above). It is for example undisputable that agrobiodiversity loss diminishes options for future breeding and agriculture. However, there is no way to take 'informed decisions' on which parts of agrobiodiversity, which races, populations, lines and varieties, eventually genotypes, genes and alleles are 'worth' maintaining and which are not. This decision depends on normative evaluations as well as on information about future needs that cannot be known at present: about tomorrow's diseases, nutrition needs, consumer demands, possible environmental events and agricultural development paths, and so on. The uncertainty inherent in the agrobiodiversity problem suggests the use of the precautionary principle as a reflexive governance strategy.

A third dimension of uncertainty relates to the effects of political interventions. The complexity of ecological, economic and social effects makes it difficult to determine what side effects agrobiodiversity conservation and utilization strategies might cause. On the one hand, agrobiodiversity strategies can have unintended impacts in the social and economic realm, and they can even cause negative feedback within agrobiodiversity itself.[19] On the other hand, non-agrobiodiversity policies have ambiguous effects on agrobiodiversity. One case in point is trade liberalisation. A reduction of trade-distorting domestic support (subsidies) might lead not only to agricultural output substitution, but also to input substitution and to output price impacts. It is very hard to assess which impact will predominate, to disentangle short-term from long-terms effects, to assess their direction and relative magnitude and therefore also their effects on agrobiodiversity (CBD 2003a). For instance, the reduction of domestic support might lead to a decline in the application of fertilizers and other agricultural chemicals and thus indirectly promote the use of more crop varieties as a means to reduce risk of pests. It might also have a countervailing impact, because production pressures lead to technological changes that induce further specialisation like mono cropping.

### Path dependencies

Path dependencies in the field of agrobiodiversity loss exist both in biological terms (relating to the problem itself) and in economic and political terms (relating to the societal capacity of reacting to the problem).

First, agrobiodiversity loss is irreversible. Once a species, race, line, variety etc. has died out, certain paths abruptly end. In other words, the plants and animals can no longer be used, either in breeding, agriculture, in landscape maintenance, or for hobby or any other purpose. A process of 'path-closing' also takes place when a breed or variety is exclusively preserved ex-situ in gene banks. Important knowledge about the animal's/plant's characteristics, utilisation, about the genetic material's traits and substances of content, are lost, rendering the further utilisation of the animals and plants unlikely.

In economic terms, innovation dynamics affect the maintenance of agrobiodiversity. There is an incentive for breeding companies to work with those genetic resources that have already been successfully developed into high-performing products by previous breeders or with which they themselves have experience. By means of their investment, breeders design a path. To the extent that knowledge is accumulated and breeding progress advances, the productivity and economic attractiveness of other varieties, lines, races or populations that are not developed, decreases (Wolff and Petschow 2004). Thus, the potential for the adaptation of crops and livestock (and implicitly of mankind) to future requirements is lost.

Finally, political path dependencies prevent a transformation of unsustainable farming practices and breeding strategies: For decades, the high-productivity, low-sustainability practices have been subsidised. The subsidies and the respective agricultural alignment have been pushed through by tight policy networks of farmer associations, the agribusiness industry, academic research and national agricultural ministries, as well as the EU Commission's DG Agriculture. In Germany, as a spearhead of agricultural 'modernisation' that assembles some 90 per cent (!) of all farmers, the Farmers' Association[20] is well represented in the administration (despite a Green Party agriculture minister 2001–2005), in political parties and their parliamentary groups, in legislative committees, advisory boards and so on (Führer 1997). The association's top functionaries are mainly big farmers that have profited most from the agroindustrialisation strategy and the EU's subsidy system. Other functionaries come from the agrochemicals, breeding, biotechnology and other agribusiness industries, ensuring their influence on the farmers' organisation. In an effort to build 'winning coalitions', agribusiness at the same time appoints leading farmers to their boards of directors or managers (Anderegg 1999: 76f).

Small and alternative farmers upholding sustainable practices have not profited from these coalitions, and yet fail to organise themselves powerfully. Organic farming is taught at only a few agricultural faculties, and the issue of agrobiodiversity is addressed at even fewer universities. Research funds for agricultural biotechnology, which is presented as a (contentious) technocratic solution for agrobiodiversity loss, almost doubled the federal budget for conventional agricultural research in 2002. In the breeding sciences, a veritable process of delegitimisation of non-molecular approaches is taking place (Wissen 2004a).

In the policy-making process at the decisive EU level,[21] the European Parliament still plays only a consultative role in the Common Agricultural Policy and its budget procedure. It has not been able to offer much resistance to the agroindustrial thrust by the Member States and the European lobby network that was created previously.[22] Against this backdrop, it is difficult to depart from a path trodden in the 1950s: the agroindustrial interests' penetration of knowledge production, agenda setting and policy-making hampers change.

## Contentious Definition of Strategic Goals and Means

The goal of agrobiodiversity protection as a contribution to sustain the long-term viability of socio-ecological systems is entangled in a web of diverging paradigms of sustainability, of conflicting values, goals and means.

Most actors in the debate refer to the overall goal of sustainable development. This stands to reason, since agrobiodiversity loss has consequences for future generations, erodes the foundations of agriculture and closes development paths. However, opinions are divided on whether intergenerational justice (WCED 1987) requires the preservation of natural capital (agrobiodiversity), or whether man-made,[23] manufactured or human capital can at least partly substitute for natural capital. This goes back to the well-known discussion of strong versus weak sustainability (Pearce and Atkinson 1995). Thus, agrobiodiversity preservation in the sense of weak sustainability is dispensable, as long as the savings that result from non-preservation are invested, for example in biotechnological progresses, agricultural or gene bank infrastructure, etc.

If the intragenerational aspect of sustainability is examined, another line of conflict appears: the weighing up of agrobiodiversity protection against another evident sustainability goal, namely the reduction of world hunger in a growing world population. The costs of agrobiodiversity maintenance are confronted with the resources needed to fight hunger. Above all, proponents of a productivity-driven food security strategy argue that only with the help of high-yielding crops and high-performing livestock, ultimately with intensive and export-oriented agriculture, can we get a grip on hunger (IFPRI 2001; ASSINSEL 1997). This line of argument however, ignores the essential function of agrobiodiversity for preserving food security (FAO 2000). In the view of many critics, there is no genuine goal conflict between food security and agrobiodiversity protection (Grandin 2003; etc group 2002; ITDG 2002; Thrupp 1997). Rather, there is a dissent in short-term versus long-term orientation, partly overshadowed by economic interests.

Beyond dissent about goals there are conflicts of means as how to best reach the goals. Most dominant approaches do not regard reflexive processes but instead focus on substantive policies (see Table 15.1). Some approaches predominantly consider existing, 'old' plant and animal genetic resources (strategies A and B in the Table), others set in with the development of 'new' agrobiodiversity. The first set of strategies can be distinguished by their stress on 'ex situ'[24] conservation (strategy A) versus the 'on-farm'[25] use of the genetic resources (strategy B). The ex situ strategy does not allow for dynamic adaptation of the existing material and is a mere 'insurance' against loss. The latter set of strategies C.1 and C.2, targeted towards developing agrobiodiversity, by aiming at changes either in current breeding strategies (C.1) or additionally in a transformation of the wider agricultural production chain (C.2). Within the breeding-oriented approach, the most contentious option proposed is certainly the use of biotechnological methods, particularly of recombinant DNA techniques in the case of plants. While parts of the research sector and especially big transnational seed breeding corporations consider the introduction of agronomic traits into plant varieties, the adding of 'well defined valuable genes' (ASSINSEL 1996; von Brook 2002: 5) an enhancement of agrobiodiversity, others reject this approach (IÖW et al. 2004a). One reason is the fear that it might ultimately promote further homogenisation of genetic

Table 15.1   Ideal types of *(non-reflexive)* approaches to agrobiodiversity maintenance

| | Approach | | | |
| --- | --- | --- | --- | --- |
| | Conservation of agrobiodiversity (A) | Use of agrobiodiversity (B) | Development of agrobiodiversity (C.1, C.2) | |
| Object | • Protection of existing plant and animal genetic resources | | Development of new varieties and lines/individuals | Protection of existing plant and animal genetic resources<br><br>Development of new varieties and lines/individuals<br><br>Development of more diverse agroecosystems |
| Implementation | 'Ex situ' conservation | 'On-farm' use | Technology-oriented transformation of breeding: Introduction of new traits through genetic engineering | Sustainable transformation of breeding[28] within agricultural production chain |

*Table 15.1* (continued)

| | Approach | | |
|---|---|---|---|
| | Conservation of agrobiodiversity (A) | Use of agrobiodiversity (B) | Development of agrobiodiversity (C.1, C.2) | |
| Segment of production chain aimed at | Post-production: <br> • Genebanks/cryo-conservation <br> • Botanic gardens, open air museums | Informal sector (conservation initiatives, hobby gardening etc.) <br> Partly: agriculture (e.g. organic farming), niche markets | Innovation system: <br> • Breeding sector | Innovation and production system: Breeding sector agriculture (on-farm), product development, processing, distribution, marketing, consumption, awareness raising |
| Scope and thrust | Segmental <br> Static | Segmental <br> Dynamic | Segmental <br> Dynamic | Holistic <br> Dynamic |
| Risk orientation | Insurance | Precaution | Risk | Precaution |

*Source:* Compilation by author

material (Graner 2003; Vangen 2003). In addition, the incalculable risks of genetic engineering stimulate a more fundamental criticism of this path (Grain 2004).[26] While Table 15.1 systematises different approaches to the maintenance of agrobiodiversity in an ideal, typical way, in reality those approaches partly overlap.[27]

## Dispersed Governance Capacities for Strategy Implementation

Sustainable transformation generally depends on drawing on governance capacities distributed between different geo-political levels, functional domains, and actors. In relation to agrobiodiversity in particular, steering potential is widely distributed between different economic actors, policy fields, and social groups, as well as over the national, EU and international level.

In the economic sphere, it is breeders, farmers, the processing industry, food retailing, and finally end consumers like households and the gastronomy that influence the demand for agrobiodiversity. Typically, most actors in the production chain feel they have no leeway for promoting agrobiodiversity. Breeders argue that they have to align their breeding targets to the demands of farmers and industry; farmers opt for the standardised high-productivity crops and livestock since these promise to raise low incomes; food processors and retailers need standardised agricultural inputs to minimise operating expenses and to be able to offer cheap foodstuff to buyers – a goal that has been politically supported for decades. Product differentiation might be a business edge, however, it is restricted to the end product; as long as there is no specific consumer demand of a relevant size it is cost-effective to keep the number of different raw materials (crops, livestock) at a minimum. On the other hand, end consumers, even if they have the respective awareness, stand little chance to put through their demand against the standardising effects of breeding, production and retail. In the end, actual economic pressures or unfavourable incentives work against agrobiodiversity. Cooperation along the production chain could help stabilise expectations and develop niche markets.

In politics, the traditional place for dealing with genetic resources is ministries of agriculture. Yet for a long time, those establishments were not responsive to the issue,[29] and frequently keep showing a narrow, production-oriented problem perspective. Environmental administrations on the other side often only cover the issue of 'wild' biodiversity. A number of further policy fields have the potential to affect agrobiodiversity positively or negatively: rural development, regional and tourism policy, consumer protection and development cooperation, trade and intellectual property law. They all pursue different primary goals, work according to different kinds of logic and possess unequal strength to assert themselves in the policy process.

The multi-level structure of national, EU and international policies further complicates things for governance that favours agrobiodiversity. Some examples: efforts of the German red–green government to introduce a harmonised budget line on genetic resource grants were thwarted by conservative State (*Länder*) governments. A facilitated registration procedure of conservation varieties cannot be introduced by EU Member States as long as the Commission delays the creation of an important implementation guideline. Multilateral provisions on plant genetic resources for food and agriculture could only be introduced after seven years of tough negotiations under the auspices of the FAO. Conflicts of interest, as well as inter- and intra-institutional friction and negative coordination practices, are crucial reasons for such multi-level complications.

Similarly, in the social realm, it is different groups like environmentalists, seed networks, hobby gardeners, or North–South activists whose activities touch on the issue of agrobiodiversity, but who do not necessarily have the explicit goal of sustaining it. It will therefore be hard to mobilise them for collective action.

## STRATEGIES OF REFLEXIVE GOVERNANCE

It is assumed that problems characterised by the governance problems outlined above can be tackled more effectively by reflexive strategies. Reflexive governance is characterised by the 'building up of capacities for social learning and responsive modulation of ongoing processes of change' (Voß and Kemp, this volume). Thereby, it takes into account the features of sustainability problems: the complexity of interlinked social, technological and ecological development, the heterogeneity of knowledge, and uncertainties as regards dynamics and effects of interventions. Reflexive governance recognises path dependencies, conflicting and changing societal value systems and goal definitions as well as the distribution of control and governance capacities between different actors, geographical levels, and functional domains.

This chapter introduces selective approaches to reflexive governance in the field of agrobiodiversity preservation and development. It has to be stressed, however, that elements of reflexive governance such as integrated knowledge production, adaptive strategies, instruments for an anticipation of systemic effects, participatory goal formulation, and interactive strategy formulation (Voß and Kemp 2004) are still rare in national and international agrobiodiversity governance.[30]

## Integrated Knowledge Production

Sustainability problems require an integrated perception of the problem, its causes and potentially successful intervention strategies. To reach this goal, knowledge production needs to draw upon different disciplines and societal actors. In the field of agrobiodiversity, some attempts of participatory and transdisciplinary research exist. In addition, the ecosystem approach adopted by the Convention on Biological Diversity gives a conceptual basis to integrated knowledge production in the field of agrobiodiversity management.

### Participatory and transdisciplinary research

One aspect of integrated knowledge production is the inclusion of practical or stakeholder knowledge. Over the past two decades, participatory research on (mainly plant) genetic diversity has developed (King 2000). The context was and still is predominantly in development projects and in CGIAR-related research on farming systems in the global South.[31] Motives for the spread of participatory research were both the recognition of the importance of farmer knowledge as well as experimentation within formal agricultural and scientific research. The main areas of participatory research are participatory plant breeding (see below),[32] and on-farm conservation. Farmer participation is crucial here, as on-farm conservation is based upon those crops that are of value to farmers, and as it makes use of farmer management skills (Jarvis et al. 1998). In situ and on-farm strategies are only successful to the extent that reseachers can correctly identify the factors affecting farmers' decisions to maintain local cultivars and can develop means to support their continued selection. A typical problem of participatory methodologies in scientific research has been the conflict between researchers and community knowledge systems. 'Participation requires increased acceptance and respect of alternative forms of knowledge, as well as a willingness on the part of researchers to accommodate and integrate different modes of perception into Western scientific paradigms' (King 2000: 3).

Another form of integrated knowledge production is transdisciplinary research. Like participatory research it is both application-oriented and directly involves practitioners, but in addition covers a broad range of disciplines. An example of this form or knowledge production was the research project 'Developing agrobiodiversity' (which constitutes the basis of this chapter).[33] The project aimed in a practically oriented way at contributing to the understanding, problematisation and mitigation of agrobiodiversity loss as a 'real world' (not merely academic) problem. It involved agriculturalists, veterinarians, ecologists, social scientists, economists and lawyers, from both research institutions and practical backgrounds, in a very integrative and comprehensive research exercise.[34] It took the project team some months to develop a joint problem perspective successfully (IÖW et al. 2004a), thus coming to grips with one of the major challenges of transdisciplinarity. Still, disciplinary and working backgrounds sometimes were strongly felt. Beyond scientific outcomes, the project resulted in a stakeholder conference, which for the first time in Germany brought together major actors beyond the 'usual suspects', ranging from FAO representatives and NGOs to multinational breeding companies and retailers. It helped to build up the discourse on agrobiodiversity loss, which is still underdeveloped in industrialised countries.

**The ecosystem approach I: integrating diverse knowledge sources**
A comprehensive framework for integrative knowledge production and biodiversity management has been elaborated by the parties of the Convention on Biological Diversity (CDB).[35] The so-called 'ecosystem approach' is a strategy for the integrated management of land, water and living resources.[36] By framing the management of living components alongside economic and social conditions, the CBD ecosystem approach goes beyond most existing ecosystem concepts (Golley 1993). It aims to integrate the ecological, economical and social sphere. Modelling ecosystem management as a social process, decision-making and management structures are at the heart of the approach. The starting point is the insight into fundamental uncertainty: 'Ecosystem processes are often non-linear, and the outcome of such processes often shows time-lags. The result is discontinuities, leading to surprise and uncertainty' (CBD 2000b). While traditional resource management perceives Nature as a pool of resources supplying economic goods and services which can be used, depleted and controlled by man, the ecosystem approach, in its 12 principles and five operational guidelines, recognises nature's dynamics and complexity, thus denying any straightforward controllability and unproblematic resource extraction. Integrated knowledge production[37] and adaptive management (see below) are recommended as appropriate means to cope with complexity, uncertainty and conflicting as well as changing social goals.

A number of the approach's principles address integrated knowledge production. First of all, there is a call to consider all forms of relevant information, including scientific and indigenous and local knowledge, innovations and practices (Principle 11). The implications for ecosystem management of different 'world views' based on different knowledge systems are explicitly recognised (CBD 2003b: 54). Principle 12 demands to 'involve all relevant sectors of society and scientific disciplines'. The complexity and potential side-effects of biodiversity management do not necessitate only multidisciplinary scientific *expertise*. Since conserving, maintaining, using and restoring ecosystems is accompanied by costs and benefits, the *interests* of all relevant sectors should be taken into account. In addition, the decentralising of management to the lowest appropriate level is propagated (Principle 2) in order to make better use of local knowledge, involve stakeholders and balance local interests with the wider public interest. One desired impact of knowledge integration efforts is that ecosystem managers can better consider (actual or potential) effects of their activities on adjacent and other ecosystems, as required by Principle 3.

The ecosystem approach represents an ideal framework for integrated knowledge production. However, its implementation in the field of agrobiodiversity needs to be promoted. Though the ecosystem approach has been transferred to agriculture and agricultural research (among others within the FAO; see Cooper 2003, Settle 2003), many of the projects conducted under this heading still neglect the dimension of knowledge integration (FAO 2002).

### Adaptivity of Strategies and Institutions

Socio-ecological transformation features uncertainties – it is always unclear whether a problem-solving strategy will indeed have the desired impact, or whether it produces unforeseen side effects. The problem itself might undergo changes as well as the societal objectives regarding its solution. Reflexive governance needs to react to these contingencies by way of flexible strategies and monitoring. In agrobiodiversity policy, the precautionary principle and adaptive management as embodied in the CBD's ecosystem approach can promote the adaptivity of strategies and institutions. While the precautionary principle provides guidelines for preventive problem treatment and thus creates opportunities for strategies to be adapted in time, adaptive management establishes feedback loops in problem treatment. It thus institutionalises the precautionary principle.

### The precautionary principle and on-farm maintenance
The precautionary principle, as recognised in the environmental policy of many Western countries as well as the EU, prescribes the preventive protection of people and the environment from risks and dangers. It demands preventive action, above all, where scientific uncertainties exist and where there is concern over possibly irreversible consequences. The precautionary principle is the basis of the adaptivity of strategies and institutions.

For the preservation of agrobiodiversity, precaution means preventing genetic erosion in the first place (IÖW et al. 2004a: 10f). This can be achieved by countering the current streamlining of breeding strategies.

Diversity automatically emerges when breeding is re-oriented from the universal use of crops and breeds towards their regional adaptation to natural habitats. It demands active agricultural (that is, on-farm) use of numerous (and genetically diverse) crops and livestock breeds and their marketing.[38] Preventing agrobiodiversity loss therefore also requires rebuilding an agricultural production system and upstream[39] and downstream[40] sectors so that they allow for diversity – for plenty of potato and diverse grain varieties, for the fatty pork of the Swabian Hall saddleback and a native lentil variety, in the fields and pastures, in food processing, and in the supermarkets. While economies of scale and corporate concentrations generally reduce such diversity, agricultural multifunctionality and the marketing of regional specialities are only a few factors that increase it. Precautionary strategies need to be bolstered by monitoring trends of agrobiodiversity loss and by researching more intensely its driving forces, risks and costs, along with possibilities for its use and utilisation. Finally, society (that is, consumers and producers) needs to be sensitised to the issue. Mainstreaming the issue in education, in agricultural training and amongst the general public is, thus, a further element of a precautionary strategy.

To date, the precautionary principle (if at all) is mainly applied with respect to on-farm maintenance. The example of biosphere reservations and the GIAHS project shall shed some light on the practice. Biosphere reserves according to UNESCO's guidelines promote sustainable economic and human development in addition to biodiversity conservation. This is to be achieved by adapted resource management and land use practices.[41] This goal qualifies biosphere reserves for the in situ and on-farm management of old varieties and rare breeds, particularly if they stem from the region. A successful example is the biosphere reserve 'Rhön' in Germany. Within an integrated regional development and tourism concept a native sheep breed ('Rhön Schaf') was re-introduced and is now being commercially marketed. In the biosphere reserve Schorfheide-Chorin in northeast Germany, the use of plant genetic resources has been promoted in collaboration of a state agency, a gene bank, local farmers and an NGO (VERN 2003).[42]

In contrast to biosphere reserves, the GIAHS Project of the FAO on Globally Important Ingenious Agricultural Heritage Systems tries to maintain rather than re-establish adapted resource management practices. Starting off with some ten pilot sites, the project serves both global awareness raising and safeguarding the selected agricultural systems with their rich autochthonous agrobiodiversity and innovative management practices. Furthermore, the capacity building of local farming communities is foreseen. Participatory elements shall warrant the project's responsiveness to local needs (FAO 2003).

The precautionary principle as yet is a concept rather than an empirical model. The element most frequently practised is on-farm maintenance. However, projects and policies commonly do not reach out to the upstream and downstream production sectors. Among other things, this is due to conflicts of goals and interest when the wider orientation of agricultural policies is put into question.

## The ecosystem approach II: adaptive management

The ecosystem approach of the Convention on Biological Diversity (CBD) not only lays the foundations for integrated knowledge production but also adopts adaptive management for agrobiodiversity maintenance. Adaptive management was first developed as a resource management tool in the 1970s (Holling 1978). Various versions have been drawn up, which all go back to the idea that management must proceed even if not all necessary information is available and not all effects of management measures are foreseeable. Management to a certain extent becomes an experiment, and learning is its core objective.[43] This requires a combination of management, research, and monitoring. It also calls for responsive management and political structures, that is, a design to overcome institutional barriers.

Within the CBD ecosystem approach, the concept of adaptive management is taken up by various principles. Very basic, Principle 1 states that management is a matter of societal choice. As societal preferences vary over time, ecosystem management needs to adapt to changing demands. Subsequently, management must recognise that change is inevitable (Principle 9): As ecosystems change, management also has to change. Adaptive management needs to anticipate change and be 'cautious in making any decision that may foreclose options, but, at the same time, consider mitigating actions to cope with long-term changes'. In addition, an operational guideline elaborates on the use of adaptive management practices. It stresses the need for learning processes and monitoring, for structures designed 'to adjust to the unexpected' and for flexibility in policy-making and implementation.[44]

One relatively simple form of adaptive management in genetic resource maintenance includes Farmer Field Schools (FFS). They are based on a season-long community-based learning methodology that is applied mainly in developing countries. Originally developed in Integrated Pest Management, it has been adapted to the management of plant genetic resources. Farmers are guided through field experiments to discover potential solutions to their field problems (Dung and SEARICE 2003). A core element includes experimental field studies that are designed and conducted by the farmer group, where varieties are evaluated, seed is rehabilitated, and preferred varieties are crossed and selected. Farmer Field Schools have proven to strengthen farmers' management, conservation and development of their crops, and skills and material are spreading quickly (ibid: 343).

## Anticipation of Long-Term Systemic Effects of Action Strategies

In order to prevent negative impacts on agrobiodiversity or even lock-in effects caused by action strategies, it is necessary to anticipate and assess indirect and long-term consequences of interventions. To date, there are no such anticipation instruments. While instruments to monitor the status and anticipate trends of agrobiodiversity do exist[45] or are envisaged,[46] none of the existing anticipation instruments examines the agrobiodiversity impacts of other policies, that is, cause–effect relations. For the future, however, agrobiodiversity issues should be considered in scenario efforts or foresight studies as they are occasionally conducted in most policy fields. Also, the agrobiodiversity needs to be integrated into instruments like Environmental or Sustainability Impact Assessments (EIAs, SIAs) and Strategic Environmental Assessments (SEAs). These instruments then need to be applied to projects, programmes, plans and policies in the realm of agriculture, food, biotechnology and development aid.

## Participatory Goal Formulation and Interactive Strategy Development

As outlined by Voß and Kemp (in this volume), successful approaches to socio-ecological transformation consistently require social agreement on goals. Such sustainability cannot be defined 'objectively' and cannot be substituted by scientific decisions as they involve subjective risk perceptions and value trade-offs. At the same time, socio-ecological transformation demands the interaction and collective action of diverse stakeholders, for example along the production chain and between political, economic and social actors. In the context of agrobiodiversity politics, the concepts of Farmers' Rights, participatory breeding and community-based resource management are approaches to participation and interaction in goal and strategy formulation. The international law concept of Farmers' Rights supports the involvement of farmers in national policies relating to plant genetic resources, thus making possible participatory goal formulation. Participatory breeding includes farmers in the strategic development of breeding goals. It also increases 'democratic' and decentralised (that is, varied) control over genetic resources. This is also the key impact of community-based forms of resource management.

### Farmers' rights

The concept of Farmers' Rights was first developed in the conflict between developing and developed countries on the question of access to genetic resources and intellectual property rights (IPRs). Farmers' Rights were meant as a countervailing right to 'classical' IPRs, valuing the knowledge system and breeding contribution of local farming communities (Girsberger 1999). Though still rather indeterminate,[47] Farmers Rights are now codified in the International Seed Treaty (ITPGR)[48] signed in 2001. Apart from provisions on the protection of traditional knowledge and the sharing of benefits arising from the utilization of plant genetic resources, Farmers' Rights include the right to participate in decision-making at the national level on matters related to the conservation and sustainable use of plant genetic resources for food and agriculture.[49] Though the implementation of Farmers' Rights is entrusted to the nation states, their codification puts pressure on national administrations to make possible participatory strategy formulation. Participation might range from the definition, elaboration, and execution of PGR policies to the design and management of state breeding or research programmes. In a wider interpretation, Farmers' Rights require nation states to strengthen farmers' participation beyond formal channels. This would mean providing them information, resources and rights in relation to genetic resources, to render their participation in goal formulation processes effective.

While the democratic nations of the North, with their established channels of interest aggregation, mostly declare no necessity to establish further means of farmer participation, there are major challenges here, too. Apart from the conventional farmers' and breeders' unions that are still privileged in many countries, participation should include alternative and ecological associations as well as NGOs that are active in the conservation of underutilised varieties. In order to enable a more interactive and integrative strategy formulation, the circle of participants may even be extended to environmental NGOs, associations of hobby gardeners, grocers' associations, biosphere reserve staff, representatives of the food industry and of distributive trade, regional/eco-tourism and gourmet associations. Informational and financial barriers to effective participation need to be removed and the participation of women to be promoted. Facilitating the farmer's voice is particularly necessary in the biotechnology debate, with genetically modified organisms posing a new threat to agrobiodiversity. Generally, it is necessary to develop rights for livestock keepers and breeders in analogy to the crop-related Farmer's Rights (Köhler-Rollefson and Wanyama 2003: 58f).

An example of participative strategy development in Germany was the drafting of the National Technical Programmes on Plant and on Animal Genetic Resources (BMVEL 2002, 2003). In both cases, the administration involved conventional breeders and researchers as well as alternative actors. The result of the consensus-driven efforts includes two overall ambitious plans of action. However, one of the reasons for achieving consensus was the absence of redistributive issues. Since the programmes do not dispose of their own budgets, decisions had less explosive force. Their implementation is subject to a budget salvo.

### Participatory and decentralised breeding

A special form of goal formulation in dealing with agricultural biodiversity is the setting of breeding goals. Here, participatory breeding facilitates farmers' stake in breeding and can increase the influence of consumers, too. To date, this approach prevails in the plant sector (Participatory Plant Breeding/PPB, Participatory Varietal Selection/PVS), though there are some projects on participatory livestock development, too.

To varying degrees, PBB and PVS make possible the influence of farmers in the analysis of local crop diversity, the setting of breeding goals, parent selection, variety release and distribution (Sthapit et al. 2003, Eyzaguirre and Iwanaga 1996). In informal seed systems, these approaches have become a customary practice which has established itself as FAO policy, too. They are based on the assumption that diversity may be both conserved and improved through cooperation between farmers and breeders/researchers.[50] Participatory breeding creates diversity, because local requirements are taken into account and also due to farmers' multi-purpose perspective in goal-setting and selection, decentralised on-farm testing, and the skill enhancement of the farmer breeders.

Participatory breeding, or respectively breeding by farmers, is almost unknown in developed countries. This is due to the special restrictions of highly industrialised and specialised agriculture: for the majority of livestock species the stages of breeding, raising/hatching, and keeping are organisationally separated from each other. Moreover, many high-performing animals are hybrids, that is, inbred lines that cannot pass on their performance characteristics. Farmers cannot reproduce them, at least not without significant losses in performance. In the case of chicken (layers) for example, farmers who decided to breed their own, commercially productive breeds would fail: the genetic resources of layer breeds are in the hands of very few transnational breeding companies. This is different with respect to cattle, where farmers still have the opportunity to breed themselves. Plant breeding also underlies specialisation and division of labour. Increasingly, intellectual property rights or biological protection systems[51] prevent even the replanting and adapting of seed by the farmer. Peasant participation in breeding is not only a promising path to locally adapted development and use of crops/livestock, but at the same time increases 'democratic' resource control by those who actually work with the resulting crops and animals (Wissen 2004b). Local adaptation is created with the help of the knowledge of local requirements imparted by experienced individuals. These forms of adaptation stand no chance when the definition of breeding goals is standardised by large breeding companies for nationwide or even international cultivation. The exact forms in which farmer participation or farmer breeding could be organised in specialised agricultural systems are dependent on the individual plant or animal species and must be consolidated further (IÖW et al. 2004a, Wiethaler et al. 2000).

Two German examples illuminate options of collaborate breeding in the case of (biodynamic) plant breeding. The Association for Biodynamic Vegetable Plant Breeding (Kultursaat) is a network of farmers, breeders, a seed company and an umbrella association. Based on the farmers' experience of crops and cultivation methods, plant breeding, the care of plants, their propagation, the testing of new varieties and maintenance is returned to farmers themselves. New vegetable varieties generated from the breeding programmes are either registered directly or given to breeders/farmers in other regions for adaptation to different growing conditions. To date, over 20 new varieties have been registered and are commonly owned (El-Hage Scialabba et al. 2002). A slightly different approach is pursued by the Cereal Breeding Research Centre in Darzau. This organisation breeds and passes on 'dynamic populations' (not homogenous varieties) to farmers who then develop farm-adapted varieties from the material (Müller 1999).

**Resource management by communities and networks**
A practice that is presently widespread (mostly) in developing countries is the community management of genetic resources. While participatory breeding aims at selection, community seed banks (CSB) focus more on the self-organised exchange and storage of seed. They are operated through a seed exchange network and managed by a group of local people who ensure seed supply, maintain the ex situ conservation, and enhance access and availability of locally adopted crops and varieties.[52] Community seed banks institutionalise exchange mechanisms common at an individual level,[53] thus helping to protect plant variety as a common property resource (Rengalakshmi et al. 2003). The continued existence of this common property resource is the basis for decentralised and self-determined goal formulation of breeding farmers. At the same time, community seed banks have effectively supported food security.

In the industrialised world, the loss of regionally adapted varieties and the wide abandonment of seed replanting due to intellectual property rights and biological protection systems prevent such approaches. However, there are private seed exchange networks that offer non-registered varieties (Dreschflegel 2003, VEN 2004, VERN 2003) – albeit for legal reasons this is restricted non-commercial use. Consequently the seeds cannot play a major role within the agricultural production system.

Beyond seed exchange networks, environmental co-operatives have evolved in the Netherlands that embark on community management of natural resources. The co-operatives are innovative associations of farmers at the local or regional level, which promote activities related to sustainable local agriculture and rural development. Though not explicitly concerned with the diversity of species, breeds and crops in the fields and barns, activities on landscape management, organic farming or the production of quality regional foods at least indirectly influence agrobiodiversity. The co-operatives emerged in the early 1990s 'in response to the crisis of high-tech agriculture, concerns over the deteriorating public image of farming and, most of all, the increasing number of environmental regulations of the government' (van der Ploeg and Renting 2002: 225). They did not only contribute to the building of new institutional relations between the state and agriculture, but successfully reduced pollution, enhanced nature management and diversified economically. For the future, environmental co-operatives could be a favourable environment for more explicit attempts of sustaining agrobiodiversity.

## CONCLUSIONS

Approaches to reflexive governance in agrobiodiversity policy are only just evolving, as is the policy field of agrobiodiversity itself. In relation to integrated knowledge production, participatory research is more common in developing countries than in the North, and transdisciplinary approaches are still rare. A promising development is the knowledge integration by way of the ecosystem approach of the Convention on Biological Diversity, which however still needs to be put into practice in agrobiodiversity management. This applies to the adaptive management approach, too. The precautionary principle may serve as another helpful and well accepted guideline to induce preventive action and thus to enhance indirectly the adaptivity of strategies. Generally speaking, so far, on-farm maintenance of neglected crops and animals (if on a small scale) has been implemented as one dimension of the precautionary principle; the dimensions relating to breeding goals, to the production chain and to awareness rising still need to be translated into public policy. While procedures to anticipate long-term systemic effects of action strategies are as yet non-existent, there are several approaches to participatory goal formulation and interactive strategy development: the abstract concept of Farmers' Rights (implemented among others by way of farmer consultation), participatory breeding and collaborative resource management. Here, too, developing countries, which still have informal seed systems, are ahead – a head start that might deteriorate as agricultural 'modernisation' carries on.

The effects and outcomes of these reflexive strategies vary. Participatory research and breeding provide more consumer (farmer) oriented, local solutions – but are partly also used to enhance farmers' acceptance of high yielding modern breeds. Adaptive management as applied in Farmer Field Schools steps up applied knowledge, learning and ownership. Participation in policy processes, as in the drafting of the German technical programmes on plant and animal genetic resources, has proven fruitful both with regard to ambitious target setting and to the fortification of an 'alternative' problem perception. However, participatory policy-making is devaluated if its results are not put into practice. This might be the case if participation is only granted as an alibi, or if implementation funds are lacking as in the case of the German Technical Programmes on genetic resources. Collaborative resource management not only builds social capital but also helps secure collective goods like agrobiodiversity and food security – which is crucial when the state does not provide the necessary assistance.

Practical problems met in the implementation of reflexive governance in agrobiodiversity policy range from lacking awareness to lacking political support and lacking funds. It is no coincidence, however, that these resources tend to lack: in many European/Western countries a decisive obstacle is the still rather firmly established network of 'hegemonial' actors that was built up after the Second World War. This 'iron triangle' of agribusiness lobby, agricultural administration and parliamentary committees which is characterised by a more or less consistent technocratic vision of agricultural development has shaped the EU Common Agricultural Policy and captured national institutions. With overproduction costs soaring and food scandals like the mad cow disease piling up, the power of the agroindustrial network has slowly started to dwindle. Still, a paradigm change towards sustainable breeding meets tough resistance as it would imply recognition that commercial breeding and the modern breeding sciences (embedded in an industrialised agricultural production chain) have critically contributed to a sustainability problem. This recognition would implicitly devaluate the knowledge, breeding 'successes', self-conception and finally the legitimacy of the sector. Alongside this immaterial devaluation, the material redistribution of resources would have to be expected, alarming vested interests and conservative forces. In order to further develop reflexive governance in agrobiodiversity maintenance, paths need to be studied and developed into how to deal effectively with such resource and legitimacy conflicts. In order to overcome antagonistic actor constellations, 'new' players need to be strengthened and windows of opportunity opened. New actors with a direct or indirect interest in agrobiodiversity for example are organic farmers. Windows of opportunity could be institutional incentives for income prospects in eco-tourism and agro-tourism or in speciality marketing (for example, labels, geographical indications or certificates of specific character for agricultural products).

Having applied the reflexive governance concept to the problem of agrobiodiversity loss and the transformation of agriculture, what insights can be drawn from this for an assessment of the reflexive governance concept itself? First, it is necessary to distinguish between the analytical framework provided by the concept and the prescriptive assumptions inherent in it.[54] Regarding the analytical framework – that is, the set of parameters and their interrelations established for the analysis of sustainability problems – the emphasis of the complex interdependence of societal, environmental and technological developments (co-evolution) and of the respective logic of different systems proves to be extremely helpful in gaining a 'realistic' understanding of agrobiodiversity loss. 'Realistic' here means to become aware of the heterogeneous dimensions of the problem,[55] instead of slicing out one particular perspective.[56]

With respect to the prescriptive assumptions of the reflexive governance concept (that is, the strategy elements recommended) it is the problem identification and investigation part ('system analysis') that is most convincing. Strategies such as promoting integrated knowledge production, designing adaptive strategies and institutions, and introducing mechanisms to anticipate long-term systemic effects are approaches that have proven their value in many problem fields. However, as the example of agrobiodiversity politics substantiates, they have so far been implemented only very selectively. This brings us to the other two strategy requirements, namely iterative participatory goal formulation and interactive strategy development. Two questions arise: (1) Will the required strategies (ranging from new forms of system analysis to participatory goal formulation and implementation) really be implemented? And (2) if implemented, will they suffice to bring about fundamental societal transformations?

Regarding the first question, the perspective of the reflexive governance concept seems to be slightly regulator-biased, assuming that state actors are equipped with political will and are 'merely' fighting against dispersed governance capacities. However, agrobiodiversity politics is one additional case where we find that governments are depreciating sustainability goals against other public goals. Therefore, we need to consider options of how political will can be strengthened. It might be fruitful to amend the regulator perspective from a bottom-up perspective, and examine, for example, under what conditions political pressure and the discourse strategies of civil society actors and social movements succeed, what role new actors entering the arena can play, and so on. Regarding the second question – whether the recommended strategies will suffice to pave the way for a more sustainable transformation – there are some well-known flaws of participatory methods that need to be worked on. For example, participatory processes as strategies to overcome political deadlocks are known to meet their limits when decisions affect third parties ('not in my backyard' politics).[57] Participatory goal formulation and interactive strategy implementation might also under-deliver when, in the course of fundamental transformations, deep societal conflicts break out: conflicts of objectives, values, and identities, reproduced in power-moulded societal discourses.

While value trade-offs are treated in the analytical framework of the reflexive governance approach, the strategic recommendations do not tackle their consequences on the implementation and success of reflexive strategies. Here, the concept could be further developed. A closer look at power imbalances and their impact on value trade-offs might help to avoid the impression that problem treatment is considered merely a matter of better institutions and procedures. It might actually be more adequate to think about governance as 'conflict regulation' rather than as 'problem treatment'.

## NOTES

1. This chapter is based on results of a research project 'Developing agrobiodiversity – impulses for sustainable crop and livestock breeding' (www.agrobiodiversitaet.net), commissioned by the German Ministry of Science. Parts of the text refer to project publications (IÖW et al. 2004a, 2004b). Special thanks to my colleagues Miriam Dross and Regine Barth for their helpful comments.
2. In Europe: agricultural/food self-sufficiency, low food prices, protection of a number of agricultural products against world market competition, adaptation of farmer income to income levels in industrial sectors.
3. Such as promoting 'rationalisation', specialisation and concentration of farming, development of the processing industry; 'scientification' and mechanisation of agriculture; deliberate uncoupling of agriculture from the natural environment by encouraging use of chemical inputs; creation of huge integrated markets in the EU; intense regulation and protection of these markets through a tight-knit web of productivity-oriented subsidisation.
4. These dimensions of agrobiodiversity are analogous to the customary definition of 'wild' biodiversity (see Wilson 1992; Doherty et al. 2000).
5. This chapter focuses on 'planned agrobiodiversity' (Vandermeer and Perfecto 1995), as opposed to the 'associated agrobiodiversity' of wild relatives, pollinators, symbionts, pests, parasites, predators, competitors and neighbouring habitats that also have a function for agriculture.
6. By the same token, 66 per cent of the mothers of European fattening pigs are crosses of the 'Large White' and 'Landrace' breeds. Only three companies supply the entire world with laying chicken lines, which primarily lead back to the one breed, the Leghorn.
7. It was aesthetic, not agronomic preferences that were decisive among other things, in the colouring of Bentheim Black Pied and Andalusian Spotted pigs.
8. The genotype is the specific genetic makeup (genome) of an individual. It acts as a code for the phenotype of that individual.

9.  Allele are different versions of the same gene that cause different specifications of a trait.
10. Article 5 (iii) and Article 8, UPOV Convention (UPOV 1991).
11. Such as disease and pest resistance, adaptation to harsh conditions and poor quality feed.
12. Famous examples of economic disasters spring from 'genetic monoculture' such as the nineteenth-century Irish potato famine and the US pest Corn Leaf Blight in 1969.
13. Food security means a state 'when all people, at all times, have physical and economic access to sufficient, safe and nutritious food to meet their dietary needs and food preferences for an active and healthy life' (FAO 2004b).
14. In the recent past, distributive conflicts have intensified between these approaches as research grants and resources for professorships are being channelled into molecular biology and genetic engineering, while subjects like taxonomy and ethnobotanics are being neglected (BMVEL 2002: 11; Swiss Biodiversity Forum 2002: 10). Severe losses of basic knowledge impend, threatening not only the monitoring of taxa but also preventing research and development of management strategies.
15. For example, with the help of methods and indicators of molecular biology, genetic variability become visible in cases where other approaches identify a high degree of uniformity.
16. For instance, the taxonomic classification of genetically heterogeneous land races is somewhat arbitrary.
17. For an impression of the opposing assessments compare, for example, Smale (1997), ASSINSEL (1996) against, for example, Thrupp (1997), Vellvé (1993), Fowler and Mooney (1990).
18. Such as the ecosystem services provided by agricultural biodiversity.
19. An example: state aid for the cultivation of old cereals (Emmer, Einkorn) in Austria led to unfair competition with non-subsidised Emmer and Einkorn in Germany, thus hampering their locally adapted cultivation and breeding in the neighbouring country.
20. Deutscher Bauernverband (DBV).
21. The Common Agricultural Policy (CAP) was established in the European Economic Community as early as 1957.
22. However, in the meantime the EP has a say in some specific agrobiodiversity matters as they fall under the heading of health and consumer politics with an EP co-decision procedure. In the 1990s, the EP successfully pushed for the first major EU initiative on agrobiodiversity, Directive 1467/94/EC on genetic resources in food and agriculture.
23. Interestingly enough, agrobiodiversity may count both as 'man-made' and as 'natural' capital. In the logic of the sustainability sciences and their capital forms typology, however, it is more to the point to interpret agrobiodiversity as 'natural' capital.
24. Conservation outside natural habitats or agricultural use, that is, in zoos, botanical gardens and above all in gene banks and by cryo-conservation.
25. The actual cultivation and husbanding, respectively, of crops and livestock.
26. In this case, the conflict of means overlaps with a conflict of values.
27. This applies especially to the 'use strategy' and the more holistic of the two 'development strategies'.
28. As opposed to the technology-oriented transformation of breeding, the envisaged changes in breeding aim at widening the breeding targets, and at reducing the universal spreading of genotypes/genetic traits, etc.
29. The FAO on the international level is an exception.
30. For an account of the conventional, predominant structures of agrobiodiversity governance, see Wolff (2004b), IÖW et al. (2004b), Raustiala and Victor (2004), Kameri-Mbote and Cullet (1999), Bragdon and Downes (1998).
31. CGIAR is the Consultative Group on International Agricultural Research, an association of public and private members supporting 16 research centres worldwide, founded in 1971. Within the reseach process, farmers have been involved in various stages, ranging from the initial documentation of genetic diversity and associated indigenous knowledge (for example, Sandoval-Nazarea 1994) to the identification of methods to assist the continued selection and maintenance of local cultivars (for example, Godbole 2000).

32. The delimitation between participatory research (knowledge production) and participatory breeding (strategy implementation) is in practice not always easy to draw.

33. The background of the project commissioned by the German Ministry of Science is a highly innovative ministry programme on socio-ecological research. The programme is, however, under political pressure to stand its ground. As elsewhere, transdisciplinary research is rather the exception than the rule in the German research scene.

34. The loss at different levels of agrobiodiversity was empirically shown for wheat, chicken and pigs in Germany. Breeding-related, economic, legal and political driving-forces as well as the dominant societal discourses were identified. See www.agrobiodiversitaet.net.

35. The CBD is an international treaty on the protection and sustainable use of biodiversity and on the fair and equitable sharing of benefits arising out of the utilisation of genetic resources. It was adopted in 1992 at the Rio summit and has 188 parties to date.

36. An 'ecosystem' as understood in the CBD means a 'dynamic complex of plant, animal and micro-organism communities and their non-living environment interacting as a functional unit' (Article 2, CBD). Unlike the understanding of 'habitats', this definition does not specify any particular spatial unit or scale.

37. A forerunner for this perspective may be seen in the literature on agroecology (Altieri 1987). With its broad perspective on optimising not the production of commodities but the agroecosystem as a whole it shifted the emphasis in agricultural research away from disciplinary approaches towards multidisciplinary research on complex interactions among and between people, crops, soil and livestock.

38. Only by this can the risks linked to agrobiodiversity loss be avoided and the ecological and agricultural benefits of agrobiodiversity realised. Also, by using agrobiodiversity, on-farm adaptivity of breeding and farming strategies to changing environmental requirements is in-built.

39. Breeding.

40. Processing, retailing, and marketing.

41. The different functions of biosphere reserves are reflected in different protection zones: core areas are devoted to long-term protection; in buffer zones, only activities compatible with the conservation objectives can take place; in an outer transition area sustainable resource management practices are promoted and developed. Stakeholder participation in designing and carrying out the reserve's functions shall be provided for (UNESCO 1996).

42. However, the financial basis of the projects is notoriously unstable.

43. Essential steps of adaptive management are the assessment of a problem, the design, implementation and monitoring of management, its evaluation and adjustment.

44. Despite the value of these principles for agrobiodiversity maintenance, the ecosystem approach within the CBD has not been applied in an integrated way to issues of agricultural biodiversity so far (Dec. VII/11, Annex II). While this is at least partly put down to the fact that agriculture is practised largely on lands under private ownership (ibid.), it might also mirror the comparatively low perception of agricultural biodiversity within the CBD.

45. For example, the State of the World's Plant Genetic Resources Report (FAO 1996) or the FAO Domestic Animal Diversity Information System.

46. For example, the measurement of effective population sizes in livestock populations in Germany (BMVEL 2003).

47. In the context of the (non-binding) International Undertaking on Plant Genetic Resources for Food and Agriculture (IU), the FAO Conference in 1989 defined Farmers' Rights as 'rights arising from the past, present and future contributions of farmers in conserving, improving, and making available plant genetic resources, particularly those in the centres of origin/diversity' (Res. 5/89). As pledge to the recognition of Breeders' Rights the FAO member states recognised Farmers' Rights. However, a substantive definition of those rights was not made. It was envisaged that the realisation of Farmers' Rights should ensure a flow of benefits from the use of plant genetic resources, to farmers and their communities. FAO Resolution 3/91 therefore laid down that 'Farmers' Rights will be implemented through international funding on plant genetic resources,

which will support plant genetic conservation and utilization programmes, particularly, but not exclusively, in the developing countries'. More radical proposals strived for developing Farmers' Rights into some form of property rights equivalent to Plant Breeders' Rights. Both Agenda 21 (1992) and the Global Plan of Action for the Conservation and Sustainable Utilization of Plant Genetic Resources for Food and Agriculture (1996) mention the objective to realise Farmers' Rights.

48. International Treaty on Plant Genetic Resources for Food and Agriculture.
49. Article 9.2, ITPGR.
50. Another rationale of PVS and PBB is the experience in developing countries that new varieties from national or international breeding programmes meet with low acceptance by farmers.
51. Hybrid breeds, and in future potentially GURTs (Genetic Use Restriction Technologies), too.
52. Seeds are distributed on a loan basis and recovered after harvest.
53. Though the introduction of high-yielding varieties and commercial crops has affected the availability of the seeds of traditional cultivars in developing countries.
54. See Table 1.1 in Voß and Kemp Chapter 1, this volume: while the middle row provides the analytical framework ('specific problem features'), the bottom row establishes prescriptive 'strategy requirements'.
55. For example, development of breeding technologies, division of labour and scientification of agriculture, emergence of the environmental and animal welfare movements, change of the farmer's role in modern societies, seed regulation, nutrition-consciousness, farmers' self-determination vs. dependence on multinational agribusiness, North–South distribution of biological diversity and of the technology to make use of it, the specific contribution of women to agrobiodiversity maintenance, international trade politics, the value but lacking remuneration of traditional knowledge, risk awareness in society, scientific discourses and curricula, rural development and global food security.
56. For example, reducing agrobiodiversity loss to a breeding problem.
57. This could be the case for example when participatory national policies on the transformation of agriculture have negative impacts on the global South.

# REFERENCES

Almekinders, C., L. Fresco and P. Struik (1995), 'The need to study variation in agroecosystems', *Netherlands Journal of Agricultural Science*, (43), 127–42.

Altieri, M. (1987), *Agroecology. The Scientific Basis of Alternative Agriculture*, Boulder, CO: Westview Press.

Anderegg, Ralf (1999), *Grundzüge der Agrarpolitik*, Munchen: Oldenbourg.

ASSINSEL (1996), 'ASSINSEL position on maintenance of and access to plant genetic resources for food and agriculture (PGRFA)', adopted in May, Geneva.

ASSINSEL (1997), 'Feeding the 8 billion and preserving the planet', Geneva.

BMVEL (Bundesministerium für Verbraucherschutz, Ernährung und Landwirtschaft) (2003), Nationales Fachprogramm Tiergenetische Ressourcen, Bonn.

BMVEL (Bundesministerium für Verbraucherschutz, Ernährung und Landwirtschaft) (2002), Nationales Fachprogramm zur Erhaltung und nachhaltigen Nutzung pflanzengenetischer Ressourcen landwirtschaftlicher und gartenbaulicher Kulturpflanzen, Bonn.

Bragdon, S. and Downes, D. (1998), 'Recent policy trends and developments related to the conservation, use and development of genetic resources', *Issues in Genetic Resources* 7, 1998.

Brookfield, H. (2001), *Exploring Agrodiversity*, New York: Columbia University Press.

CBD (2003a), 'The impact of trade liberalization on agricultural biological diversity', UNEP/CBD/COP/7/INF/14, 18 December.

CBD (2003b), Recommendations adopted by the Subsidiary Body on Technical and Technological Advice at its ninth meeting, UNEP/CBD/COP/7/4.

CBD (2000a), 'Decision V/5: Agricultural biological diversity: review of phase I of the programme of work and adoption of a multi-year work programme', in UNEP/CBD/COP/5/23, Annex III: Decisions adopted by the Conference of the Parties to the Convention on Biological Diversity at its fifth meeting, Nairobi, 15–26 May, p. 85.

CBD (2000b), 'Decision V/6: Ecosystem approach', in UNEP/CBD/COP/5/23, Annex III: Decisions adopted by the Conference of the Parties to the Convention on Biological Diversity at its fifth meeting. Nairobi, 15–26 May, p. 103.

Cooper, D. (2003), 'The ecosystem approach and agricultural biodiversity', in CIP-UPWARD (ed.), *Conservation and Sustainable Use of Agricultural Biodiversity. A Sourcebook, Vol. II*, Los Banos, Laguna, Philippines: CIP-UPWARD, pp. 56–67.

Crucible Group (1994), *People, plants and patents. The impact of intellectual property on biodiversity, conservation, trade and rural society*, Ottawa: IDRC.

Doherty, M., A. Kearns, G. Barnett, A. Sarre, D. Hochuli, H. Gibb and C. Dickman (2000), 'The interaction between habitat conditions, ecosystem processes and terrestrial biodiversity–a review', Australia: State of the Environment Second Technical Paper Series (Biodiversity), Series 2.

Dreschflegel (2003), *Saaten und Taten 2003*, Witzenhausen.

Dung, N. and SEARICE (2003), 'Applying the Farmer Field Schools Approach to Genetic Resources Conservation', in CIP-UPWARD (ed.), *Conservation and Sustainable Use of Agricultural Biodiversity. A Sourcebook, Vol. II*, Los Banos, pp. 337–43.

El-Hage Scialabba, N., C. Grandi and C. Henatsch (2002), 'Case study no. 4. Organic agriculture and genetic resources for food and agriculture', in FAO: *Biodiversity and the Ecosystem Approach in Agriculture, Forestry and Fisheries*, proceedings of a satellite event on the occasion of the ninth regular session of the Commission on Genetic Resources for Food and Agriculture, Rome, 12–3 October.

etc group (2002), 'Food Sovereignty II,' in *Genotype*, 5 June.

Eyzaguirre P. and M. Iwanaga (eds) (1996), 'Participatory Plant Breeding', proceedings of a workshop on participatory plant breeding, 26–9 July 1995 in Wageningen, the Netherlands. Rome: International Plant Genetic Resources Institute.

FAO (1993), 'Agrobiodiversity: the case for conserving domestic and related animals', FAO fact sheet on the conservation of domestic animal genetic resources, at: http://www.fao.org/docrep/v1650t/v1650t0y.htm

FAO (1996), Report on the State of the World's Plant Genetic Resources for food and agriculture, prepared for the International Technical Conference on Plant Genetic Resources Leipzig, Germany 17–23 June.

FAO (2000), 'Food Security', at: http://www.fao.org/biodiversity/sd/foodsecur.asp.

FAO (2002), 'Biodiversity and the ecosystem approach in agriculture, forestry and fisheries', proceedings of a satellite event on the occasion of the ninth regular session of the Commission on Genetic Resources for Food and Agriculture, Rome 12–13 October 2002.

FAO (2003), 'The GIAHS project', at: www.fao.org/ag/agl/agll/giahs/projsume.stm.

FAO (2004a) 'Loss of domestic animal breeds alarming', press report, 31 March.

FAO (2004b), 'The Special Programme for Food Security,' http://www.fao.org/spfs/ (September).

Fowler, C. and P. Mooney (1990), 'Shattering: food, politics, and the loss of genetic diversity', Tucson: University of Arizona Press.

Führer, Jochen (1997), Interessensvermittlung und Steuerungsproblematik im agrarpolitischen Netzwerk. Zur politischen Einflußnahme des Bauernverbandes und der hessischen Agrarverwaltung. Frankfurt/M. u.a: Peter Lang Verlag.

Girsberger, M. (1999), *Biodiversity and the Concept of Farmer's Rights in International Law*, Berne: Peter Lang Verlag.

Godbole, A. (2000), 'Participatory ethnobotanical research for biodiversity conservation: experiences from Northern Nagaland, India', in E. Friis-Hansen and B. Sthapit (eds), *Participatory approaches to conservation and use of plant genetic resources*, Rome, pp. 173–80.

Golley, F.B. (1993), *A history of the Ecosystem Concept in Ecology*, New Haven and London: Yale University Press.

Grain (2004), 'Confronting contamination. Five reasons to reject co-existence', in *Seedling*, April, 1–4.

Grandin, F. (2003), 'Seed security for Africa's farmers', in *Seedling*, October, 29–32.

Graner, A. (2003), 'Kulturpflanzenevolution: Moderne Pflanzenzüchtung als Biodiversitätssink?', *Nova Acta Leopoldina NF 87*, **328**, 147–61.

GTZ (Gesellschaft für Technische Zusammenarbeit) (2003), 'Sicherung der Agrobiodiversität im ländlichen Raum', Homepage: http://www.gtz.de/agrobiodiv/u-blick/u-blick.htm (July).

Hertler, Christine (1999), 'Aspekte der historischen Eritstehung ron Biodiversitätskonzepten in den Biowissenschaften', in Christoph Görg, Christine Hertler, Engelbert Schramm and Michael Weingarten (eds), *Zugänge Zur Biodiversität: Disziphnäre thematisierungen und Möglichkeiten integnerender Ansätze, metropolis*, Marburg, pp. 39–152.

Holling, C.S. (1978), *Adaptive Environmental Assessment and Management*, Chichester: John Wiley.

IFPRI (2001), *2020 Global Food Outlook. Trends, Alternatives, and Choices*, Washington, DC.

IÖW, Öko-Institut, FU Berlin, LAGS and Schweißfurth-Stiftung (2004a), 'Positioning paper for sustainable plant and animal breeding', joint research project 'Developing Agrobiodiversity' (www.agrobiodiversiaet.net), Berlin.

IÖW, Öko-Institut, FU Berlin, LAGS and Schweißfurth-Stiftung (2004b), Projektbericht des Verbundforschungsprojekts 'Agrobiodiversität entwickeln' in BMBF-Förderschwerpunkt Sozialökologische Forschung, Berlin.

ITDG (2002), Preserving the web of life, ITDG briefing for WSSD available at http://www.ukabc.org/itdg-weboXife.pdf.

Jahn, Thomas and Peter Wehling (1998), 'Gesellschaftliche Naturverhältnisse–Konturen eines theoretischen Konzepts', in Karl-Werner Brand (Hg), *Soziologie und Natur: Thetoretische Perspektiven*, Soziologie und Ökologie Band 2, Reine 'Soziologie und Ökologie', Opladen: Leske an Budrich, 75–93.

Jarvis, D., T. Hodgkin, P. Eyzaguirre, G. Ayad, B. Sthapit and L. Guarino (1998), 'Farmer selection, natural selection and crop genetic diversity: the need for a basic data set', proceedings of a workshop to develop tool and procedures for in situ conservation on-farm, 25–29 August 1997, Rome.

King, A. (2000), *Tools for Participatory Research on Crop and Tree Diversity*, available at http://www.ipgri.cgiar.org/themes/human/Articles/Particip-research2.doc.

Köhler-Rollefson, I. and J. Wanyama, (eds) (2003), 'The Karen Commitment', proceedings of a Conference of Indigenous Livestock Breeding Communities on Animal Genetic Resources, Karen, Kenya, 27–30 October 2003.

Müller, K.J. (1999), 'On-farm improvement and "original seeds" in Germany', in T. Gass, L. Frese, F. Begemann and E. Lipmann (eds), 'Implementation of the Global Plan of Action in Europe – Conservation and Sustainable Utilization of Plant Genetic Resources for Food and Agriculture', proceedings of the European Symposium, 30 June – 3 July 1998, Braunschweig, Germany: Rome.

Pearce, D.W. and G. Atkinson (1995), 'Measuring sustainable development', in D.W. Bromley (ed.), *The Handbook of Environmental Economics*, Oxford: Blackwell.

Perlman, Dan L. and Glenn Adelson (1997), *Biodiversity: Exploring Values and Priorities in Conservation*, Oxford: Blackwell Science.

Ploeg, Jan Douwe van der and Henk Renting (2002), 'Environmental co-operatives reconnect farming, ecology and society', in Bertus Haverkort, Katrien van't Hooft and Wim Hiemstra (eds), *Ancient Roots, New Shoots: Endogenous Development in Practice*, London: Zed Books pp. 222–7.

Raustiala, K. and D. Victor (2004), 'The Regime Complex for Plant Genetic Resources.', *International Organisation*, **58** (2).

Rengalakshmi, R., D. Dhanapal, Oliver King and T. Boopathy (2003), 'Institutionalizing traditional seed exchange networks through community seed bands in Kollihills, India,' In CIP-UPWARD (ed.), *Conservation and Sustainable Use of Agricultural Biodiversity. A Sourcebook, Vol. II*, Los Banos, Laguna, The Philippines, pp. 302–8.

Sandoval-Nazarea, V. (1994), 'Memory banking protocol: A guide for documenting indigenous knowledge associated with traditional crop varieties', Los Banos, Laguna: UPWARD, 1994 Training Document Series: 2.

Settle, W. (2003), 'Case Study No. 11. Ecosystem management in agriculture. Principles and application of the ecosystem approach', in FAO: Biodiversity and the Ecosystem Approach in Agriculture, Forestry and Fisheries. Proceedings of a satellite event on the occasion of the Ninth Regular Session of the Commission on Genetic Resources for Food and Agriculture, Rome, 12–13 October 2002.

Smale, M. (1997), 'The Green Revolution and wheat genetic diversity: some unfounded assumptions', in *World Development*, **25** (8).

Soriano Niebla, J.J. (2002), quoted in N. El-Hage Scialabba, C. Grandi and C. Henatsch, 'Case study no. 4: Organic agriculture and genetic resources for food and agriculture', in *FAO: Biodiversity and the Ecosystem Approach in Agriculture, Forestry and Fisheries*, Proceedings of a satellite event on the occasion of the Ninth Regular Session of the Commission on Genetic Resources for Food and Agriculture, Rome, 12–13 October 2002.

Sthapit, B., A. Subedi, S. Gyawali, D. Jarvis and M. Upadhaya (2003), 'In situ conservation of agricultural biodiversity through participatory plant breeding in Nepal', in CIP-UPWARD (ed.), *Conservation and Sustainable Use of Agricultural Biodiversity. A Sourcebook, Vol. II*, Los Banos, Laguna, The Philippines, pp. 311–21.

Swiss Biodiversity Forum (2002), *Visions in biodiversity research. Towards a new integrative biodiversity science*, availale at http://diversitas.mirror.ac.in/news/visions_pdf.

TAB (Büro für Technikfolgenabschätzung) (1998), 'Gentechnik, Züchtung und Biodiversität', *TAB-Arbeitsbericht*, **55**, Bonn.

Thrupp, L.A. (1997), *Linking biodiversity and agriculture: Challenges and opportunities for sustainable food security*, World Resources Institute, Washington, DC.

UNESCO (1996), 'Statutory Framework of the World Network of Biosphere Reserves', UNESCO General Conference.

UPOV (1991), 'International Convention for the Protection of New Varieties of Plants', (UPOV Convention).

Vandermeer, J. H. and I. Perfecto (1995), *Breakfast of Biodiversity: The Truth about Rainforest Destruction*, Oakland, CA: The Institute for Food and Development Policy.

Vangen, O. (2003), 'Modern breeding programmes', available at http://www.nordgen.org/download/bokartikkel-odd.doc.

Vellvé, Renée (1993), 'The decline of diversity in European agriculture', in *The Ecologist*, **23** (2): 64–9.

VEN (2004), 'Samenliste 2004: Verein zur Erhaltung der Nutzpflanzenvielfalt e.V.', Schandelah.

VERN (2003), 'Compendium: Verein zur Erhaltung und Rekultivierung von Nutzpflanzen in Brandenburg', Greiffenberg.

Von Brook, R. (2002), 'Biodiversität: Diskurs grüne Gentechnik des BMVEL'.

WCED (Word Commission on Environment and Development) (1987), *Our Common Future*, Brundtland Report.

Wetterich, F. (1999), 'Biological diversity of livestock and crops: useful classification and appropriate agri-environmental indicators', in OECD (ed.), *Agriculture and Biological Diversity: Developing Indicators for Policy Analysis*, proceedings from an OECD Expert Meeting. Zurich, Switzerland, November, pp. 40–52.

Wiethaler, C., R. Oppermann, and E. Wyss (2000), *Ökologische Pflanzenzüchtung und Biologische Vielfalt von Kulturpflanzen*, Bonn: NABU.

Wilson, Edward O. (ed.) (1988), *Biodiversity*, Washington, DC: National Academy Press.

Wissen, Markus (2004a): 'Akteure und Interessen im Problemfeld Agrobiodiversität', in Institut für ökologische Wirtschaftsforschung, Öko-Institut e.V., Schweisfurth-Stiftung, Freie Universität Berlin, Landesanstalt für Großschutzgebiete (Hrsg.): 'Agrobiodiversität entwickeln! Handlungsstrategien für eine nachhaltige Tier- und Pflanzenzucht', Endbericht, Berlin 2004, available at www.agrobiodiversitaet.net.

Wissen, Markus (2004b), 'Biodiversität und demokratische Ressourcenkontrolle – Vielfalt als Nebeneffekt', *Politische Ökologie* 90/2004, Munich: Oekan Verlag.

Wolff, F. (2004a), 'Legal factors driving agrobiodiversity loss', *Environmental Law Network International (elni), Review*, pp. 25–36.

Wolff, F. (2004b), Staatlichkeit im Wandel – Aspekte kooperativer Umweltpolitik. Munich.

Wolff, F. and Petschow, U. (2004), 'Der Konflikt um genetische Ressourcen in der Landwirtschaft', *Jahrbuch Ökologie 2005*, Munich.

# Conclusions

# 16. Reflexive governance: a view on an emerging path

## Jan-Peter Voß, René Kemp and Dierk Bauknecht

## INTRODUCTION

This concluding chapter is more than a summary of the arguments presented in the preceding chapters. One could say that we take a reflexive approach to the theme of the book. We reconsider the ideas from the Introduction in the light of the ideas it has prompted in the chapters. In this way, we can rework a concept of reflexive governance that incorporates feedback from theoretical as well as more practical areas of application. This feedback promotes learning with respect to the concept of reflexive governance. Experiences that are gathered on the basis of reflexive governance reproduce and modify the conceptual framework and shape further experience – they are an example of 'conceptual structuration', to paraphrase Giddens (1984/1986). This concluding chapter can thus be seen as a 'view on an emerging path' of thinking and practice in societal governance and problem solving.[1]

We proceed by first discussing the relationship between sustainable development and reflexive governance in more depth. Here, the initial hypothesis from the Introduction becomes substantiated by evidence from the chapters. Sustainable development serves as a label under which a fundamental transformation of governance, in the context of reflexive modernisation, is politically negotiated. Seen in this light, sustainable development is indeed more than an empty phrase; it is both a symptom and a catalyst of what Beck (1994) describes as reflexive modernisation.

A second point is a more explicit concern for the quality of the outcome of processes of reflexive governance. Does reflexive governance actually produce better results? This question refers to the need for criteria of procedural quality, since it is not possible to arrive at a solid definition of the 'right' outcome of problem handling for sustainable development. Such criteria can support an assessment of reflexive governance without getting trapped in the temptation to predefine the results for learning processes and thereby negate the very strength of the approach.

A third point is that we add to the question of the location of reflexive governance: in which types of interaction and at what level of social organisation does reflexive governance take place? In this respect, we introduce different levels as a conceptual extension to reflexive governance. This view acknowledges that the levels at which problems are addressed and the interplay of governance processes across different levels are an important dimension. In this volume, both Beck and Wolff show this aspect with respect to transnational governance as a response to the limits of political organisation in nation states. Other chapters in this volume, like those of Loibl and Whitelegg that discuss knowledge production, show how reflexive governance in research plays a role on both a macro-level of programme management and a micro-level of project management.

As a fourth point, we add a fundamental qualification to the concept of reflexive governance by introducing the efficacy paradox. This concept refers to the contradicting requirements of opening up and closing down in social problem-solving processes (see also Stirling 2005). On the one hand, problem-oriented interactions need to be opened to take account of the interaction of diverse factors, values and interests. This is necessary to produce robust knowledge and strategies. On the other hand, selection of relevant factors, decisions about ambiguous evaluations and convergence of interests are necessary to take decisions and act. The strategy elements of reflexive governance, as presented in the Introduction, address the need to open up various specialised kinds of problem solving to allow for integrated assessment and coordinated strategies. The efficacy paradox draws attention to the fact that effective governance requires these strategy elements to be complemented with appropriate strategies to reduce complexity and achieve stable strategies. The proposed way to deal with these paradoxical requirements is to combine opening up with closing down, for example, by organising problem-handling processes in sequences of opening up and closing down (compare the discussion of exploration and exploitation in March 1991).

At the conclusion of this final chapter, we summarise the concept of reflexive governance and formulate our position on its overall potential for furthering the societal search for sustainable development. As a last step towards the unfolding of the concept of reflexive governance, we outline an agenda for further research and practical experimentation.

# REFLEXIVE GOVERNANCE AND SUSTAINABLE DEVELOPMENT

Reflexive governance was presented in the Introduction to this volume as a twofold concept, both a condition of governance in the modern world and a specific strategic orientation that results from this condition. The first meaning refers to the self-confrontation of governance. This can be seen in the increasing devotion of governing capacities to problems which are themselves caused by governing. That is to say, governance to a large extent involves repair work for the unintended consequences of prior attempts at shaping societal development. This meaning of 'self-confrontation' is analogous to the meaning of reflexive modernisation as modernity confronted with itself as introduced by Beck and others (Beck et al. 1994; Beck et al. 2003).

A second meaning refers to new kinds of strategies, processes and institutions which can be observed emerging under this condition of self-confrontation. This has to do partly with the reflection of the condition of self-confrontation by unintended consequences and the development of deliberate responses to it. In the Introduction we undertook a systematic reflection of the sources for reflexivity (self-confrontation) in governance. This resulted in a set of reflexive strategies labelled integrated knowledge production, experimentation and adaptivity of strategies, anticipation of long-term effects, interactive participatory goal formulation and interactive strategy implementation.[2]

In practice, governance arrangements that include these reflexive strategies usually evolve from repeated attempts at grappling with very specific problems rather than from the theoretical recognition of reflexivity (self-confrontation). For example, interactive technology assessment aims at avoiding conflicts between advocates and opponents at a late stage of technology development; transdisciplinary research seeks to cope with the limitations of disciplinary academic science that show up when laboratory science is applied to real world problems; cooperative policy networks are a response to the interference of actor strategies that may spoil policy implementation. From within the social processes in which these new modes of governance evolve it is not always visible that the problems they address are themselves caused by existing governance structures which evoke narrow and myopic problem treatment and unintended repercussions: institutional arrangements of technology development in which development work is dissociated from social needs and contexts of use; self-referential science dynamics supported by the institutional demarcation of knowledge fields and academic peer review; or departmentalised policy making not being able to take account of interaction across policy areas. If viewed from a broader perspective, however, the emergence of various new modes of governance appears to follow a similar pattern. This becomes articulated by the concept of reflexive governance: governance learning is being shaped by the experience of unintended feedback of its own working (compare with first-order reflexivity in note 2 to this chapter). These experiences lead into adapting cognitive concepts and institutional arrangements so that they transcend the boundaries of closed-up problem solving routines. Conventional governance processes are opened up for interaction with their contexts and develop capacity for mutual adaptation of strategy and context before the damage is done. Social concerns and factors of influence that have hitherto been externalised become incorporated in problem definition and strategies. New principles such as precaution, experimentation, learning, participation and integration reflect the possibility of unintended feedback and error of any rigorous analysis and strategy by translating it into fruitful interaction with dynamic contexts of real world implementation (compare with second-order reflexivity in note 2).

While the concept of reflexivity is seldom referred to in these processes of governance learning, the concept of sustainable development plays an important role. In fact, reference to sustainable development is what governance changes in these various fields of practice have in common. The chapters in this book offer examples from research policy and management (Whitelegg; Loibl), risk assessment (Stirling), regional development (Sendzimir et al.), sectoral planning (Kemp, Loorbach; Voß et al.; Weber), technology development (Smith; van Vliet; Spaeth et al.), and agricultural policy (Grin, Wolff). Sustainable development provides a broader framework and discursive context to the particular problems in each of these problem areas. The systems perspective, together with the integration of diverging social goals and the long-term approach, are outstanding characteristic elements of sustainable development, regardless of the substantial openness of the concept. They provide a general orientation in searching for ways to handle recurrent problems and provide a legitimate reference in pushing for new governance forms. The notion of sustainable development thus serves as a catalyst for the exploration of new forms of governance – and is itself kept alive and becomes materialised by references made to it.

As such, sustainable development can be understood as the *chiffre* under which the structural changes that are sociologically conceptualised as reflexive modernisation become politically negotiated. Sustainable development is an aspect of reflexive modernisation, it works as a change agent, a vehicle and a mediator for governance changes towards reflexive governance. In this respect, sustainable development is not something empty, irrelevant or without practical value or factual implications as is sometimes claimed. Rather, it is indeed an important driver of societal change.

The notion of sustainable development has 'succeeded' to the extent that it has condensed the problem of the self-undermining side-effects of modernity into a slogan that triggers communication across different domains and levels of social action. Even if the substantial meaning is disputed, the attribute 'sustainable' always works to contextualise particular actions, concepts, strategies and so on within a broader environment. Those who claim to act in a sustainable manner are expected to justify their actions with respect to consequences in society and nature. Calling something 'sustainable' means taking into account possible side-effects – both immediate and long term – and their impact on the viability of society as a whole. As such, it can be seen as a late modern version of the concept of the common good that has now become widened to include the natural conditions of human well-being and therefore encompasses a different time structure. This is a qualitative change in the concept. Concerns for more complex interactions, ignorance, irreversibility and path dependency are introduced to the search for the common good. Sustainability signifies that what we think and do now may enable or restrict thinking and acting in the future. This becomes most visible in the degradation of global ecosystems. But it also refers to the shaping of social structures through, for example, institution building, industrial subsidies or education. In comparison to the common good, the notion of sustainable development thus strengthens a dynamic, historical understanding of society whose values and knowledge undergo change. But this also means that the agent of governance gets displaced from its Archimedean point, outside of the developmental context. Instrumental rationalisation and steering are not applicable under these conditions. In this way, references to sustainability trigger a search for new governance forms that take a learning-oriented approach towards steering.

Sustainable development and reflexive governance clearly make life more complicated and make conflicts more obvious at an early stage. What were once externalities become interdependencies and trade-offs that are explicitly considered and negotiated. The perceptions and interests of actors from other realms of society, which were bracketed out in specialised problem solving, now need to be addressed. Not surprisingly, sustainability is not easy to operationalise into consensual strategies. It has a radical impact on social institutions, practices and processes in which problems are perceived and acted upon. It calls for a fundamental reorientation of governance (see especially the chapters by Beck, Grin, Rip and Stirling, this volume).

By articulating reflexive governance as a phenomenon that is actually happening and by elaborating the rationale behind it, we take part in the process of governance change occurring under the heading of sustainable development. Reflexive governance can serve as a conceptual underpinning for diverse experiments with new forms of governance for sustainable development. It can contribute to the discussion on institutional sustainability as a possible 'fourth pillar' of sustainable development in addition to ecological, social and economic sustainability (Spangenberg, 2004). As such, reflexive governance could offer a concept by which diverse local and problem-specific processes of governance innovation can be connected with each other. It facilitates the discussion of common underlying problem structures and methodical experiences of tackling them. It could, for example, be interesting to relate the experiences with integrated knowledge production that are made in transdisciplinary research, climate policy making and technology assessment. Reflexive governance provides a common language, a cognitive platform through which reflexive governance innovations can find synergies and develop momentum in transforming established institutions (see Grin, this volume, on the role of such linkages between innovative practices).

## POLITICS AND THE QUALITY OF OUTCOMES

The elements of reflexive strategy that were presented in the Introduction refer to particular ways of organising governance processes. However, they do not prescribe any specified results that are to be achieved for sustainable development such as emissions targets or income indices. This is due to the recognition that uncertainty and ambivalence are features of the operationalisation of sustainability. For example, what is the right trade-off between emissions reduction, social equality and economic stability? Reflexive governance therefore asks for open-ended searching and learning.

If the outcome of reflexive governance cannot be defined, how can we then know if it works? One could, for pragmatic reasons, refer to politically defined goals such as the Kyoto targets for reducing greenhouse gas emissions. However, this does not resolve whether current political structures actually produce sustainable targets, or whether, for example, more substantial greenhouse gas reductions might not be necessary, as many scientists argue. To take current political goals, concepts and measures as points of reference for the evaluation of outcomes would 'short circuit' the evaluation of governance, which itself contains particular dynamics of political discourse. The potential of reflexive governance for open-ended learning with respect to goals and targets, would be blocked. What has to be evaluated is the actual working of reflexive governance arrangements, not predefined outcomes.

A concern for evaluation as such is important, however, because reflexive governance arrangements can be misused. As mentioned in many places throughout the chapters of this volume (for example, Rip, Stirling, Smith, Wolff), the reality of reflexive governance, of course, includes opportunistic behaviour, rhetoric and power struggles no less than it includes collective problem handling, dialogue and cooperation.

Therefore care needs to be taken to prevent any particular interests from dominating reflexive governance. For this purpose, one could refer to the collective interest and cooperative orientation of participating actors as a precondition for reflexive governance. In this respect, one could think of procedural settings, selection criteria for participants and the long-term perspective of sustainable development that make it possible for this precondition to be met. This would emphasise the 'rational discourse' dimension (in a Habermasian sense) of reflexive governance. At the same time, however, it would make the process vulnerable. The preconditions of rational discourse are not very widespread in reality, as many critics of Habermas argue, and their creation cannot be taken for granted.

To understand reflexive governance simply in terms of rational argumentation and consensual understanding, however, misses an important dimension of the interaction process. This is the mutual adaptation of actors' knowledge and strategies and the formation of a common understanding of problems, goals and strategies that takes place even when actors contest each other and use arguments merely strategically to gain an advantage in the power game. As long as actors are compelled to articulate and defend their problem analysis, goals and strategies with respect to a common focus such as public acceptance or a political decision to be taken, patterns of argumentation will become connected with each other because no one can afford to ignore relevant points that others bring up. The resulting patterns of strategy will be more robust than if they were dreamed up within the separate worlds of each actor alone. They are tempered in anticipatory interaction, rather than in real-time, possibly irreversible trial and error. Even if reflexive governance helps to articulate conflicts and cleavages, it furthers social learning. Its outcome represents a new shared view on reality even if it contains dissimilar problem definitions, goals and strategies. Actors may commonly refer to this reality and position themselves and others within it. Without interaction, this variety would remain unknown. Thus, in addition to operating through conscious deliberation, the reflexive strategies presented in the Introduction also work as coordination mechanisms behind actors' backs. Arie Rip nicely elaborates a similar dynamic in his treatment of 'controversies as informal technology assessment' (1986).

For mutual adaptation in controversies, however, as well as for consensus-oriented deliberation, it is important that the interaction process be open to diverse perspectives and that these perspectives be articulated on an equal footing. This is what has to be accomplished by procedural rules and moderation of searching and learning processes in reflexive governance. This is also what can be taken as criteria for process evaluations of reflexive governance.

With respect to the evaluation of outcomes, further work needs to be done on indicators that can measure structural change independently of a predefined direction or end state in which such changes would go. Change indicators would allow the effect of social learning in reflexive governance to be monitored without contradicting the open-endedness of sustainable development. They could refer to problem definitions, actor constellations, interaction practices, strategy options and so on. Indicators are necessary to avoid losing direction during long and ramified projects of transformation. Without such indicators, attempts at system innovation may become stifled after an enthusiastic starting phase because results are not immediately visible. This might happen just as important cognitive and institutional changes begin underneath the surface performance gauged by output indicators. The five strategy requirements of reflexive governance presented in the Introduction to this volume, may serve as a starting point for the development of such institutional change indicators for sustainable development.

Whatever the specific result of any further work on evaluating reflexive governance, it is important that its particular qualities are taken as a reference:

- **Achieving societal ends**:  first, reflexive strategies seek to avoid repercussions from unintended effects and second-order problems and thereby contribute more effectively than narrow problem-solving approaches to achieving societal ends. This does not happen by gaining acceptance for predetermined solutions but through the exploration of a broad set of alternatives with respect to a diverse set of criteria.
- **Learning about ends**:  second, reflexive strategies provide platforms for interaction that complement conventional political decision making. Interactions are not restricted to institutionalised policy fields, but instead evaluate and reconsider societal ends against the background of diverse concepts and values. Experiments with strategies may yield experiences that lead to a reassessment of needs and interests or to identification of other ways of meeting them.
- **Quality of problem definitions**:  third, reflexive strategies increase the quality of problem definitions by actively involving diverse viewpoints – even from actors who have limited capacities to articulate

and press for their ideas and perceptions of problems in public discourse. Participatory knowledge production and strategy development and implementation are based on insight into social pluralism and distributed intelligence – an insight that relates fundamentally to the ideal of democracy.

## SHIFTING SCALES: MULTI-LEVEL REFLEXIVE GOVERNANCE

In the Introduction, we raised the question of *how* to deal with uncertainty, ambivalence and distributed control in sustainability issues. In the very first chapter, Beck points out the need to explore also *where* such reflexive governance strategies should be located. Beck argues that collective political action is no longer restricted to nation states and the system of international relations between them. Rather, he sees reflexive governance approaches as transgressing former borders and boundaries. This is very much in line with the five strategy elements of reflexive governance that have been explored throughout the book. They are all about bringing into interaction what has formerly been separated – integrating scientific disciplines and practical knowledge through transdisciplinary knowledge production, integrating distributed action strategies and integrating long-term systemic effects into today's action. Transgressing the boundaries of the nation state is just another dimension of integration, which brings nationally-bound political processes into interaction. In this way, factors and effects that come from or go beyond the boundaries of nation states become internalised.

Yet the question of where governance should and could take place goes beyond this. It is not merely about transgressing geographical boundaries to deal with the global problem of sustainable development. Rather, it is about finding the right place and space to tackle specific problems of sustainable development – reaching from global to local approaches. Given that governance in practice is oriented towards specific problems such as the transformation of energy provision or agriculture, spaces for interaction need to be geared towards the problems and cannot be restricted to conventional institutional and geographical boundaries of problem solving. Much like transdisciplinary research projects, which draw upon disciplinary research but need to be reassembled according to the problem they have to deal with, reflexive governance cannot be limited to existing institutional settings, but may need to establish a setting that is appropriate for the relevant problem. In short, the interaction space needs to be congruent with the problem space. This congruency could be introduced as a sixth strategy element of reflexive governance that covers all three dimensions of problem solving: problem analysis, goal formulation, and strategy development and implementation.

The chapters in this volume have uncovered a number of insights as to the level of social organisation at which reflexive governance is taking place and the creation of problem-specific institutional settings. The chapter by Kemp and Loorbach provides one example of tailor-made problem-solving spaces, namely the transition arena, which they call 'a new institution for interaction' and 'an open and dynamic network in which different perspectives, different expectations and different agendas are confronted, discussed and aligned where possible'. Interestingly, the transition arena is very fluid, changing its size, task and participant profile throughout the transition management process and thereby creating a congruency between the shape of the transition arena and the problem on its agenda. Kemp and Loorbach also introduce a concept that has been referred to in several other chapters. They differentiate between three levels of socio-technical systems: macro-landscape, meso-regimes and micro-niches. Reflexive governance can in principle be located on all of these levels. Smith describes two approaches that have chosen the niche level as the appropriate place to foster system change. Other approaches, such as sustainability foresight, suggested by Voß et al., highlight the need to coordinate niche activities and developments on the regime level.

Looking at the chapters by Loibl and Whitelegg, we find another example of how reflexive governance can be placed on different levels and how these interact. While Loibl analyses reflexive governance *within* research projects, Whitelegg looks at the reflexive governance *of* research programmes. The latter includes both the governance of the programme itself – for example, the learning/adaptability of programmes or participation of stakeholders to define priority areas – and the promotion of reflexive governance within research projects. The chapter by Loibl also points us to the fractal and nested nature of reflexive governance that operate at different levels. This chapter focuses on one of the five reflexive governance strategies set out in the Introduction, namely, integrated knowledge production. Yet while exploring the practice of transdisciplinary knowledge production as an example of a reflexive strategy element in societal governance, it turns out that other reflexive strategy elements are also at work in the governance of the research process itself. Those elements are needed to deal with complexity, heterogeneity and distributed resources in transdisciplinary research processes.

While it is an important insight that reflexive governance can and must be developed on different levels, it is mainly the chapters in the section on strategies for sustainable system transformation that emphasise interactions between system levels. In their description of the transition management approach, Kemp and Loorbach, for example, describe transitions as a 'cascade of innovations at different levels', all of which may be governed by reflexive governance arrangements. In a similar vein, Voß et al. present their sustainability foresight approach as a macro nexus to connect various innovation processes with broader structural transformations on a sector level.

Shifting governance levels, linking governance levels or creating new governance spaces to grasp relevant viewpoints, factors and resources of specific sustainable development problems as they appear would therefore need to be added as a complementary requirement applying to the other five elements of reflexive strategy.

## THE EFFICACY PARADOX OF HANDLING COMPLEXITY

The previous section introduced multiple levels of problem handling as just one more dimension in which reflexive governance requires an opening up of problem-solving processes to integrate relevant factors that could be responsible for unexpected adverse results if they are not incorporated into problem definition, goals and strategies. A review of the various policy and management practices through which reflexive governance becomes implemented, however, also draws attention to an inherent problem connected to the opening up of governance processes for comprehensive problem appraisal and robust strategies: although necessary to respond adequately to the problem of sustainable development, too much complexity, ambivalence and interaction severely reduces action capacities and may block deliberate attempts at shaping societal development.

Appraisal of this situation reveals a dilemma of reflexive governance: the contradicting requirements of opening up and closing down (Stirling, 2005). Opening up is necessary to grasp adequately the factual embedding of decision making and problem solving in systemic contexts. Closing down is necessary to reduce complexity in order to avoid anomy and retain the ability to act – even if it is revealed as illusionary in its modernist form (Rip, this volume). It is a dilemma that is rooted in limited capacities to handle complexity.

The concept of sustainable development would require taking a truly holistic approach to embrace the whole world, but there are immediate restrictions. In our framework of reflexive governance these limitations are effective in all three dimensions of problem handling, but in different ways. In problem analysis, they are linked to cognitive limitations in processing complexity. In goal formulation they are linked to the need of at least temporarily defined goals for the development of action strategies. In strategy development they are linked to limited resources for the exploitation of possible options. In all three dimensions, opening up in terms of the number and heterogeneity of participating actors decreases the probability of achieving agreement and increases transaction costs.

This situation could be interpreted in such a way that it reveals the futility of sustainable development and reflexive governance and leads back to the fragmented practices of muddling through within the framework of established institutions. Isn't it better to be ignorant of systemic interactions, trade-offs and interfering strategies that cause unintended effects and second-order problems than to be unable to act at all? Reflexive strategies do not eradicate uncertainty, ignorance, ambiguity and interfering activities. Rather, they only bring them to our attention. According to such an interpretation, reflexive governance may not offer anything in terms of practical action.

This line of reasoning, however, takes us back again to where we started in the introductory chapter. It is widely acknowledged that there is a necessity for more than muddling through and there are good reasons why better results can be achieved by applying reflexive strategies. But there is no easy, straightforward way to apply the principle of opening up. Moreover, reflexive strategies include ambivalences. In principle, the underlying dilemma cannot be resolved, but a balanced employment of reflexive strategy elements can help to avoid collateral damage, undesired path dependencies, lock-ins, myopic or biased assessments or collision of actor strategies. By raising awareness of fundamental uncertainties and ambivalences, they suggest a more cautionary approach towards shaping societal development. In so doing, they can reduce the probability of second-order problems but cannot eliminate them.

The issue of the erosion of action capacities as a possible detrimental effect and limit to the opening up of governance processes is important. It qualifies the basic concept of reflexive governance as outlined in the Introduction by stating a meta-requirement to keep the balance between two extremes. Instead of one-dimensionally proposing 'the more opening up the better', it helps us refine our set of reflexive strategies by introducing a counter image of complete fluidity and openness in which any kind of strategic action must suffocate. Reflexive governance thus becomes an 'as-well-as' concept in itself, a concept that entails combining and balancing two or more truths rather than deciding for one of them (compare Beck 1993, p. 9). It is, therefore, not a question of choosing between keeping up action capacity or opening problem handling for contextualisation, but a matter of pursuing both. Against the background of the above discussion, this sounds like a paradox. We believe it is one. It can be called the 'efficacy paradox of complexity'. In order to assure the efficacy of strategies in complex contexts, it is necessary to consider a wide variety of aspects and stay flexible to adapt to unexpected events. At the same time, it is necessary to reduce the number of aspects considered and decide on certain options in order to produce output. This paradox cannot be resolved without losing out on one side or the other. With respect to action strategy, reflexive governance thus implies a dilemma.

We think that it is fruitful to recognise the paradox, not to resolve it, but to work with it as suggested by Ravetz (2003:819). 'Another approach to paradoxes, characteristic of other cultural traditions', Ravetz argues, 'is to accept them and attempt to learn from them about the limitations of one's existing intellectual structures'. In this sense, it can work like the 'ironies' suggested by Rip (this volume).

The efficacy paradox has to be faced in strategies for sustainable development. It could be one of the reasons why we have made so little progress with sustainable development. Opening up of the discussion on future societal development towards a broader set of considerations and wider system boundaries in terms of levels of policy, geographical boundaries and the inclusion of future generations goes hand in hand with increasing difficulties to act. To deal with this paradox, the typology that we develop in the following section may appear as a useful first step. It allows decision makers and analysts to deal with the paradox conceptually.

## COMBINING OPENING UP AND CLOSING DOWN IN REFLEXIVE GOVERNANCE

We propose to qualify the concept of reflexive strategies proposed in the Introduction with an explicit requirement to balance the opening up of governance processes for incorporating uncertainty, ambivalence and distributed control with a reciprocal requirement to close down governance processes to enable decision and action. This task of balancing two contradicting requirements to handle fruitfully the efficacy paradox is more of an art than a science. We cannot offer any precise method for diagnosis or a tool kit by which a specific adequate combination of opening up and closing down for each real world governance situation could be determined. Instead, what we can do is sketch out, in a very rough manner, some generic forms in which opening up and closing down can be combined. Our sketch is based on the review of empirical governance practices and theoretical discussions in the literature and the chapters of this book. It may be helpful to consider a spectrum of possibilities when designing governance strategies and institutional arrangements.

First, a differentiated look is needed at what it is that is going to be opened up or closed down. Here, we can refer to the three dimensions of problem solving against the background of which reflexive governance was discussed in the Introduction: problem analysis, goal formulation and strategy implementation. Opening up can occur in all these dimensions or in only one or two of them. For problem analysis, opening up would mean extending the system boundaries and increasing the range and diversity of factors and interactions considered in analysing problem causes, dynamics and effects of interventions. For energy forecasting, for example, this could entail an opening up of economic models to include the strategic behaviour of market actors, political processes that influence regulation, public opinion, resource exploitation and climate change. In the dimension of goal formulation, opening up refers to the revising of given targets by taking into account a broader spectrum of values and facing trade-offs that have to be made. For the energy example, this could mean simply taking into account the established goals of economic efficiency, security of supply and environmental soundness for each policy decision and not letting each ministry follow its own preferred goal. But it could also mean broadening the goal catalogue with values such as aesthetic acceptability and democratic participation in energy provision. In the dimension of strategy implementation finally, opening up refers to a widening of the range of measures and options that are considered and implemented for problem handling. In the energy example this would entail developing and experimenting with a diversity of radically new policy instruments – such as tradeable energy efficiency obligations or participatory technology development – and technologies such as solar electricity import or micro co-generation.

In principle, it is possible that governance processes are opened up in all of these dimensions at once. Problem definitions are called into question, goals are scrutinised and the set of assumed solutions is revised. One possibility to reduce the disruptive effect of opening up on strategic capabilities, however, is to focus sequentially on each of these dimensions, not on all at once. In any case, because of the interdependencies between goals, problem definitions and measures, opening up in one dimension will most likely induce similar processes in other dimensions.

Across all three dimensions of problem solving, an important aspect of opening up refers to the number and heterogeneity of actors involved in problem analysis, goal formulation or strategy development/and/ implementation. Eventually, opening up must be linked in one way or the other to extended participation, since knowledge about different problem aspects and values as well as resources for making measures and options work are distributed among different actors. Ultimately, it is the diversity of world views and problem perceptions held by different actors that is the key trigger for opening up governance processes. At the same time, however, it is also the key trigger for controversy and misunderstanding, which makes governance difficult and seemingly ineffective.

In the following paragraphs, we describe schematically different combinations of opening up and closing down. In doing this, we refer to problem analysis, goal formulation, strategy development/and/implementation and actor participation as the four aspects in which opening up and closing down can take place. In principle, there are very many different ways of combining opening up and closing down in governance and problem handling. One could therefore develop a highly differentiated typology. Here, we restrict ourselves to the presentation of four types (see Figure 16.1). Two of them are the extreme types of totally closed and totally open governance processes: 'problem solving with blinkers' and 'erosion of strategic capabilities'. These serve to delimit the spectrum of possibilities. The other two types are combinations in which a phase of opening up is followed by a phase of closing down.

In one of the types, 'sequential opening and closing', the complexity that has been built up through widening system boundaries, considering diverse values and exploring a range of alternative measures and options is pragmatically reduced again into one coherent framework of problem definition, goals and options for problem-handling. The strategy resulting from this framework can be expected to be more robust because a variety of perspectives has been explored and a context-oriented and situational adaptation of the problem-handling framework has taken place. Nevertheless, the selection and priority setting that has taken place in closing down the governance process towards one consistent strategy is still vulnerable to unexpected side-effects. Only probing the strategy under real-world conditions can disclose all its effects and hint at requirements for further revising.

The other type of opening up and closing down, 'exploring experiments', differs in that a variety of problem-handling frameworks rather than a single framework is developed into a portfolio of strategy experiments. In this way, closing down does not have to end up with one 'best possible strategy'. Instead, the uncertainty, ambivalence and diversity of options experienced in the first phase of opening up can be translated into a set of alternative frameworks of problem definition, goals and options. It is not possible to decide *a priori* which one of these frameworks is better adapted to sustainable development. Instead, they induce variation and offer experience from which society can learn what sustainable development is. The unintended side-effects from each experiment can be compared with each other. If one strategy appears impractical or too risky, others can be followed and further developed.

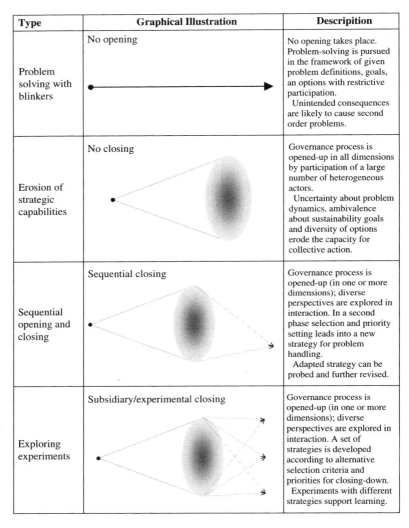

| Type | Graphical Illustration | Descripition |
|------|------------------------|--------------|
| Problem solving with blinkers | No opening | No opening takes place. Problem-solving is pursued in the framework of given problem definitions, goals, an options with restrictive participation.<br>Unintended consequences are likely to cause second order problems. |
| Erosion of strategic capabilities | No closing | Governance process is opened-up in all dimensions by participation of a large number of heterogeneous actors.<br>Uncertainty about problem dynamics, ambivalence about sustainability goals and diversity of options erode the capacity for collective action. |
| Sequential opening and closing | Sequential closing | Governance process is opened-up (in one or more dimensions); diverse perspectives are explored in interaction. In a second phase selection and priority setting leads into a new strategy for problem handling.<br>Adapted strategy can be probed and further revised. |
| Exploring experiments | Subsidiary/experimental closing | Governance process is opened-up (in one or more dimensions); diverse perspectives are explored in interaction. A set of strategies is developed according to alternative selection criteria and priorities for closing-down.<br>Experiments with different strategies support learning. |

*Figure 16.1   Types of combining opening-up and closing-down in governance*

This brief overview of different combinations of opening up and closing down in governance illustrates the efficacy paradox and indicates a direction in which ways can be found to cope with it.

## A FEW FINAL WORDS

Having arrived at the end of the book, perhaps it is good to state what we hope to have achieved. First and foremost, we hope we have generated an interest in the very idea of reflexive governance, realising that this is only a first step. Second, we hope we have shown that reflexive governance represents a radical innovation with respect to dominant 'modernist' regimes of governance and that it needs to be taken up by theorists. And third, we hope we have shown that reflexive governance is 'for real' – that it already exists in various forms.

In the Introduction we introduced five strategies which can be derived from the reflexive governance perspective (integrated knowledge production, experimentation and adaptivity of strategies, anticipation of long-term effects, interactive participatory goal formulation and interactive strategy implementation). In this concluding chapter we added the congruency of governance and problem space as a sixth strategy element. We suggest that these six strategies are central elements of a conceptual repertoire which can further the development of practices of reflexive governance. Their application injects second-order reflexivity into governance processes, leading actors to reconsider their embedding in wider system contexts and review the problem definitions, goals, options and strategies coming out of it. In this way, governance gets prepared to deal with the first-order reflexivity of modernisation, the spiralling up of problems and problem solving as a result of unexpected side-effects.

The different chapters have demonstrated that existing governance systems already include elements of reflexivity that go beyond the confrontation of social groupings with unintended consequences. There are indeed many instances, in diverse areas of practice, of new governance approaches based on the reflection and anticipation of unintended consequences, in which the handling of uncertainty, ambivalence and distributed control plays a central role. In the terminology proposed at the beginning of this chapter, one could say that there is broad evidence for the emergence of second-order reflexivity on top of the first-order reflexivity of societal development. As a fourth and final point, we hope that we have been able to show how these quite fundamental changes in society are linked to the concept of sustainable development, which plays an important role as a catalyst of social discourse and change.

An unexpected outcome of this book is the suggestion of thinking about different combinations of opening up and closing down in governance processes, which we believe is a useful scheme for thinking about the efficacy paradox and handling it in a practical way. The efficacy paradox is an intricate problem for sustainable development. In simple terms, it means that to be able to act you must reduce complexity, which, however, easily leads to the neglect of long-term system effects. On the other hand, consideration of all possible effects reduces the capacity to act. There is a clear tension and strategic dilemma. The paradox must somehow be dealt with. The different ways to combine opening up with closing down present central elements of a conceptual repertoire that helps to do this. Further research on indicators for procedural quality and for the monitoring of institutional changes towards reflexive governance is needed. This book is a first outline of a new theoretical perspective that may look rather 'impressionistic'. It may even fail to impress. Yet we believe the concepts and arguments advanced here take the discussion of reflexive modernisation firmly into the realm of governance, something we felt was unquestionably needed. Furthermore, they throw light on quite fundamental implications of the concept of sustainable development, when that concept is translated into requirements for governance: considering the long-term systemic effects of short-term, specialised solutions proves to have disruptive potential for modernist problem-solving routines. In this way, sustainable development may open the way for fundamental innovations in society and governance. Reflexive governance could be such an innovation, one that provides a conceptual framework within which dispersed innovations in governance can link up with each other and gain momentum. With this bold claim we offer the book to readers. We hope that further steps will follow and that by means of such steps, 'we make the path by walking'.

## NOTES

1. As such, however, reflexive governance is naturally embedded in a broad context of governance, management, planning and operation studies and various innovative practices linked to them. Reflexive governance bundles things in a different way while focusing on some aspects and leaving out others.
2. Stirling (this volume) introduces a variation of this understanding of reflexivity. He reserves the term reflexivity for a cognitive 'recursive loop, in which it is recognised that representations are contingent on a multiplicity of subjective perspectives, and that these subjective perspectives are themselves reconstituted by processes of representation'. Reflexivity thus refers to cognitive processes that turn attention towards themselves. In this understanding, reflexivity is always a deliberate intentional effort. A 'reflexive system of governance therefore involves explicit recognition that policy appraisals are contingent and constructed, including by commitments to the interventions that they ostensibly inform'. Although this is fruitful terminology with respect to the cognitive dimension of

governance, it does not connect easily to the occupation of modern development with itself, which appears in the repairing of the undesired side-effects of its own working. This aspect is strong in the concept of reflexive modernisation. Environmental protection and technology assessment are examples of societal governance that is oriented towards its own results without concern for the link between objective problems and subjective approaches to problem solving. This 'material' reflexivity of governance can be observed even when it is not cognitively reconstructed by the actors who conduct environmental protection or technology assessment. As for the concept of reflexive governance, we further use a notion of reflexivity that includes the unintentional – and even unreflected – self-confrontation of social action. To avoid confusion, however, it is advisable to introduce a clear differentiation between unintended reflexivity as a condition of governance – being confronted with side-effects – and its cognitive reflection and corresponding adaptation of problem-handling practices as new governance approaches that cope with side-effects by incorporating uncertainty, ambiguity and distributed control. The first form of unintended reflexivity can be labelled first-order reflexivity; the second form of reflected reflexivity can be labelled second-order reflexivity.

# REFERENCES

Beck, U. (1993), *Die Erfindung des Politischen*, Frankfurt am Main: Suhrkamp.

Beck, U. (1994), 'The reinvention of politics: towards a theory of reflexive modernization', in U. Beck, A. Giddens and S. Lash (eds), *Reflexive Modernization*, Cambridge: Polity Press, 1–55.

Beck, U., W. Bonss and C. Lau (2003), 'The theory of reflexive modernization: problematic, hypotheses and research programme', *Theory, Culture & Society*, **20**, 1–33.

Beck, U., A. Giddens and S. Lash (eds) (1994), *Reflexive Modernization-Politics, Tradition and Aesthetics in the Modern Social Order*, Cambridge: Polity Press.

Giddens, A. (1984/1986), *The Constitution of Society*, Berkeley, CA: University Press.

March, J.G. (1991), 'Exploration and exploitation in organizational learning', *Organization Science*, **2** (1), 71–87.

Ravetz, J. (2003), 'A paradoxical future for safety in the global knowledge economy', *Futures*, **35**, 811–26.

Rip, A. (1986), 'Controversies as informal technology assessment', *Knowledge: Creation, Diffusion, Utilization*, **8** (2), 349–71.

Spangenberg, J. (2004), 'Sustainability beyond environmentalism: the missing dimensions', GoSD Working Paper No. 2, May, www.gosd.net/pdf/gosd-wp 2.pdf (accessed 14 September 2005).

Stirling, A. (2005), 'Opening up or closing down: analysis, participation and power in social appraisal of technology', in M. Leach, I. Scoones and B. Wynne (eds), *Science, Citizenship and Globalisation*, London: Zed Books.

# Index